2007-2008
EVANGELICAL SUNDAY SCHOOL LESSON COMMENTARY

FIFTY-SIXTH ANNUAL VOLUME
Based on the
Evangelical Bible Lesson Series

Editorial Staff
Lance Colkmire — Editor
Tammy Hatfield — Editorial Assistant
James E. Cossey — Editor in Chief
Joseph A. Mirkovich — General Director of Publications

Lesson Exposition Writers

J. Ayodeji Adewuya	Rodney Hodge
Lance Colkmire	Joshua Rice
Jerald Daffe	Richard Keith Whitt

Published by

PATHWAY PRESS   Cleveland, Tennessee

* To place an order, call 1-800-553-8506.
* To contact the editor, call 423-478-7597.

Lesson treatments in the *Evangelical Sunday School Lesson Commentary* for 2007-2008 are based upon the outlines of the Pentecostal-Charismatic Bible Lesson Series prepared by the Pentecostal-Charismatic Curriculum Commission.

Copyright 2007

PATHWAY PRESS, Cleveland, Tennessee

ISBN: 978-1-59684-272-4

ISSN: 1555-5801

Printed in the United States of America

TABLE OF CONTENTS

INTRODUCTION TO THE 2007-2008 COMMENTARY

The *Evangelical Sunday School Lesson Commentary* contains in a single volume a full study of the Sunday school lessons for the months beginning with September 2007 and running through August 2008. The 12 months of lessons draw from both the Old Testament and the New Testament in an effort to provide balance and establish relationship between these distinct but inspired writings. The lessons in this 2007-2008 volume are drawn from the second year of a seven-year cycle, which will be completed in August 2013. (The cycle is printed in full on page 15 of this volume.)

The lessons for the *Evangelical Commentary* are based on the Evangelical Bible Lesson Series Outlines, prepared by the Pentecostal-Charismatic Curriculum Commission. (The Pentecostal-Charismatic Curriculum Commission is a member of the National Association of Evangelicals.) The lessons in this volume, taken together with the other annual volumes of lessons in the cycle, provide a valuable commentary on a wide range of Biblical subjects. Each quarter is divided into two units of study.

The 2007-2008 commentary is the work of a team of Christian scholars and writers who have developed the volume under the supervision of Pathway Press. All the major writers, introduced on the following pages, represent a team of ministers committed to a strictly Evangelical interpretation of the Scriptures. The guiding theological principles of this commentary are expressed in the following statement of faith:

1. WE BELIEVE the Bible to be the inspired, the only infallible, authoritative Word of God.

2. WE BELIEVE that there is one God, eternally existing in three persons: Father, Son, and Holy Spirit.

3. WE BELIEVE in the deity of our Lord Jesus Christ, in His virgin birth, in His sinless life, in His miracles, in His vicarious and atoning death through His shed blood, in His bodily resurrection, in His ascension to the right hand of the Father, and in His personal return in power and glory.

4. WE BELIEVE that for the salvation of lost and sinful men, personal reception of the Lord Jesus Christ and regeneration by the Holy Spirit are absolutely essential.

5. WE BELIEVE in the present ministry of the Holy Spirit by whose cleansing and indwelling the Christian is enabled to live a godly life.

6. WE BELIEVE in the personal return of the Lord Jesus Christ.

7. WE BELIEVE in the resurrection of both the saved and the lost—they that are saved, unto the resurrection of life; and they that are lost, unto the resurrection of damnation.

8. WE BELIEVE in the spiritual unity of believers in our Lord Jesus Christ.

USING THE 2007-2008 COMMENTARY

The *Evangelical Sunday School Lesson Commentary* for 2007-2008 is presented to the reader with the hope that it will become his or her weekly companion through the months ahead.

Quarterly unit themes for the 2007-2008 volume are as follows:
- Fall Quarter—Unit One: "Abraham"; Unit Two: "Great Women of the Bible"
- Winter Quarter—Unit One: "Isaac, Jacob and Joseph"; Unit Two: "Christian Discipleship"
- Spring Quarter—Unit One: "The Gospel in Romans and Galatians"; Unit Two: "Ecclesiastes"
- Summer Quarter—Unit One: "God's Deliverance and Provision (Exodus)"; Unit Two: "Great Hymns of the Bible"

The lesson sequence used in this volume is prepared by the Pentecostal-Charismatic Curriculum Commission. The specific material used in developing each lesson is written and edited under the guidance of the editorial staff of Pathway Press.

INTRODUCTION: The opening of each week's lesson features a one-page introduction. It provides background information that sets the stage for the lesson.

CONTEXT: A time and place is given for most lessons. Where there is a wide range of ideas regarding the exact time or place, we favor the majority opinion of conservative scholars.

PRINTED TEXT: The printed text is the body of Scripture designated each week for verse-by-verse study in the classroom. Drawing on the study text the teacher delves into this printed text, exploring its content with the students.

CENTRAL TRUTH and FOCUS: The central truth states the single unifying principle that the expositors attempted to clarify in each lesson. The focus describes the overall lesson goal.

DICTIONARY: A dictionary, which attempts to bring pronunciation and clarification to difficult words or phrases, is included with many lessons. Pronunciations are based on the phonetic system used by Field Enterprises Educational Corporation of Chicago and New York in *The World Book Encyclopedia*. Definitions are generally based on *The Pictorial Bible Dictionary*, published by Zondervan Publishing Company, Grand Rapids, Michigan.

EXPOSITION and LESSON OUTLINE: The heart of this commentary—and probably the heart of the teacher's instruction each week—is the exposition of the printed text. This exposition material is organized in outline form, which indicates how the material is to be divided for study.

QUOTATIONS and ILLUSTRATIONS: Each section of every lesson contains illustrations and sayings the teacher can use in connecting the lesson to daily living.

TALK ABOUT IT: Questions are printed throughout the lesson to help students explore the Scripture text and how it speaks to believers today.

CONCLUSION: Each lesson ends with a brief conclusion that makes a summarizing statement.

GOLDEN TEXT CHALLENGE: The golden text challenge for each week is a brief reflection on that single verse. The word *challenge* is used because its purpose is to help students apply this key verse to their life.

DAILY BIBLE READINGS: The daily Bible readings are included for the teacher to use in his or her own devotions throughout the week, as well as to share with members of their class.

SCRIPTURE TEXTS USED IN LESSON EXPOSITION

Genesis

12:1-20	September 2
13:1-18	September 2
14:8, 9, 10-24	September 9
15:1-6, 17, 18	September 16
16:1-5, 8-10, 15, 16	September 16
17:1-10	September 16
17:15-21	October 14
17:15-22	December 2
18:1-15, 25, 32, 33	September 23
21:1-7	October 14
21:1-8	December 2
21:6, 7	October 14
21:9-12	December 2
22:1-14	December 9
22:1-18	September 30
24:1-4, 10-15, 19, 26, 27, 50-54, 58-61	October 7
25:20-28	December 16
27:30-36, 41	December 16
28:10-22	December 16
31:3-7, 17-21	December 30
32:1-12, 24-32	December 30
34:30, 31	January 6
35:1-15	January 6
37:1-13, 18-36	January 13
39:1-9, 17-23	January 20
41:14-16, 33, 38-41	January 20
45:1-15	January 27
46:1-7	January 27
47:11, 12	January 27
50:15, 19-21	January 27

Exodus

1:8-22	June 1
2:1-25	June 1
3:1-8, 13-16, 18	June 8
4:2, 3, 6, 9-12, 19-21	June 8
11:1-10	June 15
12:21-33, 40-42	June 15
14:1-4, 10-14, 19-30	June 22
15:1-21	July 20

Exodus (con't)

16:10-18	June 29
17:1-16	June 29
18:5-26	July 6
32:1-14, 29-35	July 13

Deuteronomy

31:30	July 27
32:1-15, 30, 31, 36-43	July 27

Joshua

2:1-4, 8-14	October 21
6:17, 20, 22-25	October 21

Judges

4:4-16, 23, 24	October 28
5:1-5, 31	October 28

1 Samuel

1:1-20	November 4
2:1, 2	November 4
25:2, 3, 10-25, 30-39	November 11

Psalms

1:2, 3	February 24
22:1-18	August 3
46:1-11	August 10
47:1-9	August 10
48:1-14	August 10
103:1-22	August 17
118:19-29	August 3

Ecclesiastes

1:1-11, 16-18	May 4
2:1-4, 9-11	May 4
3:9-14	May 4
5:1-7	May 18
7:1-12	May 18
9:7-10	May 18
11:7-10	May 25
12:1-14	May 25

Matthew

1:5	October 21
6:24	February 10

Matthew (con't)

12:49, 50	February 17
20:25-28	February 10
25:34-40	February 24

Luke

8:1-3	November 18
10:38-42	November 25
14:25-27, 33	February 10
17:7-10	February 10

John

1:1-18	December 23
1:29-34	December 9
11:17-27	November 25
12:1-7	November 25
13:34, 35	February 17
15:1, 7	February 17
15:8	February 3
15:8-11	February 17
20:1-3, 10-18	November 18

Acts

2:42	February 24
2:46, 47	February 3
8:5-17	May 11
10:44-48	May 11
11:15-18	May 11
19:1-7	May 11

Romans

1:7-17	March 2
1:11, 12	February 3
1:18-23, 28, 32	March 9
2:17-29, 32	March 9
3:21-31	March 9
4:1-25	March 16
5:1-21	March 30
6:1-23	April 6
7:1-13, 21-25	April 13
8:1-4	April 13
8:5-39	April 20
12:1-21	April 27

1 Corinthians

15:20-26, 35-38, 42-57	March 23

2 Corinthians

4:5	February 10

2 Corinthians (con't)

5:18-20	February 3
6:14-18	February 17
7:1	February 17

Galatians

1:6-24	March 2
2:5-10, 15-21	March 9
3:6-14	March 16
3:16	December 2
3:19-29	March 16
3:21-31	March 9
3:26, 28, 29	March 16
4:22-31	December 2
5:1-6, 13, 14	April 13
5:16-23	April 20
6:1-10	April 27

Ephesians

4:11-13	February 3
6:18-20	February 24

Philippians

1:27-29	February 10
3:9-14	February 3
4:6, 7	February 24

Colossians

2:10-13	September 16

1 Thessalonians

3:12, 13	February 17

2 Timothy

1:11, 12	February 10
2:1, 2	February 3
3:16, 17	February 24

Hebrews

10:23-25	February 24
11:31	October 21

James

2:21-26	October 21

1 Peter

2:11, 12	February 3
2:19-23	February 10
3:1-6	October 14

2 Peter		Revelation	
3:18	February 24	4:1-11	August 24
		5:1-14	August 24
		11:15-19	August 31
1 John		19:1-10	August 31
2:15-17	February 24		
3:1-3	February 17		
4:7-11	February 17		

SCRIPTURE TEXTS USED IN GOLDEN TEXT CHALLENGE

Genesis		Ecclesiastes (con't)	
15:6	September 16	7:12	May 18
17:16	October 14	12:13	May 25
18:19	January 6		
18:27	September 23	**Matthew**	
22:12	September 30	23:12	December 30
39:21	January 20		
50:20	January 13	**Luke**	
		14:33	February 10
Exodus			
2:23	June 1	**John**	
3:10	June 8	1:14	December 23
12:13	June 15	15:8	February 3
14:13	June 22	15:15	November 25
15:2	July 20		
		Acts	
Deuteronomy		2:42	February 24
32:4	July 27	11:16	May 11
Judges		**Romans**	
5:1, 2	October 28	1:16	March 2
		5:10	March 30
1 Samuel		6:14	April 6
1:27	November 4	8:2	April 13
		8:32	December 9
		8:37	April 20
Psalms		12:2	November 18
37:5	October 7	12:10	April 27
48:1	August 10	12:21	January 27
103:1	August 17		
118:21	August 3	**1 Corinthians**	
		15:20	March 23
Proverbs			
3:5, 6	July 6	**Galatians**	
15:1, 2	November 11	2:16	March 9
20:17	December 16	3:11	March 16
		4:28	December 2
Ecclesiastes			
3:14	May 4		

Philippians
4:19   June 29

1 Timothy
2:1   July 13

2 Timothy
1:7   September 9

Hebrews
11:8   September 2
11:31   October 21

1 John
4:11   February 17

Revelation
4:11   August 24
19:1   August 31

ACKNOWLEDGMENTS

Many books and Web sites have been used in the research that has gone into the 2007-2008 *Evangelical Commentary*. The major books that have been used are listed below.

Bibles
King James Version, Oxford University Press, Oxford, England
Life Application Study Bible, Zondervan Publishing House, Grand Rapids
New American Standard Bible (*NASB*), Holman Publishers, Nashville
New International Version (*NIV*), Zondervan Publishing House, Grand Rapids
New King James Version (*NKJV*), Thomas Nelson Publishers, Nashville
The Nelson Study Bible, Thomas Nelson Publishers, Nashville
Word in Life Study Bible, Thomas Nelson Publishers, Nashville

Commentaries
Adam Clarke's Commentary, Abingdon-Cokesbury, Nashville
Barnes' Notes, BibleSoft.com
Commentaries on the Old Testament (Keil & Delitzsch), Eerdmans Publishing Co., Grand Rapids
Ellicott's Bible Commentary, Zondervan Publishing House, Grand Rapids
Expositions of Holy Scriptures, Alexander MacLaren, Eerdmans Publishing Co., Grand Rapids
Expository Thoughts on the Gospels, J.C. Ryle, Baker Books, Grand Rapids
Jamieson, Fausset and Brown Commentary, BibleSoft.com
Joseph: A Man of Integrity and Forgiveness, Charles Swindoll, Thomas Nelson Publishers, Nashville
Life Application Commentary, Tyndale House, Carol Stream, IL
Matthew Henry's Commentary, BibleSoft.com
The Bible Exposition Commentary: New Testament, Warren Wiersbe, Victor Books, Colorado Springs
The Expositor's Greek Testament, Eerdmans Publishing Co., Grand Rapids
The Interpreter's Bible, Abingdon Press, Nashville
The Pulpit Commentary, Eerdmans Publishing Co., Grand Rapids
The Wesleyan Commentary, Eerdmans Publishing Co., Grand Rapids
The Wycliffe Bible Commentary, Moody Press, Chicago
Zondervan NIV Bible Commentary, Zondervan Publishing House, Grand Rapids

Illustrations
A-Z Sparkling Illustrations, Stephen Gaukroger and Nick Mercer, Baker Books, Grand Rapids
Knight's Master Book of New Illustrations, Eerdmans Publishing Co., Grand Rapids
Notes and Quotes, The Warner Press, Anderson, IN
1,000 New Illustrations, Al Bryant, Zondervan Publishing Co., Grand Rapids
Quotable Quotations, Scripture Press Publications, Wheaton
The Encyclopedia of Religious Quotations, Fleming H. Revell Co., Old Tappan, NJ
The Speaker's Sourcebook, Zondervan Publishing House, Grand Rapids
3,000 Illustrations for Christian Service, Eerdmans Publishing Co., Grand Rapids
Who Said That?, George Sweeting, Moody Press, Chicago

Reference Books

Biblical Characters From the Old and New Testament, Alexander Whyte, Kregel Publications, Grand Rapids

Harper's Bible Dictionary, Harper and Brothers Publishers, New York

Pictorial Dictionary of the Bible, Zondervan Publishing House, Grand Rapids

Pronouncing Biblical Names, Broadman and Holman Publishers, Nashville

The Interpreter's Dictionary of the Bible, Abingdon Press, Nashville

Vine's Expository Dictionary of New Testament Words, W.E. Vine, MacDonald Publishing Company, McClean, Virginia

Evangelical Bible Lesson Series (2006–2013)

Fall Quarter September, October, November	Winter Quarter December, January, February	Spring Quarter March, April, May	Summer Quarter June July, August
Fall 2006 1 • Old Testament Survey 2 • New Testament Survey	**Winter 2006-07** 1 • Beginnings (Genesis 1–11) 2 • Basic Christian Doctrine	**Spring 2007** 1 • Teachings of Jesus in Matthew 2 • The Christian Family	**Summer 2007** 1 • Prayers in Psalms 2 • God's Providence
Fall 2007 1• Abraham (Genesis 12—25) 2 • Great Women of the Bible	**Winter 2007-08** 1• Isaac, Jacob & Joseph 2 • Discipleship	**Spring 2008** 1 • Romans & Galatians 2 • Ecclesiastes	**Summer 2008** 1 • God Delivers His People (Exodus) 2 • Great Hymns of the Bible
Fall 2008 1 • The Early Church (Acts, Part 1) 2 • Proverbs 3 • Job (Faithfulness)	**Winter 2008-09** 1 • 1 & 2 Corinthians 2 • Profiles of Faith in Christ	**Spring 2009** 1 • Mark* (The Servant Messiah) 2 • Practical Christian Living (James)	**Summer 2009** 1 • Joshua and Judges 2 • Prayers in the Psalms (Part 2)
Fall 2009 1 • The Expanding Church (Acts, Part 2) 2 • Law and Gospel (Leviticus–Deuteronomy)	**Winter 2009-10** 1 • Major Prophets (Isaiah, Jeremiah & Ezekiel) 2 • Bible Answers to Current Issues	**Spring 2010** 1 • Ephesians 2 • Commended by Christ	**Summer 2010** 1 • 1 & 2 Samuel 2 • Sin and Holiness
Fall 2010 1 • Hope Through Christ (1 & 2 Peter) 2 • The Person and Work of the Holy Spirit	**Winter 2010-11** 1 • Godly Kings of Judah (1 & 2 Kings; 1 & 2 Chronicles) 2 • Christian Ethics	**Spring 2011** 1 • Luke* 2 • Ruth & Esther	**Summer 2011** 1 • Partnership in the Gospel (Philippians) 2 • Wholeness in Christ (Colossians) 3 • Evangelism
Fall 2011 1 • Justice and Mercy (Minor Prophets) 2 • Priorities and Values	**Winter 2011-12** 1 • 1, 2, 3 John & Jude 2 • Growing Spiritually	**Spring 2012** 1 • Return From Exile (Ezra and Nehemiah) 2 • Gifts of the Spirit	**Summer 2012** 1 • 1 & 2 Thessalonians (The Second Coming) 2 • Redemption and Spiritual Renewal
Fall 2012 1 • Hebrews 2 • Who Is God? (The Nature of God)	**Winter 2012-13** 1 • Pastoral Epistles (1 & 2 Timothy, Titus, Philemon) 2 • Prayer	**Spring 2013** 1 • John* (The Son of God) 2 • The Church	**Summer 2013** 1 • Daniel and Revelation (Triumph of Christ's Kingdom) 2 • Help for Life's Journey

*Emphasize the uniqueness of each Gospel.
**Unit themes subject to revision

Introduction to Fall Quarter

"Abraham" is the theme of the first six lessons, which begin with God's calling of Abraham, include His covenant with Abraham, and conclude with Abraham's relationship with Isaac.

Expositions were written by the Reverend Joshua Rice (B.A., M.A.Th.), who is regional director of youth and Christian education for the Great Lakes Region. He is a graduate of Lee University and Columbia Theological Seminary.

The second unit, "Great Women of the Bible," features studies of the following women of faith: Sarah, Rahab, Deborah, Hannah, Abigail, Mary Magdalene, Martha and Mary. We see how God ordained women for His purposes in both the Old and New Testament.

Expositions were written by the Reverend Dr. Jerald Daffe (B.A., M.A., D.Min.), who earned his degrees from Northwest Bible College, Wheaton College Graduate School, and Western Conservative Baptist Seminary. An ordained minister in the Church of God, Dr. Daffe has served in the pastoral ministry for 10 years and has been a faculty member at Northwest Bible College and Lee University for 30 years. Dr. Daffe received the Excellence in Advising Award (1999) at Lee University. His three latest books are *Speaking in Tongues, Life Challenges for Men*, and *Revival: God's Plan for His People*.

Faith, Doubt, and Faith Again

INTRODUCTION

We live in an age where faith appears to be assaulted by doubt at every turn. For every tenant of Biblical truth there seems to be a scientist, philosopher or entertainer bent on disproving it. For this reason, as Christians we can easily withdraw into our own, tight-knit world, where we are safe from the uncertainties outside. However, this is neither necessary nor Biblical. In fact, as we turn to the life of Abraham we see that doubt is not something inherently opposed to faith; it is actually a vital part of its development.

Abraham had reasons to doubt God time and time again: when the land he was promised fell victim to famine; when he fled to Egypt only to be separated from his wife; when he was promised a massive offspring only to remain childless into his elderly years. His life illustrates a quotation by Frederick Buechner: "Doubts are the ants in the pants of faith. They keep it awake and moving" (*Wishful Thinking: A Theological ABC, Revised and Expanded Edition*).

This continual struggle with doubt is quite understandable in Abraham's case. After all, God made "impossible" promises to him, and then chose the most bizarre ways of making good on them. One sometimes wonders how Abraham kept his sanity (during the journey to murder his son, for example), much less his faith. When it was all said and done, Abraham truly had faith *in God*. That is, he believed God was ultimately trustworthy, no matter how twisted the path to His promises appeared, so Abraham continued to be faithful. As a result, he stands as the New Testament's favorite Old Testament faith hero.

The Jews appealed to their rights as children of Abraham against John the Baptist's call to repentance from the heart (Matthew 3:9). Jesus himself included Abraham in many of His teachings (Matthew 8:11; Luke 13:28; 16:23-31; John 8:39, 40). Paul cited Abraham's faith in teaching how God justifies people (Romans 4:1-3, 12-22; Galatians 3:6-18). And the writer of Hebrews declared, "Abraham, when called to go to a place he would later receive as his inheritance, obeyed and went, even though he did not know where he was going" (11:8, *NIV*). For that is faith's essence.

Unit Theme:
Abraham

Central Truth:
Developing a healthy faith in God may require wrestling with fear and doubt.

Focus:
Acknowledge that the struggle with doubt is part of our journey with God and trust Him for renewed faith.

Context:
Around 2000 B.C., events taking place in Haran, Canaan and Egypt

Golden Text:
"By faith Abraham, when he was called to go out into a place which he should after receive for an inheritance, obeyed; and he went out, not knowing whither he went" (Hebrews 11:8).

Study Outline:

I. Faith to Obey God (Genesis 12:1-9)

II. Fear and Doubt (Genesis 12:10-20)

III. Faith to Let Go (Genesis 13:1-18)

I. FAITH TO OBEY GOD (Genesis 12:1-9)

The life of Abraham teaches us that faith is linked first and foremost to obedience. Abraham did not need to be able to wrap his mind around all that God was promising him; he simply needed to act on the faith he had to trust the character of God. This initially required the abandonment of the place of stability and security Abraham had known his entire life in Haran.

A. Abraham Leaves in Faith (vv. 1, 4, 5)

1. Now the Lord had said unto Abram, Get thee out of thy country, and from thy kindred, and from thy father's house, unto a land that I will shew thee:

4. So Abram departed, as the Lord had spoken unto him; and Lot went with him: and Abram was seventy and five years old when he departed out of Haran.

5. And Abram took Sarai his wife, and Lot his brother's son, and all their substance that they had gathered, and the souls that they had gotten in Haran; and they went forth to go into the land of Canaan; and into the land of Canaan they came.

In Genesis, God's amazing plan to build a nation that would serve Him alone takes shape in germinal form. The point at which Abraham fits into the overall framework of the Biblical story is vital to understanding his significance. Abraham is the first to whom God revealed His plan to form a nation, and it was through God's only Son that this came to fulfillment. This is why the name *Abram*, a variation of the word *father* in Hebrew, was changed by God to *Abraham*, meaning "father of many" (ch. 17). When the Gospel writers constructed their genealogical records of Jesus Christ, they led all the way back to Abraham, in order to prove Jesus' authentic Jewishness (Matthew 1:1; Luke 3:34). In fact, it is with Abraham that Matthew began his Gospel story. We can faithfully say, then, that without Abram's willingness to obey the command of God, the landscape of Biblical history would look completely different. He had no way of knowing just how important he was to all of humanity at that time, but he was willing to sacrifice in order to obey God anyway.

Genesis 12:1 begins the history of God's interaction with the Jewish nation. There is no mention of how this conversation was conducted, and we would like answers to a myriad of questions: Where was Abram when God called him? What was he doing? Did he hear an audible voice or simply receive an impression in his heart? What did God describe about Himself, if anything? How did Abram know it was Yahweh? We can only guess at such details. We know one essential—it was Yahweh who called Abram.

Haran (HAY-run)—v. 4—a city that still exists on a branch of the Euphrates River

souls—v. 5—people

Sarai (SAY-ri)—v. 5—Abraham's wife; the name might have meant "contentious."

Talk About It:
1. Restate the Lord's command in verse 1 in your own words.
2. In one word, describe Abram's response to God's command (v. 4).
3. Why did Abram take everything with him?

Faith, Doubt, and Faith Again

This naming of Yahweh is an important aspect of the beginning of the story, which comes across a little fuzzily in the English translation. In short, there are numerous designations for God in the Old Testament that typically utilize either the designation *Elohim* or *Yahweh*. *Elohim*, and its shortened form *El*, mirrors our generic term for "God" (see, for instance, Genesis 1:1ff). *Yahweh*, however, is taken from the specific name of Israel's God written in four letters without vowels (*YHWH*), so as to render the sacred name unpronounceable (Christians added the vowels later in order to pronounce God's Hebrew name). English translations write "LORD" in all caps to denote this name. Often, the two designations for God are combined in the Old Testament, written in English as "the LORD God" (e.g. 2:4ff). Here in Genesis 12:1, the *YHWH* stands alone as if to accentuate the fact that it was Israel's God who distinctively called Abram.

Why is this important? The calling of Abram by the named God of Israel (not just their generic name for God) is vital because it may give us a hint as to Abram's background. We know from archaeological digs around the ancient Near East that these early peoples were extremely religious. By this time, Abram is 75 years old (v. 4), and thus has been practicing the religion of his family/clan his entire life. The alternate "gods" of the land typically focused on fertility and often demanded human sacrifice. Simply the fact that he would be open to this new God, who was downright strange compared to the gods his clan served, indicates Abram's courageous heart.

Abram needed all of the courage he could muster to have faith in this new God and then to obey Him. Yet obey he did, packing up his entire family right down to his nephew Lot and setting out from the comfortable city of Haran. This included quite a bit of property, for Abram was apparently a man of some means. For a well-to-do urban dweller, nomadic life likely had no more appeal than it would today, particularly at 75 years old. But Abram obeyed anyway by faith, providing an example for all readers of Scripture to follow. In Abram's heart, the land of security, comfort and stability was no match for this divine call from Yahweh.

> "Faith is not sense or sight, nor reason, but taking God at His word."
> —A.B. Evans

B. Abraham Worships in Faith (vv. 2, 3, 6-9)

2. And I will make of thee a great nation, and I will bless thee, and make thy name great; and thou shalt be a blessing:

3. And I will bless them that bless thee, and curse him that curseth thee: and in thee shall all families of the earth be blessed.

6. And Abram passed through the land unto the place

Sichem (SIGH-
kem)—v. 6—An
ancient city, called
Shechem in other
parts of the Old
Testament, it was
located near Mount
Gerizim in Canaan.

Sichem (SIGH-kem)—v. 6—An ancient city, called Shechem in other parts of the Old Testament, it was located near Mount Gerizim in Canaan.

Moreh (MO-rey)—v. 6—The word refers to oak trees. It was Abram's first stopping place in Canaan.

Hai (HAY-eye)—v. 8—A Canaanite city near Bethel, the word means "a heap of ruins."

Talk About It:
1. Why would God "bless" Abram (vv. 2, 3)?
2. What did God promise Abram, and how did he respond (vv. 7, 8)?

"Faith is dead to doubt, dumb to discouragement, and blind to impossibilities."
—*The Defender*

of Sichem, unto the plain of Moreh. And the Canaanite was then in the land.

7. And the Lord appeared unto Abram, and said, Unto thy seed will I give this land: and there builded he an altar unto the Lord, who appeared unto him.

8. And he removed from thence unto a mountain on the east of Bethel, and pitched his tent, having Bethel on the west, and Hai on the east: and there he builded an altar unto the Lord, and called upon the name of the Lord.

9. And Abram journeyed, going on still toward the south.

It was not only the compelling identify of Yahweh that convinced Abram to totally pull up roots and hit the road for an unknown destination, but the promise of God. Whereas some might have considered His promise too good to be true, Abram must have found it too good *not* to be true.

Abram could probably not have known, at least initially, that the promise to not only create a nation from him but also to bless all other nations through him (v. 3) referred to God's sending of the Messiah. Through Jesus Christ, salvation would reach beyond Israel, culminating in the Jerusalem Council of Acts 15 and the ministry of Paul the apostle. The fact that Israel failed to reach out to other nations on its own, resulting in its heartless religious leaders portrayed in the Gospels, no doubt weighed heavily on the heart of Jesus himself (see Matthew 23:37-39). It is part of the sweeping message of the Biblical narrative that Israel be a blessing to the entire earth, beginning with God's promise here to Abram.

After Abram departed Haran and arrived in the land of Canaan, the Lord appeared again with a specific word about his possession of that land (Genesis 12:7). This pattern clearly runs throughout the Abraham narratives in chapters 12–25, as God specifies His initial promise, fleshing it out and making it clearer. He does not give the big picture to Abram all at once, but in pieces. Abram responds by building a sacrificial altar to Yahweh, a practice he likely learned in the pagan religions of his clan, but there is no mention of an actual animal sacrifice here or when he builds the second altar between Bethel and Ai (12:8). There is explicit mention, however, of the Canaanites, said to inhabit the land "at that time" (v. 6, *NIV*). This reference, also in 13:7, may give us some insight into the author or editor of this history, who apparently compiles the material after Joshua has driven out the Canaanites. Literarily, the reference also foreshadows the coming Exodus and conquest. The reader recognizes that God's promise to Abram will directly affect the Canaanites, since God promises their land to Abram's descendants.

II. FEAR AND DOUBT (Genesis 12:10-20)

Abram's obedience to God does not remain a smooth road

for long. After God's promise is reinforced in verse 7, a famine immediately strikes the land, and things get bumpy. It has been often said that adversity proves the character of a man, and in this regard Abram quickly fails the test.

A. Abraham Falters (vv. 10-16)

10. And there was a famine in the land: and Abram went down into Egypt to sojourn there; for the famine was grievous in the land.

11. And it came to pass, when he was come near to enter into Egypt, that he said unto Sarai his wife, Behold now, I know that thou art a fair woman to look upon:

12. Therefore it shall come to pass, when the Egyptians shall see thee, that they shall say, This is his wife: and they will kill me, but they will save thee alive.

13. Say, I pray thee, thou art my sister: that it may be well with me for thy sake; and my soul shall live because of thee.

14. And it came to pass, that, when Abram was come into Egypt, the Egyptians beheld the woman that she was very fair.

15. The princes also of Pharaoh saw her, and commended her before Pharaoh: and the woman was taken into Pharaoh's house.

16. And he entreated Abram well for her sake: and he had sheep, and oxen, and he asses, and menservants, and maidservants, and she asses, and camels.

After the optimistic description of Abram's sacrificial obedience to the promise and command of God in verses 1-9, this section is a letdown in its entirety. We can only imagine Abram's frustration as he pulled up roots again and entered dangerous territory. Abram wandered from the land of Canaan, which God promised him, into Egypt, which God had not promised him. The famine, of course, gave him a good excuse, but trouble quickly mounted. As of yet, Abram did not understand the character of Yahweh, who had called him.

This story happened, of course, before the Ten Commandments were given, so deception was the order of the day. Knowing Sarai's astounding beauty firsthand, Abram was sure this could be a problem, so he devised a scheme to lie about their relationship in order to protect himself. The deception worked, but the result probably was not what Abram had expected. Sarai was quickly married off to Pharaoh himself in exchange for more wealth for Abram. The Egyptians believed Abram was her brother, and they paid him the bride price by giving him sheep, oxen, donkeys, camels and servants.

Talk About It
1. When Abram moved into Egypt, what was his fear (v. 12)?
2. What did Abram gain, and what did he lose (vv. 15, 16)?

"Fear causes people to draw back from situations; it brings on mediocrity; it dulls creativity; it sets one up to be a loser in life."
—Fran Tarkenton

B. Yahweh Saves Abram From a Place of Compromise (vv. 17-20)

17. And the Lord plagued Pharaoh and his house with great plagues because of Sarai Abram's wife.

18. And Pharaoh called Abram, and said, What is this that thou hast done unto me? why didst thou not tell me that she *was* thy wife?

19. Why saidst thou, She is my sister? so I might have taken her to me to wife: now therefore behold thy wife, take her, and go thy way.

20. And Pharaoh commanded his men concerning him: and they sent him away, and his wife, and all that he had.

From a material standpoint, the situation was comfortable again for Abram. He found a way out of God's promise due to the famine, and was living off the wealth of Egypt, but he had lost his beautiful wife. Sarai had been taken into Pharaoh's harem, where she was being prepared for entering a sexual relationship with Pharaoh. Ironically, it is Pharaoh who recognized the hand of Abram's God in the diseases spreading throughout his palace, and he apparently squeezed the truth out of Sarai before confronting Abram. Providentially, the unnamed plague that struck Pharaoh's house caused him to be in such awe of God that he would not harm a hair on Abram's head, and he even sent a delegation to help Abram's household leave Egypt. It was nothing short of the closest call, but Yahweh wasn't about to give up on Abram. The journey, the adventure, had just begun.

III. FAITH TO LET GO (Genesis 13:1-18)

A different Abram emerges in chapter 13. Seasoned by the trial and deliverance in Egypt, and still goaded on by God's promises back in Haran, he begins to recognize the supremacy of Yahweh, both in the sense that this God is serious when He makes commandments and that with equal passion He commits to His promises. Now that Abram has learned these truths (the hard way), he begins to truly trust God, and as a result God's promise to him is intensified.

A. Abram Returns to God (vv. 1-4)

1. And Abram went up out of Egypt, he, and his wife, and all that he had, and Lot with him, into the south.

2. And Abram was very rich in cattle, in silver, and in gold.

3. And he went on his journeys from the south even to Bethel, unto the place where his tent had been at the beginning, between Bethel and Hai;

4. Unto the place of the altar, which he had made there at the first: and there Abram called on the name of the Lord.

Talk About It:
What was the result of the "great plagues" God sent on Pharaoh's household?

Talk About It:
Why is it significant that Abram returned to the place he "had been at the beginning" (v. 3)?

Faith, Doubt, and Faith Again

Enriched by the bounties of Pharaoh, Genesis 13 begins another significant segment of Abram's life. This was quite a demotion from Pharaoh's lavish court, as the Negev ("the south") was known as a dry, arid region in southern Palestine. Yet for Abram, it was nothing short of a spiritual pilgrimage. In verse 4, Abram returns to the exact spot, between Ai and Bethel, where he built the altar to Yahweh in 12:8. And just as he did back then, Abram "called on the name of the Lord" (13:4). Had he been calling on the names of other gods, sinking back into those forms of worship that were all he knew for 75 years? We do not know. However, the fact that Abram turns back to God marks a major turning point in his life. However, just like his initial act of obedience when he left Haran was met with the tragedy of a famine, Abram's recommitment to Yahweh here is followed by conflict.

B. Abram Defers to Lot (vv. 5-13)

5. And Lot also, which went with Abram, had flocks, and herds, and tents.

6. And the land was not able to bear them, that they might dwell together: for their substance was great, so that they could not dwell together.

7. And there was a strife between the herdmen of Abram's cattle and the herdmen of Lot's cattle: and the Canaanite and the Perizzite dwelled then in the land.

8. And Abram said unto Lot, Let there be no strife, I pray thee, between me and thee, and between my herdmen and thy herdmen; for we be brethren.

9. Is not the whole land before thee? separate thyself, I pray thee, from me: if thou wilt take the left hand, then I will go to the right; or if thou depart to the right hand, then I will go to the left.

10. And Lot lifted up his eyes, and beheld all the plain of Jordan, that it was well watered every where, before the Lord destroyed Sodom and Gomorrah, even as the garden of the Lord, like the land of Egypt, as thou comest unto Zoar.

11. Then Lot chose him all the plain of Jordan; and Lot journeyed east: and they separated themselves the one from the other.

12. Abram dwelled in the land of Canaan, and Lot dwelled in the cities of the plain, and pitched his tent toward Sodom.

13. But the men of Sodom were wicked and sinners before the Lord exceedingly.

By all indications, sticking with Abram had been a very profitable venture for his nephew Lot. Working for the family business

Silent Trust
After the fall of Germany in World War II, rescuing forces found this quote cut into the wooden barracks of a Nazi concentration camp: "I believe in the sun even when it is not shining. I believe in love even when I do not feel it. I believe in God even when He is silent." Sometimes faith can be hard to muster during times of trial and doubt, but in fact, this is mature faith's primary breeding ground.

Perizzite (PAIR-iz-zite)—v. 7—one of the 10 tribes of Canaan whom the Israelites eventually defeated

Zoar (ZO-ahr)—v. 10—A small town near Sodom and Gomorrah

Talk About It:
1. Why couldn't Abram and Lot continue to live together?
2. Why didn't Abram take advantage of his seniority to choose the better land?

had brought him a significant portion of blessing, mostly due to his ability to breed animals successfully, and it quickly became a point of contention between the two "companies." In fact, after a while they grew so prodigious that there was simply not enough vegetation in a single area to feed all the livestock. This was not surprising in the dry regions of Palestine, and they were certainly not the only herders in the land. Disputes among their employees exacerbated the tension.

Abram stepped up and said, "Is not the whole land before you? Let's part company. If you go to the left, I'll go to the right; if you go to the right, I'll go to the left" (v. 9, *NIV*).

What had happened to Abram? A short time before, he had put into motion a scheme that enslaved his wife, made him rich, and almost killed the entire government body of Egypt. Now, however, he extends dramatic grace to his nephew, calling him "brother" (v. 8). As the patriarch of the family clan, Abram possessed the authority to make such decisions himself, but he humbly deferred to his subordinate, the lesser Lot. Whether he thought Lot would choose fairly, we cannot know. After all, Lot had become rich on the coattails of Abram. Surely he would honor his elder! Instead, he took the well-watered Jordan plains, leaving Abram with the arid Canaan desert. Lot "pitched his tent even as far as Sodom" (v. 12, *NKJV*). Sodom was known for its atrocious sin and firm opposition to Yahweh, yet Lot spread out his camp to reach that city. This reveals that Lot's heart was turned toward the flesh instead of toward Yahweh.

C. God Reinforces His Promise (vv. 14-18)

14. And the Lord said unto Abram, after that Lot was separated from him, Lift up now thine eyes, and look from the place where thou art northward, and southward, and eastward, and westward:

15. For all the land which thou seest, to thee will I give it, and to thy seed for ever.

16. And I will make thy seed as the dust of the earth: so that if a man can number the dust of the earth, then shall thy seed also be numbered.

17. Arise, walk through the land in the length of it and in the breadth of it; for I will give it unto thee.

18. Then Abram removed his tent, and came and dwelt in the plain of Mamre, which is in Hebron, and built there an altar unto the Lord.

Although Abram had just given up the eastern land to his ungrateful nephew, Yahweh immediately put that loss into perspective. The east was nothing; God would give Abram's descendants everything he could see in every direction. And for the first time, Yahweh revealed how expansive this promise

Hebron (HEE-bruhn)—v. 18—meaning "alliance," one of the oldest and most important cities of southern Palestine

would be—throughout all time. What a promise for one rather average man traipsing around in the Palestinian desert! His descendants would *always* have the rights to that land, no matter what. Then God announced that Abram's offspring would be as plentiful and uncountable as dust particles (later, in 15:5, God uses the metaphor of the stars in the sky). Since Abram was able to exercise the faith to let go, even to the point of being personally wronged by Lot, God drew near to him.

God also reckoned that Abram was ready for a new command. Abram was instructed to walk around in the land he had just seen—through its length and breadth—as an act of faith that he genuinely believed God was giving it to him and his descendants forever (13:17). This is a strange commandment to a man who was already elderly and had already traveled such great distances, but Abram packed quickly and began walking.

Chapters 12 and 13, then, depict Abram's progression from a well-to-do urban dweller to a full-fledged nomad. Why did God desire Abram to be nomadic? Could He not have accomplished His purposes by having Abram set up a city in the Promised Land? Two reasons are possible for this.

First, the nomadic life requires total dependence on God. Abram would no longer have the comforts of home to live in, only the shelter of tents and the harsh conditions of the open wilderness (which was often desert). He could not learn to depend fully on Yahweh in comfort, but only in neediness.

Second, the nomadic lifestyle requires a continual disposition of hospitality. Nomads must learn to stick together, to live in community, to welcome one another into their dwellings. They cannot survive otherwise. In fact, God's judgment on Sodom and Gomorrah is immediately connected to the city's inability to be hospitable to the visiting angels, and Lot is saved because he practices passionate hospitality toward them (19:1-7).

This preference for hospitality became the basis for many of the Ten Commandments and the Torah community laws in general. The Jews were expected to treat one another with kindness and fairness on the basis of hospitality. Later, Jesus himself commanded His disciples that when they traveled for ministry, they were to engage in hospitality with those who would provide a bed and food for them (Luke 10:7). So we see that Abram's lifestyle lay the foundation for many of the themes that come later in Scripture, including hospitality and total dependence on God.

CONCLUSION

The beginning of Abram's journey with Yahweh was fraught with difficulty and the sometimes hard, but always invaluable, lessons of faith. God gave unchanging commands to Abram,

Talk About It:
1. After Lot left, what did God do (vv. 14-16)? Why then?
2. Why did God want Abram to walk throughout Canaan (v. 17)?

"God our Father has made all things depend on faith so that whoever has faith will have everything, and whoever does not have faith will have nothing."
—Martin Luther

offered His grace at every turn, encouraging him time and time again with His precious promise that the entire earth would benefit from Abram's life and his descendants. Even before he became known as "Abraham," before God made a formal covenant with him, and before he was given any offspring whatsoever, God shaped Abram's character to get him ready for all of these things. Through Abram's faith to obey God, even through fear and doubt, and ultimately his faith to let go and trust Yahweh, he placed himself in a position to be further used of God.

Daily Devotions:
M. Obey God's Word
   Judges 6:11-16; 7:19-22
T. Let God Fight for You
   2 Chronicles 20:14-17, 20-24
W. Trust God in Adversity
   Job 1:13-22
T. Trust in God When Afraid
   Psalm 56:1-13
F. Surrender to God's Will
   Luke 1:28-38
S. Deal With Doubt
   John 20:24-29

GOLDEN TEXT CHALLENGE

"BY FAITH ABRAHAM, WHEN HE WAS CALLED TO GO OUT INTO A PLACE WHICH HE SHOULD AFTER RECEIVE FOR AN INHERITANCE, OBEYED; AND HE WENT OUT, NOT KNOWING WHITHER HE WENT" (Hebrews 11:8).

Abraham was called of God. This call consisted of a command and a promise. The command was, "Get thee out of thy country" (Genesis 12:1). The promise was that all nations would be blessed in him. Abraham obeyed the command. He went out as he was called to do. What an illustration of faith! On the first call of God, he responded with absolute obedience without regard for what it might cost him or even of what the reward consisted.

The same is required of us. Our attitude toward God must be one of complete trust.

Faith, Doubt, and Faith Again

Courage Through Faith in God

Genesis 14:1-24

The story of Abraham (who was first called Abram) is one of slow and steady progression. It begins as he carries on his normal life of paganism. In act one, Abram receives the call from God and struggles to obey and come to terms with all that this calling means for his life and his future. In act two, he travels through the ups and downs of life with Yahweh until the promise starts to take shape. Hence, the story of Abraham is the story of the nature of faith itself. Faith is not an easy, linear process where God takes us directly from one level to another. Instead, it is filled with twists, obstacles and challenges that are all as much a part of faith as righteous living and prayer. And how exciting would life be without these challenges? They must come our way in order to keep faith alive and passionate.

A particular character trait emerges in Abraham as he steadily flexes his faith muscles—courage. As he learned to trust God through the problems of famine and his ungrateful nephew, it welled up deep within his heart. This courage was produced as a response to God's leading him through these problems and as a necessity to face the challenges ahead. In order to take him to greater places in his relationship with Yahweh, Abraham would need the courage to surmount even more intimidating obstacles than before.

Paul explains this progression of faith under fire in Romans 5: "Not only so, but we also rejoice in our sufferings, because we know that suffering produces perseverance; perseverance, character; and character, hope" (vv. 3, 4, *NIV*).

In order for the graces of hope and perseverance, or courage, to develop within the recesses of the soul, suffering must occur, and for this Paul instructs us to rejoice. In Genesis 12, Abraham failed the test of suffering through his unfaithfulness to God and to Sarah during a time of famine. In chapter 14, however, he passes with flying colors, marking another vital page in his amazing spiritual journey. It will take all the courage he can muster to continue following this dangerous God, but one imagines that it was God all along granting him the courage in the first place.

Unit Theme:
Abraham

Central Truth:
Believers can overcome obstacles through faith in God.

Focus:
Affirm that overwhelming difficulties can be conquered through faith in God and respond with confidence in Him.

Context:
Around 1950-1900 B.C. in Dan, Hobah and Valley of Shaveh

Golden Text:
"God hath not given us the spirit of fear; but of power, and of love, and of a sound mind" (2 Timothy 1:7).

Study Outline:
I. Facing Overwhelming Odds (Genesis 14:1-12)
II. Courage to Act (Genesis 14:13-16)
III. Deliverance and Blessing (Genesis 14:17-24)

I. FACING OVERWHELMING ODDS (Genesis 14:1-12)

A. God-Sized Challenge (vv. 1-9)

(Genesis 14:1-7 is not included in the printed text.)

8. And there went out the king of Sodom, and the king of Gomorrah, and the king of Admah, and the king of Zeboiim, and the king of Bela (the same is Zoar;) and they joined battle with them in the vale of Siddim;

9. With Chedorlaomer the king of Elam, and with Tidal king of nations, and Amraphel king of Shinar, and Arioch king of Ellasar; four kings with five.

Genesis 14 begins on a dark, ominous note, with a long list of kings engaged in a large-scale war against one another. King Chedorlaomer ruled from Elam, a region east of Babylonia in the most strategic location of the Persian Gulf. His power was so great, however, that he ruled much of the land in Palestine also. At this point, his "rule" in Palestine did not necessarily indicate he had much, if anything, to do with the lives of its people. Instead, it denoted that he simply retained the authority to tax, and he probably enforced this authority with military might. By the time of Genesis 14, the kings under his domain decided to rebel. Note that these "kings" are associated with various cities in the land, probably indicating that they functioned more like our modern mayors, in the sense that they did not rule over an expansive territory, but a single city. Nonetheless, with cities holding the vast majority of the population, and thus the majority of the wealth, their power was real, and this renegade alliance of freedom-fighting kings felt confident that together they could throw off the heavy yoke of Chedorlaomer.

Even the writer of Genesis observes that the odds didn't look good for Chedorlaomer and his allies. Ancient readers would also have noticed that his name pays homage to a foreign god. This kind of political instability was the last thing Abram needed while trying to make a home in the land God promised him. With Chedorlaomer in power, he had been able to travel freely without worrying about bandits, looting, and other problems associated with weak central government. News of such a massive battle would likely reach the distant parts of the country quickly, and Abram had to wonder what would come of the freedom he had known in the land. Also, hadn't Yahweh promised the land *to him*? He was certainly in a strange predicament, since these pagan allies were determined to win and control it. Once again, this experience of frustration and confusion undoubtedly drew Abram to prayer, and to complete dependence on God.

B. Retribution for Lot (vv. 10-12)

10. And the vale of Siddim was full of slimepits; and the

Talk About It:

1. What was the cause of the war that was taking place?

2. What impact could this war have on Abram?

kings of Sodom and Gomorrah fled, and fell there; and they that remained fled to the mountain.

11. And they took all the goods of Sodom and Gomorrah, and all their victuals, and went their way.

12. And they took Lot, Abram's brother's son, who dwelt in Sodom, and his goods, and departed.

As the story unfolds, Lot truly develops into a tragic character in the Old Testament. One thinks of the tragedies of Shakespeare, wherein figures such as King Lear poignantly illustrate the predicament of humanity overall. Lot functions similarly, enslaved by his poor decisions at almost every turn. There are times where he shows courage and goodwill (19:3), but his ulterior motives constantly appear to be lurking just beneath the surface. It is hardly surprising, then, that Lot finds himself in a terrible situation in the sudden aftermath of the battle between the two groups of kings. Incredibly, Chedorlaomer and his allies thoroughly rout the larger force against them, to the extent that the losers foolishly flee into the Valley of Siddim and so find themselves slowed by dangerous tar pits. This gave Chedorlaomer's forces ample time to plunder Sodom and Gomorrah, stealing untold wealth and leaving the populace in tumult and destitution. But they didn't stop there. "They also carried off Abram's nephew Lot and his possessions, since he was living in Sodom" (14:12, *NIV*).

What use marauding forces would have for a town citizen goes unstated. We know, however, that Lot was a man of means, particularly due to his shrewd decision in chapter 13 to grow his livestock holdings on the best part of the land, thus insulting Abram. Perhaps his estate was so opulent that the soldiers thought it potentially profitable to have such a wealthy man in their actual possession. Someone so important might have other wealthy friends that could offer a bribe for his safe return.

Moreover, it is curious that Lot was living in Sodom in the first place. It seems that his decision to disconnect from Abram had gained him material wealth, but at the cost of his safety and even his spirit. For with the entire plain of the Jordan available to him, Lot chose the horrifically sinful city of Sodom instead. Verse 12, therefore, may represent a time of divine retribution for Lot's selfish act. When allied with Abram, Lot could live on his righteous uncle's "residual" blessing. Without Abram's guidance, however, he faced the consequences of foolish living on his own. He was helpless, aimless and hopeless, unless Abram would extend grace to him one more time.

II. COURAGE TO ACT (Genesis 14:13-16)

A. Abram's New Place of Comfort (vv. 13, 14)

13. And there came one that had escaped, and told

Siddim (SID-im)— v. 10—a broad, flat tract between hills, it was filled with asphalt pits

Talk About It:
1. What happened to the fleeing leaders and soldiers of Sodom and Gomorrah (v. 10)?
2. What happened to the goods of Sodom and Gomorrah (v. 11)?
3. How did Lot's selfish choice of the better land (13:10-13) now come back to haunt him (14:12)?

Missing Pain
An extremely rare condition called congenital analgesia results in the total failure of all pain sensors in the body. Sufferers of this disease typically die young, as death can come from infection in cuts and burns that is easily treatable in other people. The problem is that the sufferers of this disease can't feel the injury, so the pain goes unnoticed. Pain is a gift of God that allows our bodies to respond properly to injury. So also, God uses times of suffering to develop within us the character traits necessary to make us true overcomers of this world.

Mamre (MAM-ree),
Eshcol (ESH-kal)
and Aner (AH-ner)
—v. 13—three
Amorite leaders with
whom Abram made
an alliance

Talk About It:
1. How did Abram react to the news about Lot, and what does this say about him?
2. What evidence do you see of God's blessing on Abram's life (v. 14)?

Abram the Hebrew; for he dwelt in the plain of Mamre the Amorite, brother of Eshcol, and brother of Aner: and these were confederate with Abram.

14. And when Abram heard that his brother was taken captive, he armed his trained servants, born in his own house, three hundred and eighteen, and pursued them unto Dan.

It is clear that God had remarkably blessed Abram since their last encounter. In response to his obedience to God's command in 13:17, he had gained considerable ancient currency. These details are probably meant to be read against Lot's complete loss of everything, so as to illustrate the divine reward of Abram and the corollary punishment of his nephew. Abram's currency consisted of two acquisitions. To this point no coinage or money has been mentioned, because a formal monetary system had yet to be established in the world. Banks, stocks and other modern inventions didn't exist. This is why Abram's acquisition of allies was worth so much in the ancient economy. Since buying and selling were based on the barter system, defined as the ability to *trade* goods and services for other goods and services, strategic alliances with the right people were invaluable. Abram had skillfully cultivated these alliances, even as a newcomer in Hebron (referenced by the title "the Hebrew" in 14:13), building a coalition with fellow clan leaders Eshcol and Aner. This alliance not only demonstrates Abram's ability to practice hospitality, a chief objective in God's plan for his nomadic existence, but was probably instrumental in giving Abram the freedom to leave his possessions and family behind in order to rescue Lot.

Abram's second allotment of currency consisted of the actual persons born in his household. In the ancient world, households included the entire extended family, along with acquired servants, employees and others choosing to join themselves to the household. Abram's magnificent leadership skills earned him a massive household with its own militia force of 31 trained fighters. They had been trained to protect their leader, his household, and his possessions from invading bandits or small armies. Abram now commissioned them as a reconnaissance force, and they immediately left for Dan. The risk was extreme. Should Abram be unsuccessful, he would lose a major part of his wealth and the force that protected his entire household. But just like his initial calling in chapter 12 had been from a place of comfort, he put everything on the line to follow the ways of God.

"People will judge you by your actions, not your intentions. You may have a heart of gold—but so does a hard-boiled egg."
—*Christians Quoting.org*

B. Abram Again Shows Mercy (vv. 15, 16)

15. And he divided himself against them, he and his servants, by night, and smote them, and pursued them

unto Hobah, which is on the left hand of Damascus.

16. And he brought back all the goods, and also brought again his brother Lot, and his goods, and the women also, and the people.

Hobah (HOE-buh)
—v. 15—a town north of Damascus

All of this risk for his erring, ungrateful nephew! Like the father of the Prodigal Son, Abram cast all logic and pretense aside out of concern for his lost relative. This undoubtedly involved stealth and brains more than military might, for how else would they find one man in such a large land? Abram's interpersonal skills served him well as they searched from village to village, city to city. Then their opportunity came.

Talk About It:
Describe Abram's success in this campaign.

Abram took two major military risks to launch a surprise attack on his nephew's captors. First, he invaded at night. This happened millennia before the light bulb, much less nightvision goggles and other technologies that make nighttime warfare so efficient and stealthy today. In Abram's world, one wrong move meant the surprise attack was foiled, and his fledgling force would be annihilated. If anyone saw or heard the slightest movement of just one of his 318 trained men, they would be thwarted and all would be lost. The risk was intensified by his decision to divide his small force. If the enemy was tipped off and Abram's men were all together, at least they could mount some stand against them. But divided into smaller platoons, no such option would have been feasible.

Their fate rested entirely on Abram's military prowess and on faith in the living God. Thankfully, the plan worked and Lot was retrieved. Not only this, Abram did not suffer any loss. Abram's forces heroically recovered Lot's possessions, and every family and servant in his care. It is easy to focus on the bravery of Abram, since he risked his own neck, the lives of his militia, and the lives of every person in his household by launching such a mission. But more than raw courage is in view here. The miracle is that Abram risked all this for the nephew that had paid him great disrespect and turned against him.

Faith in Yahweh was rooting itself deep in Abram's heart, and his character was being shaped to look more like God. He was experiencing the attributes of God which were later revealed clearly to Moses in the giving of the Law, as Yahweh proclaimed Himself "the compassionate and gracious God, slow to anger, abounding in love and faithfulness, maintaining love to thousands, and forgiving wickedness, rebellion and sin" (Exodus 34:6, 7, *NIV*). Abram's journey with Yahweh continued to transform his attitudes and outlook.

III. DELIVERANCE AND BLESSING (Genesis 14:17-24)
A. A Potential Political Alliance (v. 17)

17. And the king of Sodom went out to meet him after

"Success seems to be connected with action. Successful men keep moving. They make mistakes, but they don't quit."
—Conrad Hilton

his return from the slaughter of Chedorlaomer, and of the kings that were with him, at the valley of Shaveh, which is the king's dale.

What a meeting is pictured in verse 17—the mighty king of Sodom deferring to the desert nomad Abram in the desert. This time it was not the king receiving homage, but instead giving it to the victor of battle. This represents a higher level of alliance Abram had yet known, as he had an opportunity to count this powerful king as his friend. This might mean protection and provision beyond what Abram had ever known. However, the king was not alone. He was overshadowed by a more important figure—one that would enhance Abram's spiritual growth.

B. A Spiritual Alliance (vv. 18-20)

18. And Melchizedek king of Salem brought forth bread and wine: and he was the priest of the most high God.

19. And he blessed him, and said, Blessed be Abram of the most high God, possessor of heaven and earth:

20. And blessed be the most high God, which hath delivered thine enemies into thy hand. And he gave him tithes of all.

The mysterious figure of Melchizedek is well known from the New Testament Book of Hebrews, where in chapters 5-7 the author connects Jesus to his priestly lineage. Apart from this reference, however, his name appears only one other time in the Old Testament (Psalm 110:4), which is the primary text the writer of Hebrews used (5:6; 7:17). Here, however, there is no comment on the later Biblical role of Melchizedek, just a short narrative of his brief interaction with Abram.

Melchizedek's reason for being present is as mysterious as the man himself. The troops of Salem, if there were any to begin with, were apparently not involved in the previous war. It is unclear what his primary job description was—king or priest. The fact that he possessed both titles hearkens back to a time when there was no modern notion of church and state. Kings were expected to be both political and religious leaders, and Melchizedek successfully fulfilled both functions. First, he offered hospitality to Abram by providing a meal. Meals were not simply means of nourishment in the ancient consciousness. They were social ceremonies through which strategic alliances were formed. Melchizedek immediately recognized a spiritual affinity with Abram, and pronounced a short blessing over him in the name of "the most high God." In this culture, words were considered to have *creative* power—that is, the ability to create new realities. Blessings were never taken lightly, as is evidenced by Jacob conning his brother Esau out of their father's blessing (Genesis 27). Interestingly,

---

Melchizedek (mel-KI-zuh-dek)—v. 18—king and priest of Salem, a place identified with Jerusalem

Talk About It:
1. Based on the blessing he gave Abram, what did Melchizedek know about God?
2. What did Abram give to Melchizedek, and why?

"The world says, 'The more you take, the more you have.' Christ says, 'The more you give, the more you are.'"
—Frederick Buechner

Melchizedek did not use the name Yahweh (which is translated into English by the capitalized LORD) in his blessing, but the more generic, shortened form of *Elohim—El*, meaning simply, "God." It was a designation used for a variety of gods, not just Yahweh. But although the divine name had probably not been revealed to Melchizedek yet, he still recognized the same, single God, Creator of all that is, the One who empowered Abram toward such an unlikely victory.

· Abram responded according to the character of generous giving that God had been forming in him. He gave the king of Salem 10 percent of all his goods. The text is not completely specific as to what this tenth entailed, but it seems likely to refer to Lot's recovered possessions in verse 16, which is the scope of the rest of the chapter. Perhaps Abram had also taken other plunder during the battle. Whatever the case, he set a precedent that is still followed today, dedicating a tithe of one's proceeds to God.

> "The blessing of God is promised to the peacemaker, but the religious negotiator had better watch his step. Darkness and light can never be brought together by talk. Some things are not negotiable."
> —A.W. Tozer

C. Alliance Avoided (vv. 21-24)

21. And the king of Sodom said unto Abram, Give me the persons, and take the goods to thyself.

22. And Abram said to the king of Sodom, I have lift up mine hand unto the Lord, the most high God, the possessor of heaven and earth,

23. That I will not take from a thread even to a shoe-latchet, and that I will not take any thing that is thine, lest thou shouldest say, I have made Abram rich:

24. Save only that which the young men have eaten, and the portion of the men which went with me, Aner, Eshcol, and Mamre; let them take their portion.

At this point in the narrative, we might think that Abram was little more than a shrewd opportunist. After all, he had allied himself with virtually anyone and everyone that has crossed his path—Pharaoh, Lot, Eshcol, Aner and Mamre. The last section of chapter 14, however, proved he was committed to godly, discriminating judgment.

The crafty king of Sodom swiftly tested the mettle of Abram, offering the terms for an alliance between them. After all, he had just watched Abram graciously offer the king of Salem a large donation, and he likely wanted a piece of the wealth. The king of Sodom proposed an efficient split of the plunder. He needed people to help rebuild his fallen city, so Abram could keep the goods. Abram, however, was not fooled. He picked up on his scheme right away.

Invoking the name of Yahweh, along with the two titles just given Him by Melchizedek (v. 22), Abram both acknowledged the validity of the alliance with Melchizedek and outright refused

Talk About It:
1. What offer did the king of Sodom make to Abram (v. 21)?
2. Why did Abram refuse the offer (vv. 22, 23)?

such a new deal. If he accepted the alliance, the king of Sodom might suppose that Abram was indebted to him, and thus ask for something more later on. Also, Abram refused to strike hands in pledge with a king who tolerated such sin in his city. Instead, Abram explained that the king of Sodom could have all the plunder left, save what his 318 trained fighting men had eaten and what belonged to his original allies—Aner, Eshcol and Mamre. Abram not only proved himself a faithful friend to his true allies, but also his exceptional character in that he decisively chose to lose riches rather than strike an alliance with the city of Sodom. He knew its evil already, and he was soon to experience it firsthand.

CONCLUSION

In Genesis 14, Abram's fledgling faith has developed into valiant courage. He proves himself unafraid of battle and of the consequences of spurning the powerful king of Sodom. After the struggles of chapters 12 and 13, the nomad is finally finding his way. Because of this, Abram receives not just another blessing from God in his heart, but an audible blessing from one of God's first priests, Melchizedek. How encouraging this must have been to the battle-scarred old man, who had endured so much to follow Yahweh. It must have reminded him once again that he was not alone.

GOLDEN TEXT CHALLENGE

"GOD HATH NOT GIVEN US THE SPIRIT OF FEAR; BUT OF POWER, AND OF LOVE, AND OF A SOUND MIND" (2 Timothy 1:7).

The spirit of power, or of courage and resolution to encounter difficulties and dangers; the *spirit of love to God*, which will carry us through the opposition we may meet with, the spirit of love to God will set us above the fear of man, and all the hurt that a man can do us; and *the spirit of a sound mind*, or quietness of mind, a peaceable enjoyment of ourselves, for we are oftentimes discouraged in our way and work by the creatures of our own fancy and imagination, which a sober, solid, thinking mind would easily answer.

The spirit God gives to his ministers is not a fearful, but a courageous spirit; it is a spirit of power, for they speak in his name who has all power, both in heaven and earth; and it is a spirit of love, for love to God and the souls of men must inflame ministers in all their service; and it is a spirit of a sound mind, for they speak the words of truth and soberness.—*Matthew Henry*

Daily Devotions:
M. Trust When
   Others Doubt
   Numbers 14:6-12
T. Dwell in God
   Psalm 91:1-7
W. Have Courage to
   Obey
   Daniel 3:13-20,
   24-26
T. Faith Brings
   Healing
   Matthew 9:18-26
F. Patiently Await
   God's Promises
   Luke 2:25-35
S. Demonstrate
   Courageous
   Faith
   Hebrews 11:32-
   40

Courage Through Faith in God

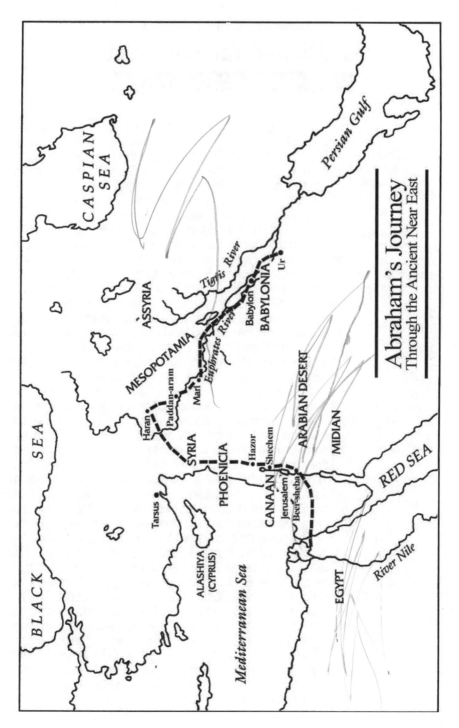

Abraham's Journey
Through the Ancient Near East

Faith and the Covenant

Genesis 15:1 through 17:13; Colossians 2:10-13

Unit Theme:
Abraham

Central Truth:
God provides everything for a covenant relationship with Him.

Focus:
Consider the establishment of God's covenant with Abraham and celebrate His faithfulness.

Context:
The events took place in Canaan around 1900 B.C.

Golden Text:
"He [Abraham] believed in the Lord; and he [God] counted it to him for righteousness" (Genesis 15:6).

Study Outline:
I. Covenant Established (Genesis 15:1-18)
II. Covenant Doubted (Genesis 16:1-16)
III. Covenant Sign Required (Genesis 17:1-13; Colossians 2:10-13)

INTRODUCTION

A simple search for the word *covenant* in the Scriptures yields an astounding 231 references; 206 of these (almost 90%) occur in the Old Testament. In the New Testament, the word is scattered throughout the Gospels, Acts, Pauline Epistles, and even Revelation, but is significantly weighted in the Book of Hebrews. Covenant is such a vital spiritual concept that it escapes no section of Scripture.

The Hebrew word for the action of creating a covenant is *carat*, which literally means "to cut." This referred to the literal bloodshed not simply associated with covenants, but required to put them into effect. Sometimes these covenants linked two people, such as that struck between David and Jonathan in 1 Samuel 20. The ancient practice of covenant-making between men involved slightly cutting one wrist and applying ash or dirt on the wound, then striking hands together so that not only was the blood mingled, but the wound was permanently scarred by a black mark. This marking was meant to forever remind the participants of the bond they had made before God.

Similarly, covenants between God and man involved the bloodshed of animal sacrifice. Often we rightly associate the practice of animal sacrifice with atonement; that is, the sins of the person are ceremonially applied to the slaughtered animal. However, the act was also to both remind and re-effect the covenant made between the one sacrificing and God. This radically distinguished the Hebrew sacrificial system from that of other pagan religions in the ancient Near East. Their sacrifices tended toward the appeasement of an angry God. Israel's was meant to remind the Jews of God's saving grace.

The centrality of covenant in Scripture appears in unlikely places that don't have animal sacrifices in primary view. The terms *Old* and *New Testament*, for instance, could equally be rendered *Old* and *New Covenant*, referring to the grounds on which God establishes relationship with His people. The ark which sat in the holiest room of the Temple and which Israel carried into battle was "of the covenant"—a constant reminder to the Jews of Yahweh who cared for them. But all of this started with a nomad named Abram, whom God chose to be the primary vessel through which He would reach all of humanity. With Abram, the initial covenant was made that would later produce Jesus himself.

I. COVENANT ESTABLISHED (Genesis 15:1-18)

The story of Abram continues in Genesis 15, beginning with the simple connecting phrase "after these things." Such phrases at the end of major scenes and chapters have the effect of moving the narrative along speedily. The writer gives us no breaks. The urgency is due to the fact that God is establishing a relationship with His chosen people starting with Abram, and it is foundational to everything else He will do in human history. So there is no time to lose. Specifically, the phrase connects chapter 15 to Abram's previous righteous alliance with God's priest Melchizedek, and his wise rejection of an alliance with the wicked city of Sodom.

A. The Covenant Established Through Abram's Faith (vv. 1-6)

1. After these things the word of the Lord came unto Abram in a vision, saying, Fear not, Abram: I am thy shield, and thy exceeding great reward.

2. And Abram said, Lord God, what wilt thou give me, seeing I go childless, and the steward of my house is this Eliezer of Damascus?

Eliezer (el-ih-EE-zur)—v. 2—Abram's chief servant

3. And Abram said, Behold, to me thou hast given no seed: and, lo, one born in my house is mine heir.

4. And, behold, the word of the Lord came unto him, saying, This shall not be thine heir; but he that shall come forth out of thine own bowels shall be thine heir.

5. And he brought him forth abroad, and said, Look now toward heaven, and tell the stars, if thou be able to number them: and he said unto him, So shall thy seed be.

6. And he believed in the Lord; and he counted it to him for righteousness.

Abram had just given up 10 percent of his plunder in order to bless the priest of God, and then untold amounts of riches in order to avoid conflict with the king of sinful Sodom. These things had not gone unnoticed by Yahweh, who assured Abram that his very life and his reward for such righteousness were secure in God's own self. This was all well and good to Abram, except for one massive problem—he had no direct heir. He confronted God head-on, contesting that he could never know this divine reward promised to him without an heir. After all, Yahweh's original word to Abram was to make him into a "great nation" (12:2). Abram's assumption was that the nation would grow from those in his household, but how he longed for a child from his own loins to fulfill the promise of God.

Yahweh had said the same thing in 13:15, 16, but perhaps it only now made perfect sense to Abram that God was speaking *literally*. He would in fact have flesh-and-blood offspring, and from that seed God would create a nation. *Surely*, Abram likely thought,

Talk About It:
1. How did God describe Himself in verse 1? Why?
2. What concern did Abram bring to God (vv. 2, 3)?
3. What was God's amazing promise (v. 5)?
4. What is the connection between faith and righteousness (v. 6)?

If God can set the stars in place, He can fulfill this promise to give me children. Genesis 15:6 says, "Abram believed the Lord, and he credited it to him as righteousness" (*NIV*).

Make no mistake—it was God who initiated things with Abram to begin with and who continued to institute His plan for the world through Abram's life. But Abram had a part to play. God initiated the plan; Abram effected it. The catalyst for all this was simple faith through and through. God peered into the heart of Abram after uttering this seemingly ridiculous promise that in his old age he would bear offspring, and God did not find doubt. He found belief. Was it that Abram *wanted* to believe so badly that he suppressed his doubt? Or did he immediately take God at His word? Abram now truly trusts this God who walks alongside him. And 20 centuries later, his act of belief became the basis for Paul's theology of justification by faith. Genesis 15:6 is quoted both in Romans 4:3 and in Galatians 3:6 as Paul explains that God found Abram righteous before the Law was given to the Jews, and God was reintroducing this Abraham-style faith in Christ.

One final word should be carefully said about Abram's belief. In the modern (or postmodern) Western world, we tend to associate belief with thinking. That is, I believe something when I mentally acknowledge its reality. The ancients had a much more comprehensive view of belief. Abram did not simply mentally assent to God's promise, *he staked the rest of his life on it.* He took the leap of his life into the arms of God by trusting that God would do what He said. This is why Paul could teach that such faith saves. And as James says (2:17), it is not distinct from action; one requires the other.

B. The Covenant Will Be Tested (vv. 7-16)

(Genesis 15:7-16 is not included in the printed text.)

After this startling announcement, God is quick to remind Abram that it is He who has allocated the Promised Land to his descendants. Even with his newfound belief, Abram wants greater evidence than God's word alone. So God instructs him to bring the elements of sacrifice, which he arranges in the traditional format. The halves of the animals are placed parallel to one another, so that a single path of blood drains out between the two rows. God's next word for Abram requires solemn, ceremonial preparation, yet even so it may be too overwhelming. So He brings Abram into a deep sleep before communicating the truth about how his offspring will come to inhabit the land. It will not be an easy path. It will be fraught with difficulty. They will be destitute strangers in another country for four centuries before God brings them back. The Amorites will be a major obstacle. This word was given to Abram to pass onto his

---

"God does not expect us to submit our faith to Him without reason, but the very limits of our reason make faith a necessity."
—Martin Luther

Talk About It:
1. How did Abram respond (v. 8) to God's promise (v. 7)?
2. What was the point of the ceremony God initiated (vv. 9, 10)?
3. Describe the "horror of great darkness" that fell upon Abram (v. 12).
4. What long-term promise did God make in verse 14?

Faith and the Covenant

descendants so that when the time of oppression in Egypt came, the people might remember that God's covenant was not null and void. Instead, God was setting them up to display His glory through them to the entire world.

C. Covenant Established Through Sacrifice (vv. 17, 18)

17. And it came to pass, that, when the sun went down, and it was dark, behold a smoking furnace, and a burning lamp that passed between those pieces. 18. In the same day the Lord made a covenant with Abram, saying, Unto thy seed have I given this land, from the river of Egypt unto the great river, the river Euphrates.

With the pieces of the sacrifice arranged in their proper place, the Lord caused a smoking pot and a blazing torch to pass along the center row created by the animal parts. These cryptic elements probably mirrored the typical tools of ancient sacrifice. The clay pot would have been used for baking, and the torch for fire. Sacrifices were usually cooked, then eaten, before the god being honored. This, however, was no ordinary sacrificial meal.

The practice of walking upon the blood flow between arranged animal halves in order to create a covenant between families is still practiced by the Middle Eastern nomadic Bedouins today—a practice reaching all the way back to Genesis 15. Here it accentuated the fact that God did not ask Abram to offer a sacrifice in order to effect a covenant, He did it Himself. Up until now in Abram's life, God had issued grand and glorious promises. To enforce the validity of these promises once and for all, God now "cut" a covenant with Abram, setting the promise in stone. Blood was shed and there was no turning back on His word. Abram's descendants could claim rightful ownership of the entire Promised Land, even when numerous other peoples oppose them.

II. COVENANT DOUBTED (Genesis 16:1-16)

We have gotten quite used to the roller-coaster progression of Abram's life. It seems that just when he is given a breakthrough word from God, the story takes a turn for the worse. After his initial calling, he fled to Egypt because of a famine. After God restored him, he was betrayed by his nephew. After rescuing Lot, he faced a sticky situation with the evil king of Sodom. Now, after God enters into solemn covenant with him, guaranteeing that a flesh-and-blood heir is on the way, the covenant couple gets impatient and acts hastily.

A. A Costly Misstep (vv. 1-5)

1. Now Sarai Abram's wife bare him no children: and

Talk About It:
1. What was the significance of the "blazing torch" (NIV) that appeared (v. 17)?
2. How specific was the covenant God made here? Why?

she had an handmaid, an Egyptian, whose name was Hagar.

2. And Sarai said unto Abram, Behold now, the Lord hath restrained me from bearing: I pray thee, go in unto my maid; it may be that I may obtain children by her. And Abram hearkened to the voice of Sarai.

3. And Sarai Abram's wife took Hagar her maid the Egyptian, after Abram had dwelt ten years in the land of Canaan, and gave her to her husband Abram to be his wife.

4. And he went in unto Hagar, and she conceived: and when she saw that she had conceived, her mistress was despised in her eyes.

5. And Sarai said unto Abram, My wrong be upon thee: I have given my maid into thy bosom; and when she saw that she had conceived, I was despised in her eyes: the Lord judge between me and thee.

The waiting must have been excruciating. Neither one of them was getting any younger, yet the miracle seemed as far away as the stars to which God had likened their offspring. Sarai, intelligent as she was, had an idea. Abram could become a father by sleeping with Hagar, the maidservant of Sarai.

Helping God out had never seemed so easy. They didn't need to wait a day longer! After all, God's promise had not specifically mentioned Sarai. It was through Abram's seed that the nation would be born. Sarai's proposal mirrored a common practice in this time period. Abram would sleep with one of the household servants in order to have a rightful heir. Although he didn't come up with the plan, Abram agreed with it.

Sometimes the ancient world seems so different from ours, and other times it looks just the same. Unsurprisingly, the sexual relationship between Abram and Hagar resulted in a strained love triangle. Because of her pregnancy, Hagar became proud and arrogant. Yet she must remain subordinate to Sarai.

Sarai was very angry, and she blamed Abram for everything. She gave him a tongue-lashing, even going so far as to invoke the sacred name of Yahweh. Their brilliant plan to see God's promise come to pass on their own terms had provided not joy, but strife upon strife. Despite this horrid mistake, God stepped onto the scene to give grace in the midst of the misunderstanding.

B. The Birth of Ishmael (vv. 6-16)
(Genesis 16:6, 7, 11-14 is not included in the printed text.)

8. And he said, Hagar, Sarai's maid, whence camest thou? and whither wilt thou go? And she said, I flee from the face of my mistress Sarai.

9. And the angel of the Lord said unto her, Return to thy

mistress, and submit thyself under her hands.

10. And the angel of the Lord said unto her, I will multiply thy seed exceedingly, that it shall not be numbered for multitude.

15. And Hagar bare Abram a son: and Abram called his son's name, which Hagar bare, Ishmael.

16. And Abram was fourscore and six years old, when Hagar bare Ishmael to Abram.

When Hagar could stand Sarai's harshness no longer, she left. In deep compassion, God dispensed "the angel of the Lord" to find her. God would not allow her to disconnect herself from Sarai and Abram and so lose out on His blessing over their household. In reward for her faithfulness, and perhaps in pity over her situation, God promised that He has heard her misery loud and clear, and her son should be named *Ishmael*, meaning "God hears." What is more, he too will become a great nation in its own right, although his birth into conflict will never be shaken loose. The nation born from him would live in constant conflict.

Scholars believe that Ishmael's descendants became the many Arab nations. If this is correct, the angel's prophecy has been completely true, as Arabs continue to live in dangerous conflict with Jews, even over the very Promised Land inhabited by Abram. Even with this forewarning, Hagar is comforted, creating a new designation for Yahweh as "You-Are-the-God-Who-Sees" (v. 13, *NKJV*).

Perhaps God made this obstacle into a stepping-stone for Abram after all. For at 86 years old, producing any child was no small feat. One imagines that Abram enjoyed a rush of pride in his new son, but also couldn't shake the stress of wondering when God would make good on the promise for Sarai also. In fact, he would wait another 13 years for the good news. God wasn't finished solidifying His covenant.

III. COVENANT SIGN REQUIRED (Genesis 17:1-13;
    Colossians 2:10-13)

Thirteen years have transpired between Genesis 16 and 17, and we are left to guess at the content of Abram's life during this interim period. We can suppose that he raised the young boy Ishmael, of course, and that he continued to wander the land God promised to his descendants. God has no qualms about taking another 13 years to shape Abram's heart in preparation for the next monumental step of his spiritual journey. The covenant divinely enacted in chapter 15 must now be divinely confirmed.

A. Covenant Confirmed (17:1-13)
    (Genesis 17:11-13 is not included in the printed text.)

1. And when Abram was ninety years old and nine, the

Ishmael (ISH-may-ell)—v. 15— Abram's firstborn son, his name meaning "God hears."

Talk About It:
1. How was the angel's promise to Hagar (vv. 10-12) similar to God's promise to Abram (15:5), and how was it different?
2. Explain Hagar's statement in verse 13, "I have now seen the One who sees me" (*NIV*).
3. Based on Abram's action in verse 15, what did he know about Hagar's encounter with God?

Lord appeared to Abram, and said unto him, I am the Almighty God; walk before me, and be thou perfect.

2. And I will make my covenant between me and thee, and will multiply thee exceedingly.

3. And Abram fell on his face: and God talked with him, saying,

4. As for me, behold, my covenant is with thee, and thou shalt be a father of many nations.

5. Neither shall thy name any more be called Abram, but thy name shall be Abraham; for a father of many nations have I made thee.

6. And I will make thee exceeding fruitful, and I will make nations of thee, and kings shall come out of thee.

7. And I will establish my covenant between me and thee and thy seed after thee in their generations for an everlasting covenant, to be a God unto thee, and to thy seed after thee.

8. And I will give unto thee, and to thy seed after thee, the land wherein thou art a stranger, all the land of Canaan, for an everlasting possession; and I will be their God.

9. And God said unto Abraham, Thou shalt keep my covenant therefore, thou, and thy seed after thee in their generations.

10. This is my covenant, which ye shall keep, between me and you and thy seed after thee; Every man child among you shall be circumcised.

Talk About It:
1. How did God tell Abram to walk and live (v. 1)? What does this mean?
2. Why did God change his name to "Abraham"?
3. Why is the word *everlasting* used twice (vv. 7, 8)?
4. What is the significance of circumcision?

The reappearance of Yahweh in Abram's old age served another distinctive purpose. The covenant had been sealed in blood by God himself in chapter 15. But now God had a rite for Abram to undergo. Perhaps doubt had again risen in Abram's heart over the truth of this covenant, so when the time was right, God steps onto the scene again to confirm the reality of the former promise.

Abraham was immediately struck by the introduction of a new designation for Yahweh—"the Almighty God" (v. 1). This name in its original Hebrew terminology is still spoken in the Christian church today: *El-Shaddai*. The name refers primarily to God's sovereignty; that is, God is the One who is in control. Therefore, He assured Abram that the covenant had not been forgotten. He would still have countless offspring, and God intended to confirm this truth once and for all.

Yahweh actually *appeared* to Abram this time. Initially he had only spoken to him (12:1), and later He appeared in a vision (15:1); but here, as in 12:7, there is some sort of an appearance of God. In response to this overwhelming epiphany, Abram fell prostrate before God. His life was about to definitively change forever.

Faith and the Covenant

First, Abram's name was changed. The old name meant "esteemed father," while the new name, *Abraham*, meant "father of many." Abraham was likely too awestruck by the presence of God to recognize the irony of the situation, for this "father of many" still had not one fully legitimate blood-heir in his household. Second, when Abraham's promised offspring arrived and the nation began to multiply, they were commanded to physically mark themselves in a distinguishing manner through circumcision.

God then gave specific instructions concerning how this circumcision was to be ceremonially carried out by all parents of newborn boys throughout every Jewish generation (17:11-13). In fact, the covenant of circumcision was to extend to any and all males under Israeli households, including servants and other employees. As God had effected the covenant through the shedding of blood in chapter 15, he expected Abraham to shed blood to confirm it here. The bloodshed on the male sex organ, symbolizing the blessed continuation and propagation of the Abrahamic race (Israel), would be a constant reminder to the people of their history and their dependence on *El-Shaddai*.

> "Faith does not operate in the realm of the possible. There is no glory in that which is humanly possible. Faith begins where man's power ends."
> **—George Muller**

B. Covenant Sign Transformed (Colossians 2:10-13)

10. And ye are complete in him, which is the head of all principality and power:

11. In whom also ye are circumcised with the circumcision made without hands, in putting off the body of the sins of the flesh by the circumcision of Christ:

12. Buried with him in baptism, wherein also ye are risen with him through the faith of the operation of God, who hath raised him from the dead.

13. And you, being dead in your sins and the uncircumcision of your flesh, hath he quickened together with him, having forgiven you all trespasses.

For thousands of years, the Jews have continued to obey God's covenant of circumcision with Abraham. In fact, mostly for health reasons, the practice of circumcision is common for Gentiles in modern developing nations, especially the United States. This makes it easy to forget that during the time of the early church, circumcision was one of the most pressing theological issues to be found. In fact, it often threatened to divide the fledgling new faith community. The Book of Galatians, for example, reveals that fundamentalist Jewish-Christian leaders had infiltrated the church by preaching that salvation depended not only on Jesus Christ, but also on the covenant of physical circumcision—a problem dealt with decisively by the Jerusalem Council in Acts 15. The apostle Paul led the charge against this unsound doctrine in both instances. In his letter to

Talk About It:
1. How is God described in verse 10, and what is He able to do?
2. How are people "buried" and "raised" in Christ (v. 12)?

Daily Devotions:
M. God Keeps His Promises
    Exodus 6:1-8
T. God Never Forgets His Promises
    Psalm 105:8-15
W. God Promised a New Covenant
    Jeremiah 31:31-34
T. Glory of the New Covenant
    2 Corinthians 3:1-11
F. God's Promises Are Certain
    Hebrews 6:13-20
S. A Better Covenant
    Hebrews 12:18-24

the Colossians, Paul explained why the covenant of circumcision was still intact, but in a different way.

It is not that the new covenant abolished the things of the old, particularly the sign of circumcision. Instead, through Christ, God had transformed the sign of circumcision from a physical, human act to a supernatural, spiritual one. Through the mystery of salvation as evidenced in baptism, Jesus himself "cuts" into our heart and marks us forever, undoing the destruction of the uncircumcised, sinful nature, and placing us in right standing with God the Father. It is amazing to think that this powerful reality began with a desert nomad named Abraham, yet it is true. Modern-day Christians are indebted to him for paying the price to be the first one to enter a covenant with Yahweh, so that Jesus could later come and enact an eternal covenant.

CONCLUSION

We cannot understand the nature of God's relationship with people as taught by Scripture without grasping the vital concept of covenant. Its rituals, as expressed in Abraham's life, can seem a little archaic to us—sacrifice, circumcision, bloodshed. Yet as the New Testament proves, these were a sign of things to come. For Jesus Christ, the ultimate sacrifice, enacted a new covenant for us through the shedding of His own blood. The story of Abraham helps us to anticipate the gospel message through his covenant with God.

GOLDEN TEXT CHALLENGE

"HE [ABRAHAM] BELIEVED IN THE LORD; AND HE [GOD] COUNTED IT TO HIM FOR RIGHTEOUSNESS" (Genesis 15:6).

The Lord saw that Abraham now understood that all His promises were received by faith and all blessings that came to people were by God's unmerited favor; they were not deserved or earned—they came purely because God wanted to bless humanity. Abraham felt his own unworthiness and inability to keep the covenant in his own strength. God counted Abraham's faith as righteousness.

The greatest blessing of all is God's gift of His Son, Jesus Christ, for the salvation of everyone who believes on Him. Just as Abraham seemed physically incapable of keeping the covenant by having children, we are spiritually incapable of pleasing God by ourselves. We can be saved only by believing that Jesus saves us.

Faith to Believe and Intercede

Genesis 18:1-33

INTRODUCTION

At the heart of a vibrant, healthy faith is basic communication. God calls us to the essential task of being in ongoing interaction with Him. In fact, the primary means by which any relationship is established and maintained is simple conversation. Relationships are grown through hours of talking.

The life of Abraham exemplifies this emphasis on communication, and sets a standard followed by the other faith heroes of the Bible. After his faith has developed to maturity, God increases His conversation with Abraham to a new level. No longer does Abraham simply listen while God talks. No longer does Abraham feel that he is just following a "voice" somewhere out there. Instead, Abraham is invited into a dynamic relationship where he is allowed to question, contest, and deal with God's terms, perhaps even with a chance of changing God's mind! We see this first in Genesis 15, where Abram finally asks God some tough questions about how exactly this covenant will take place, seeing as how there are no babies in sight and he is already an old man married to an old woman. This was less conversation, however, and more rapid-fire question-and-answer. In chapter 18 the tone of the dialogue has significantly changed, moving to a more mature level. It is here that we learn most directly about intercessory prayer within the lifestyle of faith.

Perhaps the most difficult aspect to these texts for modern Christian readers to make sense of is the nature of prayer itself. When Abraham addresses God, he is doing so in a vision, or to an angel, or to the literal presence of God himself. Therefore, his conversation with God in many ways mirrors any conversation between two people of that time. Since God has expressed Himself definitively in Jesus Christ for all times, we rarely see such experiences of physical conversation with Yahweh today. However, the conversations Abraham has with God still have the power to teach us how to pray. We learn, for instance, that we can be honest and express our feelings. We learn that God can handle our toughest questions. And most importantly, we learn that God passionately desires to be in conversation with us.

Unit Theme:
Abraham

Central Truth:
God invites His children to dialogue with Him.

Focus:
Believe God interacts with His people and welcome opportunities for intercession and fellowship with Him.

Context:
Around 1900 B.C. on the plains of Mamre and in Sodom and Gomorrah

Golden Text:
"Abraham answered and said, Behold now, I have taken upon me to speak unto the Lord, which am but dust and ashes" (Genesis 18:27).

Study Outline:
I. Faith to Welcome God (Genesis 18:1-8)
II. Called to Believe Beyond Reason (Genesis 18:9-15)
III. Faith to Intercede (Genesis 18:16-33)

I. FAITH TO WELCOME GOD (Genesis 18:1-8)

A primary tenet of salvation is that it takes simple faith to accept Jesus Christ into one's heart. This was the rallying cry of the 16th-century Protestant Reformation, as the great Christian leader Martin Luther held up the standard of *sola fida*—faith alone—for salvation, apart from the works-oriented righteousness of the Roman Church of his day. The truth is not that there is a vast chasm between faith and works, but that faith is the only means by which salvation may be received. From faith flows good works. We see this doctrine clearly represented in the life of Abraham, as his spiritual journey of faith continues to develop.

A. Strengthening Abraham's Faith (vv. 1, 2)

1. And the Lord appeared unto him in the plains of Mamre: and he sat in the tent door in the heat of the day;

2. And he lift up his eyes and looked, and, lo, three men stood by him: and when he saw them, he ran to meet them from the tent door, and bowed himself toward the ground.

Talk About It:
How did Abraham respond to the three surprise visitors, and why?

There was still more waiting. It must have been slow, painful and excruciating. In chapter 17, Abram received his new name upon believing, and then the covenant of his great offspring was confirmed through the sign of circumcision. Surely that would be the time God would bless him with the news of a son! Instead, he went back home to his tent just as clueless about how exactly this would all play out as he ever had been. Added to this was the ironic reality that his name had been changed to "father of many." Strangers probably chuckled to themselves when they met this prosperous nomad named "father of many" who had no children, save one son born to a handmaiden. But things changed for Abraham when three visitors stopped by.

Abraham had become familiar with appearances of Yahweh. For around 25 years now, God had been stepping onto the scene from time to time to remind Abraham of the original covenant that he was going to make his progeny into a great nation of people. At this point Abraham had seen God's power too often and too closely to doubt God. But the issue of his growing old was front and center in his mind. We know that Abraham was 99 years old in chapter 17 and Sarah was 90 (v. 17). However, an unstated amount of time has transpired since then and they may be much older. Abraham had not forgotten that God had promised him a son, but was his faith weakening?

This time Yahweh mysteriously visited in the form of three men. Even in the initial appearances, Abraham did not likely look at God with his physical eyes, if God can even be seen to begin with. We do not know what Abraham actually saw, if anything. Through the three men, however, Abraham could engage God's messengers physically, which must have been a welcomed

Faith to Believe and Intercede

change. At this point, more words from God were inadequate. The nomad needed to see and to touch. The fact that Yahweh visited Abraham in the form of three men may also be the first direct reference to the triune nature of God in the Scriptures. Although the word *trinity* does not appear in either Testament, Christians affirm one God eternally coexistent in three persons. There are hints of this plurality in the Creation narrative, where God says, "Let *us* make man in *our* image" (Genesis 1:26; italics added). Here, however, the divine visitation of three figures marks a new milestone in the spiritual journey of Abraham, strengthening his faith.

> "So long as we imagine it is we who have to look for God, we most often lose heart. But is the other way about— He is looking for us."
> —Simon Tugwell

B. Passionately Pursuing God (vv. 3-8)

3. And said, My Lord, if now I have found favour in thy sight, pass not away, I pray thee, from thy servant:

4. Let a little water, I pray you, be fetched, and wash your feet, and rest yourselves under the tree:

5. And I will fetch a morsel of bread, and comfort ye your hearts; after that ye shall pass on: for therefore are ye come to your servant. And they said, So do, as thou hast said.

6. And Abraham hastened into the tent unto Sarah, and said, Make ready quickly three measures of fine meal, knead it, and make cakes upon the hearth.

7. And Abraham ran unto the herd, and fetcht a calf tender and good, and gave it unto a young man; and he hasted to dress it.

8. And he took butter, and milk, and the calf which he had dressed, and set it before them; and he stood by them under the tree, and they did eat.

We do not know how and when the three men were immediately recognized by Abraham to be Yahweh's messengers, but he wasted no time in reaching out to them. Hospitality was a staple of survival in the nomadic lifestyle, and to refuse hospitality was considered highly insulting. But social graces may not have been the only reason for Abraham's ardor. Perhaps he sensed something greater was at stake.

Abraham was not completely certain about the identity of the men. He suspected they might be departing soon and thus might need the food for nourishment. But he likely hoped otherwise. Perhaps their appearance was different than anyone else he had ever seen. Whatever the case, he instructed Sarah to bake a large amount of bread and then selected his best calf to be prepared by a household servant. In addition, curds and milk were served. This meal was not only financially costly, it was prepared in great haste. Abraham apparently anticipated that something wonderful was going to happen, and he wanted to

Talk About It:
Describe all the ways Abraham expressed hospitality to his guests.

> "Do not forget to entertain strangers, for by so doing some have unwittingly entertained angels" (Hebrews 13:2, *NKJV*).

keep these three mysterious visitors in his tent for as long as possible. Hospitality became a household effort in order to obtain the blessing about to come.

II. CALLED TO BELIEVE BEYOND REASON
(Genesis 18:9-15)

Hebrews 11:1 teaches that "faith is being sure of what we hope for and certain of what we do not see" (*NIV*). Faith is not a matter of seeing and believing, but of believing in order to someday see. This is the struggle of genuine Biblical faith, and all believers have known it, especially when the object of our hope seems impossible by human calculations. The faith of Abraham teaches us to never lose faith when hearing from God, even when His word sounds unreasonable or even beyond reason itself. What is laughable at first may wind up being literally true in the end.

A. God's Unreasonable Word (vv. 9-11)

9. And they said unto him, Where is Sarah thy wife? And he said, Behold, in the tent.

10. And he said, I will certainly return unto thee according to the time of life; and, lo, Sarah thy wife shall have a son. And Sarah heard it in the tent door, which was behind him.

11. Now Abraham and Sarah were old and well stricken in age; and it ceased to be with Sarah after the manner of women.

Talk About It:
How did Sarah hear the amazing news?

At this point, the attention in the story abruptly turns to Sarah. This must have been a strange moment for Abraham, who rather than eating with his visitors was simply standing near them, listening and waiting. He hoped that they would give him the instruction or blessing he needed from God to continue to walk faithfully with Him. Instead, they ask about the whereabouts of Sarah, probably wanting her to be close enough to hear their astounding promise: "I will surely return to you about this time next year, and Sarah your wife will have a son" (v. 10, *NIV*).

Scripture is clear that they were delivering the words of Yahweh. However, the nature of these visitors remains in question. Whether they were angels or a physical manifestation of God himself is not important. The words they say were Yahweh's words, just like in the past when God spoke to Abraham without the aid of the three men. Besides, a word this radical had to come from Yahweh—the God of the impossible.

Scientists today can occasionally prescribe fertility treatments that help a woman become pregnant in her 40s, or extremely occasionally in her 50s, but not in her 90s! In the ancient world, which did not have the luxury of modern medical treatments, infertility was a common medical problem, with dire social ramifications. Infertile women were often considered cursed by the gods, and thus were made outcasts. The word from Yahweh was as wild as saying that next year Abraham would be a licensed pilot for an airline company! Such a thing had never been heard of in the world, and it was too much for Sarah to handle.

B. Laughter Before Faith (vv. 12-15)

12. Therefore Sarah laughed within herself, saying, After I am waxed old shall I have pleasure, my lord being old also?

13. And the Lord said unto Abraham, Wherefore did Sarah laugh, saying, Shall I of a surety bear a child, which am old?

14. Is any thing too hard for the Lord? At the time appointed I will return unto thee, according to the time of life, and Sarah shall have a son.

15. Then Sarah denied, saying, I laughed not; for she was afraid. And he said, Nay; but thou didst laugh.

Until now, Sarah had been waiting patiently at the entrance of the tent, modestly hiding herself but straining to hear the conversation between Abraham and the mysterious visitors. What she heard floored her, so much so that she defied the conventions of hospitality. The notion of this prophecy from the visitors was hilarious to Sarah. Laughter spilled softly from the tent at the thought of it. Her body was worn, and her husband was even older. Or perhaps she laughed at the irony of Yahweh making her wait all of this time to finally give her the pleasure of her heart.

Talk About It:
1. Why did Sarah deny that she had laughed?
2. Why is nothing "too hard for the Lord" (v. 14)?

It is strange that although Abraham received this promise from the visitors sent from Yahweh, he was relegated to a secondary position in the story after the promise was announced. Instead, everything focused on the laughter, the disbelief, the disrespect of Sarah. In the face of her behavior, God reiterated the promise again, to ensure no one had heard incorrectly. Sarah—the same elderly, laughing woman in the tent—would birth a son within the next year. After regaining her composure, Sarah was embarrassed and craftily attempted to deny her laughter. Yahweh would have none of it, and the name *Isaac*, meaning "laughter," would forever remind the Jewish nation of her response that day.

Two principles can be taken from Sarah's behavior in this passage. First, nothing is said of Abraham's reaction, but he apparently did not join in her laughter. Whether he stood in stunned silence, sat down with his face in his hands, or jumped for joy is not known, but God specifically asked him not about his own laughter, but Sarah's. This implies that it was Sarah who had the lack of faith in God's word, not Abraham. Nonetheless, her faith could not prevent the divine plan from coming to pass. God did not need Sarah to believe. Abraham's faith was enough, and Sarah could ride the coattails of this spiritual giant. As Jesus would later say, just a tiny amount of faith is enough to move mountains (Matthew 17:20), and apparently God found at least that much between the two of them.

Second, it is significant that in the spiritual journey of Sarah, laughter comes before faith. The word of God is hilariously good, so good that it always offers a choice between dismissing it as fantasy or jumping out onto the high limbs of faith. As Frederick Buechner has written:

> Maybe the most interesting part of it all is that far from getting angry at them for laughing, God told them that when the baby was born he wanted to name him *Isaac*, which in Hebrew means "laughter." So you can say that God not only tolerated their laughter but blessed it and in a sense joined in it himself, which make it a very special laughter indeed—God and man laughing together, sharing a glorious joke in which both of them are involved. It is perhaps as important to look closely into the laughter of Abraham and Sarah as it is important to look closely into the tears of Jesus (*Telling the Truth*).

The gospel, whether being proclaimed by Jesus to the world or by the visitors to the family of Abraham, is always almost too good to be true. But the power is in the "almost." For what is impossible with man is possible with God.

III. FAITH TO INTERCEDE (Genesis 18:16-33)

A dramatic break in the context and content of Genesis 18 occurs when the divine visitors finish eating and depart Abraham's tent. The ensuing conversation provides Abraham a chance to prove the merits of his faith, which is far stronger than Sarah's has just proven to be. His bargaining with Yahweh has much to teach us about the faith necessary for Biblical intercessory prayer.

A. Standing Before the Lord (vv. 16-22)

(Genesis 18:16-19 is not included in the printed text.)

20. And the Lord said, Because the cry of Sodom and Gomorrah is great, and because their sin is very grievous;

21. I will go down now, and see whether they have done altogether according to the cry of it, which is come unto me; and if not, I will know.

22. And the men turned their faces from thence, and went

> "In God you come up against something which is in every way immeasurably superior to yourself.... As long as you are proud you cannot know God."
>
> —C.S. Lewis

Faith to Believe and Intercede

toward Sodom: but Abraham stood yet before the Lord.

Abraham's fervency to receive all that he could from the divine visitors is illustrated in the fact that he continued with them after they left his tent (v. 16). Next we get a rare glimpse into the mind of God, as the visitors consulted with one another as to whether they should divulge God's news about Sodom with Abraham. The consensus was that he should be told, since Yahweh had chosen him to live righteously and justly, contrasted with the going lifestyle of Sodom. Abraham should understand God's judgment so as to avoid it. But as the men turned toward Sodom to investigate the grievous sin there, "Abraham remained standing before the Lord" (v. 22, *NIV*).

B. Interceding for a City (vv. 23-33)
(Genesis 18:26-31 is not included in the printed text.)

23. And Abraham drew near, and said, Wilt thou also destroy the righteous with the wicked?

24. Peradventure there be fifty righteous within the city: wilt thou also destroy and not spare the place for the fifty righteous that are therein?

25. That be far from thee to do after this manner, to slay the righteous with the wicked: and that the righteous should be as the wicked, that be far from thee: Shall not the Judge of all the earth do right?

32. And he said, Oh let not the Lord be angry, and I will speak yet but this once: Peradventure ten shall be found there. And he said, I will not destroy it for ten's sake.

33. And the Lord went his way, as soon as he had left communing with Abraham: and Abraham returned unto his place.

The three visitors had not explicitly stated that Sodom would be destroyed; they only claimed to be investigating to see just how bad things had become. Abraham, however, didn't need any more data to see the truth. The city was a cesspool of sin and degradation. The results of their inquiry would be dire. If the city was to be saved, he had to jump into action. He asked the Lord, "Will you sweep away the righteous with the wicked?" (v. 23, *NIV*).

There was no time for small talk. Abraham had sniffed out the fact that God was about to wipe out Sodom, and he feared for his nephew, Lot, who lived there. Surely there were other righteous households that God would not destroy. He first appeals to the character of Yahweh himself.

How audacious the old nomad had become, lecturing God on what was out of bounds! But God showed no anger, no frustration. The Lord continued to agree with Abraham's terms, which decreased from 50 righteous persons to 10 very quickly.

Talk About It:
1. Why did the Lord not hide from Abraham His plan concerning Sodom (vv. 17-19)?
2. Explain the significance of the statement, "But Abraham stood yet before the Lord" (v. 22).

"Don't put people down—unless it's on your prayer list."
—Stan Michalski

Talk About It:
1. Explain the title Abraham attributes to God in verse 25 and its meaning.
2. Why did Abraham refer to himself as "dust and ashes" (v. 27)?
3. What do you learn about intercessory prayer from verses 28-32?

This passage serves as a remarkable example of the power of intercessory prayer. Incredibly, God allowed Abraham to set the terms of God's own judgment of the city. Of course, Abraham's participation had its limits. God never withdrew his judicial right to destroy the city for its evil, and Abraham did not argue that the city was less evil than God portended. They both agreed that Sodom was a terrible place that deserved to be eradicated from the face of the earth. Abraham's intercession focused not on the justice of God toward the wicked in that city, but on God's mercy toward the righteous. If He really was a covenant-making God, then His covenant was with all righteous individuals following His ways, including those who (for whatever reason) were living in Sodom. God could not just give up on them.

This passage not only exemplifies intercessory prayer, but also elicits the discussion of a major theological concern—the manner of God's participation with humanity. Those Christians who theologically adhere to a belief system called Calvinism have historically emphasized the sovereign nature of God. For Calvinists, God is unchanging and, therefore, no person can convince God to make a better decision. God's decisions are always best and will always come to pass, for they are preset. This passage appears to open up another option, but without downplaying or decreasing the sovereignty of God. Notice that Abraham is not taking control of God or the situation in the passage. He is consistently aware of his boldness in addressing God in the first place, and completely recognizes that the decision is fully up to God. Also, we will see later that Abraham's intercession did not save Sodom. There simply were not 10 righteous people in the city, so God destroyed it anyway. Being eternal and all-knowing, God knew the outcome of Sodom during His conversation with Abraham, but He still let Abraham participate in the processes of judgment and mercy. This is true prayer—not cajoling God to do what we want but participating with Him to actualize what He wants. God saw that Abraham's heart was softened and loving toward his nephew Lot and toward even the sinful city of Sodom. God honored Abraham's contrite heart, and later saved Lot and his household.

CONCLUSION

To enjoy fellowship with God is a wonderful gift He gives to today's church, but it did not start with us. God's extension of friendship and grace to Abraham began humanity's covenant relationship with God, and still provides a relevant example for how we can remain in ongoing communication with our heavenly Father. Even when Sarah laughed in God's face, and when Abraham pled for the city of Sodom, God honored the

---

Betting on Prayer
In June 2004, *The Christian Century* reported that Christians are twice as likely as unbelievers to buy lottery tickets. These findings stunned researchers, who expected Christians to be more careful about gambling their money. They found, however, that the statistics were connected to prayer. Christians hoped that God would grant their request for instant wealth, and so acted on their faith by purchasing lottery tickets. Too often, we approach prayer as if it is a way to get our wish list granted. Instead, prayer should move us closer to the heart of God.

fact that they were committed to relationship with Him. By doing this they pleased God's heart, for He longs for our fellowship.

GOLDEN TEXT CHALLENGE

"ABRAHAM ANSWERED AND SAID, BEHOLD NOW, I HAVE TAKEN UPON ME TO SPEAK UNTO THE LORD, WHICH AM BUT DUST AND ASHES" (Genesis 18:27).

Abraham approached God with the right combination of boldness and humility. He could be bold because he was confident in the character of the Lord God and in his relationship with Him. He did what the writer of Hebrews urges us to do: "Let us therefore come boldly unto the throne of grace, that we may obtain mercy, and find grace to help in time of need" (4:16).

However, Abraham was not arrogant. He referred to himself as *dust* (the lightest particles of earth) and *ashes* (the remainders of consumed substances) in the sight of the Lord. Yet he stood in the gap on behalf of Lot and Sodom, just as God wants us to humbly yet boldly intercede on behalf of our unsaved loved ones and sin-ravaged cities.

Daily Devotions:
M. Noah Walked
   With God
   Genesis 6:5-9
T. God's Presence
   With Us
   Exodus 33:12-17
W. Nehemiah
   Pleaded for
   Judah
   Nehemiah 1:4-11
T. Jesus Interceded
   for His Disciples
   John 17:6-15
F. Walking With
   God
   1 John 1:3, 5-7
S. God With Us
   Revelation 21:1-4

Faith Tested

Genesis 22:1-18

INTRODUCTION

The reality that God tests His followers is among the most difficult to fathom fully in Scripture, especially the Old Testament. Although the New Testament gives us a clear picture of the enemy of our souls, the devil, who prowls around like "a roaring lion . . . seeking whom he may devour" (1 Peter 5:8), the Old Testament includes only a few references to Satan at all. This directly confronts our tendency to view the world through the lenses of what theologians call dualism. A dualistic view considers God locked in a cosmic battle with Satan, with everything happening to us connected to that battle. This often results in trying times being blamed solely on the devil.

In Scripture, however, more often than not it is in fact God who sends trying times our way, or at least consciously allows them. It is God who allows the Israelites to be oppressed in Egypt for four centuries. It is God who approves the Babylonians' sacking of Jerusalem in the time of Jeremiah. It is God who lets the early church experience persecution under the Roman Empire. Even in Job, where Satan plays a leading role, he acts only under the authority and command of God. In fact, he still conducts himself like an angel, coming before God, asking permission. Whether we understand the theological intricacies of it or not, Scripture clearly communicates that God is usually the One who sends trials our way to test us.

The greater question has to do with the focus of the testing. Principally, does God test us in order to get insight into our spiritual maturity? Surely not! An all-knowing, all-powerful God lacks no knowledge about our lives. Instead, God's testing allows us to benefit through victoriously emerging after a trying time through His power. These victories, even small ones, go into a sort of "spiritual bank" in our hearts and minds to draw from when greater challenges come. God knows what is in us. He wants us to know as well, so we can be confident in His ability to bring us through. These truths are graphically illustrated in perhaps the most famous story associated with Abraham's life: the near-death experience of his son Isaac.

I. AN UNTHINKABLE COMMAND (Genesis 22:1-5)

In John 6:60, many followers of Jesus abandoned Him after a particularly difficult teaching, exclaiming that it was just too much of a "hard saying." Scripture has many hard words, but perhaps no one received one more difficult than Abraham. This uncharacteristic command of Yahweh threatened every sacrifice Abraham had made to follow His plan in the first place. Thus, Genesis 22 challenges not only Abraham's faith to a new level, but the Bible reader's also.

A. A Dreadful Journey (vv. 1-3)

1. And it came to pass after these things, that God did tempt Abraham, and said unto him, Abraham: and he said, Behold, here I am.

2. And he said, Take now thy son, thine only son Isaac, whom thou lovest, and get thee into the land of Moriah; and offer him there for a burnt offering upon one of the mountains which I will tell thee of.

3. And Abraham rose up early in the morning, and saddled his ass, and took two of his young men with him, and Isaac his son, and clave the wood for the burnt offering, and rose up, and went unto the place of which God had told him.

Even the opening of this story is different from what we've become used to while reading through the life of Abraham. Typically, each individual narrative begins with the word of God simply coming to Abraham either through a vision or through unspecified means (as do most similar narratives in the Old Testament). It is assumed that Abraham somehow hears God's voice loud and clear as the word is given. Here, however, God startles His wandering nomad with an abrupt call, perhaps belying the suddenness of the instruction.

Abraham wasted no time in responding to God. He had been remarkably blessed since their last encounter, not only enjoying his new son, Isaac, but also forming a strategic alliance with Abimelech, king of Gerar (21:22-34). He finally had the raw material—Isaac—for the covenant promise of God to be fulfilled. He waited on God to explain this in further detail, but instead received an astonishing message from Yahweh: sacrifice Isaac as a burnt offering.

It is almost impossible to imagine the shock that rattled through Abraham's mind and body at the hearing of these words. The God whom he had trusted completely appeared to be turning against him. Recall that the history of God's calling of Abraham had focused on his legitimate offspring. God entered into a sacred, unbreakable covenant with him in chapter 15, confirmed it with the sign of circumcision in chapter 17, and then finally brought it to pass in chapter 21. Now the entire foundation

Talk About It:
1. In what sense does God "tempt" people (v. 1)?
2. Why do you suppose God described Isaac as He did in verse 2?
3. What is significant about Abraham rising up "early in the morning" (v. 3)?

of their relationship was being unexpectedly threatened by God himself. We can only imagine the thoughts of Abraham. Perhaps he reckoned that he had been wrong about Yahweh and His covenant; it really was breakable. Perhaps he guessed that God was judging him for again using his wife to get ahead (ch. 20), or for making a treaty at Beersheba (21:31). Perhaps he sighed a long sigh at yet another dramatic twist in this covenant story and could only wonder what Yahweh would do next. Or, perhaps he had a burning faith even at the hearing of the command that God would come through somehow again— that even if Isaac were lost, God would miraculously provide another heir. But even that optimistic thought couldn't have made it much easier to plan to kill his and Sarah's only son.

The most difficult thoughts, however, that Abraham must have wrestled with centered on Yahweh himself. Child sacrifice was prevalent among the pagan religions in the ancient Near East of his day. Abraham knew of them and may have even witnessed them in his previous life of paganism. He had been drawn to Yahweh for His love, grace and compassion, but now his thoughts turned dark. *Can Yahweh be just like those other gods? Is He any different?* For Abraham, what was at stake was the very character, nature and integrity of God. Would Yahweh prove Himself as He had in the past, or would this be the end of their covenant together?

With these questions, doubts and frustrations undoubtedly ringing in his brain, Abraham got up early and set out anyway. He even saddled his own donkey and chopped the wood himself, despite having plenty of servants who usually did these kinds of things for him. Perhaps he hoped that God would interrupt the process after Abraham got the donkey ready, or after the wood was cut. But he heard nothing—nothing except the details concerning the precise location Isaac was to be killed. Nonetheless, Abraham kept faith in the character of Yahweh, though he could not have understood what was going on, and headed toward the place of ultimate sacrifice.

B. Faith in the Fire (vv. 4, 5)

4. Then on the third day Abraham lifted up his eyes, and saw the place afar off.

5. And Abraham said unto his young men, Abide ye here with the ass; and I and the lad will go yonder and worship, and come again to you.

To properly understand Abraham's next words, we must be careful to locate this story in the larger life of Abraham. Many times people are led to doubt God's character by reading this passage without its surrounding context. Recall that Abraham had been walking with Yahweh now for over 25 years. They had a great history together of ongoing fellowship through prayer

"We are not necessarily doubting that God will do the best for us; we are wondering how painful the best will turn out to be."

—C.S. Lewis

Talk About It:
How did Abraham describe the purpose of his journey to his servants (v. 5)?

Faith Tested

and worship. Abraham had been obedient to God's commandments, and his household had prospered greatly as a result. His faith was no longer immature and fledgling; it was seasoned and rock-solid.

For three days Abraham had journeyed, hoping with every step that Yahweh would call the deal off and reward him for assenting to it up to that point. But such a word never came. Instead, the awful place of sacrifice came into view. Most ordinary men and women would never have even started the journey, much less remained strong to this point. Despite the questions swirling like a torrent in Abraham's mind, he would not discard his mature faith. Even in such a critical situation, it came through loud and clear. "He said to his servants, 'Stay here with the donkey while I and the boy go over there. We will worship and then we will come back to you'" (v. 5, NIV).

What an incredible statement of faith! Neither the servants nor Isaac knew the commandment Abraham had received, so it meant nothing to them. They probably assumed this was a routine time of worship and sacrifice, and that Isaac was brought along so as to be introduced to the family religion. But the resounding cry of veteran faith lies in Abraham's announcement that both he and Isaac "will come back." Abraham made a choice to completely trust the character of God. He threw himself into the faithful arms of Yahweh, truly believing he would not fall to the ground.

II. WITHHOLD NOTHING (Genesis 22:6-12)

The stage has now been set for a wonderfully dramatic scene. The writer of Genesis draws the reader into the story with graphic details, such as the donkey's saddle, the wood for the fire, and the servants in the journey. Obviously, the passage calls us to slow down and read carefully. Genesis here is offering careful insight into what is involved in a spiritual journey with Yahweh. Although Abraham has proven himself faithful for over 25 years, God never stops shaping him, bringing him to a place of total reliance on Him.

A. Persistent Faith (vv. 6-8)

6. And Abraham took the wood of the burnt offering, and laid it upon Isaac his son; and he took the fire in his hand, and a knife; and they went both of them together.

7. And Isaac spake unto Abraham his father, and said, My father: and he said, Here am I, my son. And he said, Behold the fire and the wood: but where is the lamb for a burnt offering?

8. And Abraham said, My son, God will provide himself a lamb for a burnt offering: so they went both of them together.

Too Loud?
Hundreds of schools are using a device to control noise levels in cafeterias. The device looks like a traffic light and measures whether noise is acceptable, loud, or too loud by signaling green, yellow, or red. God's testing in our lives works much the same way. When we go through a difficult time, we are made aware of the distractions around us that drown out the voice of God, so God can then show us the parts of our lives He wants to change.

Talk About It:
1. What was Isaac carrying, and what did Abraham carry? What was missing?
2. In what sense did it seem God had already provided "the lamb"?

"Faith has to do with things that are not seen and hope with things that are not at hand."
—Thomas Aquinas

Tension mounted as the unknowing, innocent boy noticed the strangeness of the situation. Abraham had prepared meticulously, bringing the wood, instruments of fire, and sharp knife. But they were missing the central ornament of sacrificial worship. Significantly, Isaac asked about the lamb for the burnt offering, denoting that this was the animal Abraham typically used for such sacrifices. In fact, this is the first reference to sacrificing a lamb in the Bible, and the messianic significance is potent. New windows of meaning are unlocked for the passage when we recognize that 2,000 years later, God would allow His own Son to be sacrificed as a spotless lamb for the sins of the world. Abraham, of course, knew nothing of this future aspect of salvation history, but he did not need to in order to trust God. He answered his son's question with another display of bold yet simple faith, declaring that God himself would provide the lamb.

Just as Abraham had spoken in faith to his servants by proclaiming that both he and the boy would be returning after their time of worship, he expressed the same faith to his son. Although he didn't know when or how, he knew Yahweh, and he believed that something great would happen. But even if it did not, he was bent on obeying the command of God. Abraham's maturity teaches us much about the vital balance between faith and obedience. While his faith likely wavered during the journey to the place of sacrifice, his obedience did not. As a result, his commitment to obedience positively influenced his level of faith, and he was able to make such pronouncements against all available evidence. Again, he had nothing but God to hope in.

B. Proven Faith (vv. 9-12)

9. And they came to the place which God had told him of; and Abraham built an altar there, and laid the wood in order, and bound Isaac his son, and laid him on the altar upon the wood.

10. And Abraham stretched forth his hand, and took the knife to slay his son.

11. And the angel of the Lord called unto him out of heaven, and said, Abraham, Abraham: and he said, Here am I.

12. And he said, Lay not thine hand upon the lad, neither do thou any thing unto him: for now I know that thou fearest God, seeing thou hast not withheld thy son, thine only son from me.

The previous, innocent question is all the author records of the reaction of Isaac in the story. We aren't given his age or demeanor. We don't know if he was compliant in the act, or if he struggled tooth and nail to escape his father's grasp. By any and all means necessary, Abraham would obey God, even when he didn't understand the commandment.

The process for preparing such a sacrifice was quite involved.

Talk About It:
1. Why do you suppose Isaac did not question his father as he was placed on the altar?

Faith Tested

The altar was constructed from large stones, stacked precariously on top of one another. The wood had to then be arranged so it would properly burn the sacrifice without crumpling off of the altar. And the sacrifice itself was no small animal, but a boy who wanted to live. Abraham continued to listen for a stay of execution, but none was given. He went forward with the ritual.

Many notable painters have depicted this scene throughout the history of the church, such as Laurent de LaHire's "Abraham Sacrificing Isaac" in 1650. The paintings inevitably depict an elderly Abraham lifting the sharpened blade high above the boy Isaac's neck, beginning its downward motion just as an angel is rushing onto the scene in terror. The Hebrew word *melek* means either "angel" or "messenger," leading us to wonder if this angel/messenger of Yahweh could be a reappearance of one of the three visitors in chapter 18. However, this assumption and the depiction of the painters may be dead wrong, for the Scripture does not technically record an *appearance* of the angel. Instead, Abraham hears a solitary voice call his name just as in 22:1. He may have seen nothing at all. Only this voice cries out his name twice, indicating urgency. Abraham's response is identical to verse 1: the simple, humble reply, "Here I am." He probably exhaled deeply, trembling as he spoke these words. Yet in them his strong faith shone brightly. Even after this torturous experience, he was just as eager to hear the word of the Lord, and just as ready to receive His instruction.

The execution is stayed and the drama is over. Now it is clearly known that Abraham honors God completely, even to the point of offering his only son.

The angel of the Lord said, "Do not lay a hand on the boy" (v. 12, *NIV*). Of course, Abraham's faith was not new information for God. He did not need to test him in order to discern his faith. The test was not for God's benefit, but for Abraham's. His performance, though, impressed even the angel of the Lord, who applauded his remarkable faith.

III. GOD PROVIDES (Genesis 22:13-18)

Interestingly, the passage does not end at verse 12. It certainly could, with the result that Abraham would once again be lifted up as a model of mature faith. But God was not yet finished teaching Abraham and Isaac through this experience. Also, He had a special reward for this choice servant's heart of total obedience.

A. Animal Sacrifice Preferred (v. 13)

13. And Abraham lifted up his eyes, and looked, and behold behind him a ram caught in a thicket by his horns: and Abraham went and took the ram, and offered him up for a burnt-offering in the stead of his son.

While they were reeling from this close call, even as Isaac was

2. Why was Abraham willing to sacrifice Isaac?

"Faith for my deliverance is not faith in God. Faith means, whether I am delivered or not, I will stick to my belief that God is love. There are some things learned only in a fiery furnace."
—Oswald Chambers

still bound and lying on the altar, they heard some rustling close by. Though Isaac had expected a lamb in verse 7, these did not typically roam free in the mountains. And even if they did, they could be hard to catch. Wild rams, however, could easily be caught with their horns snagging them in thorns, and this is exactly what God provided. Interestingly, the Scripture does not explicitly say God had anything to do with the ram, but Abraham was convinced it was the provision of Yahweh. Therefore, he offered it as a sacrifice. Notice the descriptive language of the sacrifice. The writer deliberately spells out the gravity of the situation: the ram was sacrificed in the direct place of Isaac, Abraham's son.

Historically, this text has been taken by the Jews to function as God explicitly setting the standard of animal sacrifice for His people Israel, as opposed to human or child sacrifice. As previously mentioned, human sacrifice was prevalent among pagan religions in the Old Testament age. By the time of the later books of the Torah, it was popular enough in Canaan to be expressly forbidden by God (Leviticus 18:21). The story of Abraham's testing provides a narrative example for all such commandments, and sets Israel apart as a community that is holy to Yahweh. Just as the sacrifice of Abel proved that Yahweh preferred costly animal sacrifices over less expensive plant offerings, so this passage proves His preference of animal rather than human sacrifice. Instead of sacrificing their firstborn son, they would consecrate him by virtue of an offering (Numbers 18:15).

"Worship is not a text but a context; it is not an isolated experience in life, but a series of live experiences."

—Gary Gulbranson

With the burnt offering of the ram, then, Abraham's original promise to his servants in Genesis 22:5 comes full circle. Both he and Isaac take the opportunity to express heartfelt worship to Yahweh before returning home.

B. Ultimate Trust Expressed (vv. 14-18)

14. And Abraham called the name of that place Jehovah-jireh: as it is said to this day, In the mount of the Lord it shall be seen.

15. And the angel of the Lord called unto Abraham out of heaven the second time,

16. And said, By myself have I sworn, saith the Lord, for because thou hast done this thing, and hast not withheld thy son, thine only son:

17. That in blessing I will bless thee, and in multiplying I will multiply thy seed as the stars of the heaven, and as the sand which is upon the sea shore; and thy seed shall possess the gate of his enemies;

18. And in thy seed shall all the nations of the earth be blessed; because thou hast obeyed my voice.

In response to the gift of the ram, which was sacrificed in place of Isaac, Abraham resounds in praise to God. It was typical to honor God by naming a place where He had been given glory, which Abraham quickly does. He also begins a tradition associated with Mount Moriah that continues through the Old Testament history. He calls that place *Jehovah-jireh*, or "The Lord Will Provide" (v. 14, *NIV*).

The marvel of this text in the history of the Old Testament is that Solomon's temple is built in this precise location: "Then Solomon began to build the house of the Lord at Jerusalem in Mount Moriah" (2 Chronicles 3:1). The place where Abraham's ancient obedience was thoroughly tested and proved eventually became the place where Israel would meet with God day after day, century after century—the place of God's holy temple.

Because of Abraham's obedience to the Lord, the angel called to him again. He introduced his word with an oath formula from Yahweh himself. As had been said before, Abraham's descendants would be innumerable. God added the analogy of the sand on the seashore to the previous comparisons to dust and stars. God would bless them not only with fruitfulness but with authority also. They would rule the cities of the Promised Land. And most significantly, the entire earth would be blessed because Abraham was completely obedient. This final promise is a direct messianic reference. Paul proclaimed that this promise to Abraham was nothing short of "the gospel in advance" (*NIV*) in Galatians 3:8. The lineage of Abraham would result in the One who would ultimately bless all the nations.

CONCLUSION

Faith must be tested in order to reach full maturity. This testing is difficult, and even stressful. However, in the end it results in a harvest of righteousness. The story of Abraham's close call with Isaac is the perfect illustration of this truth. After enduring the harsh word of Yahweh, he was rewarded with blessing upon blessing, and his faith reached completeness. Abraham knew the entire earth for all generations would be a better place because of his obedience.

GOLDEN TEXT CHALLENGE

"HE SAID, LAY NOT THINE HAND UPON THE LAD, NEITHER DO THOU ANY THING UNTO HIM: FOR NOW I KNOW THAT THOU FEAREST GOD, SEEING THOU HAST NOT WITHHELD THY SON, THINE ONLY SON FROM ME" (Genesis 22:12).

The fear of the Lord is revealed to be behind the testing of Abraham and the provision of God. Ironically Abraham's obedience shifted the focus of the situation. Abraham provided obedience and God was put to the test!

In both instances, God and Abraham were faithful. God was faithful to His covenant word and Abraham was faithful to God.

Talk About It:
1. Why did Abraham name this place "Jehovah-Jireh" (v. 14)?
2. Why does obedience bring blessing?

"Throughout the Bible, . . . when God asked a man to do something, methods, means, materials and specific directions were always provided. The man only had one thing to do: obey."
—**Elisabeth Elliot**

Daily Devotions:
M. God Tries the Heart
  1 Chronicles 29:14-18
T. Job's Faith Tested
  Job 1:12-22
W. We Can Depend on God
  Psalm 121:1-8
T. Overcoming Temptation
  Matthew 4:1-11
F. Sacrifice All for Christ
  Philippians 3:7-11
S. Persevere in Trials
  James 1:2-4, 12-14

Faith for Every Decision

Genesis 24:1-67

INTRODUCTION

At its heart, the story of Abraham is the story of God's sovereignty over the lives of those with whom He enters a covenant. From the beginning of their journey together, Abraham learned there was no use trying to discern the future. This new God offered few clues into how His promises would come to pass. So because Abraham was freed to take his focus off of his circumstances, he could fully focus on Yahweh. He could place his hope and faith in God Almighty. And this is exactly what he did. At times, his steadfast faith appeared to be making no real difference in the everyday situations of life. He still had to deal with famine, war, childlessness, violence, destruction, temptation, infidelity and marital problems. An outsider might have wondered how on earth Abraham's God was doing him any good, or perhaps assumed that God had turned against the wandering nomad. But Abraham knew better. As he continued to place his faith in Yahweh, his life maintained a firm course.

We accept God's sovereignty over the routine decisions of our lives when we put into action a major principle from the life of Abraham. His life shows us that for God, the journey is just as important as the destination. God was clear on the definition of the destination of Abraham's life from the very beginning. When He initially called Abraham, He laid it out: Abraham was to become the father of a great nation. This destination was fleshed out in greater detail as he continued to walk with God, adding the details of the blood covenant, including animal sacrifice and circumcision. But even with these additions, the destination was clear. What seemed perpetually unclear, however, was the landscape of the journey. It was full of twists, turns and unexpected occurrences. Yet it was the faith necessary for the journey that made the destination realizable in the first place. As Abraham built his faith through the ordinary decisions of life, day after day, year after year, his character was shaped so that he could reach the destination. When we recognize God's sovereignty and seek to mold our decisions to Him, we also will see His will come to pass in our lives.

I. FAITH FOR THE NEXT GENERATION (Genesis 24:1-9)

One of the most ominous scriptures in the entire Bible occurs in Judges 2:10: "After that whole generation had been gathered to their fathers, another generation grew up, who knew neither the Lord nor what he had done for Israel" (*NIV*). This sad commentary on the period of Israel's history that followed Joshua and the conquest of the Promised Land is a warning for all generations of believers. If the faith is not intentionally and carefully passed along, it will die, and generations will experience suffering, confusion and heartbreak as a result. In Genesis 24, Abraham is determined to not allow this in his lineage. He has been through too much with Yahweh to let it come to nothing.

A. Abraham Prepares to Pass on the Faith (vv. 1-4)

1. And Abraham was old, and well stricken in age: and the Lord had blessed Abraham in all things.

2. And Abraham said unto his eldest servant of his house, that ruled over all that he had, Put, I pray thee, thy hand under my thigh:

3. And I will make thee swear by the Lord, the God of heaven, and the God of the earth, that thou shalt not take a wife unto my son of the daughters of the Canaanites, among whom I dwell:

4. But thou shalt go unto my country, and to my kindred, and take a wife unto my son Isaac.

The chapter begins this time not with Yahweh giving new instruction to Abraham, but with Abraham acting on his own. We have gotten used to a word of the Lord prompting Abraham to act. But now Abraham has the experience with God and maturity to move in the right direction without a specific mandate.

Verse 1 contains a potent summary of the life of the man who, at this point, needs no more of an introduction. His specific age is not given, for he isn't identified by his age but by his relationship with the Lord. Every aspect of Abraham's life has been touched by God. What an incredible testimony to take to his grave! But for Abraham, this testimony was inadequate unless his descendants experienced the same blessing. Therefore, he gets proactive about ensuring that this will really happen.

Verse 2 introduces a solemn oath. Abraham instructs his chief servant to place his hand under his thigh, near his genitals. As mentioned in the discussion about the covenant sign of circumcision, the male sex organ was culturally significant in that day as the symbol of offspring and fruitfulness. A man's honor and the value of his life were based on the nature of his offspring. Therefore, when the most sacred of oaths were taken, one party would place his hand on or near the genitals

Talk About It:
1. How does verse 1 summarize Abraham's life?
2. Why was the selection of Isaac's wife so important?

of the other. This symbolized the gravity of the situation. For if the oath were broken, a curse would follow the lineage of the one breaking it.

Passages like this give hints as to why Abraham was considered to have lived out the tenets of the Law even before it was given (Genesis 26:5), for so much of the nomad's life reflects the later commandments in the Torah. In this case, Abraham establishes firm purity norms for his offspring by attempting to keep them separate from Canaanite culture. Abraham's oath with his chief servant became normative for the later Jewish communities in at least three ways. First, it set a precedent of holiness, defined as being consecrated and separated to the Lord. The call from Yahweh to "be holy, because I am holy," occurs throughout the Pentateuch, especially in Leviticus, and called the community to emerge from the surrounding Canaanite peoples as one consecrated to God alone.

Second, Abraham's oath set a precedent for Jewish marriage laws. Although he was living in Canaan, as commanded by God, he did not want to join his clan to any of its peoples through marriage. This would not only result in an automatic alliance, but would run the risk of introducing Canaanite religion into Abraham's offspring, thus leading them into paganism. He would have none of that, so he sent his servant back to his own country in Haran (12:4, 5). In the ancient world, interfamily marriages were typical. These marriages often took place between cousins, or between non-blood relatives who were considered part of the family clan by virtue of their connection to one of its households. As Israel grew into a nation, of course, interfamily marriages would be unnecessary, but the injunction against intermarriage with the Canaanites remained loud and clear. Both Moses and Joshua ardently commanded the people to not allow either their daughters or sons to intermarry with them (Deuteronomy 7:3; Joshua 23:12, 13). They knew it was a primary path to personal and national idolatry.

Third, Abraham's example remained a template for Israel even in their second settlement of the Promised Land. Recall that when Babylon sacked Jerusalem in 587 B.C., the Jews were exiled to Babylon. That is, they were forced to leave their land and plant roots in that pagan nation. However, when Persia defeated Babylon, King Darius allowed the Jews to return to their own land and resettle Jerusalem, led by such prominent leaders as Nehemiah and Ezra. Ezra in particular turned to the ancient Abrahamic example about intermarriage and consecration to help Israel to a new start, commanding them, "Separate yourselves from the peoples around you and from your foreign wives" (Ezra 10:11, NIV).

So the chief servant's solemn oath with Abraham was not

The Immediate or the Eternal?

As World War II was drawing to a close, C.S. Lewis, literature professor in Oxford, England, asked a group of his students, "How can you go to college and study literature when London is under siege?" Then he answered his own question: "We're always under siege. The real question is, Will you spend your life dealing with the immediate or the eternal?"

—David C. Cooper

only for their time; instead, it lay the moral foundation for the nation of Israel throughout history. Because Abraham was careful to prepare for future generations, he was rewarded with faithfulness by his chief servant and by Yahweh.

B. Abraham Prepares to Pass on the Covenant (vv. 5-9)
(Genesis 24:5-9 is not included in the printed text.)

The servant, perhaps taken aback by the intense charge given to him by Abraham, fired off a poignant question. Haran was a long way (hundreds of miles), and Abraham had not been back there in decades. Why should he assume that a family there would give up a daughter to risk her life on the long journey back, then make a home so far away from the life she had always known? Abraham was blunt. His son should not set foot in Haran at any point, under any circumstances. In order to explain his refusal to compromise, Abraham rehearsed the faithfulness of God in his life. The recounting centered on the covenant God made with him when he brought him out of Haran in the first place. Just as Yahweh made an oath with Abraham, so Abraham extended an oath to the chief servant. He should not be worried about such details, for the Lord would send a messenger to help him. If he could not convince a woman to return with him, the oath was null and void, except for the promise to never allow Isaac to take one step out of the Promised Land. The oath was sworn, and it was binding. The covenant would be passed on.

Talk About It:
1. Why was it critical that Isaac not be taken to Abraham's homeland?
2. What did the Lord say "his angel" would do (v. 7)?

II. A SPECIFIC PRAYER OF FAITH (Genesis 24:10-28)

Prayer has been a major part of Abraham's spiritual maturity and life journey, but in the story of Rebekah we are allowed to glimpse the effects of his prayer life on the members of his larger household. Abraham's offspring would later turn to such prayers to learn the ins and outs of communicating with God. Although much attention has been given in recent years to the prayer of Jabez (1 Chronicles 4:10), Genesis 24 records an equally powerful prayer by a nameless servant of Abraham (probably Eliezer—see 15:2).

A. A Servant's Prayer (vv. 10-14)

10. And the servant took ten camels of the camels of his master, and departed; for all the goods of his master were in his hand: and he arose, and went to Mesopotamia, unto the city of Nahor.

11. And he made his camels to kneel down without the city by a well of water at the time of the evening, even the time that women go out to draw water.

12. And he said, O Lord God of my master Abraham, I

Nahor (NAY-hor)—
v. 10—Abraham's brother and Rebekah's grandfather; he either lived in Haran (here referred to as "the city of Nahor") or in a town named Nahor located close to Haran.

pray thee, send me good speed this day, and shew kindness unto my master Abraham.

13. Behold, I stand here by the well of water; and the daughters of the men of the city come out to draw water:

14. And let it come to pass, that the damsel to whom I shall say, Let down thy pitcher, I pray thee, that I may drink; and she shall say, Drink, and I will give thy camels drink also: let the same be she that thou hast appointed for thy servant Isaac; and thereby shall I know that thou hast shewed kindness unto my master.

Talk About It:
1. Why did Abraham's servant take so many camels with him?
2. Describe the servant's faith.

The servant understood that the entire covenant between Yahweh and Abraham now rested on his shoulders. If Isaac was forced to take a wife from the clans of Canaan, then the promise of Abraham's offspring growing into a consecrated nation was threatened. His master had entrusted him with his dying wish, and with their oath ringing in his ears he set out across the wilderness.

He providentially arrived at dusk, when women would come and draw water to be used for the evening meal. Foreigners were not always welcome in small villages, and this foreigner had traveled a great distance. Also, he was only claiming to be a representative of his master. What if the people of the clan did not believe him? What if they thought he was a spy or an impostor?

Overwhelmed by his task and its nonexistent margin of error, the servant began to beseech Yahweh for guidance. Notice that he addressed the Lord as the "God of my master Abraham" (v. 12), and he unselfishly prayed based on the merits of Abraham. He told God that he had placed himself in the perfect position to view the daughters of the townspeople, but he had no idea which one he should approach. So he prayed, "May it be that when I say to a girl, 'Please let down your jar that I may have a drink,' and she says, 'Drink, and I'll water your camels too'—let her be the one you have chosen for your servant Isaac" (v. 14, *NIV*).

"Nothing puts feeling into prayer like a mighty good reason for saying it."
—O.A. Battista

The servant wanted things clear-cut, in unambiguous black and white. The girl that freely offered to water his camels, without any prodding, was to be the one. The servant even stated the specific phrase that he would like Yahweh to make sure that she uttered. Although a bit problematic as a model of prayer for consistent followers of Christ today, the specificity of the prayer is a wonderful example for us. We may rarely receive specific signs that quickly and easily unveil God's will for us, but we can pray specifically for help in times of need, just like Abraham's servant. We can know that God hears the smallest details we bring to His throne.

B. A Speedy Answer (vv. 15-28)
(Genesis 24:16-18, 20-25, 28 is not included in the printed text.)

15. And it came to pass, before he had done speaking, that, behold, Rebekah came out, who was born to Bethuel, son of Milcah, the wife of Nahor, Abraham's brother, with her pitcher upon her shoulder.

19. And when she had done giving him drink, she said, I will draw *water* for thy camels also, until they have done drinking.

26. And the man bowed down his head, and worshipped the Lord.

27. And he said, Blessed be the Lord God of my master Abraham, who hath not left destitute my master of his mercy and his truth: I being in the way, the Lord led me to the house of my master's brethren.

No sooner had the chief servant finished uttering this simple prayer than he glimpsed a young woman carrying a jar. The writer gives us information about the woman that the chief servant did not know. In fact, he wouldn't have even known her name. She was attractive, but what exactly drew the servant to her? Was it a gleam in her eye, a bounce in her step, or just something indefinable about her that got the servant's attention? We do not know. However, even he himself must have been surprised by how quickly things were shaping up. She emerged before his prayer was even completed. The promise of Scripture is certainly not that we will always see God's answer to our prayer immediately, but that He does hear our prayers the moment they are spoken. Sometimes, His answer appears over time. Sometimes, the answer is a simple "no." But occasionally, we find the answer to our prayers immediately.

The scene played out exactly as the chief servant had imagined it in his prayer. Hurrying to meet her before she returned to the house, he asked for a drink and then waited for her fateful reply. Finally, after he drank, she hospitably offered water for his camels. In fact, she watered every one of them. This involved considerable work, for wells at this time were often dug like mines, or found naturally in caves, so that in order to get water one would have to walk a considerable distance downhill, then back uphill carrying a heavy, full water jar. As Rebekah worked ardently at offering the man such authentic hospitality, the chief servant watched her in silence. At some point, he knew for certain that Yahweh had chosen her to return with him to Isaac. In response to this revelation, he withdrew costly gold jewelry from his supplies, presented the pieces to her, then asked about her identity. She immediately offered shelter both for him and his animals. In response to this uncommon find, the chief servant bowed down and worshiped Yahweh, pronouncing a blessing toward the God of Abraham. Rebekah, however, ran to her home to tell her parents about this mysterious and generous visitor.

Bethuel (beh-THU-el)—v. 15—nephew of Abraham, father of Rebekah

Talk About It:
1. Based on verses 18-20, describe Rebekah.
2. How long did Abraham's servant "hold his peace" (v. 21), and why?
3. How can God show "his mercy and his truth" (v. 27)?

Shot-Making Faith
Studies have shown that professional golfers actually experience less brain activity than recreational golfers while striking the ball. This may seem strange, given that professionals have their careers and income on the line with every shot. Yet they learn to put faith in their preparation and simply swing the club. When we honor God with our daily decisions, we build a record of faith that can be drawn from in the critical moments of our lives. Learning to be like Christ may seem mechanical at first, but through faith it can become as natural as a professional golfer's swing.

III. FAITH TO ACCEPT GOD'S WILL (Genesis 24:50-61)

After accepting the wonderful hospitality of Rebekah's family, but before he would eat, Abraham's chief servant lay out his proposition. He impressed them with Abraham's résumé by including the details about his exorbitant wealth and his miraculously born son (vv. 34-36). He then recounted his prayer to Yahweh, and the entire scene at the well (vv. 37-48). He spared no detail in letting them know that he was genuine, and he asked for their reply to bring to his master (v. 49).

A. Celebration of God's Providence (vv. 50-54)

50. Then Laban and Bethuel answered and said, The thing proceedeth from the Lord: we cannot speak unto thee bad or good.

51. Behold, Rebekah is before thee, take her, and go, and let her be thy master's son's wife, as the Lord hath spoken.

52. And it came to pass, that, when Abraham's servant heard their words, he worshipped the Lord, bowing himself to the earth.

53. And the servant brought forth jewels of silver, and jewels of gold, and raiment, and gave them to Rebekah: he gave also to her brother and to her mother precious things.

54. And they did eat and drink, he and the men that were with him, and tarried all night; and they rose up in the morning, and he said, Send me away unto my master.

Rebekah's brother, Laban, was drawn to the mysterious visitor at the spring when he saw the costly gifts he gave to his sister. After hearing the chief servant's story, however, his heart was softened from selfish opportunism to the recognition that God was truly at work here, and His work was greater than any of them.

Rebekah's father and brother did not directly answer the chief servant. They were simply so overwhelmed by the opportunity to have their family explicitly used for Yahweh's purposes that they readily submitted to what God was doing. The entire process had been undeniably directed by God, and who were they to object to His will? Therefore, they humbly assented.

The chief servant had been astonished by the entire experience. Perhaps he was pessimistic at first, but God had far exceeded his expectations. He threw himself on the ground to give thanks to Yahweh, knowing that his sacred mission was almost accomplished. But before the next segment began, the servant knew it was time to celebrate. He brought out expensive jewelry and clothes for Rebekah, her mother and her brother. The chief servant, his traveling companions and Rebekah's family ate and drank together.

Talk About It:
1. According to verse 50, why did Laban and Bethuel speak "Take her, and go" (v. 51)?
2. Explain the servant's action in verse 52.

This celebration was indicative of two important aspects of ancient marriage rites. First, in order to enter into a marriage contract, a dowry was a must. This is due to the fact that marriage was not primarily considered the joining of a man to a woman, but of a family to a family, a clan to a clan. Hence, the chief servant feared that no family there would join to Abraham's because it was so far removed, and so he spared no degree of detail in explaining his story to the family. To join oneself to a family far away was virtually unheard of. Second, the eating and the drinking also carried weighty significance, since feasting symbolized open, familial fellowship. The fact that Rebekah's family would eat and drink with Abraham's servants implied that the households were ready to be united in alliance. But there is still one more link in the chain necessary to complete the union.

B. The Covenant Remains Pure (vv. 55-61)
(Genesis 24:55-57 is not included in the printed text.)

58. And they called Rebekah, and said unto her, Wilt thou go with this man? And she said, I will go.

59. And they sent away Rebekah their sister, and her nurse, and Abraham's servant, and his men.

60. And they blessed Rebekah, and said unto her, Thou art our sister, be thou the mother of thousands of millions, and let thy seed possess the gate of those which hate them.

61. And Rebekah arose, and her damsels, and they rode upon the camels, and followed the man: and the servant took Rebekah, and went his way.

The celebration was the easy part, considering all the costly gifts, food and drink. But now it was decision time and the painful break had to be made. Rebekah's family knew what was at stake. If they allowed her to leave with the servant, they would probably never see her again. They would never know if she even lived to see her new groom. They would never know what kind of man Isaac was. It was much too risky, so they begged the chief servant to stay 10 more days. But he was on a mission, and he would not waste time. God's plan now hinges on the answer of the girl herself. "So they called Rebekah and asked her, 'Will you go with this man?' 'I will go,' she said" (v. 58, *NIV*).

Her response translates "I will go" from a single Hebrew word, *halak*. With one word, she took the greatest risk imaginable, pledging herself in marriage to a man she had never met, from a family she had never seen, who left her land long before she was born. Girls were often married when they reached sexual maturity, so Rebekah was likely a young teenager. In

Talk About It:
1. What did Rebekah's family request (v. 55), and how did Abraham's servant respond (v. 56)? Why?
2. Why do you suppose Rebekah was willing to go?
3. How did the blessing of Rebekah in verse 60 come to pass?

Daily Devotions:
M. Trusting God for Protection
2 Samuel 22:1-4
T. Trusting God for Guidance
Psalm 5:1-12
W. Trusting God for His Will
Psalm 40:1-8
T. Trusting God for the Impossible
Luke 1:28-38
F. Trusting the Spirit's Prompting
Acts 3:1-10
S. Trusting God in Trying Circumstances
2 Corinthians 4:8-18

response to her remarkable act of faith, her household blessed her with a blessing of fruitfulness, foreshadowing the fact that God's covenant with Abraham would find fulfillment through her progeny. She still stands today as a wonderful model of what it means to faithfully and radically accept God's will.

CONCLUSION

The life of faith is primarily a life of discerning and accepting God's will. Abraham had walked with God for many years learning this truth, but his servant experienced it in a single situation. The fact that Abraham faithfully passed on specific instructions to the chief servant regarding Isaac's marriage reflected Abraham's concern to pass on his faith to the next generation. Without their combined efforts to secure Isaac a bride who was faithful to Yahweh, their faith would not last long. But due to their obedience to God, Abraham's descendants grew into the great nation of Israel, just as Yahweh had promised.

GOLDEN TEXT CHALLENGE

"COMMIT THY WAY UNTO THE LORD; TRUST ALSO IN HIM; AND HE SHALL BRING IT TO PASS" (Psalm 37:5).

To commit our ways unto the Lord is to commit to Him everything of which we are masters—our futures, our desires, our achievements; and likewise, those things that we cannot master—our failures, our mistakes, and the circumstances in which we find ourselves. Commitment means the dethronement of our selfish wills as we completely turn our lives over to Him who is able to accomplish all things.

Trusting implicitly in His greatness, we find that the burdens of life cease to be ours and become His. We are changed from prisoners shackled by life's problems to soldiers who see their Captain doing battle for them. Trusting God is simply taking Him at His Word and believing He will do that which He has promised. It is faith in action. The effectiveness of trust depends on the object of trust. But He who created us and sustains our existence will certainly bring to pass within us the promises of His Word.

Sarah—Mother of Nations

Genesis 17:15-21; 21:1-7; 1 Peter 3:1-6

INTRODUCTION

Any series of lessons based on historical characters presents some specific challenges. First, to accurately portray the person, one needs to understand the culture in which that person lives. Though all humans experience some of the same challenges and joys, they are funneled through the guidelines and expectations of their particular society.

Second, because of their cultural setting, we cannot attempt to interpret or to judge in view of this 21st century.

A third challenge is to avoid the temptation of "story fabrication." Too frequently individuals are guilty of saying "I think . . ." or "I believe. . ." and have no Biblical or historical basis for what is being said. This usually stems from not carefully observing the two guidelines previously stated. When this occurs, we fail to teach with truth and integrity.

This series on key women in the Bible enables us to examine their characteristics and actions in a wide variety of settings. Though they come from varied backgrounds, each one contributes to God's overall plan of redemption. They definitely aren't perfect. Some fail at moments when one expects faith and strength. However, they demonstrate how God uses women as well as men in fulfilling His will.

Sarah (first called "Sarai") enters the Biblical narrative in Genesis 11:29ff. Here she is introduced as the daughter-in-law of Terah and the wife of Abraham. Later, as they are about to arrive in Egypt, Abraham's concern for his life stems from Sarah's beauty (12:11, 12). He fears Pharaoh's wanting to add her to his harem. If it were known she is married to Abraham, Pharaoh might decide to kill him. Keep in mind Sarah is at least 65 years old at this point, yet strikingly beautiful.

As we will see, Sarah, as well as Abraham, were specifically chosen by God for a divine purpose. Neither are perfect. Their faults stand out. But equally evident are God's blessings. Sarah is blessed of God to be the mother of a nation through whom the world will be blessed.

Unit Theme:
Great Women of the Bible

Central Truth:
We must be willing to respond to God's invitations.

Focus:
Examine Sarah's example and submit to God's will.

Context:
Old and New Testament passages concerning the life of Sarah

Golden Text:
"I will bless her [Sarah], and give thee [Abraham] a son also of her: yea, I will bless her, and she shall be a mother of nations" (Genesis 17:16).

Study Outline:
I. Covenant Partner (Genesis 17:15-21)
II. Woman of Promise (Genesis 21:1-7)
III. Example for Christian Women (1 Peter 3:1-6)

I. COVENANT PARTNER (Genesis 17:15-21)

A. Sarah's Inclusion (vv. 15, 16)

15. And God said unto Abraham, As for Sarai thy wife, thou shalt not call her name Sarai, but Sarah shall her name be.

16. And I will bless her, and give thee a son also of her: yea, I will bless her, and she shall be a mother of nations; kings of people shall be of her.

When God comes to Abraham to speak once again of their covenant, he and Sarah have been in Canaan for 24 years. On several occasions, as God forecast the future of a nation of descendants, Sarah was not mentioned as being the mother of those descendants and a partner sharing in the covenant. This may be one reason why Sarah chose the cultural custom of giving her handmaiden Hagar to her husband for the purpose of bearing a child in her place (Genesis 16). This does not justify her action of attempting to fulfill God's plan, but it may have been a factor.

Now when it is impossible for a birth to occur from the union of Abraham and Sarah, God comes and renews the covenant. Besides restating the previous items of countless descendants and possession of Canaan, there are two new statements. First, male circumcision is to be the sign of the covenant (vv. 9-14). Second, Sarah becomes a partner and recipient in God's plan. He changes her name from *Sarai* to *Sarah*. It probably changed the meaning slightly, from "princely" to "princess."

In verse 16 the specifics of being included in the covenant are stated. She is to be blessed by bearing a son for Abraham. He will be the beginning of the promised descendants. All the stigma of being barren will be removed. From a cultural standpoint she will have fulfilled the expected role of a wife to her husband by bearing a child, specifically a son. Sarah will also be the mother of nations. Since she has no children other than Isaac, it would seem this is a spiritual dimension reflecting the redemption which will come through Jesus Christ.

The Lord also indicates her child will have kings in his lineage of descendants. This indicates an organized nation with rulers. Most notable of them would be David and Solomon. The fact of a nation with kings further points to her being blessed as a partner in its covenant.

B. Abraham's Questions (v. 17)

17. Then Abraham fell upon his face, and laughed, and said in his heart, Shall a child be born unto him that is an hundred years old? and shall Sarah, that is ninety years old, bear?

Notice Abraham's posture. At the news of what is to come, he prostrates himself before the Lord in humility and joy. Jewish

Talk About It:
1. Why did God wait until Sarai was 89 years old to change her name?
2. Explain the phrase "mother of nations" (v. 16).

Tomorrow
Finish each day and be done with it. You have done what you could; some blunders and absurdities no doubt creep in; forget them as soon as you can. Tomorrow is a new day; you shall begin it serenely and with too high a spirit to be encumbered with your old nonsense.
—Ralph Waldo Emerson

interpreters see Abraham's laugh as one of happiness rather than doubt or disbelief. This seems to be supported by the words of Jesus as recorded in John 8:56.

The questions asked are based on the physical circumstances—age and ability to conceive a child. Sarah's inclusion as a covenant partner doesn't lessen Abraham's position or relationship with God. Rather, it seems to enhance it. The honoring of Sarah brings honor to Abraham.

A strong marriage application stands out here. Anytime one partner receives a blessing or honor, it should be seen as an item for rejoicing and happiness to both. Anytime jealousy enters in such a setting, it reflects a competitive relationship rather than a joint benefit in which the two are one.

Talk About It:
Why did God wait so long to give Abraham and Sarah a son?

"It's never too late to be what you might have become."
—**George Eliot**

C. Sarah's Blessing (vv. 18-21)

18. And Abraham said unto God, O that Ishmael might live before thee!

19. And God said, Sarah thy wife shall bear thee a son indeed; and thou shalt call his name Isaac: and I will establish my covenant with him for an everlasting covenant, and with his seed after him.

20. And as for Ishmael, I have heard thee: Behold, I have blessed him, and will make him fruitful, and will multiply him exceedingly; twelve princes shall he beget, and I will make him a great nation.

21. But my covenant will I establish with Isaac, which Sarah shall bear unto thee at this set time in the next year.

It's so easy to listen, to enjoy and then to want a different way. That seems to be the case with Abraham. Even after hearing God's plan for Sarah to be blessed with a son and he to be the father, Abraham struggles. What about Ishmael? He too is Abraham's son. Possibly for over a decade now it has been assumed he would be the covenant son, being the only child of Abraham. But now everything seems to change.

How easily this can happen in our own lives. We develop a plan, but God knows better and chooses a different path.

For a second time God plainly repeats what will happen in the near future. He is going to enable Sarah to bear a child, specifically a son. The name of this covenant child will be *Isaac*, which means "laughter." The covenant which stands between God and Abraham will be passed on to Isaac and to all his descendants. Notice this covenant stands forever. There are no time limits or lapses.

God doesn't overlook the fact of Ishmael's being Abraham's son. He too will be blessed and be the father of many descendants. The many Arab nations attest to the fulfillment of these prophetic words.

Talk About It:
Compare and contrast God's promises for Isaac with His promises for Ishmael.

The fact remains, however, the covenant child will be Sarah's son, Isaac. God indicates a timeline for Isaac's birth. Sarah's pregnancy and the birth of Isaac will be within the next year. This means a 99-year-old husband and an 89-year-old wife are able to look at each other and say, "Next year at this time we will have a baby!"

At this point only Abraham is party to this covenant information. Later when Sarah overhears what is to take place, she laughs (18:9-15). The context indicates her laughter issues from doubt rather than joy; otherwise God's rebuke would not have been necessary.

This reminds us how we sometimes have difficulty grasping the reality of God's blessing. Remember, Sarah was not the one who regularly or even occasionally encountered God. Also, from a physical standpoint she cannot conceive a child. Even at her advanced age she learns to grow in faith and accept the blessings of being a covenant partner.

II. WOMAN OF PROMISE (Genesis 21:1-7)
A. Isaac's Birth (vv. 1-5)

1. And the Lord visited Sarah as he had said, and the Lord did unto Sarah as he had spoken.

2. For Sarah conceived, and bare Abraham a son in his old age, at the set time of which God had spoken to him.

3. And Abraham called the name of his son that was born unto him, whom Sarah bare to him, Isaac.

4. And Abraham circumcised his son Isaac being eight days old, as God had commanded him.

5. And Abraham was an hundred years old, when his son Isaac was born unto him.

Once again we see the certainty of God's promises. Exactly as previously stated, Sarah conceives a child, a son. Verse 1 points specifically to this being a divine action enabling this chosen servant to experience the joy of giving birth to a son. Though humanly impossible, God enters their lives and enables Abraham and Sarah to have a child together. Abraham is 100 years old, yet he will have the opportunity to enjoy this child as he grows into manhood, marries and has children, for Abraham will live to the age of 175.

Within the first five verses of this chapter, there are three specific references to Isaac being Abraham's blood son. This further emphasizes the fulfillment of the covenant promise given a decade before. At that time God pointed out the error of Abraham's thinking Eliezer, apparently an adopted servant, would be his heir. "This man will not be your heir, but a son coming from your own body will be your heir" (Genesis 15:4, *NIV*).

When God renewed the covenant in chapter 17, He instituted

"We keep on assuming that we know the play. We do not know whether we are in Act I or Act V. We do not know who are the major and who the minor characters. The Author knows."

—C.S. Lewis

Talk About It:
1. What two divine commands did Abraham obey in these five verses?
2. What is the meaning of *circumcision*?

Sarah—Mother of Nations

circumcision as the sign of the covenant people. This action was to occur on the eighth day of the male's life. We see in 21:4 that Abraham doesn't overlook this stipulation in the euphoria of the birth of Isaac.

This reminds us of the need for our complete obedience to God's will. What good would it do for Sarah to have been blessed with the fulfilled promise and then have her husband fail to fulfill all the aspects of God's covenant?

B. Sarah's Joy (vv. 6, 7)

6. And Sarah said, God hath made me to laugh, so that all that hear will laugh with me.

7. And she said, Who would have said unto Abraham, that Sarah should have given children suck? for I have born him a son in his old age.

Most of us cannot understand the deep joy Sarah expresses when she says, "God hath made me to laugh." Only those desiring to have children, being unable to do so for many years, and then suddenly conceiving a child can possibly relate to Sarah's experience. Keep in mind she is 90 years old. If she were married at the common age of 15, she has been barren in the marriage for 75 years. Couple that with the fact of her no longer being physically able to conceive a child. Yet she is now a mother. She and her husband are the proud parents of a baby boy.

Previously Abraham laughed at the thought of him and Sarah having a son. This was a reaction to future happiness. Sarah laughed when she overheard the divine messengers stating she would bear a son, believing this to be an impossible dream. This was a laughter of doubt.

Now Sarah can laugh with joy. Others can join in this celebration and laugh with her. How appropriate for Isaac's name to mean "laughter." The sorrows and frustrations of decades of barrenness are washed away in the joyous celebration of God's promise fulfilled in Sarah.

This is the first of several Biblical accounts of women who were barren for many years. Later in our series, Hannah and the birth of Samuel will be studied. Let's consider others who were in the same situation. Isaac and Rebekah had been married for 20 years before Jacob and Esau were born (25:21). Manoah's wife was barren until she was enabled to conceive Samson (Judges 13:2, 3, 24). Not to be forgotten is the conception and birth of John the Baptist to the aged couple, Zacharias and Elizabeth (Luke 1:5-25).

When God miraculously enters our lives and changes situations, there is cause for joy. This joy needs to be expressed, allowing others to join in. Testimony of God's actions not only causes rejoicing, but also builds our individual and corporate faith.

> "God is not a deceiver, that He should offer to support us, and then, when we lean upon Him, should slip away from us."
> —**Augustine**

Talk About It:
How would Sarah's laughter be contagious?

> "Joy is the gigantic secret of the Christian."
> —**G.K. Chesterton**

III. EXAMPLE FOR CHRISTIAN WOMEN (1 Peter 3:1-6)

This passage provides some "hot topics" for discussion. Before looking at the specifics of these verses, let's review a few basic principles. First, we need to be reminded of the purpose for Scripture. Second, Timothy 3:16 specifies one purpose—to be instructed, or trained, in righteous living. Second, it is important to remember the cultural times in which Scripture was written. This gives us a better understanding, but doesn't allow us the privilege of simply discarding godly directives. Third, we must be cautious not to taint Scripture with our own feelings. Let Scripture speak for itself.

A. Marital Submission (vv. 1, 2, 6)

1. Likewise, ye wives, be in subjection to your own husbands; that, if any obey not the word, they also may without the word be won by the conversation of the wives;

2. While they behold your chaste conversation coupled with fear.

6. Even as Sara obeyed Abraham, calling him lord: whose daughters ye are, as long as ye do well, and are not afraid with any amazement.

As Peter penned these words, he used an example of a woman (Sarah) who lived about 2,000 years prior to the founding of the church. How could this be relevant? The answer is twofold. Cultural change during that time period was minimal. Structures and concepts were very similar. Also, God's principle for righteous living transcends time.

The second challenge is the cultural norms. In the patriarchal society, the husband/father stood as the legal and spiritual head of the family. Within some of the people groups, women and children were the property of the husband/father, to be treated as he willed. However, this is not the structure God originated in the Garden for Adam and Eve's relationship. Sin always degrades.

Note that women were given higher status in the Israelite society than those of their surrounding neighbors. Also, the Romans—whose empire surrounded the Mediterranean Sea—provided a greater opportunity for women than did many other people groups.

A third challenge is for us to see the complete picture of Peter's writing. Submission does not just pop into the narrative. In the previous chapter he speaks of submission to the laws of the land and of servants submitting to their masters (2:13, 18). At the beginning of the third chapter he addresses the relationship between husbands and wives. Peter does not speak of inferiority or superiority of one gender over the other.

Peter points to the need for Christian wives to continue in

---

chaste conversation coupled with fear (v. 2)— "respectful, pure behavior" (*TLB*)

Talk About It:
1. What does it mean to be "in subjection" to one's husband?
2. Why should a woman want to be considered a daughter of Sarah?

submission to their unbelieving husbands. Religious difference doesn't negate the subordination which comes due to the sin in the Garden of Eden (Genesis 3). Just because a wife becomes a believer and experiences freedom in Christ, she is not exempt from the obligation to her husband. Even the cultural norms of the time expected her to recognize the position of headship which was given to the husband.

A woman's proper actions may become the stimulus that eventually leads her unbelieving husband to come to Christ. Rebellion always causes strife and separation. In contrast are behaviors and words that are uplifting and unifying. The word translated as *conversation* in 1 Peter 3:1 means "behavior." Here we stand reminded of the power of an ongoing godly lifestyle. This form of evangelism convinces unbelievers of one's Christianity. It also provides power when words are spoken.

In verse 6 the author suddenly includes Sarah as an example to be followed. She was a partner in the covenant who conceived and bore the promised covenant son. She was greatly honored by God. Yet she continued in submission to her husband, Abraham.

Peter views all believing women as the daughters of Sarah, as they live appropriately within the headship of their husbands and "do not give way to fear" (v. 6, *NIV*). Maybe some were fearful of their submission being interpreted as inferiority. However, this should never appear in a Christian marriage where men are to love and respect their wives. Ephesians 5:25-29 and 1 Peter 3:7 describe how a husband is to love his wife. When he loves in that manner, submission isn't really an issue.

B. Inner Beauty (vv. 3-5)

3. Whose adorning let it not be that outward adorning of plaiting the hair, and of wearing of gold, or of putting on of apparel;

4. But let it be the hidden man of the heart, in that which is not corruptible, even the ornament of a meek and quiet spirit, which is in the sight of God of great price.

5. For after this manner in the old time the holy women also, who trusted in God, adorned themselves, being in subjection unto their own husbands.

Because of these verses, along with 1 Timothy 2:9, 10, some of the most conservative Holiness groups teach women are to keep away from specific actions of beautification. This translates in some instances to no cutting of their hair, having only simple hairstyles, using no cosmetics, and wearing no ornamentation. The opposite extreme interprets these verses as applying to a limited cultural directive for a particular time. Both views fall short. The first simply focuses on the "thou shalt nots" without seeing

Unmarried Humor
An elderly woman in my dad's church was commenting on her status of never having been married. She said jokingly, "I read in the Bible where Sarah called Abraham 'Lord.' I couldn't call any man 'Lord,' so I just didn't get married!"
—Jerald Daffe

plaiting (v. 3)—braiding

Talk About It:
1. How does God define beauty (v. 4)?
2. How do "holy women" live (v. 5)?

the bigger picture of the passage. The second view says such teachings are inconsistent with freedom in Christ and thus do not apply today. This view misses the bigger idea.

It would seem Peter is not opposed to caring for and beautifying the outside. Being ugly or having a sloven appearance is not a Biblical principle. The bigger issue is one's motive. What is inside a person determines who she is instead of the outer appearance. First and foremost should be the ornamentation of the inner person. A gentle spirit continues to be radiant even when one's physical beauty fades with the aging process. There is a spiritual beauty that transcends physical beauty. It shines to an even greater degree as a person consistently demonstrates a godly life.

We have no record of the specific beauty features of Sarah. There are no hints of how she wore her hair or if she wore any type of jewelry. However, the Scriptures do indicate she was a woman of beauty—both physically and spiritually. Her spiritual beauty was not due to her being chosen to participate in the covenant and become the mother of the promised son. Rather, it stemmed from her spirit and actions directed toward her husband, Abraham.

CONCLUSION

Sarah's life demonstrates how God works to accomplish the seemingly impossible. Though our faith and human understanding may be limited in some circumstances, He will take us to places of joy and fulfillment that seemed impossible. We see only the limitations, but our God knows the realities He intends.

GOLDEN TEXT CHALLENGE

"I WILL BLESS HER [SARAH], AND GIVE THEE [ABRAHAM] A SON ALSO OF HER: YEA, I WILL BLESS HER, AND SHE SHALL BE A MOTHER OF NATIONS" (Genesis 17:16).

God's covenant with Abraham was also a covenant with Abraham's wife and family. God had always planned for Sarah to be the one through whom He would fulfill His covenant. It would be from her womb that the promised heir would be born. God changed her name from *Sarai* to *Sarah*, meaning "princess." Her new name indicated the influence and leadership she would have as a person and a mother. Along with Abraham, Sarah's influence would extend to future generations—including nations and kings.

God would use Sarah particularly in her role as a mother. This is a powerful affirmation of the role and influence of women as leaders and mothers of leaders. This role may extend not only to their immediate families but also to people and nations around them.

"There is only one kind of beauty that can transcend time, and many women possess it. It is, of course, beauty of the spirit that lights the eyes. . . . Women who are interested in others and forget themselves, and who accept each stage of life gracefully, are the lasting beauties of this world—and the happiest."

—Deidre Budge

Daily Devotions:
M. Partners in
    Praise
    Exodus 15:1-3,
    20, 21
T. Faith Partners
    Ruth 1:8-18
W. Marriage
    Partners
    Proverbs 31:10-
    15, 23-28
T. Partners in
    Ministry
    Acts 18:1-3, 18,
    24-26
F. Partners in
    Service
    Romans 16:3-12
S. Reconciling
    Spiritual Partners
    Philippians 4:1-4

Sarah—Mother of Nations

Rahab—Unlikely Ally

Joshua 2:1-24; 6:17-25; Matthew 1:5; Hebrews 11:31; James 2:21-26

INTRODUCTION

Isn't it amazing to see whom God chooses for service in His kingdom? In the natural sense, humans tend to select those individuals whose appearance—looks, height, build—meets their standards. Ability and intelligence also play a part in the selection process. The best and the brightest are assumed to be the right individuals for the important tasks. In some cases, one's family name may be the factor in whether or not an individual receives a particular opportunity.

Sometimes overlooked are those who do not make a great first impression or haven't received honors and recognition. People with lower-level jobs, limited education, and a minimal range of skills are often bypassed. It is amazing the bias, prejudice and discrimination which often comes into play.

Isn't it wonderful how God doesn't use the same criteria! He sees the heart and what each person can become. He knows the potential when given the opportunity. Such is the situation when Rahab, an unlikely woman to be in the lineage of Christ, had her faith rewarded.

Rahab lived in the city of Jericho on the eastern edge of Canaan near the Jordan River. The population was probably about 3,000, with the area of the city being somewhere between 7 and 13 acres. People mainly worked outside the city and returned at night for housing and safety. Jericho was a double-walled city. The outer wall was 6 feet thick and the inner wall 12 feet. The walls stood 15 feet apart and rose 30 feet above ground.

From a human perspective, Jericho stood as a mighty fortress providing safety for its population. It is significant that God led Israel to this city as the first military target in Canaan. From a military perspective, this was brilliant strategy. By taking possession of the middle ground, the Israelites were cutting off the routes from north to south. Also, the destruction of this major fortress would send a message to the Canaanites. They would constantly have in mind the power of Israel and her God, Jehovah. However, that would not stop them from fighting against these perceived invaders.

That Rahab played a pivotal role in this story is amazing. Her occupation raises eyebrows. Her faith appears so strong while lacking so much knowledge of God. Her reward emphasizes God's grace and abundant blessings.

Unit Theme:
Great Women of the Bible

Central Truth:
God often chooses unlikely people to do His will.

Focus:
Be amazed that God chooses unlikely members for His family and rejoice in His grace.

Context:
Old and New Testament passages concerning the faith of Rahab

Golden Text:
"By faith the harlot Rahab perished not with them that believed not, when she had received the spies with peace" (Hebrews 11:31).

Study Outline:
I. Thoughtful and Courageous (Joshua 2:1-24)
II. Honored for Bravery (Joshua 6:17-25)
III. Made Righteous by Faith (Matthew 1:5; Hebrews 11:31; James 2:21-26)

I. THOUGHTFUL AND COURAGEOUS (Joshua 2:1-24)
A. The Risk (vv. 1-7)
(Joshua 2:5-7 is not included in the printed text.)
1. And Joshua the son of Nun sent out of Shittim two men to spy secretly, saying, Go view the land, even Jericho. And they went, and came into an harlot's house, named Rahab, and lodged there.

2. And it was told the king of Jericho, saying, Behold, there came men in hither to night of the children of Israel to search out the country.

3. And the king of Jericho sent unto Rahab, saying, Bring forth the men that are come to thee, which are entered into thine house: for they be come to search out all the country.

4. And the woman took the two men, and hid them, and said thus, There came men unto me, but I wist not whence they were.

Talk About It:
1. What did Joshua want the two spies to find out?
2. Why do you suppose the spies' names are not given?

Everything was ready for Israel to conquer and take possession of the Promised Land. At this point it appears God hadn't given Joshua any specific directions or battle plan. Being a military man, he understood the need for inside information prior to attacking. So Joshua sent two men to secretly gather information about the land and the city of Jericho. Upon arriving in Jericho, they stayed at the home of Rahab.

Why would these men go to the house of a prostitute? Initially, it appears questionable. Further knowledge points to the same Hebrew word being used for "female innkeeper" and "harlot." It is likely that Rahab had rooms to rent and her services could be purchased for those who so desired. Some have suggested their staying at her home would give them less visibility. Visits of strange men would not raise suspicion as would their staying in another location.

Any attempt of being incognito failed. Keep in mind the relatively small size of the city. It would be difficult not to be seen. Also, the report to the king specifically pointed to their being Israelites. Verse 3 says the king was told these men's purpose in coming—they were spies!

Immediately messengers were sent to Rahab with the directive to bring these men to the king. Would she obey the king of her city or take the risk of hiding the men who represented Israel? She decided to protect the Israelites, but what would she say in response to the king's men?

Without hesitancy Rahab glibly lied. Her story contained three separate falsehoods: (1) She claimed not to know where the men were from. (2) She stated they left just before the time of the evening gate closing. (3) She indicated a lack of knowledge as to their direction but assured that swift pursuit would

Rahab—Unlikely Ally

result in their being caught (v. 5). She was a sinner who followed the way of sin in spite of knowing something of Israel's God. Sometimes this type of action is difficult for us to understand. Yet, if we pause and think about it, we should recognize some imperfections in our lives which have been changed through the process of commitment to Christ, growth in the Word, and the empowerment of the Holy Spirit.

All along the two spies were hidden on the flat roof under bundles of flax. Since the roofs were used for storage of drying grain, the flax became a convenient hiding location. There would be no reason to search the roof having heard Rahab's story. Also, it would be logical for spies to operate under the cover of darkness and leave at that hour. All the pieces of the puzzle seemed to fall into place.

> "Courage is a special kind of knowledge: the knowledge of how to fear what ought to be feared and how not to fear what ought not to be feared."
> —Ben Gurion

B. The Request (vv. 8-14)

8. And before they were laid down, she came up unto them upon the roof;

9. And she said unto the men, I know that the Lord hath given you the land, and that your terror is fallen upon us, and that all the inhabitants of the land faint because of you.

10. For we have heard how the Lord dried up the water of the Red sea for you, when ye came out of Egypt; and what ye did unto the two kings of the Amorites, that were on the other side Jordan, Sihon and Og, whom ye utterly destroyed.

11. And as soon as we had heard these things, our hearts did melt, neither did there remain any more courage in any man, because of you: for the Lord your God, he is God in heaven above, and in earth beneath.

12. Now therefore, I pray you, swear unto me by the Lord, since I have shewed you kindness, that ye will also shew kindness unto my father's house, and give me a true token:

13. And that ye will save alive my father, and my mother, and my brethren, and my sisters, and all that they have, and deliver our lives from death.

14. And the men answered her, Our life for your's, if ye utter not this our business. And it shall be, when the Lord hath given us the land, that we will deal kindly and truly with thee.

After the king's messengers left, Rahab spoke to the men on the rooftop. In verse 9 she acknowledged God's having given Jericho to Israel and that His terror had fallen on the people. She said, "All who live in this country are melting in fear" (*NIV*). They somehow knew of the distant past when God miraculously

Talk About It:
1. How did the people of Jericho know about the Israelites' triumphs, and how did it affect them?
2. Why was Rahab's belief about the God of Israel (v. 11)?
3. What positive characteristic does verse 13 reveal about Rahab?
4. What did the spies promise Rahab in verse 14?

"Promises may get friends, but it is performance that keeps them."
—Owen Feltham

Talk About It:
1. What did the spies' response (v. 22) to Rahab's instructions (v. 16) reveal about their confidence in her?
2. What contingency did the spies add to their agreement with Rahab, and why (v. 20)?
3. Describe the spies' report to Joshua (v. 24).

opened the Red Sea for Israel. Also known to them was the immediate past as God enabled Israel to destroy the army of the Amorites (Numbers 21:21-35).

These two events on either side of a 40-year span point to God's enabling of His people. Nothing could stand in His way. As a result, the people of Jericho's courage had melted. Where there once was strength, only weakness now resided. Apparently the people sensed the hopelessness of the future.

In verse 11 of the text, Rahab made a major confession regarding the God of Israel: He is the God of the heavens and earth. This can be seen as a statement in which she abandoned the gods of Canaan for the sovereign Almighty God.

Having made a confession concerning the true God, Rahab then requested kindness for herself and her father's household. She asked that the favor shown to the spies would be returned in like kind. She provided security and safety despite the king's request. Would they return a similar act of kindness when Israel's army invaded? Rahab also requested a token or sign of this agreement. The spies responded by agreeing to spare her life and those of her family in exchange for her actions. There was one requirement: Rahab must remain silent about their actions and intent. This points to the need for Rahab to continue on the path of commitment to God and His plans for Israel.

C. The Escape (vv. 15-24)
(Joshua 2:15-24 is not included in the printed text.)
Rahab's assistance to the spies went far beyond that of the initial hiding. Next they must leave the city unnoticed. Through the use of a rope, the men were lowered to the ground outside the city walls. It's not likely this rope remained tied to the window; otherwise it would be a "dead giveaway" of the duplicity and aiding of the spies. She was, however, to place a scarlet marker of some type in the window. Symbolically it seems similar to the blood on the doorposts when the death angel passed over Egypt. The scarlet cord became the sign of security.

Rahab's thoughtfulness can be seen in her directing the spies to go to the mountains for three days. By that time those watching the fording places would have given up and gone home. The spies followed her directions and returned safely to report to Joshua.

Before leaving, the spies reminded Rahab of the requirements of safety. The scarlet marker needed to be in place. Family members were to stay in her house and not wander into the streets. She was to maintain complete silence about their activities.

These verses remind us of the need to follow God's plans

and directives. Our salvation isn't a do-it-yourself job in which we determine the parameters of belief and action. God sets the stage and writes the script.

II. HONORED FOR BRAVERY (Joshua 6:17-25)
A. The Plan (vv. 17-21)
(Joshua 6:18, 19, 21 is not included in the printed text.)

17. And the city shall be accursed, even it, and all that are therein, to the Lord: only Rahab the harlot shall live, she and all that are with her in the house, because she hid the messengers we sent.

20. So the people shouted when the priests blew with the trumpets: and it came to pass, when the people heard the sound of the trumpet, and the people shouted with a great shout, that the wall fell down flat, so that the people went up into the city, every man straight before him, and they took the city.

God's plan for the capture of Jericho combines simple obedience of the people and divine intervention. They will march, trumpets will be blown, and the people will shout. Then the walls will fall flat. This part of the lesson opens at the beginning of the seventh day as the instructions are being given. On the six previous days, the Israelites had marched silently around Jericho once each day.

Though the people of Jericho are to be killed, a specific exemption is given. Rahab, once again labeled as a prostitute, and her family are to live. Only the people inside her house are to be spared.

The saving of Rahab and her family stands as a monumental distinctive in contrast to the destruction of the people and the city itself, and the burning of its contents. There is to be no taking of spoils for the captors. Only the silver, gold, bronze and iron articles are to be taken and designated for the Lord's treasury (v. 19). Jericho will be a burnt offering to the Lord. It is of interest to note how archaeological digs have confirmed the fate of Jericho. The burned portion of the rubble is far greater than that found in other cities that were captured and spoiled.

B. The Reward (vv. 22-25)
22. But Joshua had said unto the two men that had spied out the country, Go into the harlot's house, and bring out thence the woman, and all that she hath, as ye sware unto her.

23. And the young men that were spies went in, and brought out Rahab, and her father, and her mother, and her brethren, and all that she had; and they brought out all her kindred, and left them without the camp of Israel.

Talk About It:
1. Describe the warning given to the Israelites (vv. 17, 18).
2. What caused the walls of Jericho to fall (v. 20)?
3. Why did Jericho and its people have to be utterly destroyed (v. 21)?

"Never be afraid to do what God tells you to do—it's *always* good."
—Malcolm Cronk

24. And they burnt the city with fire, and all that was therein: only the silver, and the gold, and the vessels of brass and of iron, they put into the treasury of the house of the Lord.

25. And Joshua saved Rahab the harlot alive, and her father's household, and all that she had; and she dwelleth in Israel unto this day; because she hid the messengers, which Joshua sent to spy out Jericho.

Besides saving her and her family from destruction, Rahab's reward increased. She was allowed to continue to live in the land and was incorporated into God's people. This is not the picture of an outcast being tolerated. No, Rahab was a woman who, by faith and action, bravely made a commitment to God and His people. She had heard of Israel's God and His mighty works, and when the opportunity arose, she began her walk of faith by the risky business of hiding the spies and aiding in their escape.

Something similar occurs when we accept Jesus as our Savior and Lord. With this commitment we become part of another people, God's family. We may live in the same region, but now there is a new citizenship.

III. MADE RIGHTEOUS BY FAITH
(Matthew 1:5; Hebrews 11:31; James 2:21-26)
A. Christ's Lineage (Matthew 1:5)

5. And Salmon begat Booz [Boaz] of Rachab [Rahab]; and Booz begat Obed of Ruth; and Obed begat Jesse.

Believers tend to skip over the genealogies which are recorded in the Old and New Testaments. The names are often difficult to pronounce. Yet they serve a vital part in validating other portions of Scripture and providing new information. In the New Testament, both the Gospel of Matthew and the Gospel of Luke include a genealogy of Jesus. Matthew traces Jesus' lineage through Joseph, His legal father. Luke records Jesus' lineage through Mary, His mother. Each reflects the fulfillment of the Davidic covenant (2 Samuel 7), which promised a descendant would be on His throne forever.

In Matthew's genealogy we find Rahab's inclusion. Normally women are not included in these lineage lists. Matthew includes two—Ruth and Rahab (in one verse)—and both have "a past." Ruth was not an immoral woman, but she was a Moabitess, one of the forbidden people for intermarriage. Rahab was known for her sexual immorality. We are thereby reminded that Christ does not hold the past against any person, but opens the door for restoration for those who will believe and live a new life. Christ also raises the status of women, as can be seen so often in Luke's Gospel. One example is Mary Magdalene, who moved from being demon-possessed to become an ardent follower of Jesus.

Rahab's inclusion in Christ's lineage reflects a person who had "two strikes" against her. First, she was part of the Canaanites, who were to be completely destroyed for their sins. Second, she participated in immoral sexual behavior. But when she turned to God in faith, He responded in love, acceptance and protection.

B. Rahab's Faith (Hebrews 11:31)

31. By faith the harlot Rahab perished not with them that believed not, when she had received the spies with peace.

This section (along with James 2:21-26) stands as the heart of the lesson. It pulls together two dimensions in Rahab's life—her faith and her actions. Also, these verses remind us as believers of the dual dimensions which should be evident in each of our lives.

Hebrews 11 is frequently referred to as the Hall of Faith. Inclusion in this lineup doesn't make any one of them better than believers who have lived since then. It does provide a wide variety of examples of people demonstrating faith in God regardless of the circumstances or the amount of their knowledge of God. This chapter follows a chronological order. In verse 30 the faith of Israel in God's plan of attack on Jericho is shown. Immediately following we read of Rahab's faith, which was the reason her life was spared. The writer then points to the action which resulted from her faith. She believed what she heard God had done in the past, she believed God and His people would triumph over her city and its surrounding land, and she acted on her faith.

Recognizing who the men were when they came to her home, Rahab had a choice. Would they be received in peace or revealed as spies? Receiving them in peace demanded taking a risk. There was no assurance of her personal fate when choosing to hide the two men. Only later would she enter into an agreement with the spies providing for the safety of herself and her family.

C. Living Faith (James 2:21-26)

21. Was not Abraham our father justified by works, when he had offered Isaac his son upon the altar?

22. Seest thou how faith wrought with works, and by works was faith made perfect?

23. And the Scripture was fulfilled which saith, Abraham believed God, and it was imputed unto him for righteousness: and he was called the Friend of God.

as many as 200 pseudonyms, the exact number isn't known. At her death, just 40 days short of her 95th birthday, Fanny was one of the best known women in the United States (March 24, 1820—February 12, 1915).

Talk About It:
What did the people of Jericho "not believe" (*NKJV*)?

"Faith, as Paul saw it, was a living, flaming thing leading to surrender and obedience to the commands of Christ."
—**A.W. Tozer**

24. Ye see then how that by works a man is justified, and not by faith only.

25. Likewise also was not Rahab the harlot justified by works, when she had received the messengers, and had sent them out another way?

26. For as the body without the spirit is dead, so faith without works is dead also.

Talk About It:
1. Why was Abraham called a "friend of God" (James 2:23)?
2. In what sense was Rahab "justified by works" (v. 25)?
3. Restate verse 26 in your own words.

James' writing in his classic chapter on faith and works blends and expands the concept seen in Hebrews. He used the examples of Abraham and Rahab. Faith cannot stand alone and be inactive. What one believes within must, of necessity, be reflected in activities consistent with that faith. When God called Abraham, he left his homeland and by faith went to a land he had never seen.

In Genesis 22, God directed Abraham to take his son to Mount Moriah and sacrifice him. Abraham did not ask questions. Instead, we see actions and words of faith. Abraham rose early for the journey (v. 3). He directed his servants to stay at a certain place and stated he and Isaac would return (v. 5). Abraham reassured Isaac of God's provision when asked about a lamb for sacrifice (vv. 7, 8).

In God's completed plan of salvation, we know we are justified by faith in Jesus as we confess our sins before Him. We are then declared righteous. This righteousness needs to be lived outwardly through actions/activities that reflect who we are and what we believe.

In James 2:25, the writer seems to be pointing to the uselessness of Rahab's having faith but not following through. Without her positive actions toward the spies, she would not have obtained righteousness. She would never have been in the lineage of Christ. Instead, Rahab and her relatives would have died with the rest of the city.

Verse 26 summarizes the whole concept. James says "the body without the spirit is dead." He is using the analogy of the human body and the life-giving spirit to demonstrate the relationship between faith and works. Faith then is basic to the Christian life—belief in who God is and what He can do. Righteous works reflect the vitality and reality of our faith.

One caution needs to be inserted here. Works alone do not make us righteous in the eyes of God. Neither does faith alone make us acceptable in the sight of God. Faith is the beginning. But it must be accompanied by actions that are consistent with the faith we claim.

CONCLUSION

The life of Rahab shows the tremendous contrast between one's past and future potential. The key is faith. Only when she chose to place her lot with the people of God and hold to faith in Him was she able to escape judgment. Death became life as she combined her faith and works.

GOLDEN TEXT CHALLENGE

"BY FAITH THE HARLOT RAHAB PERISHED NOT WITH THEM THAT BELIEVED NOT, WHEN SHE HAD RECEIVED THE SPIES WITH PEACE" (Hebrews 11:31).

Faith is an absolute necessity. Without it, prayers return as empty as they went out; attempt at worship is wasted time; trying to live a holy life is useless effort; and good deeds are of no effect. "Without faith it is impossible to please him" (v. 6).

Daily Devotions:
M. Grace-Filled Offer
   Genesis 7:1-10
T. Surprising
   Outcome
   Genesis 32:24-30
W. Unlikely Deliverer
   Judges 4:18-22
T. Unusual Choices
   Matthew 4:17-22
F. Amazing Grace
   1 Corinthians
   1:26-31
S. Chosen Through
   Mercy
   1 Timothy 1:12-
   17

4th Judge (handwritten)

Deborah—Leadership Model

Judges 4:4 through 5:31

Unit Theme:
Great Women of the Bible

Central Truth:
Characteristics of strong leadership include wisdom, submission and humility.

Focus:
Examine Deborah's leadership traits and submit to God's plan for our lives.

Context:
Around 1300 B.C. in the hill country of Ephraim

Golden Text:
"Then sang Deborah and Barak . . . Praise ye the Lord for the avenging of Israel, when the people willingly offered themselves" (Judges 5:1, 2).

Study Outline:
I. Wise and Available (Judges 4:4-7)
II. Submissive to God's Plan (Judges 4:8-24)
III. Humble and Grateful (Judges 5:1-31)

INTRODUCTION

Deborah provides a picture of leadership that wasn't normally seen in the society of her time. Very few women in Scripture rose to positions of national leadership. Deborah stands out due to both her spiritual and civil leadership. She was the only woman who served as a judge during those extended years of turmoil.

For the most part, the Book of Judges reflects a negative picture of God's people drifting away spiritually and then eventually experiencing God's judgment. This comes through His allowing other nations to come in and dominate their existence. At times they pillaged Israel's crops, as seen in the account of Gideon and the Midianites. Other people, such as the neighboring Philistines, dominated the nearby areas of Israel. Each time the Israelites woke up spiritually and repented, God provided leaders who made a difference in their situation.

Apparently the oppression of the Israelites wasn't always throughout the entire area of Canaan at the same time. Likewise, the reigns of the judges overlapped in time. For that reason, we should not add up the time periods of each judge and assume that number represents the entire era of the judges.

This lesson focusing on Deborah's leadership is a contemporary topic. Our society is currently in a second cycle of leadership emphasis within about a 25-year period. Leadership first came to the forefront in the early '80s. A number of books on leadership were written. Some Christian titles highlighted the leadership principles found in Nehemiah's actions in building the walls of Jerusalem. The current emphasis on leadership often draws from secular sources drawing from business concepts and principles.

It is rare to hear anyone project Deborah as an example of spiritual and civil leadership to follow. However, as will be seen in the following pages, Deborah's actions and attitude deserve careful attention.

I. WISE AND AVAILABLE (Judges 4:4-7)
A. Service as a Judge (vv. 4, 5)
   4. And Deborah, a prophetess, the wife of Lapidoth, she judged Israel at that time.
   5. And she dwelt under the palm tree of Deborah between Ramah and Bethel in mount Ephraim: and the children of Israel came up to her for judgment.

Because of the sins of the people, they were under the oppression of Jabin. He ruled over the northern portion of Canaan with Hazor being his capital city. The name *Jabin* may be a title like *Caesar, Pharaoh* or the Philistine *Abimelech.* The military power of this enemy of Israel was significant. He had 900 iron chariots under the command of Sisera (v. 3). Such a force would be very difficult, if not impossible, to defeat under normal circumstances.

The domination over Israel may be seen in verse 2, where Sisera's base of operation is noted. *Harosheth* means "woodcutting." Some have surmised the possibility of Sisera's forcing the inhabitants to serve as woodcutters. Regardless of the specifics, the length of time is definite. For 20 years God's people bowed under Jabin's oppression. Surely it must have appeared unending to them.

Then we read of Deborah's coming to the position as a judge in Israel. As can be seen in verse 1, after the death of Ehud the people had drifted into sin with its resulting consequences. Deborah faces a difficult challenge. We have no record of the circumstances or scenario in which God brought her to the judgeship; this was a divine appointment. One can only wonder what her thoughts were when God initiated this action.

Let's pause to look specifically at her task. In the Hebrew language the title *judge* indicates someone who will bring others into a right relationship. This points to the spiritual dimension even though the specific tasks were of a civil nature. The three basic functions were administration, the settlement of disputes, and military leadership. However, these tasks must not provide a picture of having sovereign authority over a geographical area. There appears to be a sense of limitation in terms of being like a king or governor.

The description of Deborah in verses 4 and 5 provides a brief picture of this, the only woman chosen to be a judge in Israel. It begins with her spiritual position as a prophetess. This distinguishes her from all the other judges. None of them were given this designation. It also speaks of her spiritual character. We also see she was a married woman with the responsibilities of being a wife. Since her age is not given, we cannot state what phase of family life she might have been experiencing.

Her location for fulfilling her duties as a judge is very specific.

Deborah (DEB-oh-rah)—v. 4—In Hebrew, her name means "bee."

Lapidoth (LAP-ih-doth)—v. 4—the husband of Deborah

Talk About It:
1. What three responsibilities did Deborah carry out (v. 4)? Why do you suppose God gave her such a heavy load?
2. According to verse 5, how did the Israelites respond to her?

Teenage Heroine

Joan of Arc (1412-1431) stands historically as a female military leader who, though only a teenager, led the armies of France in victory over the English and Burgundians. Though well aware of her inabilities and lowly status in life, she chose to follow supernatural guidance. Against all odds she became the leader of the armies of France at age 17. Her subsequent capture by the enemy led to being put to death at the stake by those claiming her to be a heretic. However, she stood as a national French heroine.

The cities of Ramah and Bethel were about four miles apart on a line north of Jerusalem. This is the same area where the prophet Samuel later judged Israel (1 Samuel 7:16). Deborah held court under a palm tree.

B. Messenger of the Lord (vv. 6, 7)

6. And she sent and called Barak the son of Abinoam out of Kedesh-naphtali, and said unto him, Hath not the Lord God of Israel commanded, saying, Go and draw toward mount Tabor, and take with thee ten thousand men of the children of Naphtali and of the children of Zebulun?

7. And I will draw unto thee to the river Kishon Sisera, the captain of Jabin's army, with his chariots and his multitude; and I will deliver him into thine hand.

In these verses we see the prophetic ministry of Deborah operating within her position as a judge of the area. The directives and results did not originate from the sharp mind of a military or civil leader. They stemmed from the Lord himself speaking through the mouth of the prophetess.

We know little about Barak, but he was God's chosen military leader for the task at hand. He lived in the city of Kedesh within the tribal lands of Naphtali. His father's name is given. But other than that bit of information, we can only make assumptions. Some have suggested his abilities and reputations as a warrior/leader had traveled southward, thus making him known to Deborah. This may or may not be true. Keep in mind that God can simply direct us to the right person even though we have no prior knowledge.

Once Barak arrived, notice the specifics of Deborah's message for him. There are no generalities which could lead to insecurity or to wrong actions. She lays out God's plan for him. Victory is guaranteed. Barak simply needs to fulfill it.

Notice the specifics. Deborah begins by identifying the source of her message. It is not self-generated. These words come from the Lord God of Israel. The direction Barak is to take is toward Mount Tabor. This mountain is distinct because of its flat top with a circumference of nearly one mile. It could serve as a fortified stronghold or as an excellent lookout post. The instructions further state the size of the fighting force and from which tribes they are to come. Since the regions being oppressed are Naphtali and Zebulun, it's only logical they should be the ones to participate in the deliverance.

In order for Barak to muster a force this size, it would appear he was known to the men of this region and trusted. After all, it would seem to be suicidal for a ground force to go against the mobilized chariots of Jabin. Of course, if Barak announced the promise of God in verse 7, the people would be foolish not to accept God's wanting to work on their behalf.

Barak (BAY-rak)— v. 6—His name means "lightning." He led the Israelites against the forces of Sisera.

Abinoam (aa-BIN-oh-am)—v. 6—the father of Barak

Kedesh-naphtali (KEY-desh NAF-tah-lye)—v. 6—A city of the Israelite tribe of Naphtali, it was appointed as a city of refuge.

Kishon (KI-shon)— v. 7—a torrent or winter stream flowing from sources on Mount Tabor and emptying into the Mediterranean Sea

Sisera (SIS-eh-rah)—v. 7—captain of the Canaanite army under King Jabin (JAY-been)

Talk About It:
1. How did God communicate to Barak (v. 6)?
2. What did God promise Barak (v. 7)?

Deborah gave the specific plan of the Lord. Sisera would be lured into a situation which would bring about his defeat. In order to attack Barak's forces, the enemy chariots would need to cross the plain through which the river Kishon flowed. In the original language of these scriptures, the word for *river* literally means "torrent bed." The Kishon would flow when flash flooding took place.

The message of the Lord clearly states this location to be where victory would take place. This victory would not be due to their superior forces. It would come from God's giving Sisera and his mighty forces into Israel's hands.

Think about putting yourself in Barak's shoes. There is a double trust issue here. He had to trust Deborah to be a true prophetess. And he must believe God would fulfill His word regardless of how impossible the task might appear.

In this case, God gave very specific directions and the results that would follow. Most of us do not experience this type of guidance in our life decisions. Yet, God is still directing us. Our faith should be no less than if everything were spelled out.

> "Courage does not look at the size or power of the enemy, but at the necessity of victory."
> —*Notes and Quotes*

II. SUBMISSION TO GOD'S PLAN (Judges 4:8-24)
A. Personal Availability (vv. 8-13)

8. And Barak said unto her, If thou wilt go with me, then I will go: but if thou wilt not go with me, then I will not go.

9. And she said, I will surely go with thee: notwithstanding, the journey that thou takest shall not be for thine honour; for the Lord shall sell Sisera into the hand of a woman. And Deborah arose, and went with Barak to Kedesh.

10. And Barak called Zebulun and Naphtali to Kedesh; and he went up with ten thousand men at his feet: and Deborah went up with him.

11. Now Heber the Kenite, which was of the children of Hobab the father in law of Moses, had severed himself from the Kenites, and pitched his tent unto the plain of Zaanaim, which is by Kedesh.

12. And they shewed Sisera that Barak the son of Abinoam was gone up to mount Tabor.

13. And Sisera gathered together all his chariots, even nine hundred chariots of iron, and all the people that were with him, from Harosheth of the Gentiles unto the river of Kishon.

Barak's response to Deborah's message indicates he accepted the plan. But he did not want to do it by himself. As we feel at times, he wanted the comfort of another human with him before fulfilling God's guaranteed plan. Moses did the same thing when God appeared to him in the desert (Exodus 3; 4). He came up

Heber (HEE-bur) the Kenite (KEY-night)—v. 11—the member of a tribe of desert nomads, the Kenites, who were known for their metalwork

plain of Zaanaim (zay-ah-NAY-ihm)—v. 11—a place on the southeastern border of the territory of Naphtali marked by an oak tree

Harosheth (ha-RO-sheth)—v. 13—the place where Sisera gathered his forces for battle

Talk About It:
1. Why did Barak insist that Deborah go with him into battle (v. 8)?

2. What did Deborah prophesy in verse 9?
3. How did Sisera know where the Israelites were gathering their troops (vv. 11, 12)?
4. Describe Sisera's strength (v. 13).

with various excuses until God said Aaron, his brother, was on the way and would be his spokesperson. Though having been given verbal assurance and a miraculous demonstration, Moses resisted until he had a family member with him.

Barak made Deborah's presence with him to be the deciding issue as to whether or not he would fulfill God's plan. Without hesitation or rebuke of Barak, Deborah agreed to accompany him. She did, however, point out there would be no personal honor in the victory for him. In spite of his being the leader and gathering the forces, there would be no acclaiming his name after Sisera's defeat. This did not seem to bother Barak. We can only speculate as to why he accepted this so readily. Probably the might of the enemy loomed before him. Or, it could be he valued the defeat of the enemy above his own personal acclaim.

In response to Barak's call for a military force, 10,000 men joined him. The engagement was not long in coming. Hearing of the gathering of rebel forces, Sisera activated his chariots and soldiers.

Here the family of Heber the Kenite enters the narrative (v. 11). Normally the nomadic Kenites lived in the wilderness south of Judah. Heber, an independent person, moved his family to the north. They were camped in a plain near Kedesh. When Sisera and his forces came where the family camped, they showed him the path that Barak's forces had taken up the mountain. Exactly as Deborah stated, Sisera moved his forces to the river of Kishon (v. 13).

B. Proper Timing (vv. 14-16)

14. And Deborah said unto Barak, Up; for this is the day in which the Lord hath delivered Sisera into thine hand: is not the Lord gone out before thee? So Barak went down from mount Tabor, and ten thousand men after him.

15. And the Lord discomfited Sisera, and all his chariots, and all his host, with the edge of the sword before Barak; so that Sisera lighted down off his chariot, and fled away on his feet.

16. But Barak pursued after the chariots, and after the host, unto Harosheth of the Gentiles: and all the host of Sisera fell upon the edge of the sword; and there was not a man left.

discomfited (v. 15)—routed

When God says "now," timing is everything. In verse 14, Deborah gives the signal. Today is the day of deliverance. In complete obedience, Barak leads his force down the mountain to meet the enemy. Their victory is overwhelming. It's not because of their tactics or fighting skill. Rather, God enters the battle and Sisera's forces are utterly confused and destroyed.

Talk About It:
1. What is the significance of the word *up* in verse 14?
2. How thorough was Sisera's defeat (v. 16)?

According to Judges 5:21, it appears God sends a flash flood which turns the plain into a muddy quagmire. The chariots are rendered useless.

Barak's army kills all of Sisera's forces. Only the leader escapes after abandoning his chariot. He literally runs for his life, hoping to find some shelter of escape. Deborah's prophetic announcement to Barak is fulfilled exactly as stated.

> "It's not the magnitude of the mess that matters; it's the measure of the man in the midst of the mess."
> —Gary Gulbranson

C. Misplaced Trust (vv. 17-24)
(Judges 4:17-22 is not included in the printed text.)

23. So God subdued on that day Jabin the king of Canaan before the children of Israel.

24. And the hand of the children of Israel prospered, and prevailed against Jabin the king of Canaan, until they had destroyed Jabin king of Canaan.

Looking for a safe haven, Sisera comes to the tent of Jael, the wife of Heber the Kenite. She invites him to come in and find safety. To enable him to rest, Jael covers him with a quilt or rug and gives Sisera milk when he requests a drink of water. Assuming his hostess will redirect anyone looking for him, Sisera goes to sleep. He never wakes again due to Jael's brutally killing him.

Talk About It:
Do you believe that Jael's actions were justified? Why or why not?

Jael's actions are debatable. On the one hand, Sisera knows the custom of never going into a woman's tent without her husband being there. Anyone who does can be killed. On the other hand, Jael's action of inviting him to come in without fear covers her intention. She doesn't hesitate to commit cold-blooded murder after having offered hospitality, which always included protection.

The end of the story results in Jael's receiving the honor of having overcome the enemy leader. "Though predicted by Deborah, the act was the result of divine foreknowledge, not of divine appointment or action" (Jamieson, Fausset and Brown). When Barak finally catches up with Sisera, it's by Jael's coming out to meet him and showing him the body.

III. HUMBLE AND GRATEFUL (Judges 5:1-31)
A. Song of Praise (vv. 1-5)

1. Then sang Deborah and Barak the son of Abinoam on that day, saying,

2. Praise ye the Lord for the avenging of Israel, when the people willingly offered themselves.

3. Hear, O ye kings; give ear, O ye princes; I, even I, will sing unto the Lord; I will sing praise to the Lord God of Israel.

4. Lord, when thou wentest out of Seir, when thou marchedst out of the field of Edom, the earth trembled,

and the heavens dropped, the clouds also dropped water. **5. The mountains melted from before the Lord, even that Sinai from before the Lord God of Israel.**

Talk About It:
1. How had "the people willingly offered themselves" (v. 2)?
2. How widely did Deborah desire her praises to be heard (v. 3)?
3. How does Deborah describe God's greatness in verses 4 and 5?

When reading through the Book of Judges, this is one chapter which we could easily bypass in favor of reading about the next judge. In doing so, we miss a poetic description of the preceding events as they recap God's deliverance. Also, failure to spend some time in this chapter robs us of reading one of the masterpieces of Hebrew poetry.

The "Song of Deborah" begins with the historical past. She calls for a remembrance of God's marvelous manifestations. It goes back to Mount Sinai where God demonstrated His power and spoke verbally to them. Then it covers the overall journey to Edom. This part of history includes God's punishment for sin as well as His provision. It also points to God's revelation of Himself.

It is easy to think of the specific events referred to here and miss the key point—praise. Deborah and Barak knew what their response needed to be. God deserved all the honor and glory. The tremendous victory over superior forces came through divine intervention. In themselves, Barak and his foot soldiers could never have accomplished such a feat.

B. Years of Peace (vv. 6-31)

(Judges 5:6-30 is not included in the printed text.)

31. So let all thine enemies perish, O Lord: but let them that love him be as the sun when he goeth forth in his might. And the land had rest forty years.

Talk About It:
1. What will eventually happen to all of God's enemies, and why?
2. What does it mean for God's people to be like the sun?

To fully appreciate the present, it is important to review the past. As Deborah continues her song or war ballad, as some call it, she reviews selected events of the past. The dire conditions that brought about the need for deliverance arose from the people's turning from God and selecting other gods (v. 8). Not only had they become defenseless spiritually, but also militarily. They had no weapons with which to defend themselves.

Hope came only when a new spirit gripped the people. They, the leaders and the people, turned to the Lord (v. 9). Though verse 7 speaks mainly of Deborah, it does emphasize the role that spiritual women play in bringing individuals, families and even nations back to their rightful relationship with God.

Deborah's song recounted how the forces of select Israel tribes were gathered and how the Lord came to fight their battle (vv. 13, 14, 18). Listed are the tribes who did not help their brothers in this encounter because they weren't asked to participate (vv. 16, 17). She sang about the death of Sisera at the hand of Jael, recounting with specifics the manner of the death (vv. 24-27). Normally the Bedouin women pitched the family tent. Tent pegs and mallets would be familiar tools to Jael.

To emphasize the misery that came upon the Lord's enemies, Deborah's song includes a picture of Sisera's mother anxiously awaiting the return of her son. Attempting to reassure, those women around her suggested the dividing of the plunder was the reason for the delayed return (vv. 28-30). But later we know she would find the true reason. Her anxiety then would turn into mourning.

Verse 31 provides a contrast between those who serve the Lord and those who are His enemies. While the enemies perish, His servants will live in strength. The key is loving God and Him alone. Though the enemies of the Lord and His people appear to be triumphant, it is only temporary. There comes a point when they will be destroyed. Sometimes we do not live to see it. Nevertheless, it will take place.

As a result of Israel's turning back to God and following Him, they enjoyed an extended period of peace. We do not know how much of this Deborah saw, since her lifespan isn't part of the narrative. Yet, it really doesn't matter. Her leadership in a time of crisis benefited the people of the area for 40 years. What a legacy!

God Is Peace
In life, troubles will come which seem as they never will pass away. The night and the storm look as though they will last forever; but calm and the morning cannot be stayed; the storm in its very nature is transient. The effort of nature, as that of the human heart, is to return to its repose, for God is peace.
—George MacDonald

CONCLUSION

The distinctive of Deborah's work as a judge stands firmly in the battle event. As a woman she would not be expected to be on the battlefield. However, she did not allow cultural norms to hinder her leadership and thereby enabled others to bring victory to God's people.

GOLDEN TEXT CHALLENGE

"THEN SANG DEBORAH AND BARAK . . . PRAISE YE THE LORD FOR THE AVENGING OF ISRAEL, WHEN THE PEOPLE WILLINGLY OFFERED THEMSELVES" (Judges 5:1, 2).

Verse 2 calls for praise to be given to the Lord. Israel, especially the northern section, had been under severe oppression for 20 years. No doubt, the only songs the people could sing were filled with frustration and mourning. Now, however, they had cause for rejoicing in the Lord. In the same way, the first response of the believer when surveying the redemption and deliverance of God should be one of praise.

The reason for praise is given next. The Lord had avenged Israel. The Hebrew word for *avenge* in this verse actually meant "to break or set loose by delivering from oppression." Deliverance from the oppression and bondage of the enemy is always cause for praise to the Lord.

The timing of their release is also given in verse 2. They were set free when they "willingly offered themselves." There

M. Support for
Leadership
Exodus 17:8-12

T. Delegation of
Authority
Exodus 18:13-24

W. Legacy of
Integrity
1 Samuel 12:1-5

T. Servant Leaders
Chosen
Acts 6:1-6

F. Motivated by
Love
2 Corinthians
5:14-21

S. Serving With
Humility
Philippians 2:1-8

are a number of words in Hebrew translated *offer*, presenting varied insights into the concept of giving an *offering*. The particular Hebrew word used here for offering emphasized the freewill nature of giving. In this verse it means the people "freely urged and gave themselves" to the Lord.

God responds to a freewill offering of ourselves. A child of God might be able to give many things to the Lord. However, God desires the believer to freely give himself or herself to the Lord. Faith brought on by manipulation and coercion is not a substitute for a genuine, voluntary giving of oneself.

Hannah—Faithful in Prayer

1 Samuel 1:1 through 2:10

INTRODUCTION

Many people become adept at crisis praying: "God help me!" or, "God, if You get me out of this, I will . . ." followed by future promises with no previous lifestyle pattern to hint the promise will be kept. God in His mercy frequently stops in and assists. It is good to seek for God's help in times of trouble. There can be no greater source of aid than our heavenly Father. However, God desires an ongoing relationship with communication on a daily basis.

It's so easy to try to follow the prayer pattern of an individual whom we respect. Or, there may be some people who attempt to impose a form of legalistic prayer on us, such as praying for one hour a day. There is no Biblical requirement for this time period. Yes, Jesus did say to His disciples, "Could you not keep watch for one hour?" But that was in a specific situation. And Paul directed the Thessalonians to "pray continually" (1 Thessalonians 5:17, *NIV*).

✗ Prayer is crucial to the sustaining of a vital life in Christ for both individual believers and the corporate church. All of us need to work on the practice of prayer without being time-conscious. The issue needs to always be fulfilling our relationship. No reasonable person will say to his or her mate, "Well, we have to talk together 10 minutes," or "Our 10 minutes are up, so let's stop." Genuine communication doesn't come from clock watching. It develops when the necessary time is spent in prayer and meditation. The consistency of our praying makes the difference.

Sometimes it seems we need to pray in order to be in a position to pray. This may be because of disobedience separating us from fellowship with God and making communication strained. It could, however, stem from our not praying on a regular basis and thus being uncomfortable with our heavenly Father.

For most of us, faithful praying doesn't automatically come with the salvation package. It comes as a result of spiritual discipline. Sometimes it takes effort to fulfill this marvelous opportunity.

Today's lesson concerns Hannah's desperate prayer for a child. More than likely, the account for our study was not the first time Hannah prayed concerning her problem. The distinctive of her prayer is how that when it was answered, she faithfully fulfilled her vow.

Unit Theme:
Great Women of the Bible

Central Truth:
God honors honest and persistent prayer.

Focus:
Understand and practice the pattern for faithful prayer.

Context:
Around the first part of the 11th century B.C., in Ramah and Shiloh

Golden Text:
"For this child I prayed; and the Lord hath given me my petition which I asked of him" (1 Samuel 1:27).

Study Outline:
I. Acknowledge the Problem (1 Samuel 1:1-8)
II. Pour Out Your Heart (1 Samuel 1:9-18)
III. Praise God for Provision (1 Samuel 1:19, 20; 2:1-10)

I. ACKNOWLEDGE THE PROBLEM (1 Samuel 1:1-8)

A. A Polygamous Marriage (vv. 1-4)

Ramathaim-zophim (rah-mah-THA-im-ZO-fim)—v. 1 —Elsewhere called "Ramah," it was the birthplace, residence and burial place of Samuel.

1. Now there was a certain man of Ramathaim-zophim, of mount Ephraim, and his name was Elkanah, the son of Jeroham, the son of Elihu, the son of Tohu, the son of Zuph, an Ephrathite:

Elkanah (El-KAY-nuh)—v. 1—Meaning "God has possessed," he was Samuel's father.

2. And he had two wives; the name of the one was Hannah, and the name of the other Peninnah: and Peninnah had children, but Hannah had no children.

Ephrathite (EF-ruh-thite)—v. 1—from the tribe of Ephraim

3. And this man went up out of his city yearly to worship and to sacrifice unto the Lord of hosts in Shiloh. And the two sons of Eli, Hophni and Phinehas, the priests of the Lord, were there.

Peninnah (Pi-NIN-uh)—v. 2—meaning "pearl," one of Elkanah's two wives

4. And when the time was that Elkanah offered, he gave to Peninnah his wife, and to all her sons and her daughters, portions.

Hophni (HOFF-nigh) and **Phinehas (FIN-ih-us)—v. 3**—the two corrupt sons of Eli the priest

This book opens with a biographical sketch of Hannah's husband. He lived in the northern part of Canaan, specifically in the region given to Ephraim. By tribal descent, Elkanah was a Levite from the family of Kohath (1 Chronicles 6:22, 23, 27, 33, 34). Immediately following the genealogy we find his marital status—he was a polygamist. Usually only kings and the wealthy had more than one wife. Knowing Elkanah was not a king suggests he was a man of material means.

As seen in other Biblical examples, this polygamous marriage had difficulties. The major cause appeared to be Hannah's barrenness. The prevailing thought was that barrenness was the result of sin. Even though Hannah was righteous, this stigma remained. Also, she had not brought honor to either her husband or herself by bearing children, specifically a son. Further complicating Hannah's situation was Peninnah's bearing children.

Talk About It:
1. List everything these four verses reveal about Elkanah.
2. How were Hannah and Peninnah different?

Elkanah stands out as a righteous man who faithfully took his family to Shiloh for the yearly celebration of Passover. The entire family—both wives and the children—went to the sanctuary (Tabernacle) for this significant worship time. Elkanah provided for each of the family so they could participate.

"Troubles are often the tools by which God fashions us for better things."
—Henry Ward Beecher

Without specifically stating it, the writer seems to point out a contrast in verse 3. Hophni and Phinehas, the sons of Eli, were the ministering priests. We see in 1 Samuel 2:22 how corrupt they were. That did not keep Elkanah from fulfilling what was right.

B. A Significant Problem (vv. 5-8)

5. But unto Hannah he gave a worthy portion; for he loved Hannah: but the Lord had shut up her womb.

6. And her adversary also provoked her sore, for to make her fret, because the Lord had shut up her womb.

7. And as he did so year by year, when she went up to

the house of the Lord, so she provoked her; therefore she wept, and did not eat.

8. Then said Elkanah her husband to her, Hannah, why weepest thou? and why eatest thou not? and why is thy heart grieved? am not I better to thee than ten sons?

Hannah was constantly aware of her being the barren wife while the other wife was enjoying the privileged status as a mother of a number of children. The yearly visit to Shiloh provided an especially stressful point in the year. Elkanah's love for Hannah never was in doubt. He gave her double portion for sacrifice, regardless of her never having given birth to any children. Neither of them knew her condition was the result of God's divine action and purpose.

The reference to Peninnah in verse 6 as Hannah's adversary indicates a distinct point of conflict. It may have been when Peninnah made a point of offering a thanks offering for being a mother and for her children. All Hannah could do was respond with weeping. Being so distraught, she could not eat.

Elkanah's love stood out as he attempted to comfort her. He had difficulty understanding her grief and heaviness of heart. Wasn't she cared for in a manner far beyond what 10 sons would be able to do? She could not be loved any more than she was right now. As a man he didn't know the sense of shame which she felt from the cultural concepts of being without a child. He also could not fully feel the tension and conflict of the visit to Shiloh as well as the rest of the year.

Hannah knew the problem with which she lived daily. She did not pretend it didn't exist and just go along as though everything was fine. Instead, we see a woman who bore such a heavy emotional load that she could not eat and openly wept.

Talk About It:
1. Why do you suppose the Lord had not allowed Hannah to bear children?
2. Why is one spouse better than two?
3. What could Elkanah not understand?

"As in nature, as in art, so in grace; it is rough treatment that gives souls, as well as stones, their luster. The more the diamond is cut, the brighter it sparkles; and in what seems hard dealing, there God has no end in view but to perfect His people."
—Thomas Guthrie

II. POUR OUT YOUR HEART (1 Samuel 1:9-18)
A. The Vow (vv. 9-11)

9. So Hannah rose up after they had eaten in Shiloh, and after they had drunk. Now Eli the priest sat upon a seat by a post of the temple of the Lord.

10. And she was in bitterness of soul, and prayed unto the Lord, and wept sore.

11. And she vowed a vow, and said, O Lord of hosts, if thou wilt indeed look on the affliction of thine handmaid, and remember me, and not forget thine handmaid, but wilt give unto thine handmaid a man child, then I will give him unto the Lord all the days of his life, and there shall no razor come upon his head.

Desperation dominates Hannah. After the family shares in a meal, she apparently leaves them and proceeds to a door of the Tabernacle. There she pours out all the bitterness and frustration

Talk About It:
1. How did Hannah's bitterness reveal itself?
2. Explain Hannah's vow.

of her situation. Her prayer is accompanied or even interrupted with intense weeping. Her burden weighs so heavily. She has only one respite—to intercede with God and hope He grants her greatest desire.

Hannah's desire for a child results in her entering an exceptionally sacrificial vow. It needs to be understood how seriously vows were to be taken. There never was the thought of "Well, I tried and just couldn't do it. God will have to understand." Not to fulfill a vow would have consequences. It would be a sin against God.

Also, any time a woman made a vow, the ruling male in her life determined whether or not she would be held to it. An unmarried woman would be under the authority of her father or other head of the family clan. A married woman would come under the authority of her husband (see Numbers 30).

More than likely, Hannah's vow took place without the knowledge of her husband, Elkanah. That was not a problem since he had the right to veto or to agree with it after the fact.

Hannah's vow contained several specifics. First, she asked for a son. To conceive and to bear a son would give her special honor in the eyes of the culture. Second, she vowed to give this child back to the Lord. He would be in the service of the Lord. We know this means taking him to live and work at the Tabernacle while still a young child (v. 24). Third, she committed him to follow the Nazarite vow. The specifics of this vow can be found in Numbers 6. A visible sign was no cutting of the hair. The person following this vow would not come in contact with the dead nor drink wine or any strong drink. The Nazarite vow could be taken for differing lengths of time. One year was a common length of time. In the case of Samuel, Hannah's son, and later account of Samson (Judges 13:2-7), this was a lifetime commitment.

B. The Rejection (vv. 12-16)

12. And it came to pass, as she continued praying before the Lord, that Eli marked her mouth.

13. Now Hannah, she spake in her heart; only her lips moved, but her voice was not heard: therefore Eli thought she had been drunken.

14. And Eli said unto her, How long wilt thou be drunken? put away thy wine from thee.

15. And Hannah answered and said, No, my lord, I am a woman of a sorrowful spirit: I have drunk neither wine nor strong drink, but have poured out my soul before the Lord.

16. Count not thine handmaid for a daughter of Belial: for out of the abundance of my complaint and grief have I spoken hitherto.

When God inclines the heart to pray, He hath an ear to hear; To Him there's music in a groan, And beauty in a tear.
—*Anonymous*

Belial (BE-lih-ul)— v. 16—worthlessness

When things couldn't be worse, suddenly it is for Hannah. In agony of soul, she prays at the door to the Tabernacle only to be observed by the high priest, Eli. This elderly priest's major difficulty isn't a loss of hearing or eyesight due to advancing age. Rather, he suffers from spiritual desensitization. He can't differentiate between drunkenness and a woman pouring out her soul to God silently. Yes, her lips move, but there is silence. She intends only God to hear the inner frustration of her condition and offered vow.

Verse 12 points to this prayer being of a longer duration. It isn't just a stop-and-go prayer. Apparently she lingers. Eli observes her and finally speaks. Having assumed her lips moving without sound are the mutterings of an intoxicated person, he pointedly charges her with drunkenness.

Hannah responds immediately. She is respectful while setting the record straight. She hasn't indulged in drink of any type which would produce drunkenness. Instead she is a woman in deep sorrow, carrying a heavy burden. Only God can change her situation.

Defending herself further, Hannah wants Eli to know she isn't a wicked woman ("a daughter of Belial," v. 16). All he observes stems from the depths of her struggle with being barren in this polygamous marriage. Regretfully, Eli is guilty of having jumped to a conclusion and speaking out of both ignorance and spiritual anemia. Notice the Scriptures do not indicate her blurting out the specifics of the situation. The spiritually insensitive Eli doesn't need to know the extent or details of the family situation. But he does need to know she is a wholesome person consumed with grief of her settings.

C. The Assurance (vv. 17, 18)

17. Then Eli answered and said, Go in peace: and the God of Israel grant thee thy petition that thou hast asked of him.

18. And she said, Let thine handmaid find grace in thy sight. So the woman went her way, and did eat, and her countenance was no more sad.

Give Eli credit for correcting his misjudgment. Confronted with his error, the high priest now offers his blessing. First, he tells Hannah to go in peace. There does come a point when, after we have poured out our heart to God, we must wait for His answer. In this case, Eli does know the God of Israel is capable of granting her request, whatever it might be. Also, Eli desires her prayer to be answered.

This point in the lesson deserves some thought. The question arises, *When do we stop interceding and wait for God's response?* There is no established time period. Sometimes the

Talk About It:
1. How and why did Eli misjudge Hannah?
2. How did Hannah explain her actions?

Lost Faith

Samuel Clemens (Mark Twain) married a Christian woman who wanted a regular family altar and mealtime prayers. After some time he said, "Livy . . . you can go on with this by yourself if you want to, but leave me out. I don't believe in your God. . . ." Years later when in dire need, he asked her to turn to her Christian faith. Her sad reply was: "I can't, Sam, I haven't any; it was destroyed a long time ago."

Talk About It:
How did Hannah change, and why?

answer comes quickly. So, how can we know? A suggestion is to pray until we have the satisfaction of knowing peace about the situation.

Verse 18 indicates Hannah's acceptance of Eli's words. No longer does she refrain from eating. When she has peace, sharing in meals becomes normal. Her facial appearance changes as well. No longer does it bear the marks of sadness. Peace permeates her being. She trusts God in His sovereignty to do what is best.

Faithfulness in prayer goes beyond the time of speaking the words. It includes believing God hears our prayers and then sitting back in faith trusting Him to do in His time the best for us. Hannah demonstrates this.

III. PRAISE GOD FOR PROVISION (1 Samuel 1:19, 20; 2:1-10)
A. Samuel's Birth (1:19, 20)

19. And they rose up in the morning early, and worshipped before the Lord, and returned, and came to their house to Ramah: and Elkanah knew Hannah his wife; and the Lord remembered her.

20. Wherefore it came to pass, when the time was come about after Hannah had conceived, that she bare a son, and called his name Samuel, saying, Because I have asked him of the Lord.

Talk About It:
1. Explain the phrase "the Lord remembered her" (v. 19).
2. Why did Hannah name her child "Samuel"?

Before returning home, the family worships. What an appropriate way to end the time spent and to begin what will become a new family dimension. After arriving home, normal family relations occur between husband and wife. God, in His mercy and sovereign will, enables Hannah to conceive. In this case, when the son is born the mother names him. The name comes from Hebrew words meaning "heard of God." She knows the child is a gift from God after her agonized prayer at Shiloh.

The rest of chapter 1 shows the events of the next few years. Hannah chose not to accompany her husband to Shiloh on the yearly pilgrimage until the child was weaned. In those days children were breast-fed until 2 or 3 years of age. The weaning of a child provided a time of celebration. It signaled a life point at which the mortality rate decreased.

The weaning of Samuel carried even more significance. After weaning of this special child, he would be given to the Lord at the next yearly trip to Shiloh. What a sacrifice! Hannah returned her only child, a son. Elkanah gave up his firstborn son of his favored wife. This is where the total picture must come into view: Except for God's intervention, there would have been no son and no opportunity to give him to the Lord.

When Hannah came to the Tabernacle, she identified herself to Eli (vv. 26, 27). She pointed to the event of several years ago

Hannah—Faithful in Prayer

when she prayed. Now she told him the distinctive request of that prayer and God's granting her request. In accordance with her vow, Hannah stood before the high priest ready to fulfill it. Have you ever wondered how surprised Eli might have been?

Verse 28 should be translated in terms of Hannah's *returning* or *giving* Samuel to God rather than "lending" him. One translation renders it, "So now I give him to the Lord. For his whole life he will be given over to the Lord" (*NIV*).

Samuel grows up being part of the Tabernacle life under the direct supervision of Eli. It doesn't seem to be the most wholesome environment in view of the spiritual degradation of Eli's sons. However, God enables Samuel to grow up to be the godly man He intended.

> "Prayer is not conquering God's reluctance, but taking hold of God's willingness."
>
> —**Phillips Brooks**

B. Hannah's Praise (2:1-10)
(1 Samuel 2:3-10 is not included in the printed text.)
1. And Hannah prayed, and said, My heart rejoiceth in the Lord, mine horn is exalted in the Lord: my mouth is enlarged over mine enemies; because I rejoice in thy salvation.

2. There is none holy as the Lord: for there is none beside thee: neither is there any rock like our God.

✱ How should we respond when God answers our prayer? With more than a simple "thanks." Praise and thanksgiving includes looking at the whole environment from which God delivers/provides.

As Hannah offers her praise, it flows from the depth of her heart in the same manner as her previous agony had been poured out. She displays a tremendous sense of joy. She sees the evidence of God's intervention in her situation. The enemy of barrenness and the slights of the other wife now are destroyed. However, before concentrating on them she emphasizes the nature of God himself. Not only does she understand He has been her salvation, but sees His holiness.

Verse 2 demonstrates an understanding of God's true nature. No one compares to Him. He supersedes any human and the concept of any false god. He stands as the immovable rock which readily becomes her fortress and refuge. This concept is seen frequently in the Psalms, including 18:2; 28:1; 62:2.

Because of God's intervention, Hannah now sees herself in terms of strength rather than weakness. Her reference to "mine horn" (v. 1) speaks of strength like an animal tossing its head with a sense of power. It is only through God's work for her that she now can speak instead of silently enduring the words of Peninnah. The miraculous birth of Samuel silences the words of pride and arrogance which surely had stung repeatedly.

The reference to warriors and their bows (v. 4) indicates how Hannah previously felt she was in a battle. The one who had

Talk About It:
1. In Hannah's song, what does she declare about herself in verses 1 and 8?
2. What does she declare about the Lord in verses 2, 3, 6 and 7?
3. What does she declare about God's enemies in verses 4, 5, 9 and 10?

been involved in a losing battle now stands with strength. No longer does she long to bear a child. Her desire is fulfilled.

In the latter portion of verse 5, Hannah speaks of the barren bearing seven children. Verse 21 records her bearing five more children after Samuel. Since these other children were not born at the time of Hannah's song, this can be seen as a prophetic statement of future births. Or, Hannah could have used the number seven in its sense of completion. Now having conceived and birthed a son, she experienced fulfillment as a wife having born a son.

In the final verses of Hannah's song of praise (vv. 6-10), we see the sovereignty of God. He lifts the very poor out of their condition and places them in positions of honor and authority. God can preserve the paths of the saints and destroy those who are the adversaries of Him and His people. No one can prevail against the great God.

Verse 10 contains a brief prophetic statement of the end times. God will "thunder" from heaven in the time of judgment, and "his anointed"—the Messiah—will reign over the earth.

CONCLUSION

In 1 Samuel 2:19-21, we read how Hannah would bring Samuel a coat she had made on her annual pilgrimage to Shiloh. She always found her son faithfully at his duties in the Tabernacle. Hannah's faithfulness to God was reproduced in Samuel.

GOLDEN TEXT CHALLENGE

"FOR THIS CHILD I PRAYED; AND THE LORD HATH GIVEN ME MY PETITION WHICH I ASKED OF HIM" (1 Samuel 1:27).

Hannah poured out her soul and made a vow to God. Then, after God's marvelous work in her life, we see the same heart faithfully pouring out words of praise in prayer. Her joy is captured in Psalm 113:9: "He settles the barren woman in her home as a happy mother of children. Praise the Lord" (*NIV*).

While Hannah prayed for a child, you may have a different request that needs to be "birthed" in your life. Faithfully take your request to God in prayer, submitting yourself to Him and His holy purpose.

"Joy can be the echo of God's life within you."
—Duane Pederson

Daily Devotions:
M. Prayer of Intercession
   Numbers 21:4-9
T. Prayer for Deliverance
   2 Kings 19:14-20
W. Prayer for Healing
   2 Kings 20:1-6
T. Prayer of Confession
   Daniel 9:4-14
F. Prayer for Mercy
   Luke 18:9-14
S. Prayer of Faith
   James 5:13-18

Hannah—Faithful in Prayer

Father rejoices

Abigail—Wise and Determined

1 Samuel 25:1-42

INTRODUCTION

Abigail definitely belongs in this study of great women of the Bible. Of the seven women being reviewed, she is the one most people are less likely to know. Scripture presents her as a beautiful, intelligent woman whose lot in life is one of being married to a rich fool. Abigail reveals how wisdom and determined action need to partner in order to save good people from disaster. Being wise in itself may not be sufficient in some situations. Without taking immediate action, it is possible to simply stand by and watch destruction that could be avoided.

Abigail's example points to the importance of the words chosen when speaking in tense situations. Harsh, loud words may become the catalyst to an unnecessary explosion. They may drive individuals to actions which will be regretted later. In contrast we see how calm, carefully calculated words can lead to a peaceful parting or solution. This lesson's golden text deserves careful attention: "A soft answer turneth away wrath: but grievous words stir up anger" (Proverbs 15:1).

Today's lesson revolves around the attitudes and actions of three persons. One doesn't hesitate to spout inflammatory words without any regard for the potential consequences. Another of the characters hears the words and, in haste, decides to retaliate in a manner with far-reaching implications. Fortunately, standing between them is a woman who immediately grasps the entire setting. Then she races to bring a peaceful end which, in the long run, will bring special benefit to her.

This lesson also provides us with another area for consideration. What should be our attitude when crisis thrusts itself upon us? It's true we have differing personalities and emotional levels. However, every one of us should strive to be "calm, cool and collected." This can be accomplished as we keep a tight rein on ourselves and allow the Holy Spirit to guide us. "Think twice before speaking once" is wise advice.

Unit Theme:
Great Women of the Bible

Central Truth:
Wise intervention can avert serious conflict.

Focus:
Analyze Abigail's response to crisis and deal wisely with conflict.

Context:
About 1031 in Carmel, a city in the mountain country of Judah

Golden Text:
"A soft answer turneth away wrath: but grievous words stir up anger" (Proverbs 15:1).

Study Outline:
I. Determined Action (1 Samuel 25:2-6, 9-19)
II. Wise Council (1 Samuel 25:20-31)
III. Courage Rewarded (1 Samuel 25:32-42)

Nabal=) (Insensato)

I. DETERMINED ACTION (1 Samuel 25:2-6, 9-19)
A. David's Request (vv. 2-6, 9)
(1 Samuel 25:4-6, 9 is not included in the printed text.)

2. And there was a man in Maon, whose possessions were in Carmel; and the man was very great, and he had three thousand sheep, and a thousand goats: and he was shearing his sheep in Carmel.

3. Now the name of the man was Nabal; and the name of his wife Abigail: and she was a woman of good understanding, and of a beautiful countenance: but the man was churlish and evil in his doings; and he was of the house of Caleb.

Talk About It:
1. Describe the differences between Nabal and his wife, Abigail (v. 3).
2. How had David's men treated Nabal's shepherds (v. 7)?
3. What request did David's men make (v. 8)?

The story of Abigail is set in the years when David and his men are fugitives from King Saul. Repeatedly Saul's forces pursue David, but he successfully eludes them in spite of the spies located in various parts of the country. On one occasion David is in the wilderness of Paran, which was located west of the southern end of the Dead Sea. This vast area proves to be a good area for raising sheep and goats. A wealthy man named Nabal uses it for his very large flocks.

Though Nabal lives in the town of Maon, he owns property at Carmel, a small nearby town. Verse 2 indicates by numbers how wealthy he is. Having this many sheep and goats will necessitate a number of shepherds to provide them with proper care. One can only imagine the effort to shear the sheep and then care for the wool. Besides the work, the shearing time also becomes a time for festivity. Nabal, more than likely, doesn't spend his time there during most of the year. Since shearing would be similar in importance to harvest for a farmer, he is there for this significant shearing event.

The difference in personality between Nabal and his wife, Abigail, are pronounced. She is both beautiful and intelligent. Her name means "whose father is joy." Then there is her husband. He is "surly and mean" (v. 3, *NIV*). You wonder if his parents gave him the name *Nabal* ("fool") or if it was conferred on him later in life. How did these two ever get together in marriage? More than likely it came about as the result of an arranged marriage.

Knowing Nabal is personally in the area, David sends 10 men to greet him and request provisions at this time of festivity. This representative group approaches him with wishes of health and long life for both himself and his household. They point to their treatment of his shepherds and that no animals are missing. This means David and his men did not simply take animals for their personal use like some fugitives would have. It also could indicate their protecting the unarmed shepherds from desert raiders. This will be verified later. It is suggested that Nabal should check the accuracy of their statements with his shepherds. Of course, that would be out of the question with such a personality as his.

Notice, David makes no specific request other than what Nabal could spare at this celebration time. This isn't a "shakedown" or a blackmail attempt.

"One can pay back the loan of gold, but one lies forever in debt to those who are kind."
—*Malay proverb*

B. Nabal's Response (vv. 10-13)

10. And Nabal answered David's servants, and said, Who is David? and who is the son of Jesse? there be many servants now a days that break away every man from his master.

11. Shall I then take my bread, and my water, and my flesh that I have killed for my shearers, and give it unto men, whom I know not whence they be?

12. So David's young men turned their way, and went again, and came and told him all those sayings.

13. And David said unto his men, Gird ye on every man his sword. And they girded on every man his sword; and David also girded on his sword: and there went up after David about four hundred men; and two hundred abode by the stuff.

Nabal's harsh dismissal of David's request demonstrates his true nature. His question "Who is this David?" provides an immediate insult. Who wouldn't know of the hero who just a few years before brought victory to Israel by defeating Goliath? How could Nabal even pretend not to know of the one whom the women sang his praises (18:7)? Nabal's response further suggests David's being a traitor to the king of Israel, a rebel. What a slap in the face to the messengers and their leader!

In view of this portrayal of David, Nabal indicates there being no reason to take provisions from his shearers and give them to David and his men. He offers no appreciation for the services rendered to his men and property. Nabal chooses to serve only himself.

Nabal's response infuriates David. He immediately orders two-thirds of his army (400 men) to strap on their swords and prepare for battle. *Ellicott's Bible Commentary* suggests, "The largeness of the force showed how terribly David was in earnest, and how bent he was on wiping out the insult of Nabal in blood. In Nabal, the rich sheep-master, the rude refuser of the fairly earned gift, David saw a deadly political advisory who would hunt him down like a wild beast." If this isn't the case, we are faced with a great difficulty in attempting to explain David's desire for such an extreme action.

C. Abigail's Efforts (vv. 14-19)

14. But one of the young men told Abigail, Nabal's wife, saying, Behold, David sent messengers out of the wilderness to

Talk About It:
1. What did Nabal imply about David (v. 10)?
2. What was his response to David's request (v. 11)?

salute our master; and he railed on them.

15. But the men were very good unto us, and we were not hurt, neither missed we any thing, as long as we were conversant with them, when we were in the fields:

16. They were a wall unto us both by night and day, all the while we were with them keeping the sheep.

17. Now therefore know and consider what thou wilt do; for evil is determined against our master, and against all his household: for he is such a son of Belial, that a man cannot speak to him.

18. Then Abigail made haste, and took two hundred loaves, and two bottles of wine, and five sheep ready dressed, and five measures of parched corn, and an hundred clusters of raisins, and two hundred cakes of figs, and laid them on asses.

19. And she said unto her servants, Go on before me; behold, I come after you. But she told not her husband Nabal.

When one of the young men inform Abigail of the events, she understands this is a crisis. Immediately she mounts an effort to avoid an unnecessary catastrophe.

It is interesting how this informant viewed what took place. David's men brought an appropriate greeting from David to Nabal. He in turn responded with no hint of expected Oriental hospitality and gratitude. Rather, Nabal hurled insults at them. This worker's description carries added weight due to his having personally seen and experienced the attitude and care of David and his men. In verse 15 he describes the protective care given by David's men to Nabal's shepherds. He describes them as being a wall shielding them day and night (v. 16).

Having shared the story, this unnamed man places the future in Abigail's hands. He knows disaster will come on them. It is possible some had attempted to speak to Nabal about the situation. But if they did, it accomplished nothing. Stubborn, obstinate, egotistical men do not change their minds! Or, if they do, it is under considerable pressure of the more powerful.

Abigail quickly gathers food supplies as a gift for David and his men. The availability of this amount of food indicates a sizeable number of individuals worked for Nabal. Once the donkeys are loaded, she sends them on ahead. Possibly she needed some extra time to be prepared properly for the meeting. All this takes place without Nabal's knowledge. More than likely he is out supervising or observing the shearing.

II. WISE COUNSEL (1 Samuel 25:20-31)
A. David's Intent (vv. 20-22)

20. And it was so, as she rode on the ass, that she came

Talk About It:
1. Describe the "wall" Nabal's servant mentions in verse 16.
2. How did the servant describe Nabal (v. 17)?
3. What risk did Abigail take (v. 19)?

At the Rough Rider Hotel in historic Medora, North Dakota, the breakfast placemats contained a variety of quotes from well-known individuals. One which stood out was from Will Rogers (1879-1935). It stated, "Never miss a good opportunity to shut up."

down by the covert of the hill, and, behold, David and his men came down against her; and she met them.

21. Now David had said, Surely in vain have I kept all that this fellow hath in the wilderness, so that nothing was missed of all that pertained unto him: and he hath requited me evil for good.

22. So and more also do God unto the enemies of David, if I leave of all that pertain to him by the morning light any that pisseth against the wall.

In these verses David's thought process becomes very evident. He realizes how worthless all his good deeds to Nabal really are. Caring for Nabal's property brought nothing more than the railing insults of a wealthy, self-centered person. This evil response deserves the most severe retribution in David's mind. He decides to attack Nabal's encampment and kill all the males. Then, David and his men could take all the needed supplies.

Talk About It:
What was David's intent, and why (vv. 21, 22)?

In this vengeful environment Abigail meets David. It is interesting how Scripture describes the exact location of their meeting. The mountain ravine provides a narrow place guaranteeing their coming face-to-face.

B. Abigail's Intercession (vv. 23-25)

23. And when Abigail saw David, she hasted, and lighted off the ass, and fell before David on her face, and bowed herself to the ground,

24. And fell at his feet, and said, Upon me, my lord, upon me let this iniquity be: and let thine handmaid, I pray thee, speak in thine audience, and hear the words of thine handmaid.

25. Let not my lord, I pray thee, regard this man of Belial, even Nabal: for as his name is, so is he; Nabal is his name, and folly is with him: but I thine handmaid saw not the young men of my lord, whom thou didst send.

Wisdom and determination evidence themselves in Abigail's actions. This is a make-or-break situation. If she can intercept and persuade David from his intended purpose, there will not be the shedding of much innocent blood. Nabal probably deserves David's wrath; however, those working for him are simply pawns in this setting.

Talk About It:
1. Explain Abigail's statement, "Upon me let this iniquity be" (v. 24).
2. How did Nabal live up to his name (v. 25)?

Recognizing who David is, Abigail immediately dismounts from her donkey and offers the bow of greatest humility. Instead of remaining on her feet and bowing either her head or from the waist, Abigail prostrates herself at David's feet. Notice her intercession. In an attempt to ward off the bloodshed and save innocent lives, she asks for the blame to be hers. Though having nothing to do with what took place, she willingly offers herself as the culprit. Only after setting the stage does she ask David to disregard the words and actions of her husband. What a contrast between Abigail's wise humility and Nabal's foolish pride.

Abigail's words in verse 25 indicate she knows the true nature of her husband. She understands him to be truly a "man of Belial"—a person who is worthless or without profit. Yes, he amasses riches, but as a person he is a "no account." Abigail points out how his name fulfills his actions. A fool makes foolish decisions.

Working as the intercessor and mediator, Abigail points to herself as being different than her husband. This is accomplished by stating she did not see the delegation of David's men when they came. Her insinuation is that things would have been different if she had.

C. Abigail's Counsel (vv. 26-31)
(1 Samuel 25:26-29 is not included in the printed text.)

30. And it shall come to pass, when the Lord shall have done to my lord according to all the good that he hath spoken concerning thee, and shall have appointed thee ruler over Israel;

31. That this shall be no grief unto thee, nor offence of heart unto my lord, either that thou hast shed blood causeless, or that my lord hath avenged himself: but when the Lord shall have dealt well with my lord, then remember thine handmaid.

A major shift now comes into the conversation. Abigail goes beyond a wife interceding for her husband and household. She suddenly becomes a messenger of the Lord. A much bigger picture comes to light as Abigail shares an understanding of God's purpose and future status of David. In verse 26 she, in essence, points to her coming as the action of the Lord keeping him from bloodshed. It's another instance of God's care and direction in David's life. For this reason the future king should be thankful.

Talk About It:
1. What would it mean for David's enemies to "be as Nabal" (v. 26)?
2. What did Abigail say the Lord would do for David (v. 27)? How did she know this?

Abigail follows with a blessing on David, which is a condemnation of all enemies in the future. This does take place during David's reign. He defeats the enemies on all sides of Israel. When the kingdom passes to his son Solomon, there is an era of peace.

✸ Whom you associate with does make a difference! In this case Abigail wants the blessing for David to spread to the men with him (v. 27). They too have been saved from killing the innocent. She wishes for the future success of David to overflow to them.

In verse 28 Abigail once again identifies herself with the actions of her husband as though they were her own. And then she moves beyond the present situation to assure David he will

Abigail—Wise and Determined

become Israel's king. The anointing of at least a decade earlier will be fulfilled. Reference to the establishment of a "sure house" speaks of a dynasty. Several years into David's reign, God assures him of an everlasting family member being on the throne (2 Samuel 7).

The Lord will partner with David and fight his battles. This doesn't take away from David's involvement and efforts. David can be assured of the inability of Saul ("a man . . . risen to pursue thee," v. 29) to thwart his rise to the throne.

Verse 31 urges David not to engage in vengeful actions which, in the future, would bring considerable grief. David would bear the stain of the blood of innocent victims on his hands. Now, thanks to the intervention of Abigail, he can face the future with a clean heart.

Abigail concludes her words with a request referring to the time when David will have ascended to the throne. What she may have had in mind can only be a matter of speculation. This writer doubts she could have ever imagined her position in the near future.

> "Colors fade, temples crumble, but wise words endure."
> —Edward Thorndike

III. COURAGE REWARDED (1 Samuel 25:32-42)
A. David's Acceptance (vv. 32-35)

32. And David said to Abigail, Blessed be the Lord God of Israel, which sent thee this day to meet me:

33. And blessed be thy advice, and blessed be thou, which hast kept me this day from coming to shed blood, and from avenging myself with mine own hand.

34. For in very deed, as the Lord God of Israel liveth, which hath kept me back from hurting thee, except thou hadst hasted and come to meet me, surely there had not been left unto Nabal by the morning light any that pisseth against the wall.

35. So David received of her hand that which she had brought him, and said unto her, Go up in peace to thine house; see, I have hearkened to thy voice, and have accepted thy person.

Abigail's plea begins an immediate positive response from David. We see instant gratitude, first to God and then to Abigail. David recognizes the hand of God in this situation. He praises this wise woman for taking action which will stop innocent bloodshed. Except for her intervention, the obliteration of Nabal and his household would surely be the result. She stands in the gap protecting both parties. Her decisive action allows life to continue.

In verse 35, David accepts the provisions from Abigail and instructs her to go home in peace. There is nothing to fear. David heeds her words and request.

> **Talk About It:**
> What did David say about Abigail and her advice (vv. 32, 33, 35)?

> "It takes a great man to give sound advice tactfully, but a greater man to accept it graciously."
> —J.C. Macaulay

B. Nabal's Death (vv. 36-38)

36. And Abigail came to Nabal; and, behold, he held a feast in his house, like the feast of a king; and Nabal's heart was merry within him, for he was very drunken: wherefore she told him nothing, less or more, until the morning light.

37. But it came to pass in the morning, when the wine was gone out of Nabal, and his wife had told him these things, that his heart died within him, and he became as a stone.

38. And it came to pass about ten days after, that the Lord smote Nabal, and he died.

Upon arriving home from intercepting David, the situation is not right for Abigail to speak to Nabal concerning her actions and David's intent. Nabal is in the middle of a feast celebrating as though he were a king. Perhaps he is celebrating another successful sheep-shearing with the resulting profit. Or he may be thinking himself to be some special person for insulting and dismissing David's messengers. Regardless of the reason, it becomes his last riotous celebration.

The next morning, once Nabal regains his sobriety, Abigail recounts the events of the previous day. Verse 37 indicates her telling him "all these things" (*NIV*). More than likely, this means she tells the story in detail and possibly recounts the exact words. (Remember, women generally tend to be able to recount the specifics of a conversation in far greater detail than men.) Apparently the stress of his foolishness, which nearly brought death to him at the hand of David, becomes too great. The description of his heart failing and becoming like a stone is probably what we would call a heart attack or stroke. He lingers for 10 days, and then dies.

Verse 38 helps us put Nabal's death in perspective. God strikes the health of this man and takes his life. The failure of Nabal isn't just rudeness and hoarding. It's his insulting and dismissing the servants of David, who is God's anointed to be the next king of Israel.

C. Abigail's Future (vv. 39-42)

(1 Samuel 25:40-42 is not included in the printed text.)

39. And when David heard that Nabal was dead, he said, Blessed be the Lord, that hath pleaded the cause of my reproach from the hand of Nabal, and hath kept his servant from evil: for the Lord hath returned the wickedness of Nabal upon his own head. And David sent and communed with Abigail, to take her to him to wife.

News of Nabal's death stimulates David to once again offer praise and thanksgiving for God's intervention. He recognizes

Talk About It
Why do you suppose Abigail's report had a deathly impact on her husband?

"I shall tell you a great secret, my friend. Do not wait for the last judgment; it takes place every day."
—Albert Camus

Abigail—Wise and Determined

the contempt and insult of Nabal deserved retaliation, but not in the way he was going to accomplish it. Instead, God allowed Nabal's own surliness to be the cause of his death.

Wasting no time and apparently with no hesitancy, David begins the negotiations for Abigail to become his wife. Following the custom of sending an intermediary, David sends his servants. However, they aren't really asking; she is expected to accept. She does, with great humility. Her bowing and offering to wash the servants' feet shows her character (v. 41). It also shows her willingness to become David's wife.

Abigail doesn't delay in going to David. There appears to be no lengthy time of putting the household in order or taking care of business. With her five maids, Abigail immediately joins David (v. 42).

We do not know the rest of the story. Becoming David's wife definitely provides a change. Instead of living in an established home in one location, Abigail now becomes part of a group who move from place to place avoiding the forces of Saul. Plus, she will not be the only wife of David. However, Abigail apparently knows the position of being David's wife is better than any of the alternatives. The woman who stopped David from making a disastrous decision is now placed under his loving care.

Talk About It
1. How did David interpret Nabal's death (v. 39)?
2. What does verse 41 reveal about Abigail?

"Humility is to make a right estimate of one's self."
—**Charles Spurgeon**

CONCLUSION

This brief glimpse into the life of Abigail speaks so loudly as to the impact a wise woman can have on the life of a man. She protected both her current husband and the man who later would become her husband. Abigail seized the information given, understood what needed to be done, and then did it.

GOLDEN TEXT CHALLENGE

"A SOFT ANSWER TURNETH AWAY WRATH: BUT GRIEVOUS WORDS STIR UP ANGER" (Proverbs 15:1).

Will we respond to the angry person positively or negatively—pleasantly or bitterly? Will we be gentle and conciliatory, or will we cause more bitterness and anger?

"A soft answer" is not a weak one. Often the most powerful response is given in the mildest tone. Even though the substance is firm, the language and spirit are gentle. Such an answer is hard to resent or refute.

When we use a soft answer, wrath is turned away. Anger is silenced. These negative emotions or attitudes cannot burn without fuel to feed them.

• What are the effects of using grievous or bitter words? Hatred, cruelty and misery. Bitterness is more powerful than wrath. While rage thunders, bitterness stabs. It creates more ill will than the angry words that provoke it.

Daily Devotions:
M. Wise Craftsmanship Exodus 31:1-6
T. Wisdom to Obey the Law Deuteronomy 4:1-9
W. Wisdom to Lead 1 Kings 4:29-34
T. Wisdom of God 1 Corinthians 1:17-25
F. Walk in Wisdom Ephesians 5:15-21
S. Wisdom From Above James 3:13-18

Mary Magdalene—Demoniac to Disciple

Luke 8:1-3; John 20:1-18

Unit Theme:
Great Women of the Bible

Central Truth:
A radically changed life is a dynamic testimony of Christ's transforming power.

Focus:
Marvel at the profound change seen in the life of Mary Magdalene and yield ourselves to Christ's transforming power.

Context:
Mary Magdalene lived during Christ's time on earth.

Golden Text:
"Be not conformed to this world: but be ye transformed by the renewing of your mind, that ye may prove what is that good, and acceptable, and perfect, will of God" (Romans 12:2).

Study Outline:
I. A Life Transformed (Luke 8:1-3)
II. Devoted Herald (John 20:1-9)
III. Seeing Christ Clearly (John 20:10-18)

INTRODUCTION

One of the great proofs of Christianity continues to be the reality of changed lives. Commitment to Christ and the empowerment of the Holy Spirit brings about transformation which amazes people even years later. In the early centuries of the church, the apologists (defenders of the faith to unbelievers) used this transformation as one of their basic arguments. Radical changes which are so widespread among believers definitely speak of a divine power.

A radically changed life most frequently is the testimony of the person who "lived a lot" by experiencing the offerings of a sinful world. These may include alcohol and drug addiction, sexual immorality, crime, and a disregard for their own health and safety. When these individuals make a commitment to Christ as Savior and Lord, the change evidences itself in a dramatic manner.

Sometimes those of us who were raised in sheltered Christian environments and did not participate in many of the sinful indulgences of our era may feel we do not have a strong testimony. But we do! We too have been transformed and made new creatures in Christ. We have been spared from the degradation and heartache so many have experienced. This is the greatest testimony of all!

All of us who accept Christ experience a radical change within. But for those who have steeped themselves in the pleasures of the world, the change is more dramatically seen by those around them. In those cases they have the opportunity to share a dynamic testimony.

Recently in an attempt to make people more visually aware of the impact of drugs, some before-and-after billboards have appeared. On the left side is a normal-looking man or woman. On the right is how they now look after being on "meth." Their teeth have rotted, their skin is splotched, and they appear to have aged 10 years or more in a short period. In marked contrast are the changes for good which come to those who receive Christ and drastically alter their lifestyles. Though we do not have a picture of Mary Magdalene before and after, it's only logical to believe she too experienced a radical transformation.

I. A LIFE TRANSFORMED (Luke 8:1-3)

A. Delivered (vv. 1, 2)

1. And it came to pass afterward, that he went throughout every city and village, preaching and shewing the glad tidings of the kingdom of God: and the twelve were with him,

2. And certain women, which had been healed of evil spirits and infirmities, Mary called Magdalene, out of whom went seven devils.

Our introduction to Mary Magdalene comes as part of a description of Christ's ministry. He and a ministry team are traveling throughout a variety of cities and villages. This particular itinerary is not recorded in any of the other Gospels. In Luke 8 the 12 disciples are not divided into teams traveling in various directions. *Ellicott's Bible Commentary* described it as follows: "The Master and the disciples formed at this period one traveling company. When they arrived at the town or village, they held a mission, the Twelve heralding His approach and inviting men to listen to Him as He taught in synagogue, market-place, or open plain."

Luke also records another company traveling as a separate group to maintain propriety within the cultural setting as well as not allowing any accusations of immoral conduct. They would arrive in advance of the Master and His disciples to make arrangements for food and lodging.

In verse 2, Luke specifically records by name one of the women in this company. The attachment of "Magdalene" to her name indicates her being from the town of Magdala. It was located on the western side of the Sea of Galilee not far from Tiberias. In just a few words it becomes evident that Mary Magdalene was the recipient of miraculous deliverances. Where previously her body was inflicted with disease, she is now healthy! At one time she was possessed by evil spirits, but now she is free and a follower of Jesus.

The seriousness of Mary Magdalene's demon possession is seen by their numbering seven. This is also recorded in Mark's Gospel (16:9). *Seven* indicates an especially aggravated or violent form of possession. What this may have meant to Mary in her past is not explained. One can only speculate.

B. Supporting (v. 3)

3. And Joanna the wife of Chuza Herod's steward, and Susanna, and many others, which ministered unto him of their substance.

Apparently a number of influential women chose to be a part of Christ's traveling ministry. They supported Him with their labor, their presence and their substance.

Talk About It:
1. From verse 1, what can you learn about Christ's ministry on earth?
2. Describe the women who assisted Jesus in His ministry.

"Thank God for that 'fine linen, clean and white, the righteousness' with which Christ covers our wounded nakedness. It becomes ours, though no thread of it was wrought in our looms."

—Alexander MacLaren

Chuza (KOO-zuh)—a business manager of Herod and the husband of Joanna

---

Herod—one of the
"Herods" who ruled
for the Romans in
Palestine

Talk About It:
How did the women
minister to Jesus?

**From Crime to
Christ**
Standing on the
platform with his
family surrounding
him, a humble indi-
vidual with tears
streaming down his
face received his
ordination certificate.
This man used to be
one of the most
feared criminals in
Lima, Peru. People
purposefully avoided
walking on his side
of the street. But on
one witnessing
team, an older lady
felt constrained of
the Holy Spirit to
walk on that side
and present the
gospel of Christ. As
a result, he is now a
pastor bringing life
rather than threaten-
ing death.

Talk About It:
Why do you sup-
pose Mary went to
the tomb so early?

Verse 3 points to the women mentioned by name as well as others possessing substantial financial resources. This appears to indicate Mary Magdalene belonged to a wealthy segment of Galilean society. She and the other women willingly financed the ministry of Jesus and His disciples.

There are so many bits of information we would like to know. For example, what type of family did Mary come from? Was she married? Did she have children? How was it possible for her to leave her home and be part of the ministry company? If she was one of the wealthy individuals, how did the family come to be one of means?

When you think of Mary Magdalene's spiritual and physical deliverance, it seems logical for her to be part of the ministry. Not only would she be thankful for her transformation, she would also want others to have the same opportunity. There is a personal application here for all of us. When we consider what salvation means to our present and future lives, we should want others to have the same experience. We do not need money to do so. Simply giving our testimony is the main thing. If we happen to be blessed with financial extras, then we should seek to support those who are ministering in ways and areas not open to us. Let us follow the Great Commission model (Matthew 28:19, 20), which reminds us to start where we are and then expand our reach.

Here is a good place to stop and emphasize the central truth of the lesson. Everyone who accepts Jesus Christ as Savior and Lord experiences a radical change. Regardless of our situation, each one of us is transformed and has a dynamic testimony. Once we were hopelessly on the path to eternal punishment, but now we are looking for eternal life with the heavenly Father. Once we were blind to the concept of true life, but now our eyes are open to truth and to the joy of having a fulfilled life in Jesus Christ.

II. DEVOTED HERALD (John 20:1-9)
A. Early Visitor (v. 1)
1. The first day of the week cometh Mary Magdalene early, when it was dark, unto the sepulchre, and seeth the stone taken away from the sepulchre.

This part of our lesson is a drastic shift from its first section. Instead of a traveling ministry, Christ's disciples are facing a cruel reality. After being arrested and abused, their Master was subjected to the cruelest form of death sentence—crucifixion. As far as they knew, He still lay dead in the tomb of Joseph of Arimathaea (Matthew 27:57-60).

After the hasty burial of Christ due to the nearing hours of the Sabbath, those having witnessed it returned home to observe the 24-hour period. Once the Sabbath was over, the women bought spices to be taken to the tomb. These embalming spices did not preserve the body. Their purpose was to help cover the odor of a decaying body. About 4 a.m. Mary Magdalene and another Mary (Matthew 28:1) came to the tomb.

This early hour for their arrival indicates the urgency they felt to provide proper care for the Master's body. Having served Him in life, they intended to continue that pattern of care even after death. Much to their amazement, even in the darkness it became evident the stone was moved from the tomb's entrance. The usual pattern of tomb construction was to have a layer of stone which rolled on a downward track to close. To open it required several individuals to roll it upward and block it.

B. The Announcement (vv. 2-9)

(John 20:4-9 is not included in the printed text.)

2. Then she runneth, and cometh to Simon Peter, and to the other disciple, whom Jesus loved, and saith unto them, They have taken away the Lord out of the sepulchre, and we know not where they have laid him.

3. Peter therefore went forth, and that other disciple, and came to the sepulchre.

Coming to the tomb at about the same time are two of the 12 disciples, Peter and John. Apparently Mary runs back to where they are with a startling announcement—the body of Jesus isn't there. She assumes someone is responsible for moving the body. Her immediate concern is not knowing where they placed Him.

In writing this account, John doesn't use the pronoun *I*. Nor does he refer to himself by name. Instead he emphasizes relationship. A closeness exists between John and the Master.

Hearing Mary's announcement, the two men run toward the tomb. This is not a time for standing around and discussing possibilities. Apparently John is the faster runner of the two, arriving first at the empty tomb. He doesn't wait for Peter to arrive before checking out the situation. Without entering he simply looks inside. Plainly visible are the linen cloths which would have been wound around the body. Immediately this showed an unusual situation. Anyone moving the body wouldn't remove the linen grave bands.

Upon arriving, Peter immediately walks inside the burial tomb. He too sees the grave wrappings simply lying there. Then he notices another significant piece of evidence. The separate face napkin, which was placed on the head in the process of preparation, is in another part of the tomb. This would indicate someone's removing it and specifically folding it. That would not be the action of a grave robber.

"Almost every day of my life I am praying that 'a jubilant pining and longing for God' might come back on the evangelical churches. We don't need to have our doctrine straightened out; we are as orthodox as the Pharisees of old. But this longing for God that brings torrents and whirlwinds of seeking and self-denial—that is almost gone from our world."
—A.W. Tozer

Talk About It:
1. Who is the "they" Mary mentions in verse 2?
2. What do you think John "believed" (v. 8)?
3. What did Peter and John not yet "know" (v. 9), and why not?

Verse 8 indicates John's also entering the tomb. Now he sees the complete picture. Faith wells up, and sorrow is drowned out as Peter and John comprehend a miraculous resurrection. Christ's past speaking of the Resurrection now can be understood. Previously they were slow of heart and understanding. But now they see what was predicted, though not fully comprehending it.

III. SEEING CHRIST CLEARLY (John 20:10-18)

A. Weeping (vv. 10-13)

10. Then the disciples went away again into their own home.

11. But Mary stood without at the sepulchre weeping: and as she wept, she stooped down, and looked into the sepulchre,

12. And seeth two angels in white sitting, the one at the head, and the other at the feet, where the body of Jesus had lain.

13. And they say unto her, Woman, why weepest thou? She saith unto them, Because they have taken away my Lord, and I know not where they have laid him.

Talk About It:
Compare Mary's actions (v. 11) with Peter and John's.

By comparing the accounts of the other Gospel writers, it appears that Mary Magdalene leaves the other two women who are with her to run back where Peter and John are still on the way. After they enter the tomb, see the signs, and are convinced of what has taken place, they return to their own homes. For some unknown reason, Mary doesn't enter the tomb while the disciples are there. One wonders whether or not some conversation passes between them. Regardless of the possibilities, one thing is for sure: Mary stands outside the tomb and weeps. She isn't demonstrating any sense of believing in a resurrected Master.

Previously Mary Magdalene saw only the opened tomb. She did not look inside. Finally, through her tears she chooses to see for herself. But it definitely is different from what Peter and John saw. Their attention was on the grave cloths. That's all there was in the tomb. In marked contrast are the angelic visitors Mary now sees. What a contrast! Once she was a woman under the domination of evil spirits. Now she enjoys the privilege of heavenly beings talking with her in the moments of sorrow.

The angels confronted Mary with a question. The content seems illogical in view of the setting—Jesus' crucifixion, His burial, and now her concept of the body being moved. Of course she would be weeping in view of what Jesus had delivered her from and her involvement in His ministry. Yet God challenged Mary to think on what she had witnessed and express how she felt about it.

Mary Magdalene—Demoniac to Disciple

In the Old Testament we see God asking Moses the seemingly insignificant question, "What is that in your hand?" (Exodus 4:2, *NIV*). Later, when the men of Ai defeated Israel, causing the people's courage to melt away, the Lord commanded Joshua, who was mourning, to "stand up"! Then He asked the question, "What are you doing down on your face?" (Joshua 7:10, *NIV*).

Each of these situations remind us of the need to think and to express oneself with the Lord. Yes, He already knows where we are in our thought process, but still wants us to speak.

Mary's response points to her perceived dilemma. Her response to the angels is consistent with what she earlier spoke to the disciples (John 20:2). The Lord's body is missing. As if it was not enough for them to have seen the suffering and death of Jesus, now the body is gone. *Who would have been so bold? Why would they have wanted to do such a deed of desecration?* No wonder she stands weeping.

Her assumption of the body's being moved was a limited, earthly perception. Lest we become too hard or judgmental on Mary, we must remember our having the advantage of looking back with all the Scriptural records. It is so easy for us to assume she should have been sensitive to the whole picture. Yet, if we are honest, we too have probably been shortsighted in some of our perceptions.

> "The Lord rewards faithfulness above fruitfulness, which puts us all on the same footing, whether famous for our effectiveness or unknown in our faithfulness."
> —John Piper

B. Meeting (vv. 14-18)

14. And when she had thus said, she turned herself back, and saw Jesus standing, and knew not that it was Jesus.

15. Jesus saith unto her, Woman, why weepest thou? whom seekest thou? She, supposing him to be the gardener, saith unto him, Sir, if thou have borne him hence, tell me where thou hast laid him, and I will take him away.

16. Jesus saith unto her, Mary. She turned herself and saith unto him, Rabboni; which is to say, Master.

17. Jesus saith unto her, Touch me not; for I am not yet ascended to my Father: but go to my brethren, and say unto them, I ascend unto my Father, and your Father; and to my God, and your God.

18. Mary Magdalene came and told the disciples that she had seen the Lord, and that he had spoken these things unto her.

There is no record of the angels responding to Mary's perceived dilemma of the Lord's missing body. For some reason she turns from them. No reason is given in Scripture. Many of the earlier Biblical commentators believe the angels motioned to indicate someone being behind Mary. When she turns,

Talk About It:
1. Why do you suppose Mary did not recognize Jesus at first?

2. What title did Mary use in addressing Jesus, and why (v. 16)?
3. In verse 17, describe the various ways Jesus referred to His heavenly Father.

Jesus stands near her, but she doesn't recognize Him. Maybe it was due to there being some difference in His resurrected body. Maybe tears dimmed her ability to focus. There also was the unexpectedness of His appearance.

Even after asking her the reason for weeping, Mary doesn't recognize the Master. It's the same question asked by the angels. Assuming He must be the gardener, since it wouldn't be logical for anyone else to be there at that hour, she asks about Jesus' body. She concludes if anyone knows, the caretaker will.

Isn't it interesting how Mary never uses Jesus' name? There's the assumption of considerable knowledge or, in her grief, she simply fails to state all the information.

Without stating it specifically, Mary implies her desire to take Jesus' body and give it a proper burial. How she would accomplish this apparently hasn't been thought through. She couldn't handle the body by herself. Also, where would she place it? All of this becomes inconsequential when Jesus simply says her name, "Mary."

Immediately Mary turns and replies with the Aramaic word *Rabboni*, meaning "Master." She hears His voice differently this time. She knows the Master's voice speaking her name. As would be expected, she apparently touches Him and holds on. It is at this point where a modern translation more accurately states Christ's response. Instead of His saying "Touch me not," the original language is better translated "Do not hold on to me." He isn't asking her not to start doing a particular action but rather to stop doing something.

It is suggested that Jesus was pointing to the fact that He was not yet ready to make a permanent ascension to the Father. She would see Him again. But for now there was a task at hand. She was to go and give the message of Jesus' resurrection and coming ascension. He told her, "Go to my brethren" (v. 17). Even though His disciples had failed Christ during His suffering, He called them His brothers.

When Mary arrives at the location of the disciples, she has a marvelous account to give. What a meeting she had experienced! Instead of bringing spices and placing them on the wrapped body of Jesus, she had met the resurrected Lord face-to-face. And she saw and spoke with angels.

Mary's experience reminds us of the spiritual experiences which can be ours when we seek our Master, the Lord Jesus Christ. The glory of God can be sensed by those who will actively seek to know Him. Paul's words to the Philippian church are appropriate here: "I want to know Christ and the power of his resurrection and the fellowship of sharing in his sufferings, becoming like him in his death" (Philippians 3:10, *NIV*).

"There is not a situation so chaotic that God cannot from that situation create something that is surpassingly good. He did it at the Creation. He did it at the Cross. He is doing it today."
—Handley Moule

CONCLUSION

Mary Magdalene provides an example of the power of God to transform a life. Regardless of the depths of sin into which one has fallen, he or she can be rescued and changed into a new creation with a new purpose in life. Mary Magdalene once suffered under the control of demons but was delivered to become a disciple. Countless similar stories can be found throughout the history of Christianity. The names are different, but the renewal is the same.

GOLDEN TEXT CHALLENGE

"BE NOT CONFORMED TO THIS WORLD: BUT BE YE TRANSFORMED BY THE RENEWING OF YOUR MIND, THAT YE MAY PROVE WHAT IS THAT GOOD, AND ACCEPTABLE, AND PERFECT, WILL OF GOD" (Romans 12:2).

The transformation here urged has its negative and positive aspect. The believer is not to be conformed to this world but transformed by a mental renewal.

This world refers to the present order of things, the age in which we live, humanity under sin—seeking its own way, separated from God, and governed by unbelief, pride, selfishness and Satan. To be *conformed* to this age is to yield oneself to it, following the line of least resistance, until one becomes like the age. Such conformation is forbidden to the believer. Demas forsook Paul, "having loved this present world [age]" (2 Timothy 4:10). Thus the Holy Spirit may be grieved, and the person polluted and paralyzed.

To be *transformed* is to be changed from within in such a way as to give external expression. As Jesus was transfigured on the mount by an unveiling of the divine glory within, so the believer is called upon to give expression to the spiritual renewal within. The renewing of the mind is the work of the Holy Spirit, and the manner in which the transformation takes place. The consequence of this transformation is "the recognition of God's will as right and fit and ideal" (*New Bible Commentary*). The Christian whose mind has been renewed "tests the reality and power of moral truth by actual experience; to others it is a region of phrase and fancy" (H.P. Liddon).

Daily Devotions:
M. From Deceiver to Prince
Genesis 32:24-30
T. From Bondage to Freedom
Deuteronomy 26:1-9
W. From Shepherd to King
1 Samuel 16:1, 7-13
T. From Death to Life
John 5:24-29
F. From Betrayer to Proclaimer
Acts 2:14-21
S. From Persecutor to Apostle
Acts 22:4-15

Mary and Martha—Friends of Jesus

Luke 10:38-42; John 11:1-27; 12:1-7

Unit Theme:
Great Women of the Bible

Central Truth:
God rejoices in all of our expressions of devotion to Him.

Focus:
Compare two styles of devotion and respect our individual ways of experiencing God.

Context:
Three accounts depicting Mary and Martha's friendship with Christ

Golden Text:
"Henceforth I call you not servants; for the servant knoweth not what his lord doeth: but I have called you friends" (John 15:15).

Study Outline:
I. Contrast in Devotion
(Luke 10:38-42)
II. Declaration of Faith
(John 11:17-27)
III. Humble Service
(John 12:1-7)

INTRODUCTION

We often use the term *friends* rather loosely. It is used to refer to people we know, though it may not reach beyond the realm of being acquainted. Some use the term in relationship to those they meet on social occasions or even business dealings. "Fair-weather" friends are those who stick by us when times are good. But when crises come, they make excuses as to their not being there with us.

Genuine friends know us for who we are—strengths as well as weaknesses—and still like us. These individuals speak "straight" to us even when it may not be what we want to hear. They laugh or cry with us depending on the situation. We don't find too many true friends throughout our lifetime.

Friendships don't automatically pop into existence. They must be cultivated and nurtured. People who are so busy "doing" often spend little time getting to really know another person who can be called a true friend.

Friends may be very much like us or very different from us. There's no set rule. Regardless, friendship brings some direct rewards. First, friends stimulate us. They push us to expand our thinking, our interests and our knowledge. Second, friends help us to feel personal value. Because of their care and relationship, we feel important and have worth. Third, friends serve us in a variety of helpful ways in accomplishing what one person or one family could not do alone. Their cooperative spirit helps out in times of need.

When speaking of friendship from a Biblical perspective, the account of Jonathan and David often surfaces. There is every reason for their not becoming friends: though Jonathan was a prince, David was a national hero for killing Goliath; though Jonathan was in line for the throne, David had been anointed by God as the next king. Yet, none of this kept them from having a binding friendship. (Read 1 Samuel 20 to see this bond between friends.)

It's easy to forget that Jesus, during His lifetime here on earth as the God-man, also needed and had friends. He had a close friendship with two sisters, Mary and Martha, and their brother, Lazarus. The details of how their friendship developed are not given. However, we do see individuals with whom Jesus felt comfortable, sought relaxation in their home, and spoke directly as the situation required.

I. CONTRAST IN DEVOTION (Luke 10:38-42)

A. The Contrast (vv. 38, 39)

38. Now it came to pass, as they went, that he entered into a certain village: and a certain woman named Martha received him into her house.

39. And she had a sister called Mary, which also sat at Jesus' feet and heard his word.

Though Luke doesn't record the name of the village, we know from other Biblical references it is Bethany (see John 11:1). Jesus lodged in this village on various occasions (see Matthew 21:17; 26:6; Mark 11:1; 14:3). Bethany is a small town on the eastern slope of the Mount of Olives, situated on the main road between Jerusalem and Transjordan. The name could hold several possible meanings, such as "the house of poverty" or "the house of unripened figs."

In various portions of Scripture, Mary, Martha and Lazarus appear as three adult siblings. Nowhere is there an inclusion of spouses or children. However, it would be unlikely that none of the three ever married. In this case, the home of Martha provides the setting for Jesus' visit and the dialogue which follows. Having received Jesus as her guest places Martha in the role of extending all the hospitality which would normally be offered. Besides, the Master was their friend.

Verse 39 introduces Mary as the sister of Martha. The specific distinction given is her desiring to be given instruction by Jesus. She takes the opportunity to listen and learn. This description of Mary does not mean Martha did not have an interest in Christ's teaching. But when Jesus arrives, Martha begins the work of hospitality while her sister, Mary, involves herself in discipleship.

B. The Concern (v. 40)

40. But Martha was cumbered about much serving, and came to him, and said, Lord, dost thou not care that my sister hath left me to serve alone? bid her therefore that she help me.

A modern translation reads, "But Martha was distracted by all the preparations that had to be made" (*NIV*). These few words of verse 40 give us a good perspective on the situation. There isn't a good-person / bad-person play here. Martha is a friend and follower of Jesus. She is concerned about proper hospitality. The narrative doesn't say who, if anyone else, happened to be traveling with Jesus. As any host can testify, company demands an extra outlay of time and effort to properly care for them.

At this point, it appears Martha has difficulty with her priority. The things to do become more important than the person. All

Talk About It:
1. How should we be like Martha?
2. How should we be like Mary?

"As the sun creates your shadow, God creates your soul, but in each case it is you who determine the shape of it."
—**Frank A. Clark**

cumbered about (v. 40)—"distracted by" (*NIV*)

Talk About It:
Describe Martha's feelings in two words.

the physical responsibilities are overshadowing the spiritual opportunity. Also, it seems unfair for Martha to be doing all the work while Mary just sits and listens to Jesus.

Why did Martha speak to Jesus about Mary's action instead of speaking directly to her sister and asking for her help? Perhaps she felt Mary's not helping was causing the meal to be late, so Jesus didn't care about mealtimes. Maybe Martha thought Jesus would tell Mary to help her sister, and the necessary help would then be given. However, let's not become lost in the possibilities and stay with what is known. Martha is distracted from what is most important.

C. The Considerations (vv. 41, 42)

41. And Jesus answered and said unto her, Martha, Martha, thou art careful and troubled about many things:

42. But one thing is needful: and Mary hath chosen that good part, which shall not be taken away from her.

It is regretful how so many people remember Martha only in terms of these verses. They do not describe the totality of her character or faith, as will be seen later in the lesson. We need individuals who are concerned about the logistics of preparation and wholeheartedly give themselves to this dimension of ministry. Where would we be without people doing the behind-the-scenes work which enables the whole program to be accomplished?

Martha's example here demonstrates how easy it is to become so wrapped up in the details that we forget the greater purpose. She becomes worried about all the things that need to be done and are either late or not accomplished at the moment. Her work for Jesus blots out the need to hear His instruction. The topic really doesn't matter. The issue continues to be hearing what He perceives to be of importance for us.

Jesus doesn't reprove her for wanting to be a hospitable hostess. He is not saying to forget the meal planning and other responsibilities of having a guest. He wants Martha to understand what is most important at the moment. There are some experiences which will last a lifetime. They need to be grasped when available.

Jesus points to Mary's having made the better choice in this case. Sitting at the feet of Jesus comes before any of the household duties of hospitality. He won't always be with them. So now is the time to bask in His presence and take in every word possible. With that in mind, we should ask, *How can I know what is the priority for the moment?*

An excellent approach is to establish principles. For example, a pastor needs to see praying as a priority before preparing to preach. All of us should see spiritual discipleship as a priority over

Talk About It:
1. How did Jesus describe Martha in verse 41?
2. What "one thing is needful" (v. 42)?

Making Friends
In an article titled "I Don't Have Any Friends and I Think I Have Discovered the Reasons," Mike Yaconelli writes: "If we are too busy to have friends, we are much too busy . . . I have decided to make some friends. It will mean I have to stay home [instead of speaking 200 times per year]. It will mean I have to spend time with someone doing absolutely nothing. It will mean I have to work at something that is not easy for me."

activities around the home. That means going to midweek service or a small-group Bible study is more important than cleaning the house or cutting the grass. Yes, the lawn should be neatly trimmed and the house kept as clean as possible, but not at the expense of growing in Christ.

II. DECLARATION OF FAITH (John 11:17-27)
A. Belief in Healing (vv. 17-22)

17. Then when Jesus came, he found that he had lain in the grave four days already.

18. Now Bethany was nigh unto Jerusalem, about fifteen furlongs off:

19. And many of the Jews came to Martha and Mary, to comfort them concerning their brother.

20. Then Martha, as soon as she heard that Jesus was coming, went and met him: but Mary sat still in the house.

21. Then said Martha unto Jesus, Lord, if thou hadst been here, my brother had not died.

22. But I know, that even now, whatsoever thou wilt ask of God, God will give it thee.

John 11 opens with the illness of Lazarus. Apparently the situation becomes so serious the sisters send word to Jesus. Though not stated, we assume they want Him to come and minister healing. Also, remember the close relationship Jesus has with these three individuals (see v. 5). Knowing what needs to take place, Jesus delays His coming to Bethany. When Jesus and the disciples arrive, Lazarus is not only dead but has been buried for four days. Friends of the family still are coming to the home to offer comfort. This seems to indicate the status with which Lazarus must have been held.

When word comes of Jesus' arrival in Bethany, it is Martha who goes out to meet Him. She is proactive. There is something to be said, so why wait? Also, it is normal to go out to meet a close friend. In verses 21 and 22 we see Martha's faith. With assurance, she states her belief in Jesus' ability to overcome illness. She has no doubt Lazarus would be alive today if Jesus had arrived on time. This means she firmly believes in Jesus' power to heal.

Martha understands healing as an event which takes away illness or disabilities from a living person. This reminds us how even people of faith need to have their perspectives of the Master's abilities to be expanded.

B. Belief in Resurrection (vv. 23, 24)

23. Jesus saith unto her, Thy brother shall rise again.

24. Martha saith unto him, I know that he shall rise again in the resurrection at the last day.

Talk About It:
1. How is Martha's personality seen in verse 20?
2. Describe Martha's confidence in Jesus (vv. 21, 22).

"Faith is not the absence of fear or doubt, but the force that gets you safely through those long, dark, waiting-room hours."
—**Merrill Womach**

With simplicity and assurance Jesus replies to Martha, stating her brother will rise again. He is speaking of an immediate healing—a healing from death. Jesus knows Lazarus will live again on this very day and be restored to his family. A marvelous miracle is about to be witnessed by everyone there.

Martha believes the words of Jesus. However, her concept of resurrection is futuristic. She foresees this taking place at the end of time. The death of her brother with the accompanying sorrow doesn't blind her to what is the hope for those who believe. She sees beyond. For that, Martha should be commended. Her example should spur every believer to be reminded of the wonderful hope we have. Life doesn't end at death.

C. Belief in Jesus (vv. 25-27)

25. Jesus said unto her, I am the resurrection, and the life: he that believeth in me, though he were dead, yet shall he live:

26. And whosoever liveth and believeth in me shall never die. Believest thou this?

27. She saith unto him, Yes, Lord: I believe that thou art the Christ, the Son of God, which should come into the world.

Talk About It:
How are both of
these statements
true—"though he
may die, he shall
live" (v. 25, *NKJV*)
and "whoever lives
and believes in Me
shall never die"
(v. 26, *NKJV*)?

In response to Martha's statement of belief, Jesus makes another "I am" declaration. He points her to a present reality instead of a future event. Jesus himself is life. The emphasis is salvation. Through belief in Christ, those who are spiritually dead in their trespasses and sins are raised to life. This life isn't just an extension of our human lives. Rather, this life extends into eternity after our having passed through physical death.

Having made this marvelous claim, Jesus puts Martha on the spot with a direct question: "Do you believe this?" (v. 26, *NKJV*). Can you imagine being in such a situation? She still grieves the death of her brother. She expresses belief in a future resurrection. Then Jesus makes a dramatic claim and wants to know if she believes in Him.

At this point we see the continued evidence of Martha being a woman of faith. Boldly she declares not only her faith but who Jesus is. She knows without hesitancy that Jesus is the promised Messiah. She knows He isn't just a good man living a godly life. This is the promised One who has come into the world for a distinct purpose—to save His people.

III. HUMBLE SERVICE (John 12:1-7)
A. A Joyful Setting (vv. 1, 2)

1. Then Jesus six days before the passover came to Bethany, where Lazarus was which had been dead, whom he raised from the dead.

2. There they made him a supper; and Martha served: but Lazarus was one of them that sat at the table with him.
The scene is clearly Bethany, where Martha, Mary and Lazarus live. Jesus' friends have gone to great effort to prepare for Him at the approaching of Passover. Though His friends don't know it, this event inaugurates the final days of the Lord's earthly ministry. It prepares the stage for His redemptive death. Particular attention is given to Lazarus. In Hebrew his name meant "God has helped." This is certainly an appropriate name for a man recently raised from the dead! The resurrection of Lazarus was clearly the event which led the Jewish authorities to finalize plans for Jesus' death.

Verse 1 specifies Lazarus as the one who had been dead. In 11:17 we are told that Lazarus had been in the grave four days prior to the arrival of Jesus (it was Jewish custom to bury the dead within 24 hours; thus, it is likely he was buried on the same day he died). This is the only recorded miracle in which Jesus raised someone from the dead who was already buried and in a physical state where decomposition would have begun to set in. Thus, the fact that he had actually been dead is reemphasized for any who doubted. The verse also mentioned again that it was Jesus who had raised Lazarus from the dead.

Thus, Lazarus' presence at the table was a source of great joy and hope. It must have been an amazing thing for those around to realize that just days earlier, Lazarus had been dead. The use of "but" (v. 2) gives the phrase in the KJV an odd connotation. It is better translated as simply "and Lazarus was one of them," expressing a statement of fact.

Verse 2 also sets a similar stage to the one in Luke 10. A supper is being prepared and served by Martha. But in this passage Martha offers no complaint toward Mary.

B. An Act of Love (v. 3)
3. Then took Mary a pound of ointment of spikenard, very costly, and anointed the feet of Jesus, and wiped his feet with her hair: and the house was filled with the odour of the ointment.
In Luke 10, Mary sat before the Master and was not deterred in her desire to hear His word. In this passage she is again before Him in an undeterred act of love and devotion.

John carefully recorded the particulars of the event. Mary had a "pound" of ointment. Following His death, a hundred pounds of ointment were used on His body (John 19:39). This pound was valued at about 300 denarii. A denarius was the equivalent of one day's wages for a laborer; thus, it would take nearly a year's salary to purchase the costly item. This explains why there was such reaction to her obvious generous deed.

Talk About It:
What is amazing about this scene?

"It is not possible . . . to trace the wonders of the Lord. When a man has finished, he is just beginning."
—Sirach

ointment of spikenard—perfume made from an oil extracted from a plant in the Himalayan Mountains

pound—"pint" (NIV)

Talk About It:
Explain Mary's unusual deed.

The "ointment of spikenard" was made from a plant from India. It was a perfumed product with a pleasing smell used for burial. It is likely that some days earlier Mary used the same concoction on the body of her dead brother. The reference to cost carries the connotation of "precious, valuable, genuine." The same word is used in 1 Peter 1:7 to describe the value of our faith that is tested and refined in the Spirit in a way greater than gold is refined. John made it very clear that Mary spared no expense or effort to express her love to Christ. Her testimony is a powerful statement of devotion. From Luke 10 we saw that she was determined to listen to Him regardless of the offense. In John 12 we see she is willing to go to great economic expense, at the risk of ridicule, for Him.

✛The house being filled with the odor of the ointment is similar to Paul's thought in 2 Corinthians 2:14-16. There the apostle gave thanks to God because he and his fellow ministers were always triumphant in Christ. As Christ triumphed in their lives, the fragrance of His knowledge was spread everywhere. Paul understood that his life was an aroma of Christ to God for those who believed and those who did not believe. For those who believed Paul's preaching of Christ, the aroma led to life; for those who rejected the message of Christ, the aroma was that of death. We should not miss the point that those who show such devoted love to Christ will indeed change the atmosphere around them.

C. A Critical Spirit (vv. 4-6)

4. Then saith one of his disciples, Judas Iscariot, Simon's son, which should betray him,

5. Why was not this ointment sold for three hundred pence, and given to the poor?

6. This he said, not that he cared for the poor; but because he was a thief, and had the bag, and bare what was put therein.

John records only Judas as the protester to Mary's actions; however, we know from Matthew and Mark that almost the entire group, including disciples, began to rebuke her. It is important to note Martha is not specifically mentioned as being one of this protesting group; she had apparently learned her lesson earlier.

Besides this passage, there are other texts in John that relate to Judas. The first is 6:64, which reveals that Jesus knew from the beginning of His ministry with the Twelve who would betray Him. His insight into people's hearts showed not only the potential for good that was in Judas, but also the potential to be seduced by evil. In verse 70, Jesus spoke openly to the Twelve that one of them was a devil. Verse 71 is John's editorial comment

Talk About It:
1. How valuable was this perfume, and what was the basis of Judas' complaint?
2. What was Judas' underlying motive?

Mary and Martha—Friends of Jesus

that identified Judas (obviously after the event). In 17:12, Jesus offered prayer for the disciples and made mention of "the son of perdition" who would be lost.

From 12:6, we know Judas had already been stealing from the money bags in his possession. That Jesus and the Twelve were given money is clear from Luke 8:3. That Judas was easily seduced by money is clear from the bribe taken in Matthew 26:14-16. In Matthew's account of the bribe, it fulfills the prophecy of Zechariah 11:12, and also takes place immediately following the anointing at Bethany! Thus, Judas was greatly offended by what he saw in Mary's act and Jesus' receptive spirit.

Earlier reference was made to the price of the ointment (John 12:3). The remark about the poor, while ostensibly gracious, was actually a ploy.

D. The Master's Rebuke (v. 7)

7. Then said Jesus, Let her alone: against the day of my burying hath she kept this.

We should think of Jesus' reply as being directed against all who spoke toward Mary. While some may have genuinely felt upset about the costly ointment and the money for the poor, there were others, like Judas, who saw only money wasted that could have been used by them.

Jesus interpreted her act to be one of preparation for His burial. Whether or not Mary actually sensed He was to soon die is beyond answer. It is clear that Jesus knew His time was at hand. He was deeply touched by her act of love, and Mark 14:6 records that He felt she had "done a beautiful thing" for Him (*NIV*).

CONCLUSION

The lives and actions of Martha and Mary demonstrate the breadth of actions which may be part of serving and experiencing God. In these accounts, it ranges from two sisters having the Master in their home to a marvelous miracle of resurrection from the dead. Both women had individual encounters providing the opportunity to verbally express their faith in who Jesus was and what He could do.

GOLDEN TEXT CHALLENGE

"HENCEFORTH I CALL YOU NOT SERVANTS; FOR THE SERVANT KNOWETH NOT WHAT HIS LORD DOETH: BUT I HAVE CALLED YOU FRIENDS" (John 15:15).

This verse records Jesus' promotion of His disciples from the status of servants to friends. Up to this time, it had been enough to take orders whether or not they understood their purpose. From now on, as His friends, they were to understand the purpose of His directions. They were now taken into His

"If the only way I can make myself look good is to criticize you, something is seriously wrong with me."
—**Warren Wiersbe**

Talk About It
How did Jesus respond to Mary's deed? Why?

"No one gives himself freely and willingly to God's service unless, having tasted [God's] fatherly love, he is drawn to love and worship Him in return."
—**John Calvin**

confidence to share in the meaning and value of Christ's instructions. The elevation to the status of friendship suggests a new intimacy which they had not known heretofore but which was now to be their own blessed experience.

Jesus still extends the offer of friendship to His followers. Not only does Jesus want to be our Master, He also wants to bring us into an intimate relationship with Himself.

Introduction to Winter Quarter

The theme for the first unit is "Isaac, Jacob and Joseph." These eight lessons focus on the relationships these three Old Testament patriarchs had with God and with their family members.

The expositions were written by the Reverend Rodney Hodge (A.B.), an ordained minister who has served as minister of music for 32 years at Northwood Temple Pentecostal Holiness Church in Fayetteville, North Carolina. He holds degrees from Emmanuel College and the University of Georgia and did graduate studies in history at the University of Georgia.

The Christmas study (lesson 4) was written by Lance Colkmire, as was the four lessons in the second unit. Lance Colkmire (B.A., M.A.) is editor of the *Evangelical Commentary* and *Real Life* young adult curriculum for Pathway Press. His latest book, *Make a Mark*, presents 25 principles of life-shaping ministry to children.

The second unit covers four aspects of Christian development: (1) goals of discipleship, (2) cost of discipleship, (3) discipleship relationships, and (4) growth in discipleship. A variety of New Testament texts are explored.

Son of Promise (Isaac)

Genesis 17:15-22; 21:1-12; Galatians 3:16; 4:22-31

Unit Theme:
Isaac, Jacob and Joseph

Central Truth:
The promises of God give hope for the future.

Focus:
Realize the prophetic significance of Isaac's life and rejoice in God's plan for believers in Christ.

Context:
Isaac was born some 2,000 years before Christ's birth.

Golden Text:
"Now we, brethren, as Isaac was, are the children of promise" (Galatians 4:28).

Study Outline:
I. Son of the Covenant (Genesis 17:15-22)

II. Progenitor of the Messiah (Genesis 21:1-12; Galatians 3:16)

III. Believers in Christ Prefigured (Galatians 4:22-31)

INTRODUCTION

Isaac was the fulfillment of the promise God made to Abraham—that he would be the father of a chosen people. Interestingly, the very first time God had spoken to Abram (his earlier name), there had been no mention of future descendants. God simply sent him from the land of his fathers on a journey. It was only after they came into Canaan that the Lord appeared to him and said, "To your descendants I will give this land" (Genesis 12:7, NKJV). Certainly the implication was that Abram would have a direct heir, although nothing was specific about Sarai being the mother.

After the separation from Lot in Genesis 13, the Lord again spoke to Abram about the land he would inherit for his descendants, but Sarai was still not mentioned. It was not until chapter 15 that Abram began to question the *how* of God's promise. God here indicated that there would be a son coming from Abram's own body. Nothing, however, was said about the necessity of the heir being born to Sarai. She had apparently been infertile throughout their marriage, a great distress to women in the ancient world. If there were no children, the woman was always blamed. Thus, Abram and Sarai took matters into their own hands when she offered her maid Hagar as a surrogate mother. This resulted in the birth of Ishmael when Abram was 86 years old and Sarai 75. This was not regarded as immoral, for Sarai would still be seen as the true mother. When the child was born, "it might be placed on the wife's body, a ritual indicating that it was born on behalf of the woman who was unable to have children herself" (*The Nelson Study Bible*).

The price that Sarai paid emotionally for having bowed to accepted cultural practices was immense. Hagar despised Sarai for using her, and then Sarai put the blame on Abram. He politely bowed to his wife's rage and let her mistreat Hagar. Providentially, the angel of the Lord appeared to Hagar to give her comfort, and a level of sanity returned to the household. The boy Ishmael was born, and assumedly an heir had been established.

We then come to Genesis 17, the text for our lesson. God obliterated the devices that had been put in place to fulfill His will. God always has ideas of His own that far exceed our manipulations. There indeed would be a son born to Sarah (her new name). Abraham (his new name) would be the father of many nations, and an everlasting covenant was established. The sign of the covenant was circumcision. Even Ishmael (who was now 13) was to undergo the rite. This was an outward sign of a thorough commitment to God. Thus, Paul would later demand that our hearts be circumcised to God as an indication of an *inward* dedication (see Romans 2:25-29).

I. SON OF THE COVENANT (Genesis 17:15-22)
A. Astonishing Promise (vv. 15, 16)

15. And God said unto Abraham, As for Sarai thy wife, thou shalt not call her name Sarai, but Sarah shall her name be.

16. And I will bless her, and give thee a son also of her: yea, I will bless her, and she shall be a mother of nations; kings of people shall be of her.

Perhaps Sarai had felt left out of the conversations over the years between God and her husband. All this talk about a covenant was fine, but every individual needs a real relationship with God that is not secondhand. This would account for her having brought Hagar into the picture. Not until chapter 18 is there an indication that she was privy to anything of divine intervention, and even there she was eavesdropping from inside the tent (v. 10). Even the promise of her bearing a son was not told to her directly.

Our text makes it explicitly clear that Abraham's heir would be born to his wife. What a blessing, especially for a woman far advanced in age. Her name would be changed to *Sarah*, although both names mean "princess." More importantly, she would be the *mother of nations*, with kings coming from her body.

Talk About It:
1. Why did God make a one-letter change to Sarai's name?
2. What promises did God make to Abraham concerning Sarah?

B. Laughter and Concern (vv. 17, 18)

17. Then Abraham fell upon his face, and laughed, and said in his heart, Shall a child be born unto him that is an hundred years old? and shall Sarah, that is ninety years old, bear?

18. And Abraham said unto God, O that Ishmael might live before thee!

That Abraham would laugh in the presence of God must be explained. Was it with an unbelieving, mocking attitude? No, because there is no rebuke here from God (though there is one to Sarah's laugh in 18:12). Abraham had just received an affirmation of all that had been promised to him, the first appearance by God to him in a number of years. This was somewhat of a culmination of his having been faithful to believe the promise. The laugh indicates that suddenly he would have to stretch his faith again. His trust in God must always be both present and future, not just past tense. "One clear purpose in Abraham's laughter is that the Hebrew expression 'he laughed' foreshadows the name 'Isaac'" (*Zondervan NIV Bible Commentary*, Vol. 1).

Abraham's laughter expressed joy at the prospect of the fulfillment of the promises to him, but that laughter suddenly turned to consternation. Why? Because apparently until this time he had assumed Ishmael was the heir through whom all

Talk About It:
1. Why did Abraham fall on his face?
2. What request did Abraham make regarding Ishmael?

"The great and Almighty author of nature, who at first established those rules which regulate the world, can as easily suspend those laws whenever His providence sees sufficient reason for such suspension."
—John Adams

promises would come. Hagar's boy was from his own body, and he naturally loved him. No wonder, then, that anxiety overcame him. It resulted in a prayer for divine favor over his first-born. "Now that God is talking with him, he thinks he has a very fair opportunity to speak a good word for Ishmael, and he will not let it slip" (*Matthew Henry's Commentary*).

C. Isaac and Ishmael (vv. 19, 20)

19. And God said, Sarah thy wife shall bear thee a son indeed; and thou shalt call his name Isaac: and I will establish my covenant with him for an everlasting covenant, and with his seed after him.

20. And as for Ishmael, I have heard thee: Behold, I have blessed him, and will make him fruitful, and will multiply him exceedingly; twelve princes shall he beget, and I will make him a great nation.

For the moment God seemed to dismiss Abraham's request for blessing Ishmael. Instead, He included the yet-to-be-born son in the everlasting covenant. He made a play on words of Abraham's laughter by declaring that the boy would be called a name meaning "laughter." Note that the emphasis is on the son that Sarah bears, and none other. God's plan all along had been for the couple to believe that the impossible could occur. Though their faith had fallen short, His promise had not.

In verse 20 we see God had not forgotten Ishmael. Remember that the Angel of the Lord had appeared to Hagar and promised that her son would be an enduring people (16:10-12). Ishmael would become a great nation of 12 tribes, in the same sense that 12 would spring forth from Isaac. It is from Ishmael that the various tribes of the Arabs descended. "These are the only people besides the Jews who have subsisted as a distinct people from the beginning, and in some respects they very much resemble each other" (*Adam Clarke's Commentary*). Though much of the Arab-Israeli conflict of our times is based on a conflict with Islam (which didn't arise until Muhammad), the fact that Ishmael was born in the first place came as a result of a certain lack of faith that God would do the impossible to make His promises come true.

D. A Set Time (vv. 21, 22)

21. But my covenant will I establish with Isaac, which Sarah shall bear unto thee at this set time in the next year.

22. And he left off talking with him, and God went up from Abraham.

In placing our trust in God's promises, we like to have timetables. If God hasn't worked within the period we think reasonable, we begin to doubt. Abraham had waited nearly 25

Talk About It:
Compare God's promises regarding Isaac with His promises for Ishmael.

Hagar Remembered
It is easy for us to look back at Hagar and feel sorry for her. She did not cause the problems in her life. Her bearing a son was not her idea. For that, both Abraham and Sarah must take the blame. Twice she fled from their household (the first time to escape Sarah's wrath, and the second at Abraham's command). However, both times God appeared to Hagar and gave promise to her life. Her son was given blessing. The people who descended from him are the Arabs, whom God loves and longs to save.

Son of Promise

years, but the promise was now given a set date of fulfillment. If the baby was to be born a year later, then there was an immediate season promised whereby both Abraham's and Sarah's bodies were to be rejuvenated to fertility.

II. PROGENITOR OF THE MESSIAH (Genesis 21:1-12; Galatians 3:16)

A. Isaac's Birth (Genesis 21:1-3)

1. And the Lord visited Sarah as he had said, and the Lord did unto Sarah as he had spoken.

2. For Sarah conceived, and bare Abraham a son in his old age, at the set time of which God had spoken to him.

3. And Abraham called the name of his son that was born unto him, whom Sarah bare to him, Isaac.

When God speaks of a specific time for promises to be fulfilled, it is certain that He will deliver. Thus He did with Abraham and Sarah. Their bodies were rejuvenated to form potent seed, conceive, and carry a pregnancy to full term.

At the end of our last point (17:22), we left Abraham and all the males of his household being circumcised as a sign of his faith in the covenant. In chapter 18 a fifth visit by the Lord (along with two angels) occurred sometime shortly thereafter. Sarah overhead the conversation concerning her bearing a child, and re-sponded by laughing in unbelief. The Lord questioned the laughter, metaphorically asked if anything was too hard for Him, and said He would return "at the appointed time" (18:14, NKJV). Finally Sarah herself had heard from God. Any faith she had expressed earlier had depended on her believing Abraham. After this visitation, Sarah no doubt began to believe with Abraham.

Thus, when we come to our present text, the realization of an old-age pregnancy had occurred. The nine months leading to Isaac's birth would have been filled with joyous anticipation. The announcement of the birth focuses on God's faithfulness to do "as he had spoken" (21:1). Every promise He makes comes true, though the wait may be long.

B. Isaac's Circumcision (vv. 4, 5)

4. And Abraham circumcised his son Isaac being eight days old, as God had commanded him.

5. And Abraham was an hundred years old, when his son Isaac was born unto him.

The pattern of Abraham's obedience continued. Earlier, all the males of his household had been circumcised, but the circumcision of Isaac carried even greater significance. "The sign of the covenant was most important for the son of promise" (*Nelson Study Bible*). What a joyous day this must have been! For the elderly couple to hold a newborn son in their arms was

Talk About It:
1. What timetable did God give Abraham?
2. Explain the phrase "God went up" (v. 22).

Talk About It:
Why are the words "said" (v. 1) and "spoken" (vv. 1, 2) so important in these verses?

"God's promises are like the stars; the darker the night the brighter they shine."
—David Nicholas

Talk About It:
What was the significance of Isaac's circumcision?

enough to further rejuvenate their bodies. This brings to mind the proverb, "Hope deferred maketh the heart sick: but when the desire cometh, it is a tree of life" (Proverbs 13:12). The very presence of an infant brings fresh life into any situation.

C. Sarah's Laughter (vv. 6-8)

6. And Sarah said, God hath made me to laugh, so that all that hear will laugh with me.

7. And she said, Who would have said unto Abraham, that Sarah should have given children suck? for I have born him a son in his old age.

8. And the child grew, and was weaned: and Abraham made a great feast the same day that Isaac was weaned.

Talk About It:
1. Explain Sarah's statement in verse 6.
2. Answer Sarah's question in verse 7.

Since realizing she was indeed pregnant, Sarah had longed for this moment. Though she had earlier been chastised for her sardonic laughter, her laughter now was out of complete joy. Not only that, the promises this boy represented meant the entire world would be blessed by his birth.

As with any child, the early months were pivotal. This was especially true in the ancient world where so many babies died unexpectedly. Thus, the time of Isaac's weaning, somewhere between his second and third year, was occasion for more rejoicing. "The child seems to have remained for the first five years under the special care of the mother (Leviticus 27:6). The son then came under the management of the father" (*Barnes' Notes*).

D. Ishmael's Mockery (vv. 9-12)

9. And Sarah saw the son of Hagar the Egyptian, which she had born unto Abraham, mocking.

10. Wherefore she said unto Abraham, Cast out this bondwoman and her son: for the son of this bondwoman shall not be heir with my son, even with Isaac.

11. And the thing was very grievous in Abraham's sight because of his son.

12. And God said unto Abraham, Let it not be grievous in thy sight because of the lad, and because of thy bondwoman; in all that Sarah hath said unto thee, hearken unto her voice; for in Isaac shall thy seed be called.

Talk About It:
1. Who mocked whom, and why (v. 9)?
2. Why did God tell Abraham to listen to Sarah (vv. 10-12)?

The occasion of Isaac coming of age was also one where his older brother, Ishmael, seemed left out of the festivities (perhaps reminiscent of the Prodigal Son story). Ishmael, now perhaps 17 years old, apparently mocked the joy being expressed by Abraham and Sarah, and may have been ridiculing Sarah for giving birth at such an old age. No matter what the boy's actual feelings, Sarah was infuriated. Her tolerance for his presence had come to an end. She possibly feared that Abraham, out of his generosity, might give the slave woman's son part of Isaac's inheritance. She insisted that both Ishmael and his mother be expelled.

"To drive them out must have been exceedingly grievous to Abraham, for he loved the boy, and for years had considered him his heir" (*Wycliffe Bible Commentary*). He was reluctant to respond to Sarah's wishes. The most joyous day of their lives had quickly turned into a very bad one. It was not acceptable to send the boy away, for when a surrogate wife had borne a son, "that mother and son could not be dismissed even if the first wife subsequently gave birth to a son" (*Nelson Study Bible*). Abraham, who seemed to constantly get himself caught in dilemmas, was now caught in another.

The Lord saved the day for Abraham by speaking for the sixth time in a direct word. He gave Abraham permission to send the mother and son away, leaving Isaac as the single heir to the covenant's fulfillment. Ishmael was promised a nation of his own. The next day Abraham sent the two away with meager provisions. This was the second time Hagar had left the household, but it would also prove to be the second time God would speak to her in her dire need. Subsequent verses show that God both provided for her and the young man, and gave them a prospering future.

> "Isaac, the object of holy laughter, was made the butt of unholy wit or profane sport. He [Ishmael] did not laugh, but he made fun."
> —Ernst Hengstenberg

E. A Single Seed (Galatians 3:16)

16. Now to Abraham and his seed were the promises made. He saith not, And to seeds, as of many; but as of one, And to thy seed, which is Christ.

Despite her bitter attitude, Sarah was right in not wanting Ishmael to receive an inheritance from Abraham. The promises of the covenant were to come through a single legitimate heir. Although Isaac was the immediate fulfillment of the covenant, the long-range one was Jesus.

Talk About It:
What is Jesus Christ called in this verse, and why?

While the Jews of Paul's day saw themselves as the fulfillment of the covenant (meaning that they were Abraham's *seeds*), they were not the *seed*. If the promises had been for all of Abraham's seeds, then indeed it might be true that the Law given through Moses was the way of salvation. However, the real promise was through a single seed, Christ, who came to bring salvation by grace. The Law was important, but the promise of blessing to all humanity given to Abraham was one of restoration to relationship with God. Also, it would not be just to the Jews, but to all people.

III. BELIEVERS IN CHRIST PREFIGURED (Galatians 4:22-31)
A. Abraham's Two Sons (vv. 22, 23)

22. For it is written, that Abraham had two sons, the one by a bondmaid, the other by a freewoman.

23. But he who was of the bondwoman was born after the flesh; but he of the freewoman was by promise.

Talk About It:
Contrast Isaac's birth with Ishmael's.

Paul was arguing with Jewish believers who said Gentile believers had to become Jewish in order to truly follow Christ. The Judaizers were proud that they were descended from Abraham, and believed the Abrahamic covenant gave them special position with God. However, John the Baptist (Matthew 3:8, 9) and Jesus (John 8:37-44) had earlier argued that just being from Abraham wasn't enough to secure salvation. Paul argues the same point, pointing to the two sons of Abraham. One son was born of a slave woman (Hagar), the other of a free woman (Sarah). "In ancient times, a mother's status affected the status of her children" (*Life Application Bible Commentary*). Also, the slave woman's son was born by ordinary means, while the free woman's son was miraculous.

Thus, Paul was distinguishing between man-made religion and the supernatural. Paul saw the Judaizers as passing themselves off as the legitimate heirs, while actually being the sons of bondage. Those following the Law are under the curse of the Law, just as Hagar suffered by being a slave. Their "religion of works and law corresponds to the natural birth of Ishmael; the religion of the Spirit, which is Christianity, corresponds to the supernatural birth of Isaac" (*Zondervan NIV Bible Commentary*).

"I have loved to hear my Lord spoken of; and wherever I have seen the print of his shoe in the earth, there I have coveted to set my foot too."
—**John Bunyan**

Agar (v. 24)—Hagar
gendereth (v. 24)—bears children

B. Two Covenants (vv. 24-27)

24. Which things are an allegory: for these are the two covenants; the one from the mount Sinai, which gendereth to bondage, which is Agar.

25. For this Agar is mount Sinai in Arabia, and answereth to Jerusalem which now is, and is in bondage with her children.

26. But Jerusalem which is above is free, which is the mother of us all.

27. For it is written, Rejoice, thou barren that bearest not; break forth and cry, thou that travailest not: for the desolate hath many more children than she which hath an husband.

Talk About It:
1. What covenant does Hagar and Ishmael represent, and how?
2. What covenant does Sarah and Isaac symbolize, and how?

Paul compares the two sons to two covenants. Agar (Hagar) represents the old covenant enacted at Mount Sinai, with her son Ishmael standing for Judaism, and Jerusalem as its center. Sarah, the free woman, represents a supernatural birth, a new covenant, and a spiritual Jerusalem. This covenant was enacted by the blood sacrifice of Jesus Christ. Sarah's son, Isaac, "stands for all who have become part of the church of the heavenly Jerusalem through faith in Christ's sacrifice" (*Zondervan NIV Bible Commentary*).

The Judaizers wanted Gentile believers to accept circumcision as a means of becoming part of the covenant. They were claiming themselves to be sons of Abraham through Isaac, though they were living like the very opposite. Paul's point was this: The Judaizers (Jews who had accepted Christ), in their insistence to force others into Judaism, were themselves products of an illegitimate covenant. "Trying to win salvation by obeying the law leads to slavery; and as the Jews persisted in this pattern, they showed themselves to be enslaved to their law" (*Life Application Commentary Series*).

Paul was trying to show the Galatians (Gentile people) that they could be included as legitimate descendants of Abraham through faith, and this was just as miraculous as had been the birth of Isaac. There were no "works" involved for such inclusion. They simply had to believe in Christ. Sarah's child had been a gracious gift, and ultimately she would have many more "children," meaning all Gentile believers. The Judaizers knew from Old Testament passages that somehow the Gentiles would come to God, but their mistake was in the assumption that these would have to first become Jews in order to be included.

C. Children of Promise (vv. 28-31)

28. Now we, brethren, as Isaac was, are the children of promise.

29. But as then he that was born after the flesh persecuted him that was born after the Spirit, even so it is now.

30. Nevertheless what saith the scripture? Cast out the bondwoman and her son: for the son of the bondwoman shall not be heir with the son of the freewoman.

31. So then, brethren, we are not children of the bondwoman, but of the free.

Paul assures the Galatian Christians that they are children of promise. They are not the proverbial "redheaded stepchildren." They have all the rights and privileges of being born free, as Isaac had been born. More importantly, they must recognize the "incompatibility of man-made and God-made religion, and respond by casting out the Judaizers" (*Zondervan NIV Bible Commentary*). There was absolutely no reason to be enslaved to Jewish laws.

Paul then speaks of persecution. Ishmael had mocked Isaac. In Paul's eyes this was persecution, and was now playing out itself again in the way his opponents (Judaizers) were persecuting him. All Jews who refused Christ (as well as Judaizer believers who insisted on believers' obeying Jewish laws) were, in essence, nothing more than Ishmaels. Anyone in slavery to the Law could not inherit the promises in Christ. In other words, being Jewish meant nothing if one did not accept Christ. Even though he was the apostle to the Gentiles, Paul still had a heart for all Jews, longing dearly for them to accept Christ.

"We are free when our lives are uncommitted, but not to be what we were intended to be. Real freedom is not freedom *from*, but freedom *for*."
—**Robert W. Young**

Talk About It:
Who are "the children of promise" (v. 28)?

"It is only when all our Christian ancestors are allowed to become our contemporaries that the real splendor of the Christian faith and the Christian life begins to dawn upon us."
—**Lynn Harold Hough**

CONCLUSION

✶ The initial promise of blessing had come to Abraham when he was 75. Ishmael was born when he was 86. The true son of the covenant didn't come until Abraham was 100. It has been said that God is never late, but He's never early either. When we review the promises of God that have not yet come to fruition in our individual lives, it is best to wait patiently, remain faithful, and not do anything to create further problems for ourselves.

GOLDEN TEXT CHALLENGE

"NOW WE, BRETHREN, AS ISAAC WAS, ARE THE CHILDREN OF PROMISE" (Galatians 4:28).

Just as Isaac was the child promised to Abraham by God, so Christians are "the children of promise." The promise made to Abraham was fulfilled by natural childbirth (through supernatural intervention), while we receive God's promise through a spiritual birth (also through supernatural intervention).

Just as it was humanly impossible for Isaac to be born when he was, so it was humanly impossible for us to be born again as children of God. While the mockers thought we could not live a born-again life, they were wrong. Through faith in Jesus Christ, we have become "children of the promise."

Bible Insight

Isaac, Jacob and Joseph

The Story of Isaac

Isaac, the son of the covenant, was a good man, but he never reached the stature of his father, Abraham, or his son Jacob. Genesis 21 records his birth, an event that precipitated the expulsion of Hagar and Ishmael. This was the beginning of an enmity that has continued passionately unto this day: Isaac's descendants were the Jews; Ishmael's were the Arabs.

Chapter 22 tells of Abraham's test to offer Isaac in human sacrifice. Spiritually, Isaac's obedience unto death was a type of the sacrificial death of Christ. Yet the incident had a practical purpose of more immediate nature. God could have known Abraham's obedient devotion without such a test, but by it God demonstrated once and forever that He neither expected nor permitted human sacrifice. Abraham lived in the midst of a people who practiced human sacrifice, and in later years the Jews would be tempted to practice it. God's last-minute intervention was a dramatic demonstration of His disapproval of the awful rite; His substitution of a ram revealed the type of burnt-offering He would accept.

Following the death of Sarah, Abraham arranged for Isaac's marriage (ch. 24). With the births of Esau and Jacob, Isaac fades from the Biblical account. Chapter 26 tells of the reconfirmation of the Abrahamic covenant to him.

The Story of Jacob

Half of the Book of Genesis concerns Jacob and his sons. The nation of Israel got its name from him, and the 12 tribes came from his 12 sons.

From their birth, Jacob and his twin brother, Esau, were rivals. The nations that sprang from them—Edom from Esau and Israel from Jacob—were always hostile to each other. Jacob first demonstrated his superiority over Esau by an unconscious act at birth (25:25, 26) and, second, by securing the family birthright from him (vv. 27-34). The birthright included succession of the father as head of the family. Although Jacob's motives for desiring the birthright were both selfish and spiritual, his possession of it was an act of faith and divine providence. God had chosen Jacob, the younger, to be the channel of the messianic promise (v. 23). Even though Jacob was sensual, cunning and deceitful, God saw a man capable of spiritual greatness.

In chapter 27 we have a strange account of family disunity, an episode in which all members of the family were wrong. *Isaac* was wrong because he tried to give his paternal blessing to Esau, even though he knew God had chosen Jacob (25:23). *Esau* was wrong because he was ready to cooperate in thwarting God's will, even after he had voluntarily sold his birthright and must surely have known that Jacob was God's choice. *Rebekah* was wrong in the methods she used to protect the interests of Jacob. *Jacob* was wrong in cooperating in her project of deceit and lying. They used wrong methods in the interest of a just and right cause.

Esau, grief-stricken and angry, would have killed Jacob, but Rebekah sent her favorite son to Haran, her former home. She never saw him again, for she died before he returned. On his way from Beersheba to Haran, a distance of 450 miles,

Jacob had his first great experience with the Lord at Bethel (ch. 28).

During and immediately after his 20 years in Haran, 12 sons were born to Jacob: Reuben, Simeon, Levi, Judah, Issachar and Zebulun (by Leah); Dan and Naphtali (by Bilhah); Gad and Asher (by Zilpah); Joseph and Benjamin (by Rachel).

Soon after leaving Haran, Jacob reached the pinnacle of his spiritual experience. Under the anxiety and pressure of an imminent meeting with Esau, he sought the protection of God. This time of confession and remembrance of the covenant led to a night of travail with God. Jacob received a new name that night: he became _Israel_, "a prince of God" (ch. 32).

The Story of Joseph

Of Jacob's 12 sons, Joseph was personally most outstanding. God revealed to Joseph at an early age that he was chosen for a special purpose (37:1-10). A series of evil things happened to Joseph, all of which worked toward his ultimate status:

1. He was hated by his brothers.
2. He was sold as a slave into Egypt.
3. He was falsely accused by a lustful woman.
4. He was unjustly locked in prison.
5. He was forgotten by one who promised to remember him.

All of these things were bad. Yet God used them together to bring about His will. When the pharaoh of Egypt had his disturbing dream, Joseph was available for its interpretation. All the evils of his life worked together for this vital moment in the history of Israel. By Joseph's interpretation of the dream and through his wise counsel, Egypt and the surrounding nations survived a time of terrible famine (ch. 41).

When his father's household was also spared from starvation, Joseph declared that God had used the evil in his life for good.—**Charles W. Conn,** *The Living Book*

Type of Christ (Isaac)

Genesis 22:1-14; John 1:29-34

INTRODUCTION

Our lesson picks up where the last one ended. After Abraham sent Hagar and Ishmael away (at Sarah's insistence and with God's permission), life settled for some years into the joyous routine of raising the child of promise. Not only was the boy the joy of his parents' lives, he was the focus of the fulfillment of the covenant God had made with Abraham. These were wonder years, years when faith was not being tested. After having waited so long for Isaac's birth, it is likely that Abraham expected no further trial. The sudden voice (the seventh visitation recorded) of the Lord commanding the sacrifice of Isaac certainly surprised Abraham. No explanation was given. We know from hindsight that this was a test—God never intended that the boy be killed. Still, Abraham didn't know this. In his mind, his son was as good as dead. We don't know how God spoke to Abraham, but there was no question in Abraham's mind. There is no mention of a tempter testing him, nor was this a figment of his imagination. All that Abraham knew was that God was his covenant partner, and that if He required the boy's life as a sacrifice, then he would certainly obey.

Isaac was likely around 16, although the historian Josephus says 25. The years of quiet upbringing had produced a complete trust by the boy in his father. He was unaware that he was the intended sacrifice during the three-day journey, and even upon arrival he offered no resistance. This illustrates him to be a type of Christ, who came to do not His own will, but the will of His Father. Isaac even carried the wood for the sacrifice, similar to Jesus' bearing His own cross. The three days they journeyed, a time in which he was figuratively already dead in his father's eyes, is a picture of the three days in the tomb before Christ's resurrection. Also, the ram which replaced Isaac prefigures the perfect Lamb being slain for the sins of all people. Equally important, Abraham represents the willingness of God the Father to give His only Son as a sacrifice. The difference was that Abraham didn't have to carry out his sacrifice, while God the Father did indeed do so.

Unit Theme:
Isaac, Jacob and Joseph

Central Truth:
Old Testament events foreshadowed the coming of Christ.

Focus:
Appreciate Isaac's experience of near-sacrifice as a foreshadow of Christ's atoning sacrifice and affirm our gratitude.

Context:
Around 2000 B.C., Abraham prepares to sacrifice his son Isaac; in A.D. 29, John declares Jesus to be the Messiah.

Golden Text:
"He that spared not his own Son, but delivered him up for us all, how shall he not with him also freely give us all things?" (Romans 8:32).

Study Outline:
I. God Requires a Sacrifice (Genesis 22:1-8)
II. God Provides a Sacrifice (Genesis 22:9-14)
III. Lamb of God, Only Son (John 1:29-34)

I. GOD REQUIRES A SACRIFICE (Genesis 22:1-8)
A. God's Command to Sacrifice Isaac (vv. 1, 2)

1. And it came to pass after these things, that God did tempt Abraham, and said unto him, Abraham: and he said, Behold, here I am.

2. And he said, Take now thy son, thine only son Isaac, whom thou lovest, and get thee into the land of Moriah; and offer him there for a burnt-offering upon one of the mountains which I will tell thee of.

Most other translations use the word *test* or *prove* instead of *tempt.* Testing was the real purpose of what took place. The question is begged as to why God would test Abraham's faith, since in His omniscience He knows everything. Perhaps Abraham needed to know for himself just how much he trusted his covenant partner. Sacrificing Isaac was the ultimate trial the patriarch could have been put through. "He must give evidence of absolute obedience and unquestioning trust in Jehovah, must even obey blindly, proceeding step by step until the faith stood out as clearly as the noonday sun" (*The Wycliffe Bible Commentary*). As Peter would later say, "You have been grieved by various trials, that the genuineness of your faith, being much more precious than gold that perishes, though it is tested by fire, may be found to praise, honor, and glory at the revelation of Jesus Christ, whom having not seen you love" (1 Peter 1:6-8, *NKJV*).

God gave Abraham specific details as to what he was to do. It was a three-day journey to Moriah. Second Chronicles 3:1 describes this as the mount where Solomon later built the great Temple, but the term may have applied to an area including an entire range of hills. Evidently, however, Abraham was aware of his specific destination. He saw a clear vision of where and what he was commanded to do.

B. Abraham's Obedience (vv. 3-5)

3. And Abraham rose up early in the morning, and saddled his ass, and took two of his young men with him, and Isaac his son, and clave the wood for the burnt-offering, and rose up, and went unto the place of which God had told him.

4. Then on the third day Abraham lifted up his eyes, and saw the place afar off.

5. And Abraham said unto his young men, Abide ye here with the ass; and I and the lad will go yonder and worship, and come again to you.

We are not told Abraham's thoughts about what had been commanded of him. Apparently he expressed his feelings to no one, least of all Sarah and Isaac. No one deemed anything

---

tempt (v. 1)—test

Talk About It:
1. How does verse 2 describe Isaac?
2. What made this command so surprising?

"The gem cannot be polished without friction, nor men perfected without trials."
—Chinese Proverb

Talk About It:
1. How did Abraham respond to God's command?
2. Whom did Abraham believe would return from Mount Moriah? Why?

Type of Christ

unusual about this trip, which even more demonstrates the man's ultimate trust in God. If God could give him a son at such a ripe old age, then He could also resurrect him. There were no limits on his faith, even though earlier detours had occurred.

The act of carrying wood indicates that the boy was not only to be killed, but his body burned. "He must not only kill his son, but kill him as a sacrifice, kill him devoutly, kill him by rule, kill him with all that pomp and ceremony, with all that sedateness and composure of mind, with which he used to offer his burnt-offerings" (*Matthew Henry's Commentary*). Why the two servants were brought along is not known. In wisdom, they were left behind when the party reached the mountain. Had they accompanied Abraham and Isaac, they would have been tempted to stop the sacrifice, believing the old man had lost his mind. "Isaac was, no doubt, the darling of the whole family" (*Matthew Henry's Commentary*). Abraham indicated to them that both he and the boy would return to them. "In the Hebrew text, these words are even more arresting than in a translation. The three verbs all show a strong determination on the part of the speaker" (*Nelson Study Bible*). In other words, Abraham was saying, "We will go, we will worship, and we will return to you."

C. Preparation for the Sacrifice (vv. 6, 7)

6. And Abraham took the wood of the burnt-offering, and laid it upon Isaac his son; and he took the fire in his hand, and a knife; and they went both of them together.

7. And Isaac spake unto Abraham his father, and said, My father: and he said, Here am I, my son. And he said, Behold the fire and the wood: but where is the lamb for a burnt-offering?

As the father and son made their way up the mountain, the silence was deafening. Certainly there had to be a question ringing in the boy's mind: Where was the lamb for sacrifice? The wood for the fire was on his own back, while his father likely carried the knife and a flint for creating a fire (or possibly a clay pot with live coals in it). The innocence of Isaac's question shows him to be a type of the perfect Lamb of God. Even as he was preparing for his own sacrifice, there was a gentle spirit of trust in his father's goodness.

D. Faith in God's Provision (v. 8)

8. And Abraham said, My son, God will provide himself a lamb for a burnt-offering: so they went both of them together.

When Isaac had finally broken the silence, Abraham was quick to reply that God would provide. These words give light to his silence. There was a faith in him that recognized God

Trust Trumps Fear
Abraham gives a clear example of one who fully trusted God. Everything in his hopes and dreams was pinned on the boy Isaac. For his son to die meant the death of his dreams. Yet, Abraham was willing to believe God's integrity and love toward him. If we are following the Lord and carrying out His purposes to the best of our abilities, we need not fear the future. He will provide all that we need. Our duty is to simply trust Him.

Talk About It:
What was wrong with this scene, according to Isaac?

Talk About It:
On a scale of 1 to 10, rate Abraham's faith in God at this point.

was not about to do him evil. If he indeed had to sacrifice his son, there would be a new joy, a resurrection, or some other wonderful thing that would manifest in his behalf. God would not renege on the covenant promises. His was not to question God, but to be obedient. In simple words, he knew God was not angry at him. Paul enlarged on this truth when he said, "He that spared not his own Son, but delivered him up for us all, how shall he not with him also freely give us all things?" (Romans 8:32).

Whether Abraham recognized it or not, there was a prophetic element to his words. It has been said that nothing ever happens in the kingdom of God until it is first spoken. Even in Creation, the earth was without form until God said, "Let there be light: and there was light" (Genesis 1:3). Prophecy must be declared before it can happen. Abraham's declaring that God would provide a lamb gave way for that provision to occur. One might imagine that at the moment Abraham spoke these words, the lamb wandering around on the mountain that would ultimately provide the sacrifice suddenly found itself caught in the thicket.

II. GOD PROVIDES A SACRIFICE (Genesis 22:9-14)
A. Isaac Bound (vv. 9, 10)

9. And they came to the place which God had told him of; and Abraham built an altar there, and laid the wood in order, and bound Isaac his son, and laid him on the altar upon the wood.

10. And Abraham stretched forth his hand, and took the knife to slay his son.

The most amazing aspect of this story is the compliance of Isaac. There was neither fight nor question from the boy. He willingly allowed himself to be bound and prepared for sacrifice. Like the Savior on an even darker day (John 10:17, 18), Isaac was willing to do his father's will. The firepot of coals was ready to ignite the wood. The knife was drawn. There seemed to be nothing to stop the horrible moment. Very often in life, problems reach the moment of desperation when no answer has arrived—yet God does come on time! The only time He didn't arrive was when Jesus cried out, "My God, my God, why hast thou forsaken me?" (Matthew 27:46). Abraham's son was ultimately spared, but God's was not.

B. The Angel Heard (vv. 11, 12)

11. And the angel of the Lord called unto him out of heaven, and said, Abraham, Abraham: and he said, Here am I.

12. And he said, Lay not thine hand upon the lad, neither

Talk About It:
1. What does Isaac's inaction say about him?
2. How far was Abraham willing to go in his obedience to God?

Type of Christ

**do thou any thing unto him: for now I know that thou fear-
est God, seeing thou hast not withheld thy son, thine only
son from me.**

At the last dramatic moment, God stepped in and spoke
from heaven to Abraham. He called Abraham's name twice.
Could it be that Abraham was so near to killing Isaac that he
had to be loudly called just to get his attention? And why did
God wait so long in stopping him? In a strange way, God was
living out with Abraham what He himself later would face with
the death of Jesus.

We don't know if Isaac heard the voice of the Lord or not.
The message was spoken specifically to Abraham. Surely,
however, the boy had heard many times the recounting of
divine visitations his father had experienced, and how he himself was a miracle child of his parents' old age. This atmosphere of trust in God's goodness had prepared him to be the
willing sacrifice. Also, if he didn't hear the divine voice now, he
certainly saw the reaction on his father's face.

In reading about the rest of Isaac's years, we do not see him
having many direct encounters with the Lord. The first is
Genesis 26:3, where God said, "I will perform the oath which I
swore to Abraham your father" (*NKJV*). Later, God appeared
again and said, "I am the God of your father Abraham; do not
fear, for I am with you. I will bless you and multiply your descendants for My servant Abraham's sake" (v. 24, *NKJV*). Though
the covenant was just as real with Isaac, the relationship of
friend to friend does not seem to have been as strong as with
Abraham.

The sacrifice of Isaac was Abraham's finest hour. He had
proved his faith and commitment to the covenant. There need
never be such a testing again in his life. He could return home
with a sense of God's presence pervading his life. "He would
never be the same again. The great promises had been
renewed, and he was assured that the covenant blessings
would come upon him and his descendants" (*The Wycliffe
Bible Commentary*).

C. The Ram Found (vv. 13, 14)

**13. And Abraham lifted up his eyes, and looked, and
behold behind him a ram caught in a thicket by his horns:
and Abraham went and took the ram, and offered him up
for a burnt-offering in the stead of his son.**

**14. And Abraham called the name of that place
Jehovah-jireh: as it is said to this day, In the mount of the
Lord it shall be seen.**

There was still the question of a sacrifice. All things were
prepared, and there was certainly reason for worship. All that

"That the Lord
Almighty . . . direct-
ly intervenes in
human affairs is
one of the plainest
statements in the
Bible."
—**Abraham
Lincoln**

Talk About It:
1. Why did
Abraham offer an
animal sacrifice to
the Lord?
2. What did
Abraham name this
location, and why?

was missing was a lamb. What we too often forget is that when God does come through for us, we should immediately worship Him with a grateful heart. Abraham had been looking toward the sound of the voice from heaven so intently that he had not looked around to see that a ram was in the thicket behind him. There apparently had not been a sound made by the ram to indicate its presence. Abraham now searched the surroundings with anticipation, apparently believing before he saw the animal that it would be there. That was certainly faith in action!

As an act of worship, Abraham gives this place of sacrifice the name *Jehovah-Jireh*. This name of God means that He will make the necessary provision for His children whatever the situation.

III. LAMB OF GOD, ONLY SON (John 1:29-34)
A. John Recognizes the Lamb of God (v. 29)
29. The next day John seeth Jesus coming unto him, and saith, Behold the Lamb of God, which taketh away the sin of the world.

Talk About It:
Why did God's Son
become "the Lamb
of God" (v. 29)?

The last words of the Old Testament came through the prophet Malachi. He had prophesied that an Elijah would come to herald the coming of the Lord (Malachi 4:5). He would open the way for the Messiah. Thus, when John the Baptist appeared on the scene, hopes were high from his preaching that certainly the Messiah was about to reveal Himself. Many thought John himself might be the promised one, something he quickly denied. John also denied that he was *the* Elijah (John 1:21), although in verse 23 he did identify himself as the herald predicted by Isaiah (40:3). Jesus would later identify him as having been "that Elijah" (see Mark 9:13).

John attracted great crowds, but left his critics confused. He didn't "seem to fit into any category familiar to the Jewish authorities, and his unusual success demanded explanation" (*Zondervan NIV Bible Commentary*). Isaiah's prophecy had gone on to say that "the glory of the Lord will be revealed, and all mankind together will see it" (40:5, *NIV*). If this was true, then something great from heaven was about to happen. John even admitted he wasn't worthy to tie the sandals of that person about to appear.

On the day John suddenly saw Jesus coming down the hill to the place on the river Jordan where he was baptizing, he declared that Jesus was the Lamb of God. John's listeners would have immediately drawn allusions from the Old Testament. First, the sacrifice of a lamb as a substitute or atonement went all the way back to Abraham's placing Isaac on the altar. Next, the Passover lamb of Exodus 12 would have come to mind. Those sacrifices were still being carried out annually in the Jerusalem temple. In addition, Isaiah 53:7 pictured the coming Redeemer as a lamb led to slaughter. By identifying Jesus as *the* Lamb of God, John was declaring Him to be the final substitutionary sacrifice that God would provide for all humanity. Even though this had been clearly prophesied by Isaiah, the Jews had not contemplated the idea that their Messiah would have to give up His life for them.

B. John Serves as the Forerunner (vv. 30, 31)

30. This is he of whom I said, After me cometh a man which is preferred before me: for he was before me.

31. And I knew him not: but that he should be made manifest to Israel, therefore am I come baptizing with water.

John knew that once the Messiah was revealed, his own personal role would be greatly diminished. However, he didn't know how much this would cost him. He was later beheaded by Herod Antipas (Mark 6:14-29). Also, John apparently did not know for certain until now that his own cousin was the Messiah. Likely he suspected such, but did not know for sure until God provided the sign of the descending dove over Jesus' head.

John also explained why he had been baptizing. Before now, only Gentiles converting to Judaism had been baptized as a sign of turning from their sins. John demanded that Jews repent for their sin and experience a moral restoration. Their sin was a presumption in thinking that just because they were descendants of Abraham, they were automatically righteous. He preached that the Jews would be purged and rejected unless they demonstrated fruits of repentance (see Luke 3:8). By preaching repentance and baptism, John was preparing the people for the coming of the Lord. Interestingly enough, the people who heeded the preaching of John were in a general sense those who turned to Jesus. Those who had refused John also refused Jesus.

C. John Testifies About Jesus (vv. 32-34)

32. And John bare record, saying, I saw the Spirit descending from heaven like a dove, and it abode upon him.

33. And I knew him not: but he that sent me to baptize with water, the same said unto me, Upon whom thou shalt see the Spirit descending, and remaining on him, the same is he which baptizeth with the Holy Ghost.

34. And I saw, and bare record that this is the Son of God.

As already stated, Jesus and John were cousins. There had been miraculous events surrounding both their births. Their

My Lord, my Love, is crucified:
Is crucified for me and you.
To bring us rebels near to God;
Believe, believe the record true.
—Charles Wesley

Talk About It:
1. Explain John's statement in verse 30 about who came first.
2. According to verse 31, why did John baptize people?

"There is a God-shaped vacuum in the heart of every man which cannot be filled by any created things, but only by God, the Creator, made known through Jesus."
—Blaise Pascal

Talk About It:
1. How did John recognize Jesus' true identity?
2. According to verse 33, what would Jesus do?

families were well acquainted, and John possibly sensed that Jesus was the Messiah, but he didn't know for sure. What he did know, however, was that he would recognize the Messiah at the right time, and he would make the grand announcement. He also knew that his baptism was one of repentance, but the One coming would baptize with the Holy Ghost. How did John *know* these things? We must remember that he was "filled with the Holy Ghost, even from his mother's womb" (Luke 1:15). Full of the Spirit, John was equipped to hear from heaven. When he saw Jesus coming, the Spirit immediately bore witness with him that this was the long-expected Lamb of God.

The baptism that John taught was one of immersion. "It pictured death, burial, and resurrection. When John the Baptist baptized Jesus, Jesus and John were picturing the 'baptism' Jesus would endure on the cross when He would die as the sacrificial Lamb of God" (*The Bible Exposition Commentary*).

CONCLUSION

The people in John the Baptist's audience were very familiar with the concept of a sacrificial lamb. This was part of their heritage, going all the way back to Abraham's near-sacrifice of Isaac. Every day—both at morning and again at evening—a lamb was sacrificed at the Temple in Jerusalem for the sins of the Jewish people. Sadly, they didn't see this as a temporary measure, even though Isaiah 53:7 had pictured the Messiah to come as being a sacrificial lamb.

The Jews did understand that sin demanded a penalty, but they satisfied themselves with the daily sacrifice of the lamb covering their sin. The wonderful truth they missed was that the Messiah would take on all sins, including the very curse of sin. Even the power of sin would be destroyed. What a shame that they missed the truth. What freedom they missed! This is why Jesus would cry out, "O Jerusalem, Jerusalem, which killest the prophets, and stonest them that are sent unto thee; how often would I have gathered thy children together, as a hen doth gather her brood under her wings, and ye would not!" (Luke 13:34).

GOLDEN TEXT CHALLENGE

"HE THAT SPARED NOT HIS OWN SON, BUT DELIVERED HIM UP FOR US ALL, HOW SHALL HE NOT WITH HIM ALSO FREELY GIVE US ALL THINGS?" (Romans 8:32).

In the previous verse, the question is raised, "If God be for us, who can be against us?" It is a rhetorical question, with the obvious answer that God is our guardian against all spiritual foes and will see us safely through. With such protection an attack from any quarter must fail.

Our Golden Text reveals that God is not only our defender but our benefactor as well. God's surrender of His own beloved Son to suffering and death carries with it all the blessings and graces needed to complete our salvation and make it rich and full here and now.

This seems to be a reference to Abraham's example of offering up his only son in obedience to God. In light of such a sacrifice, God could put complete confidence in the great father of the faithful. Likewise, we can be assured that if God would give up His Son to die for our sins, He will also give each of us every spiritual provision needful for our victorious life and ultimate glory.

Daily Devotions:
M. First Sacrifice Implied
Genesis 3:17-21
T. Sacrifices Commanded
Exodus 29:36-42
W. Unacceptable Sacrifices
Isaiah 1:11-17
T. Jesus' Self-Sacrifice
John 10:14-18
F. Christ, Our Atonement
Romans 5:6-11
S. Christ Died for All
2 Corinthians 5:14-21

Fraud and Flight (Jacob)

Genesis 25:19-34; 27:1 through 28:22

Unit Theme:
Isaac, Jacob and Joseph

Central Truth:
God's will is that we live honestly, trusting Him.

Focus:
Be warned that dishonesty has serious consequences and trust God to have our best interests at heart.

Context:
Canaan between 1943 and 1929 B.C.

Golden Text:
"Bread of deceit is sweet to a man; but afterward his mouth shall be filled with gravel" (Proverbs 20:17).

Study Outline:
I. Two Destinies Foretold (Genesis 25:20-28)
II. A Blessing Gained Dishonestly (Genesis 27:30-45)
III. Running From Sin's Consequences (Genesis 28:10-22)

INTRODUCTION

At the close of our last lesson we saw Abraham prove his commitment to the covenant God had made with him. Because of his willingness to sacrifice Isaac, no further trials came to test his faith. He did, however, have to mourn the death of Sarah some years later. She died at age 127, a long life that had allowed her to joyously raise Isaac to adulthood. Genesis 23 covers the details of her death and subsequent burial in the cave in the field at Machpelah.

Genesis 24 tells the beautiful story of Abraham sending his servant to find a wife for Isaac among his own people. Though not specifically stated, many believe this "eldest servant of his house" (v. 2) to be Eliezer, the same servant who had been named as Abraham's heir before he had a natural son. There is a sweet irony to the fact that this faithful man would be chosen to go find a wife for someone who had displaced him. In this story we see the footprints of the Lord directing the lives of those He loved. The same is true today. We may not understand much of what is happening from time to time, but when we look back, we can see just how strong God's hand has been in shaping events and circumstances.

Genesis 25 begins with the events of the final years of Abraham's life. Amazingly, he took another wife who bore him six more sons before his death at age 175. Though these sons were given gifts before his death, the bulk of Abraham's wealth went to Isaac, who was the legal firstborn and heir to the covenant. We are then given the genealogies of Ishmael and Isaac. We see that God fulfilled all His promises to Abraham. Ishmael had 12 sons who became princes, and Isaac had 12 grandsons by Jacob, which became the 12 tribes of Israel.

This brings us to our current lesson. Isaac married Rebekah when he was 40 years old, but it was 20 years later when they had children. Isaac cried out to the Lord because his wife was barren, and his cry was heard. The pregnancy, however, was so difficult that Rebekah herself entreated the Lord for help. The Lord spoke directly to her about the nations that would arise from the two sons wrestling in her womb. That wrestling is the subject of our lesson.

I. TWO DESTINIES FORETOLD (Genesis 25:20-28)

Isaac, though very much the son of promise, receives relatively little attention in the Biblical narrative. Mostly we see him repeat some of his father's own mistakes. Just like Abraham, he foolishly allowed a foreign king to believe his wife was his sister. Also, like his mother had been, his wife was barren. Both he and his father prayed for their wives, and children eventually came. From this we see that "the promised blessing through the chosen seed of Abraham is not to be accomplished merely by human effort. The fulfillment of the promise at each crucial juncture requires a specific act of God" (*Zondervan NIV Bible Commentary*).

A. Rebekah's Barrenness (vv. 20, 21)

20. And Isaac was forty years old when he took Rebekah to wife, the daughter of Bethuel the Syrian of Padan-aram, the sister to Laban the Syrian.

21. And Isaac intreated the Lord for his wife, because she was barren: and the Lord was intreated of him, and Rebekah his wife conceived.

Padan-aram (v. 20)—in the district of Mesopotamia, a plain or field surrounded by mountains

Though Isaac prayed, it was not a matter of trying to change God's mind. The Lord certainly knew that for there to be a continuation of the covenant, Rebekah would have to bear children. His purposes in withholding pregnancy were many. First, Isaac had to know that the covenant he received was a gift from God. There was nothing in him inherently righteous that he should be favored over Ishmael. In other words, Isaac could carry no pride in his position. Second, Isaac needed to learn the patient exercise of faith. Though the covenant was real, it was not automatic. Finally, would Isaac try to speed up God like his father had done? To his credit, Isaac did not resort to a concubine. He had at least learned something of the heartbreak that comes when people try to "help" God fulfill His word.

Talk About It:
What do these verses say about prayer?

"The protracted sterility of the mothers of the patriarchs, and other leading men amongst the Hebrew people, was a providential arrangement, designed to exercise faith and patience, to stimulate prayer, to inspire a conviction that the children born under extraordinary circumstances were gifts of God's grace, and specially to foreshadow the miraculous birth of the Saviour" (*Jamieson, Fausset, and Brown Commentary*).

"We should be as specific in our requests when in prayer to God as we are when we need a definite item at the market."
—Samuel Brengle

B. A Difficult Pregnancy (vv. 22, 23)

22. And the children struggled together within her; and she said, If it be so, why am I thus? And she went to enquire of the Lord.

23. And the Lord said unto her, Two nations are in thy womb, and two manner of people shall be separated from

thy bowels; and the one people shall be stronger than the other people; and the elder shall serve the younger.

Talk About It:
What did the Lord reveal to Rebekah concerning her pregnancy?

Sometimes the answers to prayers bring even greater problems. Rebekah had a very difficult pregnancy. Her inquiry of the Lord might be rephrased like this: "Lord, if this child I'm carrying is divinely ordained, why should there be such a struggle inside of me?" The fact that she went to the Lord at all implies that worship and prayer had been established among the members of Abraham's family. She might have gone to ask Isaac to consult with the Lord, but she did not. She inquired for herself. "This passage conveys to us the intimation that there was now a fixed mode and perhaps place of inquiring of the Lord" (*Barnes' Notes*).

Rebekah's inquiry did not go unanswered. The Lord spoke directly to her, likely through a vision or a dream. She was told that two children were in her womb, representing two nations that would develop. The struggle going on inside her was only a prelude to the wars that would continue between the two in their later history. From Esau would come the Edomites, and from Jacob would come the Israelites. What different peoples they became! Their customs, religion and manners were so diametrically opposed that they became perpetual enemies. The struggle in Rebekah's womb was an omen of things to come.

"Every tomorrow has two handles; we can take hold by the handle of anxiety or by the handle of faith."
—*Quotable Quotes*

The Edomites became idol worshipers, while the descendants of Jacob had a divine visitation from Jehovah while they were enslaved in Egypt. From there the religion of the Jews was firmly established through Moses. When Moses led the Israelites out of Egypt, they asked for passage through Edom, but were refused. From that time forward the history of the Edomites "is little more than the history of their wars with the Jews" (*Adam Clarke's Commentary*).

C. Parental Favorites (vv. 24-28)

24. And when her days to be delivered were fulfilled, behold, there were twins in her womb.

25. And the first came out red, all over like an hairy garment; and they called his name Esau.

Esau (v. 25)—
hairy; rough

Jacob (v. 26)—
supplanter; heel-catcher

26. And after that came his brother out, and his hand took hold on Esau's heel; and his name was called Jacob: and Isaac was threescore years old when she bare them.

27. And the boys grew: and Esau was a cunning hunter, a man of the field; and Jacob was a plain man, dwelling in tents.

28. And Isaac loved Esau, because he did eat of his venison: but Rebekah loved Jacob.

The word *behold* (v. 24) seems to indicate a surprise at there being more than one baby. Had Rebekah not told anyone of her word from the Lord? Perhaps not. Certainly the implication of the message was that the covenant would be passed down through the younger son. So why did Isaac not give more attention to Jacob? Whatever the reason, these verses provide a glimpse of life in the home of Isaac and Rebekah. The twin boys were anything but identical. Esau was a strong, ruddy, outdoors type, who loved to hunt, while Jacob was a frail, mama's boy. No wonder Isaac preferred Esau.

If Isaac did understand that the covenant would be perpetuated through Jacob, he apparently convinced himself otherwise. Esau was everything a man could want in a son, carrying the traits that Isaac himself seemed to have missed. The favoritism of the two parents was further indication of the struggle between the two brothers. "The point is not that the struggles were necessary for the accomplishment of the will of God but that God's will was accomplished in spite of the conflict" (*Zondervan NIV Bible Commentary*).

Talk About It:
1. Compare Jacob with Esau.
2. How did the parents respond to their twin sons?

> "Parents wonder why the streams are bitter when they themselves have poisoned the fountain."
> —**John Locke**

II. A BLESSING GAINED DISHONESTLY (Genesis 27:30-45)
A. Deception Exposed (vv. 30-33)

30. And it came to pass, as soon as Isaac had made an end of blessing Jacob, and Jacob was yet scarce gone out from the presence of Isaac his father, that Esau his brother came in from his hunting.

31. And he also had made savoury meat, and brought it unto his father, and said unto his father, Let my father arise, and eat of his son's venison, that thy soul may bless me.

32. And Isaac his father said unto him, Who art thou? And he said, I am thy son, thy firstborn Esau.

33. And Isaac trembled very exceedingly, and said, Who? where is he that hath taken venison, and brought it me, and I have eaten of all before thou camest, and have blessed him? yea, and he shall be blessed.

Chapter 27 begins by saying that Isaac was old and blind, and apparently felt himself to be nearing his death. In fact, however, it would be many years before he would actually expire. He lived to see Jacob return home with his two wives and children (after 20 years in Padan Aram with Laban), as well as see his two sons make a truce. That Esau would ever forgive Jacob would be a miracle in itself. The eventual meeting between the two takes place in Genesis 33. Jacob feared for his life, since Esau had a potential army of 400 men with him. However, though he harbored hostility toward his brother, God had gradually changed Esau. "In the 20 years that had intervened, the controlling hand of God had wrought changes in both men" (*Wycliffe Bible Commentary*).

Talk About It:
1. What might have happened if Esau had returned from hunting a short time earlier?
2. Describe Isaac's reaction to being deceived (v. 33).

Back to our present text, we see that Isaac was intent on Esau's receiving the primary parental blessing. This was in spite of the fact that Esau had already made poor decisions. He had traded his birthright off to Jacob for a bowl of stew. Possibly, Isaac was not privy to this failure in judgment by his favorite son. Also, Esau had married two Hittite women, a point of grief to both his parents. The entire story of Esau's giving up the birthright (25:29-34) shows what little value he had placed on it.

Isaac planned a ceremony to celebrate his blessing on Esau, and thus the desire for a meal of savory food. Rebekah overheard the plan and set her own in motion to circumvent Isaac's desires. We might call this cruel and calculating on her part, but she had, in fact, received a message from the Lord that the younger brother (her favorite) was to be dominant. The drama of the story is heightened as Esau enters just as Jacob exits, having tricked his blind father.

Isaac was suspicious of the charade that was taking place, but in the end gave his blessing to Jacob, alluding to the promise of Abraham in the final words. When Esau entered, Isaac suddenly realized he had been tricked. His frustration was heightened because he had spoken words that could not be retracted. "Isaac's words of blessing had power—indeed, they were backed by the power of the Lord" (*Nelson Study Bible*).

B. Realization of Loss (vv. 34-40)
(Genesis 27:37-40 is not included in the printed text.)

34. And when Esau heard the words of his father, he cried with a great and exceeding bitter cry, and said unto his father, Bless me, even me also, O my father.

35. And he said, Thy brother came with subtilty, and hath taken away thy blessing.

36. And he said, Is not he rightly named Jacob? for he hath supplanted me these two times: he took away my birthright; and, behold, now he hath taken away my blessing. And he said, Hast thou not reserved a blessing for me?

It is not quite clear why Esau would be so intent on receiving his father's blessing, unless his selling of the birthright to Jacob was not known to others. If that be the case, then Esau himself was guilty of trickery. What he desired was no longer his. Ultimately, Isaac blessed him as best he could, reiterating what had been revealed to Rebekah before the boys' birth—that the older would serve the younger.

Esau comes across as a whiner. Even though Jacob was a deceiver, Esau had been earlier ignorant of the sacredness of his heritage. His bitterness now only shows that he wanted his father's blessing without the responsibility. "His deep hurt that

---

Birds in their little nests agree;
And 'tis a shameful sight,
When children of one family
Fall out, and chide, and fight.
—Isaac Watts

---

have the dominion (v. 40)—"break loose" or "become restless"

Talk About It:
1. Why couldn't Isaac grant Esau's plea (vv. 34, 35)?
2. How had Jacob's actions matched his name (v. 36)?
3. Describe the blessing given to Esau.

Fraud and Flight

Jacob had outwitted him in securing the birthright, his bitter disappointment, his pathetic sobbing, and the burning shame that quickly kindled into intense hatred and desire for revenge are deeply moving" (*Wycliffe Bible Commentary*).

C. Esau's Hatred of Jacob (vv. 41-45)
(Genesis 27:42-45 is not included in the printed text.)

41. And Esau hated Jacob because of the blessing wherewith his father blessed him: and Esau said in his heart, The days of mourning for my father are at hand; then will I slay my brother Jacob.

Perhaps one reason Esau never fully pursued his hatred of Jacob was that he promised himself to wait until Isaac was dead. As stated earlier, Isaac proved to have a resilient constitution, surviving another 40 years. He lived to be 180. One might say that Esau's reluctance to kill Jacob was out of respect for Isaac, even though Esau spitefully shortly thereafter took an Ishmaelite woman for a wife.

Rebekah did her part to thwart any plans by Esau to harm Jacob. She sent Jacob to visit her brother Laban. There he could find a wife from her relatives. Rebekah and Isaac were already frustrated that Esau had taken two Hittite women for wives. "Isaac agreed with Rebekah that intermarriage with the pagan women of Canaan was dangerous. These women would bring their own false gods into the household" (*Nelson Study Bible*). Sadly for Rebekah, she would never see her favorite son again. Though he would return home with two wives and many children, she died during the intervening years.

III. RUNNING FROM SIN'S CONSEQUENCES
(Genesis 28:10-22)

A. Jacob's Dream at Bethel (vv. 10-15)

10. And Jacob went out from Beer-sheba, and went toward Haran.

11. And he lighted upon a certain place, and tarried there all night, because the sun was set; and he took of the stones of that place, and put them for his pillows, and lay down in that place to sleep.

12. And he dreamed, and behold a ladder set up on the earth, and the top of it reached to heaven: and behold the angels of God ascending and descending on it.

13. And, behold, the Lord stood above it, and said, I am the Lord God of Abraham thy father, and the God of Isaac: the land whereon thou liest, to thee will I give it, and to thy seed;

14. And thy seed shall be as the dust of the earth, and thou shalt spread abroad to the west, and to the east, and

"For sons or daughters in Biblical times, receiving their father's blessing was a momentous event. It gave these children a tremendous sense of being highly valued by their parents and even pictured a special future for them."
—**John Trent**

Talk About It:
1. What was Esau's plot (v. 41)?
2. What was Rebekah's plan for Jacob (vv. 44, 45)?

"Character is the sum and total of a person's choices."
—**P.B. Fitzwater**

Beer-sheba (v. 10)—the southern end of Judah's cultivated land

to the north, and to the south: and in thee and in thy seed shall all the families of the earth be blessed.

15. And, behold, I am with thee, and will keep thee in all places whither thou goest, and will bring thee again into this land; for I will not leave thee, until I have done that which I have spoken to thee of.

Just as with his father and his grandfather, Jacob here received a visitation of heaven confirming the covenant. Abraham's visit had come in a vision, while Isaac's had occurred more likely in a dream, as with Jacob. The sight of angels ascending and descending a ladder showed Jacob that there "actually is communication between heaven and earth. He recognized in that place that God was by his side, promising him guidance through his life, and future greatness" (*Wycliffe Bible Commentary*). This apparently was the first time in his life that he experienced the presence of God, and he was profoundly moved. The voice of the Lord, the hope, the sense of love and acceptance—these were enough to change the conniver's heart and bring him to a point of total worship.

The circumstances of the visitation were austere. As Jesus later would say of Himself, "The Son of Man has nowhere to lay His head" (Matthew 8:20, *NKJV*). Jacob was a man on the run, with no place to call home, a bounty on his life. Yet, this was by divinely appointed choice. With only a stone for a pillow, he received the most heavenly of visions. At the lowest point of life, God intervened to make him aware of his destiny. He may be utterly destitute, but above him in heaven stood the Lord, ready to help him. The ladder resting on the earth and reaching to heaven showed the "real and uninterrupted fellowship between God in heaven and His people upon earth. The angels upon it carry up the wants of men to God, and bring down the assistance and protection of God to men" (*Keil & Delitzsch Commentary on the Old Testament*).

In the dream God promised Jacob that he would be protected, his descendants would be as the dust of the earth, all the earth would be blessed by his seed, and he himself would be brought back to his home under divine protection. Certainly this final promise was the guiding principle years later in causing Jacob to leave his uncle Laban and return to face his brother, Esau.

B. Recognition of Divine Visitation (vv. 16-19)

16. And Jacob awaked out of his sleep, and he said, Surely the Lord is in this place; and I knew it not.

17. And he was afraid, and said, How dreadful is this place! this is none other but the house of God, and this is the gate of heaven.

Talk About It:
1. What do you suppose was the significance of the ladder (v. 12)?
2. How did God introduce Himself (v. 13)?
3. What promises did God make to Jacob (vv. 13-15)?

"According to Scripture, God is incomprehensible yet knowable, absolute yet personal."
—Herman Bavinck

dreadful (v. 17)—awesome

Fraud and Flight

18. And Jacob rose up early in the morning, and took the stone that he had put for his pillows, and set it up for a pillar, and poured oil upon the top of it.

19. And he called the name of that place Beth-el: but the name of that city was called Luz at the first.

Jacob awoke from his dream as a new man. Of course, much of his character was yet to be transformed. This would not occur until another major visitation years later when his name would be changed from *Jacob* ("supplanter") to *Israel* ("prince with God"). Still, Jacob now recognized that he was loved of God, and that he would be blessed in mighty ways. A holy fear of God came over him. He suddenly realized that the blessing of Isaac that had been pronounced over him carried divine authority, that Jehovah would guide, protect, and be near him to make good on the promises made in the covenant. "To that end the Lord proved to him that He was near, in such a way that the place appeared dreadful, inasmuch as the nearness of the holy God makes an alarming impression upon unholy man, and the consciousness of sin grows into the fear of death" (*Keil & Delitzsch Commentary on the Old Testament*).

Because of the weightiness of the moment, Jacob determined that where he was standing was holy ground and should be named *Bethel*, meaning "the house of God . . . the gate of heaven." It was the place where heaven was opened up to him.

C. Jacob's Vow (vv. 20-22)

20. And Jacob vowed a vow, saying, If God will be with me, and will keep me in this way that I go, and will give me bread to eat, and raiment to put on,

21. So that I come again to my father's house in peace; then shall the Lord be my God:

22. And this stone, which I have set for a pillar, shall be God's house: and of all that thou shalt give me I will surely give the tenth unto thee.

Jacob set up a stone as a memorial to the revelation he had received, and he poured oil on the stone to consecrate it. This was not an idol, but rather a reminder of the mercy that had been shown to him, a "sanctuary where intimate fellowship with God would always be possible" (*Wycliffe Bible Commentary*). He also pledged his life and a tenth of everything he would ever possess to God. His grandfather Abraham had earlier given the same portion to Melchizedek (14:20). Notice, however, that he made his promise to God conditional with the word *if*. Yes, this was a point of dedication, but Jacob still had a long way to go, as the events of the next few years would prove.

Bethel (v. 19)—
"house of God"

Luz (v. 19)—
"almond tree"

Talk About It:
1. How was Jacob's understanding of God limited (vv. 16, 17)?
2. Why did Jacob turn a "pillow" into a "pillar" (v. 18)?

Open Our Eyes
Like Jacob, we are often unaware of how much God is watching over us, protecting us, and guiding us. Often providential circumstances go unnoticed by us as we struggle with daily life. May we pray as Paul urged: "That the eyes of your heart may be enlightened in order that you may know the hope to which he has called you, the riches of his glorious inheritance in the saints, and his incomparably great power for us who believe" (Ephesians 1:18, 19, *NIV*).

Talk About It:
1. List all the promises Jacob made to God.
2. Why did Jacob make these promises?

CONCLUSION

The dream that Jacob had at Bethel was the first time in his life he "experienced God." Up to this point, all he knew of Jehovah was secondhand information. Yes, he had bought the birthright from his brother, Esau, and the promises of the covenant, but this had been so purely from selfish reasons. The heavenly visitation proved to him that God was interested in him, that there were blessings over his life, and there was a purpose in everything he did. The same is true for us.

Do you remember the first time the Holy Spirit brought conviction to your heart? That sense of dread and utter sinfulness were enough to put the fear of the Lord in your heart. Nothing would satisfy that conviction except giving your life to Christ. At the same time, there was the wooing of the Lord for you to draw near to Him because He loved you and He wanted you. Thank God that He still visits people's hearts and shows Himself to be real and ready to accept every sinner.

GOLDEN TEXT CHALLENGE

"BREAD OF DECEIT IS SWEET TO A MAN; BUT AFTERWARDS HIS MOUTH SHALL BE FILLED WITH GRAVEL" (Proverbs 20:17).

There is nothing sweet about deceit. Just ask Jacob.

At the moment when Jacob realized he had deceived his blind father and gained his brother's blessing, no doubt he sensed an adrenalin rush and a sense of sordidly sweet accomplishment. However, the sweetness soon turned gravelly when he realized he must snatch up a few of his belongings and flee for his life. How could Jacob have known that he would be gone for two decades and would never again see his dear mother?

Unlike Jacob, let's not bake the "bread of deceit," but instead cook with ingredients that never go bad.

Daily Devotions:
M. Deceived by Satan
Genesis 3:1-6, 13
T. Honestly Commanded
Leviticus 19:11-18
W. Lamenting a Deceptive Society
Jeremiah 9:1-9
T. Satan, Father of Lies
John 8:42-47
F. Manifesting the Truth
2 Corinthians 4:1-6
S. Honest Living
Colossians 3:9-15

The Incarnation (Christmas)

John 1:1-18

INTRODUCTION

One cannot read the Bible without being confronted with an astonishing phenomenon: God frequently broke through to the minds of human beings with His self-revelation. Men and women in the Bible did not reason out or discover God. Rather, He graciously disclosed Himself to them. The total Bible is the inspired record of God's self-disclosure. In other words, the divine self-revelation is embodied in the book we call the Bible.

The self-revelation of God has taken many forms, as in the following examples: (1) *theophanies*—a term meaning "a manifestation of God" (see Genesis 17:1; 18:1-3; 32:24-30); (2) names; (3) miracles; (4) special providences; (5) verbal utterances (e.g., the Ten Commandments); (6) the ministry of the prophets.

Our present lesson focuses on the Biblical event in which God's self-revelation reaches its consummation and crown—the incarnation of God the eternal Son in the person of Jesus. This divine revelation was something utterly different from every other mode of revelation. It went infinitely beyond theophany, miracle, providence, verbal utterance, and the prophetic ministry—not only in degree, but in quality also. By the Incarnation the living God himself, in His nature and person, became man without ceasing to be God.

To quote E.A. Litton, "In the person of Christ all previous manifestations of God are summed as in an epitome; the scattered rays are here concentrated in a focus; and for this reason we can expect no further, or more complete, revelation of God" (*Introduction to Dogmatic Theology*).

The Christmas lesson is taken from the beautiful and majestic prologue to the Gospel of John. In this way we are able to receive another impression of the meaning of Christmas as seen in the eternal Word. It is this Word that came to live among people as their life and their light. The transforming power of this Word enables us to become sons and daughters of God by receiving the revelation of God in Christ, the eternal Word.

Unit Theme:
Birth of Jesus Christ

Central Truth:
God's purpose in the Incarnation was to reveal Himself through Christ.

Focus:
Understand that God became flesh and receive Jesus Christ as Savior and Lord.

Context:
Written about A.D. 90-100

Golden Text:
"The Word was made flesh, and dwelt among us, (and we beheld his glory, the glory as of the only begotten of the Father,) full of grace and truth" (John 1:14).

Study Outline:
I. The Eternal Word (John 1:1-5)
II. The True Light (John 1:6-13)
III. The Word Made Flesh (John 1:14-18)

I. THE ETERNAL WORD (John 1:1-5)

A. The Word Is (vv. 1, 2)

1. In the beginning was the Word, and the Word was with God, and the Word was God.

2. The same was in the beginning with God.

Talk About It:
1. Why is Jesus called "the Word"?
2. What do these two verses reveal about Jesus?

These verses reveal three truths about the Word, which is Jesus. First, "in the beginning was the Word." This means that Jesus did not have to be created. When the earth was brought into being, He was already there because He had always been in existence. "The beginning" speaks of a dateless past where Christ was with God.

If modern science were to prove that the earth was billions of years old, that fact could not predate the existence of Christ. He as a person existed at the beginning.

The Greek expression for "Word" is *Logos*. Hobbs writes that the classical Greek used *logos* to express numerous functions:

> Heraclitus used it for the principle which maintains order in the universe. The Stoic philosophers used it for the soul of the world. . . . Upon what basis therefore did John choose the Word to personify Christ? Recalling that John in his first few verses deliberately parallels Genesis 1 throws light upon this question. In the Genesis account of Creation each new phrase is introduced with the words "And God said." Here, therefore, is the spoken or outward revelation of God. And this thought is expressed through the Greek word *logos*, or Word . . . "therefore in the beginning was always the Word."

Second, "the Word was with God." This emphasizes that God and the Word were one. One translation reads, "The Word was face-to-face with God." Another reads, "The Word saw eye to eye with God."

Third, "the Word was God." This completes a statement that has only one inevitable conclusion. If the Word was in the beginning, and was in complete company with God, obviously the Word was, by nature, essentially the same as God. This is not to say that the Word was identical with God, but that the Word was absolutely the same as God.

"Jesus Christ is all we have; He is all we need and all we want. We are shipwrecked on God and stranded on omnipotence!"
—Vance Havner

B. The Word Creates (v. 3)

3. All things were made by him; and without him was not any thing made that was made.

Not only did the Word exist before Creation, but He participated in the creation of all matter. Christianity has always believed in the creation of matter—making something out of nothing. It has likewise always believed the world belongs to

God because He created it for Himself. The existence of evil does not detract from the fact that "this is my Father's world" and that because He created it, He controls it. In time, He will have it totally as His exclusive possession.

Perhaps this is why the statement "No room at the inn" has such tragic tones. He who created the world could find no place that would receive Him at His birth. Joseph and Mary were crowded out of the inn because no one recognized that here about to tabernacle among men was the Word, the eternal God.

C. The Word Lives (v. 4)

4. In him was life; and the life was the light of men.

Barclay suggests that, as a musical composer builds on a theme which dominates his composition, here John introduces what is to become the great theme of his Gospel. This Gospel is built on the words *life* and *light*. As the Gospel begins with life, so it ends.

John says his aim in writing his Gospel is that people might "believe that Jesus is the Christ, the Son of God; and that believing ye might have *life* through his name" (20:31). Jesus regrets that people do not come to Him and accept *life* (5:40). Through Him we can have abundant *life* (10:10). He says that this *life* cannot be taken away (v. 28). He says that He is "the way, the truth, and the *life*" (14:6).

This word *life* in its various forms is used 40 times in the Gospel of John. What does it mean? It is the opposite of death. To have life in God is to become immortal with Him and to participate in the promise of everlasting life.

D. The Word Shines (v. 5)

5. And the light shineth in darkness; and the darkness comprehended it not.

The second great theme of John is the word *light*. This word appears no less than 21 times in this Gospel. Barclay suggests that it is the "light that puts chaos to flight." The light that shines in darkness causes the empty chaos to become light (Genesis 1:3). It is also a *revealing* light and a *guiding* light. As Jesus reveals to us what we are, He shows us what we can become by His grace and power.

The power of this light is so great that the darkness cannot put it out. This light of Christ shines in the hostile darkness, and the darkness tries but cannot overcome it. This darkness is a symbol of all who stand for injustice, for ignorance of the Truth, and for all those blind areas of darkness that reach for the souls of humanity. They will not triumph. The darkness is great, but the light of Christ reaches out into the darkness with a Resurrection message that Life and Light have come to men and women.

Talk About It:
Why is it important to know that God's Son was involved in creating the world?

Talk About It:
What does Christ's "light" accomplish?

Talk About It:
What does the darkness represent, and what could it not do? Why not?

"Now is the time to sing, envision, enact, and retell a story of God coming unexpectedly in the worst of times as a baby born poor, born homeless, born to die that all human life might be transformed and dreams made real. It's God's good news, but only because we already know the story of Easter."
—**John Westerhoff**

"To John, the Christless life was life in the dark. The darkness stands for life without Christ, and especially for life which has turned its back on Christ" (Barclay). Although some never believe, the fact remains: darkness has never been able to extinguish the light of the Word (see Romans 3:3, 4). It still shines even brighter in the hours of greatest moral and spiritual darkness.

II. THE TRUE LIGHT (John 1:6-13)

A. Witness (vv. 6-8)

6. There was a man sent from God, whose name was John.

7. The same came for a witness, to bear witness of the Light, that all men through him might believe.

8. He was not that Light, but was sent to bear witness of that Light.

Here John, the writer, moves from eternity into time and begins to record the historical events surrounding the coming of John the Baptist. This man, who was sent from God, was not the great Light of whom John spoke. He witnessed the reality of that Light. His coming was to be a record, a testimony, a witness to the coming of Christ.

The reason it was necessary to point out that John was not the Messiah was the tremendous attention that came to him. For over 400 years there had been no prophet in Israel until John came. While the attention he drew was predictable, he was not the Light, but one who predated the coming of Him who was the Light of the World.

B. True Light (v. 9)

9. That was the true Light, which lighteth every man that cometh into the world.

The Incarnation was an event like no other. While the prophets spoke some truth, they held their light against a background of human imperfection. The light borne by Christ was the Truth in every sense.

Like the coming of a welcomed cloud over the black bay of nothingness, Jesus brought the true Light that would light all humanity. He dissipated the shadows of *doubt*.

The Greek mind thought it near impossible to find out about God, but the Word revealed God in bold relief so all could discern Him. He dispelled shadows of *despair*; hopeless people found a new reason to live. He took away the fear of *death*. The ancients feared death above all things, but Christ brought a hope that promised life with victory over death. This indeed was the true Light.

Talk About It:
1. What was John's relationship to "the Light"?
2. How well did John carry out his mission? (see vv. 19-23).

Talk About It:
Explain the phrase "gives light to every man" (*NIV*).

God in a Manger
I see a baby wrapped in swaddling clothes. Is this the One who is clothed in the beautiful glory of unapproachable light?
Listen! He is crying. Is this the One who thunders in

C. Stranger (vv. 10, 11)

10. He was in the world, and the world was made by him, and the world knew him not.

11. He came unto his own, and his own received him not.

The Westminster Catechism says, "The lights of nature, and the works of creation and providence do so far manifest the goodness, wisdom and power of God as to leave men inexcusable." God has brought light through the prophetic word, and through the living Word; so people are without excuse. Even so, the majority of those who heard Jesus in His day and saw His miracles did not receive Him as Lord.

In ways that are just as magnificent, God is revealing Himself today, and the world does not know Him. But what better example is there than Christmas? The Baby that was born in Bethlehem as Prince of peace longs to break through the meaningless expressions of the season, but few will let Him.

D. Children of God (vv. 12, 13)

12. But as many as received him, to them gave he power to become the sons of God, even to them that believe on his name:

13. Which were born, not of blood, nor of the will of the flesh, nor of the will of man, but of God.

Not every person rejected the revelation of God in Christ. Those who did not reject Him received the remarkable ability to become "sons of God."

A man is not naturally a son of God. He is conceived in sin and born in evil. He receives an ability to become his best through the *power* of Christ. John describes this power in terms of "a right": "But to as many as did receive and welcome Him, He gave the authority (power, privilege, right) to become the children of God" (v. 12, *Amp.*). When we believe, we have a right to worship—a right to become children of God.

As if to bury any doubt about the background of these children, verse 13 adequately and completely avers that they were not born of blood, nor of the will of man, but of God. The regeneration described here is the result of the implanting of the seed of God in the heart of people who are transformed and brought to a new life in Jesus Christ.

III. THE WORD MADE FLESH (John 1:14-18)

A. Lived With Us (v. 14)

14. And the Word was made flesh, and dwelt among us, (and we beheld his glory, the glory as of the only begotten of the Father,) full of grace and truth.

The effect of this passage is staggering. It would seem enough

the heaven making the angels lower their wings? Yes, but He has emptied Himself in order to fill us.

—Guerric of Igny

Talk About It:
1. Explain the irony in verse 10.
2. Who are "his own," and how did they respond to Jesus? Why?

Talk About It:
1. What power does God offer us, and how do we receive it (v. 12)?
2. Describe the birth process pictured in verse 13.

"I do not believe that the virgin mother gave birth to a son and that He is the Lord and Savior unless, added to this, I believe the second thing; namely, that He is my Savior and Lord."

—Martin Luther

Talk About It:
1. Why was Jesus "made flesh"?
2. Why is it important for Jesus to be filled with both "grace and truth"?

that God in His majesty would even look upon humanity. But He himself *became* flesh. This means He assumed the nature of humanity and accepted all its possibility of sin. John witnessed the fact of this remarkable existence because he looked at Jesus and described Him as being "full of grace and truth."

When Mary gave birth to a Son, she brought a Baby into the world with the same human adequacies and inadequacies that every baby has. He was flesh. John saw Him as a man and wanted us to know He was man. But He was the perfect man, sensitive to all the important issues of life.

B. Brought Grace (vv. 15-17)

15. John bare witness of him, and cried, saying, This was he of whom I spake, He that cometh after me is preferred before me: for he was before me.

16. And of his fulness have all we received, and grace for grace.

17. For the law was given by Moses, but grace and truth came by Jesus Christ.

grace for grace (v. 16)—"one blessing after another" (*NIV*)

Talk About It:
1. What made Jesus greater than John, according to John?
2. How did Jesus surpass Moses (v. 17)?

One of the points the Gospel writer is making is that John the Baptist, as great a prophet as he was, occupied a secondary role to Christ. This passage conveys three great truths about Jesus, the living Word.

First, His fullness has been made available to all of us. This means that in Jesus is all the wisdom, the power, and the love of God.

Second, we have received "grace for grace," meaning "grace upon grace" (*NASB*). This strange expression actually indicates that an abundance of divine favor is extended to those who trust Him. It also indicates the boundlessness of Christ's love. When we enter into His kingdom, the blessings of God grow every day, drawing from an inexhaustible supply.

Third, John says that while the Law came by Moses, "grace and truth came by Jesus Christ." Under Moses, one had to do a thing whether he liked it or not, and whether he understood the reason or not. "But with the coming of Jesus we no longer seek to obey the law of God like slaves. We seek to answer the love of God like sons" (*Barclay*).

C. Declared Clearly (v. 18)

18. No man hath seen God at any time; the only begotten Son, which is in the bosom of the Father, he hath declared him.

A summary of the major points in John 1:1-18 is given in this verse. The phrase "No man hath seen God" highlights the deity of the Word (Christ). The Word cannot be compared with any created person or thing. The Word is God. No man has seen

God. The "seeing" symbolizes the ability to comprehend or equal the Word. God is God.

The phrase "only begotten Son, which is in the bosom of the Father" reemphasizes the intimate relationships between the members of the Godhead. The depth of the relationship is illustrated by the familiar terms *Father* and *Son*.

The phrase "he hath declared him" conveys the relationship of the Word (Christ, Logos) to the universe and especially to people. The Word has come "declaring," or revealing, God. The Greek word for "declared" literally means "to lead out or explain." The meaning in this context is to "reveal and recount." The Word is the revelation of God.

John has explained that Jesus Christ is God, intimately related to the eternal Godhead, and that He reveals God to people. In just 18 verses he describes critical principles concerning the foundation of Christianity. It is vital that Christians maintain that Christ is God, an intimate member of the Trinity, and the revelation of God. John presents these as decisive factors in following Christ. The same is true today. If Christians fail to affirm these critical points, they will miss the Christ presented in Scripture.

Talk About It:
1. Explain the phrase "in the bosom of the Father."
2. What has Jesus "declared" ["explained," *NASB*] and how?

"Despite our best efforts to keep Him out, God intrudes. The life of Jesus is bracketed by two impossibilities: a virgin's womb and an empty tomb. Jesus entered our world through a door marked 'No Entrance' and left through a door marked 'No Exit.'"
—Peter Larson

CONCLUSION

"From the human perspective, when you compare [God] to the other gods of the other religions in the world, you have to say our God is really sort of odd. He uses the most common of people, people that aren't any different from any of us here; He comes in the most common of ways, when by His Spirit an anonymous young woman is found to be with child. And the strangest thing is that He comes at all—He's not the Above-Us-God, too holy to come down. This God's love is so immense that He wants to come down. And He has proved His love by the fact that He did come down and touch our ground" (James R. Van Tholen, *Where All Hope Lies*).

GOLDEN TEXT CHALLENGE

"THE WORD WAS MADE FLESH, AND DWELT AMONG US, (AND WE BEHELD HIS GLORY, THE GLORY AS OF THE ONLY BEGOTTEN OF THE FATHER,) FULL OF GRACE AND TRUTH" (John 1:14).

The greatest fact of history is that Jesus Christ, the Son of God, lived on this earth, died for the sins of humanity, and was resurrected from the dead. The greatest hope of the world today is that He who one time dwelt among us is coming again to the earth.

What a privilege it was for the disciples to behold the glory of Christ! They saw Him perform miracles. They heard Him teach.

They saw Him transfigured on the Mount of Transfiguration. They saw Him die for the sins of all of us. They saw Him in His resurrected body, and they saw Him as He ascended to His Father.

We missed a lot by not living on this earth when Jesus was here in the flesh; but one day we too will behold His glory. We will see Him in all of His majesty and power. We will bow at His feet and worship Him, our Redeemer, our Lord. Further, as the Scriptures declare: "Beloved, now are we the sons of God, and it doth not yet appear what we shall be: but we know that, when he shall appear, we shall be like him; for we shall see him as he is" (1 John 3:2).

The disciples beheld the glory of Christ. One day we also will behold His glory. And one day all of His disciples, from the first in history to the last in history, will experience a momentous transformation—"we shall be like Him." Thank God for the plan of salvation—a plan which lifts us from a base state as a sinner in rebellion against God to an exalted state as a heavenly creature "like" the Son of God.

Humbled and Exalted (Jacob)

Genesis 31:1-21; 32:1-32

INTRODUCTION

At the end of lesson 3, Jacob was on his way to his mother's home in Padan-aram. This was not an easy journey, especially for one not accustomed to rugged outdoor living and travel. He probably had never journeyed far from his mother's tent. He now had no alternative but to run, however, and finally arrived in Haran at a well (possibly the same one where Eliezer had met Rebekah). Upon questioning local shepherds, he discovered that his uncle was still alive, and shortly thereafter his cousin Rachel appeared leading a flock of her father's sheep. Wonderfully surprised at meeting his kinfolk (indicating how frightening the journey may have been), Jacob wept, while Rachel rushed off to tell Laban of his arrival.

Laban was ecstatic to see his sister's son and was eager to receive an able-bodied worker in his household. Certainly he remembered all the gifts Eliezer had brought when he came to fetch a bride for Isaac. Also, both his daughters were ready for marriage, and Jacob was an eligible bachelor. Laban was just as much a conniver and supplanter as Jacob. "The young nephew from the hill country would learn to deal cautiously with him. In fact, Jacob would learn to outwit the chief trickster of all the 'children of the East'" (*Wycliffe Bible Commentary*).

Rachel was beautiful, and Jacob quickly fell in love with her. We know the story of how Laban tricked him into marrying Leah instead. Leah was certainly not beautiful, but her fertility in producing male children made her a force to be reckoned with. It would be one of her sons, Judah, through whom Jesus would ultimately be born. After working 14 years for Laban, Jacob finally received Rachel as his wife, but she was barren. This produced an enmity between sisters. The inclusion of Bilhah (Rachel's maid) and Zilpah (Leah's maid) as concubine wives for Jacob produced four more sons, but did little to relieve the tension in the household. Finally, however, God took away Rachel's reproach and gave her a son named Joseph. Though not the son to carry the bloodline of Jesus, this special boy later became a savior for his people.

Eventually there was trouble in paradise. Jacob now had 11 sons and one daughter. God had given him favor through a dream where he was given a secret to controlling the genetics of sheep and goats. This had made him a wealthy man—much to the expense of Laban. Our lesson picks up at this point.

Unit Theme:
Isaac, Jacob and Joseph

Central Truth:
God ordains that humility will precede exaltation.

Focus:
Recognize that God exalts those who fervently seek His blessing and submit to Him.

Context:
Around 1900 B.C., Jacob goes from Padan-aram to Peniel.

Golden Text:
"Whosoever shall exalt himself shall be abased; and he that shall humble himself shall be exalted" (Matthew 23:12).

Study Outline:
I. Homeward Bound at God's Command (Genesis 31:3-7, 17-21)
II. Humbled by Fear and Distress (Genesis 32:1-12)
III. Confronted and Exalted by God (Genesis 32:24-32)

I. HOMEWARD BOUND AT GOD'S COMMAND
(Genesis 31:3-7, 17-21)

A. The Voice of the Lord (v. 3)

3. And the Lord said unto Jacob, Return unto the land of thy fathers, and to thy kindred; and I will be with thee.

Talk About It:
How specific was God's Word to Jacob?

After Rachel bore Joseph, Jacob wanted to go home, but had he left then he would have taken only his family. He had no personal wealth, for all his labor had gone into making Laban richer. Also, his father-in-law was adamantly opposed to losing him (as well as his sons, some of whom were getting old enough to work). Laban did allow Jacob to name his wages. Jacob made an offer that Laban could not refuse. Unknown to Laban, however, Jacob had heard from God in a dream (v. 10) showing him how to selectively breed sheep and goats. "In Syria the sheep were white and the goats were black, with very few exceptions. Jacob offered to start in business at once, accepting as his the sheep that were not white and the goats that were not black, and leaving the rest to Laban" (*Wycliffe Bible Commentary*). Tricky Laban quickly removed the few multicolored specimens from his flock and hid them so that Jacob would have nothing to start with.

Whether there was any science to what Jacob had up his sleeve is dubious. More likely, this was an act of faith based on something God had shown him in a dream. As such, the results were nothing short of miraculous. More and more multicolored sheep and goats were being born. The favor of the Lord was upon Jacob, and even his reputation as a *supplanter* was blessed by God.

"Many refuse to admit to the reality of a personal God because they are unwilling to submit to His authority."
—Kurt Bruner

B. A Consultation With Two Wives (vv. 4-7)

4. And Jacob sent and called Rachel and Leah to the field unto his flock,

countenance (v. 5)—attitude

5. And said unto them, I see your father's countenance, that it is not toward me as before; but the God of my father hath been with me.

6. And ye know that with all my power I have served your father.

7. And your father hath deceived me, and changed my wages ten times; but God suffered him not to hurt me.

Talk About It:
1. Contrast the consistency of Jacob's father-in-law with the heavenly Father's consistency in regard to Jacob (vv. 5-7).

Jacob's success in genetics did nothing to gain his father-in-law's favor. He had now worked 20 years for Laban. Relations became so tense that he realized it was time to leave, especially after God commanded him to do so. Even though this meant facing Esau, Jacob now firmly believed in the divine hand over his life. He remembered the promise of the Lord to be with him (see 28:15). He consulted with his wives, and for once they were in agreement about something. Despite their ties to their home, they knew there was no inheritance for them. They also recognized the unfair treatment their husband was facing at the hand of their father. In their minds, Laban had stolen from them personally and from their children.

C. A Quiet Exit (vv. 17-19)

17. Then Jacob rose up, and set his sons and his wives upon camels;

18. And he carried away all his cattle, and all his goods which he had gotten, the cattle of his getting, which he had gotten in Padan-aram, for to go to Isaac his father in the land of Canaan.

19. And Laban went to shear his sheep: and Rachel had stolen the images that were her father's.

In one sense, Jacob didn't run away from Laban. He simply chose a time to leave when Laban was off shearing sheep. Unknown to Jacob, Rachel stole the household idols. It is not clear whether Laban was polytheistic (worshiping many gods), or henotheistic (believing in Yahweh above all other gods). Either way, the household gods of ancient households were passed down to the principal heir. Possibly Rachel was not viewing these as gods, but rather as a declaration of something rightfully belonging to Jacob. However, Jacob had nothing to do with the theft. Rachel had done this on her own. Her "covert action is matched by Jacob's deception in departing from Laban secretly" (*Zondervan NIV Bible Commentary*).

D. A Face Set Toward Home (vv. 20, 21)

20. And Jacob stole away unawares to Laban the Syrian, in that he told him not that he fled.

21. So he fled with all that he had; and he rose up, and passed over the river, and set his face toward the mount Gilead.

There was no doubt where Jacob was headed. The angry remarks of Laban's sons had made it very clear that peace could not be maintained by staying. The large party of wives, camels, children and flocks crossed the Euphrates River and headed toward Canaan. The immediate goal was Mount Gilead on the eastern side of the Jordan River. The phrase "stole away unawares" indicates that Jacob literally deceived Laban.

Some have questioned how Jacob was able to get his flocks across the Euphrates. Perhaps there were shallow places for fording known to Jacob. Some believe "that God performed a miracle for Jacob on this occasion, and that he passed over dry sod" (*Adam Clarke's Commentary*). This is not improbable; since God had commanded him to go, He would also provide the means along the way.

2. How did Jacob describe his work ethic?

O God, our help in ages past
Our hope for years to come,
Our shelter from the stormy blast,
And our eternal home.
—Isaac Watts

Talk About It:
Explain the significance of the five simple words beginning with the letter *g* in verse 18.

Talk About It:
Explain the manner and timing of Jacob's leaving Laban.

II. HUMBLED BY FEAR AND DISTRESS (Genesis 32:1-12)

A. God's Host (vv. 1, 2)

1. And Jacob went on his way, and the angels of God met him.

2. And when Jacob saw them, he said, This is God's host: and he called the name of that place Mahanaim.

Jacob was not the same man who had been forced to run away from home. He was older now, changed, had a relationship with God, and was ready to make peace with his brother and be reunited with his father. The angels who met Jacob assured him of divine help. In essence, then, they were inviting him to return. Comforted by their presence, Jacob named the place *Mahanaim*, meaning "two camps." There was an inner camp made up of Jacob and his household, and an outer company, made up of the messengers of God. This outer company formed a supernatural circle of protection around the travelers.

B. Jacob's Messengers (vv. 3-5)

3. And Jacob sent messengers before him to Esau his brother unto the land of Seir, the country of Edom.

4. And he commanded them, saying, Thus shall ye speak unto my lord Esau; Thy servant Jacob saith thus, I have sojourned with Laban, and stayed there until now:

5. And I have oxen, and asses, flocks, and menservants, and womenservants: and I have sent to tell my lord, that I may find grace in thy sight.

Despite the comfort of angels, Jacob was taking no chances with the hatred Esau might still hold for him. The last he had heard, his brother had full intentions to kill him out of revenge for the stolen blessing (as well as the birthright). At this point in the story, which is told with great suspense, the reader does not know what will happen either. In order to feel out the situation, Jacob sent messengers to his brother with a report of what had occurred in his life the past 20 years. Included was a request for grace and favor. Implied here is also a desire for mercy. Jacob was intentionally making himself vulnerable.

We might look at Jacob's precaution as being foolish. If Esau knew he was coming, then very easily he could be prepared to kill him. Jacob likely sent the message so that the Lord could work on Esau's heart before he arrived. Also, there had been no apparent communication between life in Canaan and that in Haran. Jacob was coming home with complete ignorance, even as to whether his father was still alive. The desire for some sense of what was coming outweighed the danger of letting his presence be known.

Mahanaim (may-ha-NAY-im)—v. 2—meaning "two camps" or "two hosts," an ancient town east of the Jordan River

Talk About It:
Describe Jacob's supernatural encounter.

Talk About It:
Summarize the message Jacob sent to Esau.

"I believe the first test of a truly great man is his humility."
—John Ruskin

Humbled and Exalted

C. Esau's Army (vv. 6-8)

6. And the messengers returned to Jacob, saying, We came to thy brother Esau, and also he cometh to meet thee, and four hundred men with him.

7. Then Jacob was greatly afraid and distressed: and he divided the people that was with him, and the flocks, and herds, and the camels, into two bands;

8. And said, If Esau come to the one company, and smite it, then the other company which is left shall escape.

It is unclear why Esau came from Edom toward Jacob with an army of 400 men. Perhaps he did plan to kill his brother and everyone with him! On the other hand, the army could have been simply a show of Esau's success in life. Perhaps he needed to prove that he had done well despite the loss of the family blessing. The land he occupied was Edom (also called Seir), an area south of the Dead Sea. However, if Esau's intentions were evil, then he had made the same mistake Jacob had made. Why let it be known you're coming with an army? Jacob would have time to prepare. It appears that God was working on both men's hearts. Though there might have been hatred in Esau's heart, he was also wrestling with God.

Despite all the hope he had in God, Jacob was still frightened. Very quickly his old scheming nature took over. He sent an elaborate peace offering ahead to his brother. Then he arranged his family, his possessions, and the fighting men in his company into the best posture he knew to be prepared for battle. He divided his group into two camps, so that if one were attacked and captured, the other might meanwhile escape. He was careful to take all the available precautions.

D. Jacob's Fearful Prayer (vv. 9-12)

9. And Jacob said, O God of my father Abraham, and God of my father Isaac, the Lord which saidst unto me, Return unto thy country, and to thy kindred, and I will deal well with thee:

10. I am not worthy of the least of all the mercies, and of all the truth, which thou hast shewed unto thy servant; for with my staff I passed over this Jordan; and now I am become two bands.

11. Deliver me, I pray thee, from the hand of my brother, from the hand of Esau: for I fear him, lest he will come and smite me, and the mother with the children.

12. And thou saidst, I will surely do thee good, and make thy seed as the sand of the sea, which cannot be numbered for multitude.

We are reminded here of the old adage from wartime which says, "Praise the Lord and pass the ammunition." Jacob had

Talk About It:
Explain Jacob's feelings seen in verse 7.

Talk About It:
1. In verse 9, what did Jacob ask God to remember (refer to 31:3)?
2. How had Jacob's fortunes changed since he last crossed the Jordan River (v. 10)?
3. What specific requests did Jacob make (v. 11)?

made precautions as best he could. He was ready for a fight if necessary (though the odds were not in his favor), and he certainly was fearful of such. He now turned his full attention to heaven. By mentioning both his father Isaac and his grandfather Abraham, he was appealing to all the faithful intervention God had made in their lives. In his prayer, Jacob reminded the Lord that it was divine command that had brought him to this place. With that command had come the promise of protection and victory. He then appealed to all that had been promised to him. His prayer was sincere and humble, even though there is no mention of repentance for having wronged Esau in the first place. Still, with the words "I am not worthy," he admitted that he did not deserve God's favor. All in all, he was simply casting himself on the mercy of the Lord.

Ultimately, Jacob appealed to the future promise that came with the covenant. If he and his seed were destroyed, then the multitude of descendants could not occur. Likely, here was where Jacob took heart. He knew the faithfulness that had already been demonstrated in his life. He knew God's word was good and could be trusted.

III. CONFRONTED AND EXALTED BY GOD
(Genesis 32:24-32)
A. Jacob's Wrestling Match (vv. 24, 25)

24. And Jacob was left alone; and there wrestled a man with him until the breaking of the day.

25. And when he saw that he prevailed not against him, he touched the hollow of his thigh; and the hollow of Jacob's thigh was out of joint, as he wrestled with him.

Everything in life had been a struggle for Jacob. He had been in conflict with his father, his brother, his father-in-law, and now his brother again. None of these, however, compared to the ultimate wrestling match he was about to face with the Lord. Having sent several tiers of gifts to Esau, each separated by some distance, Jacob bedded down his family in camp north of the Jabbok River (vv. 13-21). However, during the night something caused him to change his mind. He got up and sent his wives, children, and possessions across the river (vv. 22, 23). This put them in the position of being another tier between him and his brother. Was this out of cowardice on his part? Certainly not. Perhaps he felt that everyone else would be spared if he was by himself when Esau finally reached him. More likely, he simply needed to get alone to pray. Did he anticipate a meeting with an angel? It is not known, but he put himself in position for visitation.

At what point the *man* came to him is not revealed. Possibly, Jacob had fallen into some sort of dreamlike state. The ensuing

Talk About It:
1. Why do you suppose Jacob chose to be alone?
2. What would always remind Jacob of this night (v. 25)?

Humbled and Exalted

wrestling match went on for hours. Jacob knew this was a divine being, and was intent on receiving a blessing. "He who had once grasped his brother's heel now clung to the bodily form of the living God. Some believe that the man who wrestled Jacob was the preincarnate Jesus Christ" (*Nelson Study Bible*). Others believe it was the archangel Michael, who appeared in Daniel 10:13, 21; 12:1; 2 Peter 2:11; Jude 9; and Revelation 12:7. In any case, this was a divine being, and Jacob knew it.

The angel ultimately *touched* the hollow of Jacob's thigh. The Hebrew word here refers to God's special touch. The touch caused pain and a permanent limp. Probably any other man would have surrendered in defeat at this point, but not Jacob. This is the turning point in the drama. He knew that his physical seat of strength had been taken from him. What he wrestled with now was a spiritual strength, one that comes from the reliance upon God. "Henceforth Jacob now feels himself strong, not in himself, but in the Lord, and in the power of his might" (*Barnes' Notes*).

B. Jacob's Persistence (vv. 26-28)

26. And he said, Let me go, for the day breaketh. And he said, I will not let thee go, except thou bless me.

27. And he said unto him, What is thy name? And he said, Jacob.

28. And he said, Thy name shall be called no more Jacob, but Israel: for as a prince hast thou power with God and with men, and hast prevailed.

Why had there been a wrestling match in the first place? Perhaps it was because Jacob was pleading with God for protection, for success with Esau, for all the things that had been promised him. The angel, on the other hand, was wrestling against the old nature of Jacob. The conniving, supplanter spirit had to be wrestled out of Jacob before he could truly be the man God desired as a covenant partner. "When God has a new thing of a spiritual nature to bring into the experience of man, He begins with the senses. He takes man on the ground on which He finds him, and leads him through the senses to the higher things of reason, conscience, and communion with God" (*Barnes' Notes*).

Finally, after a long struggle, the visitor demanded release. Jacob refused to do so unless he blessed him. When the angel asked Jacob his name, it was not for information. It was that Jacob would speak it himself. He had been a schemer all his life, and had to admit such. Then the angel declared him to have a new name—*Israel*. This word carries two meanings. One is "he who strives with God"; the other is "prince," or "prince with

Unveiling the Unknown
God desires to make known the unknown to His children. He desires to unveil the hidden. Yet many times we are satisfied not knowing. Either we aren't willing to take the time to wait, or we aren't sure God wants us to know.
—Charles Stanley

Talk About It:
1. Why wouldn't Jacob let "the man" go?
2. Why did the man ask Jacob his name?
3. Describe the significance of Jacob's new name.

"We, through warfare prayer, have the responsibility and power to come against the strongholds Satan has in our lives and in others' lives."
—Charles Stanley

God." Because Jacob had striven with God and won, he could be assured of the blessing of God. The immediate benefit would be that he would have victory in dealing with Esau.

For the rest of his life Jacob would carry a limp, a sign of weakness in the natural. However, in the spiritual sense, it would be a reminder of the royalty he had achieved.

C. Jacob's Question (v. 29)

29. And Jacob asked him, and said, Tell me, I pray thee, thy name. And he said, Wherefore is it that thou dost ask after my name? And he blessed him there.

Talk About It:
Explain the phrase "he blessed him there."

Jacob had been asked his name. Now he asks the angel's name. The man didn't answer. "That request was denied, that he might not be too proud of his conquest, nor think he had the angel at such an advantage as to oblige him to what he pleased" (Matthew Henry). Jacob thus had to make his own assumptions as to the divine being's identity. The name he apparently gave him was spoken many years later on his deathbed. He called him "the mighty God of Jacob" (49:24).

D. Jacob's Testimony (vv. 30-32)

30. And Jacob called the name of the place Peniel: for I have seen God face to face, and my life is preserved.

31. And as he passed over Penuel the sun rose upon him, and he halted upon his thigh.

32. Therefore the children of Israel eat not of the sinew which shrank, which is upon the hollow of the thigh, unto this day: because he touched the hollow of Jacob's thigh in the sinew that shrank.

Peniel (pi-NIGH-ul)—v. **30**—"face of God"

Some believe that Jacob limped for the rest of his life, a reminder of what had occurred here. Others think he immediately recovered. If indeed he did remain impaired, "he had no reason to complain, for the honor and comfort he obtained by this struggle were abundantly sufficient to countervail the damage, though he went limping to his grave" (Matthew Henry). This was in the same sense that Paul declared, "Let no one cause me trouble, for I bear on my body the marks of Jesus" (Galatians 6:17, *NIV*). Paul rejoiced that the beatings he had endured identified him with the stripes Jesus had taken.

Talk About It:
1. How did Jacob identify his wrestling opponent?
2. Why do you suppose Jacob was left with a limp?

Just to make sure he never forgot this night, Jacob named the place *Peniel,* meaning "the face of God," because there he had truly met God. He didn't call himself a conqueror, but rather saw himself as having been shown the mercy of God.

"Safe? . . . Who said anything about safe? Course He isn't safe. But He's good. He's the King, I tell you."
—**C.S. Lewis**
(*The Lion, the Witch and the Wardrobe*)

CONCLUSION

For all his years Jacob had been a deceiver. He carried an overly firm reliance upon himself and his wits. Though commendable in some ways, it was at the same time a terrible character flaw that brought much heartache into his life. Finally, he came to a situation that he couldn't get out of on his own. His wrestling match with the angel at Peniel transformed his old nature.

What about you? Is there some character flaw that seems to keep you from the relationship with God that you desire? Perhaps it's not self-reliance but the very opposite. Are you always down on yourself, feeling totally worthless in God's sight? Do you constantly doubt God's goodness at the first sign of trouble? Are you afraid He won't come through for you?

What we all need is a wrestling match with God, a time when we refuse to let Him go until He changes us and gives us a "prosperity of soul." It is possible. John prayed for such. He said, "Beloved, I pray that you may prosper in all things and be in health, just as your soul prospers" (3 John 2, *NKJV*).

GOLDEN TEXT CHALLENGE

"WHOSOEVER SHALL EXALT HIMSELF SHALL BE ABASED; AND HE THAT SHALL HUMBLE HIMSELF SHALL BE EXALTED" (Matthew 23:12).

Here Jesus reveals the amazing truth that everyone will be exalted *and* everyone will be humbled. It's not a matter of *if* these things will happen; instead, it's a question of *when*, *where* and by *whom*.

First, let's consider those who choose to exalt themselves. They are lifting themselves up in the here and now, which means they will eventually be brought down by God himself. In the life of Jacob, we see that right after he deceitfully promoted himself to receive the blessing of the firstborn son, he almost immediately fell to the rank of a desperate fugitive.

Now, consider the person who follows Jesus' example by humbling himself. In the preceding scripture, Jesus said, "He that is greatest among you shall be your servant" (v. 11). Those who live as God's humble servants in the here and now will be exalted to a place of eternal prominence in the kingdom of Christ.

Daily Devotions:
M. Humility Rewarded
   1 Kings 3:6-15
T. Humility Prevents Judgment
   2 Chronicles 12:5-12
W. Humbled by God's Holiness
   Isaiah 6:1-8
T. Jesus Taught Humility
   Matthew 23:1-12
F. Called to Humble Repentance
   Acts 2:37-42
S. Christ Humbled and Exalted
   Philippians 2:5-11

A Family in Crisis (Jacob)

Genesis 34:1 through 35:29

Unit Theme:
Isaac, Jacob and Joseph

Central Truth:
Families need a right relationship with God.

Focus:
Acknowledge that God wants to help families in times of trouble and ask for His help.

Context:
Critical events in Jacob's life in the 1890s B.C.

Golden Text:
"For I know him, that he will command his children and his household after him, and they shall keep the way of the Lord" (Genesis 18:19).

Study Outline:
I. God Intervenes for Jacob's Family (Genesis 34:30—35:3)
II. Jacob's Family Returns to God (Genesis 35:4-8)
III. God Renews Covenant With Jacob (Genesis 35:9-15)

INTRODUCTION

Even though there had been a life-changing meeting with God just hours before, Jacob still faced the meeting with his brother, Esau, with fear and uncertainty. He set out the next morning with his family, aligned in a formation that hopefully would protect them all. His favorite wife, Rachel, and favorite son, Joseph, were in the rear. The wrestling match had not changed his prejudices and preferences. This tells us something of the Christian life. No single experience with God, as wonderful as it might be, is sufficient to vault us through our entire life. We must walk with Christ daily, letting Him change every aspect of our character. It is a lifelong process. Though much about Jacob had been deeply affected the night before, he certainly was not to be free from problems and personality flaws in the future. Our present lesson will give witness to that.

In an elaborate manner indicative of formal meetings in ancient days, Jacob bowed seven times as Esau and his 400 men came into view. This was a demonstration of complete compliance and subservience. Amazingly, Esau exhibited a wonderful spirit of acceptance. His hostility had dissipated. The question of when this change happened can be endlessly debated. Perhaps he did set out with an army of 400 men to fight his brother, and God changed his heart along the way. Another possibility is that Esau had forgiven Jacob years earlier, especially as he had become successful despite the loss of the birthright and family blessing. There was no doubting that God had blessed him. Perhaps he wanted to show Jacob that he could defeat him, but had no intentions of really doing so. Finally, we must remember that the two men were twins, and the blood bond between them was unchangeable. The 400 men were likely brought along to escort Jacob's family the remainder of their journey. Whatever the situation, God had transformed Esau's heart, just as He had done with Jacob.

Our present lesson moves ahead a few months, or perhaps a couple of years. Jacob's sons were now grown men, and rather on the strong-willed side. The entire clan had settled near the city of Shechem in Canaan. Jacob kept some distance from Shechem on purpose, for this was a city of pagan gods. Still, there was contact with the locals, and that's where the problems began.

I. GOD INTERVENES FOR JACOB'S FAMILY
(Genesis 34:30—35:3)

A. A Sister Disgraced (34:30, 31)

30. And Jacob said to Simeon and Levi, Ye have troubled me to make me to stink among the inhabitants of the land, among the Canaanites and the Perizzites: and I being few in number, they shall gather themselves together against me, and slay me; and I shall be destroyed, I and my house.

31. And they said, Should he deal with our sister as with an harlot?

Perizzites (PER-uh-zites)—v. 30—forest-dwelling people who were eventually conquered by Israel

Genesis 34, not specifically a part of our lesson, is the relating of the story of Dinah being raped and disgraced. As the only daughter of Jacob among 11 brothers, Dinah had sought friendship among the girls of the local town, only to be taken advantage of by the son of a prominent citizen. By the end of the chapter, Simeon and Levi had instigated the death of both father and son, as well as all the other men of the city. The other sons of Jacob had then joined them in pillaging everything in sight.

Talk About It:
Compare Jacob's concern with the concern of his sons Simeon and Levi.

When Jacob had heard the news of Dinah's disgrace, he had responded with a level head, even though he was consumed with rage. His sons, though seeming to do the same, planned a murderous plot. They apparently inherited some of Jacob's scheming nature. When all was said and done, Jacob was furious at his boys and rebuked them. The word *stink* (v. 30) indicated that Jacob's family had become a stench to their neighbors. The response of Simeon and Levi was not repentance, however, but rather insistence that they had only defended their sister's honor.

"The family is the most basic unit of government. As the first community to which a person is attached and the first authority under which a person learns to live, the family establishes society's most basic values."
—**Charles Colson**

B. Bethel Revisited (35:1)

1. And God said unto Jacob, Arise, go up to Beth-el, and dwell there: and make there an altar unto God, that appeared unto thee when thou fleddest from the face of Esau thy brother.

There were four prior times that God had visited Jacob. The first was at Bethel when he was escaping from Esau. The second was the vision of how to breed speckled livestock and a directive to flee from Laban. The third was the angels of God at Mahanaim. The fourth was the wrestling match at Peniel. Now, this fifth time was a summons to move on to Bethel. "Bethel was 1,010 feet higher than Shechem and situated on the road that led to Jerusalem, Bethlehem, and Hebron" (Wycliffe). It was where God had first made covenant promises to Jacob (Genesis 28:13-17). In return, Jacob had vowed that if he was brought back safely home, God would be his

Talk About It:
Why did God want Jacob to return to Bethel?

God and he would give a tenth of everything to the Lord. God had kept His part of the bargain, and now Jacob needed to complete his. Had Jacob forgotten his vow? "Seven or eight years it was now since he came to Canaan; he had purchased ground there, and had built an altar in remembrance of God's last appearance to him when he called him Israel (33:19, 20); but still Bethel is forgotten" (Matthew Henry). Life had settled into a comfortable routine until the terrible incident with his daughter, Dinah. That should have stirred Jacob, but did not seem to, so God reminded him. This was the first time in Scripture that God commanded an altar to be built for Him.

The name *Bethel* means "house of God." With the summons to move his entire family there, God was reminding Jacob that this is where they should live, not just visit. Jacob was overdue in his worship. He had "allowed 10 years to pass since his return from Mesopotamia, without performing the vow which he made at Bethel when fleeing from Esau, although he had recalled it to mind when resolving to return, and had also erected an altar in Shechem to the 'God of Israel'" (Keil & Delitzsch).

C. Jacob's Household Cleansed (vv. 2, 3)

2. Then Jacob said unto his household, and to all that were with him, Put away the strange gods that are among you, and be clean, and change your garments:

3. And let us arise, and go up to Beth-el; and I will make there an altar unto God, who answered me in the day of my distress, and was with me in the way which I went.

The only foreign gods in Jacob's household mentioned before now were those Rachel stole from her father. Any others had likely been picked up while the clan lived in Shechem. Remember that Jacob's sons had pillaged the town, taking the women and children as slaves. With these people came their gods. No matter where they came from, they had to be disposed of. The change in garments required that everyone first be bathed (cleansed). This had particular significance to Simeon and Levi, who had blood on their hands.

This was to be a holy pilgrimage. When Abraham had been willing to sacrifice Isaac, God's commendation of him was, "Now I know that you fear God" (22:12, *NKJV*). The fear God demanded was one of great reverence. Jacob was insistent that his family now approach Bethel with that same awe.

II. JACOB'S FAMILY RETURNS TO GOD (Genesis 35:4-8)

A. Strange Gods (v. 4)

4. And they gave unto Jacob all the strange gods which were in their hand, and all their earrings which were in

---

"I find that doing the will of God leaves me no time for disputing about His plans."
—George MacDonald

Talk About It:
Why did Jacob's clan need to change their clothing?

A Family in Crisis

their ears; and Jacob hid them under the oak which was by Shechem.

It is evident that God wanted more than the worship of Jacob. He wanted the entire family to know Him. Jacob was, by this time, well aware of the dysfunctional aspects of his polygamous family, and commanded his household to prepare both physically and spiritually for their meeting at Bethel.

As head of the home, every father should be responsible for the spiritual knowledge and understanding of his children. As Joshua would later say, "And if it seem evil unto you to serve the Lord, choose you this day whom ye will serve . . . but as for me and my house, we will serve the Lord" (Joshua 24:15). Sadly, it appears that Jacob had already missed his opportunity when his sons and daughter were children. We see nothing of his having communicated his covenant with the Lord to them. Neither did he prohibit the plunder they had taken in the town of Shechem, among the trinkets of which had been idolatrous emblems. Likely, this was the first entrance of Canaanite religions into his family.

The oak tree mentioned here is likely the *terebinth,* a deciduous variety known for living many years. Like stones, these were often "used to commemorate important events or to mark places of worship" (*Nelson Study Bible*). They were regarded as sacred, and as such no one would venture to dig up anything buried beneath their limbs. Not only did Jacob want the trinkets of idolatry removed, but he wanted to set up a memorial to their having done so and dedicated themselves. This was possibly the same spot where Abraham had once built an altar to the Lord (see Genesis 12:6, 7). "The burial of the idols was followed by purification through the washing of the body, as a sign of the purification of the heart from the defilement of idolatry, and by the putting on of clean and festal clothes, as a symbol of the sanctification and elevation of the heart to the Lord" (Keil & Delitzsch).

B. Supernatural Terror (v. 5)

5. And they journeyed: and the terror of God was upon the cities that were round about them, and they did not pursue after the sons of Jacob.

The energy with which Jacob now pressed his family to cleanse themselves and prepare for worship had an amazing effect on all the cities through which they passed. Certainly these locals had been preparing a united effort against Jacob for what his sons had done in Shechem, but now a "supernatural panic seized them; and thus, for the sake of the 'heir of the promise,' the protecting shield of Providence was specially held over his family" (*Jamieson, Fausset, and Brown Commentary*).

Shechem (SHEK-um)—an ancient fortified city

Talk About It:
What did Jacob bury, and why?

Talk About It:
Explain the phrase "terror of God."

"The outward lives of God's people should be indicative of the possession of inner spiritual wealth."
—Union Signal

Thus, in His demand for worship, God was not being selfish, but was actually making a pathway of safety for His chosen people through hostile territory.

C. An Altar at Bethel (vv. 6, 7)

6. So Jacob came to Luz, which is in the land of Canaan, that is, Beth-el, he and all the people that were with him.

7. And he built there an altar, and called the place El-beth-el: because there God appeared unto him, when he fled from the face of his brother.

The return to Bethel marked the end of a long, looping journey for Jacob. The name *Luz* was apparently the former one given to this territory, which had likely heretofore been unoccupied. Jacob had promised he would come back to this spot, and even though he had to be reminded, he had at last done so. When he arrived here, he knew he was walking on holy ground. God had been with him throughout his journey, and like his predecessors Abraham and Isaac had done on sacred occasions, he now built an altar to the Lord. He named the altar *El-bethel,* which means "God of Bethel." It is likely numerous sacrifices were now made, including up to one-tenth of Jacob's cattle. He had declared he would give a tenth of all he owned back to the Lord.

D. Death of an Elderly Nurse (v. 8)

Allon-bachuth (v. 8)—"the oak of weeping"

Talk About It:
What memories would this tree have for Jacob?

8. But Deborah Rebekah's nurse died, and she was buried beneath Beth-el under an oak: and the name of it was called Allon-bachuth.

Somewhere prior to this time, it is apparent that Jacob had gone to visit his father, Isaac, who was much advanced in age. His mother, Rebekah, was probably dead, though nothing is ever mentioned of such. However, her elderly nurse, Deborah, had survived her, and since Jacob had been very much a "mama's boy," she would have been dear to him. He took her to be part of his family—"to be a companion to his wives, her country-women, and an instructor to his children" (Matthew Henry). While at Bethel, Deborah died, and Jacob buried her. The very mention of this indicates a nobility on Jacob's part—that he honored her, even though she was not a member of his family. Another truth seen here is that the problems of life go on, even during the times we have dedicated to the Lord. Jacob had to grieve over Deborah's death, even as he was rejoicing in the time of visitation from heaven.

Special Attention
Perhaps the nurse Deborah had been the stabilizing person in Jacob's early chiildhood, in light of the conflict between him and his brother, as well as his parents' both playing favorites. Though she was not a blood member of

It is notable that a nurse's death would be commemorated in Scripture, while the death of Rebekah is not. After she pressured Jacob to go to Haran to find a wife from among her people,

A Family in Crisis

nothing else is recorded of Rebekah, except her burial (Genesis 49:31). "Her name is written in the dust. And is not this designed as a mark of the disapprobation of God?" (*Adam Clarke's Commentary*).

III. GOD RENEWS COVENANT WITH JACOB
(Genesis 35:9-15)

A. The Lord Appears (v. 9)

9. And God appeared unto Jacob again, when he came out of Padan-aram, and blessed him.

It is not clear as to whether anyone else witnessed the Lord's appearance to Jacob, but we would hope so. Certainly God did not have the entire clan show up at Bethel, not to be touched at all. It had been 30 years since Jacob's first encounter with the Lord at this very spot. The first had been at night in a dream, when Jacob had been promised divine protection while in a foreign land, and a safe return to his home (28:15). This new visitation came during the day, but the word from God on both occasions was the same.

Despite the divine care Jacob was granted, his relationship with the Lord had declined in the recent years. Some think that as much as eight years had passed since the reuniting with Esau. How quickly we can forget those moments when God touched us, showed us mercy, and pulled us successfully through a difficult situation. We should all "return to Bethel" and remember His goodness to us in times past.

The Lord's appearance to Jacob confirmed the Abrahamic blessing. "To Isaac and Jacob these frequent appearances of God were necessary, but they were not so to Abraham, for to him one word was sufficient—Abraham believed God" (*Adam Clarke's Commentary*).

B. The Name *Israel* Confirmed (v. 10)

10. And God said unto him, Thy name is Jacob: thy name shall not be called any more Jacob, but Israel shall be thy name: and he called his name Israel.

Although this new name had already been given to Jacob back at Peniel, God now reaffirmed the change. "The point of the second renaming was to give the name *Israel* a more neutral or even positive connotation" (*Zondervan NIV Bible Commentary*). Remember that one of the meanings of *Israel* was "he struggles with God" (see Genesis 32:28). Such negativity need be remembered no more, giving way for the more noble definition, "Prince with God." As such, Jacob would be constantly reminded of his special relationship to Jehovah, and that he should carry himself like a prince. After all, he was the heir to all that had been promised to Abraham. He would never

his family, he considered her so.

What people do we have in our lives who have been instrumental in our spiritual growth that we should honor in their later years?

Padan-aram—in the district of Mesopotamia, a plain or field surrounded by mountains

Talk About It:
What two things did God do here? How are they related?

"Seek to cultivate a buoyant, joyous sense of the crowded kindnesses of God in your daily life."
—Alexander MacLaren

Talk About It:
Why did God have to repeat the command of Genesis 32:28 in 35:10?

forget this moment. He alluded to it at the close of his life (48:3, 4) when he blessed Joseph's two sons.

C. The Lord Speaks (vv. 11-13)

11. And God said unto him, I am God Almighty: be fruitful and multiply; a nation and a company of nations shall be of thee, and kings shall come out of thy loins;

12. And the land which I gave Abraham and Isaac, to thee I will give it, and to thy seed after thee will I give the land.

13. And God went up from him in the place where he talked with him.

Everything that had been spoken to Abraham was now ratified in Jacob. Despite the visitations prior to this point, Jacob had not had the same relationship with the Lord as his grandfather had. We should remember that Abraham lived to see his grandsons. Certainly the old man had communicated with those boys (Jacob and Esau) the wonderful times of friendship with the Lord. Also, Isaac would have reminded his sons of the greatness planned for their family. Several key elements of the covenant include:

- God was active in the affairs of humanity, choosing this family through which He would reveal Himself.
- Jacob's descendants would become many, such that a multitude of nations would arise.
- Royalty would come through the bloodline. This was fulfilled in David and his descendants, but most importantly through Jesus.
- The land of Canaan would be theirs. The phrase "and to thy seed" (v. 12) indicates a perpetual right to the land— "the primeval blessing of humankind as renewed through the promise of a royal offspring and the gift of the land" (*Zondervan NIV Bible Commentary*).

Verse 13 says the Lord then left, probably with some visible display of great glory. Jacob would have to remember this moment for years, for God does not display Himself frequently or carelessly. The lives of His people are to be lived by faith. "The sweetest communions the saints have with God in this world are short and transient, and soon have an end" (Matthew Henry). Praise God that there will come a time when any sense of separation from Him will be no more. For now, "we see through a glass darkly" (1 Corinthians 13:12), but we do have the indwelling comfort of the Holy Spirit that gives us a monumental advantage over the ancient patriarchs.

D. A Stone Pillar Erected (vv. 14, 15)

14. And Jacob set up a pillar in the place where he

"God does not give us everything we want, but He does fulfill all His promises . . . leading us along the best and straightest paths to Himself."
—Dietrich Bonhoeffer

A Family in Crisis

talked with him, even a pillar of stone: and he poured a drink-offering thereon, and he poured oil thereon.

15. And Jacob called the name of the place where God spake with him, Beth-el.

To make sure he never forgot, Jacob erected another monument at Bethel—a stone pillar. This would be much more memorable than the earlier one. He confirmed the place as being the "house of God." The first monument he had anointed with oil, but this time he used both oil and a drink offering. Sadly, Bethel would later become a place of idolatry and iniquity during the days of Jeroboam. This tells us that no matter how sacred a moment one generation experiences, every succeeding generation must have its own visitation from heaven.

Talk About It:
Explain the significance of Jacob's actions.

CONCLUSION

Before Jacob's family could go to Bethel, he had to rid his wives and children of pagan religious artifacts. It seems they had picked up "foreign gods" in their short stay near the Canaanite city of Shechem. Throughout the Old Testament we see that Israel was to be a people separated unto God. In the New Testament our commission is somewhat different. We are told to "go ye therefore, and teach all nations, baptizing them in the name of the Father, and of the Son, and of the Holy Ghost" (Matthew 28:19).

It is all but impossible to keep our children's eyes from what is in the world, but they are still to "love not the world, neither the things that are in [it]" (1 John 2:15). The best way this can be accomplished is the same that God commanded of Jacob. If we teach them by our own worship of God, demonstrate a holy life before them, and put them in a place where they can learn worship, then they can experience God and discover that "greater is he that is in you, than he that is in the world" (4:4). How well are you teaching your family?

GOLDEN TEXT CHALLENGE

"FOR I KNOW HIM, THAT HE WILL COMMAND HIS CHILDREN AND HIS HOUSEHOLD AFTER HIM, AND THEY SHALL KEEP THE WAY OF THE LORD" (Genesis 18:19).

This scripture reveals the Lord's thoughts concerning Abraham. God chose to enter into covenant with him because He knew how Abraham would respond.

God would teach His ways to Abraham, who would take the teaching to heart and follow the Lord's ways. But it wouldn't stop with Abraham. Instead, Abraham would train the members of his household to "keep the way of the Lord by doing what is right and just" (*NIV*).

Nor would Abraham's influence stop with his own household.

Indeed, the nation birthed through Abraham and "all the nations of the earth" (v. 18) would be touched for the kingdom of God through Abraham's faithfulness.

Like Abraham (as well as his grandson Jacob), God wants our lives to count for His kingdom. There is no greater honor than helping others—especially our own relatives—to walk in relationship with God.

Lessons From the Life of Joseph
by Bill Isaacs

The measure of a man is his life—not his trappings or his titles. The definition of a man is his life—how he lived it, how he managed it, what he was. I believe that and I live by that. One day, my two sons will bury me in the ground and it won't matter where I ministered or what titles I held. What will linger with my two sons will be my life, our relationship, who I was. Long after I'm gone and the wall plaques have been sold in a yard sale, the measure of my life and yours will be how we lived it. That's why Joseph is so interesting to me. The quality of the man is not measured in his lineage or ancestry, but in how he lived. Joseph lived his life in alignment with his Creator and made an incredible mark for his God, the kingdom and his family.

There are seven major characters in the Book of Genesis. You can probably name all of them—Adam, Eve, Noah, Abraham, Isaac, Jacob and Joseph. There is more written about Joseph than any other character in the book. Fourteen chapters of the Bible's first book are devoted to the details and descriptions of his life. However, as I read and study his life, I am not surprised by this. Evidently, there is something God wants us to know about Joseph. His life speaks to us. We can relate to him. As you consider his life, you will see the sovereignty of God at work in the life of a man who loved God supremely. Lest you think Joseph was someone who had it all together, consider these facts:

1. *He did not choose his own parents.* Like every other child born into the world, he did not choose who his father and mother were or how his life would be influenced by them. His family was not his greatest asset. Overcoming his family members and their history was his first major hurdle. The genetic connection was a source of stress for Joseph. In order to survive and succeed, Joseph determined not to allow his family to define his character.

2. *His father was a schemer.* Jacob probably learned how to con and scheme from his mother, Rebekah, who was also deceitful. Joseph's great-uncle, Laban, Rebekah's brother, was a schemer himself, who deceived Joseph's father into marrying Leah, Rebekah's sister, first, although he did not love her. This was a household with a sordid past. Lying, deception and manipulation were the tradition in his family. Joseph was from a large family of 12 sons and one daughter born to Jacob from his two wives and two concubines. His family was not united. There was much distrust and jealousy. This was his beginning—he could easily have followed the family path, but, remarkably, he chose another course. He abandoned his family way of life and sought God's way. It was a difficult decision and not everyone understood Joseph's behavior, but God guided his steps, as He will guide yours, if you will learn the lesson of Joseph and surrender to Him in obedience.

3. *He lost his mother early in life.* Joseph's mother, Rachel, died during the birth of his younger brother, Benjamin. For the rest of his childhood, he was raised by a stepmother and his father. He was left to cope in life without his mother. Millions of adults and children, perhaps even you, know how he felt. The comforting, nurturing touch of a mother is an important part of human life. Faced to live without, we are required to adjust. Many do, but it is never easy. The loss is permanent and lingers like a hidden wound, always there and never fully healed.

There is something profoundly special about Joseph. Although my background is different from his, I have ministered to many people who can relate to his early life. Unfortunately, some were born to parents who did not have their own lives together and the children suffered because of it. Maybe you are one of them, and your life has been marked by experiences and hurts that have scarred you and you cannot seem to recover. If you are one of those persons, I know you can relate to Joseph. He suffered the hatred of his siblings, the betrayal of his family, the rejection of his peers, and yet he never lost hope for tomorrow. How can this be?

Some people never recover from one bad experience, but Joseph lived through a period of more than 13 years with one negative circumstance after another, yet he never gave up his belief in God's ultimate plan. Like Joseph, I have met others who have chosen to live above their circumstances, deciding not to allow negative situations to define them.

I know a woman whose past is not pleasant. A man who once promised to love her only, for as long as they both lived, lied. When he decided he loved another woman, he left my friend in a desperate situation, with small children to raise alone. The impact of that compromise still haunts her children, although they are grown and have their own families. Together, this lady and her family deal with the trauma of grief and pain. They are familiar with loss and sorrow. The cycle of divorce has marked a son, and this devoted woman prays and worries for the effect on her grandchildren. She and her second husband have worked, prayed and struggled at times to survive. Financial reversals from investments gone sour and other events have threatened their sanity and peace at times, but they keep going! She once remarked to me, while under the intense pressure of another attack, "You know, sometimes you just have to tell God, 'I can't handle this! I trust You because I know You love me. I don't understand, but I will not be defeated by this.' You move on, knowing that God will take care of you and your family." She is moving on with her life, although the future is hazy from a human perspective. With every day, she finds new hope and faith in God's ultimate handling of life's struggles.

Joseph was also determined to keep going. Because he did, his life is a glorious story of God's divine providence. There are some rocky roads we must travel. It will be gruesome and difficult—a road we are familiar with already.

If there is one thing the life of Joseph teaches, it is this: *Your circumstances do not have the power to define you.* You can rise above your environment. Regardless of your beginning, you can be the person God destined you to be.

Joseph sincerely believed God had placed His divine hand upon his life. The same can be true for you. The final chapters of your life have not yet been written. There is a brighter day ahead. Our sovereign God is working everything together in your life for a higher purpose. You may not see the outcome yet, and at times you may wonder what God has planned, but if you listen closely to the Savior, you will hear His constant reminder, "Don't give up."

This Bible Insight is taken from the book *Embracing Destiny: Lessons From the Life of Joseph*. It is available from Pathway Press online at *www.pathwaybookstore.com* or by calling 800-553-8506.

The Dreamer (Joseph)

Genesis 37:1-36

INTRODUCTION

God had appeared at Bethel and reaffirmed the covenant with Jacob. What a wonderful time this must have been. Yet, in spite of the blessings of divine presence, there were difficulties about to come Jacob's way. The old nurse Deborah died while they were there. Then, as soon as the clan began the journey from Bethel, Jacob's favorite wife, Rachel, went into difficult labor with a second baby. Earlier, when her first son Joseph was born, Rachel had prayed for another son (see Genesis 30:24). Apparently the midwife was cognizant of this prophetic prayer, and encouraged Rachel during the travail by saying, "Do not fear; you will have this son also" (35:17, *NKJV*). As she was dying, Rachel named the son *Ben-Oni,* which means "son of my pain."

Despite the sorrow of having lost the nurse of his childhood, and now the terrible loss of Rachel, Jacob would not allow the new baby to carry a prophetic name with negative connotations. He chose instead to call the boy *Benjamin,* which means "son of my right hand," or "son of my wealth." Jacob buried Rachel at Ephrath, which later became Bethlehem.

Once arriving at Mamre, Jacob soon had to face the death of his father, Isaac (vv. 27-29). On a good note, he and Esau were in united brotherhood as they buried their father. Thus, when we arrive at our present lesson, it is easy to understand the frame of mind Jacob was in. He was emotionally depleted and vulnerable. As such, he poured his attention into a favorite child. Interestingly, as much as he was attached to the infant Benjamin, it was Joseph that he doted over. The favoritism shown to this boy would bring tremendous grief to the entire family. We can understand why the other brothers hated him. At the same time, it is obvious that God had a hand on Joseph's destiny. That destiny was not Joseph's alone, but included every descendant of Jacob.

Genesis 37:2 says, "This is the history of Jacob" (*NKJV*). However, the attention for the remainder of Genesis is not on Jacob, but rather on Joseph.

Unit Theme:
Isaac, Jacob and Joseph

Central Truth:
God is working for good in all things.

Focus:
Know that in all things God is working for good and trust His wisdom.

Context:
About 1893 B.C. in Hebron, Shechem and Dothan

Golden Text:
"But as for you, ye thought evil against me; but God meant it unto good" (Genesis 50:20).

Study Outline:
I. Hated by Brothers (Genesis 37:1-11)
II. Object of Treachery (Genesis 37:12-24)
III. Sold Into Slavery (Genesis 37:25-36)

I. HATED BY BROTHERS (Genesis 37:1-11)

A. Joseph's Mistake (vv. 1, 2)

1. And Jacob dwelt in the land wherein his father was a stranger, in the land of Canaan.

2. These are the generations of Jacob. Joseph, being seventeen years old, was feeding the flock with his brethren; and the lad was with the sons of Bilhah, and with the sons of Zilpah, his father's wives: and Joseph brought unto his father their evil report.

Already mentioned were some of the trying problems that had come against Jacob. In addition to those, Jacob had also faced the rape of his daughter, Dinah (and the consequences it brought), as well as the scandal of his oldest son, Reuben, having sexual relations with Jacob's concubine Bilhah. In neither of these situations had he taken firm control of his family. "Jacob (Israel) was such a passive father that when he heard what his son had done, he did absolutely nothing about it" (Charles R. Swindoll, *Joseph—A Man of Integrity and Forgiveness*).

During those years Jacob also moved about frequently. When he left Laban, he first settled near Shechem. Then he returned to Bethel and renewed the covenant with the Lord. Next he traveled south to Ephrath (Bethlehem), where Rachel died in childbirth with Benjamin. Next he went to Hebron, where he buried his father. He was truly a *stranger* in the land (v. 1), although it was the very territory God had promised to him.

The phrase "generations of Jacob" (v. 2) gives the impression that he would continue to be the central focus of the narrative. However, for the rest of Genesis, Joseph takes the stage. The 17-year-old is introduced as a shepherd working with his half brothers. He is much younger, and somewhat of a tattletale. The simple incident mentioned gives a clue to the resentment the 10 other brothers held for him. It was a mistake to taunt them with the favoritism he enjoyed in his father's eyes. Some commentaries suggest that the wording here might indicate Joseph was "shepherding his brothers" (Victor P. Hamilton, *The Book of Genesis: Chapters 18-50*). If this is true, we see an early indication that Joseph was by nature a leader, one that might be deemed a type A personality.

B. Parental Favoritism (vv. 3, 4)

3. Now Israel loved Joseph more than all his children, because he was the son of his old age: and he made him a coat of many colours.

4. And when his brethren saw that their father loved him more than all his brethren, they hated him, and could not speak peaceably unto him.

Joseph was his father's favorite, partially because he was

the son of Jacob's old age (although young Benjamin was as well), but more importantly because he was Rachel's child. Perhaps Jacob never got over his resentment at being tricked into marrying Leah. This antipathy extended to her sons, as well as to the sons of Jacob's two concubines. Joseph was also different in character from the rest of the siblings. The other sons were wild bucks because of Jacob's passivity and lack of discipline in the home. No doubt, as we see the story unfold, there was an anointing on the boy's life. Joseph was the bright spot in a family filled with anger, envy, spite and deceit—all manifestations of Jacob's own *deceiving* nature.

For 17 years the brothers watched Joseph receive the loving attention they never enjoyed. This turned into rage, so much so that they could not even "speak peaceably" (v. 4) with him. It would take only one spark to set them off.

Jacob foolishly did nothing to hide his favoritism toward Joseph, creating an even more hostile environment. The coat of many colors was apparently extravagant, "reaching to the hands and feet, worn by persons not much occupied with manual labor, according to the general opinion" (*Barnes' Notes*). The fact that the coat comes up repeatedly in the story shows the extent to which the brothers had turned against Joseph. In their eyes it seemed to indicate that Joseph had been deemed heir apparent.

C. Joseph's Dreams (vv. 5-9)

5. And Joseph dreamed a dream, and he told it his brethren: and they hated him yet the more.

6. And he said unto them, Hear, I pray you, this dream which I have dreamed:

7. For, behold, we were binding sheaves in the field, and, lo, my sheaf arose, and also stood upright; and, behold, your sheaves stood round about, and made obeisance to my sheaf.

8. And his brethren said to him, Shalt thou indeed reign over us? or shalt thou indeed have dominion over us? And they hated him yet the more for his dreams, and for his words.

9. And he dreamed yet another dream, and told it his brethren, and said, Behold, I have dreamed a dream more; and, behold, the sun and the moon and the eleven stars made obeisance to me.

Joseph was oblivious to the resentment breeding against him. "His frankness in reciting his dream to his brothers marks a spirit devoid of guile, and only dimly conscious of the import of his nightly visions" (*Barnes' Notes*). Still, he should never have recounted the dreams to his brothers, even if there was

Talk About It:
1. Why did Jacob love Joseph more?
2. How much did Joseph's brothers hate him?

"Hating people is like burning down your own house to get rid of a rat."
—H.E. Foscick

made obeisance (v. 9)—bowed down

Talk About It:
1. Why did Joseph tell his brothers his dreams?
2. What questions did his brothers ask regarding his dreams (v. 8)?

no intended condescension. Both dreams ended with all the other brothers bowing at his feet. This entrenched their opinion of him as a spoiled brat. Pride was also indicated in that the dreams appeared prophetic in nature. Dreams were given far more significance in ancient culture than they are now. Joseph seemed aware that these were not just "pizza" nightmares, but contained significance for the future. The fact that there were two dreams added proof of such (see Genesis 41:32).

There is certainly something wonderful about receiving a dream from the Lord. He has a divine plan for each of us. However, there is also a proper time to reveal such dreams. Joseph should have kept his to himself. Likely, during the many years in prison, he looked back and repented over the pride that he had displayed. This would have molded a softened heart toward the brothers when he eventually was reunited with them.

D. Jacob's Passivity (vv. 10, 11)

10. And he told it to his father, and to his brethren: and his father rebuked him, and said unto him, What is this dream that thou hast dreamed? Shall I and thy mother and thy brethren indeed come to bow down ourselves to thee to the earth?

11. And his brethren envied him; but his father observed the saying.

Joseph recounted the dreams to his father as well, and even Jacob was frustrated at the pride being displayed. "The rebuke seems to imply that the dream, or the telling of it, appears to his father to indicate the lurking of a self-sufficient or ambitious spirit within the breast of the youthful Joseph" (*Barnes' Notes*). It is surprising that he didn't recognize the prophetic significance of the boy's dreams, since he had apparently seen God's hand on him. More importantly, we see here another instance of Jacob's passivity. He did nothing to chastise the boy.

II. OBJECT OF TREACHERY (Genesis 37:12-24)
A. Joseph's Obedience (vv. 12, 13)

12. And his brethren went to feed their father's flock in Shechem.

13. And Israel said unto Joseph, Do not thy brethren feed the flock in Shechem? come, and I will send thee unto them. And he said to him, Here am I.

Despite the arrogance earlier displayed, Joseph was still a willing and obedient son. His immediate response to Jacob's instruction brought the response, "Here am I" (v. 13). This phrase occurs 16 times in the Old Testament, and each time represents obedience as unto the Lord. The fact that the brothers were pasturing the sheep in Shechem is significant. This was where their

"If there is any sin more deadly than envy, it is being pleased at being envied."
—Richard Armour

Talk About It:
Explain the different responses of Joseph's dad and his brothers in verse 11.

The Dreamer

sister, Dinah, had been raped, as well as where all the succeeding events and repercussions occurred. Perhaps Jacob was afraid for their safety, and this prompted his sending Joseph to check on them.

B. Providential Meeting (vv. 14-19)
(Genesis 37:14-17 is not included in the printed text.)

18. And when they saw him afar off, even before he came near unto them, they conspired against him to slay him.

19. And they said one to another, Behold, this dreamer cometh.

Joseph apparently lost his way in the search for his brothers. In his disorientation he himself was *found* by a man who pointed him to Dothan, a town 12 miles north of Shechem (vv. 15-17). This may not seem significant, but it shows symmetry inherent to the story of Joseph. Here his brothers saw him coming and plotted to kill him. Later, in Genesis 42:7, Joseph would see his brothers coming toward him and disguised himself, "so that they did not recognize him and then planned a scheme that, at least on the surface, looked as if he intended to kill them" (*Zondervan NIV* Bible *Commentary*).

C. Conspiracy (v. 20)

20. Come now therefore, and let us slay him, and cast him into some pit, and we will say, Some evil beast hath devoured him: and we shall see what will become of his dreams.

This was likely a plot that had been concocted before, but no viable opportunity had presented itself until now. What had before been idle venting suddenly became the beginning of a horror story for Joseph. Charles Swindoll points out that "the mixture of a passive parent in a hostile family environment results in out-of-control consequences." Murder was the only thing on the brothers' minds. Again the brothers mentioned Joseph's dreams. They thought they were putting an end to any possible fulfillment of them. What an irony, for their own futures pivoted on those visions.

D. Reuben's Intervention (vv. 21-24)

21. And Reuben heard it, and he delivered him out of their hands; and said, Let us not kill him.

22. And Reuben said unto them, Shed no blood, but cast him into this pit that is in the wilderness, and lay no hand upon him; that he might rid him out of their hands, to deliver him to his father again.

23. And it came to pass, when Joseph was come unto

---

vale (v. 14)—valley

Dothan (DOE-thun)—v. 17—a town whose name means "two wells"

Talk About It:
1. Why should Jacob have known better than to send Joseph on this errand?
2. What do these verses reveal about Joseph's persistence?
3. What did Joseph's brothers call him, and why (v. 19)?

Talk About It:.
Describe Joseph's brothers' conspiracy.

"I don't believe an accident of birth makes people sisters or brothers. It makes them siblings, gives them mutuality of parentage. Sisterhood and brotherhood is a condition people have to work at."
—**Maya Angelou**

---

his brethren, that they stript Joseph out of his coat, his coat of many colours that was on him;

24. And they took him, and cast him into a pit: and the pit was empty, there was no water in it.

Despite his past failures, Reuben here showed a sense of responsibility indicative of being the eldest son. Perhaps he even saw this as a chance to prove himself before the Lord and his father as a better man than he had been in the past. Whatever the motivation, he wanted the boy spared and safely back in his father's house. To diffuse the hostile moment, he suggested that they simply throw Joseph into a pit in the wilderness. The brothers seemed to be satisfied with this, especially when they had stripped Joseph of his special robe, the symbol of his superiority over them, and cast him into the dry pit. Assumedly, they planned to let him die there.

III. SOLD INTO SLAVERY (Genesis 37:25-36)
A. Appearance of the Ishmaelites (v. 25)

25. And they sat down to eat bread: and they lifted up their eyes and looked, and, behold, a company of Ishmeelites came from Gilead with their camels bearing spicery and balm and myrrh, going to carry it down to Egypt.

As a blatant demonstration of their seared consciences, the nine brothers (with Reuben absent) sat down to eat, apparently within Joseph's earshot. They no doubt heard his pleas for mercy, but relished the upper hand they now enjoyed over him. Their despising of Joseph must have gone far deeper than just sibling rivalry. There was something "which made his character and conduct a constant censure upon theirs, and on account of which they found that they could never be at ease until they had rid themselves of his hated presence" (*Jamieson, Fausset and Brown Commentary*). The only thing that interrupted their revelry was the appearance of a passing caravan.

B. Judah's Solution (vv. 26-28)

26. And Judah said unto his brethren, What profit is it if we slay our brother, and conceal his blood?

27. Come, and let us sell him to the Ishmeelites, and let not our hand be upon him; for he is our brother and our flesh. And his brethren were content.

28. Then there passed by Midianites merchantmen; and they drew and lifted up Joseph out of the pit, and sold Joseph to the Ishmeelites for twenty pieces of silver: and they brought Joseph into Egypt.

There is no indication that Judah had communicated with Reuben, but he apparently also wished to save Joseph's life. Had he known of Reuben's plan, he might very well have kept

---

Talk About It:
1. How did Reuben differ from his brothers?
2. How significant of a role did Joseph's coat play?

"The younger brother must help to pay for the pleasures of the elder."
—Jane Austen

Talk About It:
Would you call this caravan's appearance a coincidence or providence? Why?

Midianites . . . Ishmeelites (v. 28)—Members of these two desert-dwelling peoples, both descendants of Abraham, apparently were joined together in this caravan.

The Dreamer

quiet. The appearance of the caravan gave Judah a moderate solution—don't let Joseph die, but sell him into slavery. Surely then Joseph's dream of ruling over his brothers could never be realized. Judah's idea was welcomed by the other eight brothers (since neither Reuben nor Benjamin was present). Thus, the young man was sold for 20 pieces of silver. This was the sum that "would have been paid for a handicapped slave in those days" (Swindoll). It was the same price Moses would later fix for a boy between 5 and 20 years old (see Leviticus 27:5). They were so anxious to be rid of him that they didn't bother to dicker for a higher price. It equated to two silver coins apiece for each brother in on the plot.

Though it resulted in Joseph's slavery, Judah at least saved the boy's life, and unknowingly furthered God's plan. When we look to Jacob's last words of blessing over his sons, it was Judah who took center stage in terms of the fulfillment of the covenant and the Promised Seed (see Genesis 49:8-12).

C. Reuben's Remorse (vv. 29-32)

29. And Reuben returned unto the pit; and, behold, Joseph was not in the pit; and he rent his clothes.

30. And he returned unto his brethren, and said, The child is not; and I, whither shall I go?

31. And they took Joseph's coat, and killed a kid of the goats, and dipped the coat in the blood;

32. And they sent the coat of many colours, and they brought it to their father; and said, This have we found: know now whether it be thy son's coat or no.

For unknown reasons, Reuben was not present when Joseph was sold. He was both surprised and angry when he learned of the turn of events. Possibly the others had suspected that he had planned to rescue the boy. His remorse may not have been so much for Joseph, but more that he wanted to redeem himself in his father's eyes. He might even have planned to betray his brothers for their plotting. "Thus in no uncertain terms we learn that it was Judah, not Reuben, who saved the life of Joseph" (*Zondervan NIV Bible Commentary*). Ultimately, the 10 brothers returned to their plan to lie to their father, saying that an animal had killed Joseph.

D. Jacob's Grief (vv. 33-35)

33. And he knew it, and said, It is my son's coat; an evil beast hath devoured him; Joseph is without doubt rent in pieces.

34. And Jacob rent his clothes, and put sackcloth upon his loins, and mourned for his son many days.

35. And all his sons and all his daughters rose up to

Talk About It:
1. To what did Judah appeal to change his brothers' minds (vv. 26, 27)?
2. In the scene described in verse 28, why do you suppose no dialogue is recorded?

"Our siblings. They resemble us just enough to make all their differences confusing, and no matter what we choose to make of this, we are cast in relation to them our whole lives long."
—Susan Scarf Merrell

Talk About It:
1. What is the meaning of Reuben's question (v. 30)?
2. What tone of voice did the brothers likely use in their statement to Jacob (v. 32)?

comfort him; but he refused to be comforted; and he said, For I will go down into the grave unto my son mourning. Thus his father wept for him.

Jacob recognized the bloody coat immediately, then tore off his own coat and put on one of sackcloth. In his mind he knew that Joseph was dead. If the brothers had intended to hurt their father, they had certainly succeeded. "It seems designed by them on purpose to be revenged upon him for his distinguishing love of Joseph. It was contrived on purpose to create the utmost vexation to him" (Matthew Henry). What hypocrisy on the part of these sons to let this continue, when they well knew Joseph was alive.

Underlying the obvious loss of Joseph was all the other grief Jacob had recently undergone—the loss of Rachel, the loss of Deborah, and the loss of his father. He seemed to be reaping all the years of his earlier deceiving character. He was so broken that he declared, "I will die in mourning for my son" (v. 35, *TLB*). No, he would not. Jacob would later go down to see Joseph in Egypt, and there he would die (46:3, 4).

E. Joseph's Fate (v. 36)

36. And the Midianites sold him into Egypt unto Potiphar, an officer of Pharaoh's, and captain of the guard.

The name *Potiphar* signifies an officer, but also could indicate a eunuch. This seems absurd in light of the fact that Potiphar had a wife. However, it was not "uncommon in the east for eunuchs to have wives" (*Adam Clarke's Commentary*). This would account for his wife later having such an obsession with Joseph.

We come to the end of this chapter of Joseph's story. When he got to Egypt he was sold to an Egyptian officer. There was no pride left in him now. All he could hold on to was the dreams he had been given, and the recognition that the God of his father would ultimately be faithful to rescue him.

CONCLUSION

To be gifted as a leader, but lacking maturity, can bring big problems. Some of the resentment harbored against Joseph may have come from his natural-born leadership instincts. Sadly, there seemed not to have been much potential for such in any of the other brothers, and this highlighted their frustration toward him.

Recently, I attended my high school reunion. Such gatherings are always interesting studies in human behavior. Despite the fact that this group of individuals had not seen each other in many years, the same old cliques and pecking orders quickly fell back into place. The person who "took charge" was the same one who had pushed herself to the front decades ago, and she was just as resented now as she had been then. No wonder Joseph's brothers were dreadfully fearful years later when they had to face him in Egypt. They would not have expected any change in his character. Yet, those years were used by God to mold and soften Joseph into the perfect leader—one with compassion and without resentment.

GOLDEN TEXT CHALLENGE

"BUT AS FOR YOU, YE THOUGHT EVIL AGAINST ME; BUT GOD MEANT IT UNTO GOOD" (Genesis 50:20).

Joseph spoke forgiveness to his brothers, sharing his understanding that God's providence had turned their intended evil to good by using him to save their lives and the lives of many others.

In this example of divine design, we again see that God works through unfavorable human circumstances to bless people. Joseph gave his life to God while young, and tremendous doors of service were opened for him, which he entered through severe testing to great victory.

In this situation we see the grace of God working for good people and for bad people! Joseph had been faithful to God and reaped the joy of renewed association with his family. The brothers of Joseph, whose evil would normally bring retaliation in human relationships, were given the blessing of physical bread and renewed family relationships.

The overriding point learned from Joseph's life is that God, through distressful events, provides a far more exceeding and eternal weight of glory for His children.

Daily Devotions:
M. Sin Prevented by a Dream
Genesis 20:1-7
T. God Revealed in a Dream
Genesis 28:10-17
W. Encouraged by a Dream
Judges 7:9-15
T. Instructed by a Dream
Matthew 1:18-25
F. Warned by a Dream
Matthew 2:7-12
S. Spirit-Inspired Dreams
Acts 2:14-17

The Ruler (Joseph)

Genesis 39:1-23; 41:1-57

Unit Theme:
Isaac, Jacob and Joseph

Central Truth:
Obedience to God leads to victorious living.

Focus:
Observe that God rewards obedience and do right in everything.

Context:
Events took place in Egypt about 1893 to 1882 B.C.

Golden Text:
"The Lord was with Joseph, and showed him mercy, and gave him favor in the sight of the keeper of the prison" (Genesis 39:21).

Study Outline:
I. Ruled His Conduct (Genesis 39:1-12)
II. Ruled His Circumstances (Genesis 39:13-23)
III. Ruled a Nation (Genesis 41:14-46)

INTRODUCTION

At the close of our last lesson, Joseph was in the worst of circumstances. He had been sold into slavery by his brothers to merciless foreign traders en route to Egypt. The abandoned teenage boy had no expectation of ever seeing again the one person on earth who loved him—his father. What a sense of hopelessness he must have felt. We can only imagine the tears that were shed along the way. Once in Egypt, insult was added to injury as he was likely stood naked on the auction block for all prospective buyers to examine.

At some point in his humiliation Joseph made a decision. Rather than despair over his situation, rather than harbor hatred and seething desire for revenge, he put his trust in the God of his father Jacob. From the bottom of his heart he cried out to the Lord for help. There was certainly nowhere else to turn. As Peter would say to Jesus in the New Testament, "To whom shall we go? Thou hast the words of eternal life" (John 6:68).

How many times Joseph must have rehearsed those prophetic dreams in his mind, wondering how God would help him to become all that was planned for him. What Joseph did not know was that brokenness is the place every follower of the Lord must reach. When we come to the point where God is all we have, then we are in perfect circumstances for Him to move mightily in our behalf. And that is exactly what began to happen. Genesis 39:2 says, "The Lord was with Joseph." Nothing can exceed that! Paul said, "If God be for us, who can be against us?" (Romans 8:31).

Of course Joseph had no idea where his life would lead. He was in a country with a culture and language he did not understand. There is no mention of the time passage. No indication is given as to when he was purchased by Potiphar, nor how soon the positive climb to success began to happen there. Also, the major adjustments he undoubtedly faced are not mentioned. "He had come from a rural culture, an unsophisticated people, and a home where he had been the pride and joy of his mother and the favorite child of a doting, aging father" (Swindoll). All that is apparent is that he met the challenges well, since the sovereign God of Israel was preparing the way for him.

I. RULED HIS CONDUCT (Genesis 39:1-12)
A. Joseph With Potiphar (v. 1)

1. And Joseph was brought down to Egypt; and Potiphar, an officer of Pharaoh, captain of the guard, an Egyptian, bought him of the hands of the Ishmeelites, which had brought him down thither.

The intrusion of the Judah/Tamar account (ch. 38) into the larger story of Joseph at first sight does not seem to fit into Genesis. However, it does serve several purposes in the grander scope of unveiling God's plan for humanity's redemption. First, it shows a major contrast between the morality of Joseph and that of his brothers. Second, it gives a further glimpse into the deterioration of Jacob's family. Although there were major personal changes in Jacob, he still was paying the consequences of his many years as a schemer. The payment came in the form of family problems. Judah should have known better than to marry a Canaanite woman (v. 2). Most certainly he knew better than to have sexual relations with someone he thought was a prostitute (vv. 15, 16). God's plan for a separated people was being undermined as the family intensified its assimilation into Canaanite culture. Finally, the fact that Tamar's son Pharez became the lineage from Judah through which the Messiah would be born shows the grace of God and His love for all humanity. Matthew's Gospel begins with a family tree, showing distinctly how Jesus' bloodline went all the way back to Abraham, and clearly mentions Tamar and Pharez (1:3).

In Genesis 39:1 we see that Joseph was sold to Potiphar, a high-ranking officer in the Egyptian hierarchy and the "captain of the guard." "Potiphar was nobody to fool around with; he was a man of seasoned military experience with power over life and death" (Swindoll).

B. God's Favor on Joseph (vv. 2-6)

2. And the Lord was with Joseph, and he was a prosperous man; and he was in the house of his master the Egyptian.

3. And his master saw that the Lord was with him, and that the Lord made all that he did to prosper in his hand.

4. And Joseph found grace in his sight, and he served him: and he made him overseer over his house, and all that he had he put into his hand.

5. And it came to pass from the time that he had made him overseer in his house, and over all that he had, that the Lord blessed the Egyptian's house for Joseph's sake; and the blessing of the Lord was upon all that he had in the house, and in the field.

6. And he left all that he had in Joseph's hand; and he

Potiphar (*POT-uh-fur*)—a high officer of Pharaoh and a wealthy man, his name means "dedicated to *Ra* [the Egyptian sun-god]"

Talk About It:
Why did Joseph land in Potiphar's household?

"Even though Joseph was enslaved, he never acted like a slave."
—Bill Isaacs

knew not ought he had, save the bread which he did eat. And Joseph was a goodly person, and well favoured.

Talk About It:
1. How was Joseph the slave "prosperous" (vv. 2, 3)?
2. Describe Potiphar's confidence in Joseph (vv. 4-6).

At some point Joseph recognized that the favor of God was upon his life. The more he saw this, the more he prospered. He managed to lay aside his past and focus on the present. Instead of seeing his predicament as a prison sentence, he took it as an opportunity to excel. He learned the Egyptian language and culture with ease. He adapted to his environment, but didn't let the pagan culture change his devotion to the Lord. Instead of cursing his slave master, he chose to bless him with the best effort he could put forth. Perhaps he remembered the promise that had been given to his grandfather Abraham: "In you all the families of the earth shall be blessed" (12:3, *NKJV*).

Not only did Joseph recognize God's hand on his life, but so did Potiphar. As an Egyptian polytheist, Potiphar was no follower of Jehovah, but he did see that the deity Joseph served was granting favor to the young man. Possibly there was some opportunity for Joseph to witness to his master about the God of Israel, but we don't know this. Most importantly, there was the outworking evidence of Joseph's faith—a faith expressed through hard work, diligence and a positive attitude. So much excellence was displayed that Potiphar gave Joseph complete run of the household. Note that Joseph did not finagle his way to the top. He simply served the Lord, and was rewarded for doing such. The text in hyperbolic fashion says that Potiphar had to concern himself over nothing more than the food he ate.

No real temptation came Joseph's way (except the temptation to despair) until he was successful. Failure (or life in the pits) is not the place where the devil fights us the most. No, he fights the hardest when he sees us doing well. As soon as God blesses, the devil rears his head. Success is much harder to handle than failure.

Verse 6 gives hint of problems to come by indicating that Joseph was physically attractive. He caught the eye of everyone who saw him. Beauty can be a curse as much as a blessing. It brings temptations that most people don't face. Add that to Joseph being so appealing in his success, and there is the formula for potential disaster.

> "Humility is the gateway into the grace and the favor of God."
> —**Harold Warner**

C. The Master's Wife (v. 7)

7. And it came to pass after these things, that his master's wife cast her eyes upon Joseph; and she said, Lie with me.

Joseph had inherited the good looks of his mother, Rachel (29:17). His handsomeness made him appealing to the one person the devil could use to destroy him. "Potiphar's wife could not resist the temptation to make a conquest of Joseph.

Talk About It:
When did Joseph become attractive to Potiphar's wife?

Apparently she had nothing to occupy her mind and no principles to undergird her in the hour of temptation" (*Wycliffe Bible Commentary*). To succumb to her advances was out of the question for Joseph. Though he might have been tempted, he knew absolutely that the source of his success was the Lord, and he refused to do anything to interrupt that relationship.

Joseph's refusal to fall prey to temptation reverses the trend that had occurred in earlier generations. It had been the beauty of Sarai and Rebekah that had gotten Abraham and Isaac in trouble. In those situations, it was the moral high ground of the foreign rulers that had saved the day. In Joseph's situation, it was his own moral courage. "Whereas in the preceding narratives, the focus had been on God's faithfulness in his covenant promises, in the story of Joseph attention is turned to the human response" (*Zondervan NIV Bible Commentary*). Though the earlier patriarchs never failed in their faith, they did fail in living up to high standards of that faith. Joseph never failed.

D. Joseph's Refusal (vv. 8, 9)

8. But he refused, and said unto his master's wife, Behold, my master wotteth not what is with me in the house, and he hath committed all that he hath to my hand;

9. There is none greater in this house than I; neither hath he kept back any thing from me but thee, because thou art his wife: how then can I do this great wickedness, and sin against God?

Joseph appealed to his master's wife to leave him alone—for the sake of purity. He was thinking not only of himself, but her and her husband as well. However, paramount in his mind was the potential of sinning against the Lord. He could see the consequences of letting sexual desire overtake him. "With the kindness of his master and the displeasure of God before his eyes, how could he be capable of committing an act of transgression, which would at once have distinguished him as the most ungrateful and the most worthless of men?" (*Adam Clarke's Commentary*). This is not to say the temptation wasn't attractive to Joseph. He likely could have reasoned as to how to keep such a liaison a secret. Perhaps the devil was bringing such strategies to mind.

E. Entrapment (vv. 10-12)

(Genesis 39:10-12 is not included in the printed text.)

The woman continued to harass Joseph daily. His continual refusals led her to take a love/hate view toward him. If she could not have him, then she would do her best to destroy him. "Where the unclean spirit gets possession and dominion in a soul, it is as with the possessed of the devils (Luke 8:27, 29),

Weak Point
Most of us have some area of weakness where the devil focuses his attacks. If we are to resist his attacks, we must keep our armor on, avoid the places and situations where we might be tempted, and commune with the Lord constantly. Satan will never give up, but neither should we. Like Joseph, when we cannot resist, we must flee.

wotteth not (v. 8)—"does not concern himself" (*NIV*)

Talk About It:
What would be a "great evil," and why (v. 9, *NASB*)?

"If Mrs. Potiphar had been successful in her attempts to seduce young Joseph, his destiny would have been forfeited."
—**Bill Isaacs**

Talk About It:
1. How frequently did Potiphar's wife tempt Joseph, and how did he protect himself (v. 10)?

2. Why didn't
Joseph just tell
Potiphar about his
wife's actions?
3. What does verse
12 say about bat-
tling temptation?

the clothes of modesty are thrown off and the bands and fet-
ters of shame are broken in pieces" (Matthew Henry).

Verse 11 of the text indicates that Joseph only went to the
part of the house where the master's wife was when it was
absolutely necessary. His noble refusals of her advances did
nothing but cause her to be more enticed. She cared nothing
for the sanctity of her marriage. All she was interested in was
Joseph as an object for gratifying her illicit desires. Finally the
time came when she had set a trap from which he could not
escape. Apparently no other servants were nearby to provide
witness. Seizing the opportunity, she physically forced herself
on him. When he tried to get away, she caught his outer garment. He had no choice but to slip out of it and run for his life.

II. RULED HIS CIRCUMSTANCES (Genesis 39:13-23)
A. False Charge (vv. 13-19)
(Genesis 39:13-16 is not included in the printed text.)

**17. And she spake unto him according to these words,
saying, The Hebrew servant, which thou hast brought
unto us, came in unto me to mock me:**

**18. And it came to pass, as I lifted up my voice and
cried, that he left his garment with me, and fled out.**

**19. And it came to pass, when his master heard the words
of his wife, which she spake unto him, saying, After this manner did thy servant to me; that his wrath was kindled.**

Talk About It:
1. Why did
Potiphar's wife first
accuse Joseph
before his fellow
servants (v. 14, 15)?
2. How strong was
the evidence
against Joseph?

Up until this point, Potiphar's wife must have thought Joseph
had some attraction for her that could be stirred to action. When
now it was demonstrated that he absolutely would have no part
of such, her attraction turned into scorn and hatred. The old
adage "Hell hath no fury as a woman scorned" (William Congreve)
fits this scene to perfection. She immediately began to build a
case against Joseph, calling him a Hebrew (v. 14). This is one of
the earliest written racial slurs recorded against Abraham's
descendants, but would be repeated later by the Egyptians in
43:32. The term *Israelite* had not yet been coined.

Potiphar's wife accused her husband of bringing Joseph
into the household to "mock" her (39:17) and the other women
(v. 14) living there. The Hebrew word for *mock* signifies "some
kind of familiar intercourse not allowable but between husband
and wife" (*Adam Clarke's Commentary*). The woman's scream-
ing complaint about the "Hebrew" was actually an accusation
thrown at her husband in front of the other household slaves.
Since these slaves would likely have been Egyptians, she had
a ready audience, for they would possibly have resented
Joseph's rise to success over them. This was a conniving
woman who was not afraid of her husband—no matter how
high his position.

"He that filches
from me my good
name robs me of
that which not
enriches him, and
makes me poor
indeed."
—William
Shakespeare

B. Wrongful Imprisonment (v. 20)

20. And Joseph's master took him, and put him into the prison, a place where the king's prisoners were bound: and he was there in the prison.

So Joseph's life took a turn for what seemed to be the worst—all because he was obedient to God. This is the time the devil will fight us with doubt and confusion—when we are trying our hardest, but life seems unfair. Joseph was totally innocent, but circumstantial evidence made him appear guilty. Potiphar's wife decided that if she could not have Joseph for sexual favors, she would not tolerate his presence at all. She had the position of power in the household to dominate the situation.

Potiphar was captain of the guard, so he could easily have had Joseph executed, but did not. Why? Perhaps because he didn't fully believe his wife's story. Instead, he had Joseph put in jail. This leniency may have been the one point of hope to which Joseph held. He knew how close to death he was walking.

We have the benefit of reading the entire story and knowing the outcome, but Joseph did not know how God would deliver him—or even if he would be delivered. "All [Joseph] knew at this painful moment was that he had done what was right and had suffered wrong for it. Time dragged on. Days turned into months. He was, again, unfairly rejected—forgotten—totally helpless" (Swindoll).

C. God's Favor (v. 21)

21. But the Lord was with Joseph, and shewed him mercy, and gave him favour in the sight of the keeper of the prison.

The one thing that kept Joseph going was the *favor* of the Lord. Favor is the unseen synergy of the Holy Spirit working on a person's behalf. When we find favor, we should seek favor even more. Certainly this is what Joseph did. He could look back and see the miraculous circumstances that had elevated him in Potiphar's house. Certainly the Lord could do this again, with even greater favor.

D. Elevation Within Prison (vv. 22, 23)

22. And the keeper of the prison committed to Joseph's hand all the prisoners that were in the prison; and whatsoever they did there, he was the doer of it.

23. The keeper of the prison looked not to any thing that was under his hand; because the Lord was with him, and that which he did, the Lord made it to prosper.

Joseph was learning patience and, at the same time, seeing enough of God's hand at work to be willing to wait for His timing. Joseph knew that he had not been divinely rejected.

Devilish Tactic
This is precisely Satan's custom: he first tempts men to sin, and then accuses them as having committed it, even when the temptation has been faithfully and perseveringly resisted! By this means he can trouble a tender conscience, and weaken faith by bringing confusion into the mind. . . . Hence Satan is properly called "the accuser of the brethren" (Revelation 12:10).
—**Adam Clarke**

Talk About It:
What three ways did the Lord minister to Joseph in prison?

Talk About It:
How was Joseph's position in prison similar to what it had been in Potiphar's household?

"He who acknowledges God in all his ways, has the promise that God shall direct all his steps. Joseph's captivity shall promote God's glory; and to this end God works in him, for him, by him" (*Adam Clarke's Commentary*).

Potiphar may actually have been at work here as well. Although he had to save face in front of his wife, he very well may have created a situation within the prison system where Joseph could continue to excel. The *keeper* of the prison would have been under the command of Potiphar. Had Potiphar truly hated Joseph, there would not have been any leniency extended to him.

III. RULED A NATION (Genesis 41:14-46)
A. Joseph's Opportunity (v. 14)

14. Then Pharaoh sent and called Joseph, and they brought him hastily out of the dungeon: and he shaved himself, and changed his raiment, and came in unto Pharaoh.

Chapter 40 represents the years of imprisonment, a time of development of both Joseph's character and leadership skills. Although he was a prisoner, he still excelled and rose to a position where the entire institution seemed under his charge. "Apparently Joseph's position was responsible for his being assigned to wait on the two incarcerated royal officials" (*Zondervan NIV Bible Commentary*). Both the king's butler and baker had prophetic dreams which Joseph interpreted, but the good deed on his part brought no immediate benefit. This is the way much of the good we do appears. However, there is recompense. Jesus said, "Anyone who gives you a cup of water in my name because you belong to Christ will certainly not lose his reward" (Mark 9:41, *NIV*).

Joseph's gift of interpreting dreams would finally bring reward when Pharaoh himself had a dream. The butler, who had long forgotten Joseph, suddenly had his memory stirred. Of course, Joseph knew nothing of the events taking place outside the prison until abruptly he was sent for. Recognizing that something was about to happen, Joseph had presence of mind to clean himself up in preparation for meeting the king. "The Egyptians were the only Oriental nation that liked a smooth chin. All slaves, and foreigners who were reduced to that condition, were obliged, on their arrival in that country, to conform to the cleanly habits of the natives, by shaving their beards and heads, the latter of which were covered with a close cap" (*Jamieson, Fausset and Brown Commentary*).

B. Joseph's Humility (vv. 15, 16)

15. And Pharaoh said unto Joseph, I have dreamed a

dream, and there is none that can interpret it: and I have heard say of thee, that thou canst understand a dream to interpret it.

16. And Joseph answered Pharaoh, saying, It is not in me: God shall give Pharaoh an answer of peace.

Reading between the lines we see that Pharaoh was desperate. His soothsayers and magicians had not been able to help him. Apparently the dream had caused him tremendous consternation. He knew there was significance for both himself and his nation. Otherwise, he certainly would not have been willing to reach into the dungeons and bring out a despised Hebrew to interpret his dream. The situation was much like an incurable disease. It doesn't matter whether one is rich or poor, for when disease strikes, all humans are equal.

Joseph knew the Lord was with him, but he certainly did not want to jeopardize his position with pride. He was aware that God had given him the abilities he possessed, and God could very easily take them away. He moved in absolute integrity, informing the monarch that he had no abilities in himself, but that God was the source of the answer. There was no sign of anger and resentment in him for all the years of mistreatment and imprisonment. He simply maintained the integrity he had built during his hard struggles.

C. Pharaoh's Dreams (vv. 17-32)

(Genesis 41:17-32 is not included in the printed text.)

Pharaoh repeated the dreams to Joseph, adding only the detail that the ugly cows looked no better after having eating up the healthy ones. The cow was the symbol of fruitfulness in Egypt, so the contrasting condition between the two groups was significant. Without any hesitation, Joseph interpreted the dreams, giving glory to God.

The seven good cows (and the seven good ears of corn) represented seven good years, while the seven ugly cows (and the seven bad ears) represented seven bad years to follow. Joseph then indicated to the monarch that God was being gracious to inform him of the 14 years to come—so that he could adequately prepare his nation and his people. "All the way through the answer, Joseph refers to God. Instead of calling attention to himself, he points Pharaoh to Jehovah" (Swindoll).

D. Joseph's Recommendation (vv. 33-37)

(Genesis 41:34-37 is not included in the printed text.)

33. Now therefore let Pharaoh look out a man discreet and wise, and set him over the land of Egypt.

Although it might appear so, Joseph was not presenting a

Talk About It:
What had Pharaoh heard about Joseph (v. 15), and how did Joseph correct it (v. 16)?

kine (v. 18)—cows

Talk About It:
1. Why couldn't the magicians interpret Pharaoh's dream?
2. Why was the dream "doubled unto Pharaoh twice" (v. 32)?

"The Lord giveth wisdom: out of his mouth cometh knowledge and understanding."
—**Proverbs 2:6**

Zaphnath-paaneah (*ZAF-nath-pay-ah-NEE-ah*)—v. 45— Joseph's new name referred to his role as savior of lives through the coming famine.

Talk About It:
1. What did Pharaoh recognize about Joseph (v. 38)?
2. List the symbols of Joseph's position (vv. 42, 43).

"Who are you trying to impress? Aim not for prestige, rather look for a place where you can serve. If God wants you on a higher scale, He will invite you to a higher place."
—**Dave Veerman**

résumé to apply for the job as chief administrator of Egypt's economy. He was simply continuing to give Pharaoh the word from the Lord. Egypt needed to organize itself immediately into a well-oiled machine. There were good years coming, after which there would be terrible years. The nation could not afford to be lulled into inaction by the prosperity of the first seven years.

"A wise man of superior ability must be found who could supervise agricultural production, gather tremendous stores of grain, and, in due time, make wise disposition of the amassed resources. The position would demand the best man the kingdom could afford" (*The Wycliffe Bible Commentary*).

E. Joseph's Elevation (vv. 38-46)
(Genesis 41:42-46 is not included in the printed text.)
38. And Pharaoh said unto his servants, Can we find such a one as this is, a man in whom the Spirit of God is?
39. And Pharaoh said unto Joseph, Forasmuch as God hath shewed thee all this, there is none so discreet and wise as thou art:
40. Thou shalt be over my house, and according unto thy word shall all my people be ruled: only in the throne will I be greater than thou.
41. And Pharaoh said unto Joseph, See, I have set thee over all the land of Egypt.

Talk about a job of selling oneself without really trying! Joseph had simply showed himself to be a man in tune with God. Proverbs 16:7 says, "When a man's ways are pleasing to the Lord, he makes even his enemies live at peace with him" (*NIV*).

Pharaoh was no fool. He would not be taken in by an impostor. Rather, he was wise enough to see the hand of God on Joseph's life. He elevated Joseph to the position of food administrator over the nation, and appointed him as a type of prime minister. Joseph would be in command over the entire kingdom, answerable only to Pharaoh himself. He was given special royal clothes and insignia, empowering him to issue edicts that would affect every citizen. He was given an Egyptian name with the likely meaning "The God Speaks and Lives" (*Nelson Study Bible*). Not only that, the people of the nation would bow to him as a sign of respect.

Joseph's years of earnest faithfulness were finally paying off. He had not once failed God, and neither had God failed him.

CONCLUSION

When presented with the mammoth problem of impending disaster, Pharaoh asked, "Can we find anyone like this man, one in whom is the spirit of God?" (Genesis 41:38, *NIV*).

When tragedy strikes, the world will turn to a man of God for direction. When the Oklahoma City bombing occurred, Billy Graham was called on to deliver the eulogy at the national memorial service. Here was a man respected by all for his integrity and relationship with the Lord. If we will live in constant relationship with God, the world will turn to us for a witness when it gets in trouble.

GOLDEN TEXT CHALLENGE

"THE LORD WAS WITH JOSEPH, AND SHEWED HIM MERCY, AND GAVE HIM FAVOUR IN THE SIGHT OF THE KEEPER OF THE PRISON" (Genesis 39:21).

Here we have a classic passage aptly illustrating God's overruling providence. Joseph has been sold by his jealous, hard-hearted brothers. He has, on false charges and, indeed, even because of his purity of conduct, been cast into prison. There seems to be no way out and his life is ruined.

But when a man is God's man and does God's will, he may safely leave himself in God's hand. The game is not over until the final second ticks off. So, what does God do?

God shows Joseph mercy by giving him favor in the sight of his jailer. Joseph then gains favorable notice by interpreting the dreams of the chief butler and chief baker. But his friend forgets Joseph's kindness. Joseph's train is stalled again for two full years! But God goes to work again. Pharaoh has a dream; the butler's memory is refreshed, and Joseph catapults into prominence and saves Egypt and his family—even those very brothers who had callously sold him to banishment!

See God's Old Testament commentary on Romans 8:28 in Genesis 50:20: "Ye thought evil against me; but God meant it unto good." Could it be said any better?

Daily Devotions:
M. Godly Rulers Are Needed
Exodus 18:17-26
T. God Chooses a Ruler
1 Samuel 16:1-13
W. The Messiah's Rulership
Psalm 72:1-8
T. Respect Rulers
Romans 13:1-7
F. Pray for Rulers
1 Timothy 2:1-6
S. Christ Rules Over All
Revelation 19:11-16

The Benefactor (Joseph)

Genesis 45:1-28; 46:1-7; 47:11, 12; 50:15-26

Unit Theme:
Isaac, Jacob and Joseph

Central Truth:
Perseverance in doing good will overcome evil.

Focus:
Give thanks that goodness overcomes evil and demonstrate Christlike love toward others.

Context:
About 1875 to 1855 B.C.

Golden Text:
"Be not overcome of evil, but overcome evil with good" (Romans 12:21).

Study Outline:
I. Reunited With Brothers (Genesis 45:1-15)
II. Caring for a Family (Genesis 46:1-7; 47:11, 12)
III. Acting With Love (Genesis 50:15-21)

INTRODUCTION

Finally Joseph could see the fruit of his faithfulness to God, as well as the Lord's faithfulness to him. If ever anyone had been through a struggle, it had been Joseph. Unfairly treated by his brothers, sold by them into slavery, falsely accused by Potiphar's wife, years spent in a dungeon—he could have taken on a negative attitude at any time during those years, but never did.

Now, having been elevated in a single day from prison to prime minister, Joseph could look back over his difficult years and see how God had been preparing him for this moment. He could say as the psalmist would later write, "It is good for me that I have been afflicted, that I may learn Your statutes" (Psalm 119:71, NKJV). He had learned a trust and a discernment that would prove extremely valuable in the years to come. This is what Pharaoh saw in Joseph. He said to him, "Inasmuch as God has shown you all this, there is no one as discerning and wise as you. You shall be over my house, and all my people shall be ruled according to your word; only in regard to the throne will I be greater than you" (Genesis 41:39, 40, NKJV). Pharaoh was neither stupid nor gullible. He was used to dealing with complex governmental issues and making high-level decisions. Yet, Joseph had impressed him with a wisdom that he had not seen elsewhere.

Joseph certainly was not jockeying for position for himself either. Too often we don't hear God clearly, because we have our own agendas. Joseph had grown beyond this. The sudden elevation still likely sobered him in an instant. Yes, it was wonderful to be given such a position—but now he had to produce enormous results.

What if Joseph hadn't really properly understood Pharaoh's dreams? What if after seven years of plenty, the eighth came and went with no change? What if he couldn't get the nation organized? These were real questions for Joseph to face, but he had confidence in the Lord. He "went out from Pharaoh's presence and traveled throughout Egypt" (41:46, NIV). In other words, he got to work immediately.

Now, as we approach this lesson, we find that God had blessed Joseph even more. The seven years of plenty had come and gone. Joseph had proved his abilities far beyond Pharaoh's expectations. The famine had begun and was affecting all the world, including the land of Canaan. Twenty years had passed since his brothers had sold him into slavery. God had helped Joseph move beyond his past, but now the terrible memories resurfaced when his brothers appeared before him asking to buy grain.

I. REUNITED WITH BROTHERS (Genesis 45:1-15)

A. Joseph Unrecognized (vv. 1, 2)

1. Then Joseph could not refrain himself before all them that stood by him; and he cried, Cause every man to go out from me. And there stood no man with him, while Joseph made himself known unto his brethren.

2. And he wept aloud: and the Egyptians and the house of Pharaoh heard.

The events of Genesis 42—44 heighten the drama of Joseph's unveiling his identity to his brothers and extending complete forgiveness to them. Why was there such a drawn-out ordeal? We do not know, except that God was somehow leading Joseph. We also know that sin demands a price, and despite the great mercy Joseph would grant his brothers, there was still a measure of payment they must pay for selling him into slavery more than 20 years earlier.

Talk About It:
Why couldn't Joseph control his emotions?

Joseph had presented himself to the brothers as a dispassionate Egyptian ruler who had little use for them. They were neither aware of his true identity nor that he understood every word they spoke to each other in Hebrew. However, while they were ignorant, Joseph remembered the dreams of his youth, dreams that had now come to pass, with the brothers bowing at his feet. He accused them of being spies—an outrageous idea, but nevertheless one that instilled fear into them. He asked questions that gave him information about his father and his youngest brother, Benjamin. He put them all in jail for three days, and upon their release he forced them to leave one brother (Simeon) behind in jail, while the others returned to Canaan to bring back Benjamin. All of this had the great effect of reviving the consciences of the 10 men. The years had given them some respite from what they had done to Joseph, but now they realized they were being punished for their sin (42:21, 22).

True to his old ways, Jacob had still played favorites with his offspring. He never loved the others like he did Joseph and Benjamin. However, by this time the 10 slighted brothers seemed to have felt no animosity toward Benjamin, a sign that they felt remorse for what they had done to Joseph. At first Jacob adamantly refused to let Benjamin be taken back to Egypt (despite the fact that Simeon was sitting there in jail). Ultimately, however, the famine was so deep that there was no choice (43:11-14).

When the brothers returned to Egypt with Benjamin accompanying them, they were taken to Joseph's personal residence, which only heightened their fears. Upon seeing Benjamin, Joseph had to retreat to his chamber to weep. Regaining his composure, he continued the ruse, sending them on their way with food, but also with money in each one's bag, as well as a silver cup in Benjamin's. As soon as they were out of the city, they were overtaken by Joseph's stewards, demanding their return because of theft.

Upon discovery of the cup in Benjamin's bag, the others were overwhelmed, knowing that this would be the last straw for their father to endure. Judah took the lead in entreating Joseph for mercy, even offering himself as a slave in Benjamin's place.

Thus we come to our text. Joseph was so moved by the earnest remorse he saw in his brothers that he could no longer restrain himself. He forced all to leave except his brothers, and his weeping was so loud that even Pharaoh heard it.

B. Identity Revealed (vv. 3, 4)

3. And Joseph said unto his brethren, I am Joseph; doth my father yet live? And his brethren could not answer him; for they were troubled at his presence.

4. And Joseph said unto his brethren, Come near to me, I pray you. And they came near. And he said, I am Joseph your brother, whom ye sold into Egypt.

This is one of the most dramatic moments in all Biblical history. Joseph had cleared the room of Egyptians. Since word had gone even to Pharaoh, likely there were many listening ears outside hoping for a clue as to what was wrong with the prime minister. Only he and his 11 brothers were left there. They had to wonder what was about to happen. What transpired was the last thing in the world they might have imagined. With tears rolling down his cheeks, Joseph exclaimed that he was their long-lost brother—the one they had so wrongfully abused. Since he was alone with them, and all communications to this point had been through an interpreter, he now spoke in Hebrew for the first time.

They were stunned to complete silence. *Terrified* might be a better description for 10 of them. A myriad of thoughts must have raced through their minds, not the least of which was what punishment they would now receive for a sin committed long ago. Their evil had caught up with them, and now they must pay. Benjamin was likely more confused than frightened, for he knew nothing of the wicked deeds his brothers had done. There is no indication that they had revealed such to him. He likely had the least trepidation in approaching Joseph, and certainly he was the one Joseph longed the most to embrace.

"The Hebrew phrasing for 'Come near to me' refers not just to spatial proximity, but to an intimate closeness. It is a term occasionally used for coming near for the purpose of embracing or kissing someone" (Swindoll). Joseph wanted them to come close so that they could see beyond the Egyptian garb

The Benefactor

and recognize him. He wanted to prove his identity. He was their own flesh and blood. Those were probably some of the most hesitant steps taken in history, but what they found earlier so hard to comprehend they now had to believe.

C. Purpose Accomplished (vv. 5-8)

5. Now therefore be not grieved, nor angry with yourselves, that ye sold me hither: for God did send me before you to preserve life.

6. For these two years hath the famine been in the land: and yet there are five years, in the which there shall neither be earing nor harvest.

earing (v. 6)— plowing

7. And God sent me before you to preserve you a posterity in the earth, and to save your lives by a great deliverance.

8. So now it was not you that sent me hither, but God: and he hath made me a father to Pharaoh, and lord of all his house, and a ruler throughout all the land of Egypt.

Talk About It:
1. Why does Joseph use the phrase "God sent me" three times (vv. 5, 7, 8)?
2. According to verse 7, why was Joseph in Egypt?
3. In verse 8, what three words does Joseph use to describe his God-given status?

Joseph saw the terror in his brothers' eyes and spoke quickly to relieve it. The tests he had put them through were not pleasant for him, but he had to make sure their hearts were repentant. The events of the past hours had assured him that they sorely regretted what they had done. Of course, even if they still hated him, he would still show mercy, for God had molded his character. Joseph himself was a changed man. He then explained to them that the famine still had five more years. He probably gave them a quick history of what had transpired over the past years, and how he had accurately interpreted the Pharaoh's dream.

Most importantly, Joseph explained to his brothers that God had orchestrated every event that had transpired. Even though they had meant harm to him, God had used this as a means of preserving His chosen people. These brothers were those chosen people, despite their sin. God had looked far into the future and placed Joseph in a position to meet their need in time of famine. "In describing how God had taken care of him, Joseph alluded to the brothers' initial question regarding his dreams as a young lad (Genesis 37:8). He reminded them that he had been made 'ruler of all Egypt'" (*Zondervan NIV Bible Commentary*).

D. Haste Urged (vv. 9-13)

9. Haste ye, and go up to my father, and say unto him, Thus saith thy son Joseph, God hath made me lord of all Egypt: come down unto me, tarry not:

10. And thou shalt dwell in the land of Goshen, and thou shalt be near unto me, thou, and thy children, and thy children's children, and thy flocks, and thy herds, and all that thou hast:

"That the Almighty does make use of human agencies and directly intervenes in human affairs is one of the plainest statements of the Bible. I have had so many evidences of His direction, so many instances when I have been controlled by some other power other than my own will, that I cannot doubt that this power comes from above."

—**Abraham Lincoln**

11. And there will I nourish thee; for yet there are five years of famine; lest thou, and thy household, and all that thou hast, come to poverty.

12. And, behold, your eyes see, and the eyes of my brother Benjamin, that it is my mouth that speaketh unto you.

13. And ye shall tell my father of all my glory in Egypt, and of all that ye have seen; and ye shall haste and bring down my father hither.

In the excitement of his revelation, Joseph had asked if truly his father was alive (v. 3). This showed his intense desire to see again the one person he had loved most. He now insisted that his brothers return to Canaan and bring Jacob to this place of safety he had prepared for them. Here they could all enjoy relief from the barrenness the famine had brought. Joseph had been planning this all along, for he now speaks of the land of Goshen as the spot for them to live. Joseph was a planner. He had been thinking about the future for his family, even while the masquerade was being carried out. He knew there were more tough years ahead, and it was his great privilege to provide for his entire family.

E. Love Expressed (vv. 14, 15)

14. And he fell upon his brother Benjamin's neck, and wept; and Benjamin wept upon his neck.

15. Moreover he kissed all his brethren, and wept upon them: and after that his brethren talked with him.

Joseph embraced his full brother, Benjamin. Surely he saw in him the resemblance of his mother, Rachel. Both of them wept openly. We must remember that Benjamin had more to take in than anyone else. He was reeling from the sudden revelation of what his half brothers had done to Joseph many years earlier. In any other circumstance he would likely have been ready to hate them for their sin, but this was no time for holding grudges.

Once the walls of fear had been broken, it was time for grand reunion and rejoicing. The 10 guilty brothers were suddenly free of the shame they had secretly carried for years. Grace had been extended to them in a way almost beyond belief. Neither did they mind that Joseph was most moved by the presence of his full brother, Benjamin. Great conversation followed, likely for many hours. There was twenty-some years of catching up to do.

II. CARING FOR A FAMILY (Genesis 46:1-7; 47:11, 12)
A. An Offering at Beersheba (46:1-4)

1. And Israel took his journey with all that he had, and came to Beer-sheba, and offered sacrifices unto the God of his father Isaac.

Talk About It:
1. What did Joseph want his brothers to do hastily (vv. 9, 13), and why?
2. Describe Joseph's plan for his family (vv. 10, 11).

Talk About It:
What do you suppose Joseph's brothers asked as they "talked with him" (v. 15)?

"The discretion of a man deferreth his anger; and it is his glory to pass over a transgression."
—Proverbs 19:11

The Benefactor

2. And God spake unto Israel in the visions of the night, and said, Jacob, Jacob. And he said, Here am I.

3. And he said, I am God, the God of thy father: fear not to go down into Egypt; for I will there make of thee a great nation:

4. I will go down with thee into Egypt; and I will also surely bring thee up again: and Joseph shall put his hand upon thine eyes.

Despite the promise of a good life to be had in Egypt with his long-lost son, Jacob wanted to be sure that God was in this. This was an enormous move for his family, one that would have tremendous implications. They were leaving the land God had promised them. When they got to Beersheba, near the southern border of Canaan, Jacob built an altar and offered sacrifices. That night the Lord graciously awakened Jacob with a vision, the seventh such time in their long relationship. "The fact that the names Israel and Jacob are used interchangeably indicates that the earlier negative connotations of the name Jacob have faded. Instead of meaning that Jacob 'supplants,' the name Jacob now means that God 'supplants'" (*Nelson Study Bible*).

The word from the Lord was one of assurance. God would go with them to Egypt, not to be permanent residents, but would bring them back to the Promised Land as a great nation. Joseph would also be with Jacob when he died. The length of time Jacob's descendants would spend in Egypt was not specified. Certainly the old man never dreamed it would be 400 years, but this was of no matter now. He had all the affirmation he needed. They could proceed in peace.

B. The Journey to Egypt (vv. 5-7)

5. And Jacob rose up from Beer-sheba: and the sons of Israel carried Jacob their father, and their little ones, and their wives, in the wagons which Pharaoh had sent to carry him.

6. And they took their cattle, and their goods, which they had gotten in the land of Canaan, and came into Egypt, Jacob, and all his seed with him:

7. His sons, and his sons' sons with him, his daughters, and his sons' daughters, and all his seed brought he with him into Egypt.

Having been assured by God that this was divinely intended, the entire clan set out for Egypt. Considering the fact this was during a terrible famine, we might compare the move to scenes from John Steinbeck's *The Grapes of Wrath*. With so many people, belongings and livestock, the trip likely took several weeks. It was a needy caravan making its way from a famished land to the wealth of the Egyptian prime minister's table.

Talk About It:
1. Why did God need to tell Jacob to "fear not" (v. 3)—what might have worried him?
2. In verse 4, what promises did God make to Jacob?

Leaving With God
A friend in the military told me how difficult some of the relocations were that her family had to make. She related that she once watched the moving van leave their old address headed toward their new assignment. She suddenly realized that her entire life was inside that giant 18-wheeler. When it disappeared out of sight, she felt homeless and full of trepidation. That's the way Jacob must have felt. Despite the fact that he was anxious to see Joseph, he still stopped at Beersheba to make sure God would truly have his family leave Canaan.

When we are facing changes in our life, we must first seek God's will. Having the assurance that He is leading us is the most important thing we can do.

"My authority in my home is exactly proportional to what I got fresh from God that day. I don't even have to talk about it—there's a heavenly aura when Dad's met God."
—Robert A. Cook

Rameses (*RAMseez*)—v. 11—a city in northwestern Egypt, the land of Goshen

Talk About It:
Describe the quality of Joseph's provision for his family.

requite (v. 15)—repay

Talk About It:
1. What did Joseph's brothers fear?

What a change of lifestyles for a group of nomadic shepherds! This would have been somewhere around the year 1876 B.C., probably during the Middle Kingdom and the Twelfth Dynasty. Egypt was a stable, dominating international power, with great achievements in education, architecture, and the arts.

Later in this chapter (v. 26), we are told that the total number of persons (sons and grandchildren) with Jacob came to 66. Adding Jacob, Joseph and his two sons, the number comes to 70. "Ancient Israelites regarded the number 70 as a token of God's special blessing on them" (*Nelson Study Bible*).

C. A Home in Goshen (47:11, 12)

11. And Joseph placed his father and his brethren, and gave them a possession in the land of Egypt, in the best of the land, in the land of Rameses, as Pharaoh had commanded.

12. And Joseph nourished his father, and his brethren, and all his father's household, with bread, according to their families.

Joseph had set up a plan whereby his family would be given the land of Goshen as a place of residence. This area was in the Nile delta. It was well watered and suited the lifestyle of shepherds. Interestingly, the Egyptians despised shepherds and would not want to live among such. Goshen was the part of Egypt nearest to Canaan, was thinly populated, and was somewhat separate from the Egyptian population. As such, it was perfect for keeping tensions between the two peoples from developing. More importantly, there would be less temptation for Israelites to intermarry with the local population.

Pharaoh's response to Joseph's plan was one of complete generosity. "Not only did he grant their wish and allow Joseph's brothers to settle in Goshen, he also put the brothers in charge of his own livestock, a result reminiscent of Joseph's own rise to power in the house of Pharaoh. Thus Joseph's fortune was duplicated in the fortune of his brothers" (*Zondervan NIV Bible Commentary*).

III. ACTING WITH LOVE (Genesis 50:15-21)
A. Guilt and Fear (vv. 15-18)
(Genesis 50:16-18 is not included in the printed text.)

15. And when Joseph's brethren saw that their father was dead, they said, Joseph will peradventure hate us, and will certainly requite us all the evil which we did unto him.

As the family returned to Egypt after burying Jacob in Canaan, there was great time for pause and reflection. Joseph had been a savior for the entire clan, but it had been Jacob who had held them together. He was the only one who could control his sons. He was the ultimate authority in their lives. Many families experience this. Once the patriarch or matriarch is dead, the very reason for unity seems to dissipate. Siblings divide the parent's land and belongings, often fighting over who gets what.

Not surprisingly, then, Joseph's brothers went into a panic over their futures. What if the kindness he had shown them was simply to please his father, Jacob? Would he now remember their sins and take revenge on them? To avert such, they went to Joseph humbly and again asked his forgiveness. They even committed themselves to being his servants—such was their fear.

The concept of grace still seemed foreign to the brothers. As long as Jacob had been alive, they had felt safe. He had been to them the restraining influence. "Perhaps in their own mourning of their father's passing, as their hearts were especially softened, guilt slipped in the unguarded gate of their memory and again robbed them of their fragile peace" (Swindoll). When we are fully aware of our sins and are repentant, our hearts are softened. Not only are we ripe for God to speak to us, but the devil will also speak loudly. We can take on guilt and burdens never meant for us.

B. Joseph's Reaction (vv. 19-21)

19. And Joseph said unto them, Fear not: for am I in the place of God?

20. But as for you, ye thought evil against me; but God meant it unto good, to bring to pass, as it is this day, to save much people alive.

21. Now therefore fear ye not: I will nourish you, and your little ones. And he comforted them, and spake kindly unto them.

We see once more the wonderful work that God had done in the heart of Joseph. Yes, it was a time when he could have easily demanded some retribution from his brothers. Instead, Joseph wisely put a stop to his brothers' rehearsing their past sins. He wept that they would even think him capable of revenge (v. 17). More importantly, he reminded them that this was God's plan, not his. His assurances to them express complete forgiveness, surpassed only by the words of Jesus Christ himself.

Joseph knew that only God could judge. It was not his position to do so. What he had to do was extend grace. He was simply happy to have been God's instrument, and joyful to have his family together again. This was more important than anything done to him many years earlier. His last statement says it all: "I will provide for you and your children" (v. 21, *NIV*). Like Joseph, we should guard our hearts when we have the opportunity to throw guilt on someone else, and instead extend love and fellowship.

2. Do you think Jacob actually said what Joseph's brothers claimed he said (vv. 16, 17)? Why or why not?

"Though the dungeon, the scourge, and the executioner be absent, the guilty mind can apply the goad [pointed rod] and scorch [painful burn] with blows."
—Lucretius

Talk About It:
1. What did Joseph mean by asking, "Am I in the place of God?" (v. 19).
2. Compare Romans 8:28 with Genesis 50:20.
3. What did Joseph promise in verse 21?

"Kindness is the golden chain by which society is bound together."
—Johann Von Goethe

CONCLUSION

Are you ever haunted by old sins you committed—sins that have long been forgiven and covered by the blood? There are things in your past to be ashamed of, but if you have received Christ's forgiveness, those sins are erased. You need not be like Joseph's brothers. Once their father was dead, it did not seem to matter how well Joseph had treated them for the past 17 years. They still feared he might hold a grudge. Joseph had to make fresh assurances that there was no ill will in him toward his family.

On the other side of the coin, we need to be reminded that once we have forgiven someone else for what was done against us, we should never let anger or retaliation reenter our hearts. Once forgiven, always forgiven.

GOLDEN TEXT CHALLENGE

"BE NOT OVERCOME OF EVIL, BUT OVERCOME EVIL WITH GOOD" (Romans 12:21).

The Christian must respond to evil actions with kindness. The underlying revelation is that even our enemies have needs. The Christian should be sensitive to those needs and try to meet them with Christian love. The temptation of the self-avenger is to try to capitalize on those needs and gain an advantage. Advantage is never gained in this way—only failure and self-destruction. As Thomas Wilson said, "It costs more to revenge injuries than to bear them."

The Christian's proper response to his or her enemies is that evil is overcome. This is a promise of victory over injustice and the workers of such iniquity. *Overcome* indicates not mere success but power and victory.

Bible Insight

Growing as Christian Disciples
by David Cooper

Have you ever stopped to think about why Jesus described salvation as a new birth? His message was, "You must be born again." Birth, you see, is the beginning of a growth process. We either grow or we die; we develop or we deteriorate; we advance or we retreat. To *grow* means "to increase in size, amount and degree; to come to be gradually, and to progress toward maturity." God doesn't call us to perfection—He calls us to maturity. "Let us . . . go on to maturity" (Hebrews 6:1).* Here are 10 ways:

1. Grow Down

Strong, deep roots determine the quality of growth. Paul says we need to be "rooted and built up . . . strengthened in the faith" (Colossians 2:7). We need deep spiritual roots of a tested-and-tried faith. Without them, the storms of life will uproot us.

We will face the storm of personal testing. Trouble is no respecter of persons. I once read that we should be kind to everyone we meet, because everyone is going through some kind of pain. But God is with us in our difficulties, failures and doubts. He will never leave us nor abandon us. A deeply rooted faith is confident in the faithfulness of God, knowing that nothing "will be able to separate us from the love of God that is in Christ Jesus our Lord" (Romans 8:39).

We also face the storm of temptation. Our deepest moral and ethical convictions will be challenged. We will be called upon to stand up for what we believe in the hour of temptation. Even Christ faced temptation in the desert, alone with the devil. He wasn't exempt, and neither are we. Here's the good news:

No temptation has seized you except what is common to man. And God is faithful; he will not let you be tempted beyond what you can bear. But when you are tempted, he will also provide a way out so that you can stand up under it (1 Corinthians 10:13).

We also face the storm of misguided teachings. Ours is the day of false prophets, false Christs and distorted spiritual messages. However, by developing deep roots, we will "no longer be infants, tossed back and forth by the waves, and blown here and there by every wind of teaching and by the cunning and craftiness of men in their deceitful scheming. Instead, speaking the truth in love, we will in all things grow up into him who is the Head, that is, Christ" (Ephesians 4:14, 15).

2. Grow Up

God wants us to ascend to a higher level. Healthy growth is upward in its orientation. Parents are to bring their children up, not put them down. Trees and plants grow upward toward the sun. We number grades so that students get the sense of going higher in life. We start at first grade and work toward 12th.

Here's the answer to low self-esteem and a negative image: Christ gives us a new self-image when we follow Him. He told common, ordinary people that they were going to change the world. He told us that God cares deeply about us, and that He has even numbered the hairs on our heads, so we would understand how important we are to God.

The Cross is the measure of a person's worth. You and I were worth the death of Jesus for our sins that we might have eternal life. Christ laid down His life for us so that we would know our eternal worth. Augustine said, "People travel to wonder at the heights of the mountains, at the huge waves of the seas, at the long course of the rivers, at the vast compass of the ocean, at the circular motion of the stars—and they pass by themselves without wondering."

God wants you to *grow up.* You are endowed with talent and ability. Don't ever let anyone put you *down.* God created you to move in an upward direction, not a downward spiral. So go on to the next level. Leave the status quo and reach upward to a higher place.

3. Grow In

Theodore Roosevelt said, "If you are not actively becoming the person you want to be, you are becoming the person you don't want to be." We need character growth in our moods, attitudes and temperament. Who we are is more important than what we do. We focus on the substance of our lives, not the style. We talk too much about lifestyle and not enough about life-substance.

4. Grow Out

Grow beyond yourself. Leo Tolstoy said, "Life is a place of service." We are to live the extended life, reaching out to others in service. We grow as we serve, and as we make an investment of ourselves in others.

Jesus said the kingdom of God "is like a mustard seed, which is the smallest seed you plant in the ground. Yet when planted, it grows and becomes the largest of all garden plants, with such big branches that the birds of the air can perch in its shade" (Mark 4:31, 32). The picture of the big branches is one of our lives reaching out to provide shelter for others.

5. Grow Uniquely

Here is one of the most reassuring promises God gives to parents: "Train a child in the way he should go, and when he is old he will not turn from it" (Proverbs 22:6). The word *train* actually means "to nurture and guide a child according to his unique bent."

No two people are alike. We shouldn't compare ourselves with others. "We do not dare to classify or compare ourselves with some who commend themselves. When they measure themselves by themselves and compare themselves with themselves, they are not wise" (2 Corinthians 10:12).

God always does a unique work of grace in every person. Charles Allen tells of being a young preacher and falling into depression when he read a book about how to be a great preacher. He found liberty when he decided to be himself.

6. Grow Together

Jesus sent His disciples out by twos to conduct their ministry. Christianity is community. Augustine said, "He cannot have God as his Father, who does not have the church as his mother."

Our relationships make us or break us. Our personalities are shaped through our interactions with others. "He who walks with the wise grows wise, but a companion of fools suffers harm" (Proverbs 13:20).

Every man needs four men in his life: a Paul to mentor him, a Timothy to disciple him, a Barnabas to encourage him, and a Jonathan to be a true friend.

7. Grow Right

Newly planted trees and plants need to be tied to a stake in the ground so they will grow straight instead of crooked. Christ is your stake. Your family is your stake. Mentors are your stake. The Bible is your stake. Tie yourself to these stakes so you will grow in the right direction.

Just as a people are trained correctly, they can also go through the wrong training. Such is the danger of unbiblical teachings and spiritual extremes. We are to "rightly divide the word of truth" (see 2 Timothy 2:15, *NKJV*).

Make the most of your educational opportunities and take time to make sure the training you receive is right so that you will grow right.

8. Grow Slowly

God is never in a hurry! He even took seven days to create the cosmos when He could have done so with one word. Growth takes time. We tend to want things to happen quickly. We are conditioned to the fast lane. We think God will give us an instantaneous miracle every time we hit a bump in the road. Most of the time when we pray for a miracle, we should be praying for maturity. Miracles happen quickly, maturity slowly, so we prefer miracles. Spiritual growth and personality development happen slowly over time. Small, gradual gains are made. We often take three steps forward and two steps back. But at least we're one step ahead.

Paul, the apostle, went through a long gradual development in humility, as seen in his writings. In his first letter, he introduces himself as "Paul, an apostle" (Galatians 1:1). Later, at the height of his ministry, he writes, "I am the least of the apostles" (1 Corinthians 15:9). Toward the end of his ministry, during the first Roman imprisonment, he writes, "To me, who am less than the least of all the saints" (Ephesians 3:8, *NKJV*). (A saint was the title of every believer.) Finally, in one of his last letters he admits to being the chief of sinners (see 1 Timothy 1:15).

What a downward progression—from apostle, to least of the apostles, to the least of God's people, to the chief of sinners. Or was it? Was it not rather an upward ascendancy toward authentic self-awareness, freedom from pride and closeness to God?

9. Grow Steady

Pace yourself. Running long distances is based on finding your own pace and sticking to it. Life is not a sprint, it's a marathon. "Let us run with perseverance the race marked out for us" (Hebrews 12:1).

Spiritual growth boils down to pressing on when you feel like quitting the race. "I press on to take hold of that for which Christ Jesus took hold of me" (Philippians 3:12). Great things happen little by little. Practice the spiritual disciplines of prayer, meditation of Scripture, worship, giving and service, and you will continue to grow.

10. Grow in Love

Paul says of the church: "The whole body . . . grows and builds itself up in love" (Ephesians 4:16). All true spiritual growth is growth in love. We grow in a deeper understanding of God's love, and we grow in our capacity to love others even as God loves us.

Christianity is a revolution of love. The American Red Cross was gathering supplies, medicine, clothing and food for the suffering people of Biafra. Inside one of the boxes that showed up at the collecting depot one day was a letter that read: "We have recently been converted to Christ and, because of our conversion, we want to try to help. We won't ever need these again. Can you use them for something worthwhile?" Inside the box was Ku Klux Klan sheets. The sheets were cut into strips and eventually used to bandage the wounds of the suffering in Africa.

Our heavenly Father is committed to getting us to the finish line of life and to meeting Him in eternity. As Paul said so confidently: "Being confident of this, that he who began a good work in you will carry it on to completion until the day of Christ Jesus" (Philippians 1:6).

*Unless otherwise indicated, Scripture quotations in this article are from the *New International Version*. This Bible Insight is adapted from *Ten Steps Toward a Better Life*. It is available from Pathway Press online at *www.pathwaybookstore.com* or by calling 800-553-8506.

Goals of Discipleship

John 15:8; Acts 2:46, 47; Romans 1:11, 12; 2 Corinthians 5:18-20;
Ephesians 4:11-16; Philippians 3:9-14; 2 Timothy 2:1, 2; 1 Peter 2:11, 12

INTRODUCTION

A *disciple* is "a student or follower who helps to spread his master's teachings." The original or secular word carries with it the idea of apprenticeship, similar to an apprentice in a trade like carpentry. Jesus said in Luke 6:40, "A student [disciple] is not above his teacher, but everyone who is fully trained will be like his teacher" (*NIV*). When fully discipled, His followers were to be like Him, despite their different personalities.

The disciple in Christianity is a follower of Jesus Christ, desiring to learn His ways and apply them to his life. It has been said that the one common trait each of Jesus' 12 disciples had was that they were teachable. A disciple must be open and have a desire to learn.

A life of discipleship must have at its base a life of prayer. It is the foundation of Christian growth, the learning of God's will, and the attainment of a likeness to Christ.

Prayer promotes spiritual growth as almost nothing else can, indeed as nothing else but Bible study; and true Bible study and true prayer go hand in hand. It is through prayer that sin is brought to light, even the most hidden sin. The psalmist said, "Search me, O God, and know my heart: try me, and know my thoughts: And see if there be any wicked way in me" (Psalm 139:23, 24). When God shoots the penetrating rays of His light into the innermost recesses of the heart, sins never suspected are brought into view. In answer to prayer, God washes away evil and cleanses one's sins. In answer to prayer, eyes are opened to view wondrous truths out of God's Word. In answer to prayer, wisdom is obtained to know God's way and the strength to walk in it. As a disciple meets God in prayer and gazes into His face, he is changed into His image from glory to glory (2 Corinthians 3:18).

To grow as disciples, it is important that we demonstrate faithfulness and a desire to learn and apply the Word of God. This may be done through hearing it preached and taught, reading it often, studying it, memorizing it, and meditating on the Scriptures.

If the Christian disciple does not grow spiritually, he is stagnating and is not really a disciple. The Bible, however, enables us to grow spiritually. Our spiritual growth comes from taking in the Word of God as our spiritual food. The Bible guides and directs us through life.—Homer Rhea

Unit Theme:
Christian Discipleship

Central Truth:
Practicing Christian disciplines develops Christlike character and maturity.

Focus:
Identify the goals of discipleship and encourage the development of Christlike practices.

Context:
Selected New Testament passages regarding the purpose of discipleship

Golden Text:
"Herein is my Father glorified, that ye bear much fruit; so shall ye be my disciples" (John 15:8).

Study Outline:
I. Christlike Character (John 15:8; Acts 2:46, 47; Romans 1:11, 12)
II. Spiritual Maturity (2 Corinthians 5:18-20; Philippians 3:9-14; Ephesians 4:11-16)
III. Good Deeds (2 Timothy 2:1, 2; 1 Peter 2:11, 12)

I. CHRISTLIKE CHARACTER (John 15:8; Acts 2:46, 47; Romans 1:11, 12)

A. Abide in Christ (John 15:8)

8. Herein is my Father glorified, that ye bear much fruit; so shall ye be my disciples.

Talk About It:
1. Describe the fruit God wants His children to bear.
2. What is the result of bearing such fruit, and why?

In John 15 Jesus speaks of the spiritual union He has with His followers. He is "the true vine" (v. 1), and they are the branches. The branches' life, strength, beauty and fertility come from the Vine. A believer has no life of its own apart from the Vine.

Verse 6 emphasizes the possibility of losing the vital contact with Jesus Christ that maintains the spiritual life. Words are not strong enough to describe the terrible consequences of not abiding in Christ, of refusing to live the life of faith in Him. The result will be like that of fruitless and dead branches of a vine. They are soon withered and gathered as firewood to be burned.

To abide in Christ means we will maintain a close communion with Him. We will constantly lean on Him, pour out our hearts to Him, and rely on Him as our constant companion and friend. To have His words abiding in us (v. 7) means we will keep His teachings and commandments ever before us. It means His commandments will become the guide of our lives and the rule of our daily conduct.

"The Christian is a person who makes it easy for others to believe in God."
—Robert McCheyne

Because of our relationship with Christ, we will produce "much fruit" (v. 8). This will bring glory to God. It will recommend our experience to others and cause the world to honor the God who has such servants. It also gives evidence that we are genuine disciples, and our lives will clearly prove we are followers of Christ.

B. Win Favor (Acts 2:46, 47)

46. And they, continuing daily with one accord in the temple, and breaking bread from house to house, did eat their meat with gladness and singleness of heart,

47. Praising God, and having favour with all the people. And the Lord added to the church daily such as should be saved.

Talk About It:
1. From verse 46, list all the words that describe the attitude of the early church.
2. What was happening "daily" (v. 47), and why?

Notice the steps in the growth of these believers in the early church. First, they had a knowledge they were saved with the accompanying peace with God. Next followed growth in divine truth and meaningful fellowship one with another as they shared their means with those in need. Then they were able to see others being saved. This growth produced gladness of heart. Their behavior also earned the respect of those who had not yet believed in Jesus Christ.

The early Christians, following Pentecost, praised God for the blessings they were receiving through the gift of His Son. They had been delivered from sin. They had communion with God, and they had love one for another.

It has been said that the best proof of Christianity is the

Christian life lived in an everyday environment. This the early believers did, and they had "favour with all the people." Such fruits of the Spirit as these early Christians showed are certain to find favor with all.

People who are sincere in their personal life of faith toward God are shown a certain respect. Even unbelievers appreciate it when those who profess to know Jesus Christ live like Christians. Christ does make a difference in one's life. When a person accepts Christ, there is a new sparkle in the eyes, a new sound in the voice, and a new attitude toward life. Unbelievers are quick to recognize this.

The natural result was, and always should be, that "the Lord added to the church daily those who were being saved" (v. 47, NKJV). The pure and simple life of the early Christians commended them to the people and made it easier for them to win confidence, and thus converts. However, the growth of the church, Luke reminds us, was not the work of any human agency or attractiveness, but of the Lord.

> "The church that does not gather into its fold the drunks, the harlots, the liars and the thieves does not deserve the right to welcome the saints."
> —Duke Barron

C. Be Established (Romans 1:11, 12)

11. For I long to see you, that I may impart unto you some spiritual gift, to the end ye may be established;

12. That is, that I may be comforted together with you by the mutual faith both of you and me.

Paul had never visited the church in Rome, but it was his hope to do so. He had a longing or earnest desire to be with them so he might share with them "some spiritual gift."

"*Charisma* ('spiritual gift') is a gift of 'grace' (*charis*)—'a favor' received without merit on the recipient's part. Paul uses it both in this ordinary sense (Romans 5:15, 16; 6:23), and in a special, technical sense, denoting extraordinary powers bestowed upon individuals by the Holy Spirit such as gifts of healing, speaking with tongues, prophecy, and so on (see Romans 12:6; 1 Corinthians 1:7; 12:4, 31; 1 Peter 4:10). In 1 Timothy 4:14 and 2 Timothy 1:6, it is used of the sum of the powers requisite for the discharge of the office of an evangelist" (*Vincent's Word Studies in the New Testament*).

Paul wanted to minister to the Romans so they might be "established"—confirmed in their faith in the gospel. This ministry would flow in two directions—"that you and I may be mutually encouraged by each other's faith" (v. 12, *NIV*). Paul would minister to them through his spiritual gift of teaching and preaching, and the Romans would minister to him through their giftedness.

Talk About It:
1. How can spiritual gifts help a church (v. 11)?
2. Describe the value of the "mutual faith" of believers (v. 12).

II. SPIRITUAL MATURITY (2 Corinthians 5:18-20; Philippians 3:9-14; Ephesians 4:11-16)

A. Ambassadors for Christ (2 Corinthians 5:18-20)

18. And all things are of God, who hath reconciled us to

himself by Jesus Christ, and hath given to us the ministry of reconciliation;

19. To wit, that God was in Christ, reconciling the world unto himself, not imputing their trespasses unto them; and hath committed unto us the word of reconciliation.

20. Now then we are ambassadors for Christ, as though God did beseech you by us: we pray you in Christ's stead, be ye reconciled to God.

Talk About It:
1. What is "the ministry of reconciliation" (v. 18)?
2. What does it take to be effective "ambassadors for Christ" (v. 20)?

The basis of the Christian's commission is found in the statement "all things are of God." The Christian must regard himself as receiving his or her authority and commission from God. Paul continually asserted in his writings that he was an apostle neither from man nor through man. He was called by God.

The Christian who leads another into the experience of reconciliation to God can never take credit for it. He or she has simply been God's instrument in bringing about this superb transformation. He could no more have done it than a gardener, who plants the seed and tends it, could change a single grain of corn into the perfected plant. God is the Lord of all harvests, spiritual as well as material.

Every Christian is called to be God's agent, God's minister, and is truly, if he or she is faithful, a minister of the gospel. Although the wonderful change of conversion and regeneration is the work of the Holy Spirit, it is also true that in all of this God uses human agents. God uses many methods to effect a change in human nature. He might use a song, a verse read from Scripture, or a sermon. But a human agent must sing the song, read the scripture, or preach the sermon. All of this is done to let people know that "God was in Christ, reconciling the world unto himself." This is the sum of the good news that Christians are to share throughout the world.

In verse 19, there are two reconciliations referred to by Paul. One is accomplished by God, and the other is to be secured by believers. The reconciliation on God's part was accomplished by His doing two things. Paul says, "For he hath made him to be sin for us, who knew no sin" (v. 21); then, as the result of this, the believer's sin will not be counted against him or her (Romans 4:8). The one thing became possible because of the other. In this reconciliation and return of God to the world, a foundation is laid for the return to and reconciliation of people with God.

Seeing the Gospel

A traveler once asked a man in China, "Have you ever heard the gospel?" "No," he replied, "but I have seen it. There is a man in our village who was the terror of his neighborhood. He had a violent temper. He was an opium smoker, a criminal, and a dangerous man. But the gospel has made him gentle and good. He no longer smokes opium. No, I have never heard the gospel, but I have seen it and it is very good."

—Quotable Quotes

Christ's death for us and our humble acceptance of this atonement gave God the opportunity to forget our sins. It is this message that Paul insists has been given to the Christian. He emphasizes that God has committed unto the Christian "the word of reconciliation." Words must be spoken, the gospel must be presented in some way, and the word—written or spoken—must come from some human being. It is a great responsibility, but also a glorious privilege. It is the work of an ambassador.

An ambassador is an officer of the highest rank in the diplomatic service. He or she represents the head of a sovereign state at the court or capital of another country. An ambassador is an honorable and responsible statesman.

As Christ's ambassadors, Christians are given a diplomatic mission. We are to seek people in behalf of Christ to be reconciled to God. This is why we are made ambassadors, to do what was done by the great Ambassador, Jesus Christ.

Christ voluntarily submitted to crucifixion for the personal salvation of every person. The most astonishing and challenging calling that could come to anyone is the calling to be an ambassador, a representative of this Christ who gave Himself for us.

B. Apprehended by Christ (Philippians 3:9-14)

9. And be found in him, not having mine own righteousness, which is of the law, but that which is through the faith of Christ, the righteousness which is of God by faith:

10. That I may know him, and the power of his resurrection, and the fellowship of his sufferings, being made conformable unto his death;

11. If by any means I might attain unto the resurrection of the dead.

12. Not as though I had already attained, either were already perfect: but I follow after, if that I may apprehend that for which also I am apprehended of Christ Jesus.

13. Brethren, I count not myself to have apprehended: but this one thing I do, forgetting those things which are behind, and reaching forth unto those things which are before,

14. I press toward the mark for the prize of the high calling of God in Christ Jesus.

Paul wanted to possess Jesus in a richer and more profound way; he wanted to be deeper in Him and a partaker of His righteousness. Legal righteousness or self-righteousness looks at the Law to justify it, which makes it a righteousness of the Law. The righteousness of Christ comes by faith through Christ. His righteousness enables us to keep His commandments, but that is the result of righteousness and not the sum of it.

In verse 10 Paul proceeds to show Christ as the object of spiritual knowledge and fellowship. When he speaks of *knowing* Him, he does not mean in an intellectual way, but by experience, which is a saving knowledge of Jesus Christ. Christians must know Him in the power of His resurrection, thereby finding fellowship with His sufferings and His death.

Just as the death of Christ was followed by a triumphant resurrection, so resurrection is a part of the Christian's death in

Talk About It:
1. Compare the two types of "righteousness" mentioned in verse 9. What makes one superior?
2. What experiences did Paul want to have (v. 10), and why (v. 11)?
3. What was Paul putting behind himself, and what was his focus?

Christ. Paul did not long for an intellectual understanding of the resurrection, for even an unbeliever might have that, but to experience the power of the resurrection in his own life. This reveals a powerful and continuing circumstance of life in the believer. Our death to sin and life in Christ leads us to a confident hope for resurrection and eternal life.

Verse 12 shows the sincere humility of Paul, who as a Pharisee thought himself to be blameless but now disavowed any claim of perfection. He simply asserted that he was still striving toward perfection. He twice used the word *already*, emphasizing that at this time he could not claim to have attained the high level to which he aspired or the perfection to which he strove.

To apprehend means "to seize." Paul's desire was to seize that lofty estate for which Christ seized him on the Damascus road.

In verse 13 Paul said he had put the past behind him and would not allow it to hinder his progress for the future. This means he would not allow any past experience to hinder his future course; he would not spend time regretting past mistakes or rejoicing over past victories; he would simply press on to victory.

The analogy Paul used was that of a runner in a race. No runner thinks of the ground he has already covered but concentrates on that which lies before him. If he continues to think about some obstacle that is behind him, he will certainly stumble over some obstacle that is before him. He must therefore concentrate on what is ahead and not what is behind.

In the ancient games of Greece, with which the Philippians would have been very familiar, the race was a common sport and the winner's prize was a laurel wreath. The runners strained every muscle and earnestly pressed forward that they might win the prize, which was usually presented by some dignitary or noble person. In the Christian life, Paul was pressing with the same intensity so that he might win the prize that comes from the hand of Jesus Christ. The Christian race is called "the high calling" (v. 14), which suggests the exalted life of devotion and service to which we are called. The word *press* indicates it will not be an easy way but that we must exert diligent effort to attain our goal.

> "We should draw our life's inspirations not from memory but from hope, from what is yet to come."
> —J.R. Miller

perfecting (v. 12)—"equipping" (*NASB*)

C. Gifted for Ministry (Ephesians 4:11-16)
(Ephesians 4:14-16 is not included in the printed text.)
11. And he gave some, apostles; and some, prophets; and some, evangelists; and some, pastors and teachers;
12. For the perfecting of the saints, for the work of the ministry, for the edifying of the body of Christ:

Goals of Discipleship

13. Till we all come in the unity of the faith, and of the knowledge of the Son of God, unto a perfect man, unto the measure of the stature of the fulness of Christ.

In this passage Paul challenges the readers to discipleship. He says that Christ has given gifts to the church so that the church may mature and may defend itself against heresy.

According to Ephesians 4:7, 8, the church officers listed in verse 11 are given by Christ as a gift of grace. This "gift" is different from an occasional token of God's good will that may be received, consumed and forgotten. By this gift Christ establishes order within the church so that the church may mature.

Four things can be said of this gift of grace for the church. First, the gift of grace is provided for all the saints equally. Second, the gift of grace is unfolded in different ministries. Third, the gift consists of particular servants instead of impersonal services. Last, all the ministers listed are persons who fulfill their service by speaking. (This does not exclude other types of ministry in the church. This passage is simply emphasizing these ministries.)

An *apostle* is the first minister that Paul mentioned. In its Biblical usage, the term suggests three meanings: (1) An apostle may be anyone who is sent by Christ to preach the gospel. (2) An apostle is a minister in a place where no one has preached the gospel. (3) An apostle is someone who has seen Christ and has worked in association with the 12 chosen disciples of Jesus. Earlier in the epistle (2:20; 3:5), Paul spoke of an apostle in the latter sense.

A *prophet* applies the gospel to specific contemporary circumstances, makes predictions of the immediate future, and speaks under the direct prompting of the Spirit of God (Acts 11:27, 28; 13:1ff; 21:4, 9).

An *evangelist* is a missionary. Although his or her work is narrower than that of an apostle in preaching in a new region, it does resemble the work of an apostle.

The two terms *pastors* and *teachers* mean the same person. The person could be defined as "a teaching shepherd." The teaching shepherd fulfills pastoral tasks in a congregation.

Three phrases in verse 12 are used to describe the purpose of the spiritual gifts mentioned in verse 11. The ministry of the church is given "for the perfecting [equipping] of the saints." The phrase suggests bringing disciples in the church to a place of maturity so they can fulfill their roles in the body of Christ. Thus, discipleship is not an end in itself. It is for a purpose. It is so the disciples may be fitted "for the work of the ministry." Every Christian has a work of ministry in the body of Christ. The church is built up ["the edifying of the body"] as each member uses his or her particular gifts in spiritual service to their fellow believers.

Talk About It:
1. What are "the saints"—God's people—supposed to be doing, and why (v. 12)?
2. Contrast spiritually mature people with the immature (vv. 13-15).

When the body of Christ is functioning as seen in verse 12, maturity takes place. The maturity is described in three ways (v. 13). First, it is "the unity of the faith." Where the gospel is preached, people of different backgrounds will be in one mind and one accord. Second, "the knowledge of the Son of God" refers to a closer relationship with Him. Third, fellowship with Jesus Christ means the full experience of life in Christ—"attaining to the whole measure of the fullness of Christ" (*NIV*).

There must no longer be the immaturity of children who are unstable in face of the proclaiming of heretical doctrines and fluctuating standards of life. There must be stability in the lives of Christians, as one would expect from adults (v. 14).

When the gospel is taught in love, the disciples will grow in stability and maturity. This growth is "in Christ." It is a development that recognizes that all things find their bearing in relation to Him.

From Christ, as Head, the body derives its whole capacity for growth. Each part of the body functions and grows as it is energized by God in the whole body. Each member does not seek its own growth but the growth of the whole body.

III. GOOD DEEDS (2 Timothy 2:1, 2; 1 Peter 2:11, 12)
A. Son and Teacher (2 Timothy 2:1, 2)
1. Thou therefore, my son, be strong in the grace that is in Christ Jesus.
2. And the things that thou hast heard of me among many witnesses, the same commit thou to faithful men, who shall be able to teach others also.

Timothy was Paul's "son" in the faith, being his convert as a young man. This fatherly advice is good for all young Christians. The tender spiritual growth must be strengthened, not only through receiving God's unmerited favor, but through letting God work through one's life. As one allows himself to be a channel of God's grace to others, the kingdom of God is enlarged; and the one who is the channel becomes a stronger Christian thereby.

Timothy was given wonderful opportunities to learn of Christ through firsthand contacts with people who had known Christ personally. Having heard the gospel and having received its benefits, he should feel a deep responsibility to pass on the benefits of salvation to others.

Writing from prison in Rome, Paul knew that everything depended now on his having been successful in training younger men to carry on after him; and Timothy was one of his key hopes for leadership in the church.

B. Strangers and Pilgrims (1 Peter 2:11, 12)
11. Dearly beloved, I beseech you as strangers and pilgrims,

True Maturity
No human being can consider himself mature if he narrows the use of his efforts, talents, or means to his own personal advantage. The very concept of maturity rests on the degree of inner growth that is characterized by a yearning within the individual to transcend his self-concentration by extending himself into the lives of others.
—Alvin Goeser

Talk About It:
Describe the process laid out in these verses.

"It is not what is poured into the student, but what is planted, that counts."
—Eugene Bertin

abstain from fleshly lusts, which war against the soul;

12. Having your conversation honest among the Gentiles: that, whereas they speak against you as evildoers, they may by your good works, which they shall behold, glorify God in the day of visitation.

The word *strangers* means "foreign settlers or dwellers in a strange land." The word *pilgrims* means "visitors or those who tarry for a time in a foreign country, those who do not settle permanently." Peter used these terms to indicate that his readers were just sojourners on earth; they were actually citizens of the heavenly country.

The apostle warned his readers to avoid those sinful practices that were evident in the country in which they were visiting. The lusts of the flesh are those desires which are a result of humanity's depraved nature.

In verse 12, the word *Gentiles* is used by Peter as a synonym for unsaved people. The suggestion is that unsaved people are watching Christians, speaking against them, and looking for excuses to reject the gospel. Therefore, if unsaved people are to receive a witness from Christ, Christians must live honest lives. They must talk and walk the Christian life. Albert Barnes writes:

> The "visitation" here referred to is undoubtedly that of God; and the reference is to some time when He would make a "visitation" to people for some purpose, and when the fact that the Gentiles had narrowly inspected the conduct of Christians would lead them to honor Him.
>
> The only question is, to what visitation of that kind the apostle referred. The prevailing use of the word in the New Testament would seem to lead us to suppose that the "visitation" referred to was designed to confer favors rather than to inflict punishment, and indeed the word seems to have somewhat of a technical character, and to have been familiarly used by Christians to denote God's coming to people to bless them; to pour out His Spirit upon them; to revive religion. This seems to me to be its meaning here; and, if so, the sense is, that when God appeared among people to accompany the preaching of the gospel with saving power, the result of the observed conduct of Christians would be to lead those around them to honor Him by giving up their hearts to Him.

CONCLUSION

Christ does not offer a level of salvation by which one barely makes it through heaven's gate. Instead, just as He said "Follow Me" to His original 12 disciples, He is still saying "Follow Me" to everyone today who will hear His voice. He is calling us

---

Gentiles (v. 12)—
pagans (*NIV*)

Talk About It:
1. How are Christians "strangers and pilgrims" (v. 11)?
2. What is the Christian's responsibility to the unsaved people around them (v. 12)?

"It is right for the church to be in the world; it is wrong for the world to be in the church. A boat in water is good; that is what boats are for. However, water inside the boat causes it to sink."

—Harold Lindsell

---

to a life of Christian character, spiritual maturity, and good deeds. Discipleship is not an option.

GOLDEN TEXT CHALLENGE

"HEREIN IS MY FATHER GLORIFIED, THAT YE BEAR MUCH FRUIT; SO SHALL YE BE MY DISCIPLES" (John 15:8).

If the Christian is not careful, he will become so absorbed in religious activity—doing good deeds—that he will leave no time for cultivation of the spiritual life. As a result, he will fail to remain in intimate spiritual relationship with Jesus. Then he will bear even less spiritual fruit (which, remember, is not Christian *activity* but Christian *character*, the automatic result of the life of Jesus functioning within us). And as he bears less fruit, his Father in heaven will receive less glory—most regrettably since the primary aim of the Christian should be to glorify God. If the Christian disciple would realize his necessary aim of giving the maximum amount of glory to God, he must be fruitful—through interrelationship with Jesus the Son and God the Father.

The final clause of verse 8 reveals the ultimate reward of the believer who is glorifying God in the bearing of "much fruit"— that believer will be Jesus' *disciple*. He will be a learner in close association with the Master—modeling after Him, listening to Him, growing in Him. This relationship, moreover, brings the ultimate joy, both now and hereafter, and the highest fulfillment, on earth and in heaven.

Daily Devotions:
M. Thirsting for God
Psalm 63:1-5
T. Advice for Godly Living
Proverbs 22:1-6
W. Be Contrite and Lowly
Isaiah 57:15-19
T. The Spirit, Our Teacher
John 14:23-26
F. Becoming Like Christ
Philippians 2:1-5
S. Love One Another
Colossians 3:12-16

Goals of Discipleship

Cost of Discipleship

Matthew 6:24; 20:25-28; Luke 14:25-33; 17:7-10; 2 Corinthians 4:5;
Philippians 1:27-29; 2 Timothy 1:11, 12; 1 Peter 2:19-23

INTRODUCTION

The self-sacrifice which Jesus practiced is the standard for His followers. Self-renunciation is more than the denial of something that is dear to us. The cross was an instrument of death to Jesus. Unfortunately, to some people the cross is merely a charm or an article for adornment; but to those who follow the example of Jesus, it is a symbol of death to the old life and a testimony of our fellowship with Jesus.

In Mark 8:35, Jesus uttered one of His great paradoxes: to gain life was to lose life. This calls for a radical adjustment in the thinking of His self-seeking disciples, past and present. People of the world try to find life in materialism, but people of the cross assume the responsibility of making the world morally fit and look to the future for their reward.

To "take up the cross" denotes the beginning of holiness in life. The objects of importance to the world become trivial to the life of the cross. The focus of the life of the cross is on Christ and not on accumulation or consumption of things.

Wealth is disvalued by the Bible. It is an incident to life, not an essential. The true "pearl of great price" is life under God's rule. All other treasures are handled with a detachment that neither seeks wealth nor despises it. Such is spiritual maturity. The ability to be rich without greediness or pride, or to be poor without covetousness or anxiety, is indeed a blessing. Those who have this attitude live in God's kingdom.

Unit Theme:
Christian Discipleship

Central Truth:
Discipleship calls for a costly commitment to Christ.

Focus:
Consider the costs of discipleship and commit to follow Christ.

Context:
Selected New Testament passages about carrying one's cross

Golden Text:
"Whosoever he be of you that forsaketh not all that he hath, he cannot be my disciple" (Luke 14:33).

Study Outline:
I. Sacrifice
(Matthew 6:24; 20:25-28; Luke 14:25-33)
II. Service
(Luke 17:7-10; 2 Corinthians 4:5)
III. Suffering
(Philippians 1:27-29; 2 Timothy 1:11, 12; 1 Peter 2:19-23)

I. SACRIFICE (Matthew 6:24; 20:25-28; Luke 14:25-33)
A. One Master (Matthew 6:24)

24. No man can serve two masters: for either he will hate the one, and love the other; or else he will hold to the one, and despise the other. Ye cannot serve God and mammon.

Jesus explains the choice between two masters. It is a choice between God and mammon, that is, between the Creator and material possessions. We cannot serve both.

In this verse Jesus presents a picture of a slave and a slave owner. A person can work for two employers without conflict, but a person cannot be the slave of two owners. He must be owned by one or the other. It is the same with us. We are either owned by God or our own creation.

B. Suffering Servant (Matthew 20:25-28)

25. But Jesus called them unto him, and said, Ye know that the princes of the Gentiles exercise dominion over them, and they that are great exercise authority upon them.

26. But it shall not be so among you: but whosoever will be great among you, let him be your minister;

27. And whosoever will be chief among you, let him be your servant:

28. Even as the Son of man came not to be ministered unto, but to minister, and to give his life a ransom for many.

Dominion and authority were eagerly pursued by the rulers of the Gentiles. This was common practice in the kingdoms of the earth in that day, and even today. This is the way of the non-Christian world. The disciples knew no other way to conduct government and maintain authority. Holding a false view of Christ's kingdom, the disciples assumed it would be like all others in magnifying people of authority.

Instead of adopting the lofty principle that governed the life of Christ, and which He enjoins upon His disciples, that of ministry, many adopt the opposite, that of "being ministered unto." They wish to *get* rather than to *give*, and live under the principle of everyone for himself.

Two disciples, James and John, asked for dominion over the others in a temporal kingdom (vv. 20, 21), but Jesus plainly told them that in His spiritual kingdom there is no such dominion for anybody. He indirectly conceded, however, that greatness of the right kind is possible in His kingdom, but it is based upon a different principle, that of ministry. Ambition for power degrades the disciples of the meek and lowly One, who taught "it is more blessed to give than to receive" (Acts 20:35).

Cost of Discipleship

James and John went to Jesus to achieve greatness by appointment to seats in a temporal kingdom. They were humbled by His statement that if they ever attained what they sought, it would be through lowly, unselfish service to their brethren. The rule of Christian living, reduced to its simplest terms, is this: Get others to minister unto us as little as possible, and minister unto them as much as we can. Make the fewest possible calls upon others, and render them maximum service ourselves.

In Matthew 20:28 Jesus sets Himself before His disciples as the great pattern of humility and service. When the Son of God came into the world, He did not appear in pomp and splendor, but in the lowly form of a servant. He was ministered to as a poor man by His friends, for there were those who cared for His needs, but none ministered to Him as a great man, the ruler of an earthly kingdom. He came to minister to those in distress; He became the servant of the sick and diseased, took pains to serve them, and gave His life as a ransom for all. He lived as a servant and died as a sacrifice. Our lives were forfeited to divine justice by sin, but Jesus, by surrendering His life, made atonement for sin and rescued us from ruin.

> "The high destiny of the individual is to serve rather than to rule."
> —Albert Einstein

C. True Disciple (Luke 14:25-27)

25. And there went great multitudes with him: and he turned, and said unto them,

26. If any man come to me, and hate not his father, and mother, and wife, and children, and brethren, and sisters, yea, and his own life also, he cannot be my disciple.

27. And whosoever doth not bear his cross, and come after me, cannot be my disciple.

As Jesus left the Pharisee's house, a great crowd followed Him. Turning about, Jesus addressed them and stated frankly *what it would cost them to follow Him.* Jesus in no wise despises or ignores the fundamental relationships of the home, the family, or of society; and it is only a twisted scheme of interpretation that tries to reverse the order of nature in this regard. But Jesus plainly teaches us that we are placed in more than a temporal context; we are also placed in the context of eternity. This confronts us with the even greater fact of our relationship to God.

Loyalty to Jesus Christ must take precedence over every other relationship and loyalty of life, even over one's own life. Compare Paul's statement in Acts 20:24: "Neither count I my life dear unto myself." No relationship of life may therefore compete with or take precedence over one's relationship to Christ; all of these must be "hated," that is to say, loved less, for the sake of Him whom we love supremely. Failure to crown Him Lord of all is failure to crown Him Lord at all. We must carry our cross.

Talk About It:
1. According to verse 26, how much must we love Jesus?
2. What does it mean to carry one's cross (v. 27)?

Keep in mind that a "crossbearer" in Roman society was generally a condemned criminal. The term signified utmost contempt and infamy. Yet it was the cross that Jesus kept in constant view as He journeyed toward Jerusalem during the last six months of His earthly ministry (cf. Matthew 16:21-25; Luke 9:21-24). And he who would follow Jesus must, like Him, "bear his cross"—and the pronoun *his* is emphatic and intensive, meaning "his *own* cross."

What this may eventually mean for us, as it did for the apostle Paul, is that "the world is crucified unto us, and we are crucified unto the world" (see Galatians 6:14). Cross-bearing for Jesus' sake involves vastly more than the sacrifice of certain externals; it involves death to self and all of its claims to priority.

> "If Jesus Christ be God and died for me, then no sacrifice can be too great for me to make for Him."
> —C.T. Studd

D. The Cost (vv. 28-33)

(Luke 14:28-32 is not included in the printed text.)

33. So likewise, whosoever he be of you that forsaketh not all that he hath, he cannot be my disciple.

Watchtowers were commonly found on city walls and in vineyards. The building of such a tower involved much time and money. No intelligent person would undertake to build a tower either for himself or for another without first calculating the cost carefully (v. 28). An unfinished tower would be worthless and become the laughingstock of the community. Just as a prudent builder will consider his resources against ultimate costs, so a genuine disciple, said Jesus, will consider the cost of discipleship, for it is indeed serious business to follow Christ.

He who rushes into tower building, or any other secular enterprise, without first counting the cost will sooner or later run into trouble. Jesus assumes that the builder in this case has done just that. The foundation is laid, but the man has exhausted his resources! The work must stop and the workmen must be discharged. To add to the builder's misery, the general public passes uncomplimentary judgment both upon the unfinished tower and on the shortsighted builder. The word *mock* (v. 29) means "to scoff at; to sneer." The word *man*, or *fellow* (*NIV*), is a term of utter contempt, accentuated by a sarcastic use of the pronoun *this* (v. 30).

In verse 31 we have a king whose domain is threatened by the fear of invasion. He realizes he must grapple with forces that may be superior to his own. He takes counsel, therefore, and deliberates with himself: "Can I match my 10,000 against the enemy's 20,000?" He realizes that success under such circumstances is not altogether impossible, yet very unlikely. The implication for our Lord's disciples is that in spiritual warfare they are ever confronted by evil forces that are most formidable (cf. Ephesians 6:12). Christians must take into full account the forces of evil that are arrayed against them!

Talk About It:
1. When should a person consider the cost of following Christ?
2. What is the cost of discipleship?

Verse 32 of the text shows the king is worried, realizing that his forces are inadequate. One alternative remains: He decides to send "an ambassage"—older men of sound judgment, ambassadors—to negotiate on a footing of equality with the invader. "Conditions of peace" suggests preliminary steps leading to a peaceful solution of a controversial issue. In any event, the implication is that the conditions of Christian discipleship must be faced realistically.

Our Lord's final appeal to that multitude was addressed to the individual: "whoever of you" (v. 33, *NKJV*). Here compare His last appeal to the Laodicean church: "If any man hear my voice . . ." (Revelation 3:20). Looking that enthusiastic crowd straight in the eye, Jesus challenged them: "Are any of you prepared to follow Me under the terms just defined? Then you must be ready to forsake, renounce all other claims of self." The word *forsaketh* was formerly used in Greek military camps to indicate that a soldier, having enlisted, now separates himself from all other concerns, says farewell to friends and relatives (cf. Luke 9:61), and leaves behind all his personal belongings. This is the language with which our Lord defines Christian discipleship. Are *we* prepared to face up to the implications?

II. SERVICE (Luke 17:7-10; 2 Corinthians 4:5)
A. Just Our Duty (Luke 17:7-10)

7. But which of you, having a servant plowing or feeding cattle, will say unto him by and by, when he is come from the field, Go and sit down to meat?

8. And will not rather say unto him, Make ready wherewith I may sup, and gird thyself, and serve me, till I have eaten and drunken; and afterward thou shalt eat and drink?

9. Doth he thank that servant because he did the things that were commanded him? I trow not.

10. So likewise ye, when ye shall have done all those things which are commanded you, say, We are unprofitable servants: we have done that which was our duty to do.

Jesus asks you, the listener, to put yourself in the place of the master in this parable. He says to imagine you have a servant who has been working hard in the field all day. Perhaps he has been plowing your field, or maybe he has been taking care of your sheep.

When the servant comes into the house, what will you, the master, say to him "at once" (v. 7, *NKJV*)? Will you say, "Make yourself comfortable, sit down and eat"? Or instead will you say to the servant, "Prepare my supper, get yourself ready and wait on me while I eat and drink; after that you may eat and drink"? (v. 8, *NIV*).

trow (v. 9)—think

Talk About It:
What is the primary point of this parable?

The answer is obvious. Your servant must first serve you, the master. And when he finishes feeding you, he doesn't expect you to thank him. It's not that you're a harsh master; it's just that servants *serve*—that's their responsibility.

In verse 10 Jesus applies this parable to our service to Christ, the Master of all. We are called "unprofitable servants." This means we cannot gain any favor with God by our Christian service, nor do we put Him under any obligation by serving Him. It also means that our work for God does not benefit or profit Him. He doesn't need our aid. As Eliphaz asked in Job 22:2: "Can a man be of benefit to God? Can even a wise man benefit him?" (*NIV*).

Our service to God is made possible only because He gives us the ability and opportunity to minister to Him. All we do is our duty to Him, but it can never begin to repay all He has done for us. If our service brings praise to God, that should be enough for us.

Just as the servant in the parable finally was able to rest and eat, so the day is coming when God's faithful servants will enter into eternal celebration with God. Until then, we must serve Him lovingly, faithfully and untiringly through the ability He gives us.

B. Not Ourselves (2 Corinthians 4:5)

5. For we preach not ourselves, but Christ Jesus the Lord; and ourselves your servants for Jesus' sake.

Paul was under no illusion about his own importance. The light of the gospel did not originate in him, but in Christ—the same Christ Jesus who had brought physical light to the eyes of Bartimaeus. Paul's only place was as a "slave" to those to whom he ministered in the name of Christ.

It was God who had "commanded the light to shine out of darkness" in the Creation (v. 6). This same God had brought light into the heart of Paul when He struck him down with a bright light on the road to Damascus (Acts 9:3, 4). The purpose of Paul's conversion was that he might share that light with others. It was a light which had its source in God as seen through the person of Jesus Christ, and it was a light which could dispel even the blindness imposed by Satan if people would only trust Christ as Bartimaeus had.

III. SUFFERING (Philippians 1:27-29; 2 Timothy 1:11, 12; 1 Peter 2:19-23)

A. Suffering for Christ (Philippians 1:27-29)

27. Only let your conversation be as it becometh the gospel of Christ: that whether I come and see you, or else be absent, I may hear of your affairs, that ye stand fast in one spirit, with one mind striving together for the faith of the gospel;

"We who lead often overlook that the true place of Christ-like leadership is out in the crowd rather than up at the head table."
—C. Gene Wilkes

Talk About It:
1. What kind of preaching honors God?
2. What is the right attitude for a preacher to have?

conversation (v. 27)—"manner of life" (*ASV*)

Cost of Discipleship

28. And in nothing terrified by your adversaries: which is to them an evident token of perdition, but to you of salvation, and that of God.

29. For unto you it is given in the behalf of Christ, not only to believe on him, but also to suffer for his sake.

perdition (v. 28)—"destruction" (*NASB*)

Paul urged the Philippians to have the same obedience of faith that he had. They were not to base their obedience to the gospel or faithfulness to Christ upon whether Paul should be delivered or not. They should determine to be steadfast whatever happened to Paul. That is the essence of Christian living—to be without condition, without reserve, and without hesitation. Faith in Christ must stand of itself, nothing held back, without being hindered by disappointment or adversity or discarded by prosperity. The Christian must believe in Jesus Christ and not be bent away from Him by circumstance.

Verse 29 teaches it is the lot of Christians both to believe on Christ and to suffer for Him. There will be adversaries to the faith, to be certain, but we must manifest unflinching courage in the face of all opposition. The adversity may be disappointment or discouragement or even physical harm, but we are to face them all with steadfast courage and resolve we do so for Christ's sake.

Talk About It:
1. How should Christians conduct themselves, and how can they do so (v. 27)?
2. How should believers respond to opposition, why, and what will the result be (vv. 28, 29)?

B. Steadfast in Suffering (2 Timothy 1:11, 12)

11. Whereunto I am appointed a preacher, and an apostle, and a teacher of the Gentiles.

12. For the which cause I also suffer these things: nevertheless I am not ashamed: for I know whom I have believed, and am persuaded that he is able to keep that which I have committed unto him against that day.

The hope of eternal life is a prominent promise of the gospel. It is the one great fact that gives Christians hope above all else (1 Corinthians 15:19). It was to this very gospel that Paul was appointed to be an apostle to the Gentiles. He gladly went forth into heathen lands and preached to Asians, Greeks and Romans the wonderful tidings of eternal life. He preached to people with morbid superstitions about vengeful gods and the finality of death. He preached to them about the resurrection of Christ and the hope of eternal life for His followers. These were exciting, glad tidings, which some heard and received, and others rejected with mockery and abuse (Acts 17:32).

Verse 12 of the text is probably the strongest assertion of faith to be found in the New Testament. Paul was suffering imprisonment in Rome because of his espousal of the Christian faith. He was not ashamed of this or intimidated in any way, because he was certain in the steps he had taken. Notice the numerous positive acts that lead to his certainty. He said, "I

Talk About It:
1. What price did Paul pay for being a minister of the gospel?
2. Why was Paul unashamed?

know . . . I have believed . . . [I] am persuaded . . . I have committed." Paul's certainty was not the product of passive attitudes and emotions, but he had made positive steps that resulted in absolute confidence.

First, he committed his life to Jesus Christ. Next, this commitment led to full persuasion and firmness of faith. This gave him the certainty of knowledge which eliminated shame or intimidation. The point of his statement is that one does not come to such triumphant attitudes by happenstance. It is a progression that begins with total commitment to the Lord. By committing ourselves to Him, we go step-by-step to life-sustaining assurance in Him.

It is difficult to intimidate a man who knows without doubt what the situation is. Even bound with shackles in a subterranean dungeon in the Mamertine prison, Paul was not intimidated. He was aware that he would probably be executed (4:6), but he still faced the future with confidence. He may have had the natural fear of dying, which is a dread of the unknown, but even this could not intimidate him. His life had reached the highest level of spiritual certainty, and that position began with his full commitment to the cause of Jesus Christ.

Talk About It:
How should the Christian respond to "suffering wrongfully"? Why?

What I Expected
A soldier in the East Indies, a stalwart man who had been a prizefighter, was a terror to his regiment until he was converted. Two months afterward, some of those who had been afraid of him before, began to ridicule him. One of them threw a basin of hot soup over him. The whole company gazed in breathless silence. After the soldier had wiped his scalded breast, he turned

C. Undeserved Suffering (1 Peter 2:19, 20)

19. For this is thankworthy, if a man for conscience toward God endure grief, suffering wrongfully.

20. For what glory is it, if, when ye be buffeted for your faults, ye shall take it patiently? but if, when ye do well, and suffer for it, ye take it patiently, this is acceptable with God.

Christ suffered unjustly, but His suffering brought our salvation. By our endurance of unjust suffering we identify ourselves with Him. It is not hard to endure punishment for wrongs committed, but it is very hard to endure unjust punishment. The Lord understands this and grants us His comforting presence.

D. Perfect in Suffering (vv. 21-23)

21. For even hereunto were ye called: because Christ also suffered for us, leaving us an example, that ye should follow his steps:

22. Who did no sin, neither was guile found in his mouth:

23. Who, when he was reviled, reviled not again; when he suffered, he threatened not; but committed himself to him that judgeth righteously.

The way of suffering is the way Christ went. If we follow Him we must expect to suffer some, too. His steps lead on; we are free to go forward or turn back. Let's remember that we suffered when we were in our sins also! The sinner's suffering goes unrewarded, but the Christian's suffering leads to eternal life and the end of all suffering.

Verse 22 reminds us Christ's life is the perfect example. Even in His speech He uttered no falsehood, no haughty retorts, no insults.

The tongue, though a small muscle, is the strongest in the body. The Bible says it is hard to tame (James 3:8); in fact, only God can tame it. Man will always be "tongue-tied to his sins" till he yields to God.

When a person meets insult with insult and rough talk with rough talk, he is yielding to temptation and leaning on his own resources to combat wrong treatment. The Christian way is to turn away wrath with a soft answer (Proverbs 15:1) or not to answer at all, enduring silently the bitter treatment. We need to commit ourselves to God and His intelligent care. He has His own way of dealing with the sinner who does not repent.

CONCLUSION

Jesus does not want people trying to follow Him carelessly and recklessly. Anyone who wishes to follow Christ should consider carefully the requirements and consequences of doing so. Unless we are prepared to pay the full price, go all the way, and commit everything to Christ, neither our wish nor our start will be of any avail.

GOLDEN TEXT CHALLENGE

"WHOSOEVER HE BE OF YOU THAT FORSAKETH NOT ALL THAT HE HATH, HE CANNOT BE MY DISCIPLE" (Luke 14:33).

The meaning of this statement is absolutely clear. It is enough to do away with all halfhearted service to Christ; all lukewarm commitment to Him is insufficient for His service and worship. We must surrender to Him our possessions, our desires, our plans, our ideals, our affairs, and even our interests. In short, our lives must be totally committed to Him.

In supposed obedience to this requirement, some have forsaken society in order to live for Him as hermits or recluses. This misses the point of Christian living entirely. We may have to give up worldly possessions, or even friends, especially if our service to Him requires going into distant lands. We must be prepared for any sacrifice that may be required of us. The principal point, however, is that we so commit ourselves to Him that we become spiritually and mentally free from worldly-mindedness, frivolity, covetousness and selfishness in order to serve Him absolutely.

around and said, "This is what I expected when I became a Christian!"
—*Elim Evangel*

Talk About It:
1. Why didn't Christ retaliate or make threats against His enemies?
2. Where did Christ place His trust?

Daily Devotions:
M. Disdain of the Godly
1 Samuel 17:42-46
T. Prosperity of the Wicked
Job 12:4-9
W. The Righteous Unmoved
Psalm 55:18-23
T. Suffering Brings Glory
Romans 8:14-18
F. Choosing to Suffer
Hebrews 11:23-26
S. Patience in Unjust Suffering
1 Peter 2:19-21

Discipleship Relationships

Matthew 12:49, 50; John 13:34, 35; 15:1-11; 2 Corinthians 6:14 through 7:1; 1 Thessalonians 3:12, 13; 1 John 3:1-3; 4:7-12

Unit Theme:
Christian Discipleship

Central Truth:
Discipleship flows from relationships with Christ and fellow Christians.

Focus:
Demonstrate that discipleship emerges from relationship with Christ and fellow Christians and strengthen those connections.

Context:
Selected New Testament passages regarding the Christian's relationships

Golden Text:
"Beloved, if God so loved us, we ought also to love one another" (1 John 4:11).

Study Outline:
I. United by Obedience (Matthew 12:49, 50; John 13:34, 35; 15:1-11)
II. Identified by Separation (2 Corinthians 6:14-18; 7:1; 1 Thessalonians 3:12, 13)
III. Connected by Love (1 John 3:1-3; 4:7-12)

INTRODUCTION

Friendship is a gamble. Would it be better to close the door to our souls and shield ourselves from the pain that may come from daring to love? The answer, of course, is this: The joy of friendship is worth every risk!

We turn to our great God for the example. Our world was friendless and hopeless. God could have doomed us to hell, but His grace redeemed us. Real friendships are based on grace. No one deserves friends; they come to us by grace.

So God became one of us, stepping out of His heavenly world into our circumstances. He robed Himself in human flesh and walked among men. The world welcomed its best friend into a stable, rather than a palace. His own family rejected Him. Even His best friends fled in terror before His impending death. Finally, Jesus, the Friend of sinners, was nailed to a cross and pierced by a spear. Such pain and agony no human being will ever know. Whether praying alone in Gethsemane or dying alone on the cross, our Lord knew what it was to hurt.

Was it worth the trip from heaven to earth, from God to man, and from glory to the cross? Scripture gives us His answer: "Greater love has no one than this, that he lay down his life for his friends" (John 15:13, *NIV*).

The author of Hebrews wrote: "Looking unto Jesus the author and finisher of our faith; who for the joy that was set before him endured the cross, despising the shame, and is set down at the right hand of the throne of God" (12:2). Jesus sacrificed His own comfort that we might be His friends forever.

The joy of true friendship is best realized when we are willing to suffer with and for our friends. In the end, love wins and friendships triumph. Take the risk. The pain is worth the gain.
—Ron Phillips

I. UNITED BY OBEDIENCE (Matthew 12:49, 50; John 13:34, 35; 15:1-11)

A. The Disciple's Family (Matthew 12:49, 50)

49. And he stretched forth his hand toward his disciples, and said, Behold my mother and my brethren!

50. For whosoever shall do the will of my Father which is in heaven, the same is my brother, and sister, and mother.

Jesus is surrounded by a huge crowd of people who are following Him because of the healings He has been performing. Among the crowd are religious critics watching His every move and scrutinizing His every word to try to undermine Him. As Jesus continues to minister, someone brings Him this message: "Look, Your mother and Your brothers are standing outside, seeking to speak with You" (v. 47, *NKJV*).

Mary and her other sons, all born after Jesus' birth, were trying to pull Jesus aside because of their concern for Him. "Reasons for their concern are obvious. Previously, Jesus' preaching at Nazareth had forced the family to move to Capernaum (Luke 4:16-31; John 2:12). Now He had brought the Pharisees into open and blasphemous opposition. In addition, friends had reported that the strain of this ministry was affecting His health (Mark 3:21)" (*The Wycliffe Bible Commentary*).

Jesus' reply was astonishing. He pointed to His disciples and said, "Here are my mother and my brothers!" (Matthew 12:49, *NIV*). No, Jesus was not belittling His mother. He always showed Mary love and respect, even as He hung on the cross (John 19:26, 27). Instead, Jesus was declaring that He has a family whose ties are closer than natural bonds. His spiritual family is made up of His followers, and they are made one through the indwelling of the Holy Spirit.

B. The Disciple's Mark (John 13:34, 35)

34. A new commandment I give unto you, That ye love one another; as I have loved you, that ye also love one another.

35. By this shall all men know that ye are my disciples, if ye have love one to another.

The mark of the true believer is his or her love for fellow Christians. This is the message of Jesus in these verses. Other aspects of the Christian's life, such as faith, power and prayer, are not mentioned here. As vital as these qualities are, the characteristic which identifies the believer is love.

The phrase "new commandment" did not indicate a commandment that had never existed before. It was new in relationship to the old covenant and the law in the Old Testament. The newness was made possible because of the work of Christ. His work established this new commandment.

Talk About It:
Who would Jesus say is *not* a member of His family, and why not?

"It is not said that *after* keeping God's commandments, but *in* keeping them there is great reward [Psalm 19:11]. God has linked these two things together, and no man can separate them—obedience and power."
—**F.W. Robertson**

Talk About It:
Why is love the greatest evidence that a person is a disciple of Christ?

The love Christ spoke of here is a commandment predicated on the love of Christ. His redemptive work on the cross is the drawing force behind the love of the Christian. As each believer looks at the love Christ displayed, the true motivation and standard by which he or she is to love others is seen. The love a Christian shows for others is a clear manifestation of the presence of Christ within.

Jesus knew that His departure was near. Therefore, He stressed the importance of the believers' love for one another after He was gone. Up to that time the disciples were known as those who had physically walked with Jesus. After Jesus' departure, they would be known by their love for one another.

C. The Disciple's Source (15:1-8)
(John 15:2-6 is not included in the printed text.)
1. I am the true vine, and my Father is the husbandman.
7. If ye abide in me, and my words abide in you, ye shall ask what ye will, and it shall be done unto you.
8. Herein is my Father glorified, that ye bear much fruit; so shall ye be my disciples.

In John 15, Jesus spoke of the spiritual union He has with His followers. But first, He emphasized that He is the *true* vine. The word *true* in this usage does not mean opposition to that which is false, but rather that Christ is the perfect, essential, and enduring reality, beside which other lights are but faint reflections.

The Father is a divine "husbandman" (gardener, vinedresser), showing loving concern for the branches of the Vine. This indicates His protecting care. His eye is upon and His hand tends to the weakest tendril and tenderest shoot. Identifying the Father in this role also suggests His watchfulness. Nothing escapes His eye.

The faithfulness of the Father is emphasized in the words "he purgeth it" (v. 2). No branch is allowed to run wild. He spares neither the spray nor the pruning knife. When a branch is fruitless, He tends it; if it is bearing fruit, He purges it so that it may bring forth more fruit.

Verse 4 presents Christ as the supplier and the source of all the life His branches have. This life is the gift of the Vine, and the branch has no other life. And because the Vine gives life to the branch, it is not merely the same *kind* of life; it *is* the same life.

Christians draw from Christ a continual supply of grace, strength and ability. They are joined to Christ by faith and united with Him in a mysterious union through the Holy Spirit. It is because of this relationship that they can stand strong in the faith and run the Christian race. It is all made possible through a vital union with their spiritual head, Jesus Christ.

"Love and a cough cannot be hid."
—George Herbert

Talk About It:
1. Describe God the Father's role as the "husbandman" of Christians.
2. Describe Christ's role as "the vine."
3. Describe the believers' role as "branches."

Verse 6 emphasizes the possibility of losing the vital contact with Jesus Christ that maintains the spiritual life. Words are not strong enough to describe the terrible consequences of not abiding in Christ, of refusing to live the life of faith in Him. The result will be like that of fruitless and dead branches of a vine. They are soon withered and gathered as firewood to be burned.

Those who abide in Christ do not pray in vain (v. 7). No work is too hard, and no difficulty is insurmountable. When individuals abide in Christ, they receive when they ask and they find when they seek.

Believers should bring forth fruit because it glorifies God (v. 8). It will recommend our experience to others and cause the world to honor the God who has such servants. It also gives real evidence that we are genuine disciples, and our lives will clearly prove that we are followers of Christ.

D. The Disciple's Joy (vv. 9-11)

9. As the Father hath loved me, so have I loved you: continue ye in my love.

10. If ye keep my commandments, ye shall abide in my love; even as I have kept my Father's commandments, and abide in his love.

11. These things have I spoken unto you, that my joy might remain in you, and that your joy might be full.

The uniting bond of fellowship between Christ and the Father is love. It is also the uniting bond between Jesus and His followers.

Talk About It:
What is the connection between love and joy?

The words "continue ye in my love" may be viewed as a command as well as a reminder. Jude said, "Keep yourselves in the love of God" (v. 21). Our fellowship with Christ is a fellowship of love, and obedience is the basis of this fellowship.

The secret of a happy and joyful relationship with Jesus Christ lies in the keeping of His commandments. Holy living and the assurance of fellowship with Christ are closely connected. As J.C. Ryle states, "He that expects assurance while he neglects Christ's commandments and gives way to daily inconsistencies of temper and conduct is expecting what he will never get" (*Expository Thoughts on the Gospels*).

Christ kept the Father's commandments perfectly and abides in the Father's love continually. Our attempts to keep His commandments and abide in His love are so imperfect. But His example is one that we must constantly strive to follow. It brings us joy.

Robert Law, in his book *The Emotions of Jesus*, says, "Unhappiness can never beget happiness, nor sickness health. Jesus came with glad tidings, came as the divine Physician into the world's vast hospital. He is the Lord of joy, and His crowning desire for His servants is that they may enter into the joy of their Lord."

William Barclay stated, "However hard the Christian way is, it is, both in the traveling and in the goal, the way of joy. There is always a joy in doing the right thing. When we have evaded some duty or some task, when at last we set our hand to it, joy comes to us. The Christian is the man of joy; the Christian is the laughing cavalier of Christ. A gloomy Christian is a contradiction in terms, and nothing in all religious history has done Christianity more harm than its connection with black clothes and long faces."

II. IDENTIFIED BY SEPARATION (2 Corinthians 6:14-18; 7:1; 1 Thessalonians 3:12, 13)

A. Come Out (2 Corinthians 6:14-18; 7:1)

6:14. Be ye not unequally yoked together with unbelievers: for what fellowship hath righteousness with unrighteousness? and what communion hath light with darkness?

15. And what concord hath Christ with Belial? or what part hath he that believeth with an infidel?

16. And what agreement hath the temple of God with idols? for ye are the temple of the living God; as God hath said, I will dwell in them, and walk in them; and I will be their God, and they shall be my people.

17. Wherefore come out from among them, and be ye separate, saith the Lord, and touch not the unclean thing; and I will receive you,

18. And will be a Father unto you, and ye shall be my sons and daughters, saith the Lord Almighty.

7:1. Having therefore these promises, dearly beloved, let us cleanse ourselves from all filthiness of the flesh and spirit, perfecting holiness in the fear of God.

Christians are warned not to marry or have an intimate friendship with non-Christians, called here being "unequally yoked." The marriage of a Christian to a non-Christian is immediately beset with difficulties that threaten failure. Marriage creates the closest tie on earth, that of a husband to a wife; they are no longer two, but one flesh; they must share a common life with common goals, common purposes, and common directions. Yet all of these things are different with a Christian and a non-Christian, so that such a marriage faces enormous struggles. Usually, either the Christian will fail in His Christian testimony or the non-Christian will be converted to Christian faith.

The fusion of two such persons is as difficult as the fusion of light and darkness. That is an impossibility, for the result is a compromise of the two, and what remains is neither. There can

---

"Joy is not gush; joy is not jolliness. Joy is perfect acquiescence in God's will because the soul delights itself in God himself."
—H.W. Webb-Peploe

Belial (v. 15)—"all anti-Christian pollutions personified" (Fausett)

Talk About It:
1. What is the danger of being "unequally yoked" (6:14) with an unbeliever?
2. According to verse 16, what does it mean to live as "the temple of God"?
3. What is "the unclean thing" (v. 17)?
4. What should motivate us to "cleanse ourselves" (7:1)?

be no fellowship between one who wants to enthrone Christ as Lord of all, and one whose life is set against Him. The result of marriage between a believer and a nonbeliever is almost inevitably misfortune.

Paul carries the analogy much deeper here by observing that no fellowship is possible between Christ and Belial (that is, the devil). Christ came to the earth to destroy the work of the devil, and the devil endeavored to kill Christ throughout the years of His earthly ministry. Fellowship between the two is therefore incomprehensible, as is close fellowship between sinners and Christians.

In verse 16, Paul reminds the readers they are the temple of the living God. The temple of God has no agreement with idols, for the function of idol worship is hostile to the worship of God. If harmonious worship of Jesus and Satan is impossible in a temple, it is equally impossible in a human being, for every Christian is the temple of the Lord.

God has said that He dwells in Christians, walks in them, is their living God, and they are His people (see Leviticus 26:12). The intimacy suggested here is both beautiful and absolute. A true Christian cannot become one in heart with an unbeliever. For such an arrangement to exist, the Christian partner must be so in name more than in fact, and must be willing to make innumerable compromises.

The solution is to "come out from among them, and be ye separate" (2 Corinthians 6:17; cf. Isaiah 52:11). The purpose of this stern admonition is for Christians to separate themselves from sinful practices. When we separate our lives from the profane and the unholy, we have the assurance that God is our Father and we are His children (2 Corinthians 6:18; cf. Jeremiah 31:1, 9).

Since we have "these promises" (2 Corinthians 7:1)—the promises that God will live in us, be our God, and we shall be His sons and daughters—we must "purify ourselves from everything that contaminates body and spirit, perfecting holiness out of reverence for God" (*NIV*). This takes concerted effort on our part. We are to lay aside sinful actions and conquer sinful thinking through the enablement of God's Spirit. "Perfecting holiness" indicates this is an ongoing process that must be continued until completion, carried out under a "wholesome fear of God" (*TLB*).

B. Draw Close (1 Thessalonians 3:12)

12. And the Lord make you to increase and abound in love one toward another, and toward all men, even as we do toward you.

Paul recognized that God was the source to which the Thessalonians must look if they were to fulfill the law of love in their daily life. The demonstration of their love had to begin

Talk About It:
What example did Paul set for the Thessalonians to follow?

within the brotherhood. If they wanted to let the world outside know what Christianity was all about, they needed to show them the love of Christ among themselves as brothers and sisters in the Lord.

The same principle holds true today. When the world sees that Christians can get along with each other, then they'll believe what we say. When we demonstrate our internal love within the body of Christ, then the unsaved will believe it when we say we love them.

Our love for those outside of Christ must also be evident. Our attitude and actions toward them should say that we love them and are interested in their spiritual welfare. Until people can know this, they are not likely to turn to Christ. Paul used his own love for the Thessalonians as an example of the kind of love we are to display. The apostle's love was unselfish, and so must our love for others be.

> "Living without loving is merely existing."
> —George Sweeting

C. Unblamable in Holiness (v. 13)

13. To the end he may stablish your hearts unblameable in holiness before God, even our Father, at the coming of our Lord Jesus Christ with all his saints.

Paul not only prayed that the Thessalonians would enjoy an increase in love, but also that they would be strengthened in holiness. He knew it was possible for them to have high moral standards and yet not be holy. Holiness has an essential Godward reference; it denotes the quality of being set apart for God.

> **Talk About It:**
> How can we be "unblameable" when we stand before God?

The test of our holiness will come at the second coming of Jesus. There, by the grace of the Lord, we can be presented blameless. On the other hand, we can find ourselves ashamed to face Him. John wrote: "And now, little children, abide in him; that, when he shall appear, we may have confidence, and not be ashamed before him at his coming" (1 John 2:28).

Believers are to be established before God in holiness. What God says about holiness, not human notions about it, is what is important. We are to strive to live by His standards. They are fair and just and always in our best interests. Holy living is healthy living; it is living at its very best.

> "If we are full of pride and conceit and ambition and the world, there is no room for the Spirit of God."
> —D.L. Moody

III. CONNECTED BY LOVE (1 John 3:1-3; 4:7-12)
A. The Father's Love (1 John 3:1-3)

1. Behold, what manner of love the Father hath bestowed upon us, that we should be called the sons of God: therefore the world knoweth us not, because it knew him not.

2. Beloved, now are we the sons of God, and it doth not yet appear what we shall be: but we know that, when he shall appear, we shall be like him; for we shall see him as he is.

Discipleship Relationships

3. And every man that hath this hope in him purifieth himself, even as he is pure.

Almost everywhere the love of God is mentioned in the New Testament, it is immediately related to the sacrifice of God's Son on Calvary. It is in that sacrifice for us that we see most clearly the love of God. Not only has the Lord Jesus saved us by His death for us, but God has become to us our Father in heaven and we are made children of God.

Sonship is a present possession. We are not going to be sons and daughters of God only when we get to heaven, but right now—on the earth, in these bodies of flesh, in spite of all our imperfections—we are really the children of God. We are possessors of His life and love.

In commenting on the statement "Therefore the world knoweth us not, because it knew him not," R.S. Candish said: "The world knew Him not because it knew not God whose Son He was. The world could not understand His thorough sympathy with God, His burning zeal for God; His lofty, uncompromising loyalty to God's righteous government and law. His being the Son of God was the very thing which made Him incomprehensible to the world that by wisdom knew not God. God's children live in a world that knows Him not and, therefore, the world will not know them. Though the world may refuse to acknowledge us as God's children and give us credit for being what we profess to be, still let us not lose our own sense of the reality of what we are."

We are already God's children since Christ has called us so, has adopted us in His great love, and has revealed to us the Father. The children of a wonderful Father have a wonderful future. "We shall be like him; for we shall see him as he is" (v. 2). This refers to the second coming of Christ. Paul put this concept in these words: "For now we see through a glass, darkly; but then face to face: now I know in part; but then shall I know [fully] even as also I am known" (1 Corinthians 13:12).

We will have greater powers for understanding spiritual truth when we are in our new spiritual bodies, and then shall we see Christ in all of His glory, in all of His love, in all of His infinite power and wisdom. Beholding Him and understanding all that He is, we shall be like Him; that is, like Him in holiness, in righteousness, in love, in truth, in all the purposes of our own hearts, and in our absolute obedience to the Father and His will.

The Christian's hope is the expectation of being like God. This hope is established on God's love as manifested in Christ. This hope will become a reality when Christ returns.

The Christian lives a pure life in this world, having before him or her the example of the sinless Christ and the hope of becoming like God. Obviously no one can purify oneself. Each must

Talk About It:
1. What does it mean to be "known" by the world, and why are Christians unknown by the world (v. 1)?
2. What is the identity of believers *now*, and what shall they *become* (v. 2)?
3. How do believers purify themselves?

"Remember the weekday, to keep it holy."
—Decision

be purified by Christ, whose blood alone cleanses from all sin. But that cleansing is not forced upon us. It must be sought and accepted by us.

B. The Command to Love (4:7-12)

7. Beloved, let us love one another: for love is of God; and every one that loveth is born of God, and knoweth God.

8. He that loveth not knoweth not God; for God is love.

9. In this was manifested the love of God toward us, because that God sent his only begotten Son into the world, that we might live through him.

10. Herein is love, not that we loved God, but that he loved us, and sent his Son to be the propitiation for our sins.

11. Beloved, if God so loved us, we ought also to love one another.

12. No man hath seen God at any time. If we love one another, God dwelleth in us, and his love is perfected in us.

The commandment to love one another is based on the nature of God: God is love. Until we recognize the truth that "God is love" as the foundation of our Christian life, then the command to love leaves us feeling inadequate, and under the condemnation of our shifting emotions.

The world seeks a love that is removed from Biblical morality and foundational truth. The seductive spirit of the world deceives many into thinking that if they have a loving attitude and treat people right, that is all that is necessary for salvation. But according to verse 7, only those who are born again, with sins forgiven by the blood of the Lamb, can truly love others and know God.

Verse 8 makes the reasonable claim that if those who love one another are born of God and know Him, then those who do not love do not know God. True knowledge of God is related to the reality of His love.

All this talk about love in the first century was as susceptible to misunderstanding as it is in the 21st century. Satan has his own deceptive imitation of love. This is why John added the clear words of verses 9 and 10. God's love, the foundation of Christian love for one another, is specifically revealed in the life of Jesus Christ. This means that definitions of love rooted in philosophy, ethics, commercialism, or other world religions do not reveal the fullness of God's love as revealed in the person and work of Jesus Christ.

Verse 9 asserts that the greatest manifestation of God's love toward us is found in the fact "that God sent his only begotten Son into the world." The relationship of verse 9 to John 3:16 is striking. This is not surprising, of course, as the apostle John

Talk About It:
1. How should we answer a person who argues that the Lord is not a loving God?
2. What have we never seen, yet what can we know nonetheless (v. 12)?

Discipleship Relationships

penned both verses and knew the importance of the Incarnation as the manifestation of divine love.

Divine love does not begin with our loving God. This would be trying to appease God through religion by our own means and efforts. This always fails, and the "god" addressed would be but an image made in our fashion. This is idolatry and can never be anything better than human self-assertion and self-love.

Divine love begins with the fact that God "loved us, and sent his Son to be the propitiation for our sins" (1 John 4:10). *Propitiation* means "atoning sacrifice." It is based on the fact that God is angry at sin. The Bible is clear in revealing God's rightful wrath in regard to sin.

Even in His wrath, He manifested His love. Instead of giving us eternal condemnation, He has mercifully given us salvation. He did this in the only way possible. Only the innocent blood of Jesus could meet the demands of the Father's justice and righteousness. This love paid the price for our sins. Even though He was offended by our sins and had the power to exact vengeance, God himself paid our penalty so His love could be extended to us in mercy and grace! As the old song proclaims, "Such love, such wondrous love!"

"If God so loved us" (v. 11) refers to Jesus' death on the cross, where He purchased our redemption and provided for our sanctification, baptism in the Holy Spirit, healing, and other spiritual blessings. John never referred to God's love as an abstraction but as it was revealed in the incarnation and atoning death of Jesus.

> "God's heart is overflowing with love . . . for you. Accept that love. Return that love. And share that love. Today."
> —**Woodrow Kroll**

God's love dwells within us as Christ lives within us. Thus, the outflowing of this love returns to God in adoration, worship and obedience; but also, through this "incarnation" of Christ's presence in us, this love flows out to others.

CONCLUSION

The love of God creates a powerful bond with His children. In spite of the way God's first human friends—Adam and Eve—treated Him, He provided a way for those who desire His friendship to approach Him without fear. Echoing through the Old Testament (*NIV*) are the plaintive cries of the heart of God:

- "Fear not, for I have redeemed you; I have summoned you by name; you are mine" (Isaiah 43:1).
- "With everlasting kindness I will have compassion on you" (54:8).
- "I have loved you with an everlasting love" (Jeremiah 31:3).
- "When Israel was a child, I loved him, and out of Egypt I called my son" (Hosea 11:1).
- "How can I give you up, Ephraim?" (11:8).

• "Call to me, and I will answer you" (Jeremiah 33:3).

God would pay the ultimate price of love by dying to bring His friends home. Though God was totally sufficient within the Trinity, there was something in Him that desired us. In that same way, we who are made in His image have within us a deep hunger for fellowship. That hunger includes a longing for the personal touch of God, as well as the desire to establish close relationships with our fellow believers.

Believe it. Only Jesus satisfies your loneliness with the joy of His friendship.—Ron Phillips

GOLDEN TEXT CHALLENGE

"BELOVED, IF GOD SO LOVED US, WE OUGHT ALSO TO LOVE ONE ANOTHER" (1 John 4:11).

I took up that word *love*, and I do not know how many weeks I spent in studying the passages in which it occurs, till at last I could not help loving people. I had been feeding on love so long that I was anxious to do good to everybody I came in contact with. I got full of it. It ran out my fingers. You take up the subject of love in the Bible, and you will get so full of it that all you have to do is to open your lips, and a flood of the love of God flows out!—D.L. Moody

Grow in Discipleship

Psalm 1:2, 3; Matthew 25:34-40; Acts 2:42; Ephesians 6:18-20; Philippians 4:6, 7; 2 Timothy 3:16, 17; Hebrews 10:23-25; 2 Peter 3:18; 1 John 2:15-17

INTRODUCTION

In a *Peanuts* cartoon, Lucy is walking along the road with Charlie Brown. He asks her, "Lucy, are you going to make any New Year's resolutions?"

Lucy hollers back at him, knocking him off his feet: "What? What for? What's wrong with me now? I like myself the way I am! Why should I change? What in the world is the matter with you, Charlie Brown? How could I improve? How, I ask you? How?"

Do you identify with Lucy in her response, or are there areas of your life where you need to improve? In particular, how do you need to grow spiritually?

In *Be a People Person*, John Maxwell tells of a certain kind of fish that has four eyes. These odd-looking creatures are native to the equatorial waters of the western Atlantic region. They have two-tiered eyes, with the upper and lower halves of each eyeball operating independently and having separate corneas and irises. The upper eyes protrude above the surface of the water and enable the fish to search for food and to spot enemies in the air. The lower eyes remain focused in the water, functioning in the usual fishlike fashion. These fish are *anableps*, meaning "those that look upward."

That is what Christians ought to be called—those who look upward. Paul wrote, "Set your affection on things above, not on things on the earth" (Colossians 3:2).

What are you doing to keep your thoughts turned toward God? Are you involved in a personal Bible study program? Do you give the Lord greater control over every aspect of your life each day?

In *The Strong Name*, James S. Stewart wrote:

I am growing more and more convinced that a great part of the secret of achieving steadfastness and serenity in the face of the battle of life is this—not only to commit your way to God in some high moment of conversion, but to do that very thing every morning, to go down on your knees and say, "Dear God, I do not ask to see the distant scene; but here, for the next 24 hours, in my life—I give it back to Thee, to guard, to bless, and control."

Growth in discipleship is a day-by-day process. There are no shortcuts.—Homer Rhea

---

Unit Theme:
Christian Discipleship

Central Truth:
The life of a disciple calls for growth in obedience and grace.

Focus:
Examine the discipleship process and take steps to grow as a disciple.

Context:
Selected Scripture passages about growing both in our knowledge of God and commitment to His will.

Golden Text:
"They continued steadfastly in the apostles' doctrine and fellowship, and in breaking of bread, and in prayers" (Acts 2:42).

Study Outline:
I. Do the Lord's Will (Psalm 1:2, 3; Matthew 25:34-40)
II. Pray (Acts 2:42; Ephesians 6:18-20; Philippians 4:6, 7)
III. Know What You Believe (2 Timothy 3:16, 17; Hebrews 10:23-25; 2 Peter 3:18; 1 John 2:15-17)

I. DO THE LORD'S WILL (Psalm 1:2, 3; Matthew 25:34-40)
A. Delight in the Lord (Psalm 1:2, 3)
2. But his delight is in the law of the Lord; and in his law doth he meditate day and night.

3. And he shall be like a tree planted by the rivers of water, that bringeth forth his fruit in his season; his leaf also shall not wither; and whatsoever he doeth shall prosper.

In verse 1 the person who delights in God's ways is called *blessed*—meaning "happy" and "divinely favored." The blessed person is the chosen object of God's favor. This man or woman receives and obeys the advice of God rather than that of worldly people. He or she avoids evil companionship and does not imitate the ways of non-Christian people.

The "ungodly" are those who withhold from God what rightly belongs to Him; "sinners" are those who do evil; the "scornful" not only refuse to commit themselves to God and live evilly; they also mock and deride Him and His laws (v. 1).

In verse 2 we see that the blessed person rejoices in being able to obey God's laws, and the very fairness and justness of them please him as he thinks about them, studies them, and even dreams of them because they are such a vital part of him. The ungodly person does not delight in law-keeping, but seeks to deviate from God's laws and rebels at the supposed restrictions to his misunderstood liberty.

Verse 3 says the person who trusts in God lives a full, meaningful and fruitful life. Life must be productive to be meaningful, and life is completely confusing without orientation to God. The godly person is intentionally planted where he or she can draw on the exhaustless waters of God's provision. "So the godly man; he is ever taking deeper root, growing stronger in the grace he has already received, increasing in heavenly desires, and, under the continual influence of the divine Spirit, forming those purposes from which much fruit to the glory and praise of God shall be produced" (Adam Clarke).

B. Inherit the Kingdom (Matthew 25:34-36)
34. Then shall the King say unto them on his right hand, Come, ye blessed of my Father, inherit the kingdom prepared for you from the foundation of the world:

35. For I was an hungred, and ye gave me meat: I was thirsty, and ye gave me drink: I was a stranger, and ye took me in:

36. Naked, and ye clothed me: I was sick, and ye visited me: I was in prison, and ye came unto me.

In addressing the heirs of His kingdom, the Lord assumes all His regal authority. He invites these heirs to possess a prepared inheritance. They are recognized as citizens of the messianic Kingdom and are invited to enjoy the privileges and prosperity of the divine government of the King of kings.

Talk About It:
1. What does it mean to "delight" in God's law?
2. Describe true prosperity.

"A man of meditation is happy, not for an hour or a day, but quite round the circle of all his years."
—Isaac Taylor

Talk About It:
1. What did God do "from the foundation of the world" (v. 34)?
2. List the various ministries seen in verses 35 and 36.

Immediately connected with the announcement of reward is the principle or basis on which the reward is granted. The basis is hospitality to Christ in the form of generous provision to others in the time of need.

Someone wrote, "Six of the seven works of mercy in Christian ethics are listed here. The first three are recognized duties, the last three are voluntary acts of self-forgetting love. Common humanity would move a man to relieve his bitterest foe when perishing by hunger or by thirst (see Romans 12:20). Oriental custom required at least a bare hospitality. But to clothe the naked implied a liberal and spontaneous self-sacrifice; to go to the wretched outcasts in prison was perhaps an unheard-of act of charity in those days; it was to enter places horrible and foul beyond description."

The kind of service mentioned is such that one who truly loves Christ and other people would render. It echoes the service rendered by Jesus when He was on earth and expresses that loving-kindness and compassion which are the will and purpose of God himself.

> "Make a rule, and pray God to help you to keep it, never, if possible, to lie down at night without being able to say, 'I have made one human being, at least, a little wiser, a little happier, or a little bit better this day.'"
> —Charles Kingsley

C. Minister to the Lord (vv. 37-40)

37. Then shall the righteous answer him, saying, Lord, when saw we thee an hungred, and fed thee? or thirsty, and gave thee drink?

38. When saw we thee a stranger, and took thee in? or naked, and clothed thee?

39. Or when saw we thee sick, or in prison, and came unto thee?

40. And the King shall answer and say unto them, Verily I say unto you, Inasmuch as ye have done it unto one of the least of these my brethren, ye have done it unto me.

We have here a repetition of the deeds of mercy previously mentioned. Those who have done these deeds are designated righteous in that their faith in Christ had manifested itself in works. They are surprised that what they had done was received by the Lord as if it had been done to Him personally. This response is indicative of humility. He explained that their deeds of mercy had been bestowed on the least of His brethren and therefore on Him.

Since the expression "my brethren" may refer either to the Jews, who were Christ's brethren in the flesh, or to Christians, who are His brethren in the spirit, kindness bestowed on either in the name of Christ will surely be recognized by the Lord.

Talk About It:
What will surprise "the righteous," and why?

II. PRAY (Acts 2:42; Ephesians 6:18-20; Philippians 4:6, 7)
A. Steadfast Prayer (Acts 2:42)

42. And they continued stedfastly in the apostles' doctrine and fellowship, and in breaking of bread, and in prayers.

This verse highlights four features that characterized the early church. First, they were steadfast in everything the disciples taught about Jesus Christ. Second, they were devoted to fellowship—they were united to God in Christ and to each other. Third, they regularly observed the Lord's Supper. Fourth, their devotion was marked by prayer.

French Arrington wrote:

> [Prayer] could have included Temple devotions as well as special times of prayer and thanksgiving. After Jesus was lifted up to God, they went to the Temple, praising God (Luke 24:53). Just before the outpouring of the Spirit, men and women gathered for prayer (Acts 1:14). At that time their hope was on the coming of the Spirit. . . . An immediate result of the Pentecostal outpouring of the Spirit was that they gave themselves to continuous prayer. Like their constant devotion to the apostles' teaching, to the fellowship, and to the breaking of bread, prayer, too, confirmed the Spirit's presence among the people (*The Acts of the Apostles*).

B. Intercessory Prayer (Ephesians 6:18-20)

18. Praying always with all prayer and supplication in the Spirit, and watching thereunto with all perseverance and supplication for all saints;

19. And for me, that utterance may be given unto me, that I may open my mouth boldly, to make known the mystery of the gospel,

20. For which I am an ambassador in bonds: that therein I may speak boldly, as I ought to speak.

Having been fitted with the armor of God (vv. 11-17), we stand by the practice of prayer as it is described here. We are to pray always, pray in the Spirit, and pray with all perseverance for all saints, for prayer is the Christian's ultimate resource. In every circumstance we must meet all spiritual opposition fully clothed in the armor of God and praying always in the Spirit.

In verse 19 Paul calls upon the Ephesians to pray for him. He feels restricted because of his imprisonment, yet he desires to preach the gospel boldly. His request for prayer includes a desire for the opportunity to preach and to make known the mystery of the gospel. He wishes above all else to reveal to every possible person the open secret that Jesus Christ is the Son of God and the Savior of humanity.

At the time this epistle was written, Paul was in Rome living in his own house under house arrest. In a spiritual sense, he was in the capital city of the Roman Empire as an "ambassador in bonds" (v. 20). The purpose of an ambassador is to speak for the nation and the sovereign whom he represents. Paul was an ambassador of Jesus Christ, representing the kingdom of heaven, and therefore believed it necessary that he be able to speak boldly for his Lord and His kingdom. For this to happen, he needed the prayers of God's people.

"We pray best when we are no longer aware of praying."
—Cassian

C. Thankful Praying (Philippians 4:6, 7)

6. Be careful for nothing; but in every thing by prayer and supplication with thanksgiving let your requests be made known unto God.

careful (v. 6)— anxious

7. And the peace of God, which passeth all understanding, shall keep your hearts and minds through Christ Jesus.

Someone has paraphrased verse 6 to read: "Don't worry about anything, but pray about everything." This is a good summary of what Paul was saying.

Talk About It: What should we pray about, and how should we pray?

There are numerous things that can lead to worry if we are not careful. Financial setbacks, family problems, failing health, faltering years—these and many other things can bring anxiety if we lose our perspective on life. The solution that keeps us going and enables us to overcome these troubles is prayer.

In an article that appeared in *Reader's Digest*, Dr. Alexis Carrel said he, as a physician, had witnessed miracles as people, "after all other therapy had failed, [were] lifted out of disease and melancholy by the serene effort of prayer. . . . But a constant, quieter miracle takes place hourly in the hearts of men and women who have discovered that prayer supplies them with a steady flow of sustaining power in their daily lives."

The prayer we offer in making our requests known should be mixed with praise. Thanksgiving gives the proper flavor to prayer. It indicates that the person who is praying has faith in the sufficiency of God to answer the petition being made.

"Prayer is more than verbally filling in some requisition blank. It's fellowship with God! It's communion with the Lord through praising Him, rehearsing His promises, and then sharing our needs."
—Billy Graham

When we combine prayer and praise, it leads to peace— more peace than ever thought possible, according to verse 7. At such times, we can rejoice in the fathomless serenity of the Savior's presence. As never before, we understand that God is our anchor and that the problems of life are as nothing compared to His ability to resolve them.

III. KNOW WHAT YOU BELIEVE (2 Timothy 3:16, 17; Hebrews 10:23-25; 2 Peter 3:18; 1 John 2:15-17)

A. Thoroughly Furnished (2 Timothy 3:16, 17)

16. All scripture is given by inspiration of God, and is profitable for doctrine, for reproof, for correction, for instruction in righteousness:

17. That the man of God may be perfect, throughly furnished unto all good works.

As Evangelical/Pentecostal Christians, we believe in the verbal inspiration of the Bible. This means we believe that the whole Bible is inspired by God. The Holy Spirit gave the Word without error to the Biblical writers.

There is no doubt that the apostle Paul had in mind the Old Testament when he wrote these words to Timothy. As the Holy Spirit further inspired the Gospel writers, Paul, and Peter, the church came to recognize the marks of Holy Spirit inspiration in those writings. The word *inspiration* literally means "God-breathed." Thus the Bible, composed of 66 books, is the only God-breathed book ever given. Over a period of about a thousand years, God gave His Word to Moses, the prophets, Solomon, other Israelite historians, and the New Testament apostles.

There are no other Holy Spirit-inspired writings of equal weight as the Biblical canon. A characteristic of false doctrine is the need for another inspired writing in place of the Bible or alongside the Bible. Contrary to contemporary advertisements, the Book of Mormon is not another gospel of Jesus Christ. The fact that such claim is made further reveals the falseness of this cult.

The Bible is "profitable" (useful) in four specific ways in the life of the believer. First, it is useful in establishing doctrine. Second, it is useful "for reproof." To *reprove* means to "convict." Thus, Scripture is used by the Holy Spirit to reveal our sin and error. It does not do so to condemn us but to set us free from error and lead us to the truth. Third, Scripture provides correction. The Greek for *correction* means to "set aright." This is the setting right of character and life. Finally, Scripture provides instruction that affects our thinking and living in regard to righteousness. God's Word provides practical wisdom for righteous living in all aspects of life.

B. Without Wavering (Hebrews 10:23-25)

23. Let us hold fast the profession of our faith without wavering; (for he is faithful that promised;)

24. And let us consider one another to provoke unto love and to good works:

25. Not forsaking the assembling of ourselves together, as the manner of some is; but exhorting one another: and so much the more, as ye see the day approaching.

One of the main objectives of the writer of Hebrews was to encourage Jewish converts to Christianity to continue in the faith. The Christian Jews were being persecuted by non-Christian Jews. Since the persecutions were designed to induce them to return to their former religion, the author of Hebrews stressed in the doctrinal part of the epistle the superiority of Christianity to Judaism. Having argued and settled his point, he now urged them to hold fast their profession of faith with a firmness which neither trials nor arguments of their enemies could shake.

In our day also, "let us hold fast the confession of our hope without wavering" (*NKJV*). Let us be willing to suffer persecution, let us be willing to deny ourselves, and let us be willing to forgo worldly pleasures so that we might enjoy the glorious benefits of continuing with Christ.

One of the distinguishing marks of the church is the consideration its members have for one another. *The Living Bible* paraphrases verse 24 as follows: "In response to all he has done for us, let us outdo each other in being helpful and kind to each other and in doing good." The apostle Paul said, "As we have . . . opportunity, let us do good unto all men, especially unto them who are of the household of faith" (Galatians 6:10).

In Hebrews 10:25 the writer continued his exhortation to his readers by admonishing them not to forsake the assembling of themselves together for worship. Apparently, some of the Christians were neglecting attendance at public services. Either for fear of persecution, lack of interest in the services, doubts of their benefit, or on the basis of some other excuse, they did not assemble for public worship.

The problem of nonattendance or poor attendance of religious services has recurred at different times in the history of the church. This not only affects the individuals themselves but often hinders the influence of the church as a whole. Members need the church if they are to develop spiritually; and the church needs its members if it is to be effective.

> "The most expensive piece of furniture in the church is the empty pew."
> —*Quotable Quotes*

C. Graciously Growing (2 Peter 3:18)

18. But grow in grace, and in the knowledge of our Lord and Saviour Jesus Christ. To him be glory both now and for ever. Amen.

The primary way a person can avoid falling from stability in Christ is to grow in the grace of God. The grace of God is the source of salvation and the means by which a person can remain and grow in salvation.

Growing in grace is similar to initial believing. This growth is received from God. It cannot be manufactured or earned. It does not come through mere human effort.

Christian discipleship springs from the action of God in a life. God's grace provides the ability and the motivation for growth as long as the believer continues to humbly receive that grace. The peril is that a person may depart from grace, rebelling against the will and knowledge of the Lord Jesus Christ (v. 17).

Talk About It:
In what ways must Christians grow, and how can this be accomplished?

D. Spiritual Warning (1 John 2:15-17)

15. Love not the world, neither the things that are in the world. If any man love the world, the love of the Father is not in him.

16. For all that is in the world, the lust of the flesh, and

the lust of the eyes, and the pride of life, is not of the Father, but is of the world.

17. And the world passeth away, and the lust thereof: but he that doeth the will of God abideth for ever.

John's warning to his readers is to stop loving the world. He assumed they did have some affection for the world. "World" in this passage does not refer to the world's people (John 3:16) nor to the created world (17:24), but to the old world order controlled by Satan. Included is all that goes to make up the organized system of evil on the earth. God's people are to stop letting the world establish their value.

When John mentioned "the things that are in the world," he was not necessarily referring to material items, although these may be involved. He had in mind people's behavior and their attitude toward things. George Findley writes: "The world is not made up of so many outward objects that can be specified; it is a sum of those influences emanating from men and things around us which draw us away from God" (*Fellowship in the Life Eternal*).

John was warning his readers against becoming so involved in the world that they become emotionally attached to it and come to value it as a way of life. Although Christians are of necessity in the world, they are not to be intimately related to the world. Its things, its ways, its attitudes, its spirit are not to be imitated by the people of God.

True Christians agree that John's prohibition is justified. The importance of it can be seen in three ways. First, the love of the world blocks us from fully loving God. The two loves are mutually exclusive. Like oil and water, they will not mix.

Second, none of the deceptively attractive things of the world come from the heavenly Father, the giver of every good and perfect gift (James 1:17). Those things of the world attracting fleshly desires—"the lust of the flesh"—have an evil source and purpose. Those things that catch the eye with their false promise of satisfaction—"the lust of the eyes"—have an evil source and purpose. These things that cause foolish men to strut and brag because they possess things—"the pride of life"—have an evil source and purpose. These were the bait that caught Eve. They were the snare set for Jesus, but He could not be tripped. They are the devil's trap to capture human souls. They are not from God; therefore they are not for the children of God.

Third, the world, with its lust, is doomed. The whole kingdom of evil will be cast out on the dump heap of eternity. But those who do the will of God will never see condemnation. They will dwell with God in His light forever.

Talk About It:
1. What does it mean to "love the world," and why can't Christians do so?
2. Describe some of the specific forms of lust that will pass away.
3. How can we be guaranteed of living forever?

"Worldliness is a spirit, a temperament, an attitude of the soul. It is a life without high callings, life devoid of lofty ideals. It is a gaze always horizontal and never vertical."
—**John Henry Jowett**

CONCLUSION

The three sections of this lesson are "Do the Lord's Will," "Pray," and "Know What You Believe." However, as it relates to our spiritual lives, the sequence works differently.

For us to do God's will, we first must understand what it is. This understanding comes only as we learn Bible doctrine and pray. Spiritual growth happens as we discover, apply and live in the will of God.

GOLDEN TEXT CHALLENGE

"THEY CONTINUED STEDFASTLY IN THE APOSTLES' DOCTRINE AND FELLOWSHIP, AND IN BREAKING OF BREAD, AND IN PRAYERS" (Acts 2:42).

Rather than separating to their own homes and their own private life with God after being filled with the Spirit on Pentecost, the 3,000 converts embarked on a life of fellowship. They learned together, worshiped together and prayed together.

Today, growing in Christ is still a "together" process. Of course we must pray and study God's Word on our own, but if we try to grow in Christ in isolation from His body, our growth will be stunted and malformed. As *The Living Bible* reads, we must join with "other believers in regular attendance at . . . teaching sessions and at the Communion services and prayer meetings."

Daily Devotions:
M. Walk in Truth
1 Kings 2:1-4
T. Remember the Word
Psalm 119:9-16
W. Submit to the Call
Jeremiah 1:4-10
T. God Is Faithful
1 Corinthians 10:6-13
F. Feed on the Word
Hebrews 5:8-14
S. The Humble Receive Grace
1 Peter 5:4-10

Introduction to Spring Quarter

The theme for the first unit is "The Gospel in Romans and Galatians." These eight lessons deal with the doctrinal issues of salvation, justification, reconciliation, Christian freedom, and spirituality.

The writer of this unit is the Reverend Dr. J. Ayodeji Adewuya (Ph.D., University of Manchester), who is an associate professor of New Testament at the Church of God Theological Seminary in Cleveland, Tennessee. Prior to joining the seminary, Dr. Adewuyua served as a missionary in the Philippines for 17 years. He is an active member of the Society for Biblical Literature, Wesleyan Theological Society, and the Society for Pentecostal Studies. He is the author of *Holiness and Community in 2 Corinthians 6:14—7:1.*

Lesson 4 (the Easter lesson) was compiled by Lance Colkmire (see biographical information on page 131).

The second unit is a trio of studies from Ecclesiastes. Searching for meaning, Biblical wisdom, and life's purpose are the subjects.

The writer of these three lessons as well as the Pentecost Sunday exposition (Lesson 11) is Keith Whitt (B.A., M.Div., Ph.D. cand.). Reverend Whitt has earned degrees from Lee University and the Church of God Theological Seminary, and has done doctoral work at the University of Nottingham England. An ordained bishop in the Church of God, Keith has served his denomination as a pastor for 23 years, district overseer for 12 years, and as a member of various boards and committees. He has taught courses for the Church of God Theological Seminary and Lee University External Studies.

Power of the Gospel

Romans 1:1-17; Galatians 1:6-24

INTRODUCTION

The gospel of Christ has the power to save from sin, to heal, to deliver and to transform lives. It is a message of good news to the hurting, helpless and hopeless. The apostle Paul experienced its transforming power on the road to Damascus. Christ Jesus was personally revealed to him in a life-changing way. Paul then went on to carry a powerful message that influenced the first-century world and which continues to challenge our world today.

In Paul's letter to the Romans, he focuses on the significance of the gospel, presenting it as an antidote to the sinfulness of humanity. He succinctly states the universal problem of sin that necessitates the universality of the gospel. Paul states the theme of the letter in 1:16, 17. The righteousness of God is revealed in the Lord Jesus Christ. This righteousness is the answer to God's wrath concerning humanity's sin.

In the same vein as Romans, Paul writes the letter to the Galatians, addressing questions that arose in the church concerning salvation. Is faith in Jesus Christ sufficient for salvation? Certain teachers had infiltrated the Galatian church and were teaching that adherence to the Law was also necessary for salvation. Oftentimes, people feel they need to do more than what has already been done by Christ to be saved and be brought into right relationship with God. But Paul is clear in both letters that the gospel message alone is sufficient for salvation. The power of God has been manifested in this gospel message, and Paul could boast of a firsthand experience. His life was dramatically changed by the gospel. The gospel continues to transform lives today as people believe and embrace it.

Unit Theme:
The Gospel in Romans and Galatians

Central Truth:
God's power to save from sin and change lives is revealed through the gospel.

Focus:
Investigate how the power of the gospel is manifested in our lives and personally experience its transforming message.

Context:
Paul's letter to the Romans (A.D. 56 or 57) was written a few years after his letter to the Galatians.

Golden Text:
"I am not ashamed of the gospel of Christ; for it is the power of God unto salvation to every one that believeth; to the Jew first, and also to the Greek" (Romans 1:16).

Study Outline:
I. Brings People to Faith
(Romans 1:7-15)
II. Reveals God's Righteousness
(Romans 1:16, 17)
III. Changes Lives
(Galatians 1:6-24)

I. BRINGS PEOPLE TO FAITH (Romans 1:7-15)
A. People Who Have Been Brought to Faith (v. 7a)
  7a. To all that be in Rome, beloved of God called to be saints.

Talk About It:
What makes some-
one a "saint"?

First, Paul addressed his letter to *all* believers in Rome. In doing so, Paul is making it clear that the message of the letter is applicable to all regardless of age, race, status or gender. The gospel message is relevant to all people, whether Jew or Gentile.

Second, Paul emphasizes that the recipients of the letter are those who have been brought to faith and, as such, are "loved by God" (*NIV*); in other words, *beloved*. Such description underscores the relational aspect of the gospel. Once the message is received and appropriated, a relationship with God results.

Third, the people Paul is writing to are a *called* people—called by God into a relationship with Him to fulfill a purpose and a mission. In the same manner that Christ, and subsequently the disciples, were called to fulfill a mission, so are the people of God. Once they respond to the call of the gospel, they become a people of purpose—a people chosen by God to manifest His power and presence to a sinful, dying world.

"I like your Christ;
I do not like your
Christians. Your
Christians are so
unlike your Christ."
—**Mahatma
Gandhi**

Fourth, the people Paul is writing to are called *saints*. In the Greek language the word used for *saints* (*hagioi*) here means "pure, holy, blameless and consecrated." The people of God in Rome are to be a people set apart to do the work of God. Now that they have been brought to faith, they are called to demonstrate holy living in a sinful environment. But it is more than that. They need to bring others to faith in God.

B. Requirements to Bring Others to Faith (vv. 7b-13)
  7b. Grace to you and peace from God our Father, and the Lord Jesus Christ.
  8. First, I thank my God through Jesus Christ for you all, that your faith is spoken of throughout the whole world.
  9. For God is my witness, whom I serve with my spirit in the gospel of his Son, that without ceasing I make mention of you always in my prayers;
  10. Making request, if by any means now at length I might have a prosperous journey by the will of God to come unto you.
  11. For I long to see you, that I may impart unto you some spiritual gift, to the end ye may be established;
  12. That is, that I may be comforted together with you by the mutual faith both of you and me.
  13. Now I would not have you ignorant, brethren, that oftentimes I purposed to come unto you, (but was let hitherto,) that I might have some fruit among you also, even as among other Gentiles.

In his characteristic manner, Paul offers a wish for his readers—grace and peace. Grace, apart from being the way of salvation, is also the means by which the Christian life is lived, and the source of perseverance and strength to carry on the gospel message. It is the divine influence upon the heart which is reflected in the life of the believer on a daily basis. It is a power that is available to all believers as they embrace the gospel message and carry it to others. Peace is that well-being that comes from a right relationship with God. It is the kind of peace the world cannot give. Both grace and peace come from the same source—God.

In verse 8, Paul expresses his gratitude to the Romans for their faith that is known throughout the world. Theirs is a faith-filled witness that is being spoken of everywhere. Such witnessing is necessary to bring others to faith. This includes the power of personal testimony—telling others about the transformation wrought by Christ.

In verse 9, Paul describes another requirement for bringing others to faith. It is a commitment to wholehearted service. Paul has learned that one must follow the example of Jesus Christ when proclaiming His gospel. As Jesus made Himself a servant to others, Paul understood that he must make himself a servant to those he was leading to faith in Christ. So also must all believers be servants.

Paul had a sincere affection for the people in Rome. He desired to be with them and to encourage them personally in their faith (v. 10). But due to hindrances beyond his control, he could not get to them. His means of supporting them was to "pray without ceasing" (1 Thessalonians 5:17). This is another basic element of sharing the faith with others. Believers must be willing to pray for those who need the message of salvation. The gospel message is empowered by the faithful prayers of the saints.

In verses 11-13 of the text, Paul stresses the value of fellowship as a means of supporting and encouraging one another in their walk of faith. Paul wants to impart a spiritual gift that will strengthen the Roman church. He understood that spiritual gifts were not given for an individual's personal edification nor to impress and entertain the believers, but were meant to strengthen the body. The impartation would take place within the community of believers through fellowship. In this environment, Paul also knew he would be spiritually strengthened by the Roman believers. He would reap a harvest among them, as he has elsewhere, and they would encourage him. Bringing others to faith was his primary goal in all circumstances.

C. People Who Need to Be Brought to Faith (vv. 14, 15)

14. I am debtor both to the Greeks, and to the Barbarians; both to the wise, and to the unwise.

Talk About It:
1. How were the Roman Christians making an impact beyond Rome (v. 8)?
2. What did Paul do "without ceasing" (v. 9), and why (v. 10)?
3. Why did Paul want to go to Rome (vv. 11-13)?

More Than a Philosophy
The gospel is not presented to mankind as an argument about religious principles. Nor is it offered as a philosophy of life. Christianity is a witness to certain facts—to events that have happened, to hopes that have been fulfilled, to realities that have been experienced, to a Person who has lived and died and been raised from the dead to reign forever.

—Massey H. Shepherd Jr.

Barbarians (v. 14)—"non-Greeks" (NIV)

15. So, as much as in me is, I am ready to preach the gospel to you that are at Rome also.

At the end of his introduction, Paul returns to his passion for ministry. He describes it as an *obligation* to all people. Paul understood himself as being indebted to preach the gospel to others—he owed the gospel message to them. It was not a message he wanted to take sole ownership of. It was a message with life-changing power that he felt driven to take to others, "both to the Greeks, and to the Barbarians."

The Greeks in this society considered themselves to be cultured and wise. This reinforces the fact that no one is so educated and so wise who can survive without the gospel. The word *Barbarians* refers to anyone who could not speak Greek. The Barbarians were considered to be uncivilized and foolish. Here Paul is inferring that there is none so uncivilized or unwise who cannot receive the life-saving message of the gospel.

II. REVEALS GOD'S RIGHTEOUSNESS (Romans 1:16, 17)
A. Faith Leads to God's Righteousness (v. 16)

16. For I am not ashamed of the gospel of Christ: for it is the power of God unto salvation to every one that believeth; to the Jew first, and also to the Greek.

Verses 16 and 17 contain the main theme of the Book of Romans. Paul develops the rest of the letter along this theme. He shows the power of the gospel both as the means of salvation and of obtaining the righteousness of God. Paul certainly was not ashamed of the gospel, for he preached wherever he went whether there be persecution or not. Nothing hindered him from his passion to present it. But he goes on to give the reason why he was not ashamed of it and boldly proclaimed it wherever he went. His driving force was that the gospel is *the power of God unto salvation.*

The most powerful man in the Roman Empire at this time was the emperor. But a Roman writer, Epictetus, said of him, "While the Emperor has the power to give peace from war on land and sea, he is unable to give peace from passion, grief and envy. He cannot give peace of heart, for which man longs even more than outward peace." Peace of heart cannot be brought about by the power and will of a human. Only God can give the peace that comes through salvation. Only God is strong enough to break the powers that hold humanity in bondage to Satan and his works of darkness. For this is precisely the evil from which humanity needs to be saved.

This salvation is available to everyone who has faith. During this time in history the Jews thought salvation was only for the religious, and the Greeks thought salvation was only for the wise. Paul stresses here that the only prerequisite for salvation is faith.

Power of the Gospel

It is universal in availability but not in application. No one will be automatically saved; faith is the condition for its realization.

B. God's Righteousness Leads to Life (v. 17)

17. For therein is the righteousness of God revealed from faith to faith: as it is written, The just shall live by faith.

The gospel message of salvation reveals the righteousness of God and brings people into a right relationship with Him. Being in right relationship with God leads the believer into a faith-filled life. Righteousness is a gift from God and is imparted by faith. God gives righteousness to those who believe the gospel message, and then He empowers them to live out their daily walk of faith through His righteousness. Paul connects a right relationship with God to moral accountability. Paul also describes God's righteousness as coming from a faith that is "from first to last" (*NIV*). Saving faith becomes a sustaining faith as the righteousness of God is revealed in the life of the believer.

Talk About It:
Why is the word *faith* used three times in this verse?

III. CHANGES LIVES (Galatians 1:6-24)

A. If the Believer Does Not Desert It (vv. 6-10)

6. I marvel that ye are so soon removed from him that called you into the grace of Christ unto another gospel:

7. Which is not another; but there be some that trouble you, and would pervert the gospel of Christ.

8. But though we, or an angel from heaven, preach any other gospel unto you than that which we have preached unto you, let him be accursed.

9. As we said before, so say I now again, If any man preach any other gospel unto you than that ye have received, let him be accursed.

10. For do I now persuade men, or God? or do I seek to please men? for if I yet pleased men, I should not be the servant of Christ.

accursed (v. 8)—
"eternally condemned" (*NIV*)

persuade (v. 10)—
seek the favor of

Paul writes the letter to the Galatians in response to certain interlopers who were disturbing the Christians in Galatia with their teachings about rules and regulations of Judaism. They were preaching a gospel that required submission to Mosaic Law and the rite of circumcision as additional prerequisites for salvation and inclusion in the body of Christ. If the Galatians were to submit to this teaching, it would be tantamount to admitting that salvation could have come through their own efforts of following the Law, and not through faith in Jesus Christ and the empowerment of the Holy Spirit. This perversion of the gospel was leaving the new converts in confusion.

Therefore, Paul wrote powerful words of rebuke concerning this *other* gospel that was being preached to the Galatians. He emphatically corrected the misconceptions of this false gospel

Talk About It:
1. What caused Paul to "marvel" (v. 6)?
2. Why was this "different gospel" (v. 6, *NIV*) "really no gospel at all" (v. 7, *NIV*)?
3. What was Paul seeking, and what was he not seeking (v. 10)?

and encouraged them not to desert the true gospel that had already been preached to them. He also emphasized that one cannot compromise the truths of the gospel by being a people-pleaser and still be a servant of Christ. If their motive for accepting this false gospel was to please the ones presenting it, they would also come under the same yoke of bondage to the Mosaic Law as the ones preaching this gospel.

B. If One Receives It (vv. 11, 12)

11. But I certify you, brethren, that the gospel which was preached of me is not after man.

12. For I neither received it of man, neither was I taught it, but by the revelation of Jesus Christ.

Paul declared there is no error in the gospel he preached because it is not of human origin. Instead, the gospel he preached is of divine origin and, therefore, is sufficient for salvation. Paul did not receive the gospel through instruction, but through a direct revelation from Jesus Christ. The means of its reception is faith. Hence, the gospel message is one that changes lives only when it is received by faith. As with any gift, if the present is not received, the benefits of the gift can neither be realized nor appropriated.

Talk About It:
How did Paul receive the gospel, and why did this matter (v. 12)?

C. If One Proclaims It (vv. 13-24)

13. For ye have heard of my conversation in time past in the Jews' religion, how that beyond measure I persecuted the church of God, and wasted it:

14. And profited in the Jews' religion above many my equals in mine own nation, being more exceedingly zealous of the traditions of my fathers.

15. But when it pleased God, who separated me from my mother's womb, and called me by his grace,

16. To reveal his Son in me, that I might preach him among the heathen; immediately I conferred not with flesh and blood:

17. Neither went I up to Jerusalem to them which were apostles before me; but I went into Arabia, and returned again unto Damascus.

18. Then after three years I went up to Jerusalem to see Peter, and abode with him fifteen days.

19. But other of the apostles saw I none, save James the Lord's brother.

20. Now the things which I write unto you, behold, before God, I lie not.

21. Afterwards I came into the regions of Syria and Cilicia;

22. And was unknown by face unto the churches of Judaea which were in Christ:

conversation (v. 13) —manner of living

wasted it (v. 13)— "made havoc of it" (*ASV*)

23. But they had heard only, That he which persecuted us in times past now preacheth the faith which once he destroyed.

24. And they glorified God in me.

Paul gives a personal testimony to demonstrate how God had dramatically changed his life through the gospel message. In verses 13 and 14, Paul describes his life before receiving his revelation from God concerning Christ. Prior to his Damascus-road experience, Paul neither believed nor was disposed to believe in the gospel. Instead, he fiercely opposed the gospel and its proclamation. But something happened as the Lord appeared to Paul (see Acts 9). His life was transformed by the gospel. Paul's point to the Galatians was that if the gospel message was so powerful as to be able to change one such as him who was so zealous for the Law, then this message could change their lives as well. The power in the gospel is power from God.

In verses 15 and 16, Paul explains how God revealed the truth of the gospel to him directly. For Paul, the source of human salvation lies in the loving purpose and will of God. But Paul also understood his conversion as a call not just to a personal relationship with God and its attendant blessings, but to a life of service. He understood himself as being set apart by God's grace in order that His Son might be revealed in and through him by the proclamation of the gospel. Therefore, Paul did not have to consult with anyone, even the other apostles.

In verse 17 we see that Paul considered himself to be an apostle. While the other apostles were chosen by Jesus when He lived on earth, Paul was called directly by Christ after His ascension. The apostle proclaimed the gospel was sufficient for him, demonstrating to the Galatians that it was also sufficient for them. The Galatians were not required to do anything but receive the gospel by faith. What they had received from God was sufficient to change their lives.

In the proclamation of the gospel, Paul was preaching the faith he once tried to destroy (v. 23). Paul was also an example to these believers of the power of proclamation. Everywhere Paul traveled, many lives were changed through his preaching of the gospel. If the Galatian converts wanted to see the gospel continue to change lives, they needed to proclaim what God had done for them as well. Paul was setting an example for all believers of the power of testimony.

Talk About It:
1. How does Paul describe his life before Christ (vv. 13, 14)?
2. What was God's plan for Paul's life (vv. 15, 16)?
3. How did the Christians respond to the new Paul (vv. 23, 24)?

"The gospel is not something we go to church to hear; it is something we go from church to tell."
—**Vance Havner**

CONCLUSION

The transforming power of the gospel has not changed through the centuries. To the one who receives it, the gospel will bring new life in Christ.

We find a message of hope in the gospel. This hope comes

from hearing that God has the power to save from sin and to change lives that are broken and shattered. It is a message that has remained alive through the centuries, through Holy Spirit-empowered believers proclaiming the transforming message to others who are lost and hurting. The message is found in the gospel and confirmed by our personal testimonies of how the gospel has forever changed our lives.

GOLDEN TEXT CHALLENGE

"I AM NOT ASHAMED OF THE GOSPEL OF CHRIST; FOR IT IS THE POWER OF GOD UNTO SALVATION TO EVERY ONE THAT BELIEVETH; TO THE JEW FIRST, AND ALSO TO THE GREEK" (Romans 1:16).

To have power is not necessarily to be loved. Power can subjugate people, but it cannot make them love us.

The apostle Paul knew from experience that the gospel of Christ was power. At the very time he was expressing opposition to it on his way to Damascus to imprison Christians, that power knocked him off his feet. But a strange thing happened. Instead of causing Paul to hate the One who wielded this power, it made him fall in love with Him.

In this detail lies the difference between the power of people and the power of God. God does not exercise His power to bring about mere forced obedience of the weak to the powerful, but to bring salvation.

And what is this salvation? It is the complete change of the individual's heart, disposition and nature. The gospel knocks a person down not to make him a slave, but a willing servant. It saves a person from sin which made him oppose God in the first place.

This is the great message of Romans 1:16. Why, then, should anyone be ashamed of the gospel as the power of God, when it is power that saves us from catastrophe and makes us want to follow our Captor?—**Spiros Zodhiates**

Need for the Gospel

Romans 1:18 through 3:31; Galatians 2:5-21

INTRODUCTION

There are many things we need in life. However there is only one thing that is absolutely necessary—the gospel of the Lord Jesus Christ. The gospel is indispensable for all humanity. Why is it necessary? Because there is a great barrier between humanity and God—sin. The gospel message shines a mirror into our lives, showing us our sinful condition, and revealing to us how to be reconciled with a holy God and live in relationship with Him throughout eternity.

The apostle Paul recognized his need for a Savior, submitted to God, and served Him in a powerful, world-changing ministry. He knew the gospel was a life-changing message that needed to be taken to both Jews and Gentiles, for it had transformed his life. In the Jewish mind, adherence to the Law was the basis for salvation. In Galatians, we see Paul was disturbed that the gospel message he preached to them was being subverted by Judaizers who, in addition to the gospel, required that people observe the Law in order to be saved. Therefore, Paul needed to show them that one is not brought into a right relationship with God by observing the Law but through believing in Christ. Christ was, and still is, the only way of salvation for both Jews and Gentiles.

Unit Theme:
The Gospel in Romans and Galatians

Central Truth:
The gospel reveals that the only way to have a right relationship with God is through faith in Christ.

Focus:
Recognize that everyone has sinned and trust Christ for salvation.

Context:
Paul's letters to the churches of Galatia and the church in Rome were probably written several years apart but addressed similar issues.

Golden Text:
"Knowing that a man is not justified by the works of the law, but by the faith of Jesus Christ, even we have believed in Jesus Christ, that we might be justified by the faith of Christ" (Galatians 2:16).

Study Outline:
I. All Have Sinned (Romans 1:18-23, 28-32; Galatians 2:5-10)
II. The Law Cannot Save (Romans 2:17-29; Galatians 2:15-21)
III. Only Christ Can Save (Romans 3:21-31)

I. ALL HAVE SINNED (Romans 1:18-23, 28-32;
Galatians 2:5-10)

A. Suppressing the Truth Through Wickedness
(Romans 1:18-20)

18. For the wrath of God is revealed from heaven against all ungodliness and unrighteousness of men, who hold the truth in unrighteousness;

19. Because that which may be known of God is manifest in them; for God hath shewed it unto them.

20. For the invisible things of him from the creation of the world are clearly seen, being understood by the things that are made, even his eternal power and Godhead; so that they are without excuse.

Talk About It:
1. What does it mean to "hold the truth in unrighteousness" (v. 18), and why do people do this?
2. Who is "without excuse" before God (v. 20)?

The righteousness of God is needed by humanity because the whole of humanity is sinful, morally bankrupt and desperately in need of forgiveness. But before the solution, Paul begins to show the plight of sinful humanity in a graphic manner. Sinners, whom Paul describes here as wicked, suppress the truth through their wickedness. Suppression is a deliberate attempt to "hold" back or prevent the truth from achieving its desired end. As such, sinners have no excuse in as much as they have known God through His creation, but have chosen to live according to their own standards instead of by God's holy standards.

Manford George Gutzke observes: "Whether you look at the earth or the sky, trees or animals, you know there must be a Creator. When you see a machine, you know there is a mechanic. If you see a picture, you know there is an artist. . . . These are fundamental realities. Paul says enough is known by such things to guide a man in right ways. If a person goes wrong, it is his own fault; he is without excuse." Indeed, each person is responsible for the choices he makes.

Paul said that the creation reveals God's invisible qualities to humanity. God's eternal power and divine nature are reflected in His works. The design of the universe teaches people that there is a divine Person behind its formation and operation.

B. Suppressing the Honor and Praise Due God (vv. 21, 22)

21. Because that, when they knew God, they glorified him not as God, neither were thankful; but became vain in their imaginations, and their foolish heart was darkened.

22. Professing themselves to be wise, they became fools.

Talk About It:
Why is it dangerous not to give God thanks and praise?

Not only do sinners suppress the truth about God, but they also suppress the honor and praise that is due the holy God. They do not give glory to God for His awesome character and mighty deeds. They also do not give thanks to Him for all that He has done in their lives.

Humankind owes the Creator God a debt of gratitude. Such gratitude, honor and thanksgiving, although including it, is not limited to a mere acknowledgment of God's existence. Instead, it is both a recognition of His lordship and a life spent in grateful obedience to Him day by day.

In verses 21 and 22, Paul spells out the result of the failure to recognize God for who He is. The unbelievers became futile in their thinking; that is, their thoughts were void of worth or value. Their hearts were darkened. There was no light within them. They claimed to be wise in their own eyes, but were actually fools in God's eyes. It is a foolish thing to think one is wise without recognizing and honoring God as the source of all wisdom.

> "Thou who hast given me so much, give me one more thing—a grateful heart."
> —George Herbert

C. Exchanging the Glory of God for Mortal Images (v. 23)

23. And changed the glory of the uncorruptible God into an image made like to corruptible man, and to birds, and fourfooted beasts, and creeping things.

With their minds futile and hearts darkened and devoid of true wisdom, people turn to worshiping the created rather than the Creator. Humanity was created to worship God but, because of the Fall, the worship of unbelievers is directed toward self, other creatures or other things. Because humanity has lost the true and living God, they invent their own religions. What a tragedy! To worship anything or anyone apart from God is both foolishness and sin. It separates the created from the Creator. It defiles the worship that is due God. It perverts the intended relationship between God and humanity.

Talk About It:
Describe the foolish exchange some people make.

D. Rejecting the Knowledge of God (vv. 28-32)

(Romans 1:29-31 is not included in the printed text.)

28. And even as they did not like to retain God in their knowledge, God gave them over to a reprobate mind, to do those things which are not convenient;

32. Who knowing the judgment of God, that they which commit such things are worthy of death, not only do the same, but have pleasure in them that do them.

not convenient (v. 28)—not proper; things that should not be done

Sin degrades people physically, mentally and spiritually. Because of humanity's sin, "God gave them over" (v. 28), or "gave them up" (v. 24). This sounds like clods falling on the coffin as God leaves people to follow their wicked desires. This phrase means "God delivered them over to the power of." It is used of delivering one to prison, as when Saul of Tarsus dragged Christians from their homes and "*committed* them to prison" (Acts 8:3). It was used also when Jesus was bound and *delivered* over to Pilate for sentencing (Matthew 27:2).

Men and women are not sinners because they sin; they sin because they are sinners. In Romans 1:29-31 Paul paints an

Talk About It:
1. What does it mean to become "reprobate," or "depraved" (*NIV*)?
2. Whom do depraved people approve of, and why (v. 32)?

ugly portrait of the depraved minds and hearts of people who intentionally turn away from the knowledge of God and His ways. They are "senseless, faithless, heartless, ruthless" (v. 31, *NIV*), and these deadly conditions of the heart produce every type of evil deed. Behind every specific act of sin there is a depraved mind that motivates it.

These rebellious people, made in the image of God, know that God will judge those who flout His nature and laws. Yet they set their eyes and rush madly toward self-destruction, and celebrate others who go with them.

"To take pleasure in what is sinful and vicious for its own sake, and knowing it to be such, is the last and lowest stage of human recklessness. The innate principle of self-love . . . that very easily and often blinds a man as to any impartial reflection upon himself, yet for the most part leaves his eyes open enough to judge truly of the same thing in his neighbor, and to hate that in others which he allows and cherishes in himself. And, therefore, when it shall come to this, that he approves, embraces and delights in sin as he observes it even in the person and practice of other men, this shows that the man is wholly transformed from the creature that God first made him; nay, that he has consumed those poor remainders of good that the sin of Adam left him; that lie has worn off the very remote dispositions and possibilities to virtue; and, in a word, has turned grace first, and afterward nature itself, out of doors" (Jamieson, Fausset and Brown).

E. Refusing to Yield (Galatians 2:5-10)

5. To whom we gave place by subjection, no, not for an hour; that the truth of the gospel might continue with you.

6. But of these who seemed to be somewhat, (whatsoever they were, it maketh no matter to me: God accepteth no man's person:) for they who seemed to be somewhat in conference added nothing to me:

7. But contrariwise, when they saw that the gospel of the uncircumcision was committed unto me, as the gospel of the circumcision was unto Peter;

8. (For he that wrought effectually in Peter to the apostleship of the circumcision, the same was mighty in me toward the Gentiles:)

9. And when James, Cephas, and John, who seemed to be pillars, perceived the grace that was given unto me, they gave to me and Barnabas the right hands of fellowship; that we should go unto the heathen, and they unto the circumcision.

10. Only they would that we should remember the poor; the same which I also was forward to do.

"There are certain diseases of which a constant symptom is unconsciousness that there is anything the matter. A deep-seated wound does not hurt much."
—Alexander MacLaren

an hour (v. 5)—"a moment" (*NIV*)

accepteth no man's person (v. 6)—"shows no partiality" (*NKJV*)

somewhat in conference (v. 6)—"seemed to be something" (*NKJV*)

Cephas (*SEE-fus*)—v. 9—The Syriac word for *Peter*, both words mean "rock."

forward (v. 10)—eager or anxious

Need for the Gospel

The Galatians had previously responded positively to the gospel of freedom and grace that Paul proclaimed. But it remained a crucial task for them to abide in the truth, especially in light of the Judaizers who had infiltrated the church. Paul would not give in or yield any ground to those who distorted the gospel with the Law (v. 5). Not even the so-called important men (v. 6) could sway him from the true gospel message. He was not impressed with who they were or how well they kept the Law. External appearances meant nothing to him. He knew that God looked at the heart when considering any person. True salvation could not be rendered by human efforts. He would not let the Judaizers add anything to this message of salvation. In fact, he goes on to say that they recognized he was called to preach the gospel to the Gentiles just as Peter had been called to the Jews (v. 7). Again what is reinforced here is that both Jews and Gentiles are in need of the salvation that comes through faith in Jesus Christ.

"Paul's privilege as preacher of the gospel to the Gentiles is called a *grace* (v. 9). The Jerusalem leaders recognized this grace by extending the right hand of fellowship to Paul and Barnabas. This was no mere formality, but a meaningful endorsement of the message of free grace that these two had been proclaiming among the Gentiles. The apostles endorsed also the division of labor that sent one group of evangelists to the Gentiles, the other to the Jews. However, they requested the missionaries to the Gentile world not to so divorce themselves from the Jewish believers—especially those at Jerusalem, who were notoriously poor (Romans 15:26)—as to forget their need. The proof of Paul's good faith in acceding to this request was that he raised a substantial fund among the Gentile churches for these people (1 Corinthians 16:1-4), which he and others took to Jerusalem on the occasion of his last visit" (*Wycliffe Bible Commentary*).

II. THE LAW CANNOT SAVE (Romans 2:17-29; Galatians 2:15-21)

A. Having the Law (Romans 2:17-20)

17. Behold, thou art called a Jew, and restest in the law, and makest thy boast of God,

18. And knowest his will, and approvest the things that are more excellent, being instructed out of the law;

19. And art confident that thou thyself art a guide of the blind, a light of them which are in darkness,

20. An instructor of the foolish, a teacher of babes, which hast the form of knowledge and of the truth in the law.

To begin his argument that the Law is unable to save, Paul spoke to the people who depended on the Law. They had started

Talk About It:
1. What wasn't Paul impressed with people's credentials (v. 6)?
2. What is "the gospel of the uncircumcision" (v. 7)?
3. What is "the right hand of fellowship" (v. 9), and why was it offered to Paul?

Talk About It:
1. What does it mean to "rely upon the Law" (v. 17, *NASB*)?

to rely on the Law for their righteousness or right relationship with God. They were proudly conscious of their membership in the "chosen people."

Not only were the Jews *instructed* by the Law (v. 18), they *had* the Law (v. 20). They considered themselves to be in a position over others because they possessed the Law—the embodiment of knowledge and truth—something that others did not possess. Verses 19 and 20 reflect the attitude of the Jews toward the Gentiles. The latter were regarded as blind and lost, foolish and infants; that is, people with little or no religious knowledge.

"The men who really believe in themselves are all in lunatic asylums."
—G.K. Chesterton

B. Breaking the Law (vv. 21-24)

21. Thou therefore which teachest another, teachest thou not thyself? thou that preachest a man should not steal, dost thou steal?

22. Thou that sayest a man should not commit adultery, dost thou commit adultery? thou that abhorrest idols, dost thou commit sacrilege?

23. Thou that makest thy boast of the law, through breaking the law dishonourest thou God?

24. For the name of God is blasphemed among the Gentiles through you, as it is written.

Talk About It:
1. What was wrong with the people Paul addressed here (vv. 21-23)?
2. What impact was their wrong living having on the neighboring Gentiles (v. 24)?

The Jews who claimed to be the instructors of righteousness were not paying attention to what was being taught. Instead, they were breaking the Law. They violated the very Law they used to argue they had a right relationship with God. As such, instead of the Law of Moses being their unique heritage, it had become an embarrassment. They discredited God's integrity by their disregard of His moral standard.

Paul's lifestyle was very different. For him, living the Word was more important than just speaking the Word. Merely hearing, teaching and preaching God's Word avails nothing without faith, submission and obedience to it as the will of God. Paul exhorted his readers to think more about their own behavior and less about their perceived religious advantages due to having the Law. The result of their breaking the Law was the name of God being blasphemed among the Gentiles (see Isaiah 52:5). Having and knowing the Law was not a free ticket to righteousness.

C. Boasting in Circumcision (vv. 25-29)

25. For circumcision verily profiteth, if thou keep the law: but if thou be a breaker of the law, thy circumcision is made uncircumcision.

26. Therefore if the uncircumcision keep the righteousness of the law, shall not his uncircumcision be counted for circumcision?

27. And shall not uncircumcision which is by nature, if it fulfil the law, judge thee, who by the letter and circumcision dost transgress the law?

28. For he is not a Jew, which is one outwardly; neither is that circumcision, which is outward in the flesh:

29. But he is a Jew, which is one inwardly; and circumcision is that of the heart, in the spirit, and not in the letter; whose praise is not of men, but of God.

In these verses the apostle Paul connects the topic of circumcision with the Law because, as the Jewish people relied on the Law, they also relied on their circumcision as an outward sign of God's love for them. God gave circumcision as a sign of His covenant with Abraham and his descendants. Since that time, the Jewish people valued circumcision highly because it distinguished them as the people of God. Circumcision was a biological identification card for Jewish males.

Paul argued that one is not right with God merely because he is circumcised. Circumcision is just a *sign* of who one is. It does not make a person into anything. The focus must be on the inner person—the condition of one's heart. A right relationship and standing with God originate out of an inner identity which Paul terms the "circumcision of the heart" (v. 29). And that circumcision is by the Spirit and for God's praise.

D. Not by Observing the Law (Galatians 2:15, 16)

15. We who are Jews by nature, and not sinners of the Gentiles,

16. Knowing that a man is not justified by the works of the law, but by the faith of Jesus Christ, even we have believed in Jesus Christ, that we might be justified by the faith of Christ, and not by the works of the law: for by the works of the law shall no flesh be justified.

What made the Jews believe they were a superior race and consider the non-Jews as a whole to be sinners? The answer lies in the understanding of the Jews that their holiness or separateness from other nations rested on their possession of the Mosaic Law. Such fundamental conviction brought non-Jews to a disadvantage. But Paul argued to the contrary. A person, even a Jew, is not justified by works of the Law. By believing in Jesus Christ, the Jewish Christians in Galatia had shown this to be true. All justification flows from a relationship of faith. This was the case with Abraham (3:6).

The verb *justify* in its different forms is used eight times in Galatians—three times in 2:16, and then in 2:17; 3:8, 11, 24; and 5:4. It occurs 15 times in Romans. In its triple usage in Galatians 2:16, *justified* means "to be declared righteous." If a human being could completely fulfill the law of God, this would

Talk About It:
1. Who is a genuine Jew, according to Paul?
2. What is the circumcision of the heart, and how is it received (v. 29)?

"Man talks of the survival of the fittest, but the glory of the gospel is that it transforms the unfit."
—*Quotable Quotes*

Talk About It:
How is grace better than the Law?

Talk About It:
1. Why did Christ die (v. 21)?
2. What does it mean to be "crucified with Christ" (v. 20)?

provide a case for justification in God's sight. But no mere human has ever accomplished this, so the only way for lost humanity to be made righteous is through faith in Jesus Christ, the sinless Son of God.

Being declared righteous by God has moral and ethical nuances. The gospel of free grace through faith in Christ does not relieve one from the moral requirements of Scripture. Indeed, we are enabled to lead godly lives through the indwelling Savior.

E. Dying to the Law (vv. 17-21)

17. But if, while we seek to be justified by Christ, we ourselves also are found sinners, is therefore Christ the minister of sin? God forbid.

18. For if I build again the things which I destroyed, I make myself a transgressor.

19. For I through the law am dead to the law, that I might live unto God.

20. I am crucified with Christ: nevertheless I live; yet not I, but Christ liveth in me: and the life which I now live in the flesh I live by the faith of the Son of God, who loved me, and gave himself for me.

21. I do not frustrate the grace of God: for if righteousness come by the law, then Christ is dead in vain.

In order to be justified in Christ, one must abandon the thing he is trusting in for his salvation. In the case of the Jew, this meant he must abandon the legal righteousness he was relying upon. In the mind of the Jew, such abandonment was sinful; thus, the one who acted in this way became a sinner. On that basis Christ was accused of promoting sin. Paul responded to that accusation by declaring it absolutely not true.

Every sinner must realize he is a sinner before God can help him. Until there is an awareness of one's condition, there is no sense of need for God. But when a man sees himself as God sees him, he is then ready to take the steps necessary to obtain forgiveness and to experience peace.

Giving himself as an example, Paul describes his own justification experience in terms of "death to the law." Through the Law he died to the Law. The Law enabled him to see his sin. He realized he could not keep all the Old Testament laws in his own strength. The Law he once lived for had become the Law he had died to. Now he was living for God—not only *for* God, but *in* God. He described a level of intimacy with God so deep that he had "died" with Christ on the cross and now Christ lived in him and through him. He was no longer wrapped up in the Law, but wrapped up in God through Jesus Christ. He was living by faith in Christ, who is the righteousness of God.

Need for the Gospel

III. ONLY CHRIST CAN SAVE (Romans 3:21-31)
A. Christ as the Righteousness of God (vv. 21-27)
   21. But now the righteousness of God without the law is manifested, being witnessed by the law and the prophets;
   22. Even the righteousness of God which is by faith of Jesus Christ unto all and upon all them that believe: for there is no difference:
   23. For all have sinned, and come short of the glory of God;
   24. Being justified freely by his grace through the redemption that is in Christ Jesus:
   25. Whom God hath set forth to be a propitiation through faith in his blood, to declare his righteousness for the remission of sins that are past, through the forbearance of God;

propitiation (v. 25) —"sacrifice of atonement" (*NIV*)

   26. To declare, I say, at this time his righteousness: that he might be just, and the justifier of him which believeth in Jesus.
   27. Where is boasting then? It is excluded. By what law? of works? Nay: but by the law of faith.

In these verses, Paul gives the solution to humanity's problem of unrighteousness laid out in the first three chapters of Romans. This solution is the provision God has made for the redemption of humankind. It is the fulfillment of the words spoken by the prophets in the Old Testament. The answer to the question of sin is found in Christ Jesus, who is the righteousness of God. He is the embodiment of all truth. He is the One who makes us right with God. Righteousness is God's gift to humanity, and it comes to us through what Christ did on the cross.

Talk About It:
1. What does "there is no difference" (v. 22) refer to?
2. Why is "boasting . . . excluded" (v. 27)?

Paul makes six points concerning justification and the gift of righteousness from God: (1) It is the means by which God makes humanity right with Himself. Humans are now provided a way to have fellowship with God. (2) It is a gift that is received only by faith and not by human effort. (3) Justification by faith breaks down barriers. Jews and Gentiles alike have turned away from God, and therefore both are in need of this gift of reconciliation with God. (4) This gift is available to humanity through the death of Christ. It is this act of redemption that has freed humanity from the bondage of sin, death and evil. (5) God has acted justly and righteously in justifying humanity in this manner. (6) By means of justification God is justly upholding His righteous law which humanity had broken.

"There is no man so good, who, were he to submit all his thoughts and actions to the laws, would not deserve hanging 10 times in his life."
—Montaigne

B. Faith Apart From the Law (vv. 28-31)
   28. Therefore we conclude that a man is justified by faith without the deeds of the law.
   29. Is he the God of the Jews only? is he not also of the Gentiles? Yes, of the Gentiles also:

30. Seeing it is one God, which shall justify the circumcision by faith, and uncircumcision through faith.

31. Do we then make void the law through faith? God forbid: yea, we establish the law.

In these verses Paul describes humanity's responsibility in the process of redemption. The only response necessary is acceptance of the gift by faith alone. Paul was explaining there is nothing that human beings can do to please God in order to attain salvation. But in chapter 6, Paul does assert that faith is manifested by good works in the life of the believer.

So the question is asked: What happens to the Law because of this faith—is it nullified or canceled out? Paul strongly responds with "Not at all! Rather, we uphold the law" (3:31, *NIV*). But how is the Law upheld? The word *uphold* (KJV, "establish") means "support" or "confirm." Believers are to support the Law or confirm it as the will of God. This is done through living a holy life that is pleasing to God. The motivation for service and good works is the love for God and His people. The love of God is shed abroad in the lives of God's people. The Holy Spirit is the power by which the believer is able to live out the will of God in both word and deed.

Talk About It:
1. According to verse 30, what is required from both Jews and Gentiles?
2. What does faith do for the Law, and how (v. 31)?

"The law tells me how crooked I am. Grace comes along and straightens me out."
—Martin Luther

CONCLUSION

Humanity has a need that can only be met by the Savior, Jesus Christ. That need is to be reconciled with God. To all who will receive it, the gospel brings the message of "good news" that a way has been made for reconciliation with God. The first step is to recognize the need for restoration of relationship with God. This is a universal need. The Bible tells us "all have sinned, and come short of the glory of God" (Romans 3:23). Second, we are to trust Jesus Christ for our salvation. It is impossible to perform enough good works to merit salvation. He has made the way for our redemption. All we are to do is walk in His way as the people called by His name.

GOLDEN TEXT CHALLENGE

"KNOWING THAT A MAN IS NOT JUSTIFIED BY THE WORKS OF THE LAW, BUT BY THE FAITH OF JESUS CHRIST, EVEN WE HAVE BELIEVED IN JESUS CHRIST, THAT WE MIGHT BE JUSTIFIED BY THE FAITH OF CHRIST" (Galatians 2:16).

To illustrate the power of faith, Paul compares faith in Christ with the privileges of the Jews. The Jews had been given more insight into the ways of God than any other people on earth. They had personally witnessed more of the miracles of God than any other nation ever would. They had experienced the power and mercy of God like no other group in time. The Jews had been blessed with an access to God that no other people or nation had.

Nevertheless, privilege does not purchase the blood of perfect sacrifice for sins. Even the Jews needed to confess their sins and have faith in the sacrifice of Christ. If any people could claim the works, ritual and worship that God required, it was the Jews. But even with all their background, revelation and testimony, they still could only receive salvation by faith in Christ.

Daily Devotions:

M. When a Nation Repents
1 Kings 8:46-52

T. Christ, the Ransom
Job 33:19-28

W. The Law Is Temporary
Jeremiah 3:14-18

T. Salvation in Christ
John 3:16-21

F. Grace Abounds
Romans 5:12-21

S. Christ Fulfilled the Law
Hebrews 10:1-10

Justification by Faith

Romans 4:1-25; Galatians 3:1-29

INTRODUCTION

It is not unusual to see religious organizations and groups appeal to a founder for support and validation of their views. For example, Wesleyans often appeal to the writings of John Wesley; members of the Salvation Army to William and Catherine Booth; Lutherans to Martin Luther; and Pentecostals to Seymour, Tomlinson and others. It was exactly the same with the Jews of Paul's day. They often appealed to Abraham. Unfortunately, their appeal to Abraham as the founder of the faith led to many serious distortions of God's truth, particularly the way of justification. The Jews assumed that merely being biological descendants of Abraham entitled them to right standing with God. Moreover, they associated circumcision with justification. In addition, some of the Jews focused on the Law as the means of justification. The cumulative effect of these distortions was a shift from dependence on God's work of redemption to confidence in human works of righteousness.

It is obvious that this issue is still alive today. There are many self-proclaimed Christians who base their claim on their heritage—being born in a particular religious tradition or being raised in a particular denomination. They assume that the faith of their parents was imparted to them either prior to or upon their birth. Such people are amazed at the idea that one can become right with God simply by believing in Christ. This principle was just as startling to the Jews in the first century. That is why Paul felt the need to declare that Abraham was justified by faith and not works.

I. JUSTIFICATION IS A GIFT (Romans 4:1-8; Galatians 3:6-14)
A. Abraham's Discovery (Romans 4:1-3)
1. What shall we say then that Abraham our father, as pertaining to the flesh, hath found?
2. For if Abraham were justified by works, he hath whereof to glory; but not before God.
3. For what saith the scripture? Abraham believed God, and it was counted unto him for righteousness.

Paul argues in favor of justification by faith with an appeal to Abraham, a person who lived out the righteousness he had previously described (3:27-31). This was not without reason. The Jews shaped their identity around God's covenant with Abraham. Hence, an appeal to the life and practices of their founder would carry much weight. For Paul, Abraham was an example of faith, and Paul thought it necessary to present him as a case study of the principle that a right relationship with God can only come through faith. Paul's appeal to the Scripture (Genesis 15:6) establishes that fact. Salvation, as Paul has previously declared (Romans 3:24), is by grace. If it is by works, then grace is ruled out of the picture.

Talk About It:
1. Why couldn't Abraham boast?
2. What was applied to Abraham, and why?

B. David's Discovery (vv. 4-8)
4. Now to him that worketh is the reward not reckoned of grace, but of debt.
5. But to him that worketh not, but believeth on him that justifieth the ungodly, his faith is counted for righteousness.
6. Even as David also describeth the blessedness of the man, unto whom God imputeth righteousness without works,
7. Saying, Blessed are they whose iniquities are forgiven, and whose sins are covered.
8. Blessed is the man to whom the Lord will not impute sin.

imputeth (v. 6) and **impute (v. 8)**—to reckon, credit, or take into account

The Jews as a whole were hardworking people. They would have thought it foolish for an employer to pay a worker his wage and call it a gift. No, this was money owed to the worker for his labor. However, things are different in God's economy. No matter how many good works a person does and no matter how hard he or she works in performing them, that person cannot earn justification. Instead, it is the person who puts his or her faith in God that receives salvation. That person is declared righteous by God. It is a free gift.

Paul goes on to introduce another witness—again a revered figure to the Jews—to explain the way of justification by faith. David the king represented the period of some of Israel's greatest glory. By demonstrating that David as well as Abraham was justified by

Talk About It:
1. Why is righteousness not a "wage"?
2. What three things does God do with the believer's sin (vv. 7, 8)?

faith, Paul would strengthen his case greatly. So he quoted Psalm 32:1, 2, where David spoke of a blessed individual, whose divine favor does not come by works or through human effort. Even David could not boast of his spiritual standing.

Once again Paul was presenting Scriptural support for his position concerning righteousness, faith and the Law. David recognized what a blessed state it is to know one is no longer guilty before God. Paul, Abraham and David discovered that a right relationship with God only comes by His gracious act, prompted by a willingness to trust Him.

C. The Blessing of Faith (Galatians 3:6-9)

6. Even as Abraham believed God, and it was accounted to him for righteousness.

7. Know ye therefore that they which are of faith, the same are the children of Abraham.

8. And the scripture, foreseeing that God would justify the heathen through faith, preached before the gospel unto Abraham, saying, In thee shall all nations be blessed.

9. So then they which be of faith are blessed with faithful Abraham.

In Galatians 3:6-9, Paul continues the argument he began in verses 1-5. Now Paul is beginning a journey with his readers through the Scriptures to substantiate that, from the time of Abraham, God had always intended justification to be by faith. Paul will compare the faith of the Galatians and what they received when they believed, to the faith of Abraham and what he received when he believed. Paul is deliberate in his choice of text to show that Abraham's faith, his being reckoned as righteous, and the promise of blessing all came before there was any mention whatsoever of circumcision or of Abraham's faithful and obedient action in regard to the offering of Isaac in sacrifice. Moreover, Abraham was made righteous hundreds of years before the Mosaic Law and covenant were given.

Note that it is God who reckoned Abraham to be righteous (v. 6). It was not based on anything that Abraham did. It was God who took the initiative. And "those who believe are children of Abraham" (v. 7, NIV).

In verse 8, Paul continues to assert that the Gentiles ("heathen") are included in God's covenant with Abraham and, as such, can also receive the gift of justification by faith. The justification of the Gentiles by faith is not an afterthought on God's part. It was always on His mind. Paul's purpose in this assertion is to address a misconception of the Jewish Christians at this time. Within the Judaizers' insistence that Gentile Christians be circumcised was a belief that the initial covenant was made with just the Jews, therefore one had to become a Jew to inherit the promise. Paul reinforces that those who have faith will receive the promised blessing of justification. For Paul to say the Gentiles are blessed in Abraham is to say they are blessed as he was. In other words, they are also reckoned righteous and need not surrender themselves to the requirements of the Law to be justified.

D. The Curse of the Law (vv. 10-14)

10. For as many as are of the works of the law are under the curse: for it is written, Cursed is every one that continueth not in all things which are written in the book of the law to do them.

11. But that no man is justified by the law in the sight of God, it is evident: for, The just shall live by faith.

12. And the law is not of faith: but, The man that doeth them shall live in them.

13. Christ hath redeemed us from the curse of the law, being made a curse for us: for it is written, Cursed is every one that hangeth on a tree:

14. That the blessing of Abraham might come on the Gentiles through Jesus Christ; that we might receive the promise of the Spirit through faith.

Paul has already established the positive example of Abraham's faith. He now goes on to show the inexpediency and absurdity of the idea that Abraham, and by implication the Galatians, would have to submit to the Law as the means of justification. Paul says that those who live on the basis of the works of the Law are cursed. One could not live under the Law and expect to participate in Abraham's blessing which comes only by the way of faith. In verse 11 Paul continues his forceful argument that justification is by faith alone, quoting Habakkuk 2:4.

In verse 12 Paul's indignation is not with the Law itself but with a distorted perception of the Law. He stresses that the Law was not meant to be the end but a means to an end. If fulfillment of the Law becomes one's main focus or chief goal, relationship with God will not be. The point of the Law is to show a person their need for salvation and not to become the means of salvation. Only faith in Christ, creating a covenantal relationship with God, is the means of salvation. From the vantage point of faith, one enters into a reconciled relationship with God and obeys the Law out of a love for God and others.

In verse 13, Paul introduces Christ as the One who has redeemed humanity from the curse of the Law. The blessings promised to Abraham by God come to both Jew and Gentile through Jesus Christ. Both receive the promised Holy Spirit through faith. To receive the Spirit is to have righteousness, life and all the promised benefits of the Spirit's presence.

Talk About It:
1. Who is "under the curse" (v. 10), and why?
2. What do believers "live by" (v. 11), and what do they obey (v. 12)?
3. In verse 14, what promise is made to believers?

"We are justified on account of Christ, through faith. . . . We are justified on account of His obedience during His lifetime and His death upon the cross. It is because of Him, and not because of anything we have done or will do, that we are made right with God. But the means by which we are justified is faith."
—Alister McGrath

II. JUSTIFICATION IS PROMISED TO BELIEVERS (Romans 4:9-15)

A. Circumcision as a Sign of the Promise (vv. 9-12)

9. Cometh this blessedness then upon the circumcision only, or upon the uncircumcision also? for we say that faith was reckoned to Abraham for righteousness.

10. How was it then reckoned? when he was in circumcision, or in uncircumcision? Not in circumcision, but in uncircumcision.

11. And he received the sign of circumcision, a seal of the righteousness of the faith which he had yet being uncircumcised: that he might be the father of all them that believe, though they be not circumcised; that righteousness might be imputed unto them also:

12. And the father of circumcision to them who are not of the circumcision only, but who also walk in the steps of that faith of our father Abraham, which he had being yet uncircumcised.

Many of the Jews whom Paul was addressing in Romans may have agreed with him in verse 9 that all must have faith in God to receive His righteousness. The Jewish Christians may even have believed this could apply to the Gentiles as well. The problem was that many of the Jewish Christians were still placing the requirement of circumcision on the Gentile converts for this promise of righteousness to be fulfilled in their lives as well. Paul questions them here about this blessed promise of righteousness and whom they consider its recipients to be.

The core issue that would answer this question was discerning at what point righteousness was credited to Abraham. Was it before or after his circumcision? Paul answers this question emphatically that it was before the circumcision. The significance of circumcision was its being a sign of Abraham's right relationship with God. As a person of faith, Abraham is the role model and patriarch for all believers who walk in the footsteps of faith, whether or not they have been circumcised.

B. Two Ways to Approach God (vv. 13-15)

13. For the promise, that he should be the heir of the world, was not to Abraham, or to his seed, through the law, but through the righteousness of faith.

14. For if they which are of the law be heirs, faith is made void, and the promise made of none effect:

15. Because the law worketh wrath: for where no law is, there is no transgression.

In these three verses Paul describes two ways of approaching God. One is by grace and the other by Law and works. Just as Abraham did, one can approach God through faith—

Talk About It:
1. What did Abraham's circumcision have to do with his righteousness?
2. How can righteousness be credited to us (v. 11)?

"Faith is like a channel through which the benefits of Christ flow to us."
—Alister McGrath

---

understanding that justification is a promised gift—or one can approach God through the Law. Those who choose the way of the Law have devalued faith, thus the promise God has made becomes of no value. The person who comes by trying to perfectly follow the Law will have to live under the wrath of God for his or her transgressions of the Law. The Law was given to reveal our falling short of God's standard of righteousness and can only take us so far. It cannot make us righteous.

Talk About It:
Why does "law [cause] wrath" (v. 15)?

III. BELIEVE THE PROMISE (Romans 4:16-25; Galatians 3:19-29)

A. Guaranteed by Grace (Romans 4:16, 17)

16. Therefore it is of faith, that it might be by grace; to the end the promise might be sure to all the seed; not to that only which is of the law, but to that also which is of the faith of Abraham; who is the father of us all,

17. (As it is written, I have made thee a father of many nations,) before him whom he believed, even God, who quickeneth the dead, and calleth those things which be not as though they were.

Having shown that circumcision does not produce righteousness, Paul noted that neither does the Law (vv. 13-16). In verse 16, Paul clearly states that Abraham is the "father of us all." By this he means that Gentile Christians can claim Abraham as their forefather also, not according to the flesh but according to faith. Apart from faith, the Jews had no special ground for boasting that they were Abraham's children. Abraham's justification and its attendant blessings were not based on the Law but on his faith in God; they were not earned by effort or merit on his part but were bestowed freely by God's grace. The principle on which God dealt with Abraham is applicable to his spiritual descendants who follow the example of Abraham by walking in faith.

Talk About It:
1. What is the relationship between grace and faith (v. 16)?
2. How is God characterized in verse 17?

In verse 17, Paul once again gives Scriptural support for his position concerning Abraham as our example. Abraham is the father of all believers. He is father of Jewish and Gentile Christians, not in virtue of any human relationship with them but because of his faith. This verse also answers the question of why Abraham is an important figure. The answer lies not so much in Abraham, but the One in whom Abraham believed. The object of his faith was God. The God to whom Abraham directed his faith is the God who gives life to the dead.

Anyone can have faith. Many people have faith in themselves, in friends, in institutions, or in political leaders. It was important for Paul to emphasize here that Abraham's faith rested *in God*. That faith was manifested by his complete trust in God and obedience to His will. It is safe to put our trust in God

Big Enough?
Is your God big enough? Is He big enough for your life, your problems, your needs, and your heartache? Or have you let them discourage you? . . . Our God is omnipotent. There can be no limit, boundary, or edge to His ability and His power.
—Paris Reidhead

because He has the power to raise the dead and to call things into existence that are not. He is the Creator God who is omnipotent and holy.

B. Against All Hope With All Hope (vv. 18-25)

18. Who against hope believed in hope, that he might become the father of many nations; according to that which was spoken, So shall thy seed be.

19. And being not weak in faith, he considered not his own body now dead, when he was about an hundred years old, neither yet the deadness of Sarah's womb:

20. He staggered not at the promise of God through unbelief; but was strong in faith, giving glory to God;

21. And being fully persuaded that, what he had promised, he was able also to perform.

22. And therefore it was imputed to him for righteousness.

23. Now it was not written for his sake alone, that it was imputed to him;

24. But for us also, to whom it shall be imputed, if we believe on him that raised up Jesus our Lord from the dead;

25. Who was delivered for our offences, and was raised again for our justification.

In these verses Paul uses Abraham as an illustration of faith that pleases God. He is using this example of faith to teach his readers about the nature of faith. How does faith work? Faith claims a promise and acts on it in spite of conditions which make its fulfillment seem impossible. First, Abraham's faith was a faith that, against all hope, believed in hope. Abraham and Sarah's childlessness looked like an unchangeable situation. But even with all the odds physically against him and Sarah, Abraham believed because God had made the promise. His focus was on God and not on his circumstances. Faith could bring life out of death, and reality out of what seemed not to be. Second, by giving glory to God in the midst of these circumstances, he was affirming his belief that God was bigger than the problem and had all the power to fulfill His promise. Abraham was "fully persuaded" (v. 21) that God was able to do what He said He would do. Such faith in the promise of God was not a work or human effort on Abraham's part.

Paul's conclusion in verse 22 is as strong as he could make it: Abraham's faith was credited for righteousness. Those words extend beyond Abraham to the Roman readers of the letter and to all who believe today. The statement sums up Paul's argument on justification.

The last three verses of the chapter point out that the story

---

delivered (v. 25)—
"put to death"

Talk About It:
1. Explain the phrase "who against hope believed in hope" (v. 18).
2. How are the phrases "staggered not" (v. 20) and "fully persuaded" (v. 21) connected?
3. What does God require us to believe in (vv. 24, 25)?

"There is no medicine like hope, no incentive so great, and no tonic so powerful as expectation of something better tomorrow."
—Orison Marden

of Abraham serves as an instruction to Christians. We are to exhibit the same kind of faith that Abraham did, one that is related to death and resurrection. Our faith is fixed on Jesus Christ who died but who, by the power of God, was raised from the dead and is our living Lord and Savior. There is a divine remedy for sin. A right standing with God is possible. It is by faith in Christ alone.

C. The Law and the Promise (Galatians 3:19-25)

19. Wherefore then serveth the law? It was added because of transgressions, till the seed should come to whom the promise was made; and it was ordained by angels in the hand of a mediator.

20. Now a mediator is not a mediator of one, but God is one.

21. Is the law then against the promises of God? God forbid: for if there had been a law given which could have given life, verily righteousness should have been by the law.

22. But the scripture hath concluded all under sin, that the promise by faith of Jesus Christ might be given to them that believe.

23. But before faith came, we were kept under the law, shut up unto the faith which should afterwards be revealed.

24. Wherefore the law was our schoolmaster to bring us unto Christ, that we might be justified by faith.

25. But after that faith is come, we are no longer under a schoolmaster.

In Romans 4, Paul proved his point with regards to the impotence of the Law concerning justification, and it now appears there is no place left for the Law in the scheme of things. Paul could easily have been branded as an *antinomian*—an advocate of lawlessness and unabashed libertinism. So, in Galatians 3:19, Paul asks the question, "What, then, was the purpose of the law?" (*NIV*). He says the Law was "added because of transgressions, till the seed should come." In the preceding verses, Paul revealed the identity of "the seed." He did this by writing that the promise was spoken not only to Abraham but to his "seed." Paul emphasized that the scripture did not say "seeds," for it was referring to the one Seed, Jesus Christ. So the Law was added because of transgressions prior to the new covenant being established through the blood of Christ.

Next, Paul asks whether the Law is opposed to the promises of God (v. 21). Certainly not, is his emphatic reply. The whole world was held prisoner to the law of sin and death. The only promise that could set free is that which would impart life. The Law did not have that power, but Christ does. Therefore, the promise of justification is obtained through putting one's faith in

Talk About It:
1. Why is Jesus called "the seed" (v. 19)?
2. How was the Law a guard and tutor (vv. 23-25)?

"Faith rests on the naked Word of God; that Word believed gives full assurance."
—Harry Ironside

Christ rather than in the Law. But the Law did have a purpose in God's work of salvation. The Law leads the way to Christ so that justification may be obtained through faith in Him. The Law makes a person aware of his or her transgressions and unrighteousness, and reinforces the need for God and his justification.

D. Heirs of the Promise (vv. 26-29)

26. For ye are all the children of God by faith in Christ Jesus.

27. For as many of you as have been baptized into Christ have put on Christ.

28. There is neither Jew nor Greek, there is neither bond nor free, there is neither male nor female: for ye are all one in Christ Jesus.

29. And if ye be Christ's, then are ye Abraham's seed, and heirs according to the promise.

Talk About It
1. What does baptism signify (v. 27)?
2. Describe the unity of the church (vv. 28, 29).

This chapter concludes with the good news that all who put their faith in Jesus Christ are children of God. We are adopted into the family of God and share in His inheritance. Those who become His children receive the promises made to Abraham. By being baptized into Christ and clothed with Christ, a person becomes part of Abraham's seed, receiving the covenant promises of God. Verse 28 reemphasizes that *all* believers become part of the one seed of Christ. The unity within this one seed transcends gender, nationality and socioeconomic status.

CONCLUSION

Within these passages of Scripture we find God's assurance of justification through faith in Jesus Christ alone. It sets us free from the bondage of trying to come into a right relationship with God though our own efforts. It is a gift of God available to all who will receive it. Through this act of justification God declares our sins to be forgiven and imparts His righteousness into our lives. We can be set free from the guilt of past sins and failures.

GOLDEN TEXT CHALLENGE

"THAT NO MAN IS JUSTIFIED BY THE LAW IN THE SIGHT OF GOD, IT IS EVIDENT: FOR, THE JUST SHALL LIVE BY FAITH" (Galatians 3:11).

Not only does the way of Law find its logical consequence in curse (v. 10), the Law reveals our sin and our utter helplessness to rid ourselves of its misery. The Law forces out the disease that is spreading under the skin. Such is its task. But healing it does not bring. "The Law," says Luther, "is that which lays down what man is to do; the gospel reveals whence man is to obtain help. When I place myself in the hands of the physician, one branch of art says where the disease lies, another what course to take to get quit of it. So here. The Law discovers our disease; the gospel supplies the remedy."

We become aware, in critical moments, that our evil desires are more powerful than the prohibition of Law, and are in truth first stirred up thoroughly by the prohibition. And this disposition of our heart is the decisive point for the question, Whether then the holy Law—the holy, just and good commandment—makes us holy, just and good men? The answer to this is, and remains a most decided, no.

But God in His grace has provided an answer, a way of justification. It is through the merits of His Son. . . . Jesus Christ has come into our world, allied Himself with our sinful race, merited consideration and acceptance by obedience to Law, even as far as death, and this merit of the Divine Man passes over to believers. In the Father's sight, therefore, we are regarded as just, when we believe on Christ Jesus. We have been justified through faith.—Excerpts from *Pulpit Commentary*

Daily Devotions:
M. Abraham Believed
Genesis 15:1-6
T. Salvation Assured
Isaiah 51:1-6
W. Clothed in Salvation
Isaiah 61:7-11
T. Christ Justifies All Who Believe
Acts 13:32-39
F. The Way of Salvation
Romans 10:5-13
S. Have Faith
Hebrews 11:1-3

Death Destroyed (Easter)

1 Corinthians 15:1-57

Unit Theme:
Easter

Central Truth:
Christ's resurrection guarantees victory over death for believers.

Focus:
Affirm that Christ has conquered death and celebrate our hope of eternal life.

Context:
Paul's first letter to the Corinthians was written around A.D. 55.

Golden Text:
"Now is Christ risen from the dead, and become the firstfruits of them that slept" (1 Corinthians 15:20).

Study Outline:
I. Christ's Victory Over Death (1 Corinthians 15:20-26)
II. Sharing in Christ's Victory (1 Corinthians 15:35-49)
III. Triumphant Through Christ's Victory (1 Corinthians 15:50-57)

INTRODUCTION

For centuries the words of 1 Corinthians 15 have provided great comfort and hope to Christians who have lost loved ones. This chapter offers encouragement to the bereaved that only faith in Christ's resurrection can bring. A careful study cannot but give us a new appreciation of the Easter message.

In the chapter's first 11 verses, Paul gives the evidences of Christ's resurrection by the eyewitnesses' accounts of Jesus' postresurrection appearances, among whom he numbers himself. Paul writes, "And last of all he was seen of me also, as of one born out of due time. For I am the least of the apostles . . . because I persecuted the church of God" (vv. 8, 9).

Paul teaches that Christ's resurrection, together with the remainder of the gospel, is ample proof that believers too shall rise. He uses the same argument to convince the Romans: "He that raised up Christ from the dead shall also quicken your mortal bodies by his Spirit that dwelleth in you" (Romans 8:11).

Some people in the Corinthian church believed in the resurrection of Christ, but not in the resurrection of God's people. Their belief in the resurrection of Christ designated them as Christian, but their disbelief in the resurrection of people showed their acceptance of doctrinal influences outside the church. The Sadducees and the Epicureans maintained that humanity would cease to exist after death. The Stoics taught the reabsorption of the soul after death into the Divinity from which it sprang, and therefore the final extinction of the personality.

Paul declares, "But if there is no resurrection of the dead, then Christ is not risen. And if Christ is not risen, then our preaching is empty and your faith is also empty" (1 Corinthians 15:13, 14, *NKJV*).

I. CHRIST'S VICTORY OVER DEATH (1 Corinthians 15:20-26)
A. Risen From the Dead (v. 20)

20. But now is Christ risen from the dead, and become the firstfruits of them that slept.

Paul's argument has ended, he has shown how everything would be completely upset if there is no resurrection of the dead, and he now takes for granted what he has proved before—that Christ has risen again and, as a result, all dead in Christ shall likewise rise again.

The "firstfruits" was an ancient practice under the Law (see Leviticus 23:10). There are three possible ways Paul could be applying this metaphor: (1) Just as a whole year's harvest was promised to the Lord in the firstfruits, so the power of Christ's resurrection is extended to all who believe. (2) In Christ himself the firstfruits of the resurrection was gathered. (3) The remainder of the harvest followed the firstfruits, and in like manner the dead in Christ will follow Him in the resurrection.

B. Cause of Death (vv. 21, 22)

21. For since by man came death, by man came also the resurrection of the dead.

22. For as in Adam all die, even so in Christ shall all be made alive.

Death entered the world through Adam. By transgressing the divine commandment, Adam brought upon himself the sentence of death threatened in Genesis 2:17. Such is the solidarity of the human race that the sin of the first father consigned the mass of humanity to a sinful nature from birth and, thereby, introduced a society which as a whole is alienated from God.

It is fitting, then, that since by a man corruption entered the human race, so by a Man it should be overcome. The divine remedy for our human predicament is set forth in terms of Christ's incarnation and resurrection; therefore, Paul's repeated use of the words "by man" (v. 21) points to the reality of the Incarnation. The tragedy came through a man—Adam. The triumph of resurrection comes through a Man—Christ. Christ was as truly man as was Adam.

The two uses of the word *all* in verse 22 have two different meanings. In the first usage it refers to the whole of humanity, for all are in Adam. But in the second it is more limited, applying only to all those in Christ. The resurrection of Christ secures the resurrection of His people, for as there was a relationship between the death of Adam and his descendants, so there is a relationship between the resurrection of Christ and His people.

"Shall all be made alive" (v. 22) refers to more than resurrection as such. It includes the thought of abundant life that Christ brings to all who are in Him. We die by means of Adam,

Talk About It:
According to verse 20, why are Christians *not* "miserable" (v. 19)?

Talk About It:
1. Why do "all die" (v. 22)?
2. What did the hope of resurrection require, and why?

"At death we cross from one territory to another, but we'll have no trouble with visas. Our representative is already there, preparing for our arrival. As citizens of heaven, our entrance is incontestable."
—**Erwin Lutzer**

because we are in Adam; and we live by means of Christ, because we are in Christ.

C. Destruction of Death (vv. 23-26)

23. But every man in his own order: Christ the first-fruits; afterward they that are Christ's at his coming.

24. Then cometh the end, when he shall have delivered up the kingdom to God, even the Father; when he shall have put down all rule and all authority and power.

25. For he must reign, till he hath put all enemies under his feet.

26. The last enemy that shall be destroyed is death.

Talk About It:
1. Describe the "order" in verse 23.
2. What will happen in "the end" (v. 24)?
3. Why is death called "the last enemy" (v. 26)?

Paul apparently took for granted that the error of "some" (v. 12) had been refuted and gave the Corinthians information concerning the order of resurrection. In classical Greek, the word *order* (v. 23) was used almost exclusively in a military sense to denote a detachment of troops, in order of their rank, which could be disposed according to the decision of the commanding officer. It later came into a more general use.

Here, we have two orders: Christ the firstfruits was made alive three days after His death; the other group, those who belong to Christ, will be made alive at His second coming. By *firstfruits* Paul utilized the rich imagery of the Old Testament. The firstfruits were comprised of the first sheaf of the harvest, which was brought to the Temple on the morning of the Passover and pledged the ultimate offering of the whole.

Afterward bridges the interim between Christ's resurrection and the Christians' resurrection at His second coming. The word *coming* is a compound of two Greek words and denotes both an arrival and a consequent presence with. The faithful, then, will follow the Lord at the time chosen by Him for His coming, when He will go out to meet them and take them to be with Him.

In the original language of the New Testament, the word translated "then" (v. 24) does not necessarily mean "immediately after." It indicates there could be a sequence of events; therefore, what follows takes place at an unspecified time.

The Greek word translated "end" (v. 24) has the thought of the consummation of all things—of that climax to which everything is destined to lead. The word is used here of the last event and indicates it as succession or a series of happenings. The series is mentioned in verses 25-28.

The reference to the Kingdom is worthy of note. It calls to mind the beginning of the preaching of John the Baptist and Jesus. Jesus' work is to destroy the work of the devil (1 John 3:8) and to found the kingdom of God. Christ effects the general recognition of the kingdom of God by believers and the ungodly alike ("every tongue," Philippians 2:11). This great act will complete what the

Father has committed to Him. It will mark the consummation of the exercise of His authority over the affairs of the Kingdom during the whole of the intervening periods of time.

Christ will "deliver up" (hand over) the Kingdom to God the Father after He has abolished all rule and authority (1 Corinthians 15:24). Paul's thought was that Christ will at last have complete authority over all things and all people and that He will then "deliver up" this authority, this rule, to His Father.

The only enemy named is death (v. 26). The term "last enemy" implies that death is man's special enemy. Death is used here in the full sense of the word: spiritual, temporal, and eternal death, as it came into the world because of sin. The Greek word translated "destroyed" means not so much "to annihilate" as "to rob of efficiency"; therefore, death will no longer be an effective enemy. Death will be conquered by the resurrection, for it will make our bodies imperishable.

> "Death is not a period but a comma in the story of life."
> —Amos Traver

II. SHARING IN CHRIST'S VICTORY (1 Corinthians 15:35-49)
A. As the Grain (vv. 35-38)

35. But some man will say, How are the dead raised up? and with what body do they come?

36. Thou fool, that which thou sowest is not quickened, except it die:

37. And that which thou sowest, thou sowest not that body that shall be, but bare grain, it may chance of wheat, or of some other grain:

38. But God giveth it a body as it hath pleased him, and to every seed his own body.

Paul, anticipating the rebuttal of a few skeptics, phrases their question for them. It appears a most difficult question, for the actual facts of death and dissolution seem to argue against Paul's belief, the doubters think.

This first question, "How are the dead raised up?" is answered in verse 36. The second question, "With what body do they come?" is answered in the remaining verses.

Paul recognizes that those who phrase this question would mock at belief in the resurrection on the grounds of common sense. The strong reply retorts that nothing but common sense would prove the resurrection, for the growth of a seed into a plant in nature gives clear example of it.

The plants shoot forth in the midst of rottenness, and nothing will spring up unless the seed dies. Therefore, we have a representation of the resurrection.

The assertion in verse 37 is that the body placed into the ground is not identical with the "body that shall be." This truth should help to clarify what some people have considered a problem of the

Talk About It:
1. What is foolish about the questions in verse 35?
2. What should we understand from the planting of seeds (vv. 36-38)?

3,000 Years Later
A sealed vase containing some peas was found in the tomb of a mummy in Egypt. The peas were wrinkled and hard as stones, but were planted under a glass. At the end of 30 days, they sprang into life, although they had lain dormant in the dust of a tomb for almost 3,000 years.
—Walter Knight

bodies of those destroyed by fire, torn to pieces by wild animals, or eaten by fish at sea. The truth here is that God forms the kind of body He wants as He does with any grain of seed.

In verse 38 the emphasis is on *God* and *giveth*. The gift of God comprises the new form that rises, and there is never any doubt as to what appearance that body will have, for the body will retain its own appearance as does also a grain of seed.

B. With Diversity (vv. 39-44)
(1 Corinthians 15:39-41 is not included in the printed text.)
42. So also is the resurrection of the dead. It is sown in corruption; it is raised in incorruption:

43. It is sown in dishonour; it is raised in glory: it is sown in weakness; it is raised in power:

44. It is sown a natural body; it is raised a spiritual body. There is a natural body, and there is a spiritual body.

Talk About It:
What contrasts are made between the human body and the resurrected body (vv. 42-44)?

In verse 39 the apostle points out the likeness of the substance of all flesh, but he emphasizes the differences in quality. In like comparison there is a difference in our mortal body and our resurrected body, and the difference we perceive in physical flesh is a sort of foreshadowing of the resurrection. And though we cannot fully comprehend the act, God finds no difficulty in renewing our present bodies by changing their state.

The "celestial bodies" (v. 40) are not likely the sun, moon and stars of verse 41, for this would hardly make a good comparison to "bodies terrestrial." The reference is probably to the bodies of our resurrected Lord and possibly those of the angels and glorified saints contrasted with the bodies of humanity and beast below. The Greek word for *celestial* is the same as *heavenly* in verse 48, and the New Testament never uses the word *heavenly* for any part of the material creation.

The point of the additional illustration in verse 41 is again the difference between the earthly and the resurrected body and not the probable difference between the saints themselves in glory. The heavenly bodies are of one substance, but they differ greatly one from the other in honor and splendor.

The animals differ in their flesh; the heavenly resurrected body differs from the earthly body in its consistency; the sun, moon and stars differ as to their glory. Why should we wonder, therefore, if our body puts on a more splendid quality. "Dust thou art, and unto dust shalt thou return" (Genesis 3:19). The resurrected body is raised in incorruptibility, not being subject to earthly conditions.

In 1 Corinthians 15:43, "dishonour . . . glory" tells of the contrast in the indignity of "dust to dust," and of the admiration and honor which the future body will deserve. "Weakness . . . power" speaks of the contrast of the helplessness of death of the earthly body, and of the soaring strength of the glorified body.

The *it* in verse 44, as well as in the preceding two verses, refers to man himself who goes down to death, having been limited by his natural body and its characteristics; but when *it* (man) is raised a spiritual body, he ceases to bear the image of the earthly or be limited by its humanity.

C. No More Dust (vv. 45-49)

45. And so it is written, The first man Adam was made a living soul; the last Adam was made a quickening spirit.

46. Howbeit that was not first which is spiritual, but that which is natural; and afterward that which is spiritual.

47. The first man is of the earth, earthy: the second man is the Lord from heaven.

48. As is the earthy, such are they also that are earthy: and as is the heavenly, such are they also that are heavenly.

49. And as we have borne the image of the earthy, we shall also bear the image of the heavenly.

soul (v. 45)—being

quickening (v. 45)—"life-giving" (*NIV*)

The word *Adam* signifies "made of dust." "Of the earth" (v. 47) denotes origin; the first man was simply "of the earth." "The second man" (or "the last Adam," v. 45) denotes the Lord, Jesus Christ. Though He appeared on earth, lived and died, and rose again, He is not to be thought of as originating from the earth, as is Adam, but as from heaven. "The second man is the Lord from heaven" (v. 47).

Talk About It:
1. List ways Christ was superior to Adam (vv. 45-47).
2. How can human beings "bear the image of the heavenly" (v. 49)?

Through Adam we have a terrestrial life, but through Christ we enter into a celestial life. There was no question in the mind of Paul, the Corinthian converts, or the Greeks at large that all people are earthly. But Christians are not only earthly, they are also heavenly because of their relationship to Christ. That has implications for this present life, but it also has implications for the whole world to come.

The Greek verb translated "borne" (v. 49) has the idea of bearing continually, or habitually (it is often used of wearing clothes). The bearing in question here is seen in the whole of life, not simply in some parts of it. Paul is saying, then, that just as throughout this life we have habitually borne the form of Adam, so in the life to come we shall bear that of our Lord.

The word translated "image" (v. 49) involves the double idea of representation and manifestation. Believers in their glorified state will not only resemble Him but will represent Him—as to both in His spiritual body and in His moral character. They will therefore "inherit the kingdom of God" (v. 50).

"When Jesus came, the people saw God 'with a face.' Jesus was God 'manifest in the flesh'" (1 Timothy 3:16, paraphrased).

III. TRIUMPHANT THROUGH CHRIST'S VICTORY
(1 Corinthians 15:50-57)
A. A Mystery (vv. 50, 51)

50. Now this I say, brethren, that flesh and blood cannot

Talk About It:
1. Why can't "flesh and blood . . . inherit the kingdom of God" (v. 50)?
2. Explain the phrase "We shall not all sleep" (v. 51).

"Before I started working with dying patients, I did not believe in a life after death. I now believe in a life after death, beyond a shadow of a doubt."

—Elisabeth Kuebler-Ross

Talk About It:
How will a radical change take place instantaneously?

"The only remedy for all this mass of misery is the return of our Lord Jesus Christ. Why do we not plead for it every time we hear the clock strike?"

—Lord Shaftesbury

inherit the kingdom of God; neither doth corruption inherit incorruption.

51. Behold, I shew you a mystery; We shall not all sleep, but we shall all be changed.

Behold has the effect of focusing attention on what is to follow, particularly the mystery of which Paul spoke. *Mystery*, in Paul's terminology, refers to that part of God's decree which was hidden in former times but is now revealed. The mystery explains that at the second coming of Christ there will be those who, despite their being flesh and blood, will "inherit [obtain] the kingdom of God" (v. 50). Paul also implied there are things about the resurrection body that the Corinthians did not understand.

The way Paul used the word *all* gives it great emphasis: "We shall not all sleep" (v. 51) refers to death in the same beautiful way that is seen in verse 18. That the apostle used the pronoun *we* did not mean that he was sure of being alive when Christ comes. What he said did imply that this power of expectation should work in the hearts of all believers until the event actually takes place.

B. A Moment (v. 52)

52. In a moment, in the twinkling of an eye, at the last trump: for the trumpet shall sound, and the dead shall be raised incorruptible, and we shall be changed.

The resurrection of the dead might be likened to the slow growth of a seed, but the change in the living will take place with startling suddenness. The change will occur instantaneously and completely for all Christians whether dead or alive. It is to take place in a *moment*. In the Greek, this word means the smallest particle which cannot be cut or divided, that is, the smallest possible; we get our word *atom* from it.

The last trumpet may have its meaning in a military custom of the ancient Romans of Paul's time. Three trumpet blasts were important. The first blast indicated it was time to strike tents and assemble arms. The second was a signal to fall in line by companies. The last was the call to march. If this was Paul's idea of the resurrection trumpet, it speaks to us once more of the military precision of this great event.

C. A Must (vv. 53-57)

53. For this corruptible must put on incorruption, and this mortal must put on immortality.

54. So when this corruptible shall have put on incorruption, and this mortal shall have put on immortality, then shall be brought to pass the saying that is written, Death is swallowed up in victory.

55. O death, where is thy sting? O grave, where is thy victory?

56. The sting of death is sin; and the strength of sin is the law.

57. But thanks be to God, which giveth us the victory through our Lord Jesus Christ.

The "corruptible" and the "mortal" will not continue as they are; therefore, a change *must* be made to conditions essential to the kingdom of God. The verb rendered "put on" indicates the momentary character of the event. The change will be from one kind of body to another. The main point here concerns quality of life, as is apparent from Paul's use of the term "this corruptible" instead of the pronoun *we*.

The swallowing up of death (v. 54, quoting Isaiah 25:8) expresses the complete removal of every trace of the physical effects of sin and the curse of Satan's power—the king of terrors will be vanquished by the Lord God Almighty.

For whereas sin gave death its sting and the Law gave sin its power, Christ is the end of the Law for the believer, and through Christ sin and death have been overcome. Death has, while retaining its outward form, lost its sting (v. 55, quoting Hosea 13:14) and is powerless to injure. Like a snake that has lost its venom, death has lost its poisonous sting; and once the sting is removed, the power to conquer is gone.

We owe this victory to "our Lord Jesus Christ" (v. 57). Through Him we have been reconciled to God, delivered from the yoke of the law, and carried into the realm of grace. It is through the Cross that we have forgiveness of sins, and His resurrection assures us of victory over death.

Talk About It:
1. What are "incorruption" and "immortality" (v. 53)?
2. Answer the questions in verse 55.

"Can we proclaim that Jesus is Lord as the first-century Christians did, by being living demonstrations of that truth? Does Christ control and shape our lives?"
—Charles Colson

CONCLUSION

Following this glorious outburst of eloquence, this chapter ends with a down-to-earth exhortation. Showing his love and concern for the Corinthians, Paul called them "my beloved brethren" (v. 58). Therefore, his admonition to be steadfast may well be because some of them had adhered to false doctrine (v. 12) and because the whole church was in danger of it.

Out of this comes the exhortation to Christian stability—"be ye stedfast"—which literally means being firmly seated but also implies a fixed purpose of heart, as against allurement to evil. Believers must also be unmovable, suggesting adherence to the faith, as against forces that would turn them aside from it and thus from allegiance to Christ.

"Your labour is not in vain in the Lord," Paul implored. Resurrection day will be indescribably sweet for God's own.

GOLDEN TEXT CHALLENGE

"NOW IS CHRIST RISEN FROM THE DEAD, AND BECOME THE FIRSTFRUITS OF THEM THAT SLEPT" (1 Corinthians 15:20).

Paul declared, despite the naysayers, Christ is risen from the dead! The witnesses have not been wrong. The preachers have not been false witnesses. Those who have died in the Lord have not perished. We are not without hope in this world or the next.

Christ is called "the firstfruits of them that slept." When the children of Israel entered the Promised Land and began to till the soil and plant their crops, God demanded that before the harvest was begun, a sheaf of the ripened grain was to be plucked and waved before the Lord in thanksgiving for His gift of a bountiful crop (Leviticus 23:10, 11). The sheaf was offered on the third day after the Passover. Thus, Christ was the Passover Lamb that was sacrificed, and His resurrection was the firstfruits of a harvest that was to come. The resurrection of Christ from the grave was proof of the truth of the resurrection from the dead and a pledge to all believers who have died from Adam till today that they too will be raised.

The order of the resurrection was to be thus: "Christ the first-fruits" and then "they that are Christ's at his coming" (1 Corinthians 15:23). Christ was the pattern for the resurrection from the dead. He was a sample of what was to be harvested, and those who have resurrected in the great harvest will be like Him (Philippians 3:20, 21; 1 John 3:2). Christ, by His resurrection, has replaced the first man, Adam, as the federal head and representative of the entire human race. "For as in Adam all die, even so in Christ shall all be made alive" (1 Corinthians 15:22).

Death Destroyed

Reconciliation to God

Romans 5:1-21

INTRODUCTION

In the first four chapters of the Book of Romans, Paul has focused on how a person can get right with God. Chapter 5 provides a transition between Paul's discussion on justification in the first four chapters and the exposition on sanctification in chapters 6-8. As a transition, on the one hand, it reaffirms and emphasizes the truths already presented by Paul on justification and, on the other hand, it prepares the way for a richer understanding on the new life in Christ that is evidenced through sanctification.

The basic meaning of *reconciliation* used in the title of this lesson is "restoration to friendship or harmony." This infers that there was previously a relationship that was harmonious but is now broken. That, of course, is the story of Adam and the problem of sin. Prior to the Fall in the Garden of Eden, Adam and Eve enjoyed a wonderful relationship with God and with each other. But as result of their sin, the relationship between humanity and God became damaged. As such, a decisive act was necessary for this relationship to be restored to its original state. Christ is the One who performed this necessary act, and the result was reconciliation with God, which is the topic of our study today.

Unit Theme:
The Gospel in Romans and Galatians

Central Truth:
God's grace makes it possible for sinners to be forgiven and reconciled to God.

Focus:
Realize that reconciliation to God is accomplished only through Christ and tell others of God's grace.

Context:
Paul wrote this letter to the church in Rome around A.D. 57.

Golden Text:
"If, when we were enemies, we were reconciled to God by the death of his Son; much more, being reconciled, we shall be saved by his life" (Romans 5:10).

Study Outline:
I. Motivated by God's Love (Romans 5:1-8)
II. Accomplished by Christ (Romans 5:9-11)
III. Made Available by Grace (Romans 5:12-21)

I. MOTIVATED BY GOD'S LOVE (Romans 5:1-8)
A. Finding Peace With God (v. 1)

1. Therefore being justified by faith, we have peace with God through our Lord Jesus Christ.

Paul begins this section of his letter with the inferential word *therefore*. The use of this word connects the theme of his previous writing to what he is now going to say. Paul reminds believers that, because of their faith in Christ, they have been "justified" or "made right" with God, which is the theme of 3:21—4:25. The new theme he is presenting is a description of the benefits available for those who are justified.

One of those benefits is peace with God. The Christian is free from the wrath of God. He or she has an inner peace that "surpasses all understanding" (Philippians 4:7, *NKJV*). The burden of guilt is gone. Paul says this peace with God comes only through the actions of the Lord Jesus Christ. There is no other way by which peace with God can be obtained. As the saying goes, "Know God, know peace; no God, no peace."

B. Receiving God's Grace (v. 2)

2. By whom also we have access by faith into this grace wherein we stand, and rejoice in hope of the glory of God.

To "have access" can be compared to walking into a place that was once closed off. Because of Christ's death and resurrection, the veil into the Temple's "holy of holies" was ripped in two, allowing us to come into a relationship with God (see Matthew 27:50, 51). Our standing before God is a gift of grace, and our access is by faith. "This grace" is a place of God's unconditional love given to those who do not deserve it and have not earned it. It is a place where those who believe not only have access to God's love but can stand in it. Just as undeserving Mephibosheth gained a place at David's table (2 Samuel 9), we have a place in God's presence as the objects of His concern and care.

Grace was necessary, along with faith, for believers to come into a right relationship with God. Access to grace brings the believer a position of security—a place to stand. One of the greatest blessings of our life in Christ is stability. Standing in this place of grace gives the believer reason to hope for the glory of God to come. Paul here suggests that the Christian's perspective is not only shaped by our past experiences or present circumstances, but also by hope for the future. We have no reason to discard the old hymn, "Whispering Hope." But we must realize that our hope is more than a faint whisper. It is a sure thing. What a blessing to be justified!

C. Producing Hope Through Trials (vv. 3-5)

3. And not only so, but we glory in tribulations also: knowing that tribulation worketh patience;

Talk About It:
What does it mean to "have peace with God"?

Talk About It:
Where do believers "stand," and how?

Hope . . . like the gleaming taper's light,
Adorns and cheers our way;
And still, as darker grows the night,
Emits a brighter ray.
—Oliver Goldsmith

glory (v. 3)— rejoice

4. And patience, experience; and experience, hope:

5. And hope maketh not ashamed; because the love of God is shed abroad in our hearts by the Holy Ghost which is given unto us.

What is the next benefit of being reconciled to God? Paul seems to give a strange answer. He reminds believers that they are not only to rejoice in the glory to come, but also in the sufferings ("tribulations") that will come because of walking in the way of salvation. Most people consider suffering something to be avoided at all costs, but Paul says to "rejoice" in sufferings. He then goes on to explain why. In the end it will produce good fruit in the lives of the believer, such as the ability to persevere amid all circumstances, the development of good character ("experience"), and hope in God.

Through suffering, a believer develops compassion for the sufferings of others. In the time of suffering, God pours out His love by the power of His Holy Spirit. It is this love that is used to comfort others through their time of affliction. But even in the midst of personal suffering, believers always can have hope, knowing that with God they will have the final victory. Even though at times believers may feel defeated by their troubles, they can know that God will never be defeated. Far from being destroyed by the sufferings we go through, these experiences should strengthen our hope in God.

D. Demonstrating God's Love (vv. 6-8)

6. For when we were yet without strength, in due time Christ died for the ungodly.

7. For scarcely for a righteous man will one die: yet peradventure for a good man some would even dare to die.

8. But God commendeth his love toward us, in that, while we were yet sinners, Christ died for us.

What has God done for His people? First, note that God's love is the basis of everything Christians receive from God. Second, Paul presents the picture of humanity prior to justification by faith and the ensuing reconciliation. People were powerless, ungodly and sinful. "Without strength" describes the inability of humans to solve the problem of evil by themselves. They could not change their ways and would not return to God. All were defeated by the power of sin. They had no ability within themselves to be reconciled to God.

Ungodly describes our acts. Our unrighteousness was manifested in our works or behavior. The word *sinners* (v. 8) describes our identity. Because of our unrighteousness and ungodly acts, we were separated from the holy God. Could God love people like us? The answer is provided by Christ's death. His death is the greatest evidence we have of God's love.

Talk About It:
1. Why can Christians rejoice in sufferings?
2. What is the present aspect of our future hope?

"Stand still . . . and refuse to retreat. Look at it [tribulation] as God looks at it and draw upon His power to hold up under the blast."
—**Charles Swindoll**

Talk About It:
How were we "without strength" (v. 6)?

God's Broken Heart
In the movie *The Passion of the Christ*, the crucifixion scene is brought to a close by a large teardrop that splashes down from heaven. The teardrop is a prelude to a violent storm and earthquake that drives all but Jesus' most committed disciples from the foot of the

Humans most often do not love those who are in opposition to them. When we love people, it is usually because we find something appealing or worthy of love. God's love is so different. It is a love that cannot be measured by human standards. Since God is love, it is part of His essence or nature to love. The only way we can begin to comprehend it is through Christ's death.

II. ACCOMPLISHED BY CHRIST (Romans 5:9-11)
A. Saving Us From Wrath (vv. 9, 10)

9. Much more then, being now justified by his blood, we shall be saved from wrath through him.

10. For if, when we were enemies, we were reconciled to God by the death of his Son, much more, being reconciled, we shall be saved by his life.

In verses 6-8 Paul pointed out two important facts about God's love through what has already been done: (1) where it was demonstrated—in Christ's death; and (2) the character of those He loved so much to die for—the powerless and ungodly sinners. In verses 9 and 10, Paul contrasts what God has already done to what God will do. If, in the death of Christ, God has now acted to save humanity from their broken relationship with Him and to set them right with Him, then believers have no need to fear the future day of wrath—God's final judgment (v. 9).

In verse 10, Paul reinforces that if God began to save people in their ungodly and rebellious condition, they can be confident that God will complete the work now that they are reconciled to Him and made His friends. Believers have been brought to a right standing with God based on the sacrifice on the cross, but they are saved by a *living* Savior.

B. Reconciling Us to God (v. 11)

11. And not only *so*, but we also joy in God through our Lord Jesus Christ, by whom we have now received the atonement.

Verse 11 provides a summary and climax. As a summary, Paul makes it known that God has acted. He has put away the enmity through the death of Christ. All that remains for us to do is to accept His friendship, the offer of reconciliation that He provides. As a climax, Paul talks about our rejoicing in Christ. Because we are justified by faith, we have no reason for boasting or rejoicing in ourselves. We can have no pride in achieving a right standing with God, but must attribute it all to God through Christ. Nevertheless, the Christian has something to rejoice about—"atonement" (reconciliation) with God.

III. MADE AVAILABLE BY GRACE (Romans 5:12-21)
A. The Effects of Adam's Work (vv. 12-14)

12. Wherefore, as by one man sin entered into the world,

and death by sin; and so death passed upon all men, for that all have sinned:

13. For until the law sin was in the world: but sin is not imputed when there is no law.

14. Nevertheless death reigned from Adam to Moses, even over them that had not sinned after the similitude of Adam's transgression, who is the figure of him that was to come.

similitude (v. 14)—likeness

Living in such an individualistic society has sometimes made verse 12 hard for people to grasp. Paul is stressing here that we are not just a collection of separate individuals who have little relation to one another. Instead, all human beings belong to one another because all are descended from the first man, Adam. Since we are his descendants, we are also partakers of sin and death as he was. In the same manner, there is a real connection between Christ and humankind, which means that Christ really does bring an end to people's wrong relationship with God, and brings them the new life that Paul has described from verse 1 to this point.

In verse 12, Paul shows that death came into the world through sin, and since sin came into the world through Adam, death came to all humanity because, like Adam, all have sinned. The act of disobedience by Adam and Eve disrupted the harmonious relationship and perfection God designed for His creation. Our first parents broke the trust relationship that had existed between them and God.

Verses 13 and 14 offer further explanation and evidence of the truth given in verse 12. Adam received God's command, broke it, and died. At that time death entered into the world and reigned not only over Adam but over all humanity to come. We see this in that during the time period between Adam and Moses, the people had no law to break and were still dying. So what Adam initially did was still influencing and would continue to affect all humanity. The tyranny of death began with the Fall and continued, though many did not sin in a specific act of disobedience after the manner of Adam's transgression. Through the act of the one person, all were made partakers of the same outcome. Note how Paul maintains the tension between the social and individual aspects of sin. We must realize there is personal responsibility for wrongdoing.

In the last part of verse 14, Paul prepares the way for his discourse about Christ in comparison to Adam since he refers to Adam as "a pattern of the one to come" (*NIV*).

Talk About It:
1. Why did "death spread to all men" (v. 12, *NKJV*)?
2. What changed when the Law was given (v. 13)?

"Sin is not weakness, it is a disease; it is red-handed rebellion against God, and the magnitude of that rebellion is expressed by Calvary's cross."
—**Oswald Chambers**

B. The Transgression Versus the Free Gift (vv. 15-17)

15. But not as the offence, so also is the free gift. For if through the offence of one many be dead, much more the

grace of God, and the gift by grace, which is by one man, Jesus Christ, hath abounded unto many.

16. And not as it was by one that sinned, so is the gift: for the judgment was by one to condemnation, but the free gift is of many offences unto justification.

17. For if by one man's offence death reigned by one; much more they which receive abundance of grace and of the gift of righteousness shall reign in life by one, Jesus Christ.

In verses 15-17, Paul distinguishes how great God's gift through Christ is in comparison to the trespass of Adam. Reference to Adam opens the way for Paul to present the truth about Christ and about grace in a series of striking contrasts. Adam was the antitype of Christ. Although they were alike, they were infinitely different. Paul's main concern was not to get into a lengthy discussion about Adam. Instead, he wanted to write about Christ. By describing Adam as a *type*, Paul showed that Christ is far greater than Adam. Christ lived as God intended that man should live, and He is the One who led humanity out of the ruin into which Adam led it. The results of what Christ did are ultimately greater than the effects of what Adam did. Just one sin brought death to the human race and brought all, by nature, under condemnation. But the death of Christ atoned not just one sin but for an absolutely countless number—all that have ever been committed. Through Adam, there was death from one sin. Through Christ, there is abundant forgiveness for unlimited sins.

The careful reader will note this vital phrase in verse 17: "those who receive" (*NIV*). The benefits of Christ's death are not automatic. They must be applied by faith; they must be received by each person individually.

C. The Effects of Christ's Work (vv. 18-21)

18. Therefore as by the offence of one judgment came upon all men to condemnation; even so by the righteousness of one the free gift came upon all men unto justification of life.

19. For as by one man's disobedience many were made sinners, so by the obedience of one shall many be made righteous.

20. Moreover the law entered, that the offence might abound. But where sin abounded, grace did much more abound:

21. That as sin hath reigned unto death, even so might grace reign through righteousness unto eternal life by Jesus Christ our Lord.

The consequence of Adam's trespass was condemnation

leading to death, but the benefit of Jesus' righteousness is justification leading to life. In verse 19, Paul emphasizes that if the one act of disobedience by Adam had the power to make us all sinners, so also the one act of obedience by Christ has the power to make us all righteous. Grace is more powerful than sin.

In verse 20 Paul points out the true function of the Law. His mention of the Law might be for his Jewish readers, since they might consider the Law rather than Christ as being what leads them to God. Paul explains that the Law could not make people righteous before God. It only could show how bad they were. The abundance of sin serves only to show the desperate need for grace. The Law did two things: (1) It pointed out what actions were sinful, and (2) it tempted people to disobey, making their disobedience worse since they did wrong in spite of knowing what was right.

Verse 21 pits sin against grace. The reign of sin is spreading moral chaos and spiritual doom around the world. But grace is arrayed against sin. It is mighty to save. Grace brings hope to the despairing and eternal life to the spiritually dead.

Talk About It:
1. Explain the progression from law to sin to grace (v. 20).
2. Compare the reign of sin with the reign of grace (v. 21).

"I'm not going to heaven because I've preached to great crowds of people. I'm going to heaven because Jesus died on a cross."
—Billy Graham

CONCLUSION

Reconciliation with God is accomplished only through Christ. Grace makes it possible for sinners to be forgiven and reconciled to God. When we testify to others of how we have experienced God's grace, we can motivate sinners to want to receive His love and come into a reconciled relationship with Him for eternity.

GOLDEN TEXT CHALLENGE

"IF, WHEN WE WERE ENEMIES, WE WERE RECONCILED TO GOD BY THE DEATH OF HIS SON; MUCH MORE, BEING RECONCILED, WE SHALL BE SAVED BY HIS LIFE" (Romans 5:10).

If we have been reconciled to God by the death of Christ, we will be sustained by His life. Humanity is pictured as helpless sinners and enemies of God, while God is shown to direct His love toward them in the death of Christ. In New Testament reconciliation, God is always the subject, the One who does the reconciling; humanity is always the object, the ones in need of reconciliation. The death of Christ is the means, and the ministry of reconciliation is the result (Romans 5:10, 11; 2 Corinthians 5:18-21; Ephesians 2:16; Colossians 1:20).

Paul said we are kept by the life of Christ. This life laid down is now taken up by the risen Lord, and He is the source of future salvation. The outpouring of God's love by the Holy Spirit makes this possible.

Daily Devotions:
M. God's Grace
Deuteronomy 7:6-9
T. Christ's Atonement
Isaiah 53:4-12
W. God's Love Is Everlasting
Jeremiah 31:1-6
T. Thankful for God's Grace
1 Corinthians 1:4-8
F. Christ's Purpose
Ephesians 1:3-10
S. God's Great Love
Ephesians 2:4-10

Freedom From Sinful Living

Romans 6:1-23

Unit Theme:
The Gospel in Romans and Galatians

Central Truth:
Christians are able to live righteously because Christ has freed them from sin's dominion.

Focus:
Discover how believers are set free from sin and celebrate life in Christ.

Context:
Paul wrote this letter to the church in Rome around A.D. 57.

Golden Text:
"Sin shall not have dominion over you: for ye are not under the law, but under grace" (Romans 6:14).

Study Outline:
I. Dead to Sin (Romans 6:1-7)
II. Alive in Christ (Romans 6:8-14)
III. Slaves to Righteousness (Romans 6:15-23)

INTRODUCTION

When it comes to the issue of freedom from sinful living, there are two opposite extremes. On the one side are those who find it difficult to comprehend that there is any possibility, however remote it may be, to be free from sins. In other words, they are content to remain, as they might term it, "sinning saints." On the other side are those who think that, having been justified, they can live any way they like—without boundaries—under the guise of avoiding what they understand to be legalism. Neither of these two positions is right. Both are due to faulty views of grace. While the former does not fully appreciate the possibility and power of grace, the latter depreciates grace. But, as Paul shows in Romans 6, grace enables the justified believer to lead a life that is pleasing to God—a life that enjoys freedom from sinful living, a life of victory. Grace brings freedom from bondage. We should live in holiness, as befits our calling.

"What is the purpose of holiness?" writes Dale Coulter. "Is holiness just about demonstrating loyalty to God, or is it more about a real transformation? I believe it is about the latter. God wants to transform us so that we can reflect the beauty of His perfection in our lives. When God adopts us into His family, He invites us to enter into a new way of living that is good for us. He wants *real* sons and daughters who love Him and long to be like Him. Likewise, the radical call to discipleship is really a call to be all that God has created us to be.

"When Jesus bids a man to come and die, He is really saying, 'Come to me and *live*.' We truly come to live when we reflect the beauty of God's own perfection in our lives. This will occur when we arrive at the place where our thoughts and desires no longer work against us, but, as one, push us in the right direction."

I. DEAD TO SIN (Romans 6:1-7)
A. United With Christ in His Death (vv. 1-4)
   1. What shall we say then? Shall we continue in sin, that grace may abound?
   2. God forbid. How shall we that are dead to sin, live any longer therein?
   3. Know ye not, that so many of us as were baptized into Jesus Christ were baptized into his death?
   4. Therefore we are buried with him by baptism into death: that like as Christ was raised up from the dead by the glory of the Father, even so we also should walk in newness of life.

At the beginning of chapter 6, Paul attempts to clarify any misunderstanding that may arise from his assertion in 5:20 that "where sin increased, grace increased all the more" (*NIV*). It could have been possible to reason that if salvation is by grace, then grace is really an encouragement to sin, because the more one sins, the more grace abounds. With such possible charge by his critics in mind, Paul asks the question, "Are we to continue sinning that grace might increase?" (see 6:1). For Paul such a thought is horrible. It is not only illogical but absurd. Since we died to sin through the experience of justification by faith, which is by grace, how dare we have any desire to continue in it? The notion that a justified person could continue to sin, or that the teaching of salvation by grace encourages sin, results from complete misunderstanding of what salvation is, what grace is, and what faith in Christ accomplishes in one's life.

Verses 2-4 describe what transpires at justification. Paul makes a bold assertion that believers have died to sin. This is the first affirmation of freedom that Paul makes in this chapter. It is important to remember that these verses are describing not what Christians *should* be like but what, in reality, they *are* like. By stressing believers' new situation in terms of dying to sin, Paul is emphasizing that there is no reason for Christians to go on sinning.

Being a Christian should no longer be about what we do or don't do, but it should be about what we *are*. Our old relationship with sin has come to an end. When someone physically dies they can no longer have a relationship with those who are left living. It is the same thing for us who have died to sin. We can no longer have a relationship to sin. Does this mean that we *cannot* sin? No. It only means that we *need* not sin, and *should* not.

To illustrate his point, Paul refers to baptism as a picture of spiritual regeneration. It is a declaration of a personal faith in Christ, who died, was buried, and rose again from the dead. Thus, baptism represents the believer's confession of having died to sin and

Talk About It:
1. Can a genuine Christian "continue in sin" (v. 1)? Why or why not?
2. What is the connection between water baptism and death (v. 3)?
3. How and why is resurrection expressed through water baptism (v. 4)?

"The verb *baptize* means 'to immerse, dip, plunge.' To portray the union of the believer with Christ in His death and resurrection, Paul refers to the immersion of the Christian in water."
—French Arrington

being raised up spiritually to a new life. We declare by baptism that we have experienced a spiritual resurrection by the power of God. As such, we pledge to walk in newness of life. We are under a solemn obligation to make the Christian life true to Christian baptism. Our manner of life—words, actions, private and public behavior, relationships and dealings with others, and all moral practices—is to show the reality of our relation to Christ.

B. United With Christ in His Resurrection (vv. 5-7)

5. For if we have been planted together in the likeness of his death, we shall be also in the likeness of his resurrection:

6. Knowing this, that our old man is crucified with him, that the body of sin might be destroyed, that henceforth we should not serve sin.

7. For he that is dead is freed from sin.

Although Paul couches the believer's situation in end-times terms, it is nevertheless clear that he has in view the present risen life of the believer. Paul is more concerned with the present participation of the believer in the life of the risen Christ than with the future. This is confirmed later in verse 11, where he says, "Count yourselves dead to sin but alive to God in Christ Jesus" (*NIV*). Dying to sin involves a spiritual participation in the crucifixion of Christ that causes a change in the believer. When a person is justified, he or she experiences a transformation that affects the old self, which was identified with Adam. That body of sin is done away with (v. 6) in order that a new life might be imparted by the power of the Holy Spirit.

In these verses, as in Galatians 2:20, Paul uses passive verbs to describe the death to the old self, with the believer being the recipient of the action. God is the One who frees us from sin (Romans 6:7). It is He who brings eternal life (5:21).

Oliver McMahan writes, "The believer may still wrestle with temptation and sin, but he is not bound to it. The Christian does not have to come under the control or domination of sin. Sin is not a necessary part of the Christian's life. As Paul said, the person crucified with Christ does not 'serve sin,' for he is freed from its slavery."

II. ALIVE IN CHRIST (Romans 6:8-14)

A. Christ as Our Example (vv. 8-10)

8. Now if we be dead with Christ, we believe that we shall also live with him:

9. Knowing that Christ being raised from the dead dieth no more; death hath no more dominion over him.

10. For in that he died, he died unto sin once: but in that he liveth, he liveth unto God.

Talk About It:
1. What does it mean to be "planted together" with Christ (v. 5)?
2. What is meant by the term "old man" (v. 6)? How is it to be dealt with?

"We are too Christian really to enjoy sinning, and too fond of sinning really to enjoy Christianity. Most of us know perfectly well what we ought to do; our trouble is that we do not want to do it."
—Peter Marshall

Freedom From Sinful Living

Death and resurrection cannot be separated. The one pre-supposes the other. If the believer's dying to sin is real, as Christ's death was, so resurrection to newness of life is real, as Christ's resurrection was. The change that takes place in con-version is radical; it is a once-for-all experience.

Christ died once, and death no longer holds sway or has dominion over Him. When He died, He died in relation to sin. Believers have experienced the benefits of Christ's death—redemption from sin and reconciliation with God—and now enjoy the benefits of His resurrection, knowing the power of the risen Christ to effect sanctification in their life. Thus Paul answers the question: *What does it mean to be risen with Christ?* As we have been partakers of His death, we are now partakers of His new life. Guilt and separation from God has now been replaced with fellowship and right relationship with God. In the past we lived against God and apart from Him; now we live *for* God and *with* Him. It is nothing we have achieved on our own but only through being united with Christ.

B. Dead to Sin and Alive in Christ (vv. 11-14)

11. Likewise reckon ye also yourselves to be dead indeed unto sin, but alive unto God through Jesus Christ our Lord.

12. Let not sin therefore reign in your mortal body, that ye should obey it in the lusts thereof.

13. Neither yield ye your members as instruments of unrighteousness unto sin: but yield yourselves unto God, as those that are alive from the dead, and your members as instruments of righteousness unto God.

14. For sin shall not have dominion over you: for ye are not under the law, but under grace.

Believers are to count ("reckon") themselves dead to sin and alive to God. This requires an understanding of what has hap-pened. Paul is recommending that believers not consider their feelings but to consider rather what they know to be true. Just as God declares us to be what we could never make of our-selves, we must count ourselves to have ended our relation with sin, even if it seems unimaginable to us by human stan-dards. It is often difficult for us to grasp the reality of our new being in Christ. However, the same faith which believes that God is the justifier must be exercised in believing that He is the One who transforms our beings into conformity with "the image of His Son" (8:29).

In 6:12-14, Paul highlights the moral obligation of believers based on who they now are in Christ. They are now trans-formed people and need to act accordingly. This means to stop acting like a sinner because, as believers, they are now free

Talk About It:
1. What cannot happen to Christ again (v. 9)?
2. How should we live (v. 10)?

"Death may be the king of terrors, but Jesus is the King of kings."
—D.L. Moody

reckon (v. 11)— consider

members (v. 13)— "the parts of your body" (*NIV*)

Talk About It:
1. What happens when sin reigns in a person's life (v. 12)?
2. How can we be victorious over sin (vv. 13, 14)?

from the servitude of sin. Sanctification is the rightful expectation of justification, and this passage emphasizes personal responsibility. Holiness of life is possible because one has become a Christian. But it is not an automatic result of justification or conversion, hence the need for the strong exhortations that Paul gives here. There is no promise here that precludes the believer from being tempted by sin again, but there is an assurance that God, and not sin, is the believer's new master. If the believer chooses, on a daily basis, to let God be in control of his or her members—eyes, mouth feet, and so on—he or she can enjoy freedom from sinful living.

III. SLAVES TO RIGHTEOUSNESS (Romans 6:15-23)
A. Slavery to the One You Obey (vv. 15-18)

15. What then? shall we sin, because we are not under the law, but under grace? God forbid.

16. Know ye not, that to whom ye yield yourselves servants to obey, his servants ye are to whom ye obey; whether of sin unto death, or of obedience unto righteousness?

17. But God be thanked, that ye were the servants of sin, but ye have obeyed from the heart that form of doctrine which was delivered you.

18. Being then made free from sin, ye became the servants of righteousness.

People who are no longer under the Law but under grace have been brought into a relationship of *service*, meaning heart obedience. In verse 15, Paul raises a question similar to the one asked in verse 1. Again, he is responding to an objection to justification by faith. The contention is that salvation on such basis allows sin. To such objection, Paul answers again, "By no means!"

Paul goes further to clarify this misconception by the use of the analogy of slavery in verses 16-18. He stresses that people will have a master, but it is their choice as to who their master will be. The choice is between God and sin: Shall they be slaves to sin or to righteousness? To willfully sin is no longer an option if people are to remain a slave to Christ. If they willfully sin, they are giving themselves back over to sin as a master leading to death. He then concludes these verses with a thanksgiving that they have made the right choice by entrusting themselves to the apostolic teaching, therefore choosing to become slaves of righteousness.

Verses 17 and 18 also present a testimony of the impact of the "good news" in the lives of sinners. Paul reminds the Galatians they were once slaves to sin but they heard the good news and obeyed its teaching, and now are slaves to righteousness. In this

Talk About It:
1. According to verse 16, what two options do we have, and what are their outcomes?
2. Describe the change that took place in the people to whom Paul was writing (vv. 17, 18).

Freedom From Sinful Living

old life, when they were servants of sin, they neither responded to the demands of holy living and purity nor recognized the
obligation to righteousness. Having been set free from sin, they
became the servants of God, and the outcome of their life was
sanctification "and the end everlasting life" (v. 22). That is why
Paul breaks out in thanksgiving. Believers have experienced
an indescribable, life-changing encounter.

B. Slavery Leading to Eternal Life (vv. 19-23)

**19. I speak after the manner of men because of the infir-
mity of your flesh: for as ye have yielded your members
servants to uncleanness and to iniquity unto iniquity;
even so now yield your members servants to righteousness unto holiness.**

**20. For when ye were the servants of sin, ye were free
from righteousness.**

**21. What fruit had ye then in those things whereof ye
are now ashamed? for the end of those things is death.**

**22. But now being made free from sin, and become ser-
vants to God, ye have your fruit unto holiness, and the end
everlasting life.**

**23. For the wages of sin is death; but the gift of God is
eternal life through Jesus Christ our Lord.**

In verse 19, Paul said he was putting this teaching in a way
that the Romans could understand and receive, and then he
used the human body as an analogy. Just as the Romans used
to offer the parts of their body in slavery to impurity, now they had
the ability to offer the parts of their body to righteousness. These
believers already knew how to offer the parts of their body to
something—they just need to change what that something was.

The word *iniquity* (v. 19) comes from a Greek word meaning "lawless." It emphasizes the rebellion of the sinner against
the life God demands. The phrase "iniquity unto iniquity"
means that the purpose of the sinner is lawlessness—rebellion
simply for the purpose of breeding more rebellion.

By comparison, the goals of Christians are revealed in the
phrase "servants to righteousness unto holiness." *Holiness*
refers to "consecration" or "devotion." It reflects commitment to
the ways of God. The righteous life serves to reflect a deep
devotion to God. It must be remembered that this life of righteousness and the resulting holiness unto God are not the
result of human effort. They come only through Christ and are
applied to the believer by faith.

In verses 20-22, Paul contrasts the old slavery with the new
slavery. Comparatively both forms of slavery offer a master, a
freedom, a benefit and an end result. The first slavery has sin
as its master, is free from the control of righteousness, and has

---

infirmity (v. 19)—
weakness

iniquity unto iniq-
uity (v. 19)—"ever-
increasing wicked-
ness" (*NIV*)

fruit (v. 21)—bene-
fit

Talk About It:
1. Answer the
question in verse
21.
2. What are the
benefits of serving
God (v. 22)?
3. Why is one thing
called a "gift," and
the other "wages"
(v. 23)?

Daily Devotions:
M. God Removes Transgressions Psalm 103:6-14
T. God's Servant Psalm 116:12-19
W. God's Way Is Just Ezekiel 18:20-30
T. Be More Righteous Matthew 5:17-20
F. Life Through Christ John 5:24-29
S. Christ's Example 1 Peter 2:21-25

"benefits" that result in death. The second slavery has God as its master, is free from the control of sin, and includes a benefit of holiness which results in eternal life. In verse 23, Paul concludes his comparison of both forms of slavery by reinforcing their end results. Death or life are the results the believer has to choose from. Eternal life is seen as a gift, while death is wages earned from a life of sin.

CONCLUSION

Freedom from sinful living is not only provided through Christ's death on the cross, but also made possible by the believer's participation in Christ's death and resurrection. The power of sin has been broken by death, and the purchase price has been paid by the work of Christ on the cross. Therefore righteousness is expected of the Christian. Moreover, living free from sin requires a daily choice to remain "in Christ" rather than "in sin."

The lesson clearly shows that we have a choice with regards to who our master should be, what we will be free from, what benefits we will partake of, and whether we will experience life or death. While we cannot lead free, overcoming lives in our own strength, we can rely on the One who can set us free. This relying on Christ is an act of faith. It is also an act of our will to remain in Him.

GOLDEN TEXT CHALLENGE

"SIN SHALL NOT HAVE DOMINION OVER YOU: FOR YE ARE NOT UNDER THE LAW, BUT UNDER GRACE" (Romans 6:14).

If we have been born again and therefore have new life in us, sin will not have dominion over us. This is true because we are not under Law, but under grace. We are no longer trying to satisfy the demands of the Law but are trying to be worthy of the gifts of love; and there is no inspiration in the world like love. As Denney put it, "It is not restraint but inspiration which liberates from sin; not Mount Sinai but Mount Calvary which makes saints."

Our inspiration comes not from the fear of what God will do to us, but from gratitude for what God has done for us.

April 13, 2008 (Lesson 7)

Law and Liberty

Romans 7:1 through 8:4; Galatians 5:1-14

INTRODUCTION

Throughout history people of all religions have tried to earn divine approval by their actions. With the Old Testament's emphasis on the Law, many people thought they could earn God's approval by keeping the Law, and thereby avoid the punishment and death brought on by disobedience. As a result, most Jews accepted God's law as the "way of life," or if they failed to keep it, as "the way of death." Yet they often overlooked the importance of the heart (see Psalms 7:10; 40:8; 139:23). Those who think this way are under the Law.

When Martin Luther, the great Reformer, visited Rome in 1510, several years before he understood the meaning of the gospel and justification by faith, he crawled up the "holy staircase" on his hands and knees, kissing the steps and saying the Lord's Prayer on each step as he climbed. He had been told that such action would please God and earn a special blessing from Him. Martin Luther later wrote: "It is not from works that we are set free by the faith of Christ, but from the belief in works, that is from foolishly presuming to seek justification through works. Faith redeems our consciences, makes them upright, and preserves them, since by it we recognize the truth that justification does not depend on our works, although good works neither can nor ought to be absent, just as we cannot exist without food and drink and all the functions of this mortal body."

God's law condemns us because we have broken it, but now that we belong to Christ we are right with God apart from the Law. We have liberty to do the will of God. Although the believer is now free from the Law as a way of earning God's approval, it is still an important part of his or her life.

Unit Theme:
The Gospel in Romans and Galatians

Central Truth:
Christians live in the liberty of God's righteousness only by the power of the Holy Spirit.

Focus:
Explain how Christians relate to the Law, and live according to the Spirit.

Context:
Paul's letters to the churches of Galatia and the church in Rome were probably written several years apart but addressed similar issues.

Golden Text:
"The law of the Spirit of life in Christ Jesus hath made me free from the law of sin and death" (Romans 8:2).

Study Outline:
I. Freedom From Legalism (Romans 7:1-6; Galatians 5:1-6)
II. Purpose of the Law (Romans 7:7-13)
III. Law of the Spirit (Romans 7:21—8:4; Galatians 5:13, 14)

I. FREEDOM FROM LEGALISM (Romans 7:1-6; Galatians 5:1-6)

A. An Illustration From Marriage (Romans 7:1-3)

1. Know ye not, brethren, (for I speak to them that know the law,) how that the law hath dominion over a man as long as he liveth?

2. For the woman which hath an husband is bound by the law to her husband so long as he liveth; but if the husband be dead, she is loosed from the law of her husband.

3. So then if, while her husband liveth, she be married to another man, she shall be called an adulteress: but if her husband be dead, she is free from that law; so that she is no adulteress, though she be married to another man.

Talk About It:
What point is Paul making in verses 1-3?

Paul begins his teaching about being free from the Law by using an illustration from the law of marriage, something that was well known to both Jews and Gentiles living in Rome. Death brings about a release from bondage—a law can only rule over a person as long as the person is alive. A wife whose husband dies is free from the law which bound her to him. She is free to start a new life with another man. Paul's point is clear. Christians are now free from the Law; they are free for eternal life with Christ. Although the Law does not die, believers have died to the Law of Moses through Christ.

B. Freedom Through Death (vv. 4-6)

4. Wherefore, my brethren, ye also are become dead to the law by the body of Christ; that ye should be married to another, even to him who is raised from the dead, that we should bring forth fruit unto God.

5. For when we were in the flesh, the motions of sins, which were by the law, did work in our members to bring forth fruit unto death.

6. But now we are delivered from the law, that being dead wherein we were held; that we should serve in newness of spirit, and not in the oldness of the letter.

Talk About It:
1. To whom are Christians "married" (v. 4), and what is the result?
2. How does verse 6 contrast a person's life before and after meeting Christ?

Paul further explains the purpose of the marriage analogy. Jews and many others remain under the Law for as long as they endeavor to secure God's approval by obedience to the Law. But, in fact, the Law only reveals sin for what it is and punishes it with death (v. 5). It can never give victory over sin and death. But we who belong to Christ have already died with Him; and because He rose from the dead, we share His new life and live for God (v. 4).

Obeying the Law is not a way to be right with God, but is a result of the new Spirit-led life in Christ. Although believers do obey the Law, they now do so not in order to gain life or acceptance with God. Instead, we do so as a result of the new life

Law and Liberty

which God has given us through Christ. In this new life we are led by the Holy Spirit.

T.S. Lockyer, in *Pulpit Commentary*, wrote: "Dead to the Law, we live to Christ. The one has no more claim; the other every claim. We are joined to Him now, indissolubly one. The plentitude of spiritual power is ours in Him. No law of the letter restrains, but a law of the Spirit inspires; His Spirit, which He hath 'poured forth' (Acts 2:33), which He hath 'poured out upon us richly' (Titus 3:6). Is it not so? A law written on the heart—the law of liberty, the law of love. And being thus filled with power, through faith in Him, we bring forth fruit unto God. The old union, with the law, wrought fruit, but it was fruit unto death. Its very holiness, as a mere exterior restraint in contact with our carnal nature, was an excitant to sin. Fruit unto death! Yes, for sowing to the flesh, we reaped corruption. But now, God's law works in us, as a quickening power. God's love is our very life; and the fruit is unto life, unto God!"

C. Freedom Through Christ (Galatians 5:1)

1. Stand fast therefore in the liberty wherewith Christ hath made us free, and be not entangled again with the yoke of bondage.

Apparently some of Paul's new converts in Galatia were being influenced by false teaching that required circumcision, along with the gospel, for salvation. Here he emphasizes that Christ has set the believer free for freedom and not for bondage. Returning to obedience to the Law as a prerequisite for salvation was going back to a life that is in bondage to the Law. In the next clause, Paul uses the word *entangled*, or "burdened" (*NIV*). To return to the Law produces a life that is heavy-laden. It is such a burdened life that Paul compares it to a yoke of slavery—a life with no freedom.

Hope is offered by Paul in the form of an admonition: "Stand fast." The believer can make a conscious decision to stand firm in the freedom that Christ has empowered His children to have.

D. Freedom Through Choice (vv. 2-6)

2. Behold, I Paul say unto you, that if ye be circumcised, Christ shall profit you nothing.

3. For I testify again to every man that is circumcised, that he is a debtor to do the whole law.

4. Christ is become of no effect unto you, whosoever of you are justified by the law; ye are fallen from grace.

5. For we through the Spirit wait for the hope of righteousness by faith.

6. For in Jesus Christ neither circumcision availeth any thing, nor uncircumcision; but faith which worketh by love.

"The best argument for Christianity is Christians: their joy, their certainty, their completeness. But the strongest argument against Christianity is also Christians— when they are somber and joyless, when they are self-righteous and smug . . . when they are narrow and repressive, then Christianity dies a thousand deaths."
—**Sheldon Vanauken**

Talk About It:
How must Christians "stand fast," and why?

Talk About It:
1. Why can't someone be "justified by the law" (v. 4)?
2. Name two things faith does in the believer (vv. 5, 6).

In verse 2, Paul stresses his point by using the expression "Mark my words!" (*NIV*). This statement prepares the reader for the statements to follow. He tells his confused converts that if they decide to get circumcised, they are making a statement that the Law is required for salvation—thus nullifying what Christ has already done. In verse 3 he explains that if the Galatians comply with this one aspect of the Law—circumcision—they will be obligated to obey all of the Law. Of course, that is impossible for any person to do completely.

In verse 4, Paul speaks to those who are "trying" (*NIV*) to be justified by the Law. It is a fruitless endeavor, for freedom can never be experienced by one's obedience to the Law. If they continue to do this, Paul warns they will become "alienated" (*NIV*), or separated, from Christ—the One who has saved them. He goes on to describe them as having "fallen from grace." The word *fallen* implies that the believers left a higher place of privilege and right relationship with God. They had substituted their faith in Christ with faith in legalistic observances of the Law. Falling away from grace also means they had abandoned the truth of God's grace that brings salvation and life. They were no longer living "in Christ" (v. 6).

In verses 5 and 6 Paul stresses how valuable faith is. Believing in Christ, with the help of the Spirit, is necessary; "trying to be justified" (v. 4, *NIV*) is not. The condition of being circumcised or uncircumcised carries no value as compared to faith. It is faith that leads to righteousness. And in righteousness there is hope because it signifies our relationship with God—"faith expressing itself through love" (v. 6, *NIV*).

"If any man ascribes anything of salvation, even the very least thing, to the free will of man, he knows nothing of grace, and he has not learned Jesus Christ rightly."
—Martin Luther

II. PURPOSE OF THE LAW (Romans 7:7-13)

A. Produces Awareness of Sin (vv. 7, 8)

7. What shall we say then? Is the law sin? God forbid. Nay, I had not known sin, but by the law: for I had not known lust, except the law had said, Thou shalt not covet.

8. But sin, taking occasion by the commandment, wrought in me all manner of concupiscence. For without the law sin was dead.

Talk About It:
1. What purpose did the Old Testament law serve?
2. How does sin take advantage of God's laws?

Paul's writings in the opening verses of Romans 7 would have led to the question, "Is the Law sin?" Therefore, he asks this question with an answer in mind. The Law is neither bad nor is it sin. To clarify, Paul uses his own experiences with the effects of the Law: (1) The Law benefited him by revealing that many of his thoughts and actions were wrong. Something can't be changed unless one knows it needs to be changed. Therefore, the Law was good because it helped him to identify wrongs in his life. (2) The Law increased his desire for things he should not have. (3) The Law condemned Paul for the sin in his life. It taught him that the life he was living—which he thought was pleasing to God—was actually grievous to the Lord.

B. Produces Death (vv. 9-13)

9. For I was alive without the law once: but when the commandment came, sin revived, and I died.

10. And the commandment, which was ordained to life, I found to be unto death.

11. For sin, taking occasion by the commandment, deceived me, and by it slew me.

12. Wherefore the law is holy, and the commandment holy, and just, and good.

13. Was then that which is good made death unto me? God forbid. But sin, that it might appear sin, working death in me by that which is good; that sin by the commandment might become exceeding sinful.

The condemnation brought by the Law revealed to Paul that he was spiritually dead—he was alienated from God. Once he knew the Law, there were no excuses for his behavior that went against God's wishes. Sin was in his life all along, but he only saw it clearly when he realized how God wanted him to live.

The main point in this section is the impotence of the Law as it relates to salvation. The purpose of the Law is to point out sin, awaken the conscience, and make humans aware of moral obligations and spiritual need. It shows that sin is "exceeding sinful" (v. 13).

Exceeding sinful means "in an excessive degree; to the utmost possible extent," wrote Albert Barnes. "The sense here is, that by the giving of the command, and its application to the mind, sin was completely developed; it was excited, inflamed, aggravated, and showed to be excessively malignant and deadly. It was not a dormant, slumbering principle; but it was awfully opposed to God and His Law. Calvin has well expressed the sense: 'It was proper that the enormity of sin should be revealed by the Law; because unless sin should break forth by some dreadful and enormous excess (as they say), it would not be known to be sin. This excess exhibits itself the more violently, while it turns life into death. The sentiment of the whole is that the tendency of the Law is to excite the dormant sin of the bosom into active existence, and to reveal its true nature. It is desirable that that should be done, and as that is all that the Law accomplishes, it is not adapted to sanctify the soul."

III. LAW OF THE SPIRIT (Romans 7:21—8:4; Galatians 5:13, 14)
A. Life Under the Law (Romans 7:21-25)

21. I find then a law, that, when I would do good, evil is present with me.

Talk About It:
1. How does verse 12 describe God's laws?
2. How was sin made "exceeding [or utterly] sinful" (v. 13)? Why did this need to happen?

22. For I delight in the law of God after the inward man:

23. But I see another law in my members, warring against the law of my mind, and bringing me into captivity to the law of sin which is in my members.

24. O wretched man that I am! who shall deliver me from the body of this death?

25. I thank God through Jesus Christ our Lord. So then with the mind I myself serve the law of God; but with the flesh the law of sin.

Paul addresses the problem of humanity outside Christ, particularly as one tries to please God by means of observing the Law. It is a life of struggle, and Paul describes such a person as "wretched." Without doubt, this passage describes Paul's pre-conversion experience; yet it's a description that fits all humans outside Christ who want to live right. But all hope is not lost. The answer to the malady of sin is found in Christ. Life in Christ is a victorious walk that can overcome the desires of the flesh.

Paul identifies the Conqueror, the victory and the battleground in verse 25. The Conqueror is Jesus Christ. The victory comes through God's work in the believer's mind. The battleground where sin lies defeated is Paul's flesh. Sin is defeated "through Jesus Christ our Lord."

B. Life According to the Spirit (8:1-4)

1. There is therefore now no condemnation to them which are in Christ Jesus, who walk not after the flesh, but after the Spirit.

2. For the law of the Spirit of life in Christ Jesus hath made me free from the law of sin and death.

3. For what the law could not do, in that it was weak through the flesh, God sending his own Son in the likeness of sinful flesh, and for sin, condemned sin in the flesh:

4. That the righteousness of the law might be fulfilled in us, who walk not after the flesh, but after the Spirit.

Although Paul rejoiced in the deliverance that comes through Christ (7:25), he still has more to say about the question in verse 24: "Who will rescue me from this body of death?" (NIV). The answer in 8:1 echoes the theme of 5:1: Those who have been "justified by faith" (5:1) are "them which are in Christ Jesus" (8:1). There is no condemnation to them—they have been liberated. They have received life in the Spirit.

Victory, joy, and freedom from sin and condemnation come through the accomplishments of Christ and by the power of the indwelling Holy Spirit. The Holy Spirit is an empowering presence within believers, enabling them to overcome sin. This life-giving ministry comes into full operation once a believer has fully surrendered to the Holy Spirit and begins obeying His

---

Talk About It:
1. What did Paul say about his "inward man" (v. 22)?
2. Why did Paul feel like a "prisoner" (v. 23, NIV)?
3. Where did Paul find hope? (vv. 24, 25)?

"I have more trouble with D.L. Moody than with any other man I ever met."
—D.L. Moody

for sin (v. 3)—"an offering for sin" (NASB)

Talk About It:
1. Explain the phrase "no condemnation" (v. 1).
2. Why did God's Son have to put on "the likeness of sinful flesh" (v. 3)?
3. If we "live according to the Spirit" (v. 4, NIV), what can we do?

Law and Liberty

promptings. It is then that victory over sin is established in the believer's life.

Life in the Spirit is a life of spiritual freedom. That freedom has its source in Christ. The Law was impotent, helpless to make us good. So God sent His Son in the likeness of sinful flesh, but without sin, to deal with the problem of sin. God's purpose is clear: "that the righteous requirements of the law might be fully met in us" (v. 4, *NIV*). Believers can fulfill the requirements of the Law by the power of the Holy Spirit.

C. Law of Love (Galatians 5:13, 14)

13. For, brethren, ye have been called unto liberty; only use not liberty for an occasion to the flesh, but by love serve one another.

14. For all the law is fulfilled in one word, even in this; Thou shalt love thy neighbour as thyself.

Believers have been set at liberty through the death of Christ and can now live victoriously over sin, not by fulfilling the Law but by the power of the Spirit. The question now is, Are they free from every law? Paul declares that believers are free from seeing the Law as a prerequisite for salvation. Next, he instructs believers not to misuse their freedom by indulging their flesh once again with sin. The believers' freedom is not without boundaries or limitations. Believers must not use their freedom as an opportunity to serve the flesh. Instead, freedom must be expressed in loving service to fellow believers.

What an irony! The believer's freedom consists of willing servitude—servitude that focuses on the welfare of another. This freedom has stringent moral obligations—not the obligations of the Law but the obligations of love. By loving and serving one another through love, believers fulfill the intent of the Law.

CONCLUSION

We do not obey the Law to gain life. Instead, obedience to the Law is now a result of the new life God has given to us through Christ. In this new life we are led by the Holy Spirit and empowered by Him to conquer evil and sin and to live according to the Law. Not only does the Holy Spirit enable us to have victory over sin, but He also gives us power to proclaim the good news wherever and to whomever God leads.

GOLDEN TEXT CHALLENGE

"THE LAW OF THE SPIRIT OF LIFE IN CHRIST JESUS HATH MADE ME FREE FROM THE LAW OF SIN AND DEATH" (Romans 8:2).

This verse sets forth the liberty which the believer enjoys in Christ Jesus. Every sinner is faced with condemnation. He is

---

"We may not understand how the Spirit works, but the effect of the Spirit on the lives of men is there for all to see. . . . No man can disregard a religion and a faith and a power which is able to make bad men good."
—**William Barclay**

Talk About It:
What has God given us the freedom to do?

Did you know the world is dying
For a little bit of love?
Everywhere we hear them sighing
For a little bit of love.
—**Anonymous**

---

under the sentence of death because he has disobeyed God and rejected Christ. When he comes to Christ, that doom is gone, his sins are forgiven, and he no longer lives under the rule of sin that kills. The old, vicious circle of sin and death is broken. What the Law could not do, and what people could not do, God did. He sent His own Son in the likeness of sinful flesh to atone for sin. In so doing, He signed the death warrant of sin in our nature. We, who were the servants of sin, can now yield ourselves to God as instruments of righteousness (see Romans 6:13). Every ability God has given us can now be used for God's glory. All that sin has tampered with can now be restored to the use God intended for it.

All of this is true because the new spiritual principle by which we are governed in Christ is the law of the Spirit of life—that is, the life-giving Spirit. Again and again, Christ spoke of this principle of life: "Search the scriptures; for in them ye think ye have eternal life: and they are they which testify of me. And ye will not come to me, that ye might have life" (John 5:39, 40). "The thief cometh not, but for to steal, and to kill, and to destroy: I am come that they might have life, and that they might have it more abundantly" (10:10). "I am the resurrection, and the life: he that believeth in me, though he were dead, yet shall he live: And whosoever liveth and believeth in me shall never die. Believest thou this?" (11:25, 26).

Victorious Christian Living

Romans 8:5-39; Galatians 5:16-26

INTRODUCTION

God intends that we live victoriously. Romans 8 and Galatians 5 show us how. Victorious Christian living is elusive—even impossible—if we trust in our own abilities. We must live by the power of the indwelling Holy Spirit and in an ever-deepening, always widening experience of the great and marvelous grace and unconditional love God has for us in Jesus Christ. These chapters describe the new life of the believer who is led by the Holy Spirit. This life is characterized by the Spirit, not the flesh, controlling the believer.

French Arrington writes: "Romans 8:14 says believers are *led by the Spirit*. The Spirit manifests the Christlike life in us as we are led by Him. He inspires our hearts and minds to do what is good and right. As we allow ourselves to be led by Him, He adorns our lives with graces that identify us as God's children.

"Galatians 5:16 says believers *walk in the Spirit*. It is similar to being led by the Spirit, but in the New Testament, walking emphasizes a way of life. As we walk in the power of the Spirit, we march in line with Him and walk the steps that the Spirit walks. As we follow the Spirit, the fruit of the Spirit flourishes in our lives."

The fruit of the Spirit (vv. 22, 23) abounds instead of the works of the flesh (vv. 19-21). Specifically, this means the Spirit-controlled mind is filled with love, joy and peace instead of hatred, envy and jealousy. The Spirit-controlled heart acts with patience, kindness and goodness instead of with impurity, debauchery and idolatry. The Spirit-controlled person practices faithfulness, gentleness and self-control instead of sexual immorality, fits of rage, drunkenness and the like.

Unit Theme:
The Gospel in Romans and Galatians

Central Truth:
God helps believers live victoriously.

Focus:
Acknowledge that God provides all we need for victorious living and accept His help.

Context:
Paul's letters to the churches of Galatia and the church in Rome were probably written several years apart but addressed similar issues.

Golden Text:
"We are more than conquerors through him that loved us" (Romans 8:37).

Study Outline:
I. The Spirit Leads Us (Romans 8:5-17; Galatians 5:16-23)
II. The Spirit Helps Us (Romans 8:18-27)
III. God Is for Us (Romans 8:28-39)

A. Who's in Control? (Romans 8:5-8)

5. For they that are after the flesh do mind the things of the flesh; but they that are after the Spirit the things of the Spirit.

6. For to be carnally minded is death; but to be spiritually minded is life and peace.

7. Because the carnal mind is enmity against God: for it is not subject to the law of God, neither indeed can be.

8. So then they that are in the flesh cannot please God.

Beginning in verse 5, Paul shows what is involved in the new way of living in the Spirit that he has just discussed in the preceding verses. How does the Spirit bring about sanctification? It begins, Paul argues, as the Holy Spirit produces a new mind-set (vv. 5-8); those who live according to the Spirit have their mind set on the things of the Spirit.

There is a huge difference between those who belong to Christ and those who do not. They live in two different spheres of existence—flesh (the carnal, sinful nature) and Spirit. To be in the flesh is to be a non-Christian, living under sin's power (vv. 8, 9). To be in the Spirit is to be a Christian, living under the control and guiding influence of the Holy Spirit. To live according to the flesh is to live by the standards, values and dictates of the flesh. To live according to the Spirit is to conduct our lives according to the standards and resources of the life-giving Spirit in us. To have our mind focused or directed only upon the things of self means being alienated from God, who is the only source of true life. The result is death now in this life (condemnation and evil) and consequently eternal death.

Paul further describes the mind directed toward the flesh (non-Christian) in relation to God (vv. 7, 8). People who are controlled by the flesh are alienated from God, even hostile to Him. They do not submit to God's law, either by choice or inner compulsion.

B. Fruit of the Flesh (Galatians 5:16-21)

16. This I say then, Walk in the Spirit, and ye shall not fulfil the lust of the flesh.

17. For the flesh lusteth against the Spirit, and the Spirit against the flesh: and these are contrary the one to the other: so that ye cannot do the things that ye would.

18. But if ye be led of the Spirit, ye are not under the law.

19. Now the works of the flesh are manifest, which are these; Adultery, fornication, uncleanness, lasciviousness,

20. Idolatry, witchcraft, hatred, variance, emulations, wrath, strife, seditions, heresies,

21. Envyings, murders, drunkenness, revellings, and

---

enmity (v. 7)— hostile

Talk About It:
Describe the differences between the carnally minded person and the spiritually minded person (vv. 5-8).

"God has a program of character development for each one of us. He wants others to look at our lives and say, 'He walks with God, for he lives like Christ.'"
—**Erwin Lutzer**

lusteth against (v. 17)—"desires what is contrary" (*NIV*)

uncleanness (v. 19)—"impurity" (*NASB*)

lasciviousness (v. 19)—"sensuality" (*NASB*)

---

such like: of the which I tell you before, as I have also told you in time past, that they which do such things shall not inherit the kingdom of God.

As he does in Romans 8, Paul contrasts life in the flesh with that of the Spirit. He begins his discourse by demonstrating that the Spirit and sin are absolutely incompatible. By living in the Spirit, one does not gratify the desires of the flesh. Believers are capable of conquering the sinful nature only as they follow the direction and prompting of the Spirit.

In verse 18, he encourages believers to be *led* by the Spirit. To live by the Spirit is to be led by the Spirit. In verses 19-21, Paul enumerates what being led by the Spirit does *not* mean as he lists the manifestations of a life lived according to the flesh. This list is quite specific: "sexual immorality, impurity and debauchery; idolatry and witchcraft; hatred, discord, jealousy, fits of rage, selfish ambition, dissensions, factions and envy; drunkenness, orgies, and the like" (*NIV*). A person who lives according to the flesh will not inherit the kingdom of God.

C. The Spirit Is in Control (Romans 8:9-11; Galatians 5:22, 23)

Romans 8:9. But ye are not in the flesh, but in the Spirit, if so be that the Spirit of God dwell in you. Now if any man have not the Spirit of Christ, he is none of his.

10. And if Christ be in you, the body is dead because of sin; but the Spirit is life because of righteousness.

11. But if the Spirit of him that raised up Jesus from the dead dwell in you, he that raised up Christ from the dead shall also quicken your mortal bodies by his Spirit that dwelleth in you.

Galatians 5:22. But the fruit of the Spirit is love, joy, peace, longsuffering, gentleness, goodness, faith,

23. Meekness, temperance: against such there is no law.

The Spirit-led life of holiness is adamantly opposed and utterly incompatible with the flesh! Believers must remember that they have the Spirit of Christ living within them. This empowers them to live according to the Spirit's direction. Hence, in Galatians 5:22, 23, Paul says that believers know they are living by the Spirit if they manifest the fruit of the Spirit.

Scholars have attempted to categorize the nine aspects of the fruit of the Spirit into three groups of three. The first three comprise the Christian's state of mind and heart. The second triad contains special qualities that affect one's interaction with his/her neighbor. The third exhibits the principles that guide the believer's conduct. Each triad seems to build upon the former. This list is representative of what comes from being led by the Spirit in a pursuit of holiness. Paul certainly meant for the "fruit

variance (v. 20)— "discord" (*NIV*)

emulations (v. 20) —jealousy

revellings (v. 21) —"orgies" (*NIV*)

Talk About It:
1. What does it mean to "walk in the Spirit" (v. 16)?
2. Why do you suppose Paul gave a detailed list of some of the "works of the flesh"?

Talk About It:
Explain the phrase "against such there is no law" (Galatians 5:23).

"When we look at other Christians, let's not dwell on the burned-out stumps of their former life. Instead, let's celebrate and affirm the exciting new growth in their lives."
—*Christians Quoting*

of the Spirit" to be a contrast to the preceding "works of the flesh."

D. Children of God (Romans 8:12-17)

12. Therefore, brethren, we are debtors, not to the flesh, to live after the flesh.

13. For if ye live after the flesh, ye shall die: but if ye through the Spirit do mortify the deeds of the body, ye shall live.

14. For as many as are led by the Spirit of God, they are the sons of God.

15. For ye have not received the spirit of bondage again to fear; but ye have received the Spirit of adoption, whereby we cry, Abba, Father.

16. The Spirit itself beareth witness with our spirit, that we are the children of God:

17. And if children, then heirs; heirs of God, and jointheirs with Christ; if so be that we suffer with him, that we may be also glorified together.

There are obligations as well as privileges of living in the Spirit. The indwelling Spirit of God offers the believer new possibilities of existence. Believers are obliged to live this way. We owe something to the One who has redeemed us and set us free. It is a way of expressing our gratitude toward God for all that He has done for us through Jesus Christ. As verse 13 shows, it is not only an obligation to live according to the Spirit, but it is also fruitful and beneficial. To live by the Spirit is to really live. A person lives by the Spirit as he or she maintains an attitude of obedience to the Lord and leads a sacrificial life. This is done by putting to death the misdeeds of the body. These misdeeds include evil thoughts, words or actions that easily beset us as human beings.

Another benefit of living according to the Spirit is stated in verse 14. The believer is a "son" (child) of God. In verses 15-17, Paul describes what being a child of God means. The believer is no longer a slave to fear. He or she has confidence in their relationship with God. Under the Law, the highest possible relationship that one could have known or enjoyed was that of servitude. But praise God that, under grace, the relationship is one of sonship—a filial relationship of love characterized by joyous and grateful obedience. By using the term *Abba* to describe God as a Father, Paul is emphasizing the closeness and intimacy of that relationship we can have with the heavenly Father.

II. THE SPIRIT HELPS US (Romans 8:18-27)

A. All Creation Groans (vv. 18-22)

18. For I reckon that the sufferings of this present time

Talk About It:
1. What obligation do Christians have, and to what are they not indebted (vv. 12, 13)?
2. What are the blessings of being a child of God (vv. 14-16)?
3. What does it mean to be "co-heirs with Christ" (v. 17, *NIV*)?

"God passionately yearns to be in a loving relationship with the people He created."
—**Bill Hybels**

Victorious Christian Living

are not worthy to be compared with the glory which shall be revealed in us.

19. For the earnest expectation of the creature waiteth for the manifestation of the sons of God.

20. For the creature was made subject to vanity, not willingly, but by reason of him who hath subjected the same in hope,

21. Because the creature itself also shall be delivered from the bondage of corruption into the glorious liberty of the children of God.

22. For we know that the whole creation groaneth and travaileth in pain together until now.

the creature (v. 19) —the creation

vanity (v. 20)— futility or frustration

travaileth in pain (v. 22)—"suffers the pains of childbirth" (NASB)

A new life in Christ is not a problem-free life. This is the thrust of the second half of Romans 8. The new life in Christ, led by His Spirit, does include glory but will also include suffering. Like Jesus, we suffer, but in our suffering we have true comfort. In order to triumph over sufferings the believer is to *consider* them carefully, as Paul does here.

The attitude with which one approaches suffering matters very much. Paul encourages believers to remember where the journey is leading—to a greater glory. Believers can endure a journey beset with hardships if they keep in mind the joy that awaits them at the end of their journey—a joy that is found in the welcome awaiting them on their arrival home.

Paul's point is to let believers know their personal sufferings are only a part of the suffering that the whole creation is enduring. Creation experiences "frustration" (NIV), or "futility" (NASB), because it cannot attain the purpose for which God had intended for it (v. 20). But there is hope. That's because the divine judgment upon creation was not God's last word. When God subjected creation to frustration, it was done in hope that it would one day be restored. In verse 21, Paul looked forward to all of creation's freedom and liberation. In fact, in verse 22 Paul describes all creation groaning and travailing until that day of full restoration. That groaning is in response to the negative effects humanity's rebellion had on the creation. The hope is that one day there will be a new heaven and a new earth—a restoration of all things according to God's will (see Revelation 21:1-4).

Talk About It:
1. How should verse 18 encourage the suffering Christian?
2. What is all of creation desperately longing for (vv. 19-22)?

"Suffering, although it is a burden, is a useful burden, like the splints used in orthopedic treatment."

—**Soren Kierkegaard**

B. God's Children Groan (vv. 23-25)

23. And not only they, but ourselves also, which have the firstfruits of the Spirit, even we ourselves groan within ourselves, waiting for the adoption, to wit, the redemption of our body.

24. For we are saved by hope: but hope that is seen is not hope: for what a man seeth, why doth he yet hope for?

25. But if we hope for that we see not, then do we with patience wait for it.

Talk About It:
1. What are "the firstfruits of the Spirit" (v. 23)?
2. What role does hope play in the Christian's life (vv. 24, 25)?

Creation can do nothing but groan and hope. Christians also do not escape this frustration in their spiritual conflicts. Life and pain are realities of Christian existence. As such, we too must then wait, groan and hope, but unlike creation, we have the first-fruits of the Spirit. The indwelling Spirit is our foretaste of heavenly glory, the anticipation of our future redemption. The Spirit is our assurance of God's better day. Believers continue to hope because the restoration has begun with Christ's redemptive work and will be completely manifested at the resurrection.

C. The Spirit Groans (vv. 26, 27)

26. Likewise the Spirit also helpeth our infirmities: for we know not what we should pray for as we ought: but the Spirit itself maketh intercession for us with groanings which cannot be uttered.

27. And he that searcheth the hearts knoweth what is the mind of the Spirit, because he maketh intercession for the saints according to the will of God.

Talk About It:
1. Why do we sometimes not know "how to pray as we should" (v. 26, *NASB*)?
2. Describe the Holy Spirit's ministry of intercession (vv. 26, 27).

Not only does creation groan and believers groan, but the Spirit also groans. This is done *for* us and *with* us. Jesus is interceding in heaven on our behalf, and the Spirit is interceding within us on earth—we are not alone. The Spirit is with us in our weakness and will help us to pray. As our advocate, the Holy Spirit not only creates hope in us, but also provides help for our infirmities. Though our prayers may be sometimes inexpressible, they are not unintelligible to God.

French Arrington writes: "These verses depict the Holy Spirit's praying through believers on their behalf as they pray in tongues. The words or groanings that flow from the Spirit through the soul of the believer touch the heart of God. As God's children, we are aided by the Spirit in our weakness, that is, we are edified as the Holy Spirit prays through us in a language we do not know. At times we may not know how to pray and to praise God, but the Holy Spirit can give us the words to say. Through speaking in other tongues, we may express prayer and praise beyond the limits of our native language, interceding on behalf of circumstances that God knows, but we do not."

"Keep praying, but be thankful that God's answers are wiser than your prayers."
—William Culbertson

III. GOD IS FOR US (Romans 8:28-39)

A. Working for Our Good (vv. 28-30)

28. And we know that all things work together for good to them that love God, to them who are the called according to his purpose.

29. For whom he did foreknow, he also did predestinate to be conformed to the image of his Son, that he might be the firstborn among many brethren.

30. Moreover whom he did predestinate, them he also

called: and whom he called, them he also justified: and whom he justified, them he also glorified. These verses give the believer another reason for patiently enduring suffering. Paul assures the believer that there is a greater purpose to suffering than is readily apparent. God can and will bring good out of the believer's trials and afflictions. This good means that all things contribute to the believer's final glorification and conformity to Christ. But there is a condition placed on this promise. This assurance is only available to those who love God and have been called according to His purpose.

Those who love God are those whom, from eternity, God knew would choose to receive His salvation and thus walk step-by-step to heaven. By His amazing grace, they were "predestined to be conformed to the likeness of his Son" (v. 29, NIV). Paul does not deny that a believer can fall away before glorification. Neither does he suggest that many are called by God who are never justified. The point is that predestination, calling, justification and glorification are the steps by which God leads His children to heaven. All our experiences are working for our good in God's eternal plan.

B. Giving Us All Things (vv. 31-36)

31. What shall we then say to these things? If God be for us, who can be against us?

32. He that spared not his own Son, but delivered him up for us all, how shall he not with him also freely give us all things?

33. Who shall lay any thing to the charge of God's elect? It is God that justifieth.

34. Who is he that condemneth? It is Christ that died, yea rather, that is risen again, who is even at the right hand of God, who also maketh intercession for us.

35. Who shall separate us from the love of Christ? shall tribulation, or distress, or persecution, or famine, or nakedness, or peril, or sword?

36. As it is written, For thy sake we are killed all the day long; we are accounted as sheep for the slaughter.

The concluding verses of Romans 8 continue to provide an immense assurance to believers in the midst of sufferings. Paul had reminded his readers of what God had done. Now he asks a series of rhetorical questions which reassure believers that they have nothing to fear. Paul's key statement in this section is, "God is for us." The assertion that "God is for us" is most fully demonstrated in God's giving up of His Son for us.

Paul argues from the greater to the lesser in verses 31 and 32: If God has made the greatest sacrifice, won't He also give us lesser things? However, in verse 33, Paul moves from the

Talk About It:
1. What does God promise about "all things" in a believer's life (v. 28)?
2. How is Jesus "the firstborn among many brethren" (v. 29)?
3. Describe four actions God does on behalf of His children (v. 30).

"Inside the will of God, there is no failure. Outside the will of God, there is no success."
—**Bernard Edinger**

Talk About It:
1. What are the "all things" referred to in verse 32, and what makes them free to believers?
2. How is Jesus ministering to believers right now (v. 34)?
3. If we are in "the love of Christ," why might we face the things listed (vv. 35, 36)?

lesser to the greater: If mere mortals falsely accuse us, can't we trust in the love and mercy of the God who justifies us? If God would give up His Son, we can be assured He will give us all we may need on our journey of life. If God has justified us, making us right with Him, no one can place any other charges against us. God is the supreme authority and judge over all matters. If Jesus does not condemn us and is our advocate before the Father interceding on our behalf, who can possibly condemn us?

We must not think it strange if adversities and persecution come our way. It does not mean that God does not love us. In fact, it is a normal result of being a Christian. Adversities have been, are, and will continue to be part of the experiences of those who love God and live according to His ways. The calamities that believers face are not a proof of abandonment by God.

C. Conquering Through Christ (vv. 37-39)

37. Nay, in all these things we are more than conquerors through him that loved us.

38. For I am persuaded, that neither death, nor life, nor angels, nor principalities, nor powers, nor things present, nor things to come,

39. Nor height, nor depth, nor any other creature, shall be able to separate us from the love of God, which is in Christ Jesus our Lord.

We need not be discouraged by the negative situations we face in life. We can live victoriously, always remembering that we are "more than conquerors" through Him who loved us. Nothing can separate us from His love.

These verses do not suggest the doctrine of unconditional security. That doctrine absolves believers of responsible, holy living by proclaiming that no matter how we live, we'll make it to heaven. That teaching is unbiblical. Instead, our emphasis must be the same as Paul's—the sufficiency of God's grace. There is grace enough to save us, empower us for holy living, and keep us safe as we make our pilgrimage to heaven. Whether we face fallen angels, future uncertainties, or formidable evil powers, nothing will stop God from loving us, and nothing can conquer us as long as we are relying on God's matchless grace.

CONCLUSION

God can and has provided all that we need to live victoriously. It is a matter of accepting His help that is always available to us. Sometimes that help comes through His Word or His presence as manifested within our community of faith as we assemble together to worship God. The key is to not remain alone but to avail ourselves of the strength that is always through Christ's church.

To live "in Christ" means to live in fellowship with His body of believers. Part of being in covenant relationship with God is being in covenant relationships with other believers. A covenant relationship requires commitment, compassion and connection. We must remain connected to God and other believers through the cords of love. The church becomes a powerful witness to the world when they see believers living together in unity and victory.

GOLDEN TEXT CHALLENGE

"WE ARE MORE THAN CONQUERORS THROUGH HIM THAT LOVED US" (Romans 8:37).

Some victories are so costly that it would have been better if the battles had not been fought. One such victory is reported when an aide said to his commanding general, "Well, General, we won!" The general looked out over the carnage of the battlefield and shook his head. "Yes," he said, "we won. But one more victory like that and we're through!"

Dr. J.B. Chapman illustrated the meaning of "more than conquerors" by a reference to the contest between David and Goliath. When David went out to meet the giant, he carried five stones in his shepherd's pouch. He stunned and killed the Philistine with the use of just one.

Had four other giants appeared, David would have been ready for them also. To have used all his arsenal would have constituted him a "conqueror." The margin of reserve made him "more than a conqueror."

Paul gives two lists of possible enemies the Christian soul must face. One list concerns visible and tangible enemies (v. 35). The other list describes the spiritual and invisible forces arrayed against us (vv. 38, 39).

Because nothing—visible or invisible, tangible or spiritual—can separate us from the love of God in Christ Jesus, we are assured of the kind of triumph that makes us not only victors, but "more than conquerors."

Daily Devotions:
M. Elders Helped Moses
Numbers 11:10-17
T. God Helps Israel
2 Samuel 3:3-14
W. A Plea for Help
Psalm 31:1-5
T. The Holy Spirit Promised
John 14:15-18
F. Philip Led by the Spirit
Acts 8:26-29
S. Help When Tempted
Hebrews 2:14-18

Living as a Christian

Romans 12:1-21; Galatians 6:1-10

Unit Theme:
The Gospel in Romans and Galatians

Central Truth:
Living as a Christian involves striving to please God and treating others with love and kindness.

Focus:
Consider how Christians are to treat others and practice brotherly love.

Context:
Paul's letters to the churches of Galatia and the church in Rome were probably written several years apart but addressed similar issues.

Golden Text:
"Be kindly affectioned one to another with brotherly love; in honour preferring one another" (Romans 12:10).

Study Outline:
I. Do God's Will (Romans 12:1-8)
II. Love Others Sincerely (Romans 12:9-21)
III. Do Good to All (Galatians 6:1-10)

INTRODUCTION

Nothing should be more important for Christians than a deepening conviction that the righteousness they have received by faith is to be demonstrated in daily life. An undeniable proof and testimony to the reality of Christian experience is a Christlike life. The believer's new life must find its expression through a right attitude toward oneself and others, through Christian love, through consideration for others, through moral integrity and purity, and in strict regard for one's Christian influence. The righteousness of God must be reflected both in the personal life of the Christian and in the wider community. These concerns constitute the burden of Paul's exhortations in Romans 12 and Galatians 6.

Romans 12 immediately challenges the believer to serve. Paul argues persuasively that service is not optional but is the reflection of genuine faith. If God is working in a believer's life, then the evidence of that work will be demonstrated in service to Him. Paul was always practical, and this chapter is no exception. After calling believers to service, he tells them how they must serve. Good intentions are inadequate; they must be translated into actual service.

In Galatians 6, Paul describes how believers will be rewarded for their service unto the Lord. A spiritual harvest will be reaped by those who do "not become weary in doing good" (v. 9, *NIV*).

I. DO GOD'S WILL (Romans 12:1-8)

A. By Being Transformed (vv. 1, 2)

1. I beseech you therefore, brethren, by the mercies of God, that ye present your bodies a living sacrifice, holy, acceptable unto God, which is your reasonable service.

2. And be not conformed to this world: but be ye transformed by the renewing of your mind, that ye may prove what is that good, and acceptable, and perfect, will of God.

These two verses summarize the ethical implications and response that Christians are to make in view of God's mercies of which Paul has spoken in the preceding chapters. They do not only set the tone and framework for the rest of the chapter but also provide the basis of Christian ethics. The word *therefore* connects the previous chapters to those that follow.

Paul begins by using the language of sacrifice. For Christians, true worship does not consist of animal sacrifices, neither in praising God only in church services, as important as that is. Christians must worship God with their bodies; that is, in all the activities of body and mind in daily life. It is important that all our behaviors be in accord with God's will. The pattern to be established is living according to God's standards, thus making our behavior holy and pleasing to God.

Paul then exhorts believers not to be conformed to the present age. Rather, we should be transformed and live as befitting people of the coming age. A choice must be made. We can either choose to conform to the thought patterns of this world or to the thought patterns of God. Instead of yielding to the influences that tend to shape us into the likeness of things around us, we must daily move in the opposite direction. The transformation that Paul urges is to come through the constant renewing of the mind. This comes by employing all the means of grace available to believers—the Holy Spirit, God's Word, prayer and the Christian community.

B. By Using Your Gifts (vv. 3-8)

3. For I say, through the grace given unto me, to every man that is among you, not to think of himself more highly than he ought to think; but to think soberly, according as God hath dealt to every man the measure of faith.

4. For as we have many members in one body, and all members have not the same office:

5. So we, being many, are one body in Christ, and every one members one of another.

6. Having then gifts differing according to the grace that is given to us, whether prophecy, let us prophesy according to the proportion of faith;

7. Or ministry, let us wait on our ministering: or he that teacheth, on teaching;

---

reasonable service (v. 1)—spiritual act of worship

Talk About It:
1. According to verse 1, what is genuine worship?
2. How can you discern God's will for your life (v. 2)?
3. How does verse 2 describe the will of God?

"Those who are wise consider how God responds to their worship."
—**David Mains**

same office (v. 4) —"same function" (*NIV*)

---

8. Or he that exhorteth, on exhortation: he that giveth, let him do it with simplicity; he that ruleth, with diligence; he that sheweth mercy, with cheerfulness.

Paul, on the basis of grace and full devotion, makes an appeal to the believers to translate the righteousness of God into their personal lives. The Christian life must be marked by humility. It is not only important for Christians to have a right attitude toward God, they must also have a right attitude toward themselves. Believers must guard against exalting themselves. But they must also avoid a self-deprecation or mock humility.

Although the church is one body, it is comprised of different members. None is useless, and none is more important than the other. In the body of Christ, its members have different functions and gifts. We should exercise all these for the edification of the church. In order to live the Christian life as God intends, believers must understand how intertwined their lives are with each other.

Paul does not intend to make an exhaustive list of spiritual giftings, for many such empowerments arise with the varying needs of the church. However, in 1 Corinthians 12:27, 28, a more detailed enumeration is given. In that passage, as well as the present one, Paul refers not so much to natural talents and personality leanings, but rather to specific functional giftings of the Holy Spirit for individuals' use for the larger body's benefit. However, even these direct callings most often take advantage of natural leanings. Prophets are generally required to be strong, bold and verbally articulate. Exhorters will have a natural love for people. Teachers need to have clear, organized thoughts and the ability to present them. Those who are comforters to the hurting and bereaved should be very caring and compassionate.

Sometimes, however, God does call individuals to areas they might not naturally lean toward. However, He will prepare them for that ministry. For instance, those who never showed compassion for the bereaved will have a change of perspective when they themselves experience a loss. God will use the experiences of life to shape a personality into a useful vessel to fill a ministry need.

II. LOVE OTHERS SINCERELY (Romans 12:9-21)
A. By Being Devoted to One Another (vv. 9-13)

9. Let love be without dissimulation. Abhor that which is evil; cleave to that which is good.

10. Be kindly affectioned one to another with brotherly love; in honour preferring one another;

11. Not slothful in business; fervent in spirit; serving the Lord;

Talk About It:
1. What is the proper way to think of oneself (v. 3)?
2. How are Christians "members one of another" (v. 5)?
3. Why are the spiritual gifts called "gifts" (v. 6)?
4. How should our spiritual gifts affect our lives (vv. 6-8)?

"When we describe 'church,' we like to say that it is a gift-evoking, gift-bearing community. . . . This is why 'church' implies a people; no one enters into the fullness of His being except in community with other persons."
—Elizabeth O'Connor

dissimulation (v. 9)—hypocrisy

business (v. 11)—diligence

12. Rejoicing in hope; patient in tribulation; continuing instant in prayer;

13. Distributing to the necessity of saints; given to hospitality.

Love must be the guiding principle in the Christian life. In these verses we see how all Christians, regardless of their functions and gifts, are to behave lovingly all the time. The problem today is discerning how much our actions are being governed by selfishness and how much by love for others. And we wonder how love should act in particular situations. This passage helps explain what love is and how it should manifest itself in various circumstances:

1. It must be sincere. Our love for others must be like God's love for us. People are to be loved strictly for who they are and not for what they do.

2. Godly love seeks after goodness. It has affinity toward all that is good, but antipathy for all that is evil.

3. Genuine love is brotherly, recognizing that we are members of God's family regardless of status, gender or race.

4. Godly love shows deference to others.

5. Genuine love is zealous in service, rejecting slothfulness and laziness.

6. It's a hopeful and steadfast love.

7. God's love is hospitable, ministering to needs of the saints and showing hospitality toward fellow Christians and strangers.

B. By Living in Harmony With One Another (vv. 14-21)

14. Bless them which persecute you: bless, and curse not.

15. Rejoice with them that do rejoice, and weep with them that weep.

16. Be of the same mind one toward another. Mind not high things, but condescend to men of low estate. Be not wise in your own conceits.

17. Recompense to no man evil for evil. Provide things honest in the sight of all men.

18. If it be possible, as much as lieth in you, live peaceably with all men.

19. Dearly beloved, avenge not yourselves, but rather give place unto wrath: for it is written, Vengeance is mine; I will repay, saith the Lord.

20. Therefore if thine enemy hunger, feed him; if he thirst, give him drink: for in so doing thou shalt heap coals of fire on his head.

21. Be not overcome of evil, but overcome evil with good.

The Christian, although in the world but not of the world, remains obligated to show love to those outside the faith. So Paul now relates the principle of love to the Christian's relationship to

---

instant (v. 12)— "steadfastly" (*NKJV*)

Talk About It:
1. How can we "abhor that which is evil" (v. 9) in daily living?
2. What does "preferring one another" (v. 10) mean, and why must Christians do so?
3. According to verses 11-13, what characteristics should mark believers?

"The question is not, 'How much may I indulge in and still be saved?' God forbid! I must rather ask, 'What about Christ's will and the example I set for my fellow Christians?'"
—Robert A. Cook

conceits (v. 16)— "opinion" (*NKJV*)

provide things honest (v. 17)— "do what is right" (*NIV*)

---

1. Practically speaking, how can we "bless" people who persecute us (v. 14)?
2. How should a Christian act toward people in a lower social class (v. 16)?
3. How far should we go to live at peace with others (v. 18)?
4. According to verse 20, how can we carry out the command of verse 21?

"Three men are my friends: he that loves me, he that hates me, and he that is indifferent to me. Who loves me teaches me tenderness. Who hates me teaches me caution. Who is indifferent to me teaches me self-reliance."
—*These Times*

those who are outside the Christian fold—people in the marketplace and public square, and even enemies. The acid test for genuine love is found in one's relationship with those who are enemies. In this section, Paul argues for a love that is astounding—a love that is known for its resilient ability to direct itself to those whom we might regard as adversaries.

A person's initial or instinctive response to maltreatment or persecution is either to curse or retaliate. However, Paul argues otherwise. The appropriate behavior is to bless and not to curse. Believers are to forgive wrongs and insults. We are also to share both in the fortunes and misfortunes of others. In so doing we demonstrate unselfish interest and reveal the spirit of Christ. It is obvious that it is difficult to love one's enemies (v. 14), but it can be equally difficult to show true sympathy as described in verse 15. Mourning with those who are heartbroken is not so hard, but rejoicing at others' successes can be difficult.

Verse 16 says we must associate with those who are lowly. We must neither shy away from humble tasks nor avoid those whose status in life is lower than ours. We should be careful not to be misled by our preferences—to that which flatters our pride. Living in harmony with others requires that we relate to one another as equals. In every situation we must do the right thing, because people are watching us and are influenced by the decisions we make and the actions we take.

If we have enemies, which is sometimes impossible to avoid, Paul gives three principles for dealing with them (vv. 17-21). First, like Jesus, we should never try to pay back (get even) with them for their wrongs. Such repayment amounts to vengeance, and that must be left to God. Our victory over evil consists in our refusal to become a party to the promotion of evil by accepting our injury without resentment. Maintaining harmony also requires not repaying evil with more evil. The only way to overcome evil is with good.

Second, we should try to help our enemy. An act of kindness toward an enemy may lead that person to recognize the evil of his or her own life, ultimately leading to a change of heart. Third, if this happens, we succeed in changing an enemy into a friend. By this means, evil is destroyed and turned into good.

III. DO GOOD TO ALL (Galatians 6:1-10)
A. To Fulfill Responsibility (vv. 1-6)
1. Brethren, if a man be overtaken in a fault, ye which are spiritual, restore such an one in the spirit of meekness; considering thyself, lest thou also be tempted.
2. Bear ye one another's burdens, and so fulfil the law of Christ.

3. For if a man think himself to be something, when he is nothing, he deceiveth himself.

4. But let every man prove his own work, and then shall he have rejoicing in himself alone, and not in another.

5. For every man shall bear his own burden.

6. Let him that is taught in the word communicate unto him that teacheth in all good things.

How should believers treat one another, and how should they behave in the body of Christ? Paul ties the answer to how we see ourselves. We belong to one another and should help one another. None of us are totally self-reliant. During struggles and temptations we need to come to the aid of each other. Fallen Christians are not to be slapped around, reviled, humiliated, or avoided. Instead we must help to restore the fallen in the spirit of gentleness.

We must also bear one another's burdens, helping the weary to shoulder their load. Bearing each other's burdens is to care for those who are in need financially, emotionally, physically or relationally. Many people carry great loads that weigh them down like boulders. Tragedies of life such as death, divorce, sickness and poverty come to everyone. During these times of crisis, people need help to carry a load that is too heavy for them to carry alone. Such concern for others is faith in action—a love that is similar to Christ's love. This is why Paul refers to it as "the law of Christ" (v. 2). This was not a law that Christ issued, but a law that He lived. It is covenant law expressing itself through love. If believers think they are unable to love in this capacity, they must remember it is the Spirit of Christ living within them that will empower them to fulfill it.

Paul next highlights a person's responsibility to oneself. Being part of a burden-bearing community does not support irresponsibility and laziness on the part of any individual member. Each person within the community must take responsibility for their own life and not burden others with the things they are able to do or should be doing for themselves.

Verse 4 warns believers not to compare themselves with other believers. Paul wrote of the false teachers in Corinth, "But they measuring themselves by themselves, and comparing themselves among themselves, are not wise" (2 Corinthians 10:12). It is not by comparative goodness that our character is measured. God, the perfect Judge, measures us by His standards which are laid out in His Word. So that is the measure we must use in evaluating ourselves.

One of those Biblical measuring sticks is in verse 6 of the text, where believers are commanded to make proper provision for the minister who leads and teaches them. Today it is the duty of the church to provide for its pastor. Ministers are the Lord's captains,

communicate (v. 6)—share

Talk About It:
1. How should we respond when a fellow Christian falls into sin (v. 1)?
2. To what "law of Christ" does verse 2 refer?
3. How can we deceive ourselves (v. 3), and how can we overcome this (v. 4)?
4. What does verse 5 mean?
5. With whom must we share, and why (v. 6)?

"You damage yourself and your relations with other people if you think either too much or too little of yourself. Take a modest, realistic view of yourself. And don't wear a false front because you want to seem to be what you're not."
—**Marion Jacobsen**

and therefore are not to go to war at their own cost. In return, ministers must diligently carry out their responsibilities.

B. To Reap a Harvest (vv. 7-10)

7. Be not deceived; God is not mocked: for whatsoever a man soweth, that shall he also reap.

8. For he that soweth to his flesh shall of the flesh reap corruption; but he that soweth to the Spirit shall of the Spirit reap life everlasting.

9. And let us not be weary in well doing: for in due season we shall reap, if we faint not.

10. As we have therefore opportunity, let us do good unto all men, especially unto them who are of the household of faith.

In verses 7 and 8, Paul presents a traditional Biblical principle that contains both a warning and an admonition. Paul draws on harvest law to address the social and financial responsibility of believers. A believer cannot claim to be living for God while sowing to the flesh. The two are incompatible, and to think otherwise is deceptive. Believers can be assured that they will reap what they sow. Those who sow to the flesh will reap death, while those who sow to the Spirit will reap eternal life.

In verses 9 and 10, Paul makes a broad application of the principle he has just outlined. Although Paul never shies away from telling people of the futility of earning God's favor by means of good works, he does point out the duties of those whose lives have been transformed by grace. They are to engage in "doing good" (v. 9, *NIV*). Following the sowing phase comes a season of waiting that must take place before one can partake of the fruit of the harvest. Paul encourages believers not to get weary and lose hope during this time, because they are not yet reaping the benefits of their wise choices. He promises that if they are patient and do not give up, they will reap a harvest in due time. He concludes in verse 10 that as Spirit-filled and Spirit-led believers, they are to continue to do good to all people, especially to fellow Christians.

Talk About It:
1. How do some people think God can be "mocked" (v. 7)?
2. Explain the phrase "sows to his own flesh" (v. 8, *NASB)*, and the result of such sowing.
3. Who will reap a good harvest (vv. 9, 10)?

"If you want to get a sure crop, and a big yield, sow wild oats."
—Josh Billings

CONCLUSION

Living as a Christian bears an example to the world of who Jesus is. When believers dwell together in unity and love, the world is provided a powerful witness of Christ's love for all. We, as followers of Christ, are expected to love our brothers and sisters in the Lord and to do good to all. It is part of God's will for those within His family.

GOLDEN TEXT CHALLENGE

"BE KINDLY AFFECTIONED ONE TO ANOTHER WITH

BROTHERLY LOVE; IN HONOUR PREFERRING ONE ANOTHER" (Romans 12:10).

God has brought those of us who know Him into a closely knit family. And whether we have known the warmth of natural family love, we can all experience the closeness and affection of a more perfect spiritual fellowship.

Our relationship with one another, as members of the Christian family, is based on "brotherly love"—the kind of love brothers feel. In the original language, the word for "kindly affectioned" means the mutual love of parents and children, or of husbands and wives.

The love we have for our family in the Lord, then, is like the tender affection that exists within the home. What warmth lies therein! What sense of security this family love yields! What eagerness is begotten in our hearts thereby to serve one another!

Daily Devotions:
M. Cain's Bad Choice
Genesis 4:3-12
T. A Godly Lifestyle
Psalm 15:1-5
W. David's Example of Doing Good
Psalm 35:11-14
T. Return Good for Evil
Matthew 5:43-48
F. Love Rewarded
Matthew 25:31-40
S. Jesus Does God's Will
John 6:35-40

Searching for Meaning

Ecclesiastes 1:1-11, 16 through 2:11; 3:9-14

Unit Theme:
Ecclesiastes

Central Truth:
We find the true meaning and purpose of our lives only in a right relationship with God.

Focus:
Assess the futility of life without God and find fulfillment in His purpose.

Context:
Ecclesiastes is generally associated with the reign of Solomon (972-932 B.C.).

Golden Text:
"I know that, whatsoever God doeth, it shall be for ever: nothing can be put to it, nor anything taken from it: and God doeth it, that men should fear before him" (Ecclesiastes 3:14).

Study Outline:
I. Meaninglessness of Life (Ecclesiastes 1:1-11)
II. Quest for Meaning (Ecclesiastes 1:16—2:11)
III. God Gives Meaning to Life (Ecclesiastes 3:9-14)

INTRODUCTION

Scripture can be challenging to one's theology! Of course, our theology *is* based on Scripture; however, about the time we feel confident in our beliefs and understanding of the Bible, we read a book like Ecclesiastes and it challenges our neatly packaged belief system. For example, we may think writers of Scripture should never express anything negative, except for momentary doubts that are quickly vanquished by confidence in God. Then along comes the writer of Ecclesiastes with expressions that cause us great discomfort—by saying things that we may feel at times, but would never express publicly. People of God are not supposed to feel this way! Or, are they?

Studying Ecclesiastes and other difficult books requires us to remember three basic facts. First, we must remember the Bible is real. It shows real people, "warts" and all. It does not gloss over David's infidelities to God and humanity (2 Samuel 11; 12), Moses' anger (Numbers 20:11, 12), Job's depression (Job 7), or even Jesus' own discouragement (John 6:66, 67) and despair (Matthew 27:46). We benefit more from examining the real issues of life and the way they affect us (positively and negatively) than from quick fixes and simple solutions that leave us empty and frustrated. It is in our times of need that we are most willing to "wrestle" with God, as Jacob did (Genesis 32:24-26). Thus, God has chosen to include sections of Scripture that, at first glance, seem to be contrary to the message of the Bible.

Second, studying the Bible requires understanding how a verse or passage fits into the context of the chapter, book, theme, and the overall message of the Bible. In examining Ecclesiastes and its initial pessimistic message, we must look at the overall message of the book. This requires looking at the themes, even if that means jumping around in the book, rather than a front-to-back examination. As well, this pessimism should be viewed in light of the Bible's complete message. Failure to look at how the pieces fit into the bigger picture can cause frustration and disappointment. This is true of studying Scripture and reflecting upon life.

Third, the Bible is a revelation from and of God. Revelation is progressive. That is, God reveals more of Himself, and we have a greater understanding of Him and His ways now than did Solomon. Therefore, we must not judge the early believers too harshly. We do not walk in their shoes or knowledge.

I. MEANINGLESSNESS OF LIFE (Ecclesiastes 1:1-11)

A. The Person (v. 1)

1. The words of the Preacher, the son of David, king in Jerusalem.

Ecclesiastes comes from the Greek word meaning "assembly" and the Hebrew equivalent (*qahal*) meaning "to gather." This concept was used by the New Testament writers to illustrate the nature of "the church" (1 Corinthians 1:2). It is with this foundation that the writer introduces himself as "the Preacher." The term carries more depth than that of one who proclaims what he has read or heard. It connotes the idea of exhortation and instruction from one who is learned, wise, experienced and penitent, who has been gathered back into the fold and now wishes to help gather others.

The writer further identifies himself as "the son of David, king in Jerusalem." Taken at face value, Solomon is the logical choice to fulfill these characteristics. Nowhere in the book is Solomon named; however, the writer's references to his life seem to indicate his perspective and circumstances (e.g., 1:16; 2:7, 8).

> "Colors fade, temples crumble, empires fall, but wise words endure."
> —Edward Thorndike

B. The Proposition (v. 2)

2. Vanity of vanities, saith the Preacher, vanity of vanities; all is vanity.

The theme, or better, the provocative proposition (a thought-provoking statement used as a foundation for teaching truth; see 12:11) on which the rest of the book centers is stated in verse 2 and is restated in 12:8. *Vanity* literally means "breath" or "vapor," and is used figuratively to refer to something temporal, transient and unstable. Warm breath on a cold night can be seen momentarily, but cannot be grasped or used for a lasting purpose. Here, *vanity* carries the idea of "futility" or "emptiness." Solomon's wording indicates it is not just emptiness or meaninglessness that is in mind, but the highest degree of futility or insignificance. Life itself has no meaning or purpose.

Does this concept reflect the past understanding of the Preacher, or the present reality of a disillusioned and bitter monarch? Is this a statement of one in despair, or that of a teacher seeking to lead his students to understand the illusiveness and emptiness of life apart from a deeper meaning and guiding force of God? The answer is not given here, but is found in the conclusion of the book (see 12:8-14). Solomon intentionally sets up this proposition, then expounds upon and illustrates it in the following verses with the intent to make the readers reflect upon their own situation and need for a vital relationship with God.

Talk About It:
1. Why is the word *vanity* used five times in verse 2?
2. If you fully believed Solomon's statement in verse 2, how would you live?

> "To live without hope is to cease to live. Hell is hopelessness. It is no accident that above the entrance to Dante's hell is the inscription, 'Leave behind all hope, you who enter here.'"
> —Fedor Dostoevski

C. The Problem (vv. 3-11)

3. What profit hath a man of all his labour which he taketh under the sun?

4. One generation passeth away, and another generation cometh: but the earth abideth for ever.

5. The sun also ariseth, and the sun goeth down, and hasteth to his place where he arose.

6. The wind goeth toward the south, and turneth about unto the north; it whirleth about continually, and the wind returneth again according to his circuits.

7. All the rivers run into the sea; yet the sea is not full; unto the place from whence the rivers come, thither they return again.

8. All things are full of labour; man cannot utter it: the eye is not satisfied with seeing, nor the ear filled with hearing.

9. The thing that hath been, it is that which shall be; and that which is done is that which shall be done: and there is no new thing under the sun.

10. Is there any thing whereof it may be said, See, this is new? it hath been already of old time, which was before us.

11. There is no remembrance of former things; neither shall there be any remembrance of things that are to come with those that shall come after.

Talk About It:
1. How are the sun, the wind and the rivers alike (vv. 5-7)?
2. Answer the question in verse 10, and explain your answer.

In verse 3, Solomon questions what profit there is in all our labor. At first glance this seems to be at odds with Proverbs 14:23, where hard work is praised. *Profit* here means "advantage" or "excellence." The idea is this: When we have expended our time and energy to make a living, what is the intrinsic worth that stands out? Certainly, we must work and make a living, but that is not *the* defining attribute of humanity. We are not characterized by what we do for a living, but who we are. Our real value or "profit" comes from character and relationship, not from an unhealthy work ethic that sacrifices our character and threatens our relationships with God, family, and others to "get ahead." To illustrate that he is speaking of all humanity and not just his personal life, Solomon uses the phrase "under the sun," which he goes on to use nearly 30 more times in Ecclesiastes to convey every aspect of life and is universal in its appeal.

To further illustrate his point, the Preacher uses a series of four natural occurrences to convey the nature of life as mere existence:

1. We only live "one generation," then we are replaced by "another" (v. 4).

2. The sun rises and sets in a monotonous daily routine (v. 5).

3. The wind blows according to its natural cycle (v. 6).

4. The water supply runs to the sea to evaporate, then is rained out over the earth to start the process all over again (v. 7).

In all these things we see "labor" in its most fundamental form, yet our senses are not satisfied (v. 8). We realize there must be more than going through the motions of life. As important as work, stability and dependability are, they are not enough

Searching for Meaning

to satisfy the deeper, spiritual nature of humanity.

Whatever we do, it really isn't new (vv. 9, 10). It is built upon the foundation of the work of others before us—a fact we fail to recognize and a fact that those who follow us will fail to realize also (v. 11). It is tempting to argue in this fast-paced age of technology that there are all kinds of new things; however, even these are based on the foundations of others. For example, the computer operates on the binary system, utilized by the ancient Egyptians, but which finds its origins in the solar system that God created. Only God does "a new thing" (Isaiah 43:19), and only in Him do "all things . . . become new" (2 Corinthians 5:17).

> "There is little difference in people, but that little difference makes a big difference. That little difference is attitude. The big difference is whether it is positive or negative."
> —Clement Stone

II. QUEST FOR MEANING (Ecclesiastes 1:16—2:11)

A. The Pursuit of Wisdom (1:16-18)

16. I communed with mine own heart, saying, Lo, I am come to great estate, and have gotten more wisdom than all they that have been before me in Jerusalem: yea, my heart had great experience of wisdom and knowledge.

17. And I gave my heart to know wisdom, and to know madness and folly: I perceived that this also is vexation of spirit.

18. For in much wisdom is much grief: and he that increaseth knowledge increaseth sorrow.

> vexation of spirit (v. 17, NIV)—"chasing after the wind"

Solomon reveals some of his inner thoughts that indicate his personal quests and conquests. He notes that he has "attained [literally, "grown into"] greatness" (v. 16, NKJV). This has to do with more than the accumulation of wealth. It speaks of his power and influence as well. Further, he has achieved "more wisdom than all who were before me in Jerusalem" (v. 16, NKJV). This statement has been characterized in two ways. First, some commentators diminish the value of this statement by pointing out that Solomon was preceded only by his father, David, in ruling Jerusalem, so his claim is a bit arrogant. This view forgets about the positive aspects of the reign of Saul (1 Samuel 9—12), who, though he did not capture Jerusalem, did rule Israel. Second, others view this as a statement that refers not only to the kings of Israel, but also to Jerusalem's present and previous inhabitants. It could even be a reference to those who ruled over Jerusalem prior to its conquest by David (see 2 Samuel 5:6-9).

> Talk About It: How do wisdom and knowledge produce "grief" and "sorrow" (v. 18)?

Regardless, in the very center of who Solomon is ("my heart"), he has become fully aware of "wisdom and knowledge" (Ecclesiastes 1:16). In its purest form, this is the ability to integrate insight gained from life experience and the accumulation of facts (whether through self-learning, teaching by others, and/or revelation from God) in an intelligent manner that is true to our redeemed character, and that benefits humanity and pleases God—a worthy pursuit for us all.

Apart from God, the pursuit of wisdom leads to "madness" (irrational thought that affects behavior) and "folly" (moral and spiritual decline, or the opposite of wisdom). The result is "grasping for the wind" (v. 17, *NKJV*). This is an idiomatic way of saying that it results in a "vexation of spirit." One cannot grasp the wind. The harder one tries, the more frustration there is. This is an excellent picture of wisdom and knowledge lacking a proper grounding in God.

At first glance, verse 18 causes us uneasiness, because there is "grief" (that results in anger and vexation) in "wisdom" and there is "sorrow" (that results in physical and/or emotional pain) in "knowledge." Knowledge and wisdom are a heavy burden to bear. It is tempting to treat this verse as a true statement only if that knowledge is separated from God. However, that is too simplistic. Consider a child's perspective. As he or she is cared for and protected by the parents, the world is secure and simple. But as he or she begins to experience more of life and learns that the world extends beyond the parents' control and protection, there is grief and sorrow that accompanies that knowledge (mentally and experientially). Unfortunately, this is one of the curses of a fallen world—a world that will be redeemed (Isaiah 32—35), the curses broken (Revelation 22:3), and the sorrowful comforted (21:4).

B. The Pursuit of Pleasure (2:1-3)

1. I said in mine heart, Go to now, I will prove thee with mirth, therefore enjoy pleasure: and, behold, this also is vanity.

2. I said of laughter, It is mad: and of mirth, What doeth it?

3. I sought in mine heart to give myself unto wine, yet acquainting mine heart with wisdom; and to lay hold on folly, till I might see what was that good for the sons of men, which they should do under the heaven all the days of their life.

Since intellectual pursuits did not satisfy Solomon, he chose to utilize pleasure as an instrument to find meaning in life. Specifically, he mentions testing his heart with three things. First, he utilized "mirth" (v. 1). This is not just gladness or joy, but pursuing those things that a person believes will produce gladness. Sometimes we get what we want, but not what we expect. As Solomon discovered and asked, "What does it [mirth] accomplish?" (v. 2, *NKJV*). Second, he engaged in "laughter." The idea is that of boastfulness, something that makes claims beyond its ability to produce. Laughter is used by God to produce wellness in us physically, mentally, emotionally and spiritually (Proverbs 17:22); but to the soul separate from God, it is "madness." Third, Solomon said wine was used to

Talk About It:
1. Why doesn't pleasure bring lasting satisfaction?
2. Answer the question in verse 2, "Laughter . . . is foolish. And what does pleasure accomplish?" (*NIV*).
3. What did Solomon try to discover (v. 3)?

"gratify my flesh" (Ecclesiastes 2:3, *NKJV*). However, Solomon makes it clear he was not engaging in abandoned drunkenness, as this pursuit was subjected to wisdom. He understood that "wine is a mocker, strong drink is a brawler, and whoever is led astray by it is not wise" (Proverbs 20:1, *NKJV*). Like sin in general, it will take people to places they do not want to go. Solomon found that this pursuit did not provide the answers he needed and sought.

C. The Pursuit of Possessions (vv. 4-8)
(Ecclesiastes 2:5-7 is not included in the printed text.)
4. I made me great works; I builded me houses; I planted me vineyards.
8. I gathered me also silver and gold, and the peculiar treasure of kings and of the provinces: I gat me men singers and women singers, and the delights of the sons of men, as musical instruments, and that of all sorts.

Solomon continues to elaborate on the things he tried in an effort to find meaning in his existence. These were not just ordinary houses that he built, but edifices worthy of a king, such as a palace (1 Kings 7:1-12) and a temple (2 Chronicles 3; 8:1). The vineyards, gardens, orchards and pools (Ecclesiastes 2:4-6) were, no doubt, just as magnificent. It is said that the three pools near Bethlehem, where two of the pools flowed into a third, together held 40 million gallons of water. To these things he added servants and herds that were greater than those before him in Jerusalem (v. 7). In addition, he "gathered" for his personal pleasure "silver and gold and the special treasures of kings," including singers and musicians (v. 8, *NKJV*). Yet, meaning was not to be found in these. Charles Marshall, a wealthy coal-mine operator, once said, "Those who think money won't make you happy have never had any. It just won't keep you happy."

D. The Pursuit of Power (v. 9)
9. So I was great, and increased more than all that were before me in Jerusalem: also my wisdom remained with me.

Solomon's quests were not totally in vain. He was successful in the accumulation of the things he pursued, including power. He became great to the point that it brought attention, fame, power and, consequently, more wealth to him (see 1 Kings 10:1-13). Greatness, however, is not the same as goodness.

E. The Pursuit of Meaning (vv. 10, 11)
10. And whatsoever mine eyes desired I kept not from them, I withheld not my heart from any joy; for my heart rejoiced in all my labour: and this was my portion of all my labour.
11. Then I looked on all the works that my hands had

"I never knew what joy was like until I gave up pursuing happiness, or cared to live until I chose to die. For these two discoveries I am beholden to Jesus."
—Malcolm Muggeridge

the delights of the sons of men (v. 8)—a harem

Talk About It:
According to verses 4-8, what things did Solomon try in his pursuit of meaning and satisfaction?

Talk About It:
What "remained" with Solomon, and why was this important?

Talk About It:
How did Solomon feel about all of his labors? Why?

"What shadows we are, and what shadows we pursue!"
—Edmund Burke

the world (v. 11)— eternity

Talk About It:
1. Explain the phrase, "He [God] has made everything beautiful in its time" (v. 11, *NIV*).
2. Why has God placed "eternity" in people's heart (v. 11, *NIV*)?

wrought, and on the labour that I had laboured to do: and, behold, all was vanity and vexation of spirit, and there was no profit under the sun.

It is easy for the "have-nots" (the poor and disenfranchised) to be negative concerning the world; however, Solomon was among the "haves" (the upwardly mobile) as he explains. His provocative proposition (1:2; 2:11) is not based on a limited view of the world, but on having experienced the best of the world at the time, and still finding that the things far too many lust after and sell their souls to attain (power, money and pleasure) do not satisfy the longing of the soul. He pursued whatever his heart desired (v. 10) and tried whatever he could conceive, yet it all was without meaning and profit (v. 11).

III. GOD GIVES MEANING TO LIFE (Ecclesiastes 3:9-14)
A. The Profit of Labor (vv. 9-11)

9. What profit hath he that worketh in that wherein he laboureth?

10. I have seen the travail, which God hath given to the sons of men to be exercised in it.

11. He hath made every thing beautiful in his time: also he hath set the world in their heart, so that no man can find out the work that God maketh from the beginning to the end.

In verse 9, the Preacher restates the question examined thus far in the book: What is the excellence or value of all our efforts in this thing we call life? In verse 10, he provides a hint of the direction he has been taking all along: it is a gift from God entrusted to us to help us fulfill our destinies in life and Christ. We want to know all the details of God's plans for us—and we want to know it now—but that would lead us to dependency upon our knowledge of the plan of God, rather than dependency upon the God of the plan. We must fulfill our destinies, even if that means doing things we would rather not do (duty). God expects and demands faithfulness. As the omniscient One (1 John 3:20), He already knows whether we will be faithful or not (Job 23:10). Sometimes, we must prove to ourselves through our struggles that we will remain faithful in spite of the toil, turmoil and turbulence in our lives. Often, it is in the daily routines, or even in the midst of doing things we would rather avoid, that we encounter God and find the answers, strength and renewal we desperately need. He indeed makes everything beautiful in its time (Ecclesiastes 3:11). This is not a reference confined to physical beauty, but the beauty of events as God works behind the scenes (and sometimes in public ways) to bring about beauty from ashes, joy for those mourning, and praise for those weighed down (Isaiah 61:3).

It cannot just be doing things, or even doing the right things at the wrong time. It must be the right thing at the right time—God's plan in God's time. Herein lies the rub—discerning both God's plan and God's time for our lives. We must trust Him with our lives, just as we trust Him with our souls. God is not a God of chaos and confusion, but a God of order and carefully executed plans (see Jeremiah 29:11; 1 Corinthians 2:9; 14:33, 40; Genesis 41:32). We must discern the time, determine the best course of action, and deliver our best efforts, even if we do not see the end of the matter (see Daniel 7:28).

B. The Profit of Worship (vv. 12-14)

12. I know that there is no good in them, but for a man to rejoice, and to do good in his life.

13. And also that every man should eat and drink, and enjoy the good of all his labour, it is the gift of God.

14. I know that, whatsoever God doeth, it shall be for ever: nothing can be put to it, nor any thing taken from it: and God doeth it, that men should fear before him.

Verse 12 says there is no intrinsic value ("no good") in labor and life apart from God. Our task and our privilege is to embrace the destiny that God has given to us in a twofold manner. First, we must rejoice in what we do. This is not putting on a public smile and muttering under our breaths because of what we are called to do. It is an attitude that emanates from the heart and affects our entire disposition. It is an attitude that is derived from God during time spent with Him. Second, it is a determination to make our lives count and accomplish good for ourselves, our families, friends, community, church and the kingdom of God. It is a disposition that seizes life and enjoys it as the gift of God (v. 13). In brief, it is doing what we do as unto the Lord (Colossians 3:17). It is worshiping the Lord with all our lives (Psalm 103:1).

We accomplish as we fulfill the admonition of Jesus to "lay up . . . treasures in heaven" (literally, "treasure up treasure," Matthew 6:20). Our work will not only be tested on earth, but it will also be tested by fire at the end of our lives (1 Corinthians 3:10-15). This is not a test we want to fail—or even receive just a passing grade.

What God does, He does with eternity and our best in mind (Ecclesiastes 3:14). We seek His will instead of our own desires, based on a limited view of eternity. Coming to this conclusion with our hearts, minds and bodies requires a total surrender to Him. For He truly knows best.

Talk About It:
1. What is a "gift of God" (v. 13)?
2. According to verse 14, what should cause us to "fear" (revere) God?

"God has no deficiencies that I might be required to supply. He is complete in Himself. . . . God is a mountain spring, not a watering trough."
—**John Piper**

CONCLUSION

Every one of us is faced with times of wondering if our lives count. Is there a purpose to what we do? Does God know

Daily Devotions:
M. Life's Brevity
    Job 7:1-10
T. Man's Vanity
    Psalm 39:4-6
W. Life Valued
    Isaiah 38:16-20
T. Life's Purpose
    Acts 17:22-28
F. To Live Is Christ
    Philippians 1:19-21
S. Futile Boasting
    James 4:13-16

where we are? Does He even care? These questions are part of the normal process of maturity and growth. There is no sin in the questions. The sin is in harboring the questions in our hearts, rather than taking them to God. He can handle our questions—in fact, He wants to handle them. We just need to give Him the opportunity and watch our lives make a difference.

GOLDEN TEXT CHALLENGE

"I KNOW THAT, WHATSOEVER GOD DOETH, IT SHALL BE FOR EVER: NOTHING CAN BE PUT TO IT, NOR ANY THING TAKEN FROM IT: AND GOD DOETH IT, THAT MEN SHOULD FEAR BEFORE HIM" (Ecclesiastes 3:14).

"That which is affirmed here is true of God's directing and guiding events in the natural world, as well as of the announcements of His will and His controlling and directing providence in the history of human affairs. All this is removed beyond the power of the creature to alter it. The meaning is not that one ought not to add to or to take from it, but that such a thing cannot be done. And this unchangeableness characterizing the arrangements of God has this as its aim, that men should fear Him" (Keil & Delitzsch).

"Whatever [God] has done, He intended to be a means of impressing a just sense of His being, providence, mercy, and judgments, upon the souls of men," said Adam Clarke. "A proper consideration of God's works has a tendency to make man a religious creature; that is, to impress his mind with a sense of the existence of the Supreme Being, and the reverence that is due to Him."

Pentecostal Experience Continues

Acts 8:5-17; 10:44-48; 11:1-18; 19:1-7

INTRODUCTION

God chose 120 faithful disciples to fill with the Spirit and scatter them to the four corners of the world. It all started in the very city that rejected Jesus. They received power to "be witnesses" through the Spirit (Acts 1:8). They moved from Jerusalem (their city), to Judea (the surrounding area), to Samaria (the area of those with whom they did not have a good relationship; see John 4:9), "and to the end of the earth" (NKJV). It began with the Twelve (see Acts 1:26), the 120 (1:15), the 3,000 (2:41), the 5,000 (4:4), and spread throughout the world from there.

The modern Pentecostal church has a tremendous challenge and opportunity. Pentecostalism is in danger of losing its passion, vision and relevance. We cannot be so concerned with protecting and trying to relive the past that we fail to examine the present and seek God for effective ways to minister to this generation through the power of the Holy Spirit. We must understand the difference between Pentecost (the giving of the Spirit to the church) and Pentecostalism (the movement that seeks to live out the power of the Spirit). Pentecost remains the same. Pentecostalism must continue to change. Harvey Cox examines Pentecostalism as an outsider and notes that we have been quite adept at adapting the message of Christ to the culture in which we live, whether in America or Africa. The message has never changed: we preach the King, who laid down His life; the Savior, who rose from the dead to impart salvation; and the Lord, who lives and is real today. We do this through the power of the Spirit, whose mission is to lift up Christ and help us to do the same to this generation (John 14:26; 16:13-15). We must proclaim the timeless message in a timely way.

Must we seek God with sincerity and determination? Can we reach a generation and culture that has little interest in organized religion? Will we be required to get out of the comfort of our "boat" (see Matthew 14:28-32) and step onto the troubled waters? Yes! The Book of Acts presents the experience of the early church's mission to a world that parallels our own in many ways. They preached Christ! And the Spirit enabled them to do so in ways that touched their world with Pentecost. The message has not changed, nor has the Spirit who empowers it.

Unit Theme:
Pentecost

Central Truth:
God's will is that every believer in Christ be baptized in the Holy Spirit.

Focus:
Acknowledge that God still gives the Holy Spirit, and invite the Spirit into our lives.

Context:
Various accounts in Acts of people receiving the baptism in the Spirit

Golden Text:
"Then remembered I the word of the Lord, how that he said, John indeed baptized with water; but ye shall be baptized with the Holy Ghost" (Acts 11:16).

Study Outline:
I. Converts Receive the Spirit (Acts 8:5-17)
II. Gentiles Receive the Spirit (Acts 10:44-48; 11:15-18)
III. Disciples Receive the Spirit (Acts 19:1-7)

I. CONVERTS RECEIVE THE SPIRIT (Acts 8:5-17)

A. The Samaritan Crusade (vv. 5-8)

5. Then Philip went down to the city of Samaria, and preached Christ unto them.

6. And the people with one accord gave heed unto those things which Philip spake, hearing and seeing the miracles which he did.

7. For unclean spirits, crying with loud voice, came out of many that were possessed with them: and many taken with palsies, and that were lame, were healed.

8. And there was great joy in that city.

Stephen had been stoned (Acts 7) and the church was in the midst of great persecution (8:1). Because of this, most of the church was compelled to leave Jerusalem. With them went the message of Christ (v. 4). It is during periods of persecution, rather than comfort, that the church grows the most. Persecution will get us out of our comfort zones—quickly! Philip was among those who were scattered (v. 5). Little is known of this interesting man outside of this chapter. He was one of the seven chosen to take care of the business of the early church, so that the apostles could devote themselves to the Word and prayer (6:3-6). He is later identified as "Philip the evangelist," with four prophesying daughters (21:8, 9). This tells us that his faithfulness in taking care of what some wrongly consider the more mundane aspects of the church led to other open doors of opportunity. It also reveals that he was a father of influence and raised his family in the faith.

In his travels, Philip went either to the capital city of Samaria or a city in Samaria. The text is unclear. No doubt, wherever it was, it was a place that provided an opportunity for the gospel to spread to other cities and regions. Samaria was a region between Judea (southern province of Israel) and Galilee (northern province of Israel), inhabited by the descendants of Jews who intermarried with Gentiles and served false gods during the Exile (2 Kings 17:24-41). The Jews and the Samaritans (regarded as half-Jews) had a rather contemptuous relationship (John 4:9). Nevertheless, Philip "preached Christ" to the Samaritans. The content of the early church's preaching was the proclamation that Jesus is the Christ, or Messiah (e.g., Acts 5:42; 8:12; 10:36; 28:31). The message is still the same: He is the Savior, Sanctifier, Spirit Baptizer, Healer, and soon-coming King.

Philip's audience was receptive and hungry. They listened carefully ("gave heed") to his message and observed the miracles and signs that followed his message (v. 6). Specifically, those bound or "possessed" by "unclean [evil] spirits" were set free (v. 7; see Mark 16:17-20). Those who were paralyzed and crippled ("lame") "were healed." These signs were also a characteristic of

Talk About It:
1. What did the crowds do "with one accord" (v. 6)?
2. What caused "great joy in that city" (v. 8)?

"The evangelistic harvest is always urgent. The destiny of men and nations is always being decided. . . . God will hold us responsible as to how well we fulfill our responsibilities to this age and take advantage of our opportunities."
—Billy Graham

Pentecostal Experience Continues

Jesus' ministry (Matthew 4:24; 11:5). The message and miracles brought "great joy" to the Samaritans (Acts 8:8).

B. The Sorcerer's Encounter (vv. 9-13)

9. But there was a certain man, called Simon, which beforetime in the same city used sorcery, and bewitched the people of Samaria, giving out that himself was some great one:

10. To whom they all gave heed, from the least to the greatest, saying, This man is the great power of God.

11. And to him they had regard, because that of long time he had bewitched them with sorceries.

12. But when they believed Philip preaching the things concerning the kingdom of God, and the name of Jesus Christ, they were baptized, both men and women.

13. Then Simon himself believed also: and when he was baptized, he continued with Philip, and wondered, beholding the miracles and signs which were done.

Philip's ministry was not the first time that miracles had occurred in the city. A man named Simon (also called Simon Magus) used witchcraft and magic ("sorcery") to astonish ("bewitch") the residents of the city (vv. 9, 11). The people attributed his actions to God (v. 10), but his concern was to draw attention to himself (v. 9b). However, when the real power of God appeared, the Samaritans were convinced and chose to be baptized (v. 12). In verse 13 we see Simon "believed also" and observed with amazement the miracles that followed the Word. What is unclear, especially in light of verses 18-24, is whether Simon believed in the man (Philip), the miracles, or the God of the miracles (see John 2:23, 24; 4:48)—an issue we all need to examine from time to time.

As Acts 8 reveals, we must be discerning when examining the signs that follow a person's ministry. Jesus warned that deceivers would come with "great signs and wonders" in an attempt to fool God's people (Matthew 24:24). We know that Satan presents himself as "an angel of light" for that purpose (2 Corinthians 11:13-15). Several questions can help clarify the validity of a person's ministry, along with a sensitivity of what the Spirit is speaking to the church:

1. Is the preaching based clearly and solely upon Scripture?

2. Does the person's character and conduct reflect a holy lifestyle?

3. Do the miracles, signs or prophecies bring unity and joy, or division and confusion?

4. Who receives the glory—the servant, the miracles, or God?

We must neither be so hardened that we attribute all wonders

Talk About It:
1. What were Simon's claims (v. 9), and how did the Samaritans respond (vv. 10, 11)?
2. How did Philip's ministry affect Simon (vv. 12, 13)?

to the devil, nor so gullible that we accept everything that comes our way. Miracles are signs, not ends within themselves. We must walk in the Spirit and let Him lead us to the truth (John 4:23; 16:13).

C. The Spirit Received (vv. 14-17)

14. Now when the apostles which were at Jerusalem heard that Samaria had received the word of God, they sent unto them Peter and John:

15. Who, when they were come down, prayed for them, that they might receive the Holy Ghost:

16. (For as yet he was fallen upon none of them: only they were baptized in the name of the Lord Jesus.)

17. Then laid they their hands on them, and they received the Holy Ghost.

When word of this move of God made its way back to Jerusalem, the apostles (the Twelve) "sent" Peter and John to Samaria with a purpose. No doubt, their mission was twofold: first, to assess the spiritual needs (v. 14), since submission, accountability and oversight are Biblical (Hebrews 13:7, 17); and second, to pray for the Samaritans that "they might receive the Holy Ghost" (Acts 8:15), since none had yet been baptized into Him. They had only been baptized (immersed) in water "in the name of the Lord Jesus" (v. 16; see treatment of baptismal "formulas" in next section).

Talk About It:
Why did Peter and John go to Samaria, and what was the result?

Peter and John "laid . . . hands on them" (v. 17). This is a means of contact, not a magical act. Laying on of hands is an act of faith and obedience in blessing others (Matthew 19:13), praying for the sick (Acts 9:12), commissioning servants of God (13:3), believing that God will impart gifts (1 Timothy 4:14), as well as baptize individuals in the Spirit (Acts 9:17; 19:6). These examples make it clear there is nothing supernatural in the hands of the one ministering. The power resides in God, who honors the faith and obedience of the person.

The Hungry Receive
A couple in one church I pastored had been seeking the baptism in the Spirit for years. When they finally got hungry enough, they asked God to fill them anyway He chose. Within days, she was filled while driving down the street. Her husband was thrilled for her and discouraged for himself, but would not give up. A few days later, as his feet hit the floor, while getting out of bed, he was filled with the Spirit. Hunger prompts willingness and receptivity!

The Samaritans "received the Holy Spirit" (8:17, NKJV), after the apostles laid hands on them. This is not the only way to receive the baptism in the Spirit (see Acts 2:4; 10:44). It is not the apostles or any other people who impart to us the Spirit. Jesus is the One who baptizes us into the Spirit (Matthew 3:11). The language depicts a powerful spiritual event in our lives. We are *immersed* into the presence and power of the Spirit. An Old Testament parallel is found in Judges 6:34, where the Hebrew says, "The Spirit of the Lord came upon Gideon."

Though there is no mention in Acts 8 of the Samaritans speaking in tongues, it seems to be implied. Simon saw something he could not conjure or imitate when the Samaritans received the Spirit (vv. 19, 20). However, while speaking in tongues is a vital part of this experience, we do not seek tongues; instead, we seek the Giver of the Spirit. Christ does not give us this experience so we can speak in tongues. He baptizes us into power for service (Acts 1:8). The question of the hour is, What are we doing with the power He has given us?

II. GENTILES RECEIVE THE SPIRIT (Acts 10:44-48; 11:15-18)
A. A New Chapter (10:44-48)

44. While Peter yet spake these words, the Holy Ghost fell on all them which heard the word.

45. And they of the circumcision which believed were astonished, as many as came with Peter, because that on the Gentiles also was poured out the gift of the Holy Ghost.

46. For they heard them speak with tongues, and magnify God. Then answered Peter,

47. Can any man forbid water, that these should not be baptized, which have received the Holy Ghost as well as we?

48. And he commanded them to be baptized in the name of the Lord. Then prayed they him to tarry certain days.

At the beginning of Acts 10, we find a man named Cornelius, a Gentile centurion, who believed there was a God ("feared God," v. 2) and knew about Jesus (v. 37), praying, fasting, and seeking a fuller revelation of who God is (vv. 1-4, 30-33). In a vision, he was told to summon the apostle Peter, which he did (vv. 5, 22, 23). Meantime, Peter was at Simon the tanner's house, where God was preparing him through a vision for ministry to these Gentiles (vv. 9-16). When God works on one end, He also works on the other.

When Peter arrived, he preached "peace through Jesus Christ" (v. 36, *NKJV*) and His redemptive provision. As he expounded on Jesus' anointed life and miraculous ministry (vv. 37, 38), efficacious death (v. 39), triumphant resurrection (vv. 40, 41), commission to His followers (v. 42), and the confirmation of His redemptive, messianic ministry by Scripture (v. 43), "the Holy Spirit fell upon all those who heard the word" (v. 44, *NKJV*). This is a powerful reminder of the transforming power of the Word and how our willingness to partner with God can bring awesome results to those in need.

The gift of the Spirit, which had only been received by Jews at Pentecost, and half-Jews in Samaria, was now received by Gentiles. Gentiles were the "unclean" and despised people who had oppressed Israel since her beginning (at the time of this event Rome occupied the land), and now God had chosen to bless them. The Jews ("the circumcision") were amazed to the point of bewilderment ("astonished") that God chose not only to save the Gentiles, but fill them with the Spirit (v. 45). His grace,

Talk About It:
1. When did the Holy Spirit come upon the people (v. 44)?
2. Why were the Jewish believers "astonished" (vv. 45, 46)?

mercy and love are indeed incomprehensible to our finite minds!

Those who accompanied Peter heard the Gentiles "speak with tongues, and magnify God" (v. 46). This is an excellent depiction of what tongues should accomplish—lift God up, extol His virtues and character, and enlarge the perception of God ("magnify"). Tongues are a means of communicating with God (1 Corinthians 14:14); they are not meant to be the culmination of what it means to be Spirit-filled. We must seek to glorify God, not the manifestation; we must desire to edify the church and win the lost (see vv. 6-25), rather than allow this gift to become an instrument of division in the body of Christ (see 13:1). This is not meant to diminish their value (see 14:5, 18), but rather that we might see their true value and walk therein.

It was after their conversion and Spirit baptism that they were baptized with water (Acts 10:47). This passage clearly reveals that baptism is not a prerequisite for salvation, but rather the reverse: salvation is required for water baptism. Some make much of Acts' emphasis on baptism "in the name of Jesus" (2:38; 8:16; 19:5). First, a primary purpose of Luke's record in Acts is to reveal that the early church accepted the deity of Jesus Christ. Those baptized were immersed into His presence, character and power. It was not just a formula pronounced over them, but a real event. Second, Jesus taught that we are to be baptized into the name (presence, character and power) of the Father and of the Son and of the Holy Spirit (Matthew 28:19). Certainly, the apostles were aware of this commandment. Third, *The Didache*, a first-century Christian letter of instruction, reaffirms that the early church baptized according to the instruction of Jesus and sees no contradiction with the accounts of Acts. Therefore, one must conclude that they were baptized according to Jesus' command, but Luke's emphasis is to reveal they accepted Christ for who He is—the Son of God.

B. A New Problem (11:15-18)

15. And as I began to speak, the Holy Ghost fell on them, as on us at the beginning.

16. Then remembered I the word of the Lord, how that he said, John indeed baptized with water; but ye shall be baptized with the Holy Ghost.

17. Forasmuch then as God gave them the like gift as he did unto us, who believed on the Lord Jesus Christ; what was I, that I could withstand God?

18. When they heard these things, they held their peace, and glorified God, saying, Then hath God also to the Gentiles granted repentance unto life.

Just like Samaria, word was received in Jerusalem of the events at the house of Cornelius (see v. 1). Some were displeased

Talk About It:
1. Explain the significance of the phrases "as on us" (v. 15) and "the like gift" (v. 17).
2. Respond to Peter's question in verse 17.

Pentecostal Experience Continues

that Peter had ministered to and fellowshipped with Gentiles (vv. 2, 3). Peter recounted the God-ordained events that led to the ministry event (vv. 4-14) and the reception of the Holy Spirit by the hearers (v. 15). He noted (1) they had the same experience as those in Jerusalem at Pentecost (Acts 2:1-4); (2) the experience lined up with the "word of the Lord" (11:16); and, (3) who are we to stand in the way of God and His plan (v. 17)? His words do not appear to be bitter or argumentative (contrary to Peter's nature), but a heartfelt account of what God was doing in his life.

Our personal testimony is a powerful tool. People may not agree with our theology, but they cannot discount what we have experienced. If it is of God, He will confirm it to them, which is what happened in Jerusalem (v. 18). The event brought glory to God.

III. DISCIPLES RECEIVE THE SPIRIT (Acts 19:1-7)
A. A New Doctrine (vv. 1, 2)

1. And it came to pass, that, while Apollos was at Corinth, Paul having passed through the upper coasts came to Ephesus: and finding certain disciples,

2. He said unto them, Have ye received the Holy Ghost since ye believed? And they said unto him, We have not so much as heard whether there be any Holy Ghost.

On his third missionary journey, Paul took the more direct route to Ephesus across the mountainous region ("upper coasts"), rather than the easier, lower route. Ephesus was a pagan city but crucial for the spread of the gospel, since it was located on major trade routes. The temple of Diana was located there, one of the seven ancient wonders of the world. Soon after his arrival, Paul encountered "certain disciples" (v. 1). In light of the verses that follow, some have suggested these disciples were (1) Jews; (2) early disciples of John, who had never been converted to Christianity; or (3) "Christians" in a special class, who were not quite Christian. However, in Acts, "disciples" is used exclusively for Christians, individually and corporately. To place them in a special category would limit the efficacy of the blood of Jesus. It is apparent they were in need of further instruction and training.

Talk About It:
Why do you suppose Paul asked the question in verse 2?

Paul begins to inquire of their spiritual understanding and formation by asking about their salvation and Holy Spirit baptism. He specifically asks them if they had received the Holy Spirit "since" ("when" or "after") they believed.

Acts 2:38 reveals the order as repentance, baptism, then Spirit baptism. In 8:12-17 the Samaritans repented and were baptized by Philip, but did not receive the Spirit until the apostles laid hands on them. This pattern is seen in the conversion of Paul, who first believed on the Lord but did not receive Spirit baptism until Ananias prayed for him; then he was baptized in water (9:1-18). Cornelius and his household repented and were filled with the Spirit while hearing the preached Word, then submitted to water baptism (10:44-48). It is clear that becoming a Christian and being filled with the Spirit are separate and distinct, yet the expectation of the Spirit's enduement and manifestation is to be anticipated and sought at the time of salvation.

If the Ephesian "disciples" had never heard about the Holy Spirit (19:2), then it would seem impossible that they were Christians, or even true disciples of John, who had proclaimed that the coming Messiah would baptize individuals in the Holy Spirit (John 1:33). They must have had some knowledge of the Holy Spirit. The Old Testament and John the Baptist both testify of the Spirit's existence. It seems probable that they had not heard of the fulfillment of the promise recorded in Acts 2. They had not heard that He had been *given* at Pentecost.

B. A New Understanding (vv. 3, 4)

3. And he said unto them, Unto what then were ye baptized? And they said, Unto John's baptism.

4. Then said Paul, John verily baptized with the baptism of repentance, saying unto the people, that they should believe on him which should come after him, that is, on Christ Jesus.

Their answer prompts Paul to ask another question, this time concerning their baptism (v. 3). It is apparent that Paul knew they had been baptized. He was asking for clarification that would help him understand the boundaries of their spiritual formation, then he could correct any problems through his skillful use of the Scripture. A proper foundation was very important to Paul (see Galatians 1:6-9; 2 Timothy 2:19).

Upon hearing that they had been baptized in John's "baptism of repentance," Paul explained to them that John's preaching focused on faith in Christ alone (Acts 19:4). It is unfortunate that space did not allow Luke to include the full content of Paul's proclamation to these disciples. It is evident, however, that Paul wanted to make sure they were no longer deficient in their understanding of the nature of John's ministry or God's provision. So often, we think we know where we are spiritually until events or people cause us to examine carefully our standing with God.

C. A New Baptism (vv. 5-7)

5. When they heard this, they were baptized in the name of the Lord Jesus.

6. And when Paul had laid his hands upon them, the

Talk About It:
What did the baptism of John anticipate?

Holy Ghost came on them; and they spake with tongues, and prophesied.

7. And all the men were about twelve.

After hearing Paul's preaching, they were moved to be baptized again. They wanted to be certain their spiritual foundation and standing were secure and not deficient in any way—an excellent example. This is the only place in the New Testament that re-baptism is mentioned, though it has been a common practice in Pentecostalism in light of this passage. They were immersed by Paul (or perhaps by a companion of Paul's) and baptized "in the name of the Lord Jesus" (v. 5). No doubt the Trinitarian pronouncement was used in compliance with Matthew 28:19. The emphasis here and throughout Acts is that those baptized were making a public proclamation that Jesus is the Messiah, *the* Savior.

Paul then laid his hands upon them and prayed that they would receive the promise of the Father (see Luke 24:49). The prayer was answered, and the Holy Spirit came upon them with manifestations consistent with those described throughout Acts and the Pauline Epistles. This event is subsequent to belief, even if one rejects these disciples as believers prior to this divine encounter with Paul.

They began to speak "with tongues, and prophesied" (Acts 19:6). *Prophesy* ("to proclaim divine revelation") can be *foretelling*, that is, revealing events to come. It can also be *forthtelling*, or a revelation of pertinent information concerning the present, as we see in Acts. This was not a onetime or temporary manifestation. The Greek tense used indicates that this became a normal part of their Christian experience, as it should be in ours. This Spirit event did not make them Christians. It resulted from a prior acceptance of Christ as Savior. They were now prepared for service (1:8). Baptism in the Spirit is not the climax of the Christian experience, but rather the beginning of our journey of holiness, service and worship, as the verse implies.

The disciples "were about twelve" in number and are distinguished as "men" (19:7). Luke often uses "about," even when being specific (see Acts 1:15; 10:3). Either there were no women and children in the group, or Luke defines the group by the number of males, a common first-century practice (cf. Matthew 14:21). We do know, however, that women were active in prophecy in the early church (Acts 2:18; 21:9; 1 Corinthians 11:5).

Talk About It:
1. What did the Ephesians' response in verse 5 say about them?
2. What happened when the Holy Spirit "came on them" (v. 6)?

The Yielded Tongue
The willingness to yield our tongues to God may indicate a more profound surrender than almost any other act. The tongue is the primary instrument of expression of the human personality, and until God has dominion over the tongue, His control over us is relatively slight.
—Don Basham

CONCLUSION

The power of Pentecost is still relevant for today. God still wants to change hearts and transform lives. In all three accounts in today's lesson, the groups who received the Spirit did so on their own turf, not in a church setting. We must be willing to go to places that we do not normally go, minister to people with whom we may not be comfortable, and allow God to get the glory as they receive the blessings. And we get to be part of it! Isn't God good?

GOLDEN TEXT CHALLENGE

"THEN REMEMBERED I THE WORD OF THE LORD, HOW THAT HE SAID, JOHN INDEED BAPTIZED WITH WATER; BUT YE SHALL BE BAPTIZED WITH THE HOLY GHOST" (Acts 11:16).

As the people in Cornelius' household spoke in tongues, Peter remembered the words of Jesus regarding people being baptized in the Holy Spirit. This promise is found in Acts 1:5. It is a word from the risen Lord to His church. It also served to authenticate the ministry of Peter as preaching baptism in the Spirit rather than John's baptism of repentance which took place in water.

The household of Cornelius was already prepared to receive the fullness of the gospel. As a God-fearer, Cornelius' heart had already turned in repentance from the ways of sin to the ways of God. Thus, the preaching of Christ served to clarify what God had done in his life and also prepared him for the baptism in the Holy Spirit.

Today, it is still God's will for us to be saved from our sins, to follow Christ's example by being baptized in water, and to receive the gift of the baptism in the Holy Spirit.

Daily Devotions:
M. Spirit-Inspired Judge
Judges 6:34-40
T. Spirit-Inspired Levite
2 Chronicles 20:14-19
W. Spirit-Inspired Prophet
Ezekiel 11:1-5
T. Spirit-Inspired Mother
Luke 1:39-45
F. Spirit-Inspired Father
Luke 1:67-79
S. Spirit-Inspired Martyr
Acts 7:54-60

Wisdom From the Preacher

Ecclesiastes 5:1-7; 7:1-12; 9:7-12

INTRODUCTION

The writer of Ecclesiastes ("the Preacher") lays a foundation early in the book that reveals the world apart from a right relationship with God is illusory and void of meaning and purpose. Solomon reveals that in his own pursuit to find meaning and peace in life, he has tried to find satisfaction in wisdom and knowledge and discovered that his intellect still required fulfillment. He tried to placate his inner yearnings with pleasure (wine, 2:3; song, v. 8; whatever he desired, v. 10), but that too left him empty and frustrated ("vexation of spirit," or "grasping for the wind," v. 17). He accumulated possessions and power fitting of a king and gained the attention of other wealthy monarchs (1 Kings 10:1-13), but that too failed to fill the God-sized hole in his soul. He found that it is only when our pursuits take place within the boundaries of a vibrant relationship with God that there is any meaning in life, purpose to what we do, and satisfaction with who we are (Ecclesiastes 3:9-15).

Solomon's struggles may be more public than many of ours, but they are not much different. Ours may put on "different clothes," but underneath, the problem is still the same. We all want our lives to count for something. We want the daily routine to be more than a rut. We want to know that when we leave this world, we will leave behind something that will benefit others. In Christ we find the fulfillment of our desires. This is the message we must communicate to the contemporary world seeking the same things Solomon did.

Even as Christians, we may find ourselves wondering about the purpose of our existence. We understand that in Christ we are saved, commissioned and complete; yet, there are times when we wrestle with the intrinsic value of our activities and labor. Some of the greatest Christian workers of all times have struggled with this. After all, if Satan can get us to question the value of what we are doing and who we are, he can cause us to question the need to continue our courses in life. Ecclesiastes has a message for both the sinner seeking satisfaction and the saint seeking to know that what he or she does is worth continuing.

Unit Theme:
Ecclesiastes

Central Truth:
Life is a gift from God to be enjoyed and lived for Him.

Focus:
Identify and cultivate attitudes that make life meaningful.

Context:
Ecclesiastes is generally associated with the reign of Solomon (972-932 B.C.).

Golden Text:
"For wisdom is a defence, and money is a defence: but the excellency of knowledge is, that wisdom giveth life to them that have it" (Ecclesiastes 7:12).

Study Outline:
I. Reverence God (Ecclesiastes 5:1-7)
II. Keep a Proper Perspective (Ecclesiastes 7:1-12)
III. Enjoy Life (Ecclesiastes 9:7-12)

I. REVERENCE GOD (Ecclesiastes 5:1-7)

A. Guard Your Steps (vv. 1-3)

1. Keep thy foot when thou goest to the house of God, and be more ready to hear, than to give the sacrifice of fools: for they consider not that they do evil.

2. Be not rash with thy mouth, and let not thine heart be hasty to utter any thing before God: for God is in heaven, and thou upon earth: therefore let thy words be few.

3. For a dream cometh through the multitude of business; and a fool's voice is known by multitude of words.

"Guard your steps" (*NIV*), or "walk prudently" (*NKJV*), is a command that warns us to be vigilant whenever we enter "the house of God" (v. 1). It brings to mind the idea of the military guarding a city to make certain that no one enters improperly or misbehaves while there. It also conveys the idea of choosing carefully the path you take. This is not an admonition to refrain from entering the public place of worship, but rather a stern reminder that we are not there to impress people or fulfill a rote obligation by going through the motions without thinking about what we are doing. It communicates the need to prepare ourselves for an encounter with God *before* we enter His house, realize why we are there, and *be* there while we are there. It is not a time to make out shopping lists, balance checkbooks, flip through the hymnal, clip fingernails, or make mental notes of things that need to be done elsewhere. It is a time to enter humbly and expectantly, encounter and *really* hear ("draw near to hear," *NKJV*) from the Creator of life, the Savior who laid down His life for us, and the Spirit who imparts life. He will be present. The question is, will we be there in more than body?

To do less is to offer "the sacrifice of fools" (v. 1). This may be connected to Malachi 1:6-14, where the reader is admonished about offering blemished sacrifices (less than our appropriate best). It is a reminder that Abel's sacrifice was an act of worship, but Cain's was an act of sin (Genesis 4:3-7). Sadly, the sacrifice of fools comes from one who is not even aware that what he or she does is evil. Fools rile against evil far off, while ignoring the sin in their own life and evil in their immediate area of influence (Matthew 7:3-5).

Solomon further emphasizes his concern in verse 2 of the lesson text. God does not desire thoughtless participation. Some suggest this may be the foundation for the teaching of Jesus in Luke 18:9-14. It is a pertinent reminder of the need for examining our attitudes in worship, whether in a temple, a church, or a prayer closet. Further, we must not be "rash" or careless with our words. The goal is not to speak a multitude of empty words, but to have an intimate encounter with God (see Matthew 6:7, 8). We are the creation "upon earth" coming

Talk About It:
1. According to verse 1, what should our attitude be at the place of worship?
2. What should worshipers be slow to do, and why (v. 2)?

before the Creator "in heaven." We are the needy coming to the Giver. If we do all the speaking, we will miss what God has to say to us; "therefore let [our] words be few" (Ecclesiastes 5:2).

The anxieties of life often follow us to bed and cause us to dream about our activities and problems. A prayer can be the same way. Solomon wrote, "As a dream comes when there are many cares, so the speech of a fool when there are many words" (v. 3, *NIV*). A prayer may be uttered in anxiety and, in an effort to cover for a lack of something to say, a person may say too much—and usually the wrong thing! Such is the prayer of a fool. It is better to contemplate and choose our words carefully and thoughtfully, than to pray just to be praying. This is not meant to discourage heartfelt prayers that flow from the heart rather than the head, but rather to guard against careless, meaningless and perfunctory prayers.

B. Guard Your Intentions (vv. 4-7)

4. When thou vowest a vow unto God, defer not to pay it; for he hath no pleasure in fools: pay that which thou hast vowed.

5. Better is it that thou shouldest not vow, than that thou shouldest vow and not pay.

6. Suffer not thy mouth to cause thy flesh to sin; neither say thou before the angel, that it was an error: wherefore should God be angry at thy voice, and destroy the work of thine hands?

7. For in the multitude of dreams and many words there are also divers vanities: but fear thou God.

Contrary to a few radical televangelists, a vow can include, but is not limited to, money. It can be a pledge of money or a promise to do something. In times of trouble and distress, all kinds of promises to God have been made. When the problem is resolved, those promises might be ignored or forgotten, but not by God! A literal reading of verse 4 is, "Whoever vows a vow unto God must not delay to complete the peace offering, for He has no pleasure in fools. Complete the offering you promised."

Usually, it is greed or lack of faith that hinders a person from giving what is due to God. Realize that a vow is more than a promise. It is a bond on the soul with spiritual implications (Numbers 30:2). Lack of fulfillment offends two parties. First, it is disrespectful of and an insult to God. Second, it is a self-inflicted injury, for God will be recompensed (see Acts 5:4). We must consider our promises carefully. As Solomon points out, it is better never to promise than to promise and not fulfill it (Ecclesiastes 5:5).

We must refrain from allowing what we say ("mouth") to

> "We get to know people by talking with them. We get to know God in like manner. The highest result of prayer is not deliverance from evil, or the securing of some coveted thing, but knowledge of God."
> —*The Kneeling Christian*

divers vanities (v. 7)—"emptiness" (*NASB*)

Talk About It:
1. According to verse 5, what is "better"? Why?
2. How are dreams and words alike (v. 7)?

**precious ointment
(v. 1)**—"fine per-
fume" (*NIV*)

Talk About It:
1. Why is "a good
name" (v. 1) so
valuable?
2. How is sorrow
better than laughter
(vv. 2-4)?

affect negatively our actions and entire being ("flesh"). Once
the promise is made, there is no recanting it (v. 6). The "angel"
("messenger of God," *NKJV*) could be either a priest who was
responsible for collecting the payments or vows due to the
Temple, or an angel who witnesses the promise made to God
and will be a witness at the judgment of words uttered but not
fulfilled. God is not looking for vain dreams and lofty words (v.
7). He is looking for a people to do His will (Matthew 7:21; 1 John
2:17). That begins with keeping our word to God. Indeed, obedience is better than sacrifice (1 Samuel 15:22).

II. KEEP A PROPER PERSPECTIVE (Ecclesiastes 7:1-12)
A. Look Deeper (vv. 1-4)
**1. A good name is better than precious ointment; and
the day of death than the day of one's birth.**
**2. It is better to go to the house of mourning, than to go
to the house of feasting: for that is the end of all men; and
the living will lay it to his heart.**
**3. Sorrow is better than laughter: for by the sadness of
the countenance the heart is made better.**
**4. The heart of the wise is in the house of mourning; but
the heart of fools is in the house of mirth.**

The Preacher proclaims some practical and paradoxical
truths that are better comprehended as we put them into
action, after we look deeper to see their real value (see Psalm
119:133; Isaiah 30:21). Also, they must be understood in light
of the verses prior to this section: "For who knoweth what is
good for man in this life?" (Ecclesiastes 6:12). Only God does!
He does not desire for us to walk through life as robots, following an ingrained program, but to live out our destinies with a
sense of fulfillment.

Solomon declares that "a good name is better than precious
ointment" (7:1). There are at least two ways to understand this.
First, an excellent and well-earned reputation outranks a life
masked with perfumes (see John 19:40). Some would rather
cover their flaws with "perfume" than earn a good reputation.
Second, a good name precedes and provides a type of anointing. "Precious ointment" was used to anoint prophets (1 Kings
19:16), priests (Exodus 30:25-30), and kings (1 Kings 1:39)
chosen for service. Thus, our good character, as reflected in a
good name, produces a precious ointment in our lives. One
can put on the precious ointment without the character, but this
will be discovered by others. However, when the anointing
flows from a good life, others are blessed too. Grammatically,
either of these two meanings are possible, as the word translated "better" can also mean "before."

The second half of verse 1 of the text can also be viewed

two ways. First, carefully protecting a good name throughout life until the day of death—being a person of integrity—fulfills the destiny imparted by God at the day of our birth. Thus, the day of death is a culmination and celebration of one's life. Second, the day of one's birth begins a life under the effects of the curse of sin; however, for the person who finds a right relationship with God, the day of death brings him or her into the presence of the Savior (2 Corinthians 5:8).

No one enjoys attending funerals. They remind us that we live in a fallen world, and that the effects of sin are far-reaching and painful. Funerals underscore that life is temporary and unpredictable. However, according to Ecclesiastes 7:2, the complexities and tragedies of life ("house of mourning") provide more meaning for us than "feasting" (food, drink, laughter). Mourning can be sobering and cause proper reflection ("the living will lay it to his heart") about where our lives are headed, what remains to be done (or redone), how we will be remembered, and where we will spend eternity. The next two verses confirm this.

The "heart," which is used here to mean much more than emotions, is made "better" by "a sad countenance" (v. 3, *NKJV*). When we share in the sorrows of others, a deeper covenant relationship develops with them (see Genesis 32:11-13; Romans 12:15), as well as with God, because we are doing His work (see 2 Corinthians 1:3, 4). Those who only frequent "the house of mirth" (Ecclesiastes 7:4) take life less seriously, miss both the inner reflection and the connection with others, as well as the opportunity to be the hand of Christ extended.

> "Death is the big flaw. Sometimes we can postpone it, lessen its physical pains, deny its existence, but we can't escape it."
> —*Quotable Quotes*

B. Listen Carefully (vv. 5-7)

5. It is better to hear the rebuke of the wise, than for a man to hear the song of fools.

6. For as the crackling of thorns under a pot, so is the laughter of the fool: this also is vanity.

7. Surely oppression maketh a wise man mad; and a gift destroyeth the heart.

We learn more from those who rebuke us than those who pat us on the back (v. 5). Rebukes are never enjoyable, and the term used here often carries the idea of "strong reprimand and actions." Criticism stings; however, we must really listen—that is, examine the truth of the "wise" critic (not all critics are wise or intend to help us). We must also apply the truth to our lives, and move past the sting. Failure to do this last step will lead to bitterness, which is more dangerous than any criticism we might receive from a person of experience. The rebuke has more lasting benefit than a temporary lift of the spirits from a "song"—especially "the song of fools."

a gift (v. 7)—a bribe

Talk About It:
1. To what should we listen, and what should we ignore (vv. 5, 6)?
2. What can happen to a wise person, and how (v. 7)?

"The laughter of the fool" (v. 6) reminds us that most people are uncomfortable with silence. Yet noise, by nature, distracts (such as the "crackling of [burning] thorns") and hinders us from deep contemplation and fulfilling the task at hand. We need listening time with wise people and with the all-wise God to make our lives richer.

"Oppression" (the act of defrauding) is a powerful force (v. 7). The Hebrew term is fairly broad in meaning—"to wrong, do violence, extort, cause distress, to crush"—but it almost always is a wrong done by one in a position of strength, influence or authority (see Ecclesiastes 5:8; Proverbs 22:16). Positions of influence are not for personal gain, whether through oppression or "bribes" (Ecclesiastes 7:7, *NKJV*). Leaders are placed in those positions (formal and informal) to make a difference in the lives of others, not to make life easier for themselves. Oppression is such a powerful force that it even "destroys a wise man's reason" (*NKJV*). The wise have a difficult time adequately explaining the delay of God in dealing with oppression and the desire of the oppressor to take advantage of others—especially if they are the ones being oppressed.

When we are in the midst of oppression, knowing that the oppressors "will get what is coming to them" addresses the intellectual aspect, but still leaves the emotions to be comforted. Defrauding a person is an act that God takes personally (Proverbs 14:31); thus we, as people of grace, must extend grace, comfort and love to those who are being oppressed. The world is full of them.

C. Love Wisdom (vv. 8-12)

8. Better is the end of a thing than the beginning thereof: and the patient in spirit is better than the proud in spirit.

9. Be not hasty in thy spirit to be angry: for anger resteth in the bosom of fools.

10. Say not thou, What is the cause that the former days were better than these? for thou dost not enquire wisely concerning this.

11. Wisdom is good with an inheritance: and by it there is profit to them that see the sun.

12. For wisdom is a defence, and money is a defence: but the excellency of knowledge is, that wisdom giveth life to them that have it.

The themes of the previous verses are revisited, expanded and illustrated from different perspectives. Just as the culmination of a person's life should be better than the beginning (v. 1b), so are events in life. Things can begin with a less-than-promising outlook, but end in a very positive way (v. 8). For example, Israel's oppression by Pharaoh ended with the Exodus event through

Talk About It:
1. How do verses 8 and 9 describe the value of patience?
2. What should we not say, and why not (v. 10)?

Wisdom From the Preacher

the mighty hand of God. Fulfilled destinies require humility, diligence and patience, whether over a lifetime or through a single difficult event. Someone has said that we want to hand God a million dollars and boast in our deed, but God hands it back and says, "Give it to Me a quarter at a time."

An initial reading of verse 9 appears to suggest that anger is a forbidden thing, yet we know that God gets angry (Psalm 74:1) and Jesus certainly got angry enough to cleanse the Temple with a whip (Matthew 21:12, 13). These examples and Ephesians 4:26 ("'Be angry, and do not sin': do not let the sun go down on your wrath," *NKJV*) help us to properly understand Ecclesiastes 7:9. Anger can be a productive thing: we should be angry when people are oppressed. However, if we get angry without thinking ("hasty in thy spirit"), remain angry ("resteth in the bosom"), or get angry over the wrong things ("of fools"), it will negatively affect our behavior and attitude.

In verse 10, Solomon addresses a common affliction in many congregations—"used-to-be-itis." In this postmodern age with its cynicism and loss of respect for religion, many churches' past looks better than their present. It is natural to long for the former "glory days"—natural, but wrong! Solomon clearly reveals again that it is unwise to yearn for and live in the past. It is not possible to return to those days. Jesus said, "No man, having put his hand to the plough, and looking back, is fit for the kingdom of God" (Luke 9:62). Often we interpret this as a reference to looking back at our life before Christ, but Jesus' point is to leave the past behind us and go forward from this point. We must learn from the past but live in the present. A person generally heads in the direction he or she is looking. If we keep looking back, we cannot move forward in an effective manner. The greatest task of today's church is to determine a way to minister the everlasting gospel to those who have no interest in religion. After all, religion is not our goal—relationship is! A fresh examination of Jesus' methods of evangelism and ministry is in order.

Finally, Solomon reminds us there are things more valuable than money (Ecclesiastes 7:11, 12). Inheritances can bless or curse people. Some inherit great wealth (or not so great wealth) and it changes them. Soon, the wealth is gone and the damage to relationships is done. The use of money must be guided with wisdom. Money is a tool—nothing more, nothing less. It is how we view it and what we do with it that matters—and reveals the nature of our relationship with God. In the end, wisdom will provide a better life than money.

III. ENJOY LIFE (Ecclesiastes 9:7-12)
A. Passion for Life (vv. 7-9)
   7. Go thy way, eat thy bread with joy, and drink thy wine

3. How does verse 12 compare wisdom and money?

"The past always looks better than it was; it's only pleasant because it isn't here."
—*Finley Dunne*

with a merry heart; for God now accepteth thy works.

8. Let thy garments be always white; and let thy head lack no ointment.

9. Live joyfully with the wife whom thou lovest all the days of the life of thy vanity, which he hath given thee under the sun, all the days of thy vanity: for that is thy portion in this life, and in thy labour which thou takest under the sun.

Talk About It:
1. What are some of the things in life we should enjoy (vv. 7, 9)?
2. How did Solomon tell his readers to express their joy (v. 8)?

Readers of Ecclesiastes will have noticed by now that Solomon's thoughts are rather circular. He examines issues, pointing out the dangers, then returns to them later to emphasize the positive aspects, when placed within the boundaries of God's will and our relationship with Him. In the verses prior to this passage, Solomon points out: (1) God is concerned with every aspect of our lives (9:1). (2) Good and bad things happen to the just and the unjust (vv. 2, 3). (3) Death comes to all, and only what we do in this life counts (vv. 4-6). He reemphasizes these things in our passage.

Within a right relationship with God, we must make the most out of life. We are to enjoy the fruit of our labor (bread and wine) with "joy" and a "merry heart," for this is the will of God (v. 7). We are to be content and peacefully enjoying the fullness of life with God. In doing so, we are to remain pure and stay true to our covenants with God and others (v. 8). The white garments and oil are signs of consecration *and* rejoicing. It is possible and preferable to be holy and happy! We are to rejoice in and enjoy the relationships that are a part of our lives (v. 9). Specifically, Solomon admonishes those who are married to "live joyfully with" and love their spouse ("wife"). He reminds us that our marriages require effort, just as careers do. There is no cruise control in the marital relationship. And the care of one's spouse is an act of worship offered unto God.

"Joys are our wings; sorrows our spurs."
—Richter

B. Passion for Work (v. 10)

10. Whatsoever thy hand findeth to do, do it with thy might; for there is no work, nor device, nor knowledge, nor wisdom, in the grave, whither thou goest.

Of all the people on the face of Planet Earth, Christians should be known as people of passion. God has not called us to halfhearted attempts and failures, but to do whatever we do with all our strength and to the best of our ability. Christians should be the best at whatever they do. We only have one life to leave a legacy. What legacy shall we leave?

Talk About It:
How should we approach life, and why?

C. Time and Chance (vv. 11, 12)

11. I returned, and saw under the sun, that the race is not to the swift, nor the battle to the strong, neither yet

bread to the wise, nor yet riches to men of understanding, nor yet favour to men of skill; but time and chance happeneth to them all.

12. For man also knoweth not his time: as the fishes that are taken in an evil net, and as the birds that are caught in the snare; so are the sons of men snared in an evil time, when it falleth suddenly upon them.

Solomon recognized no matter how fast, strong, wise, brilliant or educated we might be, we cannot control all the situations life will bring. The fast sometimes lose the race, the strong sometimes lose the battle, the wise don't always eat well, the intelligent aren't always wealthy, and the educated are not always popular. The psalmist said, "No king is saved by the size of his army; no warrior escapes by his great strength. . . . We wait in hope for the Lord; he is our help and our shield" (Psalm 33:16, 20, *NIV*).

We are provided with "time" and opportunities wherein we should make the most of our strengths and abilities, but "chance" also comes into play (Ecclesiastes 9:11). Just as a fish is suddenly caught in a net and a bird is trapped by a surprise snare, so unexpected difficulties sometimes ensnare people regardless of our status or skills (v. 12). However, God is never caught off guard. If not one sparrow can fall to the ground without divine permission (Matthew 10:29), we can be confident nothing random can happen to us without God allowing it. Chance yields to God's providence.

> **Everything Matters**
> A contractor was interviewing painters for his crew. When he sat down with one painter, the person wanted to know if he was looking for someone to just paint apartments or carefully paint custom houses. My friend replied, "If you have more than one level of quality, you can't work for me. Everything we do is seen and counts!"

CONCLUSION

We have two options: we can cruise through life, cursing our failures and blaming others; or we can approach life with the power and provision God has put into us. We can operate as fools or the wise. In the end, we will stand before God and excuses will not stand under His scrutiny. We must choose this day to do all of life for His glory.

GOLDEN TEXT CHALLENGE

"FOR WISDOM IS A DEFENCE, AND MONEY IS A DEFENCE: BUT THE EXCELLENCY OF KNOWLEDGE IS, THAT WISDOM GIVETH LIFE TO THEM THAT HAVE IT" (Ecclesiastes 7:12).

In the arid Middle Eastern world where the writer of Ecclesiastes lived, proper protection from the sun's relentless heat was critical. In this verse, he used the imagery of a tent covering to say that wisdom and money are alike in that they both provide shelter for people. The *New American Standard Bible* reads, "For wisdom is protection just as money is protection."

There is a significant difference, however. The protection

offered by wisdom is superior to that which money can provide. Here are three ways:

1. Money comes and money goes, but wisdom is not affected by the economy.

2. Money provides material goods for daily living, but godly wisdom gives life to those who have it. Jesus said, "Man shall not live by bread alone, but by every word that proceeds from the mouth of God" (Matthew 4:4, *NKJV*).

3. Money has only temporary benefits, while wisdom brings eternal blessings.

The Purpose of Life

Ecclesiastes 11:7 through 12:14

INTRODUCTION

"'Vanity of vanities,' says the Preacher; 'vanity of vanities, all is vanity'" (Ecclesiastes 1:2; 12:8, *NKJV*) is one of the first verses that comes to mind when thinking of this book. Ecclesiastes is often approached with uncertainty and not considered particularly edifying. As we have seen in previous lessons, this need not be the case. Does it require looking beyond the surface to determine the meaning? Is more than a casual reading required to benefit from its truths? Can its message help us understand our place in the kingdom and history (or better, "His story")? The answer to all these questions is yes.

The world outside of the church doors is not looking for easy answers that leave them empty. Hurting people do not want someone to tell them everything will be fine, while ignoring the reason for their hurt (see James 2:15-17). They are looking for honesty, genuineness, true spirituality, and lasting relationships. In Ecclesiastes in particular, and the Bible in general, we find these things. Solomon opens his heart to share his struggles, searches, failures and successes. He explores the issues of life in a practical and philosophical approach. His reasoning can be challenging to follow at times, but the primary message comes through clearly: Apart from God, everything loses its meaning. Only in Him can we find the purpose of life, for we were created to honor Him.

We must remember that Solomon was writing approximately 3,000 years ago and his style reflects that. It also reveals a certain brilliance and distinct comprehension of God's truth. It is worth the extra effort to mine for nuggets of gold. Its verses have been quoted, paraphrased, or alluded to by most of the New Testament writers. It reaffirms to us that God's Word is timeless. Its truths stand the test of time. It may not answer every question we have, but it provides the principles we need to live victoriously while we search for the answers. It also serves as the roadmap to the One who is the solution to our struggles and the center of all truth—the One who loves us unconditionally. *This* is the message the world is searching to find and needs to hear from us.

Unit Theme:
Ecclesiastes

Central Truth:
The purpose of life is to love and serve the Lord.

Focus:
Highlight what God expects of each person in all stages of life and serve Him faithfully every day.

Context:
Ecclesiastes is generally associated with the reign of Solomon (972-932 B.C.).

Golden Text:
"Let us hear the conclusion of the whole matter: Fear God, and keep his commandments: for this is the whole duty of man" (Ecclesiastes 12:13).

Study Outline:
I. Youthful Vitality and Accountability (Ecclesiastes 11:7—12:1)
II. Frustrations of Mortality (Ecclesiastes 12:2-8)
III. Life's Ultimate Purpose (Ecclesiastes 12:9-14)

I. YOUTHFUL VITALITY AND ACCOUNTABILITY
(Ecclesiastes 11:7—12:1)

A. Be Positive (11:7-10)

7. Truly the light is sweet, and a pleasant thing it is for the eyes to behold the sun:

8. But if a man live many years, and rejoice in them all; yet let him remember the days of darkness; for they shall be many. All that cometh is vanity.

9. Rejoice, O young man, in thy youth; and let thy heart cheer thee in the days of thy youth, and walk in the ways of thine heart, and in the sight of thine eyes: but know thou, that for all these things God will bring thee into judgment.

10. Therefore remove sorrow from thy heart, and put away evil from thy flesh: for childhood and youth are vanity.

Passivity is not an option for the child of God. We cannot walk through life with a stoic philosophy ("what will be will be"). We still believe in the power of prayer to touch the heart of God, who can change any situation. In the verses that immediately precede this section, the Preacher addressed the need to be prepared for and live with faith in the future in spite of the uncertainties of life (see vv. 1-6).

Just as difficulties are to be expected in life, so are the good times (v. 7). When the sun is shining (physically and metaphorically), life seems better and more agreeable ("sweet"). It is a joy to experience the good times. However, human nature seems predisposed to look at (and for) the negative aspects of life, rather than the positive. Some people live as "perpetual martyrs." That is, they are always looking for something bad to happen and seem most content when it does! Solomon reminds us here that we are to expect and enjoy the good times.

We are not to ignore the difficulties we have experienced and overcome ("days of darkness," v. 8). We learn from them, understand that we are who we are because of them, and realize they will not cease ("shall be many") until we depart this life. Difficulties may appear to be meaningless ("vanity"), but God turns even the tragedies of believers' lives into something beneficial (see Romans 8:28). However, Solomon may be hinting at something else. We may also understand *vanity* here in its purest form, "a fleeting breath." Thus, Solomon is also conveying the need to remember the swiftness of life and how soon we find ourselves at its end. "That which approaches comes like a quick breath" is a possible translation.

The admonition to enjoy life continues in Ecclesiastes 11:9. Specifically, the following counsel is given to those in their youth: (1) "Rejoice" in the days you are living; (2) have a pleasant disposition and attitude ("heart cheer"); (3) follow the course ("walk") that your heart believes is right; and (4) pursue the desires you see. This seems to be reckless advice to give to the young (or anyone!), but it is constrained by the knowledge that they (and all of us) will give an account to God at the Day of Judgment (see John 5:22; 2 Corinthians 5:10; Revelation 20:11-15) for the manner in which they fulfill these.

One of Solomon's key themes is here reemphasized: Live life to the fullest, but do so within a right relationship with God. Thus, grief and anger ("sorrow") are to be turned aside ("put away"), and immoral behavior ("evil") is not to be fulfilled in the body or spirit ("flesh"), for "childhood and youth are vanity"—they will pass quickly as a fleeting breath (v. 10).

B. Be Different (12:1)

1. Remember now thy Creator in the days of thy youth, while the evil days come not, nor the years draw nigh, when thou shalt say, I have no pleasure in them.

The frailty of being young is the belief that one is going to live forever and there is plenty of time to consider the weightier matters of life. Solomon amplifies his thoughts from the previous verses and reminds the young that they are to seek God even in their youth. This is important advice. Most of the "vices" with which people struggle originate in their youth. What begins as a natural curiosity leads to experimentation, which leads to further indulgence, which leads to bondage and death (see James 1:13-16). This will become a vicious downward cycle throughout life, if the cycle is not broken through the redemptive power of the blood of Christ.

Many Christians admit that "the sin which so easily ensnares" them (see Hebrews 12:1) stems from something they tried as a youth. Thus, it is imperative that we teach young (and not so young) people to seek God early in life and not open doors that cannot be closed again. One can receive forgiveness for a sin, but sin's effects are harder to overcome and may not be reversible. Life is complicated enough ("evil days,") and its effects can diminish our zest and zeal ("have no pleasure," Ecclesiastes 12:1). We must establish a firm foundation early in life if we are to enjoy all the gifts and beauty the Creator has designed for us.

II. FRUSTRATIONS OF MORTALITY (Ecclesiastes 12:2-8)
A. Seasons of Life (vv. 2-5)

2. While the sun, or the light, or the moon, or the stars, be not darkened, nor the clouds return after the rain:

3. In the day when the keepers of the house shall tremble, and the strong men shall bow themselves, and the grinders cease because they are few, and those that look out of the windows be darkened,

long home (v. 5)— eternal home

Talk About It:
1. List ways the aging human body is compared with a house in verses 3 and 4.
2. According to verse 5, what are some of the negative results of aging?

4. And the doors shall be shut in the streets, when the sound of the grinding is low, and he shall rise up at the voice of the bird, and all the daughters of musick shall be brought low;

5. Also when they shall be afraid of that which is high, and fears shall be in the way, and the almond tree shall flourish, and the grasshopper shall be a burden, and desire shall fail: because man goeth to his long home, and the mourners go about the streets.

This passage mixes *literal* (things that mean what they say) and *allegorical* (symbolic representations that point to the truth intended) elements to present its message. It is a difficult passage to interpret because of these mixed elements. One commentator has catalogued 176 possible interpretations! Perhaps that is Solomon's point. Scripture is alive and can speak to us differently, depending on our needs and circumstances—all while staying true to the intended meaning. Of course, Scripture is not of "private interpretation" (2 Peter 1:20), so our understanding of a passage is subject to the confirmation of those who are mature in the faith. Further, doctrines and determinations should not be made on the basis of one verse or passage. Scripture confirms itself. Here we will focus on the most likely applications.

Just as there are seasons in nature, there are seasons of life (v. 2). When the "sun" shines (youth and vitality), even the "moon and stars" (approaching maturity) do not look dark. The spring showers, however, soon give way to lasting rain, and the "clouds do not return" to the upper skies "after the rain" (*NKJV*). It is a picture of the onset of a life that starts out sunny (full of life and light), but gives way to "the rain" (the drearier aspects of growing old). It becomes more difficult to ignore life's concerns and problems, as well as the aches and pains (physical and emotional).

The idea of youth giving way to age is further illustrated through the image of a house that is preserved or maintained by its "keepers," but as their strength dissipates ("tremble") they are no longer able to keep up the house as they once did. Age takes its toll on the knees and back ("bow down"), as well as the teeth ("grinders"). The eyes "grow dim" (v. 3, *NKJV*), the sounds are harder to hear and distinguish, and the ability to sleep soundly and through the night is greatly diminished ("rise up at the sound of a bird," v. 4, *NKJV*). The sounds once enjoyed ("daughters of music") bring less pleasure ("are brought low)."

Verse 5 says heights become more fearful, and the hustle and bustle of life becomes more bothersome. The almond tree (in Palestine) blossoms in a blaze of white (reminiscent of white hair) in midwinter. Unlike the almond tree, there is no approaching spring for the elderly. Even something as small as a grasshopper becomes a burden, and "desire" for favorite or pleasurable things "no longer is stirred" (*NIV*). The end result for the aged one is the final journey to his or her "eternal home" (*NKJV*). There is mourning by those who are left, but soon they return to their own lives ("go about the streets"). No doubt this was written toward the end of Solomon's life, as he contemplated his own mortality. It is a sobering reminder to live life like we are going to die soon.

B. End of Life (vv. 6-8)

6. Or ever the silver cord be loosed, or the golden bowl be broken, or the pitcher be broken at the fountain, or the wheel broken at the cistern.

7. Then shall the dust return to the earth as it was: and the spirit shall return unto God who gave it.

8. Vanity of vanities, saith the preacher; all is vanity.

The word *ever* (meaning "before") points back to the first verse, thus, the *New King James* inserts "Remember your Creator" to help clarify the meaning (v. 6). We are to live in covenant relationship with God before death so there is no fear when it approaches us. Solomon gives two pictures of death in this verse to remind us of its suddenness and permanency.

Talk About It:
How does verse 7 describe death?

First, we must cling to God before "the silver cord be loosed." This is the cord that held an oil lamp. If it were severed, the "golden bowl" would crash violently to the ground. Second, there can be no water drawn from a well ("fountain") if the "pitcher" used for drawing water is shattered. Also, water cannot be drawn if the wheel is broken that holds the rope and allows the pitcher to be lowered into the well. Some have seen verse 6 as a depiction of various parts of the body. That is, the cord symbolizes the spine, the bowl depicts the head, the pitcher characterizes the heart, and the wheel represents the organs. Obviously, this verse can be understood in different ways, but the primary point is clear: Life on earth is temporary and fragile.

At death the components of our being return to their respective places (v. 7). Genesis 2:7 says, "The Lord God formed man of the dust of the ground, and breathed into his nostrils the breath of life; and man became a living being" (*NKJV*). The body was created from the dust, and the spirit (life-force) came via the breath of God. Theologians point out that ontologically (in our being), humanity is a *trichotomy* (consisting of three essential parts)—body, soul and spirit. Technically, we are a body and soul and have a spirit, but are not a spirit. The soul resides with the body only so long as we have the life-force from God. The soul is the seat of intelligence, emotion, and volition or will. It is the soul that distinguishes us from the rest of creation, determines our personality, and makes us human. The soul is that which is satisfied only through a relationship with God (Proverbs 20:27), because it is the gift God has given to us (Job 33:4).

Life is in the hand of God, who ultimately determines the time of our end (Ecclesiastes 12:7). There are certain things we can do to help prolong it within God's plan, such as being obedient to parents (Ephesians 6:1-3) and to God (Proverbs 3:1, 2); praying (Psalm 91:15, 16); weighing carefully our attitudes and the resulting expressions (Proverbs 18:21); hating evil (28:16); and exercising (1 Timothy 4:8—better translated, "Bodily exercise profits for a little while."). In the end, our life span is determined by God (Job 14:5), and we must live with and by that knowledge. To Him we shall give an account (Ecclesiastes 11:9).

Once again, Solomon warns the reader that life is empty, meaningless, frustrating and fleeting ("vanity") apart from God (12:8). As one stands back and looks at the imagery of life, growing old and facing death, as presented in this lesson, it is a stark reminder that it is easier to come to God in one's youth than to wait until later in life, when the heart is hardened by the cares of this world. As Solomon points out, we must choose carefully and correctly.

III. LIFE'S ULTIMATE PURPOSE (Ecclesiastes 12:9-14)
A. Communicating Truth (vv. 9, 10)

9. And moreover, because the preacher was wise, he still taught the people knowledge; yea, he gave good heed, and sought out, and set in order many proverbs.

10. The preacher sought to find out acceptable words: and that which was written was upright, even words of truth.

Some see this as an epilogue appended to Ecclesiastes by a disciple of Solomon, which is certainly possible and in no way affects the quality of inspiration or authenticity of the material as God's Word (2 Timothy 3:16). However, there is no reason to believe it did not come from Solomon himself. He knew he was wise (Ecclesiastes 1:16; 2:9), and he knew his wisdom was a gift from God (1 Kings 3:12). It is not a boast, but a statement of fact, just as Elijah, the prophet, proclaimed he was speaking for God (2 Chronicles 21:12).

Even though Solomon's wisdom was a gift of God, he was neither prideful nor presumptuous. That is, he did not consider it a gift that was his alone; instead, he shared it with others that they might benefit from his teaching and gain "knowledge" (information that results in discernment). Nor did he presume that his gift was sufficient in itself. He did not assume that God had excused him from further educating himself and preparing himself for additional ministry because he was blessed with a gift. He reflected upon ("gave good heed"), searched out, arranged and made known ("set in order") "many proverbs" (Ecclesiastes 12:9). Solomon diligently searched and chose acceptable words to offer as an act of worship to God and a blessing to the hearers (v. 10). He wanted truth to prevail and did not twist it to suit his purposes. He understood that he had been entrusted with a gift and that it carried an awesome responsibility; thus, he utilized the revelation he received from God (wisdom) and the abilities God had given him to prepare himself to be a vessel through whom God could touch others.

Preparation is not a sin. Preparation does not stifle the Spirit. Quite the contrary! An examination of Jesus' life reveals One who prepared Himself for 30 years before beginning His ministry. Preplanning is not a bad thing. God prepared a message for us before the creation of the world (Matthew 13:35). We "inherit the kingdom prepared for [us] from the foundation of the world" (25:34). In fact, Christ was slain for us in the mind and heart of God long before there ever was a sinner (Revelation 13:8). God had the whole plan of salvation worked out before the world was formed (Hebrews 4:3). God prepared and so should we. Laziness, pride in our heritage, and complacency are not spirituality, but neither should our preparation take precedence over the moving of God's Spirit. We must learn to offer an "unblemished" (suitable and proper) sacrifice to the Lord and allow Him to place it upon the altar for His glory. Like Solomon, we must strive to give God something to work with, and then allow Him to work.

> "For the ignorant, old age is a winter; for the learned, it is a harvest."
> —Jewish proverb

B. Communicating Knowledge (vv. 11, 12)

11. The words of the wise are as goads, and as nails fastened by the masters of assemblies, which are given from one shepherd.

12. And further, by these, my son, be admonished: of making many books there is no end; and much study is a weariness of the flesh.

Wise words are like "goads" (v. 11). Ancient goads were sticks that had been stripped of bark and sharpened at one end, so that an uncooperative animal could be prompted to move in the proper direction (see Acts 9:5). Usually, the other end had a piece of flat iron affixed to it that was used to scrape off any dirt that clogged the plow and prevented it from doing the job properly. This is a powerful image. The "words of the wise" serve to move us in the right direction at the right time and help us remove things from our lives that would hinder us in our pursuit of God's will and the ministry He has placed in our hearts.

Talk About It:
1. How are wise words like "goads," and how are they like "nails" (v. 11)?
2. What warning is given in verse 12?

Further, "the words of scholars are like well-driven nails" (*NKJV*). They serve to anchor us to the place where we need to be. The work of these "scholars," who bring us wisdom and insight from God's Word, is just as important as the words of the prophet, for they too are inspired "by one Shepherd." Wisdom comes from Him, regardless of the vessel He uses to bring it to us. This is confirmed by James: "But the wisdom that is from above is first pure, then peaceable, gentle, willing to yield, full of mercy and good fruits, without partiality and without hypocrisy" (James 3:17, *NKJV*).

Finally, Solomon communicates to the reader or learner ("my son") a solemn teaching that carries a hint of warning ("be admonished") concerning ever-expanding knowledge (Ecclesiastes 12:12). A visit to the library or bookstore (secular *and* Christian) will illustrate Solomon's point: there are a multitude of legitimate subjects concerning which books have been written, and there are a large number of books that should not be read. We must choose what we read carefully, lest our study becomes exhausting and draining ("wearisome," *NKJV*). This does not mean, however, that we should always avoid works from authors with whom we disagree, for we can learn more from them than from those with whom we agree. They make us examine our positions, the foundation for those beliefs, and their validity. It does mean, however, that we must be selective, because we cannot read everything, nor should we. While the task of study can be wearisome to the flesh, its culmination should cause us to be refreshed in spirit and intellect.

C. Keeping Commandments (vv. 13, 14)

13. Let us hear the conclusion of the whole matter: Fear God, and keep his commandments: for this is the whole duty of man.

14. For God shall bring every work into judgment, with every secret thing, whether it be good, or whether it be evil.

Solomon closes this candid and thought-provoking book with a summary that encapsulates its entirety. In the end, when all is said and done, we must reverence God with a constant awareness of who He is ("fear God") and listen to and observe all His instruction ("keep His commandments"), for this is why humanity exists ("the whole duty of man"); that is, it is our highest form of worship to honor and obey Him.

The awareness that our judgment by God will include every secret thing, both good and evil, should never leave our subconsciousness (v. 14). It should guide all we think, speak and do. We should not walk in constant terror, however, for mercy always precedes judgment, and God always has our best interest at heart. He just wants *us* to have our best interests (and His) at heart.

Talk About It:
1. What is "the whole duty of man" (v. 13)?
2. What awaits every human being (v. 14)?

CONCLUSION

Life is a gift from God and should be lived with passion, zest and fullness. It should be lived in a way that brings honor to God and benefit to us. It frustrates us, scares us, and daunts us at times because of its swiftness and complexities. Yet, as we walk day by day with God, we are victorious in each new day.

GOLDEN TEXT CHALLENGE

"LET US HEAR THE CONCLUSION OF THE WHOLE MATTER: FEAR GOD, AND KEEP HIS COMMANDMENTS: FOR THIS IS THE WHOLE DUTY OF MAN" (Ecclesiastes 12:13).

I learned at an early age what fear of a father could mean. My perception, however, was distorted by my youthfulness. If I disobeyed my father, I knew the consequences would be physically uncomfortable. Therefore I obeyed the laws my father established in order to avoid being disciplined. It was from this obedience that I learned to appreciate the real meaning of fearing my father. His laws were imposed upon me to protect me from dangerous activities, to protect me from bad influences, to develop respect for him and to express his sincere love for me. This is similar to our fear of God, our heavenly Father. It is a fear that demonstrates God's desire to protect us from the spiritual dangers and evil influences of this world, to instill within us an awe for His majesty, and to express His divine love for us.

Fear generates a lot of energy, negative and positive. It is negative energy when we become so afraid of something that we lose control of the situation, like the man in the parable who received one talent and was afraid to use it (Matthew 25:25). Fear is positive, however, when it delivers us from all other fears. Thus, fear is conquered by faith (Psalm 112:7). This is the fear of God that Solomon has exhorted us to demonstrate before our God.

The Hebrews of the Old Testament demonstrated this concept to the best of their ability. They expressed their reverence and honor for God by fearing Him in their heart. And rightfully so, for the Bible lays great stress upon the condition of the heart. The heart determines what we really are because it is the origin, or fountain, of moral actions.

The fear of God in our heart is reverence of God's majesty. It causes our actions to be positive as we honor God, keep His commandments, and are obedient. This is the "beginning of wisdom" (Psalm 111:10).

Daily Devotions:
M. Consequences of Sin
Genesis 3:14-24
T. Choose Life
Deuteronomy 30:11-20
W. Youth Renewed
Psalm 103:1-5
T. Treasures for Life
Luke 12:13-21
F. Life Through Christ
Romans 6:5-11
S. Flee Youthful Desires
2 Timothy 2:22-26

Introduction to Summer Quarter

G od's Deliverance and Provision," as seen in the Book of Exodus, is the theme of the first unit. Truths are drawn from the experiences of Moses and the children of Israel in Egypt and the wilderness.

The expositions were written by the Reverend Joshua Rice (see biographical information on page 16).

The second unit is "Great Hymns of the Bible." These studies of divinely inspired poetry come from the Books of Exodus, Deuteronomy, the Psalms and Revelation.

The expositions were written by the Reverend Rodney Hodge (see biographical information on page 131).

The Need for Deliverance

Exodus 1:1 through 2:25

INTRODUCTION

No single event is as responsible for shaping the character of Old Testament and modern Israel and its Scriptures as the great exodus from Egypt. Although Israel's cycle of oppression-prayer-deliverance continues throughout the Old Testament, and becomes the basis for Jesus' gospel and the early Christian message to oppressed Israel, the theological, moral and political matrix that undergirds the nation's experience derives directly from the story of Moses. In fact, the Ten Commandments and the Torah are embedded within Israel's experience of oppression and deliverance in and from Egypt. This is why the exhortation to "remember" occurs 16 times in Deuteronomy, which represents Moses' final address to Israel and the close of the Pentateuch. "Remember that you were slaves in Egypt and that the Lord your God brought you out of there with a mighty hand and an outstretched arm" (5:15, *NIV*).

On first glance, it may seem strange that the ethos of Old and New Testament Israel is more affected by the stories of Exodus than those of Genesis. It is not as though the Genesis narratives are not central to ancient Jewish experience, as we see in the New Testament's emphasis on Abraham, Isaac, Jacob and Joseph. The difference is that while in Genesis God often delivered individual patriarchs and their households from times of peril, in Exodus God delivers a nation. Therefore, Exodus was key to the formation of a national identity. This is similar to any nation whose roots are traced to some sort of revolution or a rebellion against an oppressive regime. Exodus is a book of national revolution, yet with vital applications to individuals.

Still today, movements to end oppression sometimes derive a theological foundation from the story of deliverance in Exodus. For example, Dr. Martin Luther King led African-Americans to equal rights under the law via the premise that God had heard the cries of oppressed, poor blacks across the United States. Whatever the specific applications of Exodus, the book demonstrates once and for all that Yahweh is the God of care and freedom.

Unit Theme:
God's Deliverance and Provision (Exodus)

Central Truth:
God provides deliverance for those who call on Him.

Focus:
Explain the need for deliverance from bondage and trust God to set us free.

Context:
In the land of Goshen in northeaster Egypt, God raises up a leader among the Hebrews; about 1520–1480 B.C.

Golden Text:
"It came to pass in the process of time, that the king of Egypt died: and the children of Israel sighed by reason of the bondage, and they cried, and their cry came up unto God by reason of the bondage" (Exodus 2:23).

Study Outline:
I. Beginning of Bondage (Exodus 1:8-22)
II. The Deliverer Rescued (Exodus 2:1-10)
III. The Deliverer Set Apart (Exodus 2:11-25)

I. BEGINNING OF BONDAGE (Exodus 1:8-22)

A simple word search for *exodus* in almost any English translation of the Bible yields no occurrences in the Old Testament, and only one in the New Testament (Hebrews 11:22, *NIV*). This is because the word is Greek with no direct Hebrew corollary. (Remember that the New Testament is written in Greek, and the Old Testament in Hebrew.) In both languages, the word signifies a departure, closure, or even death. In the Septuagint—the Greek translation of the Old Testament read by Greek-speaking Jews during the time of the New Testament—the word appears almost a dozen times, referring to a group of people "leaving" a place (Exodus 19:1) or even the "end" of the year (23:16), in addition to Israel's specific deliverance from Egypt (Numbers 33:38). It is only later on that the word comes to have explicit theological meaning as a summary of Israel's deliverance.

A. Joseph's Clan Multiplies (vv. 8-14)

8. Now there arose up a new king over Egypt, which knew not Joseph.

9. And he said unto his people, Behold, the people of the children of Israel are more and mightier than we:

10. Come on, let us deal wisely with them; lest they multiply, and it come to pass, that, when there falleth out any war, they join also unto our enemies, and fight against us, and so get them up out of the land.

11. Therefore they did set over them taskmasters to afflict them with their burdens. And they built for Pharaoh treasure cities, Pithom and Raamses.

12. But the more they afflicted them, the more they multiplied and grew. And they were grieved because of the children of Israel.

13. And the Egyptians made the children of Israel to serve with rigour:

14. And they made their lives bitter with hard bondage, in morter, and in brick, and in all manner of service in the field: all their service, wherein they made them serve, was with rigour.

Exodus begins with some information that helps the reader make the transition from Genesis. The Book of Genesis concludes with the death of Joseph just after his pronouncement that his people will one day be assisted by God to possess the land promised to their father, Jacob (50:24-26). Recall that Jacob's clan was given special permission to immigrate to the best lands in Egypt during a regional famine (45:10). Exodus begins, then, with the names of the sons of Jacob—renamed *Israel*—and the number of their household

Pithom (PIE-thom) and Raamses (RAM-uh-seez)—v. 11—two Egyptian storage cities built by the Israelites for their oppressors

Talk About It:
1. What was the concern of Egypt's new king regarding the Israelites (vv. 8-10)?
2. Describe the life of the Israelites under the new king (vv. 11-14).

that originally immigrated (1:1-5). From these 70 or so Israelites, a nation was growing.

For a while, the multiplication of Joseph's clan was no problem. They spread throughout Goshen and perhaps other parts of Egypt, living their lives and preserving the traditions and worship of the patriarchs. However, when a new pharaoh who knew nothing of Joseph's loyalty to the Egyptian aristocracy came to power, horrible things began for the Israelites. This begs the question, How could this new pharaoh be ignorant of Joseph? After all, he had been personally responsible for saving the royal court and the rest of the nation from certain death through famine several generations earlier. One imagines that the story of his great act would be written in the annals of Egyptian history and passed onto future generations. But the new pharaoh has never even heard of him and knows little or nothing about his God.

The main concern of this new Pharaoh is the growth rate of the Israelite clans (Exodus 1:9, 10). This posed two problems for the Egyptians. The first problem was theological. Egyptian religion, along with other religions of the ancient Near East including Baalism, was extremely focused on fertility. In an agricultural economy, everyone is dependent upon the fertility of the land and the family for survival, and this need bleeds into almost all religions, including that of the Old Testament. Yahweh is different, however, because He is focused more on *morality* than fertility. In Egyptian culture, the Israelites' ability to healthily bear numerous children would make them appear blessed by the gods who brought fertility. Had they been Egyptian, this would likely have been celebrated. But they were not. And Egypt certainly didn't want to compete with a people blessed by a powerful rival Deity.

This fear led to Pharaoh's second problem with the Israelites, which was a military one. As the dominant empire of the time, Egypt was in constant danger from invading armies and internal revolution. In the event of war, whether from outside or inside the empire, why would Israel side with Egypt? They were required to give 20 percent of their crops to the government (Genesis 47:26)—no small amount for an agrarian society. The answer for Pharaoh, then, became a machine of oppression to stop the Israelites from growing larger. An added benefit, of course, was cheap labor. The Israelites were used to build cities to store Pharaoh's royal provisions and luxuries. Exodus 1:14 says, "In all their hard labor the Egyptians used them ruthlessly" (*NIV*).

Nevertheless, the Egyptians grew more fearful of the Israelites. The harder they worked them, the more they grew. The harsh conditions they were under certainly weren't conducive to bearing healthy children, so this was probably

Painful Plan

If God exempted Christians from pain, pastors and ministers could stop preaching. TV preachers could cancel their air time, and lay people could stop witnessing. Nonbelievers would throng to the church and wear out the carpeted aisles to the altar, for Christianity would be the modern-day panacea, a gold-plated insurance policy for happiness. However, that is not God's plan.

—George Sweeting

attributed to an act of their God, Yahweh. Pharaoh realized he had to stop this growth or he would have a major public relations problem, not to mention a national security threat; so he turned to a group of common women who were to become the unlikely heroines of an oppressed people.

B. The Nation's Unlikely Heroes (vv. 15-22)

Shiphrah (SHIF-ruh) and . . . Puah (POO-uh)—v. 15 —two midwives whom Pharaoh ordered to kill Hebrew males at their birth

lively (v. 19)—"vigorous" (NIV)

Talk About It:
1. Why didn't the midwives obey Pharaoh's decree?
2. How did God honor the midwives?
3. Why did Pharaoh order that baby girls be spared?

15. And the king of Egypt spake to the Hebrew midwives, of which the name of the one was Shiphrah, and the name of the other Puah:

16. And he said, When ye do the office of a midwife to the Hebrew women, and see them upon the stools; if it be a son, then ye shall kill him: but if it be a daughter, then she shall live.

17. But the midwives feared God, and did not as the king of Egypt commanded them, but saved the men children alive.

18. And the king of Egypt called for the midwives, and said unto them, Why have ye done this thing, and have saved the men children alive?

19. And the midwives said unto Pharaoh, Because the Hebrew women are not as the Egyptian women; for they are lively, and are delivered ere the midwives come in unto them.

20. Therefore God dealt well with the midwives: and the people multiplied, and waxed very mighty.

21. And it came to pass, because the midwives feared God, that he made them houses.

22. And Pharaoh charged all his people, saying, Every son that is born ye shall cast into the river, and every daughter ye shall save alive.

Pharaoh was relentless in his pursuit of the goal of stopping Israel's growth, and his next solution was horribly practical. He found the two midwives responsible for assisting the majority of Israelite births. With two professionals like this as his employees, he could take care of the growth issue, perhaps even without the Israelites realizing what he was doing. After all, the midwives could discretely suffocate boys just after birth and attribute it to a medical problem.

Even under the direct command of the most powerful ruler in the world, the Israelite midwives refused to comply. They feared and honored God too much to kill innocent children. It is interesting that the chapter focuses first on Pharaoh's fear of the Israelites, then on the Israelite midwives' fear of Yahweh. When called in to account for the lack of decline in the male birth rate, the midwives were indignant. In fact, they practically laughed in Pharaoh's face, denigrating the strength of Egyptian women compared to Israel's women. As a result, Pharaoh looked even

The Need for Deliverance

more ridiculous as his plan backfired again. Not only did the Israelites continue to be blessed with increase, the midwives themselves were defiantly having children of their own ("God made them houses," v. 21). Pharaoh and the Egyptian religion were losing face quickly as the Israelites multiplied. It seemed that the fertility cults of Egypt were working incorrectly!

For Pharaoh, the time for half-measures was over. No longer was his new command to only his slave masters or Israelite midwives. Now the edict goes out to all his people under slavery. They were to commit murder themselves by drowning every newborn boy (v. 22). To have a son meant that the family name, honor and household would carry on to further generations. Pharaoh tried to cut off this possibility for every Israelite family. He began a process of slow genocide, but (just like the midwives) among the people of God there will always be those who resist the work of the Enemy.

II. THE DELIVERER RESCUED (Exodus 2:1-10)

The Scriptures are packed with stories of unlikely beginnings for future leaders. The men, women and teenagers whom God has raised up throughout the centuries are rarely those with everything going for them. Instead, they often seem to be born into the most difficult conditions. In Exodus 2, God chooses a deliverer who barely survives infanthood, and then winds up living with the enemy.

A. A Bold Move (vv. 1-4)

1. And there went a man of the house of Levi, and took to wife a daughter of Levi.

2. And the woman conceived, and bare a son: and when she saw him that he was a goodly child, she hid him three months.

3. And when she could not longer hide him, she took for him an ark of bulrushes, and daubed it with slime and with pitch, and put the child therein; and she laid it in the flags by the river's brink.

4. And his sister stood afar off, to wit what would be done to him.

The Torah-keeping Jews who originally read these texts would immediately recognize the significance of the fact that the son born here is of pure Levite descent. Later, when Israel is reconstituted as an independent nation, the tribe of Levi is anointed as the priestly tribe to minister in the Temple. By all indications, that tradition begins here, with Moses as the first type of Levitical priest. We see a piece of this tradition even in the Gospels, where those leaders opposed to Jesus call themselves "Moses' disciples" (John 9:28). The fact of his bloodline is filled with theological import for ancient and modern Jews.

This unnamed woman in Exodus 2:2 (identified as

goodly (v. 2)— beautiful

slime (v. 3)—tar
flags (v. 3)—reeds

Talk About It:
What was ironic about the place (2:3) Moses' mother placed her child (see 1:22)?

Jochebed in 6:20) makes the bold and life-threatening decision to hide her new son, after recognizing that he is a "goodly" child. The Hebrew word here is *tob*—the same word used in the Creation story in Genesis 1, in which God pronounces that what He has made is "good." But what exactly is the goodness that this mother sees in her child? We are not told. We are left to imagine that when she looked at him, her heart welled up with some hope that his life had a purpose, and for that she risked everything. Carefully building a basket, she released him to the dangers of the elements and the care of Yahweh. As far as she knew, this was the last time she would see her son. Her bravery, and her willingness to take the ultimate risk, prove invaluable for generations to come.

B. God's Unforeseeable Plan (vv. 5-10)

5. And the daughter of Pharaoh came down to wash herself at the river; and her maidens walked along by the river's side; and when she saw the ark among the flags, she sent her maid to fetch it.

6. And when she had opened it, she saw the child: and, behold, the babe wept. And she had compassion on him, and said, This is one of the Hebrews' children.

7. Then said his sister to Pharaoh's daughter, Shall I go and call to thee a nurse of the Hebrew women, that she may nurse the child for thee?

8. And Pharaoh's daughter said to her, Go. And the maid went and called the child's mother.

9. And Pharaoh's daughter said unto her, Take this child away, and nurse it for me, and I will give thee thy wages. And the woman took the child, and nursed it.

10. And the child grew, and she brought him unto Pharaoh's daughter, and he became her son. And she called his name Moses: and she said, Because I drew him out of the water.

The Nile River plays prominently in this narrative, since it was the command of Pharaoh that male babies be thrown specifically there. It was also the river that sustained life and irrigation for the people of Egypt. But for the Hebrew slaves, it was a place of weeping and torment. The situation turned to hope, however, when a princess caught a glimpse of a Jewish basket.

The source of this information appears to be Moses' older sister (Miriam) standing at a distance, who later tells the community of the wonderful event. As is the case with many primitive communities, the village water supply functioned in multiple ways—irrigation, drinking and bathing. So here, Pharaoh's daughter bathed in the Nile, attended by her entourage, who stayed on the riverbank for her protection. Seeing the basket,

Talk About It:
1. How did the discovery of verse 6 affect Pharaoh's daughter?
2. Describe the double blessing Moses' mother received (v. 9).

she had a servant retrieve it, and she recognized him as an Israelite. She called the baby a Hebrew, but something was different about this one. We don't know why she was suddenly moved with compassion. Perhaps she was physically unable to have children. Perhaps she saw her father's oppression for what it was. Whatever the reason, she connected with the child at a deep level. This was the hand of God.

When Pharaoh's daughter discovered the child, Moses' sister moved quickly to the scene. Thinking quickly and shrewdly, she offered to find a Hebrew woman to nurse the child. Wet-nurses were common in the ancient world, so Moses' sister didn't need to give her identity away. She didn't know the princess's motives, so she mentioned nothing of being related to the baby. But when given permission, she naturally took him back to their mother.

When Moses grew older, he was taken back to Pharaoh's daughter, who adopted him. The age of Moses at this time of transition is not specified. Nursing could easily last two or more years, so it was likely time enough for the mother and child to bond deeply. So much is not said in this verse, perhaps because it is too painful to imagine this woman sacrificing so much to only give her son away again. In a new home he received a new name based on the place where he was saved from certain death. Just as Moses was drawn from the waters of death, he would one day lead his people out of the land of destruction.

III. THE DELIVERER SET APART (Exodus 2:11-25)

It would be a long time before the baby in the basket became the servant-leader of the nation. There was much forming and maturing that needed to take place in Moses' heart. But the stage had been set, and the way God sets apart Moses in his adult years is as miraculous as the way He saved him as a baby in the Nile.

A. Moses' Sacred Discontent (vv. 11-14)

11. And it came to pass in those days, when Moses was grown, that he went out unto his brethren, and looked on their burdens: and he spied an Egyptian smiting an Hebrew, one of his brethren.

12. And he looked this way and that way, and when he saw that there was no man, he slew the Egyptian, and hid him in the sand.

13. And when he went out the second day, behold, two men of the Hebrews strove together: and he said to him that did the wrong, Wherefore smitest thou thy fellow?

14. And he said, Who made thee a prince and a judge

Freedom Road
Perhaps there is no more famous modern-day "Moses" than Mahatma Gandhi. Initially a well-respected young lawyer, he was troubled by the oppression of the British Empire in India. After leading the nonviolent revolution resulting in a free India, he summed up the process: "First they ignore you. Then they laugh at you. Then they fight you. Then you win." It is also an accurate summary of Moses' life and God's deliverance of the Israelites from Egyptian slavery.

over us? intendest thou to kill me, as thou killedst the Egyptian? And Moses feared, and said, Surely this thing is known.

The narrative takes a lengthy jump into time. Now we join Moses after he has "grown" (v. 11). The Hebrew word here can connote both age and status, and being raised in the Egyptian court means Moses definitely had the second. We marvel at God's plan to have him raised so royally, especially given the fact that the Scriptures give no details of his palace upbringing. We can reasonably guess, however, that Moses was schooled both in the leadership and the culture of Egypt. This would serve him in two ways. First, God knew that at one point he would lead a great nation. Of course, he would lead differently than Pharaoh, so perhaps he was learning many things *not* to do, along with vital administrative abilities he would need. Second, God knew that he would later be involved in "diplomatic relations" with Pharaoh. Israel's deliverer needed a keen insight into the customs of Egypt in order to deal properly with their leader.

The text does not say Moses realized he was a Hebrew. Perhaps his adoptive mother told him; perhaps she did not. On this day, however, he was watching the concentration camp in action. There he witnessed the violent beating of a Hebrew by an Egyptian, and something rose from within Moses. According to Acts 7:23-25, he identified with the Hebrew as a brother. Whatever the case, he rose up, killed and buried the Egyptian slave master. Moses was filled with a sacred discontent, one that indicated the purpose God had for his life—to overturn injustice. However, that purpose would not be fulfilled under his own power, one Egyptian at a time. It would not be the result of a violent, military overthrow of the Egyptian regime. Moses found this out quick enough when the story of his deed became widespread.

B. Yahweh's Faithfulness to Moses (vv. 15-22)

15. Now when Pharaoh heard this thing, he sought to slay Moses. But Moses fled from the face of Pharaoh, and dwelt in the land of Midian: and he sat down by a well.

16. Now the priest of Midian had seven daughters: and they came and drew water, and filled the troughs to water their father's flock.

17. And the shepherds came and drove them away: but Moses stood up and helped them, and watered their flock.

18. And when they came to Reuel their father, he said, How is it that ye are come so soon to day?

19. And they said, An Egyptian delivered us out of the hand of the shepherds, and also drew water enough for us, and watered the flock.

Talk About It:
1. Do you think a court today would call this killing a "justifiable homicide"? Why or why not?
2. What caused Moses to fear?

"We are free to sin, but not to control sin's consequences."
—J. Kenneth Kimberlin

Reuel (ROO-el)—v. 18—a priest of Midian and herdsman, better known as *Jethro*

Zipporah (zip-POE-ruh)—v. 21—A daughter of Jethro, she married Moses.

20. And he said unto his daughters, And where is he? why is it that ye have left the man? call him, that he may eat bread.

21. And Moses was content to dwell with the man: and he gave Moses Zipporah his daughter.

22. And she bare him a son, and he called his name Gershom: for he said, I have been a stranger in a strange land.

The consequences of Moses' actions were more than just a bad reputation. His life was quickly on the line. Because of his hot-headed murder of an Egyptian citizen (and government employee), Pharaoh put out a warrant for Moses. All of his potential as a future ruler of Egypt had been destroyed in a single crime, and he fled eastward to Midian, where he pondered his next move. Little did he know, however, that Yahweh was looking out for him.

Though impulsive as ever, Moses' heart for victims of injustice was again expressed as he heroically fought off shepherds who were harassing some young girls. Remaining at the well unsure about his future, God moved on Reuel (or Jethro; see 3:1) to offer hospitality to this wandering person wearing the garb of the Egyptians. The bond they formed turned into a wedding, and in the naming of his son, Moses accepted his lot in life (v. 22). He supposed that he would live out his days as an alien in Midian with his new family. Of course, God had other plans.

C. Yahweh's Faithfulness to Israel (vv. 23-25)

23. And it came to pass in process of time, that the king of Egypt died: and the children of Israel sighed by reason of the bondage, and they cried, and their cry came up unto God by reason of the bondage.

24. And God heard their groaning, and God remembered his covenant with Abraham, with Isaac, and with Jacob.

25. And God looked upon the children of Israel, and God had respect unto them.

This tumultuous period of Moses' life ends not with more commentary on him, but with a glimpse into the heart of Yahweh. The situation in Egypt became more desperate than ever. Pharaoh died, sparking some hope for the Israelites, but it came to nothing. Their harsh slavery continued. But God heard, God remembered, and God was concerned. Specifically, God remembered the covenant He made with Abraham—another vital link to Genesis. God did not forget this covenant. It never exited His mind. In fact, it was about to come to fruition in the reality of Moses' life and leadership.

Gershom (GUR-shom)—v. 22—
Firstborn son of Moses, his name means "sojourner."

Talk About It:
1. How did Moses display heroic qualities (vv. 16, 17)?
2. How did Jethro's daughters describe Moses (v. 19), and why?
3. Why did Moses name his son "Gershom" (v. 22)?

"Some must follow, and some command, though all are made of clay."
—Henry Longfellow

had respect (v. 25)—"took notice"

Talk About It:
1. What two significant events does verse 23 describe?
2. What is the connection between "groaning" and "covenant" in verse 24?

CONCLUSION

The story of Moses is one that reminds us of the prevailing purposes of God. The chips were stacked against the Israelites in every conceivable way. They were slaves under a murderous maniac intent on their extinction. Moses himself was a victim of the violent regime, until he was miraculously saved. Then, in adulthood, he was miraculously preserved again. Through the twists and turns of his early life, the heart of Yahweh remained constant and steady, groaning with His people and preparing for their deliverance.

GOLDEN TEXT CHALLENGE

"IT CAME TO PASS IN THE PROCESS OF TIME, THAT THE KING OF EGYPT DIED: AND THE CHILDREN OF ISRAEL SIGHED BY REASON OF THE BONDAGE, AND THEY CRIED, AND THEIR CRY CAME UP UNTO GOD BY REASON OF THE BONDAGE" (Exodus 2:23).

"The process of time" was nearly 40 years. During those decades, Moses led his new life as a desert shepherd, while the Hebrews continued suffering in Egypt. Now, at last, the Israelites, whose worship had been influenced by the idolatry of Egypt (Ezekiel 20:8), not only groaned because of their suffering, but also cried out to Almighty God for help.

God heard the Israelites, remembered His covenant with them, and was concerned about them (Exodus 2:24, 25). He would step into Israel's situation and write the new chapter of their history—deliverance from slavery.

If we are in covenant relationship with God through Jesus Christ, we can confidently cry out to Him for help in the middle of our misery, knowing He hears us, is concerned about us, and will act according to the promises He has given us.

God Chooses a Deliverer

Exodus 3:1 through 4:23

INTRODUCTION

The revelation of God's character in the Scriptures consistently portrays His prerogative to choose particular human beings for His purposes. A theological quandary, however, has always existed over the manner in which God makes these choices. After all, looking through the Bible it becomes clear that God chooses all kinds of people. He may use the wealthy and powerful like Solomon, or the poor and nameless like Gideon. He may raise up a leader out of obscurity like Peter, or choose one from the ranks of government leadership like Moses. One thing Yahweh demands in order to use those He chooses is *humility*. The story of Moses' calling illustrates this poignantly, as God takes His time in breaking Moses' spirit in order to make him usable.

This reality of God's prerogative to choose is made plain in Genesis, which sets the stage for the calling of Moses in Exodus. Noah was called because of his righteousness, but there is no such commentary on others. Abram, for instance, was called without any stated reason, and he was likely worshiping other gods of the ancient Near East at the time. Jacob was called and preferred over Esau, even though he was a deceiver. And it was Jacob's name that God changed to *Israel*! Reflecting on God's ability to choose, it is no wonder Paul later proclaimed that "God's gifts and his call are irrevocable" (Romans 11:29, *NIV*). The one God chooses is chosen, period.

In fact, it is this issue of calling that became the first major impasse for the early Christian church. Initially, of course, the faith was a Jewish phenomenon, and the earliest Christians worshiped in the synagogues as a small sect of Judaism. As more and more Gentiles accepted salvation in Jesus Christ, however, the Jewish leaders of the church had a complex problem on their hands. How much of the Jewish character of the new Christian faith were they to expect the Gentiles to follow? More importantly, why was the faith growing faster among Gentiles than Jews? Paul's answer in Romans 9 is simple—God chooses whom He wants, and we must respond to His choice. He is not responsible for catering to our cultural tastes.

Unit Theme:
God's Deliverance and Provision (Exodus)

Central Truth:
God prepares and sends those He calls.

Focus:
Hear and respond to God's call.

Context:
Around 1440 God reveals Himself to Moses.

Golden Text:
"Come now therefore, and I will send thee unto Pharaoh, that thou mayest bring forth my people the children of Israel out of Egypt" (Exodus 3:10).

Study Outline:
I. God Calls Moses (Exodus 3:1-12)
II. God Prepares Moses (Exodus 3:13—4:9)
III. God Sends Moses (Exodus 4:10-23)

I. GOD CALLS MOSES (Exodus 3:1-12)

Moses likely assumed that the course of his life had been effectively set. He had fled Egypt years ago and now dwelt in peace and safety with his new clan. Tradition has it that the first third of Moses' life was spent in Egypt, the second third in Midian, and the final third in leading the children of Israel. Thus, God's call to Moses took place relatively late in his life, and brought him back from obscurity for a great challenge bound to bring even greater fame. The catch is that Moses wasn't interested.

A. Curiosity and Fear (vv. 1-6)

Horeb (HO-reb)—
v. 1—Meaning
"dry" or "desert," it's
the *mountain of
God* in the Sinai
Peninsula where
God gave the Law
to Israel.

1. Now Moses kept the flock of Jethro his father in law, the priest of Midian: and he led the flock to the backside of the desert, and came to the mountain of God, even to Horeb.

2. And the angel of the Lord appeared unto him in a flame of fire out of the midst of a bush: and he looked, and, behold, the bush burned with fire, and the bush was not consumed.

3. And Moses said, I will now turn aside, and see this great sight, why the bush is not burnt.

4. And when the Lord saw that he turned aside to see, God called unto him out of the midst of the bush, and said, Moses, Moses. And he said, Here am I.

5. And he said, Draw not nigh hither: put off thy shoes from off thy feet, for the place whereon thou standest is holy ground.

6. Moreover he said, I am the God of thy father, the God of Abraham, the God of Isaac, and the God of Jacob. And Moses hid his face; for he was afraid to look upon God.

Exodus 3 picks up where chapter 2 leaves off, with Moses settled into the life of a shepherd. He is long removed from the luxuries and independence of his former life in the Egyptian royal court, for he now works as a laboring employee in his father-in-law's household. Interestingly, we finally get his employer's name, *Jethro* (named *Reuel* in 2:18). We also know that Moses' father-in-law is a priest, but this helps little in uncovering much data about the shadowy figure, since the deity he serves is unnamed. Being in Midian, away from the Jews in Egypt, it is uncertain how much he could have known about the traditions of Yahweh. Nonetheless, Scripture presents Jethro as a righteous man, and Moses seems content to serve him.

Talk About It:
1. Why didn't the fire burn up the bush?
2. Why was the ground "holy" (v. 5)?
3. How did God identify Himself (v. 6) and why?

Moses' life of tranquillity is quickly shattered with something he certainly could never have expected—an angelic encounter. Ancient Jewish ears would perk up at this reference to "the angel of the Lord" (3:2). This is the same divine messenger who

God Chooses a Deliverer

had ministered to Abraham and his household (see Genesis 16:7-11; 22:11). That the angel of the Lord was intricately involved with the one with whom God established His covenant proves the angel's importance. What is more, this is the only appearance of this angel in Exodus. The messenger will not appear again to anyone until Balaam in Numbers 22. Although almost as shadowy as Jethro, the angel of the Lord seems to serve a special function in the heavenly economy, and appears only at critical moments in the Old Testament history.

Although pop culture has often portrayed this meeting as between only Moses and a burning bush, perhaps with a voice emanating from the shrub, the Scripture says the angel of the Lord appeared to him somehow within the flames. We can only guess what form this took. Perhaps there was a divine presence visible within the flames; perhaps there was only a voice from the flames. Regardless, it was the flames that grabbed Moses' attention. In a hot, arid region like Midian, small brush fires were not uncommon. This one, however, seemed to burn on and on, so the shepherd walked an indeterminate length to examine it. Curiosity drew Moses to the burning bush, but this curiosity would quickly turn into a gasping fear.

In verse 4 the narrator uses the sacred name of God, Yahweh—translated into English as "the Lord"—to specifically designate the God who was calling Moses. We do not know if Moses had previously worshiped Yahweh, but he was obviously at least familiar with the God of the enslaved Hebrews. To clear up any confusion, Yahweh let him know exactly who He is. He is the God of the Jewish patriarchs, and we can only imagine the emotions that struck Moses' heart.

B. Yahweh's Benevolent Heart (vv. 7-12)
(Exodus 3:9-12 is not included in the printed text.)

7. And the Lord said, I have surely seen the affliction of my people which are in Egypt, and have heard their cry by reason of their taskmasters; for I know their sorrows;

8. And I am come down to deliver them out of the hand of the Egyptians, and to bring them up out of that land unto a good land and a large, unto a land flowing with milk and honey; unto the place of the Canaanites, and the Hittites, and the Amorites, and the Perizzites, and the Hivites, and the Jebusites.

In the experience of Moses, it is hard to imagine the gap between verses 6 and 7. The God of Israel had identified Himself. Moses waited breathlessly for the message to come. To Moses' relief, God revealed His benevolent heart toward Israel, then toward Moses himself.

We benefit as much as Moses from these simple verses

> "We shall never learn to know ourselves except by endeavoring to know God; for, beholding His greatness, we realize our own littleness."
> **—Teresa of Avila**

Talk About It:
1. Why had God "seen" and "heard," and what was His response (vv. 7-9)?
2. Did Moses doubt that it was God speaking to him? Did he doubt God's plan?
3. What "token" ("sign," *NIV*) did God offer Moses (v. 12)?

that reveal the depths of God's heart for human suffering. He had seen the "affliction" (misery) of His people. The Hebrew word for "affliction" is *aniy,* and can also mean "poverty." God had seen the harsh reality of the Jews right down to their economic situation. He had seen the brutality of the slave masters and Israel's intense suffering. So He had come to rescue them and bring the entire nation to a great land. The reader of Genesis will quickly notice that this is the precise promise originally given to Abram at the making of the covenant in Genesis 15:18-21. This underlines the progressive nature of the Old Testament. A promise given may take centuries to reach its fulfillment, but Yahweh is a God who perpetually remembers and acts on His promises.

God stuns Moses by saying he has been chosen to represent Israel before the mighty Pharaoh. Moses humbly replies, "Who am I, that I should go to Pharaoh and bring the Israelites out of Egypt?" (v. 11, *NIV*). Yahweh answers, "Certainly I will be with thee" (v. 12). And then the Lord promises that one day Moses will again stand where he is now, but this time leading the Israelites on their way to the Promised Land.

II. GOD PREPARES MOSES (Exodus 3:13–4:9)

At this point, the argument has already begun. The moment God finishes telling him the best news in the world for the children of Israel, Moses begins contesting the divine plan. Who is he to accept such a challenge? After assuring him that not only will God make good on His word but will bring the oppressed nation back to this very spot to prove it, Moses points out a second problem.

A. God Reveals His Divine Name (vv. 13-15)

13. And Moses said unto God, Behold, when I come unto the children of Israel, and shall say unto them, The God of your fathers hath sent me unto you; and they shall say to me, What is his name? what shall I say unto them?

14. And God said unto Moses, I AM THAT I AM: and he said, Thus shalt thou say unto the children of Israel, I AM hath sent me unto you.

15. And God said moreover unto Moses, Thus shalt thou say unto the children of Israel, The Lord God of your fathers, the God of Abraham, the God of Isaac, and the God of Jacob, hath sent me unto you: this is my name for ever, and this is my memorial unto all generations.

God constantly uses human error to reveal His glory. The significance of these verses cannot be overestimated, not only because they represent the revelation of God's true name, but because of the context. For the revelation comes about not by Moses' great faith in God, but his lack of it.

Talk About It:
1. What did Moses know the Israelites would ask him (v. 13)?
2. What is God's "memorial unto all generations" (v. 15)?

God Chooses a Deliverer

Moses realizes that getting Pharaoh to pay him any attention will take a miracle all on its own, and the whole idea will be automatically derailed if the Israelites refuse to rally behind him. He asks God what to do if the Jews start plying him with questions. After all, they might suspect he is just an Egyptian spy. He still has the leftover Egyptian accent and mannerisms. But if he knows the sacred name of their God, perhaps they'll listen. So God lets Moses in on the secret: "I Am Who I Am. . . . 'I Am has sent me to you'" (v. 14, *NIV*).

Here stands the unprecedented revelation of God's sacred name for His people throughout time. The translation is not easy, but there is a vital connection between God's name and verse 12. The construction of "I will be" when God promises to be with Moses in verse 12 is identical to the "I Am" here in verse 14. The term is a first-person verb of being. It can similarly be rendered "I exist." And it is this verb that is altered to become the noun that later is called *Yahweh*—something like, "the existing One." When Moses spoke this name to the Israelites (we do not know how it was pronounced then), they would know he was legitimate. What is more, although Moses doesn't get this point at the time, the name of God answers Moses' weaknesses. That is, God says, "I Am," while Moses says, "I am not." But before Moses can offer another excuse, Yahweh tells him exactly how this will all play out.

> "When God would make His name known to mankind, He could find no better word than 'I AM.' 'I am that I am,' says God, 'I change not.' Everyone and everything else measures from that fixed point."
> —A.W. Tozer

B. God Reveals His Divine Plan (vv. 16-22)

(Exodus 3:17, 19-22 is not included in the printed text.)

16. Go, and gather the elders of Israel together, and say unto them, The Lord God of your fathers, the God of Abraham, of Isaac, and of Jacob, appeared unto me, saying, I have surely visited you, and seen that which is done to you in Egypt:

18. And they shall hearken to thy voice: and thou shalt come, thou and the elders of Israel, unto the king of Egypt, and ye shall say unto him, The Lord God of the Hebrews hath met with us: and now let us go, we beseech thee, three days' journey into the wilderness, that we may sacrifice to the Lord our God.

Moses is to tell Israel's elders the plain truth with no frills. He is to give them the account of his encounter with Yahweh by name. He can expect the elders to hear him and rally around him. Then comes the really tough sell. Moses and the leaders of the slaves are then to request a meeting with Pharaoh and ask not for freedom, but for a short reprieve to conduct sacrifices. Incredibly, God tells Moses to jump through this hoop although He knows what Pharaoh will do!

Sometimes readers of Scripture are troubled by the references

Talk About It:
1. What message was Moses to give to the elders of Israel (vv. 16, 17)?
2. How specifically did God describe the events that would transpire in Egypt (vv. 18-22), and why?

that God himself "hardened" Pharaoh's heart when the plagues begin in chapter 7. However, chapter 3 shows God's mercy, as He clearly gives Pharaoh a choice to lessen Israel's hardship. Should Pharaoh respond agreeably, perhaps a peaceful negotiation can be arranged. It is amazing that, despite the way in which God knows the future of Pharaoh, His foreknowledge does not affect Pharaoh's choice. In fact, the damage God will do will be so widespread that the Egyptians will beg them to leave, and give away their wealth in response.

C. God Reveals His Divine Signs (4:1-9)
(Exodus 4:1, 4, 5, 7, 8 is not included in the printed text.)
2. And the Lord said unto him, What is that in thine hand? And he said, A rod.
3. And he said, Cast it on the ground. And he cast it on the ground, and it became a serpent; and Moses fled from before it.
6. And the Lord said furthermore unto him, Put now thine hand into thy bosom. And he put his hand into his bosom: and when he took it out, behold, his hand was leprous as snow.
9. And it shall come to pass, if they will not believe also these two signs, neither hearken unto thy voice, that thou shalt take of the water of the river, and pour it upon the dry land: and the water which thou takest out of the river shall become blood upon the dry land.

Talk About It:
1. What was Moses' fear (v. 1)?
2. Why did Moses have a rod? Why and how did God choose to use it?
3. Describe the other two signs God gave to Moses.

After the unveiling of the entire plan to free God's people, one would think Moses would be full of astonishment and wonder. After all, he was speaking to God himself through a fiery shrub. But this wasn't enough for the broken shepherd. His mind brought up excuse after excuse, beginning with the obvious—"But suppose they will not believe me" (v. 1, *NKJV*). Who could believe such a story? Who would think that after four centuries of enslavement the Egyptians will let their slaves walk out of the country with all the treasures they can carry? Yahweh, ever compassionate, understood Moses' doubt, and asked what he was holding in his hand.

At this point in the narrative, Moses' world is being turned upside down . . . again. He barely survived birth . . . later escaped from capital punishment . . . and then learned to survive in desert heat. He had given away a prince's throne to tend sheep because he had stood up for an abused Israelite. Now God has shown up and commanded him to throw even his staff on the ground—the tool he used to make a living. When the staff miraculously becomes a snake, Moses is instructed to pick it up "by the tail" (v. 4)—a command any shepherd would know meant certain death, as snakes should always be picked up near the

God Chooses a Deliverer

head. Nonetheless, when Moses obeys, the snake becomes a staff again. If that isn't enough, Moses' physical hand can be made leprous and clean again, like switching a light bulb on and off. And if still that doesn't impress anyone, God will also endue him with the ability to turn water into blood. We have no comment from Moses on these marvels, but his next question indicates that he felt they aren't enough.

III. GOD SENDS MOSES (Exodus 4:10-23)

Moses had been groomed for this mission during his time in the desert, and God deemed him finally ready. His reluctance was a sign of his brokenness and humility—exactly the qualities God wanted. In his former life Moses had killed an Egyptian with his own hands, but now was the time to rise up in the face of oppression in God's way. His original life in Egypt took place long before. Now he only wanted to live out his days in peace. Yet this was a hope that God would not allow to materialize. Moses had been irrevocably chosen whether he liked it or not.

A. God's Final Commandment (vv. 10-17)

(Exodus 4:13-17 is not included in the printed text.)

10. And Moses said unto the Lord, O my Lord, I am not eloquent, neither heretofore, nor since thou hast spoken unto thy servant: but I am slow of speech, and of a slow tongue.

11. And the Lord said unto him, Who hath made man's mouth? or who maketh the dumb, or deaf, or the seeing, or the blind? have not I the Lord?

12. Now therefore go, and I will be with thy mouth, and teach thee what thou shalt say.

Almost by definition, positions of political leadership require at least a decent level of public-speaking ability. Most national leaders are exceptional orators. Here Moses has been called to the art of persuasion toward two large nations, no less. Again, he thinks Yahweh has tapped the wrong man and speaks his mind: "O Lord, I have never been eloquent. . . . I am slow of speech and tongue" (v. 10, *NIV*). Apparently, after 40 years in Midian, Moses was no longer fluent in Egyptian, as he had been before (see Acts 7:22).

Literally in the Hebrew wording, Moses first objected that he had never been "a man of speech." His living as a shepherd obviously did not require extensive verbal acrobatics. Not only was he weak at crafting speeches, even if he could pen them he couldn't deliver them, because his tongue was "slow." The Hebrew literally reads that he had a "heavy" mouth and tongue. It is the same word used to describe the "weightiness" or the

"Do the thing you fear most and the death of fear is certain."
—**Mark Twain**

Talk About It:
1. What excuse did Moses give (v. 10), and how did God answer it (vv. 11, 12)?
2. In verse 13, what did Moses ask God to do?
3. What role did God allow Moses' brother to play (vv. 14-16)?

"glory" of God's presence. But God won't have any of Moses' excuses. Yahweh's response was direct.

Until now, Yahweh's answers had been compassionate and patient. Now it was time for Moses to once again remember who he was speaking with. This was not one of the hundreds of minor gods the Egyptians believed in. This is the one God who created all things, including the speech and hearing capacities of humanity. Therefore Yahweh was uniquely qualified to help Moses craft speeches and deliver them. When Moses objected again, still wanting out of the plan, God was displeased. He had offered Moses the fulfillment of the great purpose for his life, but Moses wanted to reject it in favor of sheepherding. Therefore, God would pair him with Aaron to help him speak. Because Moses spurned God's offer to help him speak, his brother Aaron would do it for him. The former would have been better for Moses' overall influence, but God would not violate the shepherd's will.

B. Moses' Departure (vv. 18-23)
(Exodus 4:18, 22, 23 is not included in the printed text.)
19. And the Lord said unto Moses in Midian, Go, return into Egypt: for all the men are dead which sought thy life.
20. And Moses took his wife and his sons, and set them upon an ass, and he returned to the land of Egypt: and Moses took the rod of God in his hand.
21. And the Lord said unto Moses, When thou goest to return into Egypt, see that thou do all those wonders before Pharaoh, which I have put in thine hand: but I will harden his heart, that he shall not let the people go.

Expectedly, God wins out in the end. Despite Moses' endless excuses, he knows that he has been chosen by a God who will not relent nor change His mind. Acquiring permission from his employer to check on the status of his own people, he is unsure that many will even be alive. He had seen their hard labor and knew their tough conditions decades ago. He also knows it was always Pharaoh's plan to exterminate their entire race. At least God tells him that the government officials who knew about his crime of murder had passed away, which must have given him a little comfort. Also, he had the miracle-working "staff of God" (v. 20, *NIV*).

On the way there, as he ponders what he will say to Pharaoh, much less the Israelites, God graciously gives him an effective communication device. In fact, He gives Moses a short parable that will make the point quickly and poignantly in Pharaoh's mind (vv. 22, 23). Armed with this parable and the staff, Moses with his family sets off on the long journey. His faith has been tested and proven, and he will need every ounce of it to fulfill God's mission.

CONCLUSION

Yahweh is a God who calls a people, and who calls individuals from a people. Often it is easy to focus on one or the other, therefore becoming either too individualistic or too communalistic. In God's way of doing things, both of these always work together. The relationship of Moses and Israel to God is an excellent illustration of these principles. God passionately cares about both the individual and the nation, and uses the relationship between them to reveal His nature to the world.

GOLDEN TEXT CHALLENGE

"COME NOW THEREFORE, AND I WILL SEND THEE UNTO PHARAOH, THAT THOU MAYEST BRING FORTH MY PEOPLE THE CHILDREN OF ISRAEL OUT OF EGYPT" (Exodus 3:10).

Although God had the power to deliver His people directly, He chose to work through a human instrument. He selected Moses as the leader of His people.

In undertaking this task, Moses had two things going for him: he was commissioned of God, and he was assured of victory. If he faced difficulties along the way, he could remind himself that the Lord had said, "I will send you to Pharaoh" (*NKJV*). If there were times when the outcome of his efforts seemed to be in doubt, he could recall the words of the Lord: "That you may bring My people, the children of Israel, out of Egypt" (*NKJV*).

When God calls a person, He makes His will clear and assures him or her of divine help in carrying out His commission. Consider God's call of Saul of Tarsus. He told him: "I have appeared to you for this purpose, to make you a minister and a witness both of the things which you have seen and of the things which I will yet reveal to you" (Acts 26:16, *NKJV*).

Daily Devotions:
M. God Calls Samuel
   1 Samuel 3:1-10
T. God Anoints David
   1 Samuel 16:1-13
W. God Commissions Isaiah
   Isaiah 6:1-10
T. The Great Commission
   Matthew 28:16-20
F. Jesus Sends the Disciples
   Luke 10:1-9
S. Paul's Charge to Timothy
   1 Timothy 1:18-20

God Delivers by the Blood

Exodus 11:1 through 12:51

Unit Theme:
God's Deliverance
and Provision
(Exodus)

Central Truth:
God delivers His
people and sets
them free.

Focus:
Consider the signifi-
cance of the blood in
deliverance and
accept God's provi-
sion.

Context:
Events in and around
the Egyptian city of
Rameses about
1440 B.C.

Golden Text:
"When I see the
blood, I will pass
over you, and the
plague shall not be
upon you to destroy
you, when I smite the
land of Egypt"
(Exodus 12:13).

Study Outline:
I. Severe Judgment
   (Exodus 11:1-10)
II. Deliverance
   Provided
   (Exodus 12:21-28)
III. Exodus to
   Freedom
   (Exodus 12:29-42)

INTRODUCTION

Perhaps no other principle of Scripture is more puzzling to modern people than blood sacrifice. Beginning with Abel in Genesis 4, animal sacrifice has been an integral custom of the faith of the people of God. By the time the Law is given, the sacrificial tradition is a complex system involving holidays, particular sins, specific animals, and precise ways of sacrific-ing those animals.

How exactly does the slaughter of an animal bring one into better relationship with the Deity? Why would God require such an act by His followers in the Old Testament? Although in the Old Testament there are numerous answers to these questions, as different sacrifices functioned in different ways, in the New Testament the custom of animal sacrifice is illumi-nated for its symbolic power.

It is the anonymous writer of Hebrews who sheds the most light on the overall plan of God inherent in the sacrificial sys-tem. This writer meticulously works through many major motifs of the Old Testament—Sabbath, the high priesthood, Melchizedek, the Tabernacle—showing how these pointed the way to the coming messianic age. In chapters 8-10, the writer discusses the manner in which Jesus' death inaugurat-ed this messianic age through the imputation of the new covenant prophesied specifically by Jeremiah. Whereas Jesus the Great High Priest became the mediator of this new covenant with-out the usual blood of animal sacrifice, blood was still required. Even though Christ offered the gift of a perfectly lived life, "without the shedding of blood there is no forgiveness" (9:22, *NIV*). Therefore, Jesus' very blood became the effecting agent of a new covenant.

God has created the life systems of the earth in such a way that life sustains life. Every time we sit down to eat a meal, we are in a sense involved in a sacrifice, for something living—plant or animal—had to die in order for us to be nourished. In the Book of Exodus, the blood of the Passover is another example of this principle. The children of Israel were distinguished from the Egyptians based on the blood of lambs. Of course, this looked forward to a time centuries later when the blood of the Lamb conquered every evil power once and for all.

I. SEVERE JUDGMENT (Exodus 11:1-10)

After Moses' journey back to his Egyptian homeland from Midian, the doubting shepherd saw the wonders of God beyond his wildest dreams. Everything happened just as Yahweh said it would, with the addition of some major challenges. These included tougher labor on the Israelite slaves when forced to produce bricks without straw, and the unexpected ability of Pharaoh's royal magicians to copy his staff-into-a-snake miracle through either sleight-of-hand or the black arts. Despite this shaky start to the liberation movement, once the plagues began, the momentum shifted in Moses' direction. Yet it took a final devastating act of divine judgment to get the slaves moving toward the Promised Land.

A. The Israelites Win Favor (vv. 1-3)

1. And the Lord said unto Moses, Yet will I bring one plague more upon Pharaoh, and upon Egypt; afterwards he will let you go hence: when he shall let you go, he shall surely thrust you out hence altogether.

2. Speak now in the ears of the people, and let every man borrow of his neighbour, and every woman of her neighbour, jewels of silver, and jewels of gold.

borrow (v. 2)—ask

3. And the Lord gave the people favour in the sight of the Egyptians. Moreover the man Moses was very great in the land of Egypt, in the sight of Pharaoh's servants, and in the sight of the people.

Despite experiencing the horrific judgment of God through a long series of terrible plagues, Pharaoh's heart was still as hardened as ever. Flies, gnats and locusts had destroyed the season's crops, so that the starvation of countless civilians was imminent. The Egyptians could not turn to livestock to take the harvest's place; the animals had been ravaged too. Even a thick darkness that penetrated the land for three days did nothing to stop Pharaoh's determination. We can only guess at his motivation at this point. After all, this is the same ruler who, against all common logic, asked that the plague of frogs remain one more day before being given reprieve (8:10). By all indications, a mixture of pride and vain hope in Egypt's gods and goddesses probably kept Pharaoh hoping for a miracle, even as his predicament grew worse and worse.

Finally it seems that even Yahweh had had enough of Egypt's misery. It was out of both judgment and mercy that He chose to act one final time. Pharaoh could have relented after each plague, but now it was clear that it would take death in his own family (and even then he would change his mind). When this final plague hit, Israel could expect to be escorted out by Pharaoh and the Egyptians themselves. In fact, by this time the

Talk About It:
1. Why would "let you go" become "thrust you out" (v. 1)?
2. How did the Egyptians view Moses and the Israelites?

Egyptians revered their Israeli slaves, so that the Jews could look forward to leaving with the lush bounties of Egypt in tow. Even Pharaoh's officials esteemed Moses now. Before they had merely laughed at him. Now they knew he was a man of God. It seems that everyone in the land knew that—everyone, that is, except Pharaoh.

This situation foreshadowed the governing structure of Israel. There was never talk of Moses becoming a king, and when Samuel eventually anointed Saul as the first king of Israel hundreds of years later, he did so reluctantly. This opposition toward monarchy began with the Israelites' experience in Egypt, where they witnessed one man, Pharaoh, leading his nation into ruin. Even after judgment finally visited his house, Pharaoh led his soldiers into total destruction.

B. The Firstborn Are Killed (vv. 4-10)

4. And Moses said, Thus saith the Lord, About midnight will I go out into the midst of Egypt:

5. And all the firstborn in the land of Egypt shall die, from the firstborn of Pharaoh that sitteth upon his throne, even unto the firstborn of the maidservant that is behind the mill; and all the firstborn of beasts.

6. And there shall be a great cry throughout all the land of Egypt, such as there was none like it, nor shall be like it any more.

move his tongue (v. 7)—bark

7. But against any of the children of Israel shall not a dog move his tongue, against man or beast: that ye may know how that the Lord doth put a difference between the Egyptians and Israel.

8. And all these thy servants shall come down unto me, and bow down themselves unto me, saying, Get thee out, and all the people that follow thee: and after that I will go out. And he went out from Pharaoh in a great anger.

9. And the Lord said unto Moses, Pharaoh shall not hearken unto you; that my wonders may be multiplied in the land of Egypt.

10. And Moses and Aaron did all these wonders before Pharaoh: and the Lord hardened Pharaoh's heart, so that he would not let the children of Israel go out of his land.

Talk About It:
1. Why do you suppose God would send the final plague "about midnight" (v. 4)?
2. How widespread would this plague be among the Egyptians (v. 5) and why?

Modern notions of God tend to emphasize His lovingkindness at the expense of His awe-inspiring power. Many people today imagine God as an essentially benevolent Santa Claus beyond the sky who is interested only in the personal happiness of individuals. This, of course, is not the God of the Bible. Yes, He is a God whose mercies are new every morning, but He also honors human choice and holds the scales of justice in His hands. Should those scales tip too far in one

God Delivers by the Blood

direction in the life of a nation, history shows many times that God corrects them, sometimes with a terrible fury.

In verse 4 it is initially unclear to whom Moses is speaking. Only when Moses departs angrily at the end of his proclamation (v. 8) do we know for certain that he is once again in Pharaoh's court. This verdict, he says, will be final and horrifying. He looks at the same court which he once loved so much and gives them disastrous news: they will all lose their firstborn son, as will every home in Egypt. And lest they think the plague is an earthly disease caused by nature alone, not one Jew will suffer loss. Their dogs won't even bark. That will finally be the last straw for Pharaoh to release the slaves from their bondage, and he will go down in history as a prideful, arrogant lunatic.

For the first time in the plague narratives, Moses has had enough. He recognizes that these needless deaths could be stopped, for Yahweh is a gracious and compassionate God. After all that Pharaoh has seen, how can he doubt Moses' words will come to pass? Thousands of innocent children and young men will die because of his recklessness. Because of this, the Scripture is emphatic that Moses was "hot with anger" (v. 8, *NIV*). The Hebrew literally reads that he had a "burning nose" or "burning face," since anger was thought to reside in the center of the face. Even so, God had told him that Pharaoh would resist, and that God would gain glory from the culmination of these wonders. So Pharaoh stays hardened, and the Israelites begin to prepare for their liberation from centuries of bondage.

3. Explain the "difference" ("distinction," *NIV*) God wanted to show (v. 7).
4. Why was Moses "in a great anger" when he left Pharaoh (v. 8)?

II. DELIVERANCE PROVIDED (Exodus 12:21-28)

In Exodus 12, the time for the Passover had come. God desired to effectively communicate to Moses, Aaron and the Israelites the sacred nature of what they were about to experience. This was not just another plague; it was to be commemorated throughout the history of Israel as the inauguration of their freedom. In the United States, we might look to the Declaration of Independence on July 4, 1776, for a parallel with regard to the initiation of our freedom. The Jews today still look to that first Passover. God proclaimed it was so vital to their formation as a nation that it was to stand as the beginning of their annual calendar, since they would no longer live under the calendar of the Egyptians. In future generations it would be celebrated in festivals across Israel, marked by the eating of foods that reminded them of their bondage. More importantly, this first Passover foreshadowed a day long in the future when a greater Lamb would be sacrificed to avert divine judgment once and for all.

A. The Passover Lamb (vv. 21-23)

21. Then Moses called for all the elders of Israel, and

> "Wherever there is danger, there lurks opportunity; whenever there is opportunity, there lurks danger. The two are inseparable; they go together."
> —**Earl Nightingale**

said unto them, Draw out and take you a lamb according
to your families, and kill the passover.

22. And ye shall take a bunch of hyssop, and dip it in
the blood that is in the bason, and strike the lintel and the
two side posts with the blood that is in the bason; and
none of you shall go out at the door of his house until the
morning.

23. For the Lord will pass through to smite the
Egyptians; and when he seeth the blood upon the lintel,
and on the two side posts, the Lord will pass over the
door, and will not suffer the destroyer to come in unto
your houses to smite you.

Talk About It:
1. Explain the
phrase "kill the
passover" (v. 21).
2. Since the Lord
knew the Israelite
homes from the
Egyptian homes,
why the require-
ments of verses 22
and 23?

God's instructions regarding the first Passover were so specific because they were setting a precedent for generations to
commemorate the first month of every Jewish year. Therefore
God was lengthy in His directives to Moses and Aaron. Moses
had the responsibility of summing up these directions so that
the people could properly follow them. He chose to speak to
the elders of the people, who would then take the word directly to the Israelite households.

Even the selection of the lamb had Yahweh's stamp on it,
since He provided for the poor by ordering that larger households share their lambs (v. 4). *Hyssop* was a reed-like plant
suitable for use as a sort of paintbrush. Once the blood had
been applied to the doorframe, every Jew was to stay inside.
Later on, the doorframes of Jewish homes became the place
where God's Word was inscribed (Deuteronomy 6:9). Here,
however, they held the blood of the lamb, for the blood alone
was their protection.

Atoning Blood
It was one of the
most gripping trials
of recent years. All
evidence pointed to
the fact that Scott
Peterson of
California had brutal-
ly murdered his wife
and unborn child
due to an extramari-
tal affair. A jury
agreed, and he was
sentenced to death.
The mother of Laci,
Scott's deceased
wife, had one chilling
thing to say to him
on the stand: "You
deserve to burn in
hell for all eternity."
In fact, we all do. But
thankfully, Jesus'
blood was enough
to atone for our sins.
Jesus took our place
so we can live eter-
nally.

The disciples of Jesus during New Testament times were
quick to recognize the correlation between the Passover celebration and Christ's crucifixion. In one of the earliest documents
of the New Testament, Paul encouraged new believers to keep
the spirit of the Passover festival by ridding themselves of mal-
ice, wickedness and boasting in their hearts. He based this on
a simple assertion: "For Christ, our Passover lamb, has been
sacrificed" (1 Corinthians 5:7, *NIV*). This may have been a simple phrase used in the earliest hymns, readings or liturgies of
the fledgling church. We can easily see why this connection
had such an appeal—the New Testament concept of atonement. In the Old Testament, atonement is what takes place theologically whenever sacrifice for sins is offered. That is, the
nature and consequences of the sin that inevitably bring about
the wrath of God are covered over—they are transmitted to the
object of sacrifice. This is exactly what took place on the cross,
as Paul wrote in Romans 3:25. In His mercy, God dealt with the
sins of human history once and for all at the Cross. Because of

God Delivers by the Blood

Jesus' death, God's wrath is turned away from repentant sinners and instead placed on Jesus' body. His suffering opened the door to abundant life and peace with God for all of eternity.

B. The Passover Tradition (vv. 24-28)

24. And ye shall observe this thing for an ordinance to thee and to thy sons for ever.

25. And it shall come to pass, when ye be come to the land which the Lord will give you, according as he hath promised, that ye shall keep this service.

26. And it shall come to pass, when your children shall say unto you, What mean ye by this service?

27. That ye shall say, It is the sacrifice of the Lord's passover, who passed over the houses of the children of Israel in Egypt, when he smote the Egyptians, and delivered our houses. And the people bowed the head and worshipped.

28. And the children of Israel went away, and did as the Lord had commanded Moses and Aaron, so did they.

Next, Moses summarized the tradition that the Passover was effecting from this point on in Israelite culture. God gave it to him in verses 14-20, and Moses (or perhaps Aaron, speaking on his behalf) added an attention-grabbing rhetorical advice so the slaves could better digest and remember the commandment. He essentially said that by preserving the Passover tradition, the centering point of the nation would be preserved. Celebrating the Passover year after year was not for the sake of custom or tradition only, but for the sake of the next generation of Israel. For the children would curiously ask them about the meaning of the festival, and they would have ample opportunity to ensure that it was not forgotten.

It is important to recognize that the Passover tradition played a prominent role in the life and ministry of Jesus Christ. Jesus was a faithful, Law-keeping Jew, and as such He annually celebrated Passover. In John's Gospel, Jesus' began His public ministry at the Passover (2:13, 23). In the synoptic Gospels, the Last Supper comes about within Jesus' tradition of celebrating the Passover (Matthew 26:17; Mark 14:12; Luke 22:8). In fact, there is a vital connection between Holy Communion and Passover. Jesus appropriated the theological power of the Passover to then introduce the new covenant He was effecting through His body and His blood. This is why in John's Gospel, Jesus is depicted as dying precisely at the time of the lamb sacrifice during the Passover commemoration (19:14).

Going back to the Exodus 12 account, the elders, along with any other Israelites hearing Moses and Aaron, bowed down and worshiped Yahweh (v. 27). He had heard their prayers and

Talk About It:
1. How would this event become a teaching tool (vv. 26, 27)?
2. Who "bowed low and worshiped" (v. 27, *NASB*), and why?
3. How did the Israelites respond to God's instructions (v. 28)?

"Faith and obedience are bound up in the same bundle; he that obeys God trusts God; and he that trusts God obeys God. He that is without faith is without works, and he that is without works is without faith."
—**Charles Spurgeon**

the prayers of their ancestors. Although they did not (and we do not) know exactly why God waited over 400 years to liberate them, this probably mattered little in their hearts. Finally, the time had come. Therefore, they meticulously followed the instructions given to them.

III. EXODUS TO FREEDOM (Exodus 12:29-42)

For the past eight chapters, the pace has been fairly painstaking. From the call of Moses, to the inital response of the Pharaoh and the Israelites, to plague after plague, the narrative takes its time in providing crucial details. Now, however, the pace picks up. With the exodus to freedom on the horizon, things begin moving speedily along. Just as God said, the final plague is the worst and thus the last blow for Pharaoh . . . at least until the Israelites get well out of town.

A. Judgment Executed (vv. 29, 30)

29. And it came to pass, that at midnight the Lord smote all the firstborn in the land of Egypt, from the firstborn of Pharaoh that sat on his throne unto the firstborn of the captive that was in the dungeon; and all the firstborn of cattle.

30. And Pharaoh rose up in the night, he, and all his servants, and all the Egyptians; and there was a great cry in Egypt; for there was not a house where there was not one dead.

Talk About It:
How do you suppose the Israelites were affected by the "great cry" that arose from the Egyptians?

We can only wonder in horror at how the executions actually took place. We do not know if God spoke death over the land and each of them happened instantaneously at midnight. We do not know if the death angel made his rounds from house to house beginning at midnight. We do not know if the victims suffered, or if the breath immediately rushed from their lungs. The narrative moves quickly in the same way God moved quickly. At the midnight hour, the deaths began and were finished quickly. God spared neither the royal court, the average peasant, nor the imprisoned criminal. Even the firstborn of whatever was left of the livestock after the plague of chapter 9 were killed—another massive blow to the survival of the economy of Egypt. The response can hardly be imagined.

Whether the Israelites heard the screams of their Egyptian neighbors we do not know. But house by house, the wailing took place. Pharaoh gathered his officials in the "situation room," but nothing could be done. Because there was no house without a death, we can suppose that houses without a young son lost the father. God's terrible judgment had been finally executed, although He never desired it to come to this. This consequence was chosen by Pharaoh.

"The vague and tenuous hope that God is too kind to punish the ungodly has become a deadly opiate for the consciences of millions."
—A.W. Tozer

God Delivers by the Blood

B. Free at Last (vv. 31-39)

(Exodus 12:34-39 is not included in the printed text.)

31. And he called for Moses and Aaron by night, and said, Rise up, and get you forth from among my people, both ye and the children of Israel; and go, serve the Lord, as ye have said.

32. Also take your flocks and your herds, as ye have said, and be gone; and bless me also.

33. And the Egyptians were urgent upon the people, that they might send them out of the land in haste; for they said, We be all dead men.

This time, unlike with the plague of frogs, Pharaoh wasted no time in responding to this national disaster. The proud ruler of the greatest empire of his day was reduced to a pathetic beggar. His first word—*cum* in Hebrew, which means in its imperative tense "Rise!" or "Get up!"—indicated his urgency. He was done wheeling and dealing. He could not stand against Moses, Aaron and their God any longer. He wanted all of the Hebrew slaves out of there now, along with their wealth in livestock, which likely represented most of the scarce food left in Egypt. His final request makes him sound like a character in one of William Shakespeare's tragedies. He asked for a blessing from the shepherd, symbolizing the utter destitution of his heart. He had lost his son and the glory of his kingdom. He actually had the gall, after everything he had put the Israelites through, to turn to Moses for a blessing. He was pitiful, and his people were right behind him, urging the Israelites to leave before they all died (v. 33).

The Exodus was happening so quickly that the Israelites had no time to either eat or store the dough of their unleavened bread. They swiftly heaved it onto their backs wrapped in their own clothes and set off, but not before obeying Moses by asking the Egyptians to open up their closets and load them up with their valuables (vv. 34, 35). Plundering armies were common in those days, but this was a plundering unlike any known before. The Egyptians actually gave their booty away without coercion from the plunderers. After all they had seen, they feared the Hebrews' God too much to do anything less.

As the narrative leads toward the summary, we are given the number of Hebrew slaves who marched out that Passover day. With 600,000 men (v. 37), we can estimate their total at well over 2 million when women and children are added. Also, "a mixed multitude went up also with them" (v. 38). These were probably native and foreign slaves who took this opportunity to flee Egypt, and later caused Moses much grief (Numbers 11:4). The Israelites journeyed to Succoth, the place where their patriarch Jacob had made his early home (Genesis 33:17). There they waited for Moses' next move.

Succoth (SUK-oth)—v. 37— Meaning "booths," this was Israel's first camping place after leaving Egypt.

victual (v. 39)— food

Talk About It:
1. What is the significance of Pharaoh's repeated statement, "as ye have said" (vv. 31, 32)?
2. Explain Pharaoh's statement, "Bless me also" (v. 32).
3. Why did the Egyptians insist that the Israelites leave immediately (v. 33)?
4. Explain the statement "They spoiled the Egyptians" (v. 36).

"History is a story written by the finger of God."
—C.S. Lewis

C. Narrator's Summary (vv. 40-42)

40. Now the sojourning of the children of Israel, who dwelt in Egypt, was four hundred and thirty years.

41. And it came to pass at the end of the four hundred and thirty years, even the selfsame day it came to pass, that all the hosts of the Lord went out from the land of Egypt.

42. It is a night to be much observed unto the Lord for bringing them out from the land of Egypt: this is that night of the Lord to be observed of all the children of Israel in their generations.

Talk About It:
1. What is the significance of the Israelites leaving Egypt "at the end of the 430 years, to the very day" (v. 41, *NIV*)?
2. What are the Israelites called in verse 41, and why?

A great transition has occurred in the life of Israel, thus the narrative needs to make a transition. This takes place via a summary by the narrator, who is simply a literary device that gives the reader important details and helps communicate the stories. This is vital in a book like Exodus where so many different kinds of materials and traditions are compiled (narrative history, law, songs, etc.). Here, the narrator puts Israel's enslavement in Egypt into a historical perspective as a newly liberated nation.

In verse 41, military language is used to begin this new era in Israel's history. They march out as Yahweh's "hosts" ("divisions," *NIV*), akin to infantry troops. Because of this, Jews stay up late on the Passover holiday to remember the swiftness with which God delivered them in the middle of the night.

CONCLUSION

Through the blood of the lamb painted onto their doorposts, the children of Israel averted the terror of the death plague and moved into a new era of freedom. It would take many years to rid themselves of the mentality of slavery, but that cannot overshadow the joy of God's liberating work. In the New Testament, the blood of Jesus the Lamb moves saved sinners into a new era of freedom through the sanctifying work of the Holy Spirit. So we see how the Old and New Testaments work in tandem to reveal the character and plan of God throughout history and in our lives today.

GOLDEN TEXT CHALLENGE

"WHEN I SEE THE BLOOD, I WILL PASS OVER YOU, AND THE PLAGUE SHALL NOT BE UPON YOU TO DESTROY YOU, WHEN I SMITE THE LAND OF EGYPT" (Exodus 12:13).

The judgment of death to the firstborn of both people and beast was placed against the nation of Egypt. This served as a condemnation of a non-covenant and offending people. The sentence of death rested upon the firstborn because he represented the family in terms of leadership and in the perpetuation of the nation.

The sentence of death upon the firstborn was also Jehovah's judgment against the false gods of Egypt. The hope of Egypt had been that they would prove their gods were more powerful than Jehovah. Since this sentence included the house of Pharaoh, for he was considered a god, and since many of the false gods of Egypt were symbolized by various animals, God struck the most powerful and meaningful blow of the conflict against the false deities, thereby executing judgments against all the gods of Egypt. Only those houses which had the sign of blood upon them would be "passed over."

The shedding of blood was essential, even for Israel, to escape the sentence of death and judgment. While Israel was the covenant nation, and was an obedient nation, they had no hope of escape from the sentence of death and judgment without covenant and atonement provisions.

JOURNEYS OF ISRAEL
(Under Moses' Leadership)

THE GREAT SEA
(Mediterranean)

406

Miraculous Deliverance

Exodus 14:1-31

INTRODUCTION

The past century of world history has clearly shown the high cost of freedom. Especially when looking back at the two world wars in Europe, we see the work of deliverance was long and bloody. Perhaps Donald Rumsfeld, the former United States secretary of defense, said it best when confronting the difficulties of the American progress in Iraq: "Freedom's untidy." These two simple words speak volumes about the effort it takes to free a nation. In the Old Testament, even with God acting as the commander in chief, Israel still found herself frequently needing deliverance.

Bible scholars often refer to a "cycle" that took place in the history of Israel throughout the Book of Judges. It began with apostasy on the part of Israel. They would forsake Yahweh and begin to serve the man-made gods of the neighboring pagan peoples. This resulted in some sort of national crisis. When the heat became too painful to handle, the Jews would cry out to Yahweh. God would then raise up a leader to deliver them, and they typically served Him faithfully throughout the life of that leader. After the leader's death, the cycle would start over. And even though God knew they would fail again, He never failed to deliver them.

The God of the Bible is unquestionably a delivering God with the power to liberate from all oppression. This divine character trait is highlighted in God's deliverance of the children of Israel from the hands of Pharaoh in Egypt. Yet, even their freedom then was "untidy." Even with a God who performed unmistakable miracles at every turn, things were not easy or linear. In fact, the process was fraught with bumps and perils. First, Moses' initial meeting with Pharaoh went sour. Then, the plagues only had a hardening effect on the ruler. Finally, when Pharaoh appeared to be broken, he changed his mind and the Israelites needed to be delivered again. Through it all, Moses and the Israelites learned that Yahweh could ultimately be trusted as a delivering God.

Unit Theme:
God's Deliverance and Provision (Exodus)

Central Truth:
God's greatest miracle on our behalf is deliverance from sin.

Focus:
Recognize and proclaim God's power to provide miraculous deliverance.

Context:
Around 1440 B.C., the Israelites leave Egypt.

Golden Text:
"Fear ye not, stand still, and see the salvation of the Lord, which he will shew to you to day" (Exodus 14:13).

Study Outline:
I. Pursued by the Enemy (Exodus 14:1-12)
II. The Salvation of the Lord (Exodus 14:13-23)
III. The Enemy Destroyed (Exodus 14:24-31)

I. PURSUED BY THE ENEMY (Exodus 14:1-12)

Between the sudden midnight exodus of the Israelites following the terrible plague on the Egyptians' firstborn sons and the journey toward the Red Sea, Exodus 12:43–13:16 provides an interlude. It may seem strange to modern readers that the action of the story is stopped for some rather tedious information regarding Passover laws, but such constructions served an important purpose to its early readers. That is, significant traditions, customs and laws for the people were interspersed within exciting narrative history. This way, the stories kept the reader engaged enough to listen closely to the traditions, and the traditions were given renewed life by being explicitly connected to their originating point. Here in chapter 14 the action heats up again, and the Israelites look to God alone for yet another experience of miraculous deliverance.

A. God Hardens Pharaoh's Heart (vv. 1-9)

(Exodus 14:5-9 is not included in the printed text.)

1. And the Lord spake unto Moses, saying,

2. Speak unto the children of Israel, that they turn and encamp before Pi-hahiroth, between Migdol and the sea, over against Baal-zephon: before it shall ye encamp by the sea.

3. For Pharaoh will say of the children of Israel, They are entangled in the land, the wilderness hath shut them in.

4. And I will harden Pharaoh's heart, that he shall follow after them; and I will be honoured upon Pharaoh, and upon all his host; that the Egyptians may know that I am the Lord. And they did so.

This chapter—one of the most famous in the Bible—begins with more specific instructions which pass on from God to Moses to the children of Israel. Moses is not the monarch calling the shots for Israel. Instead, Moses is wholly dependent on Yahweh in the leadership of the nation. Every step of the way, it is God who directs the actions of His people. Many times, all Moses and Aaron must do is relay the message.

In chapter 13, we find out that from the beginning God has planned to lead the children of Israel to the edge of the Red Sea (v. 18). There was a shorter route, but God does not want to frighten His fledgling nation with the possibility of a threatening army from the Philistine country (v. 17). He has other plans for revealing His glory. Note that the place of Israel's encampment is directly across from a city named after Egypt's chief god, Baal (14:2). Although loaded down with the plunder of Egypt, the Jews are still in enemy territory. It will take a miracle to bring them out.

Pi-hahiroth (pi-ha-HI-roth)—v. 2—the place where Israel camped before crossing the Red Sea

Migdol (v. 2)—meaning "watchtower" or "fortress," a place west of the Red Sea

Baal-zephon (BAY-uhl-ZEE-fon)—v. 2—a place belonging to Egypt on the border of the Red Sea; means "Baal of winter"

with an high hand (v. 8)—boldly

Despite the fact that Egypt lies in waste, Pharaoh still fails to get the point. He refuses to let go of his pride and to accept failure. He will not acknowledge that Israel's God has proven Himself greater than those of the Egyptian cults. As a result, Yahweh means business again, and this time it will be ultimate and final. The instructions He gives to Israel regarding moving their encampments are strange indeed. Using an unmistakable mass of cloud by day and one of fire by night, He leads them to a position that no human general would ever desire. Basically, the Israelites are trapped by the Red Sea on one side and the hot desert on the other. But this is only a flanking position—a decoy to take care of Pharaoh and his army once and for all. This is important not only for God's name to gain glory, but also for the literal future protection of the Israelites. Remember, they are traveling with over 2 million people. Even if they have weeks or months of a head start, Pharaoh could quickly make up that ground with a small invading force and attack their rear. Re-enslavement or death in the desert is a constant fear of the Jews, necessitating this gruesome act of God toward the Egyptians.

Readers of the Bible have spilled much ink over God's relationship with Pharaoh as presented in Exodus. When God initially called Moses, we saw that He gave Pharaoh an opportunity to accept a preliminary and relatively low-cost request to allow the Jews three days to worship, even though God knew Pharaoh would reject it. With each horrible plague, Pharaoh had ample opportunity to say "Enough!" and to let the Israelites go. So it is within this context whereby Pharaoh is given a conscious choice that we must read these verses. All in all, God has been more than patient with the Egyptian monarch.

Nonetheless, the words of the passage do refer to God playing an active part in the heart of Pharaoh. Yet again, *his heart is already hardened*. It has been hardened from the beginning; and as we know from our own experiences with sin, when we are hard we are stubborn. When we are stubborn, we often make illogical decisions. Regardless, though, of Pharaoh's condition, Yahweh will make His name great through the ruler's stupidity. The entire Egyptian army will fall, thus ensuring Israel's future protection as a viable nation and securing glory for Yahweh. When hostile neighboring peoples hear about Yahweh and His victory over Pharaoh, they'll be inclined to steer clear of His people.

Beginning at verse 5, Pharaoh again acts just as God has said he will. His motivation at this point appears to be economic—they have just lost the cheapest labor in the land. We cannot know what was left of the army, but there were many who certainly hoped for revenge over this people they considered responsible for the destruction of their households and their nation.

Talk About It:
1. What wrong idea did Pharaoh have (v. 3)?
2. What was God's purpose in this situation (v. 4)?
3. Describe the Egyptians' change of heart (v. 5).

"Our lives are shaped by the decisions we make. . . . The decisions we make are shaped by the condition of our heart."
—**Carla Galanos**

B. The Israelites Lose Faith (vv. 10-12)

10. And when Pharaoh drew nigh, the children of Israel lifted up their eyes, and, behold, the Egyptians marched after them; and they were sore afraid: and the children of Israel cried out unto the Lord.

11. And they said unto Moses, Because there were no graves in Egypt, hast thou taken us away to die in the wilderness? wherefore hast thou dealt thus with us, to carry us forth out of Egypt?

12. Is not this the word that we did tell thee in Egypt, saying, Let us alone, that we may serve the Egyptians? For it had been better for us to serve the Egyptians, than that we should die in the wilderness.

With an extremely sophisticated army, trained to function as a unified, sleek, speedy fighting machine, Pharaoh reaches the Israelites quickly enough. Understandably, the Jews are terrified and cry out to the Lord for help. Even with the pillar of cloud still standing right in front of their eyes, and with the smell of the burning pillar of fire from the previous night lingering in their nostrils, they quickly lose faith. Moses takes the brunt of their anger (a pattern throughout Exodus), and they even recall their initial rejection of his entire proposal in the first place. When their faith is tested, they immediately long for Egypt.

Exodus will revisit Israel's mentality of slavery over and over again as the nation makes its journey toward the Promised Land. Keep in mind that we are talking about a way of life not just of one generation, but of numerous generations of Jews stretching back over 400 years. The rigors and dependencies of slavery are embedded in their consciousness. All that they know is generational dysfunction. Just because God has set them free does not mean they know how to function as free people. This passage shows us that they are far from ready. Nonetheless, God in His patience continues to lead them toward freedom and maturity.

II. THE SALVATION OF THE LORD (Exodus 14:13-23)

It is not only God who has the opportunity to display His greatness; Moses also has something to prove at this critical juncture. Will he join in the Israelites' faithlessness and relinquish his responsibility to lead them onward, or will he remain steadfast in devotion to the Lord, even if it seems like blind loyalty? It is a moment for the history books, and a lesson in leadership for all people throughout time.

A. Moses Rallies the People (vv. 13, 14)

13. And Moses said unto the people, Fear ye not, stand still, and see the salvation of the Lord, which he will shew

Talk About It:
1. Describe the nature of the Israelites' cry to God (v. 10).
2. How did the Israelites feel about Moses' leadership (vv. 11, 12)?

"Some people are so afraid to die that they never begin to live."
—Henry Van Dyke

to you to day: for the Egyptians whom ye have seen to day, ye shall see them again no more for ever.

14. The Lord shall fight for you, and ye shall hold your peace.

There is no time to lose. With the Egyptian army gaining ground quickly, threatening to close the Israelites in for good, definitive orders must be given. Moses hardly seems like the same weak, frightened shepherd of Midian as he rises to the challenge. He is assuming the mantle of leadership like never before. Moses rings out an exhortation that can be found throughout the Scriptures after him: "Whatever you do, don't fear!" Although God has not revealed the details of the plan to Moses yet, Israel's leader believes they have not been led into the desert to die.

Moses exhorts, "The Lord will fight for you; you need only to be still" (v. 14, *NIV*). Obviously, there has been a major change of strategy. In 13:18, we find out that the Israelites were originally armed for battle, apparently with weaponry they were able to obtain from Egypt. When the fighting men in the group see the approaching Egyptian army, they no doubt ready themselves for a showdown. Moses, however, discerns that the situation will not be resolved in this way. In fact, the strategy is the opposite of warfare; it is nothing at all. Yahweh will fight on their behalf if they can only be still. This was God's plan even though there was a real army with real weapons heading straight at them; a real army filled with armed chariots, armored cavalry, and thousands of infantry wielding swords and spears.

Talk About It:
Describe the two uses of the word *see* in verse 13.

"Faith is the refusal to panic."
—D. Martyn Lloyd-Jones

B. God Rallies Moses (vv. 15-18)
(Exodus 14:15-18 is not included in the printed text.)

There must be a gap of time existing between verses 14 and 15. Previously, Moses was exhorting the people heroically, standing up for faith in the midst of their doubt. But here God is the One encouraging Moses, who has turned to fretfully crying out to Him along with the rest of the Jews. No doubt Moses was looking for more specific instructions, and God grants them. Moses needed to quit his wailing and reach for the staff of God. The same staff that worked wonders in Egypt will remain reliable in the wilderness. There is no new formula for success here. Therefore, when the staff is stretched out toward the Red Sea, it will begin to part, just enough so that Israel can start moving to the other side on dry ground. God then repeats His original commitment to gain glory through Pharaoh and his army, but exactly how, He does not reveal.

Talk About It:
1. Do you think God's command to "go forward" (v. 15) was surprising to Moses? Why or why not?
2. What was the significance of Moses holding out his rod and his hand?
3. What was so important about the honor God would gain in this miracle?

C. The Red Sea Separates (vv. 19-23)
19. And the angel of God, which went before the camp of

Israel, removed and went behind them; and the pillar of the cloud went from before their face, and stood behind them:

20. And it came between the camp of the Egyptians and the camp of Israel; and it was a cloud and darkness to them, but it gave light by night to these: so that the one came not near the other all the night.

21. And Moses stretched out his hand over the sea; and the Lord caused the sea to go back by a strong east wind all that night, and made the sea dry land, and the waters were divided.

22. And the children of Israel went into the midst of the sea upon the dry ground: and the waters were a wall unto them on their right hand, and on their left.

23. And the Egyptians pursued, and went in after them to the midst of the sea, even all Pharaoh's horses, his chariots, and his horsemen.

What happens next is completely unexpected. It is a part of God's plan that He does allow Moses to know in advance. The large pillar of cloud follows God's angel to form a wall between the Egyptians and the Jews. In fact, this supernatural wall provides light to Israel throughout the night, which must have been a welcome relief to them. Had they been forced to encamp in the dark, who knows what panic might have led them to do! Instead, they are totally separated from the Egyptians. But this was not so they can rest, but so they can get moving.

Although movies depict the parting of the Red Sea occurring in an instant, there appears to be some significant time involved. For instance, the Scripture is clear that God uses nature—a strong east wind—to accomplish the parting of the water. This may have been a few yards of dry ground at a time, or the entire path at once. But the wind was ongoing, so a path through the sea stayed dry. We are correct to guess that the path was large, as some 2 million people had to cross it speedily. With the angel of God creating the diversion between the Israelites and the Egyptians, escaping was not difficult. But suddenly the angel relents without warning.

God had told Moses He would gain glory at the expense of Pharaoh, but there is no reason to assume Moses expected things would turn in this direction. Simply stopping the army in its tracks brought glory to God, but now it is seen that God has more in store. Pharaoh's actions seem the height of lunacy after all the Egyptians had seen. Nonetheless, they likely reason that Israel's God will not return the waters with the Jews still making the crossing, so they race toward their foes with suicidal abandon.

III. THE ENEMY DESTROYED (Exodus 14:24-31)

The chase is on as the Egyptian army tears into the Red

Talk About It
1. What two purposes did the cloud serve (v. 20)?
2. How do you suppose the Israelites felt as they walked through the divided sea?
3. What do you suppose was the Egyptian army's attitude as they rushed after the Israelites?

"We shall not grow wiser before we learn that much that we have done was very foolish."
—F.A. Hayek

Sea in pursuit of the Israelites' rear guard. Presumably, Moses has stationed some of Israel's strongest fighting men at the rear of the traveling party, but Scripture doesn't say this. It simply doesn't need to. For the Jews do not need to even unsheathe a sword to achieve one of the greatest military feats ever recorded in human history.

A. A Battle With God (vv. 24, 25)

24. And it came to pass, that in the morning watch the Lord looked unto the host of the Egyptians through the pillar of fire and of the cloud, and troubled the host of the Egyptians,

25. And took off their chariot wheels, that they drave them heavily: so that the Egyptians said, Let us flee from the face of Israel; for the Lord fighteth for them against the Egyptians.

in the morning watch (v. 24)—at sunrise

The "morning watch" refers to the period just before daybreak, and God waits this long to definitively act. Waiting this long gives the Egyptian army ample time to move in its entirety into the flood zone. But in order to widen the ever-closing gap between the Egyptians and God's people, He takes action quickly, throwing the army into a strange chaos. The main Hebrew tradition has it that God took the wheels right off the chariots. Some other versions of the ancient manuscripts, the Septuagint for example, recount that God jammed the chariot wheels, implying perhaps that they sank in the mud of the seabed. Whatever the case, the Egyptians suddenly realize they are not pursuing a defenseless people. Instead, they are involved in the futile attempt to outwit a powerful God. Therefore, they forget about fighting and run for the shore. Of course, it is too late.

Talk About It:
What caused the Egyptians to change their mind about pursuing Israel?

B. The Annihilation of Egypt (vv. 26-28)

26. And the Lord said unto Moses, Stretch out thine hand over the sea, that the waters may come again upon the Egyptians, upon their chariots, and upon their horsemen.

27. And Moses stretched forth his hand over the sea, and the sea returned to his strength when the morning appeared; and the Egyptians fled against it; and the Lord overthrew the Egyptians in the midst of the sea.

28. And the waters returned, and covered the chariots, and the horsemen, and all the host of Pharaoh that came into the sea after them; there remained not so much as one of them.

Once again, as Moses' staff played a key role in initially parting the waters, God gives similar instructions for completing the mission. What happens next cannot be considered complacently; these were the real lives of real people whom God

Talk About It:
How complete was the Lord's victory over Egypt?

cared about. Yet they had made a critical error against all odds to disrespectfully oppose the God of Israel.

A single Hebrew letter, which can mean either "to" or "from," marks the translation decision here as to whether the Egyptians were fleeing into the sea or away from the sea. If into the sea, this is indicative of the spirit of confusion with which God struck them. However, it seems likely based on previous verses that they are running for their lives toward the shore. Whichever it was, it did not matter. There is nowhere to escape, and just as the sunrise peaks over the horizon, Moses makes his move and the army vanishes. Not one can swim well enough to survive the bone-crushing torrent of water that heaps upon them again and again as the Red Sea resumes its normal levels. It is a grisly scene indeed.

C. The Response of the Israelites (vv. 29-31)

29. But the children of Israel walked upon dry land in the midst of the sea; and the waters were a wall unto them on their right hand, and on their left.

30. Thus the Lord saved Israel that day out of the hand of the Egyptians; and Israel saw the Egyptians dead upon the sea shore.

31. And Israel saw that great work which the Lord did upon the Egyptians: and the people feared the Lord, and believed the Lord, and his servant Moses.

Talk About It:
What impact did this miracle have upon the Israelites?

Barely believing their eyes and the remarkable power of their God, the Israelites sense that this horrific part of their history has finally ended. They can finally breathe easily through the knowledge that the tyrant is dead—killed at the hand of their almighty God. In fact, verse 29 is one of summary, as the story wraps up.

Soon the corpses of the Egyptians begin washing onto the beach, watered by the tide. Undoubtedly, they were everywhere with terrified looks of death remaining on their faces. Finally, justice has been accomplished.

It is easy to grimace at the violence of such passages, but Yahweh is unalterably a God of justice, and justice sometimes requires violence both then and now. The same nation who enslaved a people and oppressed them for over 400 years finally receives recompense for their actions. It is a heavy blow, not only to the members of the Egyptian army but to Egypt as a whole. For though a new pharaoh could quickly be established, a new army would be years in the making. In the meantime, the nation would be the laughingstock of its enemies, open to invading attackers, plunderers and bandits. The great nation has fallen at last.

As a result, verse 31 reads that the people place their trust both in the Lord and in Moses. This should not be overlooked, for

Monument to Freedom
In the throes of Soviet rule, ordinary Lithuanians erected a strange and beautiful monument still standing today. The "Hill of Crosses" became both a spiritual and political protest against atheistic communism. Although repeatedly bulldozed by the communists, the crosses continued to arrive by the thousands. Today, this hill serves as a monument to freedom for Lithuanians.

it inaugurates the combination of theology and politics in the life of Israel. There was no concept of a separation of church and state then in any nation. Instead, the natural consequence of God's work is both theological and political. As the rest of Exodus shows, the children of Israel will be stretched in both arenas of their faith.

CONCLUSION

Previously, God delivered the children of Israel by the blood of lambs. Now He has done it through a supernatural power over nature itself. No wonder Jesus' disciples marvel and worship when Jesus calms the storm; such an act probably brought to mind Exodus 14. Theologically, what happened then rings true in our Christian experience today—God still miraculously delivers from bondage and will bring about His justice for the oppressed in time. Our responsibility, just like that of the ancient Israelites, is to have faith, to be still at times, and to join God in His work.

GOLDEN TEXT CHALLENGE

"FEAR YE NOT, STAND STILL, AND SEE THE SALVATION OF THE LORD, WHICH HE WILL SHEW TO YOU TO DAY" (Exodus 14:13).

God gives His leaders encouraging words for discouraging times. While we cannot always stay away from life's troubles, we can stay above our fears. Moses' first response, "Fear not," was a word of comfort to the wavering Hebrews. The Bible repeats that same command exactly 365 times—one for each day of the year. Without a doubt He is telling us not to fear. We can be sure, on the promise of His Word, that "perfect love casteth out fear" (1 John 4:18).

Another word of comfort was the command to "stand still" and see the deliverance of the Lord. Sometimes we miss God's best blessings because we intrude ourselves in His way. We feel we must always be "doing something." We feel we *must* make it happen! If we could only learn to rely on Him who is able to deliver! Charles Spurgeon commented on this thought: "Despair whispers, 'Lie down and die; give it all up.' Cowardice says, 'Retreat; go back to the worldling's way of action.' Precipitancy cries, 'Do something; to stand still and wait is sheer idleness.' Presumption boasts, 'If the sea be before you, march into it and expect a miracle.' But faith listens neither to Presumption, Despair, Cowardice, nor to Precipitancy. It hears God say, 'Stand still.' It will not be long before [He] shall say to you as distinctly as Moses said it to the people of Israel, 'Go forward!'"

The Israelites were assured of deliverance. In the process, their enemies were to be utterly destroyed. "If God himself bring His people into straits, He will Himself discover a way to bring them out again" (*Matthew Henry's Commentary*).

Daily Devotions:
M. God Will Deliver Again
   Joshua 3:5-17
T. Remember God's Miraculous Power
   Psalm 106:6-12
W. God Is Able to Deliver
   Daniel 3:13-25
T. Pray for Deliverance
   Matthew 6:9-13
F. Miracles of Deliverance
   Acts 19:11-20
S. Hope for Deliverance
   2 Corinthians 1:3-11

God Provides for His People

Exodus 16:1 through 17:16

Unit Theme:
God's Deliverance and Provision (Exodus)

Central Truth:
God will provide for those who trust in Him.

Focus:
Realize that God provides for His people and rejoice in His sufficiency.

Context:
Around 1440 B.C., God makes supernatural provision for the Israelites in the desert.

Golden Text:
"My God shall supply all your need according to his riches in glory by Christ Jesus" (Philippians 4:19).

Study Outline:
I. God Provides Food
   (Exodus 16:6-18)
II. God Provides Water
   (Exodus 17:1-7)
III. God Provides Victory
   (Exodus 17:8-16)

INTRODUCTION

The Bible is a book of economics as well as a book of theology or spiritual truths. It is filled with commandments and teachings that primarily deal with finances. Two of the Ten Commandments—prohibitions against stealing and coveting—are explicitly economic in nature. In other places in the Torah are regulations regarding appropriate interest rates, property transactions, wedding costs, and so on. By the time of the New Testament, Jesus' teachings and parables deal with economic realities more than any other subject. Many times God asks His people to put their money where their mouths are.

Yet this emphasis on finances does not stem primarily from the need for God's people to live upright and generous lives. In fact, the economics of Scripture are a natural outgrowth of God's character as a God of both miraculous and ongoing provision. Early on, it is Abraham who recognizes Yahweh as the God who provides (Genesis 22:8). After God supplies a ram to make a sacrifice in place of his son, Isaac, Abraham gives the mountain a new name: *Jehovah Jireh*—"The Lord Will Provide" (v. 14, *NIV*). In fact, *Jireh* is a Hebrew verb that also means "sees." So Yahweh is a God who not only sees, but acts in response to human need. His very nature is to provide for the physical and spiritual needs of His children.

In recent years, this divine characteristic has been twisted into the "prosperity gospel." Although God's provision *sometimes* results in prosperity, the Scriptural promise of provision does not guarantee overabundance. In fact, there are many Biblical warnings concerning the temptations and fallacies of wealth. It is not that financial abundance is inherently evil or wrong, but that God knows that such a lifestyle sometimes brings with it complications that can easily hinder one from doing the work of God in the world. Consider Jesus' exhortation in Matthew 6:33: "Seek ye first the kingdom of God, and his righteousness; and all these things shall be added unto you." What are "these things"? In the context of the Sermon on the Mount, they are the basic necessities of life—food, clothing and shelter. Because we serve *Jehovah Jireh* and His Son, Jesus Christ, we can place our trust in Him to provide for our needs.

I. GOD PROVIDES FOOD (Exodus 16:6-18)

A short time has passed since the children of Israel walked through the parted waters of the Red Sea. Their faith was experientially strengthened by this incredible miracle, and as a result Exodus 14:31 says they begin to trust both God and Moses. This trust erupts into a song that comprises most of chapter 15. But the joy that filled their hearts as a result of the destruction of Pharaoh and his army is soon to vanish, as they fail to find water. When God solves that problem, the obvious next one is food. Since like a little child Israel has never had to take care of herself, God proves Himself to be *Jehovah Jireh*—the Lord who provides—in order to teach them total dependency on Him.

A. God Hears Israel's Grumbling (vv. 6-12)

(Exodus 16:6-9 is not included in the printed text.)

10. And it came to pass, as Aaron spake unto the whole congregation of the children of Israel, that they looked toward the wilderness, and, behold, the glory of the Lord appeared in the cloud.

11. And the Lord spake unto Moses, saying,

12. I have heard the murmurings of the children of Israel: speak unto them, saying, At even ye shall eat flesh, and in the morning ye shall be filled with bread; and ye shall know that I am the Lord your God.

Replenished by their stay in Elim, where fresh water springs quenched their thirst and gave them strength (15:27), the Israelites restart their desert trek about a month after leaving Egypt. However, they have had little to eat in this month, and the euphoria of freedom is quickly wearing off, giving way to the pangs of physical hunger. As a result, they blame Moses and Aaron. After all, these leaders are the ones ultimately responsible for the success or failure of the whole venture. Should the nation be allowed to starve, the story will end as a tragedy, not as an expression of God's transcendent power.

Moses is just as helpless as everyone else until God gives him instructions. In what will be a pattern in their life together, Moses simply passes on these divine directions, adding his own commentary as he sees it necessary. But Moses' and Aaron's message to the Israelites in verses 6-8 comes out more like a violent scolding. In a word, they are sick to death of the people's grumbling. The Hebrew word for *grumbling/murmuring* indicates the Israelites were obstinate; they were persistent in their complaining.

The problem of grumbling is also seen in the New Testament. The crowds and disciples frequently grumbled about the words and behavior of Jesus. The early church encountered its first internal problem when the Grecian Jews complained that their

Talk About It:
1. What did the Israelites still not fully comprehend (v. 6)?
2. What were their "murmurings" (v. 7) about (see v. 3)?
3. What did Moses say the people were really doing (v. 8)?
4. What did God promise to do (v. 12)?

widows were not receiving the proper distribution of charitable food (Acts 6:1). Paul made reference to the Exodus story and offered, along with James, this basic commandment to the early church: "Do not grumble" (1 Corinthians 10:10; James 5:9, *NIV*). In a sense, the sin of Israel that receives the harshest judgment throughout the pages of Scripture is this murmuring.

Moses' first instruction to the people has a tone of sheer anger. He and Aaron get God's point across, but not without coming off as vindictive. In Exodus 16:10, as Aaron tells the people to come near the Lord because He has heard their murmurings, the glory of the Lord appears. Whether to comfort Moses, to correct Israel, or simply to show everyone there who was still in charge, the glory of Yahweh somehow appears in the cloud which the nation is following, and Moses receives God's word a second time.

Verse 11—"The Lord said to Moses" (*NIV*)—is among the shortest in the Bible. Of course, these pages were not originally written with verses, and we don't know why a later editor placed them as such. But it seems quite fitting here, given the need Moses had for encouragement and reassurance from God. The message is not new information at all. It is simply a more succinct version of what God has already told Moses in verses 4 and 5. Nonetheless, it likely calms Moses' disheveled soul, and apparently he carries through with the Lord's instruction to give the Israelites the second message, without inserting his personal frustration.

B. God Provides an Unknown Food (vv. 13-16)

13. And it came to pass, that at even the quails came up, and covered the camp: and in the morning the dew lay round about the host.

14. And when the dew that lay was gone up, behold, upon the face of the wilderness there lay a small round thing, as small as the hoar frost on the ground.

15. And when the children of Israel saw it, they said one to another, It is manna: for they wist not what it was. And Moses said unto them, This is the bread which the Lord hath given you to eat.

16. This is the thing which the Lord hath commanded, Gather of it every man according to his eating, an omer for every man, according to the number of your persons; take ye every man for them which are in his tents.

Moses is in need of another show of divine favor that reminds everyone he is still God's chosen leader. It is disheartening that such signs are necessary, for the Israelites have already seen so many wonders. After all, this is the man who championed their cause in Egypt and led them out among

---

"If the men of our time had their way, God would be on the carpet all the time offering soothing explanations to angry questions."
—Walter Farrell

hoar—v. 14—frost

omer—v. 16—about two quarts

Talk About It:
1. Describe the miraculous provision seen in verses 13 and 14.
2. What was the heaven-sent food called, and why (v. 15)?

God Provides for His People

incredible miracles. Yet they are still taking baby steps in their new identity as an independent nation, so God continues to publicly support their leader. God doesn't simply send manna. He certainly could have, but He chooses to make Moses His instrument to first let the Israelites know He will be sending them food. The integral use of Moses serves to keep him continually before the people as their God-ordained leader.

"In the morning there was a layer of dew around the camp. When the dew was gone, thin flakes like frost appeared on the ground" (vv. 13, 14, *NIV*). Dew in itself would be quite a wonder in such a desert region. But it was the flaky residue left behind that was even more amazing. One can imagine the anticipation of the Israelites during this time. Moses had told them that God was about to miraculously provide both bread and meat. Instead, they found these small, quaint chips on the ground. They had never seen anything quite like this before, so they said to themselves what anyone would say: "What is it?" The Hebrew word for this question is *man*, so the name sticks in its noun form—*manna*.

Before the Jews began snatching up the manna, Moses gave the specific instructions of the Lord. They were to take as much as they needed; however, the Lord had prescribed that need as an *omer* per person and no more. An *omer* was a Hebrew amount of measurement weighing about 10 percent of an *ephah*. Each person was to pick up enough manna to fill what amounts to our contemporary 2-liter bottle.

C. God Measures the Manna (vv. 17, 18)

17. And the children of Israel did so, and gathered, some more, some less.

18. And when they did mete it with an omer, he that gathered much had nothing over, and he that gathered little had no lack; they gathered every man according to his eating.

mete—v. 18—measured

First, the writer tells us that the people followed Moses' instructions perfectly and everything was fine. "The Israelites did as they were told" (v. 17, *NIV*). It looked like a huge win for Moses. When the people needed water, God provided through His servant Moses. Now the same pattern was followed with regard to the people's food. Everything happened just as Moses said it would, and the people were filled and content. Next, however, he commanded them to refrain from keeping any of the manna overnight. No sooner did the words come out of his mouth before some of the people ran back to their tents to stow manna away, thus bringing an infestation of smelly maggots into the camp (v. 20). So the cycle continued, with Moses battling for his leadership to be obeyed.

No More Fog

The captain of a ship transporting the great English preacher George Mueller tells the story of a terrible fog that halted their progress. Afraid he might be late for his meeting in Canada, Mueller brought the captain into the hull of the ship to pray. The captain was incredulous, telling Mueller they could never make it in time. After a simple, perhaps two-sentence prayer, Mueller told the captain to ready the ship for immediate departure. When they went out on the deck, the fog had lifted.

"Is there any greater need today than that we get to grips with the living God, that we understand the discipline of God, that we learn the truth of God, that we accept the will of

Through all of this, we're given a beautiful scene of God holding the hand of His fledgling people like a child. He could have saved everyone a lot of work by providing a larger portion of food all at once. Instead, the Israelites had to faithfully arise each morning to pick up just enough manna for the day. In this way they learned to depend on God for their daily bread, not just for the "larger" miracles of spectacular deliverance. The God who parted the Red Sea was also the One who placed tiny flakes in the morning dew.

II. GOD PROVIDES WATER (Exodus 17:1-7)

The conflict between Moses and the people he is leading just keeps on coming. Like waves in the ocean, the minute one problem ends, a new one begins. There seems to be no rest for the great liberator, who must feel as though he is aging with each passing day. After being disobeyed by those who kept their manna overnight, thus risking disease in the camp, he is again defied by those who break the Lord's command by exiting their tents on the Sabbath in order to search for more manna (16:25-27). These problems could have turned Moses' eyes off the great miracle of God's provision, but he does not let them detract from its significance. In fact, he commemorates God's work by storing some of the manna in a jar to be passed onto future generations, so that no one will forget Jehovah Jireh (vv. 32-34). This decision also foreshadows a coming day when the manna will cease—when Israel will be mature enough to stand on her own two feet. Yet for Moses, that day will be a long time away.

A. Further Conflict With Moses (vv. 1-4)

wilderness of Sin (v. 1)—desert land between Elim and Sinai

Rephidim (REF-uh-dim)—v. 1—a place in the desert where the Israelites had hoped to find water

1. And all the congregation of the children of Israel journeyed from the wilderness of Sin, after their journeys, according to the commandment of the Lord, and pitched in Rephidim: and there was no water for the people to drink.

2. Wherefore the people did chide with Moses, and said, Give us water that we may drink. And Moses said unto them, Why chide ye with me? wherefore do ye tempt the Lord?

3. And the people thirsted there for water; and the people murmured against Moses, and said, Wherefore is this that thou hast brought us up out of Egypt, to kill us and our children and our cattle with thirst?

4. And Moses cried unto the Lord, saying, What shall I do unto this people? they be almost ready to stone me.

Although the manna appeared each morning, regardless of where the Israelites stopped on their journey, water was tougher to come by. They depended on finding the occasional oasis in the desert. After setting out from the region of Sin, however, they found no water anywhere. Once again, their parched tongues turned into weapons to attack Moses. This time, rather than grumbling, the Scripture says they "quarreled" (v. 2, NIV) with their leader. The Hebrew word here is riv; it refers to a struggle, striving or controversy. It is a more active word than murmur, in that now the Israelites were blatantly opposing Moses to his face, making bold demands for water.

The Israelites appeared to be approaching Moses as if the miracles he did with the staff of God were under his own power. Recall that Moses threw a piece of wood into the bitter water of Marah, making it drinkable (15:23-25), three days after their march through the Red Sea, and apparently the Israelites thought Moses could and should do such things on demand. His response was telling: they were not opposing his power, but God's (17:2). Then the grumbling started again, and Moses cried out to the Lord in exasperation. Moses feared for his life at the whim of this temperamental people.

Talk About It:
1. What does it mean to "tempt the Lord" (v. 2)?
2. When a need arose, what pattern did the Israelites fall back into and why?

"It is more dangerous to trifle with God than to bare your chest to a blizzard, or play with a rattlesnake."
—**Wilbur Nelson**

B. Another Answer From God (vv. 5-7)

5. And the Lord said unto Moses, Go on before the people, and take with thee of the elders of Israel; and thy rod, wherewith thou smotest the river, take in thine hand, and go.

6. Behold, I will stand before thee there upon the rock in Horeb; and thou shalt smite the rock, and there shall come water out of it, that the people may drink. And Moses did so in the sight of the elders of Israel.

7. And he called the name of the place Massah, and Meribah, because of the chiding of the children of Israel, and because they tempted the Lord, saying, Is the Lord among us, or not?

At this point, God was specific with His instruction to Moses. The leader was more stressed than he ever had been, afraid that he might suffer violence at the hands of an angry mob. Therefore, God surrounded him with others to encourage him and strengthen his resolve. The Lord said, "Walk on ahead of the people. Take with you some of the elders of Israel" (v. 5, NIV).

Moses had been busying himself in the center of the people's strife. That was not the proper place for him. He should be at the forefront of the people, so God commanded him to move to that place of leadership. Equally important, Moses had faced this latest challenge alone. There is not even a mention of Aaron in the passage, unlike chapter 16, where Moses and Aaron faced the problem of food side by side. Therefore, God commanded Moses to take some of Israel's respected elders with him. The people needed to see they were not just rebelling against Moses, but they were rebelling against the seasoned God-followers of Israel—those who had suffered the brutal treatment at the hands

Massah and Meribah (v. 7)— two names for the same place, with *Massah* meaning "temptation" and *Meribah* meaning "contention"

Talk About It:
1. Why did the Lord have elders accompany Moses to the rock?
2. What question were the Israelites asking (v. 7)?

of the Egyptians alongside them. When they saw these old soldiers rally around Moses, they would be more inclined to do the same. But this wasn't all. Like a soldier puts his trust in a proven, battle-ready weapon, Moses again reached for the staff of God—the symbol of God's calling and power on his life. God reminded him it was the same staff that worked the initial wonders back in Egypt, and Moses could still trust God with the same ardor now. He would prove it with a miracle.

With the elders perhaps standing close enough to feel the stirring of air as Moses swung his stick, he did something that must have made him look crazy at first. We do not know how quickly the water came or whether Moses had to hit the rock more than once. We do know he had great faith in God's word to do something so odd. Water does not flow from rocks, of course. But this time Moses brought the elders in on the action to witness firsthand God's provision. God helped Moses get intentional about bringing a team around him—a lesson Moses had a hard time learning. After the miracle, Moses gave the place two names, not for remembering God's provision of water, but because of the Israelites' obsessive quarreling and testing. *Massah* means "testing," and *Meribah* means "quarreling." Had the water not come just in time, Moses might not have survived.

> "Leadership is a matter of having people look at you and gain confidence, seeing how you react. If you're in control, they're in control."
> —**Tom Landry**

III. GOD PROVIDES VICTORY (Exodus 17:8-16)

At this point in the Book of Exodus, Israel has faced numerous challenges, some of which have seemed insurmountable. The largest, of course, was Egypt in all her strength and power, but there have been many others along the way. Finding the basic necessities of food, water and shelter has been a dilemma. Getting along with their leadership has caused problems at every turn. Yet a new challenge breaks out right after their thirst is quenched by water from the rock. It is a challenge they will face dozens of times if they are to successfully make it into the Promised Land. It is the challenge of a hostile neighbor with a trained fighting force.

A. A New Partnership (vv. 8-13)

8. Then came Amalek, and fought with Israel in Rephidim.

9. And Moses said unto Joshua, Choose us out men, and go out, fight with Amalek: to morrow I will stand on the top of the hill with the rod of God in mine hand.

10. So Joshua did as Moses had said to him, and fought with Amalek: and Moses, Aaron, and Hur went up to the top of the hill.

11. And it came to pass, when Moses held up his hand, that Israel prevailed: and when he let down his hand, Amalek prevailed.

God Provides for His People

12. But Moses' hands were heavy; and they took a stone, and put it under him, and he sat thereon; and Aaron and Hur stayed up his hands, the one on the one side, and the other on the other side; and his hands were steady until the going down of the sun.

13. And Joshua discomfited Amalek and his people with the edge of the sword.

Around Rephidim, the peace of the Israelite camp was broken by an attack of the Amalekites. After all, the Israelites were carrying around the plunder of Egypt in broad daylight. From Deuteronomy 25:17-19, we learn that Amalek first attacked the stragglers at Israel's rear, harassing those too weak to defend themselves. Apparently they persisted in this and kept camping near Israel without attacking the main camp.

Moses knew his people must decisively retaliate to prevent further attack. Although they were not to be a people of vengeance, they could not stand back and be humiliated. If they do, they would not survive.

Once again, Moses turned to the staff and to his God to deliver them from this dangerous situation. He also empowered a new leader in Israel to select a viable fighting force. Finally, Moses was beginning to learn the important task of delegation. He could not do all the work himself. Yet he would be integrally involved in the next day's battle, surveying the scene and beseeching God for a favorable outcome. The battle would be twofold. Joshua would head up its military component, and Moses its spiritual component.

In addition to Joshua, a new partner was brought onto Moses' administrative team. If this man named Hur is the same one as in Exodus 31, he was a skilled craftsman who became responsible for overseeing the construction of the Tabernacle. The job of Hur and Aaron was more than symbolic. When Moses held his hands toward heaven, Joshua's army surged ahead. Aaron and Hur came alongside Moses to help him hold up his hands, and the Israelites were victorious. What a morale booster for Israel! They had been slaves all these years, and suddenly, with little to no training, God gave them a military victory.

B. A Curse on the Amalekites (vv. 14-16)

14. And the Lord said unto Moses, Write this for a memorial in a book, and rehearse it in the ears of Joshua: for I will utterly put out the remembrance of Amalek from under heaven.

15. And Moses built an altar, and called the name of it Jehovah-nissi:

16. For he said, Because the Lord hath sworn that the Lord will have war with Amalek from generation to generation.

The invasion of the Amalekites incensed and angered the

discomfited (v. 13)—overcame

Talk About It:
What was the significance of Moses' uplifted hands (v. 11)?

"The will to persevere is often the difference between failure and success."
—David Sarnoff

Jehovah-nissi (v. 15)—"The Lord is my banner."

Talk About It:
1. What prophetic message was written down, and why (v. 14)?
2. What does it mean for God to be *Jehovah-nissi* (our banner)?

heart of Yahweh. They attempted unprovoked to destroy His people, so God demanded that a proclamation be written down. Even Joshua should hear what God had to say, as he would be ultimately responsible for carrying out this word from God. Also, Moses built an altar and was moved toward a new designation for God's character—*Jehovah Nissi*. *Nissi* refers to a banner, the type which might be carried before an army to signal war. Such wars were bound to continue with the Amalekites until they were completely defeated; for this grievous sin would not be forgotten by God.

It was many generations before Israel completed the destruction of the Amalekites. It was almost completed in the days of Saul (1 Samuel 15), continued under David (27:8, 9; 30:1-20), and apparently finished in Hezekiah's day (1 Chronicles 4:41-43).

CONCLUSION

It is clear that during their journey in the wilderness the Israelites simply did not understand much about the character of their God. They knew Him as a God of power and authority because of their deliverance from Egypt, but they had difficulty knowing Him as a God of detailed provision. He had to continually teach them this truth through the provision of water, food, administrative leadership and military strength. Only as the Israelites learned to trust His unfailing provision would their mission to take the Promised Land be ultimately successful.

GOLDEN TEXT CHALLENGE

"MY GOD SHALL SUPPLY ALL YOUR NEED ACCORDING TO HIS RICHES IN GLORY BY CHRIST JESUS" (Philippians 4:19).

The Christians in Philippi had been generous to the apostle Paul and his ministry. Even in "the early days of [their] acquaintance with the gospel" (v. 15, *NIV*), they supported Paul financially when no other church did so. "Again and again" they had ministered to Paul's needs (v. 16). In verse 18 he thanks them for their most recent gifts, which he calls "sweet . . . acceptable, wellpleasing to God." Their generosity was not overlooked by God, who would credit it to their "account" (v. 17).

So in our Golden Text, Paul pronounces a blessing on the Philippians. He declares that God will meet their needs, drawing from the "glorious riches" (*NIV*) Christ Jesus has in His account. The Philippians had not been *giving to get*, yet Paul assured them that God saw their generosity and would supply their every need.

Daily Devotions:
M. The Lord Will Provide
Genesis 22:6-14
T. Miraculous Provision
2 Kings 4:1-7
W. Remember God's Provision
Psalm 78:9-16
T. Seek God's Kingdom First
Matthew 6:25-34
F. Christ Provides for the Multitude
Matthew 14:13-21
S. God Supplies Our Needs
Philippians 4:10-19

God Provides Structure for Success

Exodus 18:1-27

INTRODUCTION

One of the greatest dangers Moses faced was the temptation to become a one-man show. The shepherd who begged God to choose someone else for his role became the unmistakable leader of a massive nation, and their quick descent from Egypt left no time to put administrative structures in place. Remember, all the Israelites knew of government was the Egyptian monarchy. Therefore, it was natural that Moses unintentionally would slide into that role. However, it would not work over the long term.

The amazing thing about the character of Moses is that, with all of this power consolidated into his position, he never became prideful. He was driven by the pure purpose of serving God and His people. He could have stifled the grumbling in the camp by executing those stirring up the crowds against him, but this did not appear to cross his mind. Though he did get frustrated and exhausted by the difficult task of leadership, he refused to become a harsh dictator. One can see why he was called "more humble than anyone else on the face of the earth" (Numbers 12:3, *NIV*). He was an extraordinary man.

Although we may try to divide God's work between what is "spiritual" and what is "practical," Scripture makes no such distinction. Building proper and effective structures that channel the work of God in appropriate directions is spiritual work. In the New Testament, this is accomplished through the distribution of spiritual gifts. There, gifts of administration and servanthood stand side by side those of miracles and prophecy. Without the vital structures that keep the people of God moving forward, other aspects of God's kingdom will never even be tapped.

These structures usually originate when a leader learns to listen to the wise counsel of others. In fact, perhaps the most powerful leader of the Old Testament, King Solomon, constantly praised the desire for wise counsel in his proverbs. As Moses learned this important discipline, an effective government was formed in Israel, thus bringing her one step closer to the identity God planned for her.

Unit Theme:
God's Deliverance and Provision (Exodus)

Central Truth:
God gives success to those who heed His counsel.

Focus:
Affirm that God wills success and effectiveness for His people and embrace His plans.

Context:
In the land of Horeb, God enables Moses to survive a leadership crisis.

Golden Text:
"Trust in the Lord with all thine heart; and lean not unto thine own understanding. In all thy ways acknowledge him, and he shall direct thy paths" (Proverbs 3:5, 6).

Study Outline:
I. Begin With Reflection and Praise (Exodus 18:1-12)
II. Recognize Human Limitations (Exodus 18:13-18)
III. Heed Godly Counsel (Exodus 18:19-27)

I. BEGIN WITH REFLECTION AND PRAISE (Exodus 18:1-12)

Exhilarated and exhausted by the military defeat over the Amalekites, it is time for Moses and Israel to regroup. This will ultimately involve the practical retooling of Moses' command structure, but there are some steps that must be taken first to get there. A period of reflection and praise allows Israel's leadership some downtime to recall what God has done, which calms their frenetic pace long enough to get them thinking about how to lead the nation better. This begins with Moses' glad reunion with his family.

A. Jethro Visits Moses (vv. 1-8)

(Exodus 18:1-4 is not included in the printed text.)

5. And Jethro, Moses' father in law, came with his sons and his wife unto Moses into the wilderness, where he encamped at the mount of God:

6. And he said unto Moses, I thy father in law Jethro am come unto thee, and thy wife, and her two sons with her.

7. And Moses went out to meet his father in law, and did obeisance, and kissed him; and they asked each other of their welfare; and they came into the tent.

8. And Moses told his father in law all that the Lord had done unto Pharaoh and to the Egyptians for Israel's sake, and all the travail that had come upon them by the way, and how the Lord delivered them.

Jethro finally reentered Moses' life after a long hiatus. It had been many months since Moses originally left the peace of his father-in-law's household to pursue God's wild mission to free Israel, but Jethro had been following their progress as best he could from Midian. Undoubtedly everyone in the land was talking about these things, and there was probably significant economic disruption due to the sudden fall of a great world power. Accompanying Jethro was Moses' wife, Zipporah, and their two sons. Before now, there had been no direct clue in the narrative to cue us to the fact that Moses had been separated from his family all this time. We know from Exodus 4:20 that they made the initial journey to Egypt with him. Perhaps Zipporah went away after a crisis involving the circumcision of one of their sons (vv. 24-26). Or perhaps Moses sent them away because he knew their lives could be threatened when things heated up in Egypt. Maybe Zipporah left when the plagues started. Whatever the reason for the separation, the family was now reunited. Remember that Moses' affection for his father-in-law was fervent; the man saved his life and brought him into his family after he fled from Egypt. Moses expressed his respect for Jethro by bowing down face-first on the ground; kissing him; and then the two exchanged a ceremonial greeting before entering into the

---

Gershom (GUR-shum)—v. 3— Moses' first son, his name means "sojourner."

Eliezer (el-ih-EE-zur)—v. 4—Moses' second son, his name means "God of help."

Talk About It:
1. How do you suppose Jethro had "heard of everything God had done for Moses" (v. 1, *NIV*)?
2. What do verses 7 and 8 reveal about Moses' relationship with his father-in-law?

Upright Heads
A proud lawyer once asked a successful farmer, "Why don't you

---

God Provides Structure for Success

tent together. There, they caught up on all that Moses had experienced. It must have been a dizzying amount of information.

Finally, Moses was receiving a break from the demands of leadership. He got a chance to say whatever his heart needed to say to someone he was not responsible to lead. At last he had a friend with whom he could speak unhindered. He could tell him not only about the good times but the bad times. He could vent his frustrations. With this welcomed reprieve, Moses gave him the entire story, not only the great things God had done but also the terrible times of hardship he had encountered. Things had changed in huge proportions since he used to tend Jethro's sheep. Israelites were a lot harder to tend.

B. Jethro Exalts the Lord (vv. 9-12)

9. And Jethro rejoiced for all the goodness which the Lord had done to Israel, whom he had delivered out of the hand of the Egyptians.

10. And Jethro said, Blessed be the Lord, who hath delivered you out of the hand of the Egyptians, and out of the hand of Pharaoh, who hath delivered the people from under the hand of the Egyptians.

11. Now I know that the Lord is greater than all gods: for in the thing wherein they dealt proudly he was above them.

12. And Jethro, Moses' father in law, took a burnt-offering and sacrifices for God: and Aaron came, and all the elders of Israel, to eat bread with Moses' father in law before God.

Although Jethro had heard of some of Israel's exploits, he could hardly believe his ears as Moses recounted miracle after miracle. All that he had heard was true, and then some! There were the plagues in Egypt, the parting of the Red Sea, the water from the rock, and perhaps they munched on some miraculous manna leftover from that morning. When Jethro had heard all of the stories, he resounded in praise to God. In a ceremonial blessing, much like we might hear from Middle Easterners today, Jethro summarized the acts of God and praised Yahweh for them.

Verse 11 is curious—only "now" did Jethro recognize the power of Yahweh over and against all other gods. When we first met Jethro, we saw he was a priest (3:1), but we do not know for which god he performed his priestly duties. Notice that he did not proclaim that Yahweh is the only God and all others are only statues, but that Yahweh is greater than other gods.

In response to Yahweh's amazing acts in the midst of Israel, Jethro offered multiple sacrifices, solidifying his household's alignment with Yahweh. He would worship no other gods anymore. As

Talk About It:
1. What did Israel's deliverance from Egypt reveal about the Lord (v. 11)?
2. How did Jethro express his faith in the Lord (vv. 9, 10, 12)?

was customary after a sacrifice, a meal ensued with Israel's elders. Sacrifices were not only for the purpose of worship, but also fellowship, since to share the meal table with another was a sacred act of unity. What a joyous and replenishing meal this must have been for the weary Israelite leaders.

II. RECOGNIZE HUMAN LIMITATIONS (Exodus 18:13-18)

The refreshing meeting with Jethro should have clued Moses in to his own limitations. After all, he is exhausted. The work and the frustrations never stop. The challenge seems to grow more and more difficult with the fickle Israelites. But Moses has yet to recognize his physical, emotional and spiritual boundaries as a human leader. Though empowered by God, he is still human and must operate physically as such. Fortunately, Jethro's visit will continue to minister to Moses' situation. Ironically, it takes a Midianite to help the Israelites form an effective judicial system.

A. Loving Rebuke (vv. 13, 14)

13. And it came to pass on the morrow, that Moses sat to judge the people: and the people stood by Moses from the morning unto the evening.

14. And when Moses' father in law saw all that he did to the people, he said, What is this thing that thou doest to the people? why sittest thou thyself alone, and all the people stand by thee from morning unto even?

Talk About It:
Describe a typical day in Moses' life, as seen in verse 13.

Although giving him a short time of rest, Moses' meeting with Jethro fails to change his perspective on leadership. The next morning he resumes his place at the national tribunal, and there he sits all day long. Case after case is brought before him. He alone is the national supreme court. One person claims his neighbor stole some of his livestock. Another claims his enemy attacked him violently. Another claims her manna keeps mysteriously disappearing and suspects an estranged family member. In modern courts, judges take frequent breaks. Such is the mental stress of listening to detailed arguments all day long. Moses gets no break, acting as an arbitrator between squabbling Israelites from dawn until dusk.

Jethro cannot believe his eyes. With Moses tied to the judge's seat, important administrative duties are being left undone. The work of judging every squabble is unsuited to the nation's leader, and after a long day of judging, Jethro rebukes Moses' actions. He should not be the only judge for some 2 million Israelites. That kind of workload is bound to incapacitate the nation and eventually Moses himself. Neither is being served by the arrangement.

B. Answer and Advice (vv. 15-18)

15. And Moses said unto his father in law, Because the people come unto me to enquire of God:

Always Working
A first grader became curious because her father brought home a briefcase full of papers every evening. Her mother explained, "Daddy has so much to do that he can't finish it all at the office. That's why he has to bring work home at night." "Well then," asked the child innocently, "why don't they put him in a slower group?"
—Charles Swindoll (*Growing Strong*)

16. When they have a matter, they come unto me; and I judge between one and another, and I do make them know the statutes of God, and his laws.

17. And Moses' father in law said unto him, The thing that thou doest is not good.

18. Thou wilt surely wear away, both thou, and this people that is with thee: for this thing is too heavy for thee; thou art not able to perform it thyself alone.

Without a written law, Moses is the only expert when it comes to Yahweh's decrees. Therefore, Moses sees himself as the only person able to properly discern God's will. This may seem arrogant, but not even the Ten Commandments have been given yet. It is a difficult task to hash out the complexities of law when so many subjective judgment calls need to be made. Moses is probably the only one trusted to make those calls, or at least the only one with the charismatic authority to enforce them. So everything goes to and through him. Jethro, however, sees no excuse for this arrangement. Moses is unnecessarily punishing both himself and Israel.

As a wealthy householder who is used to administrating multiple employees and various branches of agricultural business, Jethro quickly and easily discerns Moses' folly. This practice is good for nobody. It will "wear away" not only Moses but also those seeking to know the Lord's will. The Hebrew word translated as "wear away" is *nabal*, and this is its only appearance in the Book of Exodus. Its next use is by Moses himself in Deuteronomy 32:6, where it has the connotation of foolishness. It is elsewhere used to describe leaves that droop and fall off of trees. Jethro essentially tells Moses that this administrative structure is foolish, as it will eventually waste him away. He cannot isolate himself and try to do everything on his own.

Jesus later says that the heart of God longs to leave the 99 sheep to search for the one (Luke 15:4-7). We are to do the same. However, this is different from sacrificing the 99 sheep for the one. Moses risks doing just this with his micro-managing style of leadership. It is time for him to think larger.

III. HEED GODLY COUNSEL (Exodus 18:19-27)

Moses stands at a critical juncture, both in his leadership over Israel and in his relationship with his father-in-law. After all, the Midianite has been rather presumptuous to rebuke the esteemed leader of Israel. This is the same leader who, by the power of God, has brought the children of Israel out of Egypt; surely that is good for something! Moses' character, however, is being tested, and it will shine forth in its spiritual maturity.

Talk About It:
1. Why did Moses think he had to be Israel's sole judge?
2. What warning did Jethro give Moses?

"Don't tell me how hard you work. Tell me how much you get done."
—**James Ling**

19. Hearken now unto my voice, I will give thee counsel, and God shall be with thee: Be thou for the people to God-ward, that thou mayest bring the causes unto God:

20. And thou shalt teach them ordinances and laws, and shalt shew them the way wherein they must walk, and the work that they must do.

Talk About It:
What role should Moses fill for the Israelites, according to Jethro (vv. 19, 20)?

While the narrative presents Jethro as the person of greater wisdom—the man who seems to have all the answers—we also see him exercise great tact in his communication with Moses, respecting his revered position.

Jethro honors both Moses' ability to choose and his calling to function as the nation's chief leader. He tells Moses exactly what he should do without pulling any punches—Jethro will offer some advice. After that, it is between Moses and God to decide what to do with it. Jethro will not press the issue another inch.

"I not only use all the brains I have but all I can borrow."
—Woodrow Wilson

His first piece of advice is affirming to Moses. Moses' heart is right to recognize that he is the people's representative before God, and this involves the alleviation of disputes among other things. Furthermore, Moses' position involves teaching and interpreting the decrees and laws of God, so that they may be applied to specific situations. Jethro basically repeats back Moses' first answer to him, stating that he is right about the heart of the matter. However, Jethro has a much more effective plan for getting the job done.

B. Jethro's Plan (vv. 21-23)

21. Moreover thou shalt provide out of all the people able men, such as fear God, men of truth, hating covetousness; and place such over them, to be rulers of thousands, and rulers of hundreds, rulers of fifties, and rulers of tens:

22. And let them judge the people at all seasons: and it shall be, that every great matter they shall bring unto thee, but every small matter they shall judge: so shall it be easier for thyself, and they shall bear the burden with thee.

23. If thou shalt do this thing, and God command thee so, then thou shalt be able to endure, and all this people shall also go to their place in peace.

Talk About It:
1. What kind of men did Jethro say Moses should choose to help him (v. 21)?

According to Jethro, Moses has simply underestimated the caliber of leadership that exists in Israel. Sure they had been slaves for generations, but this does not mean they are all incompetent. In fact, with 2 million slaves it is likely that the Egyptians used many of them as leaders and foremen, entrusting them with responsibilities. Ancient slavery was quite different than the later form of slavery in the Americas, in that slaves then could sometimes enjoy higher status if they proved themselves competent administrators. Jethro has hung around in the camp long enough to see capable men everywhere, and he tells Moses so.

Moses is apparently guilty of tunnel vision. Caught up in the rigors of governing day to day, he tended toward isolating himself in the midst of the stress. Although he shows no signs of developing a self-centered messiah complex, perhaps Jethro knows that this is inevitably the next step of such behavior. Therefore, he gives a detailed plan for installing a hierarchy of officials over various segments of the population. They will judge disputes straightway up the chain. That is, if an official over 10s hears a difficult case, he can refer it to the official above him over 50s, and so on. If necessary, the case could then go to a judge over 100s, and then a judge over 1,000s. That way, Moses will only be responsible for hearing the most difficult cases requiring his personal expertise in God's decrees. Of course, all of this will be made much easier with the subsequent giving of the Law, but that remains to occur.

Jethro lays out a win-win situation, but it will still take the command of God to put it into effect. Although the scheme may be well devised by human standards, it will be useless without God's approval. If after conversing with God, Moses finds divine endorsement, everyone will win. The *New International Version* reads that Moses "will be able to stand the strain" (v. 23). It can also be interpreted "endure," but perhaps Jethro is simply referring to Moses' habit of literally sitting in the tribunal seat all day long. Instead of that, he'll be able to stand up and work on other aspects of the new government. In addition, the people will leave the judge's seat satisfied. The Hebrew word here is *shalom*, which is one of the most important concepts in the Old Testament language. It refers to a lifestyle of peace, well-being, wholeness and completeness. This is how the Israelites will feel when they leave the judge's court, rather than the frustration caused when Moses tried to do everything himself.

C. Moses' Humility (vv. 24-27)
(Exodus 18:27 is not included in the printed text.)

24. So Moses hearkened to the voice of his father in law, and did all that he had said.

25. And Moses chose able men out of all Israel, and made them heads over the people, rulers of thousands, rulers of hundreds, rulers of fifties, and rulers of tens.

26. And they judged the people at all seasons: the hard causes they brought unto Moses, but every small matter they judged themselves.

There is no record that Jethro had ever administrated a huge enterprise. There is no reason to believe that Jethro had ever

2. Explain the phrase "if . . . God command thee so" (v. 23).

Vision and Structure
In the 1988 United States presidential campaign, governor Michael Dukakis declared, "This election isn't about ideology. It's about competence." Although he lost that election, his point is important. Just because a leader is morally right doesn't mean he or she is disciplined enough to reach stated objectives. God's people must not only have a divine vision, but also the structure to see the vision come to pass.

seen a burning bush or any other miracle of Yahweh. So Moses stands at a critical juncture. As the leader of Israel, he can ignore the advice of his father-in-law. But instead, Moses "listened to his father-in-law and did everything he said" (v. 24, *NIV*).

What humility resided in the heart of Israel's leader! As the story of Exodus continues, we see more clearly why God called Moses to lead the children of Israel not when Moses was young and strong, but when he was an experienced shepherd who wanted nothing to do with leadership. God needed someone without a big ego, and here Moses exemplified his humility again, by first simply listening to his father-in-law. Moses did not have to listen. He was a busy, powerful man. Yet he carefully listened to everything Jethro had to say, and it all sounded right to him, so he followed his advice.

Moses executed the plan exactly as Jethro gave it to him, installing four levels of officials to serve as judges six days per week. Moses functioned as the chief justice, hearing any cases that were too difficult for the lower magistrates. We are not given the nature of these complex cases, but they could have involved many of the things in our courts today. Just because the Israelites were moving from place to place does not mean that normal life was prevented. They went about their everyday business of raising livestock, marrying off their sons and daughters, engaging in business transactions, and living their lives. Also, like any other nation, Israel was not devoid of thieves, criminals, adulterers and murderers. Presumably, the courts also dealt with those guilty of such crimes.

In the end, Jethro returned to his own country an unlikely and unknown hero of the Israelite people. In all likelihood, not many people recognized him as the one putting the structures in place that would allow the nation and its leadership to properly function for four decades in the wilderness, and beyond that in their settlement of the Promised Land. Equally impressive was Moses' political savvy to know a good idea when he heard it. The narrative continually lets us know that despite the difficult challenges Moses faced, he was still God's man; for his heart was humble toward God and toward Israel.

> "My best friend is the one who brings out the best in me."
> —**Henry Ford**

CONCLUSION

The story of Exodus is a story of tremendous success. God gave Moses an incredible vision for a free nation that would serve God alone, and this vision slowly came to pass. Wise administrative structures helped bring it to life, as evidenced in chapter 18. Without the nitty-gritty tools of solid government, Israel probably would have never made it to the Promised Land. But with a listening leader who was not afraid to take risks, Israel steadily moved down the path God laid out for her.

GOLDEN TEXT CHALLENGE

"TRUST IN THE LORD WITH ALL THINE HEART; AND LEAN NOT UNTO THINE OWN UNDERSTANDING. IN ALL THY WAYS ACKNOWLEDGE HIM, AND HE SHALL DIRECT THY PATHS" (Proverbs 3:5, 6).

The word *trust* implies a decisive act that will affect our outward actions by changing our motives. The heart is the seat of all of our fear, our consciousness and unconsciousness; and it must be turned toward the Lord.

So trust is an act—a responsible action. And responsible behavior is the root, not the result, of happiness.

"Why not trust our own understanding?" someone may ask. The answer is that our reasoning is limited by our cultural and educational background. We tend to see things only in a subjective manner.

Others may ask, "What's in it for me? How does this affect *my* household? *my* city? *my* state? *my* politics?" In politics there is a term for this shortsightedness; it is called "pork barreling." The politician, at the expense of the entire country, often offers his particular district certain benefits.

The artist knows about this egotistical manner of people. He knows that when a person looks at a picture, he often places himself at the center of each painting. So, consistently, the middle portion of each canvas—often referred to as the "magic middle"—becomes the most important area to place something the artist wants to be readily seen or understood. The Christian learns to place God at the center of situations.

As we trust the Lord, He gives us the language of purpose. He gives us long-range stability. He gives us long-range viewpoints. He integrates our life with those around us for His glory, and He uses each for the benefit of all. So when we compare trusting our understanding with trusting in the Lord, we find that the Lord gives us stability in place of a life blown like chaff by every situation. The Lord gives us purpose instead of aimless wandering up blind alleys looking for answers. The Lord gives us a long-range viewpoint in lieu of a clouded eye which cannot decide why we are here, where we came from, or what our particular purpose is. The Lord integrates our lives—both within and without. Our own understanding leaves us at war with ourselves, with other people, and with the world in general.

Daily Devotions:
M. Prayer for Wisdom
1 Kings 3:6-14
T. Delight in the Lord
Psalm 37:1-6
W. Trust in the Lord
Proverbs 3:1-10
T. Structure for Service
Acts 6:1-8
F. Renewed for Effective Service
Romans 12:1-13
S. The Approved Worker
2 Timothy 2:14-26

God Hears Sincere Intercession

Exodus 32:1-35

Unit Theme:
God's Deliverance and Provision (Exodus)

Central Truth:
God will respond to our sincere intercession.

Focus:
Intercede for those who need it and believe God will answer.

Context:
Around 1440 B.C. near the foot of Mount Sinai

Golden Text:
"I exhort therefore, that, first of all, supplications, prayers, intercessions, and giving of thanks, be made for all men" (1 Timothy 2:1).

Study Outline:
I. Quick to Turn From God
   (Exodus 32:1-10)
II. Intercession for God's Mercy
   (Exodus 32:11-14)
III. God's Just Judgment
   (Exodus 32:29-35)

INTRODUCTION

One of the greatest theological debates throughout the history of the Protestant church is that between Calvinism and Arminianism. The former is identified with John Calvin (1509-1564), the Swiss reformer who possessed a high view of God's sovereignty along with a low view of human choice. For Calvin, texts such as Romans 9 were interpreted to mean that God's plan cannot be countered or swayed by individuals who play a predetermined part in that plan, which they have no choice over, including their individual salvation. Jacob Arminius (1560-1609), a professor at Leiden University in Holland, opposed this view and instead emphasized the free choice of humanity in the face of God's offering. For Arminius, Scripture clearly offers people a choice with which God will not interfere, and we are thus integrally involved in unfolding the plan of God through making decisions. The debate between Calvinism and Arminianism cuts to the heart of a Scriptural view of intercessory prayer, which is the focus of today's lesson.

For Calvin, prayer is an exercise that brings one into alignment with God. It is not an exercise of swaying God to act in a certain way, for His plans cannot be swayed. Although there are pieces of the truth in both Calvinism and Arminianism, when it comes to intercessory prayer, the Old Testament history records something far different from Calvin's view of prayer. Of course, prayer does bring us into alignment with God's plan, but Yahweh is also in a dynamic relationship with His people, and those people have a say in how their history plays out.

We see this demonstrated in the life of Abraham, Moses and eventually Jesus. The One who hung on the cross testified to His ability to call down 12 legions of angels to fight on His behalf (Matthew 26:53). That is, He recognized His choice to reject the cross. God would have let Him. But for our sake, He did not make that choice.

Understanding the free will God has given us not only makes the Scriptures exciting, but our lives as well. For through intercessory prayer we are not passive observers of God's plan, but dynamic participants.

I. QUICK TO TURN FROM GOD (Exodus 32:1-10)

The action sequence of the Exodus narrative now resumes after almost 11 chapters that recount the various laws Moses received on Mount Sinai. These laws include detailed regulations concerning slaves, injuries, property, festivals, Sabbath keeping, priestly garments, sacrifices and the construction of the Tabernacle. They begin, though, with the vital Ten Commandments. Ironically, while Moses is communing with God, the Israelites are breaking faith with Him. What is worse, Aaron is fully compliant in their awful rebellion.

A. The Golden Calf (vv. 1-6)

1. And when the people saw that Moses delayed to come down out of the mount, the people gathered themselves together unto Aaron, and said unto him, Up, make us gods, which shall go before us; for as for this Moses, the man that brought us up out of the land of Egypt, we wot not what is become of him.

2. And Aaron said unto them, Break off the golden earrings, which are in the ears of your wives, of your sons, and of your daughters, and bring them unto me.

3. And all the people brake off the golden earrings which were in their ears, and brought them unto Aaron.

4. And he received them at their hand, and fashioned it with a graving tool, after he had made it a molten calf: and they said, These be thy gods, O Israel, which brought thee up out of the land of Egypt.

5. And when Aaron saw it, he built an altar before it; and Aaron made proclamation, and said, To morrow is a feast to the Lord.

6. And they rose up early on the morrow, and offered burnt-offerings, and brought peace-offerings; and the people sat down to eat and to drink, and rose up to play.

The problem begins when Moses stays on Mount Sinai for a long time. We know from Exodus 24:18 that he has been there 40 days and nights, but presumably that is 40 days from that point only. He had already been there an indeterminate amount of time before this, so it may have amounted to many days or weeks beyond the 40 days, to several months in all. One thing is certain: it was enough time for the Jews to grow restless, nervous and rash. It also gave the dissenters an opportunity to vent their frustration with the absent leader. While they acknowledge Moses as the one responsible for liberating them from Egyptian slavery, they have lost hope. They do not know if he will ever come back, and Aaron is not a strong leader like Moses.

Whether it is out of fear or pride, we do not know. Perhaps

wot (v. 1)—know

play (v. 6)—indulge in lewd acts

Talk About It:
1. How did Moses' long absence affect the Israelites (v. 1)?
2. What purpose did the golden calf serve?
3. What was right about this "feast to the Lord" (v. 5)? What was wrong with it?

Aaron fears the angry mob that the people are quickly becoming. Perhaps he sees his chance to take over the reigns of Israel in the absence of Moses, supposing he can lead better. Perhaps he agrees with them that Moses may have disappeared forever and he is as nervous as anyone. Whatever the case, Aaron heads up the operation by taking a collection of the golden items that were recently plundered from Egypt. How ironic that the booty from Egypt moves the Israelites toward a new form of bondage.

The work of fashioning a metal idol was laborious. It involved heating the gold pieces until they reached liquid form, carefully pouring away any dross, and then slowly forming the quickly-hardening mass into a recognizable shape. Aaron chooses a calf, which was quite typical for idols then, because a calf was a symbol of agricultural fertility and thus wealth. Later on in Israel's history they will be tempted to worship Baal, who is represented as a bull. When Aaron's sculpture is complete, the people lift up a resounding cry, proclaiming the idol their almighty god. The Hebrew uses the plural "gods" (32:4), and this is noted in most English translations. Often in the Hebrew language, when referring to divine personages it is a sign of reverence and awe to use the plural. Therefore, since the Scripture records only one idol made, which was undoubtedly massive, the Hebrew plural is probably functioning in this manner.

When the cry goes up, Aaron again springs into action, building an altar and announcing a festival to Yahweh the next day. This shows that Aaron and the people are not seeking to turn away from Yahweh to a rival god, but to represent Yahweh in the bull itself. Their sin is not apostasy, but idol worship. In fact, they are breaking the second commandment that no images should be used to represent the Lord (20:4, 5)—breaking it just after Moses gave it to them. They don't want to worship an invisible God anymore, but one they can see—one that will make them look powerful and accepted among neighboring peoples. So they carry it out just as Aaron planned.

The horror of verse 6—"they sat down to eat and drink and got up to indulge in revelry" (32:6, *NIV*)—resonates into Christian history, as Paul quotes it to the Corinthians who were dabbling in all sorts of sinful things (1 Corinthians 10:7). The freed slaves paraded in front of the statue like a bunch of Egyptians and sacrificed their offerings to the golden bull, made out of their own jewelry. In fact, they had a full-blown pagan feast that day with all sorts of sexual immorality. But Yahweh was not far off. He sees the entire debacle.

"God made man of the dust of the earth and man makes a god of the dust of the earth."
—Thomas Watson

B. God's Imminent Judgment (vv. 7-10)

7. And the Lord said unto Moses, Go, get thee down;

for thy people, which thou broughtest out of the land of Egypt, have corrupted themselves:

8. They have turned aside quickly out of the way which I commanded them: they have made them a molten calf, and have worshipped it, and have sacrificed thereunto, and said, These be thy gods, O Israel, which have brought thee up out of the land of Egypt.

9. And the Lord said unto Moses, I have seen this people, and, behold, it is a stiffnecked people:

10. Now therefore let me alone, that my wrath may wax hot against them, and that I may consume them: and I will make of thee a great nation.

The narrative depicts God's omniscience—His "all-knowing-ness"—by recalling His conversation with Moses. In fact, God lets Moses in on all that His people have done in his absence. God calls the Jews "your people" (*NKJV*) as if disconnecting Himself from their actions. They are not acting like His people, but like poor humanity at its worst. The people have become "corrupt" (see v. 7). The Hebrew word here is used in the same form in Genesis 13:10 to describe the "destruction" of Sodom and Gomorrah. The people have committed an act worthy of their destruction by turning away from God's straightforward and essential commandment against graven images. What is worse, God breaks the heart of Moses by informing him that the Israelites have worshiped and sacrificed to the calf, declaring it the same God who led them from slavery.

Seeing Moses' despair, the Lord prepares to deal harshly with the rebellious Israelites. God's denunciation of the Israelites is emphatic in the literal Hebrew. After stating that He has "seen" these people in the deepest sense, the Hebrew adds an emphatic word, *hinah*, translated here as "behold" (Exodus 32:9). This word comes directly before God's characterization of them as "a stiffnecked people." This term brings three Hebrew words together and occurs throughout the Scriptures. Stephen even uses its Greek form in his denunciation of the Jews before his martyrdom (Acts 7:51). But the term shows up first in the Bible right here in the mouth of God.

What God proposes is nothing new. After the inhabitants of the earth became so corrupt that God could bear it no more, He wiped the slate clean in the days of Noah and started over. Perhaps it was time for Him to do the same with Israel—this obstinate people who didn't care to appreciate all that the Lord had done for them. Instead, they wanted the Lord to be just like the worthless fertility gods in Egypt. Of course, Yahweh will have none of that. He proposes that He will accomplish the great dream of a godly nation beginning with Moses alone. After all, this is the God who promised the same thing to

Talk About It:
1. What had the Israelites done "quickly" (v. 8; see 20:4)?
2. What plan did God present to Moses in verse 10?

The Golden Calf
From Sinai we
 have heard Thee
 speak,
And from mount
 Calv'ry too;
And yet to idols oft
 we seek,
While Thou art in
 our view.
Lord, save us from
 our golden calves,
Our sin with grief
 we own;
We would no more
 be Thine by
 halves,
But live to Thee
 alone.
 —John Newton

Abraham, and He could definitely do it again. Moses' measured response, moreover, has much to teach about the power of prayer.

II. INTERCESSION FOR GOD'S MERCY (Exodus 32:11-14)

There is no time to lose for Moses. On the one hand, the Israelites are indulging in every kind of revelry imaginable at the base of the mountain. The worship of the golden calf continues unimpeded. On the other, God has threatened to erase their memory from the face of the earth and to start the whole process over again. Moses' humble heart and quick thinking provides a pattern for intercessory prayer for God-followers throughout time.

A. Remember the Egyptians (vv. 11, 12)

11. And Moses besought the Lord his God, and said, Lord, why doth thy wrath wax hot against thy people, which thou hast brought forth out of the land of Egypt with great power, and with a mighty hand?

mischief (v. 12)—
"evil intent" (NIV)

12. Wherefore should the Egyptians speak, and say, For mischief did he bring them out, to slay them in the mountains, and to consume them from the face of the earth? Turn from thy fierce wrath, and repent of this evil against thy people.

Talk About It:
Explain how Moses could ask God to "repent" (v. 12).

This passage sounds strange, at best, to modern ears. Why would an all-knowing God propose such a drastic means of dealing with Israel's sin if He can be talked out of it? Two points here will navigate us through. First, the divine economy is very different from the human economy. God works in ways that the human mind at its best cannot always comprehend even in metaphor, and this may be one of those instances that will never make sense to the human perception. We have not been created with the intellect to grasp all eternal realities. Second, modern notions of God tend to be based on a later, Greek mind-set that considers God as a static character. That is, for many people God's perfection means He is a rather unemotional and unmoved being. This is simply not the God of the Scriptures. In the Ten Commandments, God has just proclaimed himself *Yahweh Kana*—"a jealous God" (20:5). The word denotes a God who is moved and full of vibrant passions. This should not lead us to believe God is impulsive or cruel, but that He is a dynamic being who is infinitely passionate about His character and emotional about His children.

Lotto Prayer?
In April 2004, a woman winning a $2.4-million casino jackpot said the following: "It was divine intervention. . . . I had just looked up at the $2 million and said a little prayer . . . when I hit the jackpot" (Newsweek). Such a statement

Knowing this, Moses appeals to the character of the Lord, that He might stem the tide of the coming judgment. The word for "favor" (v. 11, NIV) is the figurative meaning of its literal Hebrew word translated "face." Moses responds by seeking the face of the Lord by asking two questions. In the first question, he asks how God can be this angry with the people He chose to bring out of Egypt. After all, He knew their character then and still chose them.

Just as Yahweh referred to the Israelites as Moses' people in verse 7, Moses now turns the phrase around, reminding God that they are still His people. He is willing to be bold with God to receive his request.

Moses' second question gets a lot more specific. He appeals to God's mercy on the basis of the Egyptian response. After Yahweh has proven Himself greater than the Egyptian empire with her gods, He and His people will become nothing but a laughingstock in Egypt if the Israelites are destroyed. Surely that is not justice—surely the people who enslaved Israel for four centuries do not deserve that kind of satisfaction. Therefore, Moses reasons, God must not destroy the nation.

B. Remember the Patriarchs (vv. 13, 14)

13. Remember Abraham, Isaac, and Israel, thy servants, to whom thou swarest by thine own self, and saidst unto them, I will multiply your seed as the stars of heaven, and all this land that I have spoken of will I give unto your seed, and they shall inherit it for ever.

14. And the Lord repented of the evil which he thought to do unto his people.

Hebrew prayer often takes the form of reminding God of His previous salvation history. Our faith is a historical faith in that each generation builds on the faith of another. We do not need new revelations to understand how to follow God; we need the old ones found in Scripture. Moses turns to this history in his final plea for God to relent.

Moses' logic is not perfect. God had not threatened to wipe all Israelites off the face of the earth, but to build the nation He promised to the patriarchs using Moses, who was a Israelite. However, it would take centuries to replenish their population beginning with one family again, and Moses sees that the divine promise to the patriarchs is already being accomplished and should not be started over. Therefore he appeals to Abraham, Isaac and Jacob, and especially the covenant God made with Abraham. For their sake God must not destroy the people, especially when the Israelites are finally on their way to inherit the land He promised to the patriarchs.

Wonderfully, the Lord listens to His human servant. For the sake of Moses, the patriarchs and His own name, He will show mercy. His judgment, though, cannot be stopped, for the Israelites must learn to follow His commands if they are to survive. Should they continue to carry around the mentality of

displays a misunderstanding of intercessory prayer. Prayer is not something that is disconnected from a godly lifestyle or a means to personal gain. Intercessory prayer aligns us with God's purposes, not our own.

Talk About It:
1. Why did Moses bring up the names of Abraham, Isaac and Jacob?
2. How did God "change His mind" (see v. 14, *NASB*)?

"More things are wrought by prayer than this world dreams of."
—**Alfred, Lord Tennyson**

Egypt in their hearts, the entire journey will fail, not to mention the settlement of the Promised Land. There is judgment to pay, but it will be a correcting judgment, steering the Israelites back toward the path of God.

III. GOD'S JUST JUDGMENT (Exodus 32:29-35)

It must have felt like the longest walk of Moses' life—longer even than the one to Egypt from Midian so many months ago. Midway down the mountain, the tablets in hand, he begins to hear a raucous noise in the camp. Joshua believes it is a noise of war, but Moses knows better (vv. 17, 18). It is not chaos he hears, but the rejoicing of a ceremony, and Moses is so angry he breaks the tablets containing the Ten Commandments (v. 19). Next he destroys the golden calf, grinds it into powder, pours the powder into water, and forces the Israelites to drink it (v. 20). Livid at Aaron for allowing this to happen, he rallies the Levites to function as agents of God's judgment. But the greater judgment is still to come.

A. Moses Intercedes Again (vv. 29-32)

29. For Moses had said, Consecrate yourselves to day to the Lord, even every man upon his son, and upon his brother; that he may bestow upon you a blessing this day.

30. And it came to pass on the morrow, that Moses said unto the people, Ye have sinned a great sin: and now I will go up unto the Lord; peradventure I shall make an atonement for your sin.

31. And Moses returned unto the Lord, and said, Oh, this people have sinned a great sin, and have made them gods of gold.

32. Yet now, if thou wilt forgive their sin; and if not, blot me, I pray thee, out of thy book which thou hast written.

Moses' first audience is with the Levites, the only tribe who rally to him on behalf of Yahweh. They are given the grisly task of fatally stabbing the worst of the idol worshipers—about 3,000 Israelites (vv. 26-28). Moses recognizes the special calling on this tribe and commends them for going through with the grim task.

As a result of their heroic service, even though it meant death to some of their fellow Jews, the Levites will be henceforth set apart to the Lord's service. Practically, the blessing of the Lord for their righteousness will secure them the esteemed place of the priestly class of Israel. Their heroism is no small thing. They showed great courage to be the only people to rally around Moses—the only ones not to participate in the golden calf spectacle. Instead, because of their holiness, they will experience the divine blessing of the real God. And they will stand on His behalf for generations to come.

Talk About It:
1. In verse 29, why were the Levites praised for being "against [their] own sons and brothers" (NIV)?
2. According to verse 30, what was Moses not sure he would be able to do for the Israelites?
3. Describe the leadership of Moses, based on verse 32.

Moses waits overnight before addressing the Israelites at large. One imagines it was a sleepless night for the leader. He has to enforce a punishment for their behavior, but he also hopes for divine mercy. Without knowing what to do, he returns to converse with the Lord.

Moses makes no bones about the gravity of the situation to the Israelites. The outcome of their actions is up in the air. Nonetheless, he takes personal responsibility for attempting to find atonement. Perhaps God will accept a sacrifice. He is equally graphic toward God himself, not covering up the evil perpetrated by the people. Moses does not justify their actions with the argument that they *meant* the golden calf to be only a stand-in for Yahweh. No, he calls them idol worshipers. But if God will not forgive them, then Moses should himself be blotted out from the divine book.

It is unclear exactly which book Moses and God are talking about. Perhaps it is some heavenly book that Moses has learned about on the mountain. However, in the context of the narrative, the book probably refers to the "book of the covenant" which Moses has just received for the nation (24:7). Moses asks to be removed from his connection with the Book of the Covenant in exchange for divine forgiveness for Israel. He offers himself in their place.

B. The Lord Judges (vv. 33-35)

33. And the Lord said unto Moses, Whosoever hath sinned against me, him will I blot out of my book.

34. Therefore now go, lead the people unto the place of which I have spoken unto thee: behold, mine Angel shall go before thee: nevertheless in the day when I visit I will visit their sin upon them.

35. And the Lord plagued the people, because they made the calf, which Aaron made.

God will not allow Moses to assume responsibility for sins he did not commit. Those who refuse to follow God's laws will be denied the benefits of God's laws, pure and simple. This may be what it means to be blotted out from the book. God finally sends Moses on his way, commanding him to lead the people behind the angel who controls the pillar of cloud and fire. Moses' request for unmitigated forgiveness cannot be granted; the people will experience judgment.

Judgment comes in the form of an undescribed plague. Usually when death is involved there is a number given by the writer, so it is likely that this plague mimicked one of the nonfatal plagues of Egypt. One wonders if God uses one of the very plagues of Egypt as if to remind the Israelites of His power there. One connection is explicit—Aaron's name is forever

Talk About It:
1. What does verse 33 reveal about God's justice?
2. How did God judge His people?

marred by the act of crafting the idolatrous golden calf. Yet God's mercy is also evident in that Aaron's calling is not obliterated. He moves past his sin, later functioning as high priest. For a time, the people experience true repentance and move on toward God's calling for them.

CONCLUSION

The story of Israel's exodus from Egypt toward Canaan is no pretty, linear process from glory to glory. There are almost too many drastic mistakes, bumps and challenges to count. The two things that stay steady are the heart of God and the heart of Moses. Moses is not perfect, of course, but the relationship with God he cultivates in the leadership process keeps Israel on the journey. He is an intercessor extraordinaire because he depends on God to make any progress whatsoever. Without Moses' dedication to seeking God's face, Israel would have never made it to the Promised Land.

GOLDEN TEXT CHALLENGE

"I EXHORT THEREFORE, THAT, FIRST OF ALL, SUPPLICATIONS, PRAYERS, INTERCESSIONS, AND GIVING OF THANKS, BE MADE FOR ALL MEN" (1 Timothy 2:1).

Paul emphasized that his instructions regarding prayer should be primary ("first of all"). Although prayer life in the New Testament was in many ways an extension of the prayer life of the Old Testament, it is marked by notable differences. In the church, prayer was an intensely personal practice, not the more formal and stately forms found in the Old Testament. Also, in the Old Testament the priest generally prayed for the people. In the church, prayer was encouraged by all people (v. 8).

Four kinds of prayer are mentioned in the Golden Text. Prayer is not a single form of communication with God; praying takes many forms and is brought about by many different circumstances.

The first form is *prayers of supplication*, which generally consist of appeals for desired favors. We supplicate in prayer for forgiveness, for blessings, for material provision, and for numerous other favors from the hand of God.

A second form of prayer is simply called *prayers*. This refers to being in constant communication with God. It is a recognition of His sovereignty, His holiness and our dependence upon Him. We communicate with God in order to retain the spiritual strength for daily Christian living.

A third form of praying is *intercession*, which means praying on behalf of others. When we pray for the needs of friends, relatives, neighbors, leaders, the lost, and others, we are said to be interceding on their behalf.

A fourth form of prayer is *giving thanks*. This is praying without making requests or appeal for favors, but simply worshiping and adoring our heavenly Father. When we come into His presence with praise and thanksgiving rather than in petition, we are attaining the highest form of prayer. It is communication with God in which we acknowledge Him as sovereign and ourselves as His creatures. We seek only to bring Him adoration and praise.

The phrase "be made for all men" is given because the instruction is for the minister's prayer for his people. While the guidelines of Paul are important for all Christian everywhere, the specific purpose for these instructions is to assist ministers in praying for their people.

"Redeemed"

Exodus 15:1-21

Unit Theme:
Great Hymns of the Bible

Central Truth:
We should praise God continually for redemption.

Focus:
Reflect on God's provision of salvation and exalt Him.

Context:
After the Israelites cross the Red Sea (c. 1450 B.C.), Moses leads them in singing unto the Lord.

Golden Text:
"The Lord is my strength and song, and he is become my salvation" (Exodus 15:2).

Study Outline:
I. Song of Salvation (Exodus 15:1-7)
II. Song of Mercy (Exodus 15:8-13)
III. Song of Triumph (Exodus 15:14-21)

INTRODUCTION

Our text, a psalm written by Moses after the crossing of the Red Sea, is the first great song of praise and worship of Jehovah recorded in the Bible. "Scripture links this triumphal paean with the song of a greater redemption, as on the shores of the eternal sea, at the final and glorious triumph over all enemies, the redeemed sing 'the song of Moses . . . and the song of the Lamb' (Revelation 15:3)" (*Wycliffe Bible Commentary*). This is one of three psalms composed by Moses (see also Deuteronomy 31:22, 30; 32:1-43; Psalm 90), and is a powerful ode to the absolute supremacy of God over Pharaoh's armies. This was a celebration by the entire nation of Israel, but also one of a community of believers. The Lord had proved Himself in the most dramatic of ways and was totally worthy of worship.

The mood here is an amazing contrast to the one the Israelites had felt when they arrived at the Red Sea. With the sea in front of them and Pharaoh's army marching straight toward their backs, terror had gripped them. Their fate seemed to be either death by drowning or death by the sword. Seeing no way out, Exodus 14:10 declares, "The children of Israel cried out unto the Lord." Though this sounds noble, it was not a cry of faith, but rather one of bitterness and betrayal. They immediately turned against Moses with vicious accusation.

In an effort to regain order, Moses responded by exclaiming prophetically, "Do not be afraid. Stand still, and see the salvation of the Lord, which He will accomplish for you today. For the Egyptians whom you see today, you shall see again no more forever. The Lord will fight for you, and you shall hold your peace" (vv. 13, 14, *NKJV*). Moses told the people to *stand still.* Yet, immediately the Lord corrected him by saying, "Tell the children of Israel to go forward. But lift up your rod, and stretch out your hand over the sea and divide it" (vv. 15, 16, *NKJV*). This was no time to stand still, but rather one to march straight into the sea and watch a miracle take place.

After crossing the sea, the children of Israel sang with joy at the wonders of God's great victory. What they should have done, however, was sing this song before they crossed the sea. To sing of what God does after He does so doesn't require faith and allegiance. The Israelites would prove their own fickleness within days, completely forgetting what they had just seen occur here.

I. SONG OF SALVATION (Exodus 15:1-7)

A. National Song (v. 1)

1. Then sang Moses and the children of Israel this song unto the Lord, and spake, saying, I will sing unto the Lord, for he hath triumphed gloriously: the horse and his rider hath he thrown into the sea.

This was a universal song sung by everyone that day on the west side of the Red Sea. No one could deny what God had done. Even the naysayers of Israel had to admit He was on their side. This is the first time in the Bible that singing is mentioned. The people were expressing their joy by such. Singing is a most natural way to express exultation. "Singing is as much the language of holy joy as praying is of holy desire" (*Matthew Henry's Commentary*).

Moses himself led the people. What a relief for him! He had personally carried such weight for so long, and though he had experienced wonderful interchange and relationship with the Lord, the people had not. The opening of the Red Sea was a divine affirmation of his leadership. How wonderful as well that he was setting the example for others to follow in worship. Too often today ministers leave the "worshiping" to the congregation, while they wait for their turn to deliver a message, assuming that their role is more important.

The reason for the song cannot be overemphasized. Some 2 million people had been gloriously delivered from Egyptian bondage. The descendants of Abraham had become a nation, one belonging to God, whom no earthly power (exemplified by Pharaoh) could defy. This was a victory to be remembered in the years and centuries to come—an ever-present example of God's intervention in behalf of His people as they faced new conflicts with the powers of this world.

The phrase "horse and his rider" sounds as though it would refer purely to men on horses, but it actually applies to a much larger grouping. Exodus 14:9 indicates that "all the horses and chariots of Pharaoh, and his horsemen, and his army" pursued the Israelites. It would appear that virtually the entire manpower of Egypt's military was included in the massacre.

B. Strength and Song (v. 2)

2. The Lord is my strength and song, and he is become my salvation: he is my God, and I will prepare him an habitation; my father's God, and I will exalt him.

Even though the occasion for the song has to do with the judgment God had just inflicted on the heathen world (personified by Pharaoh), the substance is praise and adoration of the Lord. "Since every individual had cause, so every individual gave utterance to his feelings of gratitude; and never before

Talk About It:
What "glorious triumph" did Moses sing about?

Real Reverence
The fear of the Lord is "honor, esteem, value, respect and reverence of Him above anything or anyone else. It is to love what He loves and hate what He hates" (John Bevere, *Driven by Eternity*). If we truly fear the Lord, what concerns Him will become our concern. If we fear Him, we will "tremble at his word" (Isaiah 66:5). This means we will obey Him, even when we don't understand, even when everything inside us says to do something different, and even when we see no benefits from obeying.
—**Rodney Hodge**

prepare him an habitation (v. 2)—praise Him

had the divine praises been celebrated on earth by so vast a multitude under the influence of such intensely elevated devotion" (*Jamieson, Fausset and Brown Commentary*). The phrase "strength and song" is an unusual pairing of words. The word *song* carries no connotation of power or might. However, with the Egyptians pursuing them and the sea in front of them, God had surprised the people with His powerful deliverance. Thus, He was the reason for them to sing. In other words, He had become their song! The words of this verse have an ascending theme. "He who has God for his strength, will have Him for his song; and he to whom Yahweh has become salvation, will exalt His name" (*Adam Clarke's Commentary*). Anyone can sing the praises of the Lord, but unless he or she has experienced God in a personal way (especially deliverance from sin), that person will be singing an empty song. The theme of "strength and song" is repeated in Psalm 118:14 and Isaiah 12:2. In both verses, God is pictured as being ready to deliver the writers from their troubles.

The concept of preparing the Lord "an habitation" (Exodus 15:2) comes well before God had revealed His plans to Moses for building the Tabernacle. Perhaps Moses was speaking prophetically. Most modern translations, however, simply render this line differently, usually as "I will praise Him." The place God most wants to inhabit is the human heart.

C. Man of War (v. 3)

3. The Lord is a man of war: the Lord is his name.

With poetic liberty, Moses describes the Lord as a *man,* but certainly not with the intent of diminishing His awesome power. "Man had no part in the victory; the battle was the Lord's" (*Barnes' Notes*). Human language is what humans have to express their thoughts, and often the words available are woefully inadequate. Still, the thought here is that Yahweh is a powerful warrior, encountering the Egyptian army in a military conquest.

In an age when there were many heathen gods, the Lord is exalted above all of them. The living God was making His name known to all humanity, and salvation could be found in Him alone.

D. Pharaoh's Army (vv. 4, 5)

4. Pharaoh's chariots and his host hath he cast into the sea: his chosen captains also are drowned in the Red sea.

5. The depths have covered them: they sank into the bottom as a stone.

In one fatal swoop, the entire military might of Egypt had been destroyed. "On such an expedition it is likely that the principal Egyptian nobility accompanied their king, and that the overthrow they met with here had reduced Egypt to the lowest extremity" (*Adam Clarke's Commentary*). The vulnerability to which that nation was left was extreme. They had no protection. It is interesting to speculate over the fear that came over that land. Their manpower was gone. It would take at least a generation to recover, not to mention the possibility of other nations invading. Adam Clarke makes an interesting observation, noting that had Moses been ambitious for power, he could have planned an invasion of Egypt and literally taken the land. However possible that might have been, Canaan was the land God had given His people, not Egypt.

E. God's Greatness (vv. 6, 7)

6. Thy right hand, O Lord, is become glorious in power: thy right hand, O Lord, hath dashed in pieces the enemy.

7. And in the greatness of thine excellency thou hast overthrown them that rose up against thee: thou sentest forth thy wrath, which consumed them as stubble.

The "right hand" is considered to be the strong hand. Throughout the Exodus story the powerful right hand of God is seen. This was a way of describing His presence on behalf of His people. There is also a closeness indicated here. God was not far away, but close among His people. The phrase "greatness of thine excellency" is another metaphor for describing the wonders of God. Again, human language is limited in its ability to give God all the praise He deserves.

The concept of the wrath of God is demonstrated in that God is stirred to wrath when His people are mistreated. Another side of God's wrath is seen by the writer of Hebrews: "It is a fearful thing to fall into the hands of the living God" (10:31).

> "The task ahead of us is never as great as the Power behind us."
> —*Christians Quoting*

II. SONG OF MERCY (Exodus 15:8-13)

A. Supernatural Blast (v. 8)

8. And with the blast of thy nostrils the waters were gathered together, the floods stood upright as an heap, and the depths were congealed in the heart of the sea.

Moses continues with flowery language and figures of speech to express the power of God acting on Israel's behalf. Somehow a strong east wind had forced the waters to part, piling up on either side and clearing the way for their open path. That powerful blast is depicted as coming from the Lord's nostrils. No details are given as to what kind of damage might have been done to land areas surrounding the Red Sea as the water became dammed up. A similar situation would occur some 40 years later with Joshua as Israel crossed the Jordan River into the Promised Land. Joshua 3:13 records, "As soon as the

Talk About It:
What did God accomplish with His breath (v. 8)? What else can His breath accomplish (see Genesis 2:7; Psalm 18:15; Isaiah 11:4; John 20:22)?

priests who carry the ark of the Lord—the Lord of all the earth—set foot in the Jordan, its waters flowing downstream will be cut off and stand up in a heap" (*NIV*). Verse 16 of that chapter says that the waters upstream began to pile up, cutting off a town called Adam.

B. Pharaoh's Arrogance (vv. 9, 10)

9. The enemy said, I will pursue, I will overtake, I will divide the spoil; my lust shall be satisfied upon them; I will draw my sword, my hand shall destroy them.

10. Thou didst blow with thy wind, the sea covered them: they sank as lead in the mighty waters.

Once Pharaoh had determined to make pursuit, his arrogance increased exponentially. What folly there is in fighting against the living God! Six choppy phrases in verse 9 "almost stimulate the heavy, breathless heaving of the Egyptians" *(Zondervan NIV Bible Commentary)* as they rushed faster and faster to overtake the escaping Israelites. Everything changes with verse 10, however. With a single gust of God's breath, the Egyptians sank into the waters of the Red Sea. Back in Exodus 14:28, we were told only that "the waters returned," thus trapping the Egyptians. Here we see it was because the wind blew. "A sudden change in the direction of the wind would bring back at once the masses of water heaped up on the north" (*Barnes' Notes*).

C. Incomparable Lord (v. 11)

11. Who is like unto thee, O Lord, among the gods? who is like thee, glorious in holiness, fearful in praises, doing wonders?

The Israelites had just left Egypt, a polytheistic land of statues and giant temples, none of which had ever helped them. These idols had not even come to the aid of the Egyptians, as seen by the effect of the 10 plagues. Now, the Israelites are inspired afresh to sing the praises of the one God who stands above all.

"Fearful in praises" speaks of a glorious holiness that can only be approached with awe and reverence. However, this fear of the Lord was not meant to drive the Israelites away from God, but rather for God to reveal Himself to them, so that He might have fellowship with them, just as He had with Moses. Later, we see this invitation at Mount Sinai when Moses says to the people, "Do not fear; for God has come to test you, and that His fear may be before you, so that you may not sin" (Exodus 20:20, *NKJV*). Sadly, the people draw back and refuse to come close to God. They do not distinguish the difference between being afraid of God and having the fear of the Lord.

There are 30 references to the "fear of the Lord" in the King

Talk About It:
Explain the character of God given in these phrases: "majestic in holiness, awesome in glory, working wonders" (v. 11, *NIV*).

James Version. They do not focus on being afraid, but rather on reverently approaching God in awe. This is perfectly seen in Psalm 19:9, where David declares, "The fear of the Lord is clean, enduring for ever: the judgments of the Lord are true and righteous altogether."

D. Singing to the Lord (vv. 12, 13)

12. Thou stretchedst out thy right hand, the earth swallowed them.

13. Thou in thy mercy hast led forth the people which thou hast redeemed: thou hast guided them in thy strength unto thy holy habitation.

Verses 1-5 were sung in the third person. Starting with verse 6, and epitomized here, the text is in the second person. The people changed from singing *about* the Lord's greatness to singing directly to Him. In a sense, this displays the difference between *praise* and *worship*. To praise is to sing the glories of God. To worship is to sing to Him about Himself.

There are two themes here: (1) the destruction of enemies and (2) the preservation and leading of God's people. The heroic deeds of God in destroying Israel's enemy were a "pledge that God would fulfill His promise of giving the land" (*Zondervan NIV Bible Commentary*). The phrase "the earth swallowed them" indicates a possible earthquake as the waters returned, thus not only drowning the Egyptians, but swallowing them up as well. Psalm 77:18 seems to verify this when it says "the earth trembled and shook." Contrasting this, the people of God were safe and secure, despite the phenomenal acts of nature.

Verse 13 of the text speaks of a "holy habitation" to which God was leading His people. This was not Sinai, nor was it Canaan alone, but as we shall see in verse 17, to a place of intimacy with Him. God's people are His inheritance.

III. SONG OF TRIUMPH (Exodus 15:14-21)

A. Fear and Dread (vv. 14-16)

14. The people shall hear, and be afraid: sorrow shall take hold on the inhabitants of Palestina.

15. Then the dukes of Edom shall be amazed; the mighty men of Moab, trembling shall take hold upon them; all the inhabitants of Canaan shall melt away.

16. Fear and dread shall fall upon them; by the greatness of thine arm they shall be as still as a stone; till thy people pass over, O Lord, till the people pass over, which thou hast purchased.

The news of Israel's deliverance quickly spread abroad. Four of Israel's future enemies are listed: Palestina (Philistia),

Talk About It:
1. What effect would the news of Israel's triumphs have on other nations? Why was this important?
2. How had Israel been "purchased" (v. 16)?

Edom, Moab and Canaan. The great manifestations of nature would have immediately drawn their attention. The news of the Egyptian army's demise would have taken a bit longer to spread, but still traveled fast. It is noteworthy that no nation tried to take advantage of Egypt in her weakened condition, possibly because of fears of similar divine retribution. The fear instilled was not a temporary one, but was still strong some 40 years later. This is indicated when Rahab helps the two spies in Jericho (see Joshua 2:9-11). She knows of the deliverance from Egypt, of the subsequent victories over the Amorites, and the fact that God has made it clear He is giving the land of Canaan to the Israelites. She speaks of the nations' reactions by saying, "As soon as we had heard these things, our hearts did melt, neither did there remain any more courage in any man, because of you: for the Lord your God, he is God in heaven above, and in earth beneath" (v. 11).

In Exodus 15:16, the pairing of two words, *fear* and *dread*, makes for one strong idea—overwhelming terror. As already stated, the fear and dread that came upon the surrounding nations would last "till thy people pass over." Notice that this phrase is repeated. The Hebrew language makes emphasis of a thought by repeating it. There would be terror among the other nations until God had safely brought His people into the Promised Land. One commentary interprets it, "'They shall be as still as a stone'—literally, struck dumb with astonishment and terror; i.e., petrified" (*Jamieson, Fausset and Brown*).

The expression "thine arm" (v. 16) is interchangeable with "right hand" in verses 6 and 12. The word *purchased* is simply another way of stating the theme of this lesson—"*redeemed.*" Other meanings for this word include "to acquire," "to possess," and "to create." All these things God had done in bringing the people out and making a nation of them.

"When you have nothing left but God, then you become aware that God is enough."
—Maude Royden

B. Eternal Reign (vv. 17-19)

17. Thou shalt bring them in, and plant them in the mountain of thine inheritance, in the place, O Lord, which thou hast made for thee to dwell in, in the Sanctuary, O Lord, which thy hands have established.

18. The Lord shall reign for ever and ever.

19. For the horse of Pharaoh went in with his chariots and with his horsemen into the sea, and the Lord brought again the waters of the sea upon them; but the children of Israel went on dry land in the midst of the sea.

God would not stop until the work of bringing the people to the place of His planning for them was complete. "Based on God's parallel handling of Pharaoh and the nations that would oppose their entrance into Canaan, Israel may now anticipate the fulfillment of the patriarchal promise that they would be given—in that future day when the Lord would reign forever—the land of Canaan as an inheritance" (*Zondervan NIV Bible Commentary*). The best way to build hope and faith for the future is to review the divine providence God has showed in our lives in the past.

As seen by the destruction of Pharaoh and his army, the people can look forward to the time when the Lord will reign forever. These earthly monarchs were but temporary leaders. They would pass away, but the Lord reigns forever. "The words are expressive of God's everlasting dominion, not only in the world, but in the church; not only under the Law, but also under the Gospel; not only in time, but through eternity" (*Adam Clarke's Commentary*).

C. Miriam's Song (vv. 20, 21)

20. And Miriam the prophetess, the sister of Aaron, took a timbrel in her hand; and all the women went out after her with timbrels and with dances.

21. And Miriam answered them, Sing ye to the Lord, for he hath triumphed gloriously; the horse and his rider hath he thrown into the sea.

The narrative changes here from Moses' song to that of Miriam. She is called a "prophetess." It was already known that she was the sister of Aaron and Moses, although this is the first mention of her by name. Because of the wording, she appears to rank only with Aaron and not with Moses. This becomes clear in Numbers 12 when she and Aaron speak out against Moses. "As a prophetess, Miriam spoke authoritatively from God. However, neither she nor her brother Aaron was ever Moses' equal in intimacy with God" (*Nelson Study Bible*). In the present situation, she was divinely inspired to lead the women in an antiphonal response to the song of Moses.

CONCLUSION

The Israelites sang of God being "glorious in holiness" and "fearful in praises" (Exodus 15:11). He was so holy and fearful that, in their minds, He was also inapproachable. When the Lord showed up later in such power at Mount Sinai, they were equally afraid. They didn't understand that this display of power was not to harm them, but to instill awe in them so that they would refrain from sinning. They didn't understand the *fear of the Lord*. Adam hid in the Garden because he had a sin to hide from God. A Biblical fear of the Lord causes us to run to God, not run away.

When the Israelites were so afraid at Mount Sinai, Moses assured them that God wanted the same relationship with

Talk About It:
List Miriam's identity, position and actions.

What Is Worship?
Worship is to feel in your heart and express in some appropriate manner a humbling but delightful sense of admiring awe and astonished wonder and overpowering love in the presence of that most ancient Mystery, that Majesty which philosophers call the First Cause, but which we call "Our Father which art in heaven."
—A.W. Tozer

them that he was enjoying. He said, "Do not be afraid. God has come to test you, so that the fear of God will be with you to keep you from sinning" (20:20, *NIV*). They failed to understand how much God really loved them and wanted their fellowship. Do we fail the same way by hiding our sins and running from Him? It is far better to confess them, and draw near to Him. Then we can sing the song of the redeemed.

Daily Devotions:
M. My Redeemer Lives
Job 19:23-29
T. Let the Redeemed Say So
Psalm 107:1-9
W. Abundant Redemption
Psalm 130:1-8
T. Look for Redemption
Luke 21:25-33
F. Redeemed by Christ
Ephesians 1:7-14
S. Song of the Redeemed
Revelation 14:1-5

GOLDEN TEXT CHALLENGE

"THE LORD IS MY STRENGTH AND SONG, AND HE IS BECOME MY SALVATION" (Exodus 15:2).

Moses and the children of Israel had just been saved from the swords of the Egyptians through the jaw-dropping congealing of the Red Sea and then its sudden return to normal. They felt the miraculous wind . . . they saw the Red Sea divided . . . they heard the cry of the drowning soldiers. Now they praised God for rescuing them through His awesome strength.

As Christians, we have never seen the "sword" that our great enemy, the devil, held over our head when we were enslaved by sin. However, we did feel the wind of God's Spirit as He brought conviction upon us and drew us to Christ. As we called out to Christ for salvation, we sensed a supernatural "dividing" taking place—God separating us from our sins. And perhaps we "heard" the cry of our old sinful nature as we repented of our life of sin.

God is our strength and our song! Do we regularly pause to worship Him for the miracle of salvation He has worked in our life?

"Redeemed"

"The Solid Rock"

INTRODUCTION

A new generation of Israelites was finally about to enter the land of Canaan. Outside of Moses, Joshua and Caleb, there was not a person in the midst over the age of 59. The rebellion and disbelief by the older generation 40 years earlier at Kadesh Barnea (see Numbers 13:1–14:45) had resulted in everyone 20 years old and older being sentenced to die in the wilderness (14:29, 30).

Recognizing that his own days were numbered, Moses gathered the people together to rehearse their history and show how God had been faithful, establish this new generation into covenant with the Lord, and pass the mantle of leadership on to Joshua. Those in their 40s and 50s could remember seeing the wondrous things God had done, while those younger could recognize their every need had been met. None of this generation was responsible for the sins of their parents, yet they had been forced to wait all this time to enter Canaan. God had not forgotten them, and now they were about to inherit the blessings their parents had missed. Even Moses himself would not cross the Jordan. His one incident of disobedience (Numbers 20:10-13) had cost him dearly. Still, he recognized that God had a long-term plan, and this next generation was key to this coming to pass. No matter how strong one generation's personal commitment might be, faith in and love of God must be taught to the next generation so that they develop their own walk with God.

Moses made one statement that is key to understanding our lesson. He said, "The secret things belong to the Lord our God, but those things which are revealed belong to us and to our children forever, that we may do all the words of this law" (29:29, *NKJV*). God had revealed His will for His people, and this was for all generations to come. There was no reason for it to be lost—but it must be taught.

This brings us to the present lesson. As he came to the end of his life, Moses had real doubts as to future generations remaining faithful to God. To ensure that his warnings would be remembered, he put them into song. This was not just his song, however, for it was the Lord's song. God had given him the words (see 31:19-22). Put in the poetic form of song, they would be easily remembered as a testimony against a people who would later so easily abandon all they had been taught.

Unit Theme:
Great Hymns of the Bible

Central Truth:
God is the solid foundation on which to build our lives.

Focus:
Proclaim that God is the Solid Rock and build a relationship with Him.

Context:
Around 1400 B.C. in the land of Moab, Moses passes on the reigns of leadership and gives promise to God.

Golden Text:
"He [God] is the Rock, his work is perfect: for all his ways are judgment: a God of truth and without iniquity, just and right is he" (Deuteronomy 32:4).

Study Outline:
I. Rock of Truth (Deuteronomy 31:30—32:6)
II. Rock of Salvation (Deuteronomy 32:7-15)
III. Rock of Justice (Deuteronomy 32:30, 31, 36-43)

I. ROCK OF TRUTH (Deuteronomy 31:30—32:6)

A. Leadership Transfer (31:30)

30. And Moses spake in the ears of all the congregation of Israel the words of this song, until they were ended.

Talk About It:
Why did Moses present his final teachings to the Israelites in the form of a song?

The reigns of leadership had just been publicly handed from Moses to Joshua. Moses spoke words of encouragement over Joshua of the Lord's faithfulness (vv. 7, 8). Then he delivered a copy of the Law (what is now known as Deuteronomy) to the priests and commanded a reading of it every seven years before all the people (vv. 9-13). God had spoken clearly as to how the people were to live. His will had been made known to all, but the coming generations must know it as well. Even foreigners living among them were to hear it.

Moses and Joshua were then called by the Lord into the Tent of Meeting, where He told them that the people would forsake Him, and that His anger would be aroused against them. "Thus Joshua too was warned to resist the tendency of the people to turn to foreign gods" (*Zondervan NIV Bible Commentary*). The solemnity of the event was heightened by the Lord appearing in a pillar of cloud. Even more solemnly, the two men were told to write down a song and teach it to the Israelites, and then have them sing it with enough repetition that it would be fixed in their minds (see vv. 14-22).

"A song is a lot like a handshake. You have to stick it out there and see if anybody grabs it."
—Roger Miller

Our text indicates that Moses spoke the words of the song before the entire assembly. In later years it is not known whether it was sung, or read as a poetic recitation. Most importantly, it was a warning against forsaking God when affluence came.

B. A Summons (32:1, 2)

1. Give ear, O ye heavens, and I will speak; and hear, O earth, the words of my mouth.

2. My doctrine shall drop as the rain, my speech shall distil as the dew, as the small rain upon the tender herb, and as the showers upon the grass.

Talk About It:
How did Moses want his teaching to be like rain and dew?

By summoning the heavens and the earth to listen, Moses was making all creation a witness to those he was about to tell the people. His words are similar to what he used in Deuteronomy 30:19, but now with poetic grandeur. This had the effect of intensifying an impact on the original hearers. The song declared heaven and earth would testify against them if they did not heed its words. The central theme is presented: "The Lord is blameless and righteous in His doings, but Israel acts corruptly and perversely" (Keil & Delitzsch).

Because of the importance of the words, Moses said they would be like rain or dew, with the power to refresh, fertilize and enliven. In many parts of the world, dew provides more moisture than rain. Without the dew nothing will grow. Moses' hope was that his song from God would be like dew on the people, helping them to grow in their dedication to the Lord.

C. The Lord's Greatness (vv. 3, 4)

3. Because I will publish the name of the Lord: ascribe ye greatness unto our God.

4. He is the Rock, his work is perfect: for all his ways are judgment: a God of truth and without iniquity, just and right is he.

In the ancient world of polytheism, this song proclaimed the *name* of the one true God. Moses had already declared the Lord's name throughout Deuteronomy. The third commandment had stated that using this name in vain would bring punishment. The people were to make oaths only in this name, and the priests were to bless the people in the Lord's name (Numbers 6:22-27; Deuteronomy 10:8; 21:5). Thus, it was the glorious name of the Lord that Moses wanted the people to revere, because His name signified His person—the God of creation, the God of history, the God of covenant, the God who was (and still is) faithful to all He promises.

Talk About It:
How does verse 4 describe the acts of God? How does it describe God's character?

Anyone with true wisdom will ultimately find himself ascribing praise to the Lord. The great argument of our day is that religion and science cannot coexist, but true scientists find themselves recognizing the Creator through the wonder of what they discover in science, and thus give Him the glory.

The use of the metaphor "the Rock" (32:4) declares the strength and enduring stability of God. He can be depended on; He can be built upon.

D. Israel's Indictment (vv. 5, 6)

5. They have corrupted themselves, their spot is not the spot of his children: they are a perverse and crooked generation.

6. Do ye thus requite the Lord, O foolish people and unwise? is not he thy father that hath bought thee? hath he not made thee, and established thee?

spot (v. 5)—blemish

requite (v. 6)—repay

Everything just stated about the faithfulness of God is now contrasted with the perverseness and corruption of the Israelites. The Lord had always been righteous and just in His handling of Israel, but they had responded corruptly by rejecting Him. This was seen most blatantly in their worship of the golden calf, making them "a warped and crooked generation" who were "no longer [God's] children" (v. 5, *NIV*). While the present audience was not responsible for the sins of their parents, they were, of necessity, the conduit through which the message had to be passed on. The song was a prophetic testimony of later generations of Israel. "It is true that the persons

Talk About It:
1. What had God done for the Israelites (v. 6)?
2. What had the Israelites become (v. 5)?

Careless Soul
The careless soul receives the Father's gifts as if it were a

the sons of Adam (v. 8)—"all mankind" (*NIV*)

Talk About It:
1. What had Moses wanted the Israelites to remember, and why?
2. What do these verses say about God's sovereignty?

addressed in this ode are not the contemporaries of Moses, but the Israelites in Canaan, when they had grown haughty in the midst of the rich abundance of its blessings, and had fallen away from the Lord, so that the times when God led the people through the wilderness to Canaan are represented as days long past away" (Keil & Delitzsch).

Verse 6 speaks of God as Israel's father. The Israelites understood the concept of being God's children, yet rarely stated such. It was not celebrated until Jesus came. He used the phrase "your heavenly Father" five times in the Gospels.

II. ROCK OF SALVATION (Deuteronomy 32:7-15)
A. The Lord's Portion (vv. 7-9)

7. Remember the days of old, consider the years of many generations: ask thy father, and he will shew thee; thy elders, and they will tell thee.

8. When the Most High divided to the nations their inheritance, when he separated the sons of Adam, he set the bounds of the people according to the number of the children of Israel.

9. For the Lord's portion is his people; Jacob is the lot of his inheritance.

The people were to remember the Lord's goodness in preparing an inheritance for Abraham's descendants. Israel was His elect people. God was sovereign over everything, including the division of the earth into nations. "While it is the Lord's will for many nations to exist, He has favored Israel with His special grace, promises, and covenant" (*Nelson Study Bible*). Canaan was to be the inheritance set aside for this favored people.

Moses here seemed to have prophetically transported himself many years into the future. As such, he then spoke to a people who may have forgotten how gracious God had been to give this special land to their forefathers. These would be people who had drifted from God, and would be thus punished by God.

In verse 9, the Lord declares His people are His portion. Israel (here called "Jacob") was the people He had chosen for Himself, His own nation. The psalmist would later say, "You are my portion, O Lord; I have said that I would keep Your words" (Psalm 119:57, *NKJV*). "As holy souls take God for their portion, so God takes them for His portion. He represents Himself as happy in His followers; and they are infinitely happy in, and satisfied with, God as their portion" (*Adam Clarke's Commentary*).

Looking back, we see that God called Abraham. Abraham was not seeking God. God simply chose him as the beginning of a great nation. We also know that Abraham became known as the "Friend of God" (James 2:23).

B. The Lord's Care of Israel (vv. 10-12)

10. He found him in a desert land, and in the waste howling wilderness; he led him about, he instructed him, he kept him as the apple of his eye.

11. As an eagle stirreth up her nest, fluttereth over her young, spreadeth abroad her wings, taketh them, beareth them on her wings:

12. So the Lord alone did lead him, and there was no strange god with him.

Despite the fact that Abraham was not looking for God, He still found this man (and his descendants) in a "desert land." Probably more specifically, the indication here was that of coming to Israel's rescue while in bondage to the Egyptians, and even more so in their later desolate situation while enduring the 40 years of wilderness wandering. "Moses focused on the people as an unorganized body in an inhospitable environment at the time God entered into the covenant-treaty with them" (*Zondervan NIV Bible Commentary*). During this season the Lord surrounded the people with His protection. One easily thinks of the cloud that guided them by day and the pillar of fire by night. The cloud shielded the people from the heat of the sun, while the pillar of fire warmed them from the cold desert night.

The comparison to a mother eagle is interesting. The eagle stirs up the nest so the eaglets will not remain comfortably there. They must learn to fly. The dismantled nest forces them into the open air space. However, though, the parent catches the fluttering young with outspread wings. In the same sense, the Lord brought Israel out of the misery of Egypt (the dismantled nest) into the Sinai desert, but did not leave them without help.

Verse 12 indicates that the idol gods of the Egyptians (as well as those of the Canaanites) were worthless in this endeavor. God alone was responsible for the development of Israel as a nation.

C. Blessings in Canaan (vv. 13-15)

13. He made him ride on the high places of the earth, that he might eat the increase of the fields; and he made him to suck honey out of the rock, and oil out of the flinty rock;

14. Butter of kine, and milk of sheep, with fat of lambs, and rams of the breed of Bashan, and goats, with the fat of kidneys of wheat; and thou didst drink the pure blood of the grape.

15. But Jeshurun waxed fat, and kicked: thou art waxen fat, thou art grown thick, thou art covered with fatness; then he forsook God which made him, and lightly esteemed the Rock of his salvation.

Talk About It:
1. How had the Lord been like an eagle to Israel (vv. 10, 11)?
2. What point is emphatically made in verse 12?

The Lord my pastor shall prepare and feed me with a shepherd's care; His presence shall my wants supply, and guard me with a watchful eye.
—**Joseph Addison**

kine (v. 14)—cows
fat of kidneys of wheat (v. 14)—"the finest of wheat"
Bashan (BAY-shan)—v. 14—fertile plain east of the Jordan River
Jeshurun (JESH-u-run)—v. 15—a poetic name for the nation of Israel

Talk About It:
1. Describe the blessings awaiting Israel in the Promised Land (vv. 13, 14).
2. How would Israel treat "the Rock" (v. 15), and what kind of feelings would this arouse in Him (v. 16)?

"Ingratitude denotes spiritual immaturity. Infants do not always appreciate what parents do for them. They have short memories. Their concern is not what you did for me yesterday, but what are you doing for me today."
—*Contact*

Talk About It:
Answer the question this verse poses.

repent himself (v. 36)—"have compassion" (*NIV*)

The mouths of those listening to the song must have watered at this point, for these people were still eating manna. They had not yet crossed into the Land of Promise. Again, Moses was transported to a future time and was looking backward at the wonderful provisions that were to be found in Canaan. Everything from livestock to bountiful crops, to honey and oil, and to bountiful grape arbors are mentioned as blessings of the land.

The blessings in the Promised Land eventually caused the people to forget the source of the blessings. "After eating fine foods and drinking choice red wine, Israel . . . grew fat, that is, became affluent and then, rather than being thankful, kicked!" (*Zondervan NIV Bible Commentary*).

Jeshurun (v. 15) was a pet name for Israel. The word means "uprightness," and describes what Israel should have become. The phrase "lightly esteemed" refers to how the people acted toward God. It means they "scoffed" (*RSV*) and "rejected" (*NIV*) the Lord. This term also occurs in 1 Samuel 2:30, but there God referred to those who despise Him as being "lightly esteemed" in His eyes. To be in such a condition is a dangerous thing, for there is little to hold back God's wrath.

III. ROCK OF JUSTICE (Deuteronomy 32:30, 31, 36-43)
A. Abandoned by the Rock (v. 30)

30. How should one chase a thousand, and two put ten thousand to flight, except their Rock had sold them, and the Lord had shut them up?

Without God, Israel was nothing. All the glorious deliverances of the past were totally of His doing. Yet the people could not comprehend their own destiny. Somehow they felt they had accomplished something on their own. The text poses a rhetorical question. Another way of saying this might be, "No single enemy warrior could put a thousand Israelite soldiers to flight, unless God had abandoned Israel." Interestingly, Joshua reversed this thought when the people had conquered Canaan. He said, "One man of you shall chase a thousand: for the Lord your God, he it is that fighteth for you, as he hath promised you" (Joshua 23:10). Joshua immediately, however, gave them warning of what would happen if they adopted the ways of the Canaanites.

B. Blessed Through Judgment (vv. 31, 36-38)

31. For their rock is not as our Rock, even our enemies themselves being judges.

36. For the Lord shall judge his people, and repent himself for his servants, when he seeth that their power is gone, and there is none shut up, or left.

37. And he shall say, Where are their gods, their rock in whom they trusted,

38. Which did eat the fat of their sacrifices, and drank the wine of their drink-offerings? let them rise up and help you, and be your protection.

Lest any enemy of Israel think that a victory achieved over Israel was due to its own strength, and thus refuse to give the glory to the Lord, Moses made it clear that God would limit any slaughter of Israel. Israel was still His people, even though He might have to put them under terrible judgment. "The preservation of a remnant from annihilation is thus rooted in God's jealousy for His own glory. At the same time, the ultimate vindication of His people, which the preservation of a remnant provides for, arises from God's compassion for them" (*Wycliffe Bible Commentary*).

Verse 36 is strong in saying the Lord will judge His people—no one else will. This is much like the way two siblings fight each other, yet come to each other's rescue when attacked by an outsider. The Lord's judgment was an expression of His compassion for Israel—both the land and the people. It was obvious, however, that Israel would never come to her senses until all her power was gone—when she was so decimated that it seemed no one was left. At this point, God would ask where were the idol gods they had trusted. The sacrifices that should have been offered up to God had instead been given to gods that could not help them.

C. Wounder and Healer (v. 39)

39. See now that I, even I, am he, and there is no god with me: I kill, and I make alive; I wound, and I heal: neither is there any that can deliver out of my hand.

The Lord here makes a personal assertion—He is the one and only true God. There are no other real gods. All others are lifeless creations. The statement is emboldened by the repetition of the pronoun "I." The Lord gives life and takes life. He would wound Israel, and He would also heal her. He asserts that no enemy of Israel is out of His control. "Because He is totally free to do what He wants, only He can either curse or bless, wound or heal, kill or give life" (*Nelson Study Bible*).

No one has the right to condemn the Lord's actions, for only He knows all. While His judgments may seem at times to be unfair, they are nonetheless fully just, for He alone discerns the hearts of men, seeing every motive, and only He can judge how people must be treated. The bottom line is this—the Lord is good. The psalmist declared, "O taste and see that the Lord is good: blessed is the man that trusteth in him" (Psalm 34:8). We need never fear that God will deal with us unjustly.

Talk About It:
1. What did even Israel's enemies admit (v. 31)?
2. What would God ask about gods (vv. 37, 38)?

"People fashion God after their own understanding. They make their god first and worship him afterwards."
—Oscar Wilde

Talk About It:
Why does God both wound and heal?

The motive of God's heart is redemption. He never allows hurts just to cause pain. He made this clear through the prophet Hosea when He said: "For I will be like a lion to Ephraim, and like a young lion to the house of Judah. I, even I, will tear them and go away; I will take them away, and no one shall rescue. I will return again to My place till they acknowledge their offense. Then they will seek My face; in their affliction they will earnestly seek Me" (5:14, 15, *NKJV*). It is a shame if we do not seek the Lord's face until we have been driven to our knees. Some might see God as capricious for being willing to let His children hurt, yet He always has our best interests in mind.

God is God—therefore He is the ultimate judge of good and evil. None of His creation has the right to condemn His actions. As He said through Isaiah, "Indeed before the day was, I am He; and there is no one who can deliver out of My hand; I work, and who will reverse it?" (43:13, *NKJV*).

D. Vengeful Warrior (vv. 40-43)

40. For I lift up my hand to heaven, and say, I live for ever.

41. If I whet my glittering sword, and mine hand take hold on judgment; I will render vengeance to mine enemies, and will reward them that hate me.

42. I will make mine arrows drunk with blood, and my sword shall devour flesh; and that with the blood of the slain and of the captives, from the beginning of revenges upon the enemy.

43. Rejoice, O ye nations, with his people: for he will avenge the blood of his servants, and will render vengeance to his adversaries, and will be merciful unto his land, and to his people.

Verse 40 shows the Lord taking an oath. Just as He added an oath to the promises made in the Abrahamic covenant, here He swears by Himself that His judgments will be certain and terrible against all who oppose Him. Inherent here is the idea that He will right all wrongs. No evil will be left unjudged. "The Lord will show Himself as the only true God, who slays and makes alive, etc. He will take vengeance upon His enemies, avenge the blood of His servants, and expiate His land, His people" (Keil & Delitzsch).

All those who truly love the Lord can take comfort in the severity of His actions. Verse 43 implies that a Messiah for all nations would come. Israel never understood that they were the people through whom God would send a Redeemer—not just for them, but for all humanity. Thus, they suffered in their rebellions. They did not understand their own purpose for existence. Still, God would redeem them. "Israel shall be long scattered, peeled, and

---

"Here is a God who has both firmness and feeling. If we cannot comprehend we can perhaps apprehend, at least enough to adore."
—Dale Davis

whet (v. 41)— sharpen

Talk About It:
On whom will God take vengeance, and why (vv. 40-42)?

"The ancient man approached God (or even the gods) as the accused person approaches his judge. For the modern man the roles are reversed. He is the judge: God is in the dock [on trial]."
—C.S. Lewis

"The Solid Rock"

punished, but they shall have mercy in the latter times; they also shall rejoice with the Gentiles in the common salvation purchased by the blood of the Savior of all mankind" (*Adam Clarke's Commentary*).

CONCLUSION

I recently overheard two schoolteachers talking about discipline in their classrooms. They both agreed that at the beginning of the school year they had to lay down strict rules, rules that were both clear and had consequences if not obeyed. The teachers commented that they could loosen the rules during the course of the school year as good relationship with the students developed, but they could never go back and make the rules stronger if they lost control in the classroom. There is a spiritual lesson to be learned here.

Paul wrote to the Romans, "Therefore consider the goodness and severity of God: on those who fell, severity; but toward you, goodness, if you continue in His goodness. Otherwise you also will be cut off" (11:22, *NKJV*). God is both good and severe—because He loves us. He lays down strict rules. If left to our fleshly ways, we will do ourselves more harm than good, and thus He must be severe. If all He shows us is kindness, like the students in a classroom, we will abuse the grace and try to take advantage of His goodness for selfish purposes.

GOLDEN TEXT CHALLENGE

"HE [GOD] IS THE ROCK, HIS WORK IS PERFECT: FOR ALL HIS WAYS ARE JUDGMENT: A GOD OF TRUTH AND WITHOUT INIQUITY, JUST AND RIGHT IS HE" (Deuteronomy 32:4).

Imagine that everything in this verse were untrue about our God. It would then read like this: "He is unstable as sand, His work is full of errors; He is unjust, a God of deception and full of wrongs, unfair and unrighteous is He."

How frightening our world would be if any of this was true. He would then be like the mythological gods of the Romans and Greeks, whose power was divine, but whose character was filled with flaws. He would play games with us, as those gods did, using us as pawns in his perverse acts of pleasures. We would be hopeless and helpless creatures.

Thinking of how terrible life would be under the reign of a capricious supreme being should motivate us to continually worship God for who He really is. Our God's character is as perfect as His power! He is the perfect, just, sinless and righteous Rock.

Daily Devotions:
M. Song of Truth
   2 Samuel 22:1-4
T. Rock of Refuge
   Psalm 31:1-8
W. Lead Me to the Rock
   Psalm 61:1-8
T. Christ Will Declare Justice
   Matthew 12:14-21
F. Christ Is the Truth
   John 14:5-13
S. Our Great God and Savior
   Titus 2:11-15

"O What a Savior"

Psalms 22:1-18; 118:19-29

Unit Theme:
Great Hymns of the Bible

Central Truth:
Christ suffered and died to save sinners.

Focus:
Reflect on the passion of Christ and exalt Him as Savior.

Context:
Two psalms giving praise to the coming Messiah

Golden Text:
"I will praise thee: for thou hast heard me, and art become my salvation" (Psalm 118:21).

Study Outline:
I. Forsaken Savior (Psalm 22:1-8)
II. Suffering Savior (Psalm 22:9-18)
III. Exalted Savior (Psalm 118:19-29)

INTRODUCTION

Once settled into the Promised Land, Israel fell into a terrible pattern of behavior. As God blessed His people, they would forget Him and indulge in the heathen lifestyles of the Canaanites. He would then let them be overrun by their enemies and suffer terribly for a period. When they finally came to their senses, they would cry out to Him for help. He would then send a deliverer (known as a "judge") to rescue them. They would regain a level of prosperity and soon start the vicious cycle all over again.

Eventually the Israelites cried out for a king, wanting to be like the nations around them. This was an insult to the Lord. He confided to Samuel, "Heed the voice of the people in all that they say to you; for they have not rejected you, but they have rejected Me, that I should not reign over them" (1 Samuel 8:7, NKJV). True to form, the first king, Saul, chose a path of disobedience to God. If the Israelites were unwilling to serve the faultless Lord as king, they certainly weren't ready to submit to a human king who had many faults.

Graciously, God was already planning a king for His people, one of His own choosing. A young shepherd boy, David, was the anointed ruler through whom an eternal dynasty would be established. This brings us to the first text for this lesson. Psalm 22 was composed by David during the years he was running from Saul. It is a plaintive cry of one in desperate circumstances. David was going through everything God said would come upon the Israelites when they forsook Him. Yet, he was not suffering because of any personal rebellion against the Lord. His was the anguish of one who was innocent, but still feeling that God had forsaken him. In the middle of his lament, he turns to give praise to God.

Our second text comes from Psalm 118, a song of praise to the Lord declaring that His mercies are forever enduring, and that He does come to aid His people in their distress. It is a testimony of confidence in the Lord. It verifies what Moses had sung earlier—that God is a Rock who can be trusted.

Both psalms are messianic in nature; that is, they show a prophetic picture of what Jesus later would endure. David's struggles in Psalm 22 were a picture of a greater struggle Jesus would suffer to secure humanity's redemption, while the stone which was rejected by the builders in Psalm 118 was symbolic of Jesus being rejected, only to become the chief cornerstone of salvation.

I. FORSAKEN SAVIOR (Psalm 22:1-8)

A. David's Distress (v. 1)

1. My God, my God, why hast thou forsaken me? why art thou so far from helping me, and from the words of my roaring?

Although we will quickly see that much of this psalm is a foreshadowing of Christ's suffering at Calvary, we first view it as David's own lament at the suffering he was going through at the hand of King Saul. David poured out his heart with three questions: (1) Why was he forsaken? (2) Why was there no attempt to rescue him? (3) Why had the Lord not heard his cry? These are the sincere feelings of anyone who has felt alone and in trouble. David still spoke of the Lord as "my God," knowing that the Lord was nearby. He had not lost faith. He simply needed to express the cry of his heart. "The language is abrupt, and is uttered without any previous intimation of what would produce or cause it. It comes from the midst of suffering—from one enduring intense agony—as if a new form of sorrow suddenly came upon him which he was unable to endure" (*Barnes' Notes*). The question "Why?" indicates a conscious innocence on David's part. There was nothing he had done to deserve such treatment.

At the same time, the cry expressed here was prophetic of Christ's suffering at Calvary. Jesus lifted His lament to the Father with the same words. Matthew 27:46 says, "About the ninth hour Jesus cried with a loud voice, saying, Eli, Eli, lama sabachthani? that is to say, My God, my God, why hast thou forsaken me?" This occurred some three hours after the strange darkness began to cover the land at noon. The word *roaring* (Psalm 22:1) means "groaning."

The irony of the passage is that David was not forsaken, but Christ truly was. The Father would not rescue Him, for that would abort the reason for having come to the earth as a man in the first place. "He bore the burden of the world's atonement by Himself. He was overwhelmed with grief, and crushed with pain, for the sins of the world, as well as the agonies of the cross, had come upon Him" (*Barnes' Notes*). This was not the cry just of physical suffering. It was the cry of One who had taken on an overwhelming burden for someone else—no, for everyone else.

B. A Continuous Cry (v. 2)

2. O my God, I cry in the daytime, but thou hearest not; and in the night season, and am not silent.

David's lament was a continuous cry by day and night. In the midst of it all, he still recognized the holiness of God, that He should be praised. He knew there would eventually come an

---

roaring—groaning

Talk About It:
1. Describe the psalmist's feelings.
2. Compare this verse with Jesus' cry on the cross (Matthew 27:46). Why did Jesus feel that way?

Perfect Prophecy
Psalm 22 portrays the Lord's suffering some 1,000 years before it actually happened. Verse 1 shows Him as being forsaken (fulfilled in Matthew 27:46); verses 7 and 8 point out the ridicule by His enemies (Matthew 27:39, 43); verse 14 describes bones pulled out of joint (John 19:34); verse 16 speaks of pierced feet (Luke 24:39, 40); verse 18 mentions His garments being divided (Matthew 27:35); and verses 27 and 28 describe the ends of the earth turning to the Lord and His ultimate rule over all the nations.

Talk About It:
What was David doing day and night?

answer, despite the prolonged absence of such. "God 'hears' every cry; but the answer to a prayer is sometimes withheld or delayed, as if He did not hear the voice of the suppliant" (*Barnes' Notes*). This was affirmed centuries later when the answer to Daniel's prayer was delayed (see Daniel 10:12, 13).

Just as David's cry was in the night season, Jesus' most intense prayer recorded in Scripture was in the Garden of Gethsemane on the night before His crucifixion. <u>The phrase "not silent" (Psalm 22:2) indicates a loud incessant cry. Most often we think of Jesus' prayer in the Garden as being a quiet supplication, barely audible.</u> This would seem plausible, since the disciples fell asleep. However, Jesus likely poured out a loud and deep lament. The fact that His prayer is recorded in the Gospels indicates that some of His words were heard.

Too often we feel that our prayers should be controlled, quiet requests to the Lord, devoid of our true feelings. However, there is nothing wrong with unleashing all our deepest feelings and pains upon the Lord. If Jesus did this, so can we. There is release in pouring our hearts out to Him.

Also, the abandonment Jesus felt, both in the Garden and on the cross, was not just the result of immediate circumstances. He had long known where His life was leading. The sorrows and trials He endured from the rejection of His family, friends and His people were part of the long continuous cry that culminated at the cross.

C. The Lord's Faithfulness (vv. 3-5)

3. But thou art holy, O thou that inhabitest the praises of Israel.

4. Our fathers trusted in thee: they trusted, and thou didst deliver them.

5. They cried unto thee, and were delivered: they trusted in thee, and were not confounded.

Deep inside his being, David recognized that God was holy and would ultimately deliver him. The track record was too good to deny. This was a friendship that could endure the present trials. His situation seemed hopeless, but there had been other times that seemed just as bad, yet the Lord had come through.

When Jesus had endured His horrible period of abandonment, cut off from the Father and left alone, He knew joy was coming. The writer of Hebrews said, "Looking unto Jesus the author and finisher of our faith; who for the joy that was set before him endured the cross, despising the shame, and is set down at the right hand of the throne of God" (12:2).

While on the cross, Jesus faced a "black hole" of separation from the Father. He could feel nothing of the Father's presence. Instead, what He did feel was the enormous weight of humanity's

inhabitest (v. 3)— "are enthroned upon" (*NASB*)

Talk About It:
1. Explain the phrase "You are holy" (v. 3, *NKJV*).
2. What did the psalmist remember about God?

sins. How often do we come across moments, hours, days, or even long seasons when it seems that nothing is worth living for? Praying is like talking to a brick wall. At these times we must rely on God's promise, as well as reviewing the wonderful times in the past when we experienced the joy of His presence.

D. No Longer Human (vv. 6-8)

6. But I am a worm, and no man; a reproach of men, and despised of the people.

7. All they that see me laugh me to scorn: they shoot out the lip, they shake the head, saying,

8. He trusted on the Lord that he would deliver him: let him deliver him, seeing he delighted in him.

David's suffering caused him to feel so abased that he was no longer a person, but more like a worm. David's enemies ridiculed him by saying if God was really on his side he would not be suffering. This was the view later held by most Jews during Jesus' ministry. Blessing equated to God's approval. Disease, distress and misfortune must then be a sign of God's disapproval. Thus, to trust God in the midst of suffering was foolishness to them. This accounts for much of the verbal abuse Jesus had to take from His tormentors during the Crucifixion (see Matthew 27:27-31, 39-44).

II. SUFFERING SAVIOR (Psalm 22:9-18)
A. But Thou (vv. 9-11)

9. But thou art he that took me out of the womb: thou didst make me hope when I was upon my mother's breasts.

10. I was cast upon thee from the womb: thou art my God from my mother's belly.

11. Be not far from me; for trouble is near; for there is none to help.

In the midst of all the trouble and taunts coming at him, David turns his attention to say, "But thou. . . ." The ultimate response to distress is to reflect on the faithfulness of God. David changed his focus from himself to God's sovereignty and love of His own. "From birth he has owed his life to God, and from birth the Lord has been his covenant God and has shown him His love" (*Zondervan NIV Bible Commentary*). Nothing has changed, because God doesn't change—despite any present circumstance. The Lord is unchangeable and will not leave His children alone and without help.

The same focus was taken by David in Psalm 3, though the circumstances were different. There he was running to escape from his rebellious son, Absalom. David cried, "Many there be which say of my soul, There is no help for him in God. . . . But thou,

> "Praising God is one of the highest and purest acts of religion. In prayer we act like men; in praise we act like angels."
> —Thomas Watson

Talk About It:
1. Why did David feel like "a worm" (v. 6)?
2. Compare the taunts David endured with those used against Jesus (Matthew 27:41-44).

Talk About It:
1. What was David's relationship with God before he was born (v. 10) and after his birth (v. 9)?
2. How much was David now dependent on God (v. 11)?

O Lord, art a shield for me; my glory, and the lifter up of mine head" (3:2, 3). Notice the same phrase, "But thou." This event was many years after Psalm 22, but the same Lord was just as faithful. The wise response to difficult situations is not to doubt God's goodness but to reaffirm a lifelong faith in the Almighty.

One can sense the tug-of-war going on in David. He feels the weight of persecution, turns his attention to God's faithfulness, but then turns around and cries, "Be not far from me" (22:11). We are no different. The moment we take our attention from God's faithfulness in the past, the reality of present circumstances strikes us in the face. Still, we don't give up, but endure until the Lord does come to help.

B. Raging Enemies (vv. 12, 13)

12. Many bulls have compassed me: strong bulls of Bashan have beset me round.

13. They gaped upon me with their mouths, as a ravening and a roaring lion.

David saw his enemies as ferocious beasts—bulls and lions. The "bulls of Bashan" were cattle known for their immense size. They were grown in the lush areas of what is today known as the Golan Heights. The lions were not so fierce for their size, but for their open mouths and ferocious teeth—ready to pounce upon prey. Of course, both these animals were metaphors for David's real human enemies, all intent on cruelty and hatred of godliness.

When the Messiah was arrested, His enemies "roared" against Him. "The more they roared for His destruction, the more He cried to His God" (Jamieson, Fausset and Brown).

Talk About It:
How were David's enemies like wild bulls?

C. Inner Alienation (vv. 14, 15)

14. I am poured out like water, and all my bones are out of joint: my heart is like wax; it is melted in the midst of my bowels.

15. My strength is dried up like a potsherd; and my tongue cleaveth to my jaws; and thou hast brought me into the dust of death.

The alienation David experiences makes an immense effect on his physical body. He feels all life has been drained from him, like the emptying of a water jug. "The bones, heart, strength, and tongue fail him, not because of any serious disease, but because of a traumatic response to being hated and alienated" (*Zondervan NIV Bible Commentary*). The dryness of the tongue is even more poignant when applied to Jesus' suffering. We remember the point at which He cried, "I thirst" (John 19:28; also see Psalm 69:21). His mouth was so dry that He could hardly speak, His tongue glued to the roof of His

potsherd (v. 15)—"sun-baked clay" (*TLB*)

Talk About It:
How were these prophetic verses fulfilled in Christ's suffering (see John 19:16-18, 28)?

mouth. All of David's anguish symbolically represents Jesus as the blood drained from His body from the beatings and nail wounds. For David, death was not forthcoming, but for Jesus, there was no reprieve.

D. Wicked Assembly (vv. 16-18)

16. For dogs have compassed me: the assembly of the wicked have inclosed me: they pierced my hands and my feet.

17. I may tell all my bones: they look and stare upon me.

18. They part my garments among them, and cast lots upon my vesture.

Dogs are the third reference to animals in this psalm. They may not seem so vicious to us, but Israelites never kept dogs as pets. Most were wild pack animals. The picture given here is of a helpless victim being viciously attacked by something akin to wolves. The reference to "bones" indicates David was thin and emaciated from lack of food, without enough strength to ward off his attackers. The reference to pierced hands and feet speaks explicitly of Jesus' crucifixion. For David this was merely a figure of speech, but for Christ it was an accurate portrayal of His suffering.

The casting of lots for Jesus' garments by the soldiers at the cross is pictured in verse 18. It is amazing that David could sense this a thousand years earlier. David prophetically felt some of the suffering Jesus went through. David's suffering was real, but we know he ultimately was delivered and rose to the throne of Israel. Still, he felt the Lord's pain.

Today, the Holy Spirit sometimes allows believers to sense the pain of another person so they might identify with his or her suffering, and thus be led to pray for the healing of that person. Paul wrote, "Bear ye one another's burdens, and so fulfill the law of Christ" (Galatians 6:2).

III. EXALTED SAVIOR (Psalm 118:19-29)

Psalm 118 is radically different from Psalm 22. It is pure praise of the living God. It is part of a group of psalms traditionally used at Passover. It was sung by the throngs as Jesus entered Jerusalem on Palm Sunday (Matthew 21:9). It was probably even sung by Jesus at the Last Supper. It reflects on the confidence that can be had in the Lord because of His enduring mercy, on God's ability to deliver His people in time of trouble, and on the complete righteousness of God. Verse 19 gives a declaration by the psalmist that he would enter the gates of the city with praise to the Lord.

Though not part of our study text, verse 17 states, "I shall not die, but live, and declare the works of the Lord." This psalm is

Talk About It:
How were these prophetic verses fulfilled in Christ's suffering (see Matthew 27:20-23, 35-39)?

May I be willing,
    Lord, to bear
Daily my cross for
    Thee;
Even Thy cup of
    grief to share,
Thou hast borne all
    for me.
    —Jennie Evelyn
        Hussey

not attributed to David, but this particular verse is a testimony of one who had come through the fire. David had been in imminent danger, his enemies thick around him, and death seemed inevitable, yet he did not die. He ultimately had the assurance that God would vindicate him and deliver him.

A. The Gates of Righteousness (vv. 19-21)

19. Open to me the gates of righteousness: I will go into them, and I will praise the Lord:

20. This gate of the Lord, into which the righteous shall enter.

21. I will praise thee: for thou hast heard me, and art become my salvation.

Only the "righteous"—those devoted to God and intent on worshiping Him—were allowed to enter these gates into the Temple. But who is righteous? We can refer to Psalm 24:3, which asks, "Who may ascend into the hill of the Lord? Or who may stand in His holy place? He who has clean hands and a pure heart, who has not lifted up his soul to an idol, nor sworn deceitfully" (*NKJV*). Obviously, there is no one righteous enough to ascend the holy hill on his or her own merit except the King of Glory himself. Only Jesus Christ could enter the "gate of the Lord" (118:20) of His own accord. However, Jesus said, "I am the door: by me if any man enter in, he shall be saved, and shall go in and out, and find pasture" (John 10:9). Jesus is the gate by which the door leading to salvation has been opened. By faith and trust in Christ, we can all now enter the gates of righteousness.

The "gates of righteousness" (Psalm 118:19) might also be seen in light of the millennial Jerusalem, "whose walls are salvation, and whose gates are praise (Isaiah 60:10, 18); and again the type of the heavenly Jerusalem's gates of pearl and wall of jasper (Revelation 21:10-13, 18, 21)" (Jamieson, Fausset and Brown).

B. The Cornerstone (vv. 22, 23)

22. The stone which the builders refused is become the head stone of the corner.

23. This is the Lord's doing; it is marvellous in our eyes.

A *cornerstone* is "the stone at the corner of two walls that unites them: specifically, the stone built into one corner of the foundation of an edifice as the actual or nominal starting point of a building" (*New Unger's Bible Dictionary*). Jesus identified Himself as the cornerstone of the Kingdom in Matthew 21:42. Paul said, "Now therefore ye are no more strangers and foreigners, but fellowcitizens with the saints, and of the household of God; and are built upon the foundation of the apostles and

"O What a Savior"

prophets, Jesus Christ himself being the chief corner stone" (Ephesians 2:19, 20). Christ is the foundational stone of our redemption, our faith, our hope for the future. Though having been rejected by His own, He nevertheless was elevated to the right hand of God. "The Cross, the symbol of Jesus' rejection, has become the symbol of our salvation" (*Nelson Study Bible*).

The two walls that a cornerstone unites might be seen as the reconciliation between God and people, as well as the offering of salvation in the new covenant to both Jews and Gentiles. The Kingdom which Jesus brought unites all believers into one fellowship with God.

C. The Day of Thanksgiving (vv. 24-27)

24. This is the day which the Lord hath made; we will rejoice and be glad in it.

25. Save now, I beseech thee, O Lord: O Lord, I beseech thee, send now prosperity.

26. Blessed be he that cometh in the name of the Lord: we have blessed you out of the house of the Lord.

27. God is the Lord, which hath shewed us light: bind the sacrifice with cords, even unto the horns of the altar.

We often sing verse 24 as a song of thanksgiving for the particular day we are enjoying. In a broader sense, it is the day of salvation. It is the day in which the psalmist rejoices because he did not expect to see it. He had been in danger, but God had spared him. "It was so full of joy, so unexpected, so bright, so cheerful, that it appeared to be a new day coming fresh from the hand of the Almighty, unlike the other days of the year" (*Barnes' Notes*). Because he can now rejoice, he also asks the Lord for greater days ahead, days of prosperity and blessing.

The words "Save now" (v. 25) are more familiarly translated as *Hosanna*. Had the people not shouted "Hosanna" as Jesus entered Jerusalem (Matthew 21:9), the stones would have had to cry out (Luke 19:40).

It had been long understood by the Jews that the Messiah would be the One who revealed the Father to them. As Jesus entered Jerusalem on Palm Sunday, the crowds truly believed He was the One who had come "in the name of the Lord." They were ready to celebrate this special day by worshiping at the holy altar.

D. The Declaration (vv. 28, 29)

28. Thou art my God, and I will praise thee: thou art my God, I will exalt thee.

29. O give thanks unto the Lord; for he is good: for his mercy endureth for ever.

Just as the song began by singing the enduring mercies and

prosperity (v. 25)— "success" (*NIV*)

horns (v. 27)— projections from the four corners of the sacrificial altar

Talk About It:
1. Why should we "rejoice and be glad" today?
2. Why was the altar central to Old Testament worship?

"Praise shall conclude that work which prayer began." —**William Jenkyn**

Talk About It:
Why should we
sing about God's
mercy?

goodness of the Lord, it closes with the same. Because He is the Lord God, His people owe Him thanks. They must exalt Him for His never-ending goodness and love.

CONCLUSION

While hanging on the cross, Jesus could have called angels to come and free Him. He could have put Himself right back into the presence of His Father. He knew, however, there was no shortcut to victory. The Father had promised Him the kingdoms of the world (Psalm 2:7, 8), but there was a price to pay.

On the night before His crucifixion, Jesus said, "I tell you the truth, unless a kernel of wheat falls to the ground and dies, it remains only a single seed. But if it dies, it produces many seeds" (John 12:24, *NIV*). Because of the "joy that was set before him" (Hebrews 12:2), Jesus chose to suffer the abandonment while carrying the weight of our sins—because He knew there was great joy to come. We must keep this in mind. No matter what we Christians endure, there is a great future awaiting us.

GOLDEN TEXT CHALLENGE

"I WILL PRAISE THEE: FOR THOU HAST HEARD ME, AND ART BECOME MY SALVATION" (Psalm 118:21).

Whether driving a Batmobile or flying through the sky without a plane, the question with superheroes is always, "Will they get there in time?" In the climactic scene, a person or a city or even the entire world is in peril, and as Batman or Superman tries to make the rescue, someone like the Riddler or something like kryptonite always tries to get in the way.

In the real world, there are no superheroes, but there is a supernatural Rescuer, and He outshines those fictional figures in every way. When we face a crisis, we do not have to question whether or not the Savior hears our cries. The psalmist said, "I will praise You, for You have answered me" (*NKJV*).

He does more than hear us—we never have to wonder whether or not He will arrive on time. That's because He is already present with us in our dilemma. While He may not extend His hand to us in the exact time or way we hope or expect, if our trust is in Him, He will be our salvation.

Daily Devotions:
M. Redeemed by
   the Savior
   Isaiah 43:1-7
T. No Other Savior
   Isaiah 45:18-25
W. Wounded
   Savior
   Isaiah 53:1-12
T. Crucified Savior
   Matthew 27:26-
   37
F. Abandoned
   Savior
   Matthew 27:38-
   50
S. Witness of the
   Savior
   Acts 5:24-32

"Great Is the Lord"

Psalms 46:1 through 48:14

INTRODUCTION

Our text of three psalms form a trilogy of praise. While Psalms 46 and 48 both focus on God's special love for Jerusalem, Psalm 47 presents a grand ascent of the King of kings to His throne (be it the earthly Jerusalem or the ultimate heavenly one). Together, the three sing praise to God and His specially designated city of dwelling.

Psalm 46 is known as one of the Zion hymns, because it celebrates God's presence in Jerusalem—frequently called Zion. The original fortress city had been a Jebusite stronghold, but David captured it and made it his capital (renaming it the City of David). Eventually Zion became a symbol of God's presence in His temple.

One likely context for the writing of Psalm 46 was the siege of Jerusalem in 701 B.C. by Sennacherib, king of Assyria. King Hezekiah of Judah valiantly withstood this tyranny by trusting in the Lord, and also by carefully shoring up defenses of the city itself. The northern kingdom of Israel had already fallen to Assyria in 722 B.C., and it seemed inevitable that Judah would also fall. Hezekiah turned to the Lord and prayed earnestly. The crux of his prayer was this: "Now therefore, O Lord our God, I pray, save us from his [Sennacherib's] hand, that all the kingdoms of the earth may know that You are the Lord God, You alone" (2 Kings 19:19, *NKJV*). The Lord miraculously answered this prayer by sending an angel who destroyed 185,000 Assyrian soldiers.

Psalm 47 celebrates confidence in God and His enthronement as King over the entire earth. In a sense, it is prophetic of the future reign of Christ. A possible occasion for its writing was Jehoshaphat's victory over Moab, Ammon, Edom and the Arabians. This evil alliance had combined to drive Judah out of its inheritance (the land of Judah and especially Jerusalem; see 2 Chronicles 20:11). The Lord directed Jehoshaphat to send choirs of Levites into the wilderness singing praise to the Lord. When they began to sing, the Lord set ambushes against the enemy, again leaving dead bodies.

Psalm 48 again celebrates God's dwelling in Zion. For the Israelites, Jerusalem was where God dwelled, even though they knew Him to be omnipresent. The city became synonymous with the Lord's presence. This psalm was apparently composed to celebrate the captives returning from Babylon, and was perhaps sung at the dedication of the second Temple, "in order to return thanks to the Lord for the restoration of their political state, and the reestablishment of their worship" (*Adam Clarke's Commentary*).

Unit Theme:
Great Hymns of the Bible

Central Truth:
God is our king and His kingdom will endure forever.

Focus:
Contemplate the greatness of God and praise Him forever.

Context:
Three psalms of praise to God written by the descendants of Korah

Golden Text:
"Great is the Lord, and greatly to be praised in the city of our God, in the mountain of his holiness" (Psalm 48:1).

Study Outline:
I. A Present Help (Psalm 46:1-11)
II. King of the Earth (Psalm 47:1-9)
III. Our God Forever (Psalm 48:1-14)

I. A PRESENT HELP (Psalm 46:1-11)

Psalm 46 is divided into three poetic movements, each closing with the word *Selah,* a musical term probably indicating an instrumental interlude. The psalm is introduced by the phrase "To the chief Musician for the sons of Korah, a song upon Alamoth." The word *Alamoth* may refer to how the song was to be sung, possibly by a high-pitched or soprano voice. The first movement, verses 1-3, is a general statement celebrating God as the people's defense. The second movement, verses 4-7, shows God as a defense even as the nations rage. The third movement, verses 8-11, celebrates the Lord even when He brings judgment.

A. Refuge and Strength (vv. 1-3)

1. God is our refuge and strength, a very present help in trouble.

2. Therefore will not we fear, though the earth be removed, and though the mountains be carried into the midst of the sea;

3. Though the waters thereof roar and be troubled, though the mountains shake with the swelling thereof. Selah.

Of the many praise songs that have been written from this text, none are as famous as Martin Luther's "A Mighty Fortress Is Our God." Verses 1, 7 and 11 portray the Lord as Israel's great God. Although He is God over the whole earth, He is at the same time very personally the God of the Israelites. He is the source of their strength.

Luther used the term *fortress* in his song, a word not used here, but found in 2 Samuel 22:2; Psalms 18:2; 31:3; 71:3; 91:2; 144:2; and Jeremiah 16:19. God is like a fortress "in an isolated, elevated place, where people built a stronghold against the enemy" (*Zondervan NIV Bible Commentary*). Matthew Henry gives an excellent summarization when he says, "God is our strength, to bear us up under our burdens, to fit us for all our services and sufferings; He will by His grace put strength into us, and on Him we may stay ourselves." Proverbs 18:10 declares, "The name of the Lord is a strong tower: the righteous runneth into it, and is safe." We may rely on God's strength as if it were our own.

The word *therefore* in Psalm 46:2 indicates a logical deduction. Since God is such a strong helper, there is nothing to fear in any present distress—not even in the face of worldwide catastrophe. This was true for Noah, who found a place of refuge in the Flood. Wycliffe said, "The idea of a worldwide catastrophe was drawn from the writings of the prophets. It furnishes the background for assuring the people that God will be present whatever the outward circumstances."

very present (v. 1)—"ever-present" (*NIV*)

Talk About It:
How should Christians respond to natural disasters? Why?

Coming Peace
We can look back at the newsreels of the 1940s and see the determination with which the Americans, the British, and the other allies united to win World War II. Despite the tough battle campaigns, casualties and protracted years, there were smiles on faces—because the people believed eventually they would win. There was a confidence that they were on the right side fighting against evil. World War II did

What seems to be described by the psalmist is a gigantic earthquake or flood, or a symbolic reference to political upheaval or war. It might even be applied to the heralding of the messianic age. The world of Judaism was shaken when Jesus appeared on the scene. His first coming made for a social upheaval, while His second will bring a variety of cosmic changes.

B. A River of Blessing (vv. 4-7)

4. There is a river, the streams whereof shall make glad the city of God, the holy place of the tabernacles of the most High.

5. God is in the midst of her; she shall not be moved: God shall help her, and that right early.

6. The heathen raged, the kingdoms were moved: he uttered his voice, the earth melted.

7. The Lord of hosts is with us; the God of Jacob is our refuge. Selah.

There is no river near Jerusalem, so this probably suggests a peace and calm in contrast to the rough waters of the ocean. A *river* is a Biblical metaphor for blessing and restoration. "While the ocean rages, and foams, and dashes against the mountains as if it would overturn them, the state of Jerusalem, the city of God, was well represented by a calm and gently-flowing river; a river of full banks, diffusing joy and fertility and beauty wherever it flowed" (*Barnes' Notes*). Though there is no river in Jerusalem, this may possibly be an illusion to a tunnel that King Hezekiah constructed through solid rock under the city to bring water from the Gihon Spring into a cistern inside the city walls. That cistern became known as the Pool of Siloam, and it provided water for the city during times of enemy siege. Certainly having this water helped the people survive more than once and "made glad the city of God." Hezekiah cleverly also closed up all the springs outside the city (2 Chronicles 32:2-4) to keep his enemies from having a water supply while laying siege.

Verse 6 of the text speaks of people and nations being agitated like the waves of the ocean. This might refer to the various foreign powers that rose and fell throughout Israel's history, nations who constantly seemed drawn to attack Israel. Note that the northern kingdom of Israel fell to the Assyrians, while Judah later fell to the Babylonians. At the same time, Egypt was a frequent enemy. Enemies came and went, but God constantly was the source of help for His chosen people: "He uttered his voice, the earth melted" (v. 6).

Verse 7 is repeated in verse 11. It might be compared to a chorus, or refrain, in a song. It might well have originally also appeared between verses 3 and 4. Notice that the word *Selah*

not end all wars, but the day of peace is coming. Psalm 46:9 says, God "makes wars cease to the end of the earth" (*NKJV*).

the heathen (v. 6)—the nations

Talk About It:
1. What does the "river" in verse 4 represent?
2. How powerful is God's voice (v. 6)?

Talk About It:
1. Describe the different acts of God depicted in verses 8 and 9.
2. What does it mean to "be still" (v. 10), and why is it important to do so?
3. In verse 10, what does God declare as a certainty?

Our Strength
There was an excellent nature movie made in the 1980s called *The Bear.* It was the story of a grizzly cub whose mother had been killed in a landslide. The cub was grudgingly adopted by an old male bear. At one point in the story the little cub gets cornered by a mountain lion, who sees dinner in front of him. The little cub does the only thing it can do—it stands on its hind legs and starts to growl ferociously. Suddenly,

---

appears at each of these breaks. It occurs 71 times in the Psalms, but its meaning is unclear. It was likely either a symbol for an interlude where the singing stopped but the orchestra continued, or the equivalent of saying *Amen*, as we would in a church service today. Whatever the meaning, verse 7 affirms God's control of the heavens as well as the armies of the earth. The use of *Jacob* is simply another way of saying *Israel* (remember that his name was changed to this). "The God who appeared to Jacob in his distress, and saved him out of all his troubles, appeared also for us his descendants, and has amply proved to us that he has not forgotten his covenant" (*Adam Clarke's Commentary*).

C. Still Before God (vv. 8-11)

8. Come, behold the works of the Lord, what desolations he hath made in the earth.

9. He maketh wars to cease unto the end of the earth; he breaketh the bow, and cutteth the spear in sunder; he burneth the chariot in the fire.

10. Be still, and know that I am God: I will be exalted among the heathen, I will be exalted in the earth.

11. The Lord of hosts is with us; the God of Jacob is our refuge. Selah.

Verses 8 and 9 exhort all the godly and wise to consider the works of the Lord. In doing so, they will recognize that He will at some point in the future bring a complete cessation to wars, and afterward instigate an era of peace for the entire world. "Since God's people have reason to be glad in distress because of God's presence, how much greater will be their joy when the causes of distress are no more!" (*Zondervan NIV Bible Commentary*). In other words, we can rejoice now amid all the problems of our lives and our world, and we can look forward to even greater rejoicing when the wars cease.

The admonition "Be still, and know that I am God" (v. 10) is often thought of in a devotional sense—that is, to get by oneself and reflect on His goodness. In essence, it is seen as a call to quiet and reverent worship. However, Adam Clarke says it is a call to "cease from your labor for a season, that ye may deeply reflect on the severity and goodness of God—severity to those who are brought down and destroyed; goodness to you who are raised up and exalted." This is not a preparation for worship, but a warning of impending judgment. It is like standing before a judge who has just declared one guilty, and now awaiting the impending doom of hearing what the sentence will be. This command was particularly appropriate for the Assyrian hosts under Sennacherib who had laid siege to Jerusalem. The angel of the Lord suddenly swooped down on them and destroyed the entire army, leaving dead bodies strewn everywhere, much like a powerful bomb would do today.

II. KING OF THE EARTH (Psalm 47:1-9)
A. Clapping and Shouting (vv. 1-4)

1. O clap your hands, all ye people; shout unto God with the voice of triumph.

2. For the Lord most high is terrible; he is a great King over all the earth.

3. He shall subdue the people under us, and the nations under our feet.

4. He shall choose our inheritance for us, the excellency of Jacob whom he loved. Selah.

Psalm 47 is another psalm attributed to the sons of Korah. It was probably sung at many of the coronations of the 19 kings of Judah crowned after Solomon's death. While an earthly king might be celebrated, the real emphasis is on the eternal King ascending His throne to rule forever. It anticipates a future time when the Lord will reign absolutely over all the earth, over Jews and Gentiles alike.

The possible occasion for the psalm's composition was the miraculous intervention by the Lord in behalf of King Jehoshaphat when a coalition of nations came against him. The Lord spoke through Jahaziel, a Levite, to tell the king: "You will not have to fight this battle. Take up your positions; stand firm and see the deliverance the Lord will give you, O Judah and Jerusalem. Do not be afraid; do not be discouraged. Go out to face them tomorrow, and the Lord will be with you" (2 Chronicles 20:17, *NIV*). In response to this word from the Lord, the people praised God with loud voices. The next morning, Jehoshaphat sent choirs (all descendants of Korah) ahead of the people to sing praises to the Lord. In response, the Lord set an ambush for the coalition of enemies. These all turned on each other and massacred each other's forces. Jehoshaphat and his people were able to plunder so much treasure that it took three days to haul it all back into Jerusalem. As they marched toward the city, they sang again in triumph. "They entered Jerusalem and went to the temple of the Lord with harps and lutes and trumpets. The fear of God came upon all the kingdoms of the countries when they heard how the Lord had fought against the enemies of Israel" (vv. 28, 29, *NIV*).

It is obvious from this story that the Lord was moved by the exuberance of worship raised up to Him (vv. 18, 19). Psalm 47 shows clapping of hands and shouting praises to be legitimate expressions of adoration. We need never be ashamed to use our bodies and our voices to express our love and gratitude to God. There is tremendous power to be found when a group of believers express

the mountain lion backs away as if frightened by the brave antics of the cub. The cub appears proud of himself for having stood his ground, until the camera backs away to show the giant grizzly papa bear poised behind him. This is the way God is to us. He is our strength in troubled times.

terrible (v. 2)— awesome

Talk About It:
1. When are clapping and shouting appropriate ways to praise God (vv. 1, 2)?
2. What role does God play concerning the earth's nations (vv. 3, 4)?

Talk About It:
1. Why is the same phrase repeated four times in verse 6?
2. What does it mean to "sing . . . praises with understanding" (v. 7)?

themselves as such corporately. This psalm also envisions a time in the future when the whole world will sing, shout, clap, dance, and so forth, in praise to the King over the whole earth. "The kingdom of God will only be established when the 'nations' on earth join with the heavenly choirs, celebrating his universal and everlasting kingship" (*Zondervan NIV Bible Commentary*).

Back in the days of Samuel, the last of the judges, the people balked at having the Lord as their king. They wanted an earthly king like other nations. Interestingly enough, this psalm finds the people acknowledging God as the "great King" (v. 2). They declare Him to be the only King with absolute power, authority and righteousness, remembering how He subdued other nations with their false gods (v. 3) and gave Israel the land He promised them (v. 4).

B. The Enthronement of the King (vv. 5-7)

5. God is gone up with a shout, the Lord with the sound of a trumpet.

6. Sing praises to God, sing praises: sing praises unto our King, sing praises.

7. For God is the King of all the earth: sing ye praises with understanding.

These verses celebrate the enthronement of God as King over all. They anticipate a time in the future when there will be no more competition and battling for that position. "He seats Himself on the throne, all who see Him in heaven and earth shout aloud in triumph" (*Nelson Study Bible*). The call to sing praises is repeated, indicating something akin to what Isaiah witnessed when he saw the Lord: "And one cried unto another, and said, Holy, holy, holy, is the Lord of hosts: the whole earth is full of his glory" (Isaiah 6:3).

From a prophetic perspective, these verses bring another picture to mind—the ascension of Christ in Acts 1:8-11. His followers saw Him ascend *up* out of their sight, but Daniel saw Him in a vision arriving at His destination—the throne prepared for Him in heaven. Note the comparison to our present text: "I saw . . . one like the Son of man [coming] with the clouds of heaven, and came to the Ancient of days, and they brought him near before him. And there was given him dominion, and glory, and a kingdom, that all people, nations, and languages, should serve him: his dominion is an everlasting dominion, which shall not pass away, and his kingdom that which shall not be destroyed" (Daniel 7:13, 14). All people and nations will one day bow at His feet.

C. Universal Acknowledgment (vv. 8, 9)

8. God reigneth over the heathen: God sitteth upon the throne of his holiness.

9. The princes of the people are gathered together, even the people of the God of Abraham: for the shields of the earth belong unto God: he is greatly exalted.

These verses return to reflect on the Lord's reign on the earth. "The heathen" refers to the nations, over whom God reigns from His holy throne. The "shields" are the leaders of the nations—the kings and princes who protect the nations. God is calling to Himself people from every nation to form one body on the earth. This is what Jesus ordered in the Great Commission: "Go therefore and make disciples of all the nations" (Matthew 28:19, *NKJV*).

Talk About It:
1. What makes God's throne holy?
2. What are "the shields of the earth," to whom do they belong, and why (v. 9)?

III. OUR GOD FOREVER (Psalm 48:1-14)
A. The City of God (vv. 1-3)

1. Great is the Lord, and greatly to be praised in the city of our God, in the mountain of his holiness.

2. Beautiful for situation, the joy of the whole earth, is mount Zion, on the sides of the north, the city of the great King.

3. God is known in her palaces for a refuge.

Psalm 48 is a reiteration of the earlier two psalms in the trilogy. The concepts of God as our refuge and God as our great King are recapitulated here. Also, the two themes of God's greatness and His glorious city are set as complementary. As stated earlier, Jerusalem as the dwelling place of the Lord cannot be separated from Judaism. The city is "beautiful," not because of location or physical attraction, but because the Lord descends to dwell there in His temple. There are higher mountains in Judah with better views of the landscape, but none retain such symbolism. Jesus himself acknowledged the city's importance when He said, "Do not swear at all: either by heaven, for it is God's throne; or by the earth, for it is his footstool; or by Jerusalem, for it is the city of the Great King" (Matthew 5:34, 35, *NIV*).

The idea that the city would be the "joy of the whole earth" speaks prophetically of a time still to come. Today it is certainly the focus of the world's attention, but more because it divides the nations (by being the center of Judaism, Christianity and Islam) instead of uniting them. Nevertheless, it is still the symbol of an eternal kingdom that the Lord will establish one day.

In the same sense that Jerusalem of itself was not holy, neither were the Jews as a people chosen by God because of any inherent beauty or attribute. They simply were the means of drawing all nations to Himself.

Talk About It:
1. Why did the psalmist call Jerusalem ("Mount Zion") "the joy of the whole earth" (v. 2)?
2. What was God known as (v. 3)?

"O God, Thou hast made us for Thyself, and our hearts are restless until they find their rest in Thee."
—Augustine

B. The Kings Assembled (vv. 4-8)

4. For, lo, the kings were assembled, they passed by together.

passed by (v. 4)—advanced

ships of Tarshish
(v. 7)—well-built
ships which trans-
ported valuable
goods across the
sea

5. They saw it, and so they marvelled; they were troubled, and hasted away.

6. Fear took hold upon them there, and pain, as of a woman in travail.

7. Thou breakest the ships of Tarshish with an east wind.

8. As we have heard, so have we seen in the city of the Lord of hosts, in the city of our God: God will establish it for ever. Selah.

These verses speak of the strength and impregnability of Jerusalem—because it was God's dwelling place. From a historical perspective, we see that many times nations and kings tried to conquer Jerusalem. They envied the prosperity of the people, as well as the riches of the Temple. David (God's chosen king) had built a great nation, which was then passed on to Solomon. No foreign power could prevail, for God was with His people. The mighty deliverances that God brought for Hezekiah and Jehoshaphat illustrate this perfectly. It was not until God's people themselves became a stench in His nostrils that He let the city fall.

Verse 8 says "God will establish it for ever." Jerusalem will be permanently set as the Lord's capital. Revelation 21:10 says, "And he carried me away in the spirit to a great and high mountain, and shewed me that great city, the holy Jerusalem, descending out of heaven from God."

Talk About It:
What had the earth's kings heard about, what did they now see with their own eyes, and how did it affect them (vv. 5-8)?

C. The Temple of God (vv. 9-14)

9. We have thought of thy lovingkindness, O God, in the midst of thy temple.

10. According to thy name, O God, so is thy praise unto the ends of the earth: thy right hand is full of righteousness.

11. Let mount Zion rejoice, let the daughters of Judah be glad, because of thy judgments.

12. Walk about Zion, and go round about her: tell the towers thereof.

13. Mark ye well her bulwarks, consider her palaces; that ye may tell it to the generation following.

14. For this God is our God for ever and ever: he will be our guide even unto death.

Talk About It:
1. What is it important to meditate upon (v. 9), and why?
2. What did the psalmist want to "tell . . . the generation following" (v. 13)?
3. What will God do for His followers "even unto death" (v. 14)?

Imagine yourself making your first visit to the Vatican in Rome, or going to the Wailing Wall in Jerusalem. There is an awe and majesty that fills the heart from just being there. These verses portray someone coming to the Temple and reflecting on God's mighty works and long history of faithfulness to His people. The natural reaction is one of praise. The visiting worshiper declares God's righteousness and the benefits of living

"Great Is the Lord"

under His glorious rule. He also rejoices in God's judgments, for they are always right. Even death need not be feared, for the Lord will be his guide. Adam Clarke summarizes this excellently: "See her courts chambers, altars, and so forth; make an exact register of the whole, that ye may have to tell to your children how Jerusalem was built in troublesome times; how God restored you; and how he put it into the hearts of the pagan to assist to build, beautify, and adorn the temple of our God."

> "In God there is no *was* or *will be*, but a continuous and unbroken *is*. In Him history and prophecy are one and the same."
> **—A.W. Tozer**

CONCLUSION

The final verse of Psalm 48 is a fitting conclusion to this trilogy of psalms. If God is "our God," we will worship and serve Him "forever and ever." He will always be our guide. It is our responsibility to pass on our knowledge of God and His faithfulness "to the next generation" (v. 13, *NIV*).

GOLDEN TEXT CHALLENGE

"GREAT IS THE LORD, AND GREATLY TO BE PRAISED IN THE CITY OF OUR GOD, IN THE MOUNTAIN OF HIS HOLINESS" (Psalm 48:1).

The Lord chose Jerusalem as the place for the Temple to be built, and He frequently saved the city from enemies intent on overtaking it. So the psalmist declared that the Lord was to be greatly praised "in the city of our God, his holy mountain" (*NIV*).

Centuries later, when a Samaritan woman reminded Jesus that the Jews said God must be worshiped in Jerusalem (John 4:20), Jesus replied, "Yet a time is coming and has now come when the true worshipers will worship the Father in spirit and truth" (v. 23, *NIV*). That time is *now*.

While it is important that we regularly come together in a "temple" (church) to worship God with fellow believers, that is but one aspect of our life of worship. Trustful, spiritual worshipers are aware that God's Spirit is everywhere, and they seek to glorify Him throughout the day, be it Sunday or Monday or Friday. Our great God is worthy of great praise.

Daily Devotions:
M. The Lord Is King
   Psalm 20:1-9
T. God of Refuge
   Psalm 62:5-12
W. Coming King
   Zechariah 14:1-9
T. Find Grace to Help
   Hebrews 4:14-16
F. The Lord, Our Helper
   Hebrews 13:5-8
S. King of Kings
   Revelation 19:11-16

"Bless the Lord, O My Soul"

Psalm 103:1-22

Unit Theme:
Great Hymns of the Bible

Central Truth:
It is good to praise God for the benefits of His mercy and love.

Focus:
Recall the blessings of God and give Him thanks.

Context:
A psalm of David

Golden Text:
"Bless the Lord, O my soul: and all that is within me, bless his holy name" (Psalm 103:1).

Study Outline:
I. Remember God's Benefits (Psalm 103:1-5)
II. Declare God's Mercy (Psalm 103:6-14)
III. Rejoice in God's Love (Psalm 103:15-22)

INTRODUCTION

Though the Psalms were written as a basis of worship for Israel and her people, they have been used just as widely by Christians over the last 2,000 years. Every emotion is dealt with here. The various experiences of Abraham's descendants, both good and bad, provide a historical backdrop and reference for later readers to apply to their own particular situations. The writers of the Psalms were motivated by a desire to respond to the Lord verbally from their deepest beings. These are timeless scriptures, because they deal with universal human experience.

In the psalms David wrote, there are times when he seems to be shouting at the Lord in frustration, other times begging Him for help, while other times pleading for mercy. Despair, loneliness, suffering and fear are freely expressed, along with joy, thanksgiving, wonder and peace. There is no restraint in the Psalms. What readers have found through the ages, however, is that there is a release that comes from venting to the Lord.

Interestingly enough, while every feeling is expressed, feelings are not the ultimate reality. David expressed painful emotions during his years while running from Saul, but we know that he ultimately was made king of Israel. His sentiments at the time of writing were reality to him, but they weren't finality. The free expression, however, indicated that he had a friend in the Lord close enough to listen to his cry. "Through relationship with God we can move from fear to trust, from alienation to comfort, from envy and jealousy to joy. Many of the psalms actually trace the process by which feelings are transformed and brought into harmony with reality" (Lawrence O. Richards, *Illustrated Bible Handbook*).

Thus, we see the appeal of the Psalms. The God who loves and accepts us is willing to let us vent our deepest thoughts to Him—without fear of judgment. God is not shocked by anything we might say. He simply wants us to tell Him everything!

Many of the Psalms were written to be sung, and were used at every festival and special occasion in Jewish life. They are still sung today. Our particular text, Psalm 103, has had scores of renditions down through the centuries. It appears to have originally been written by David after some mercy was granted to him by the Lord. "This merciful interposition filled the heart of the psalmist with emotions of gratitude and praise, and led him to call on his own soul (vv. 1, 2), and all the angels (v. 20), and the hosts of heaven (v. 21), and all the works of God everywhere (v. 22) to unite in celebrating his praise" (*Barnes' Notes*).

I. REMEMBER GOD'S BENEFITS (Psalm 103:1-5)

A. Blessing the Lord (vv. 1, 2)

1. Bless the Lord, O my soul: and all that is within me, bless his holy name.

2. Bless the Lord, O my soul, and forget not all his benefits.

These opening verses are spoken in the first person as the psalmist stirs his heart to praise God in thanksgiving. Before entreating others to join him, he concentrates on himself. To "bless the Lord" is to give praise to Him with strong affection. It is "to remember that He is the source of all our blessings" (*Nelson Study Bible*). We normally think of blessing a person as doing some special deed for him or her, such as giving a gift or lending a helping hand in time of need. We might bless also as we flow under the anointing of the Spirit, using the gifts the Lord has granted us. However, what can we do to bless our Maker, who already has everything? The answer becomes clear: To "bless the Lord" is to praise Him for what He has already done for us!

In the Old Testament, the Lord himself allowed a means by which His blessing might be conferred on others. He told Moses to tell Aaron and his sons (the priests of Israel), "This is how you are to bless the Israelites. Say to them: 'The Lord bless you and keep you; the Lord make his face shine upon you and be gracious to you; the Lord turn his face toward you and give you peace'" (Numbers 6:23-26, *NIV*). In the New Testament, Peter said believers are all part of "a chosen generation, a royal priesthood" (1 Peter 2:9). As such, then, we have the same privileges as Aaron and his sons. We can confer the blessing of God on others—more specifically, those within the household of faith. We do this by the good deeds we do for them, as well as simply blessing them with the words of our mouth. Thus, we can bless the Lord with our praise, and we can bless others with the Lord's blessing.

The word *soul* (*nephesh*) appears 780 times in the Hebrew Bible (*Vine's Expository Dictionary of Biblical Words*). In the King James Version it appears only 458 times, because that translation uses 28 different English words for the one Hebrew word. Carrying a variety of nuances, the word generally refers to the essence of life, or one's innermost being. It is "equivalent to mind or heart: my mental and moral powers, as capable of understanding and appreciating His favors" (*Barnes' Notes*). We were created to praise the Lord and enjoy His fellowship, contemplating on the wonders of all that God does. Thus, to bless the Lord is to do precisely what we were created to do. The phrase "all that is within me" (Psalm 103:1) denotes that God is worthy of adoration from every fiber of our being. The

Talk About It:
1. To whom is the psalmist talking in these two verses?
2. What does it mean to "bless the Lord"?

Twin Quests
God's quest to be glorified and our quest to be satisfied reach their goal in one experience: our delight in God overflows in praise. For God, praise is the sweet echo of His own excellence in the hearts of His people. For us, praise is the summit of satisfaction that comes from living in fellowship with God.
—John Piper

repeating of the phrase "Bless the Lord, O my soul" (v. 2) denotes emphasis. A statement in Hebrew that needs to be emphasized is simply repeated.

B. Forgiveness and Healing (v. 3)

3. Who forgiveth all thine iniquities; who healeth all thy diseases.

Divine forgiveness includes removing both the sin and the remembrance of it. David said, "Blessed is he whose transgressions are forgiven, whose sins are covered. Blessed is the man whose sin the Lord does not count against him" (Psalm 32:1, 2, *NIV*). Forgiveness does not mean one will not have to face at least some consequence for his sin. David suffered greatly the remainder of his life for his adultery with Bathsheba and the murder of her husband, Uriah. Upon repentance, David was completely forgiven, but the prophet Nathan said to him, "The Lord has taken away your sin. You are not going to die. But because by doing this you have made the enemies of the Lord show utter contempt, the son born to you will die" (2 Samuel 12:13, 14, *NIV*). David's relationship with the Lord was restored, but he still had to endure many problems resulting from his sin.

The healing of diseases was first promised in Exodus 15:26, conditional upon keeping the commandments and statutes of the Lord. In Numbers 12:13, Moses pleaded for the healing of his sister, Miriam, from leprosy (which was a result of her sin). In 21:7-9, he set up the fiery serpent on a pole for the healing of the people from snakebites (again, the result of their sin). In both these situations there was repentance for the sins committed. However, as we look into the New Testament, Jesus did not heal people contingent upon the spiritual situation, but purely out of their need.

Notice that in verse 3 the psalmist changes from the first person ("my") to the second person ("thy"). He started by stirring his own heart, and now he challenges his readers to do likewise.

C. Salvation and Satisfaction (vv. 4, 5)

4. Who redeemeth thy life from destruction; who crowneth thee with lovingkindness and tender mercies;

5. Who satisfieth thy mouth with good things; so that thy youth is renewed like the eagle's.

Most of us can look back over our lives and see mistakes, stupid decisions, failures in the flesh, and so forth, and recognize that only the Lord's mercy and protection kept us from ruining ourselves. In verse 4, David reflects that the Lord had not only saved him from destruction, but He had exalted (or

Talk About It:
Why is the word *all* used twice in this verse?

"Not long before she died in 1988, in a moment of surprising candor in television history, Marghanita Laski, one of our best-known secular humanists and novelists, said, 'What I envy most about you Christians is your forgiveness; I have nobody to forgive me.'"
—John Stott

mouth (v. 5)— "desires" (*NIV*)

Talk About It:
1. Why do we need to be redeemed?

"Bless the Lord, O My Soul"

crowned) him with royalty. The idea of being "crowned" infers not only that God is the ultimate source of blessing, but that He sees value and dignity in His children. "Lovingkindness" speaks of the Lord's loyalty and trustworthiness toward His own. "Tender mercies" indicates the Lord's ability to empathize with our feelings and infirmities. This was amazing insight on David's part, since Jesus had not yet come to prove these qualities to the world.

In verse 5 David says God "satisfies" us. Much meaning can be found in family and friends, a life's work that is enjoyable and has benefit to others, and community service—but still a yearning is left. This can only be satiated by a relationship with the Lord. Just as there are foods we can eat that simply don't meet the body's demand, many of life's endeavors are just as fruitless. The Lord, however, can fulfill our deepest longings. One of those is for long and strong life. The eagle is a symbol of such. Eagles are known to live many years and can go long periods without food. The psalmist here, "sustained by the bounty of God in his old age . . . became, as it were, young again" (*Barnes' Notes*).

II. DECLARE GOD'S MERCY (Psalm 103:6-14)
A. Helper of the Oppressed (v. 6)

6. The Lord executeth righteousness and judgment for all that are oppressed.

Throughout history there have been tremendous abuses of people by wicked rulers in powerful positions. The thirst for power is one of the worst consequences of humanity's fall, and the devil has used this to destroy multitudes of people. Think about the millions who died because of Hitler's quest for power during World War II. In contrast, "the Lord works righteousness and justice" (*NIV*).

In Psalm 9:9 we read, "The Lord [is] a refuge for the oppressed." However, He is much more than that, for He executes justice for every wrong that has been committed. Psalm 72:4 says He will "break in pieces the oppressor." The Lord himself is the avenger, not us. In Deuteronomy 32:35, the Lord declares, "It is mine to avenge; I will repay. In due time their foot will slip; their day of disaster is near and their doom rushes upon them" (*NIV*).

B. Revelation of the Lord (vv. 7-10)

7. He made known his ways unto Moses, his acts unto the children of Israel.

8. The Lord is merciful and gracious, slow to anger, and plenteous in mercy.

9. He will not always chide: neither will he keep his anger for ever.

2. How does God want to "crown" us?
3. What does it mean to have one's "youth . . . renewed like the eagle's" (v. 5)?

"When God and His glory are made our end, we shall find a silent likeness pass in upon us; the beauty of God will, by degrees, enter upon our soul."

—Stephen Charnock

Talk About It:
Who are the "oppressed," and what does the Lord do for them?

chide (v. 9)— "accuse" (*NIV*)

10. He hath not dealt with us after our sins; nor rewarded us according to our iniquities.

The word *ways* (v. 7) is a reference to the Law. The Law was given to Moses as a means of showing the people right from wrong. They had lived under Egyptian domination for hundreds of years and did not know the ways of God. They were not so much *immoral* as they were *amoral*.

David here is thankful for God's law. Psalm 119:165 says, "Great peace have they who love your law, and nothing can make them stumble" (*NIV*). The Law gave an anchor for well-ordered living and conduct. Through obedience to the Law, the children of Israel could have peace, even in the middle of trouble and disappointment. Of course, they also found that real righteousness could not be produced by obedience to the Law. That required relationship. Every hero of the Old Testament was known for his faith and love of the Lord, not merely for his obedience to the Law. This was the fallacy of some Pharisees in Jesus' day. They forgot the virtues of love, kindness and caring, and concentrated only on obeying the minute legalisms of the Law.

After rejoicing in the Law that was revealed to Moses, David rejoices in the revelation of God himself that Moses had received. In Exodus 33:18, Moses had asked the Lord to show Him His glory. This was an amazing request, given that no one had ever experienced anything like the revelation Moses had already received. Still, Moses knew if he was to lead the Israelites, he needed an even greater sense of God's presence. This request was realized in 34:4-8. As the Lord's backside passed before Moses (who was shielded in the cleft of a rock), He proclaimed, "The Lord God, merciful and gracious, longsuffering, and abundant in goodness and truth" (v. 6). David, in Psalm 103:8-10, is speaking forth the essence of this revelation. Although the Lord becomes angry at sin, He is still merciful and does not hold His anger for long. His mercy is greater than His anger. For this David rejoices, having himself been the recipient of divine mercy.

C. The Love of a Father (vv. 11-14)

11. For as the heaven is high above the earth, so great is his mercy toward them that fear him.

12. As far as the east is from the west, so far hath he removed our transgressions from us.

13. Like as a father pitieth his children, so the Lord pitieth them that fear him.

14. For he knoweth our frame; he remembereth that we are dust.

David here compares the love of God for those who fear

Talk About It:
1. Why is Moses suddenly mentioned?
2. How is the Lord "slow" (v. 8), and why?
3. What would happen if God "dealt with us" and "punished us" (*NKJV*) as we deserve (v. 10)?

Unbreakable Word

We sometimes speak of people being only as good as their word, and we remember the times when legal agreements could be sealed with something as simple as a handshake. Because of the Lord's faithfulness, David rejoiced in the covenant God made with His people. A covenant is much deeper than a contract. Contracts have a time limitation, but a covenant is permanent. David knew God would never break His word.

pitieth (v. 13)— has compassion

Him to the distance between earth and heaven (v. 11). In other words, it is incalculable. That love is expressed in His mercy—in forgiving their sins, blessing them, giving them grace, and taking care of them in their needs. In verse 12, David amplifies Moses' revelation. God had spoken to Moses of "forgiving iniquity and transgression and sin" (Exodus 34:7). David declares that forgiven sins have been removed as far as the east is from the west! Again, this is an impossible distance to calculate. If God forgives us, then we should never take on the guilt again. He has removed it. However, the love of God is discriminating. These wonderful blessings are only for those who fear Him.

It is illustrative of David's relationship with the Lord that he compares Him to a *father* (v. 13). The concept of God as a heavenly Father was not clear in the Old Testament—except to those who knew Him as such, and these included David. Jesus spoke of "your heavenly Father" several times in the Gospels (see Matthew 6:14, 26, 32). The Father has compassion ("pitieth") on us, knowing we live in mortal bodies made from the dust of the earth.

III. REJOICE IN GOD'S LOVE (Psalm 103:15-22)

A. Transitory Existence (vv. 15, 16)

15. As for man, his days are as grass: as a flower of the field, so he flourisheth.

16. For the wind passeth over it, and it is gone; and the place thereof shall know it no more.

The last part of verse 14 speaks of man as being dust. The thought is continued here to show that our existence is brief at best. We are like a blade of grass, or a flower. Both are here today and gone tomorrow. This is in amazing contrast to the Lord, who is eternal. "The continuance of God's loving-kindness stands in the sharpest contrast possible to man's transitoriness" (*Wycliffe Bible Commentary*). The word *flourisheth* implies a blossom, fresh and beautiful—but soon to fade away. The concept of the afterlife was still vague in the Old Testament. At death everyone went to *sheol* (the Hebrew term; in Greek it was *hades*). This was understood to be an underground region, gloomy and shadowy. Both the righteous and unrighteous went there, but there was a division. Those who were wicked were punished, while the righteous enjoyed rewards.

The revelation of an eternal home in heaven came with Jesus. He told Nicodemus "that whosoever believeth in him [Jesus] should not perish, but have everlasting life" (John 3:16). We should bless the Lord every day for a better revelation of what is promised to us after death. There is a clear distinction between eternal life with Christ and eternal damnation.

Talk About It:
1. How great is God's mercy (v. 11)?
2. How far is "the east . . . from the west" (v. 12)?
3. What does God "remember" about us (v. 14), and why does this matter?

"God loves us the way we are, but too much to leave us that way."
—Leighton Ford

Talk About It:
Is the message of verses 15 and 16 encouraging or discouraging? Why?

"When I consider the short duration of my life, swallowed up in the eternity before and after, the little space which I fill, and even can see, engulfed in the immensity of space of which I am ignorant, and which knows me not, I am frightened, and am astonished being here rather than there, why now rather than then."
—Blaise Pascal

B. Covenant Keepers (vv. 17, 18)

17. But the mercy of the Lord is from everlasting to everlasting upon them that fear him, and his righteousness unto children's children;

18. To such as keep his covenant, and to those that remember his commandments to do them.

Talk About It:
1. How can our walk with God influence future generations (v. 17)?
2. How does verse 18 challenge us to live?

Despite the uncertainties of what death might bring, David still rejoiced, knowing that God would be eternally faithful to those who loved Him. He also knew that wherever death took him, God would be there. In Psalm 139:8, he said, "If I ascend up into heaven, thou art there: if I make my bed in hell, behold, thou art there." Because of the mercy of the Lord, David had no fear for the future—because he was in covenant with the Lord. The word *mercy* here might be translated as "loyal love." David had done many things wrong in his life, but knowing that the Lord's mercy never ends, he could count on a future. In contrast, there were no promises of blessing to those who *remain* unfaithful—meaning that everyone fails at some time or another. David failed at times, but he also repented, and God restored him.

"Young people set their watches, for right time or for wrong, by the watches of their elders."
—*Anonymous*

One great benefit of keeping God's law was that faithfulness would produce fruit for the next generations. "Our only hope that we or our children will be partakers of the blessings of the covenant is to be found in the fact that we ourselves are faithful to God" (*Barnes' Notes*).

C. The Lord's Throne (vv. 19-22)

19. The Lord hath prepared his throne in the heavens; and his kingdom ruleth over all.

20. Bless the Lord, ye his angels, that excel in strength, that do his commandments, hearkening unto the voice of his word.

21. Bless ye the Lord, all ye his hosts; ye ministers of his, that do his pleasure.

22. Bless the Lord, all his works in all places of his dominion: bless the Lord, O my soul.

Talk About It:
1. How does verse 19 describe God's kingdom?
2. What is the role of angels (vv. 20, 21)?
3. How do God's "works" praise Him?

David now draws attention to the Lord's kingdom. "His *throne* may be in heaven but His kingdom extends to all creation" (*Zondervan NIV Bible Commentary*). Thus, His rule is the only one that matters. Worldly kingdoms might come and go, but the Lord reigns forever.

The concept of the Kingdom was greater revealed to us by Jesus. Part of His mission was to show us that the kingdom of heaven extends everywhere, including the earth. Of course, it will not be fully revealed until He returns, but in the meantime we have been given authority to manifest many of its attributes into our daily lives. He told us, "Whatever you bind on earth will be bound in heaven, and whatever you loose on earth will be loosed in heaven" (Matthew 18:18, *NKJV*). Whenever He fed the multitudes, Jesus reached into the invisible spiritual realm of that Kingdom and manifested the abundance of food to the hungry people there in the natural realm. Miracles, divine healings, and so forth, are manifestations of God's invisible kingdom superimposing itself over the natural realm.

In Psalm 103:20-22, David calls on the heavenly hosts to join with all of creation in praising God. The psalmist's call to the angels has its parallel only in Psalm 148. The heavenly creatures are always loyal to the Lord, and God's people here on earth should follow their example.

In conclusion, David returns once more to exhorting his own soul, which he modestly includes among God's "works" mentioned in verse 22. So his final phrase mirrors his opening words: "Bless the Lord, O my soul."

> "Millions of spiritual creatures walk the earth unseen, both when we wake and when we sleep."
> —**John Milton**

CONCLUSION

How often have we given lip service to the Lord by reciting "Bless the Lord!" or "Bless Your name!" as we begin our prayer time. Sometimes our praises are spoken so much in routine that we don't realize what we are saying. To "bless the Lord" is to remember and remind ourselves that He is the source of every good thing in our lives. More often than not, however, we aren't even thinking about the great things He has already done, but are focused on those problems facing us. The best way to face the future is to remember the faithfulness of the past. Let us continually "bless the Lord" by reviewing the mercies and blessings He has extended to us.

GOLDEN TEXT CHALLENGE

"BLESS THE LORD, O MY SOUL: AND ALL THAT IS WITHIN ME, BLESS HIS HOLY NAME" (Psalm 103:1).

Contemplating the many benefits he received from God, the psalmist was caught up into a rapture of joy. He exhorted his soul and innermost being to praise the Lord.

By stirring up himself to gratitude, the psalmist gave a lesson to all believers of the duty incumbent on us. For doubtless the negligence in offering praise to God for His bountiful blessings rests on all of us and we need the reminder to offer praise. John Calvin said, "The Holy Spirit indirectly upbraids us on account of our not being more diligent in praising God, and at the same time points out the remedy, that every person may look into himself and correct his own sluggishness."

Not content with merely calling upon his soul—by which he most likely meant the seat of understanding and affection—to bless Jehovah, the psalmist also included "all that is within me."

With this comment, he addressed his mind and heart and all the faculties of both. The Hebrew mind was keenly aware of the admonition of the Lord in Deuteronomy 6:5: "Thou shalt love the Lord thy God with all thine heart, and with all thy soul, and with all thy might." Throughout the Bible the diligence with which devout Jews praised the Lord is in evidence.

"Thou Art Worthy"

Revelation 4:1 through 5:14

INTRODUCTION

The Book of Revelation was written when the first-century church was facing persecution from outside, as well as struggles from within. Rome was becoming increasingly antagonistic to the gospel (as demonstrated by the execution of both Paul and Peter, as well as the exile of John), and many churches faced suffering, spiritual warfare, heresy, sinful practices among their members, and even spiritual apathy. All of these problems are exposed in the seven letters of Revelation 2 and 3.

With this backdrop in mind, the initial readers of Revelation were hungry for encouragement and hope. They needed to be reminded that God is sovereign—greater than any power anywhere. He controls all of history, as well as everything in the future. Even though Satan may exert temporary havoc on the earth, Christ will be victorious. Faithful believers will be protected from divine judgment on the world. They will inherit eternal life, and will reign with Christ.

Just as the first readers of Revelation received hope, so can we today. With nuclear proliferation and the prospects of mass destruction, the blatant rise of terrorism, the violent hatred brought on by false religions, and the ever-increasing knowledge that evil is out of control, we thirst for the same encouragement that the first-century believers longed for. We must see freshly that Christ really is in control, and that we have a destiny to share with Him in His ultimate reign.

Some of the prophecies in Revelation had an immediate fulfillment in the early church age, but they also have a long-range fulfillment. This is typical of Biblical prophecy. We see the great spectacles John described as culminating in the future. Perilous world conditions can easily be seen as ratifying such a conclusion.

Jesus admonished His saints to be watchful and prayerful during perilous times "that you may be counted worthy to escape all these things that will come to pass, and to stand before the Son of Man" (Luke 21:36, *NKJV*). This verse gives us a great clue to understanding our present passage and lesson. In clarification, we must understand that the Book of Revelation falls into an outline of three parts. John was instructed in 1:19, "Write the things which thou hast seen, and the things which are, and the things which shall be hereafter." The things "thou hast seen" are found in chapter 1. The things "which are" are found in chapters 2 and 3. The things "which shall be hereafter" begin with chapter 4 and continue through chapter 22.

Unit Theme:
Great Hymns of the Bible

Central Truth:
Christ, the Lamb of God, is worthy of all praise.

Focus:
Acknowledge that Christ is worthy and worship Him.

Context:
The Revelation was recorded by John the apostle while on the island of Patmos around A.D. 96.

Golden Text:
"Thou art worthy, O Lord, to receive glory and honour and power: for thou hast created all things, and for thy pleasure they are and were created" (Revelation 4:11).

Study Outline:
I. Worthy of Praise (Revelation 4:1-11)
II. Worthy to Open the Book (Revelation 5:1-10)
III. Worthy Is the Lamb (Revelation 5:11-14)

I. WORTHY OF PRAISE (Revelation 4:1-11)

A. The Throne of Heaven (vv. 1-3)

1. After this I looked, and, behold, a door was opened in heaven: and the first voice which I heard was as it were of a trumpet talking with me; which said, Come up hither, and I will shew thee things which must be hereafter.

2. And immediately I was in the spirit: and, behold, a throne was set in heaven, and one sat on the throne.

3. And he that sat was to look upon like a jasper and a sardine stone: and there was a rainbow round about the throne, in sight like unto an emerald.

Talk About It:
1. What is the significance of the statement "A door was opened in heaven" (v. 1)?
2. Explain the statement "At once I was in the Spirit" (v. 2, *NIV*).
3. What is the significance of the "rainbow round about the throne" (v. 3)?

Our text for this lesson marks the beginning of the things to come. Revelation 4:1 uses the phrase "after this" and the word *hereafter.* Sandwiched between the two is the phrase "come up hither." This is so "similar to that which the church anticipates at the Rapture that many have connected the two expressions. It is clear from the context that this is not an explicit reference to the rapture of the church, as John was not actually translated; in fact he was still in his natural body on the island of Patmos" (John F. Walvoord, *The Revelation of Jesus Christ*). John was in heaven only temporarily through his vision. Still, it seems that this represents the natural order of events. In other words, what John was seeing at this point was the end of the church age, that the saints have been caught away to be with the Lord, and that they are catching their first view of the throne of God. Thus, from this point on in Revelation, all things are viewed from the perspective of eternity. To come to this conclusion, we point out that God promises that His wrath will not fall upon believers. First Thessalonians 5:9 says, "For God did not appoint us to suffer wrath but to receive salvation through our Lord Jesus Christ" (*NIV*). He was careful to remove Noah and his family (Genesis 6—8) and Lot (ch. 19) before sending destruction.

Much like Isaiah (Isaiah 6), John here is caught up into the realm of the Spirit and sees heaven. He is in the very presence of God. "The reference to heaven is not to the atmospheric heavens nor to the starry heavens, but to that which is beyond the natural eye which the best of telescopes cannot reveal. This is the third heaven, the immediate presence of God" (Walvoord). The voice he hears is the same he heard in 1:10. The invitation to "come up hither" requires no effort on his part, but of itself transports him. The prophecies he will now see indicate things to happen in the future, as indicated by the word *hereafter.* Since the word *church* (which occurs so often in chapters 2 and 3) is not mentioned again until 22:16, it might be argued that the saints are now in heaven and are not part of the events that will transpire on earth as described in much of the rest of the book. People who come to know the Lord on earth during this period "are described as saved Israelites or saved Gentiles, never by terms which are characteristic of the church, the body of Christ" (Walvoord).

The precious stones John saw in his description of the Lord seem to have some meaning. *Jasper* is like clear crystal, or what we would call a diamond. This might refer to the purity of God. The *sardine stone*—similar to a ruby, a beautiful red—might indicate the blood of redemption. The rainbow of *emerald* green conveys the idea of the Lord's "encircling brilliance." Since the rainbow first appeared at the covenant with Noah indicating that the earth would never again be destroyed by flood, it represents God's unchanging mercy.

The One sitting on the throne is God the Father, since Christ is represented separately as the Lamb. This might seem contradictory, since Christ on the throne is mentioned in 3:21. A simple explanation is resolved by the unity of the Trinity. Jesus said, "He that hath seen me hath seen the Father" (John 14:9). Also, Christ is said to be "seated at the right hand of God" (Colossians 3:1, *NIV*).

B. Around the Throne (vv. 4-6a)

4. And round about the throne were four and twenty seats: and upon the seats I saw four and twenty elders sitting, clothed in white raiment; and they had on their heads crowns of gold.

5. And out of the throne proceeded lightnings and thunderings and voices: and there were seven lamps of fire burning before the throne, which are the seven Spirits of God.

6a. And before the throne there was a sea of glass like unto crystal.

John's attention is drawn to the 24 elders sitting on thrones surrounding the grand throne. They are clothed in white and have crowns of gold. Interestingly, there were 24 orders of priests during the days of David and Solomon. Each order was represented by one priest in conclaves and meetings. "When these priests met together, even though there were only 24, they represented the whole priesthood and at the same time the whole of the nation of Israel" (Walvoord). In the New Testament, Peter describes the saints as a "holy priesthood" (1 Peter 2:5). It is possible then, that the elders here are a picture of the redeemed saints of all time, both Jew and Gentile. Another possibility is that they represent the 12 tribes of Israel and the 12 disciples. Whatever the situation, they are dressed in white, indicating that their earthly labors are finished. Their crowns of gold speak of having received a glorious reward, having overcome by the blood of the Lamb.

The lightning and thunder signifies here (as well as other

Talk About It:
1. What are the elders wearing, and why?
2. Describe the various sights and sounds John experienced at the throne (vv. 5, 6).

In 1715 King Louis XIV of France died after a reign of 72 years. He had called himself "the Great." As his body lay in state in a golden coffin, orders were given that the cathedral should be very dimly lit with only a special candle set above his coffin, to dramatize his greatness. When Bishop Massilon began to speak at the funeral, he snuffed out the candle and said, "Only God is great."

places in Revelation) that something important is about to happen. This also happened at Sinai when God gave the Law (see Exodus 19:16). Here, the indication is that judgment and wrath are coming. The seven lamps before the throne indicate both the omniscience and omnipresence of the Holy Spirit. The Holy Spirit is not seen in human figure, since He is a spirit. When the Spirit descended on Christ at His baptism, He appeared as a dove. At Pentecost, the form was "cloven tongues . . . of fire" (Acts 2:3). The number *seven* is symbolic of the perfection of the Spirit.

The "sea of glass" likely doesn't mean that John is speaking about a body of water or glass. Rather, he is referring symbolically to the appearance of the surface before the throne. There is depth and transparency, calmness and stability, clarity and strength in the reign of God.

C. The Four Living Creatures (vv. 6b-9)

6b. And in the midst of the throne, and round about the throne, were four beasts full of eyes before and behind.

7. And the first beast was like a lion, and the second beast like a calf, and the third beast had a face as a man, and the fourth beast was like a flying eagle.

8. And the four beasts had each of them six wings about him; and they were full of eyes within: and they rest not day and night, saying, Holy, holy, holy, Lord God Almighty, which was, and is, and is to come.

9. And when those beasts give glory and honour and thanks to him that sat on the throne, who liveth for ever and ever.

John's rapt attention is drawn to the four living creatures in the midst of the throne. They are strange beings in that they are full of eyes and wings. In addition, they are seen separately as a lion, a calf, a man, and a flying eagle. Their purpose seems to be to constantly ascribe holiness to the Lord. There is an interesting correlation here. The four faces of the creatures match the four Gospel letters. Matthew wrote to the Jews, and often spoke of Christ as the *Lion* of Judah. Mark wrote to the pragmatic Romans, portraying Christ as the perfect *servant*, much like an ox. Luke wrote to the sophisticated Greek mind, thus portraying the Lord as the perfect *man*. Finally, John wrote of the deity of Christ, showing Him soaring like an *eagle.*

The four creatures have a distinct ministry. They give constant praise to the holiness of God and His eternity. They are also similar to what Ezekiel saw (Ezekiel 1:4-10), as well as the six-winged seraphim Isaiah saw (Isaiah 6:2, 3), and might be identified as *cherubim,* or angels whose role is to bring honor and glory to God. Their song—"Holy, holy, holy, Lord God Almighty,

Talk About It:
1. Describe the ministry of the four beasts.
2. What does it mean to call God "Holy, holy, holy" (v. 8)?

which was, and is, and is to come" (Revelation 4:8)—has been sung by saints over the last 2,000 years countless times.

D. The Worship of the Elders and the Creatures (vv. 10, 11)

10. The four and twenty elders fall down before him that sat on the throne, and worship him that liveth for ever and ever, and cast their crowns before the throne, saying,

11. Thou art worthy, O Lord, to receive glory and honour and power: for thou hast created all things, and for thy pleasure they are and were created.

The creatures never rest in their worship and ascription of holiness to God, but periodically the elders join them. The word *worship* comes from the Old English word *worthship,* and denotes ascribing worth to one who is deserving. Bowing, lying prostrate before, building altars, speaking praise, lifting one's hands unto—all these are means of expressing worship. The elders give their worship by falling prostrate and casting their crowns before the throne. By casting their crowns, they testify that it was by God's grace, mercy and salvation made available through Christ that they were able to overcome.

Talk About It:
1. What do the elders do with their crowns, and why?
2. Why should "all things" glorify God (v. 11)?

Matthew Henry said the reason for their adoration of God is threefold: "(1) He is the Creator of all things, the first cause; and none but the Creator of all things should be adored; no made thing can be the object of religious worship. (2) He is the preserver of all things, and His preservation is a continual creation; they are created still by the sustaining power of God. All beings but God are dependent upon the will and power of God, and no dependent being must be set up as an object of religious worship. (3) He is the final cause of all things at His pleasure, so He made them for His pleasure, to deal with them as He pleases and to glorify Himself by them one way or other."

II. WORTHY TO OPEN THE BOOK (Revelation 5:1-10)
A. Reason to Weep (vv. 1-4)

1. And I saw in the right hand of him that sat on the throne a book written within and on the backside, sealed with seven seals.

2. And I saw a strong angel proclaiming with a loud voice, Who is worthy to open the book, and to loose the seals thereof?

3. And no man in heaven, nor in earth, neither under the earth, was able to open the book, neither to look thereon.

4. And I wept much, because no man was found worthy to open and to read the book, neither to look thereon.

John was introduced to a book containing the prophecies of the events that would unfold in the rest of Revelation. The book, which was probably a scroll, was sealed with seven seals. Its

Talk About It:
1. Why do you suppose this book was so tightly sealed?
2. What could not be found, and why not?

being in the right hand of the Father sitting on the throne gave it supreme importance. The seals must be broken in succession in order to be unrolled and read. "Roman law required a will to be sealed seven times as illustrated in the wills left by Augustus and Vespasian for their successors" (Walvoord).

The "strong angel" (v. 2) is a powerful being. His role is similar to that of a court bailiff. He doesn't merely say something—he proclaims it for all to hear. The proclamation is in the form of a question: Who has the authority to loose the seals and open the book? The silence that follows indicates that no one in heaven nor on earth has such authority. John then records that he wept, perhaps not even knowing why. This dramatic moment impresses upon him the importance of the contents of the book and the revelation it contains.

The scroll contains the "mystery of God" that Old Testament prophets foretold centuries earlier (see Revelation 10:7). It unveils the entire puzzle of the universe, and how history will culminate for all the earth and its inhabitants. It unfolds God's ultimate work in renewing His creation, once again making a perfect state for humanity to live in fellowship with the Creator.

"There are 256 names given in the Bible for the Lord Jesus Christ, and I suppose this was because He was infinitely beyond all that any one name could express."
—Billy Sunday

B. The Worthy Lamb (vv. 5-8)

5. And one of the elders saith unto me, Weep not: behold, the Lion of the tribe of Juda, the Root of David, hath prevailed to open the book, and to loose the seven seals thereof.

6. And I beheld, and, lo, in the midst of the throne and of the four beasts, and in the midst of the elders, stood a Lamb as it had been slain, having seven horns and seven eyes, which are the seven Spirits of God sent forth into all the earth.

7. And he came and took the book out of the right hand of him that sat upon the throne.

vials (v. 8)—bowls

8. And when he had taken the book, the four beasts and four and twenty elders fell down before the Lamb, having every one of them harps, and golden vials full of odours, which are the prayers of saints.

Suddenly and unexpectedly, one of the elders speaks to John, admonishing him not to weep, for the "Lion of the tribe of Judah" is able to open the book. If indeed the 24 elders are made up of the 12 tribal leaders of Israel and the 12 apostles, then this elder might be Judah himself. Judah was called a lion by Jacob in Genesis 49:9, 10. Here it was prophesied that the Messiah would come from Judah. The phrase "Root of David" comes from the prophecy of Isaiah 11:1, indicating that the Messiah would be of David's lineage. The lion symbolizes the strength of Christ at His second coming, being majestic and

Talk About It
1. Explain the three names given to Christ in verses 5 and 6.
2. What do the elders' actions in verse 8 say about Christ?
3. What is in the golden bowls, and why (v. 8)?

"Thou Art Worthy"

sovereign. At the sound of this title, John must have gotten excited. He turns, likely expecting to see the Lion, or at least see Jesus as he had known Him in His earthly ministry.

Instead, John sees a "slain" Lamb with the marks of death still written on His body. These will remain on Christ's body for all eternity. It has been said that the only one who will live in heaven with a less-than-perfect body will be the eternally perfect One himself.

This "Lamb, looking as if it had been slain" (Revelation 5:6, *NIV*), has seven horns and seven eyes. The horns represent omnipotence, while the eyes indicate omniscience. The beasts and the elders all fall down in adoration and worship. Thus, Christ is shown to be equal with the Father. Only God may be worshiped (see 19:10).

The beasts and the elders each hold a bowl full of incense (v. 8), which represents the prayers of saints offered through the ages. The sincere prayers of God's people are never lost. Their answers may be postponed, but every one will eventually be answered. We should remember this every time we pray. The opening of our hearts to the Lord is so precious to Him that He keeps our prayers as treasures.

C. A New Song (vv. 9, 10)

9. And they sung a new song, saying, Thou art worthy to take the book, and to open the seals thereof: for thou wast slain, and hast redeemed us to God by thy blood out of every kindred, and tongue, and people, and nation;

10. And hast made us unto our God kings and priests: and we shall reign on the earth.

Verse 8 also told us that the beasts and the elders each had harps. The trumpet and the harp are the only instruments mentioned in heavenly worship. It is not stated that the harps are played, but it is implied. When the people of Judah were carried off into Babylonian captivity, they hung up their harps in sorrow (Psalm 137:1-4), signifying that they no longer had anything to celebrate in music. Here, however, we see every reason for God's people to rejoice. Along with their worship, they sing a new song. It recounts all the work Christ accomplished, for which He is to be praised. He was slain as the perfect Lamb, redeeming with His blood those who believe. He brings them into His kingdom, makes them priests, and appoints them to reign on the earth.

The song gives every bit of glory to the Lamb. He is the only One worthy of praise. Believers should always remember this, making certain that beautiful voices and talent not tempt them to take any credit for themselves.

Only One

Henry Morris wrote, "But what is this remarkable scroll? It is nothing less than the title deed to the earth itself." Throughout history men have tried to "open the scroll" but failed. Nebuchadnezzar, Alexander the Great, the Caesars of the Roman Empire, Napoleon, Hitler—all had a thirst for power, much the same as what brought on Lucifer's fall. Even the godly people of history who did great things were not able to reverse the downward spiral of sin on the planet. There is only One who is worthy to open the scroll and finally bring evil to an end.

Talk About It:
1. What made this "a new song" (v. 9)?
2. What does Christ do for the "redeemed"?

III. WORTHY IS THE LAMB (Revelation 5:11-14)

A. Throngs of Angels (v. 11)

11. And I beheld, and I heard the voice of many angels round about the throne and the beasts and the elders: and the number of them was ten thousand times ten thousand, and thousands of thousands.

Talk About It:
Why do you suppose God created so many angels?

There is nothing more wonderful than to be involved in a large convocation of believers and to hear them all worshiping and praying in unity. In the scene that John sees, the Lamb takes the scroll from the Father, evoking a scene of ecstasy from all present. The angelic hosts break out into spontaneous praise. The time has finally arrived for evildoers to be judged and their power taken away from them. The number of angelic hosts present is staggering—10,000 times 10,000 (equaling 100 million) plus 1,000 times 1,000 (1 million). Angels are spiritual beings created to help carry out God's work in all His creation. Their great numbers indicate the fantastic scope of what John was witnessing. John had seen Jesus beaten and crucified. In fact, he was the only disciple who stayed at the cross. Now he sees millions encircling Him with worship and praise.

B. The Praise of All Heaven (vv. 12-14)

12. Saying with a loud voice, Worthy is the Lamb that was slain to receive power, and riches, and wisdom, and strength, and honour, and glory, and blessing.

13. And every creature which is in heaven, and on the earth, and under the earth, and such as are in the sea, and all that are in them, heard I saying, Blessing, and honour, and glory, and power, be unto him that sitteth upon the throne, and unto the Lamb for ever and ever.

14. And the four beasts said, Amen. And the four and twenty elders fell down and worshipped him that liveth for ever and ever.

Talk About It:
1. What is the Lamb worthy to receive, and why?
2. What did John hear "every creature" doing (v. 13)?

In concentric circles with the Lamb at the center, the throngs of heaven join in singing. The words they sing speak of seven attributes ascribed to the Lamb—power, riches, wisdom, strength, honor, glory and blessing—for which He deserves their worship and adoration. This unparalleled scene of praise sets up the scenes which will follow, in which the seven-sealed book will be unrolled.

Added to the mighty chorus in heaven is the praise of every creature on the earth and in the sea. This is a reiteration of Psalm 148:7-12, where we read, "Praise the Lord from the earth, you great sea creatures and all ocean depths, lightning and hail, snow and clouds, stormy winds that do his bidding, you mountains and all hills, fruit trees and all cedars, wild animals and all cattle, small creatures and flying birds, kings of the earth and all nations, you princes and all rulers on earth, young men and maidens, old men and children" (*NIV*).

Believers today can draw magnificent hope from the fact that they will personally see the same scene that was unfolded prophetically in Revelation 4 and 5 for the apostle John. We will be part of the glorious throng praising God around the throne.

> "It is clear that there is one main message creation has to communicate to human beings, namely, the glory of God. Not primarily the glory of creation, but the glory of God."
> —**John Piper**

CONCLUSION

Jesus said, "All authority in heaven and on earth has been given to me. Therefore go and make disciples of all nations" (Matthew 28:18, 19, *NIV*). In other words, Jesus took back what the devil had stolen from Adam and gave it again to us. Now, if redeemed men and women have the right to disciple even nations, why is the world degenerating to a point that evil is so rampant that Jesus must "open the scroll" and bring things to an end? After all, didn't He say we would do "even greater things" (John 14:12, *NIV*) than He had done?

The answer lies in a number of facts: Evil is still on the earth, the devil is fighting harder as his time gets shorter, fallen human nature has not changed, the earth itself is degenerating, and the human population is multiplying faster than ever. There are more people alive today than in all the centuries prior put together. Still, this should not stop us from moving in power. Jesus said, "The kingdom of heaven suffers violence, and the violent take it by force" (Matthew 11:12, *NKJV*).

Even though we read Revelation and see a terrible time to come on the earth, there is a generation rising that also sees the opportunity to win millions to Christ throughout the nations. The scope of the problem should not discourage us at all from doing greater things and bringing as many as possible into the Kingdom.

GOLDEN TEXT CHALLENGE

"THOU ART WORTHY, O LORD, TO RECEIVE GLORY AND HONOUR AND POWER: FOR THOU HAST CREATED ALL THINGS, AND FOR THY PLEASURE THEY ARE AND WERE CREATED" (Revelation 4:11).

Here the worthiness of the Lamb of God is associated with Creation. Everything that has been created is Jesus' handiwork, and has been made for His pleasure. Our ultimate purpose in living is to give Him pleasure because He is worthy. The things we get puffed up about and boast that we "created" are not creations at all. They are merely new discoveries, new arrangements, and rearrangements of materials and ideas He has already provided. Jesus deserves our praise and worship because He alone is Creator.

This verse shows heaven's praise is intelligent, flowing from the understanding of who God is. The closer we are to the throne and the presence of the Lord, the more intelligent our praise becomes. Worshipers extol Him because He is worthy of glory—we ascribe praise to Him. He is worthy of honor—we approach Him as worthy of all our respect. He is worthy of power—we recognize the infinite authority resident in the One on the throne.

"Thou Art Worthy"

"Alleluia"

Revelation 11:15-19; 19:1-10

INTRODUCTION

As stated in our last lesson, the Book of Revelation falls into an outline as given in 1:19. The first section, the "things which thou hast seen," is found in chapter 1. The "things which are" are seen in chapters 2 and 3, and the "things which shall be hereafter" begin with chapter 4. This third section continues to the end of the book. A further breakdown of the third point is useful for setting up our present lesson:

A. Worship in heaven, the subject of our last lesson (4:1—5:14)
B. Seven seals (6:1—8:5)
C. Seven trumpets (8:6—11:19)
D. Seven wonders (or signs) (12:1—14:20)
E. Seven bowls (15:1—16:21)
F. The final judgment and the triumph of Christ (17:1—20:15)
G. A new heaven and new earth (21:1—22:5)
H. Conclusion (22:6-21)

In the sections devoted to groups of seven items (B–E), a pattern becomes obvious. Six of the seven in each group unleash major actions. Then there is a pause during which God's people are encouraged to persevere and remain faithful. The seventh item then unfolds and gives rise to the next seven. This climaxes with the concluding defeat of evil and ultimate victory of Christ.

The first of the two texts for our lesson is Revelation 11:15-19. When the seventh trumpet sounds, John suddenly hears voices in heaven announcing that the kingdoms of the earth have become the kingdoms of Christ, and that from this point on, He will reign forever. Even though there are other judgments coming, the end is in sight. The inhabitants of heaven, and earth as well, have been plainly shown that God is in control, holding ultimate power over all things. The announcement of the reign of the King occurs here, but the final breaking of the enemies' hold over the world does not occur until the return of Christ in 19:11. "This event is so certain that the angels sang of it as though it had already occurred. They were shouting that the whole world has now become Christ's kingdom. These voices were declaring the triumph of Christ and His establishment on the throne, reigning forever and ever" (*The Life Application Commentary Series*).

Unit Theme:
Great Hymns of the Bible

Central Truth:
Christ will come again and the redeemed will reign with Him forever.

Focus:
Proclaim that Christ will reign and anticipate His kingdom rule.

Context:
The Revelation was recorded by John the apostle while on the island of Patmos around A.D. 96.

Golden Text:
"I heard a great voice of much people in heaven, saying, Alleluia; Salvation, and glory, and honour, and power, unto the Lord our God" (Revelation 19:1).

Study Outline:
I. Christ's Kingdom Is Supreme (Revelation 11:15-19)
II. Our God Reigns (Revelation 19:1-6)
III. United With Christ Forever (Revelation 19:7-10)

I. CHRIST'S KINGDOM IS SUPREME (Revelation 11:15-19)

If a thing is certain, we can rejoice in it. Despite any present struggle, trial or disaster we might be going through, the Word declares that God will triumph and vindicate His people. This is the message of the Book of Revelation. The words of Hannah Whitall Smith are relevant here: "It is of vital importance for us to understand that the Bible is a statement, not of theories, but of facts; and that things are not true because they are in the Bible, but they are only in the Bible because they are true" (*The God of All Comfort, The God Who Is Enough*).

A. Victory Proclamation (v. 15)

15. And the seventh angel sounded; and there were great voices in heaven, saying, The kingdoms of this world are become the kingdoms of our Lord, and of his Christ; and he shall reign for ever and ever.

Talk About It:
What will happen to the nations of the world?

The "great voices" heard here are probably the heavenly choirs. Prior to this moment, the proclamations have been made by a single voice, but here it is by the throngs. The phrase "the kingdoms of this world" is better translated in the singular *kingdom*. It is true that the world is presently under the control of Satan, because Christ has not yet returned to claim His rights. We might draw a parallel from the parable of the wicked vinedressers, who were under the influence of the Evil One (Matthew 21:33-41; Mark 12:1-12; Luke 20:9-16). When the master returned, he destroyed them. There was never any question that he would return and claim what was rightfully his.

In the same sense, even though Satan exerts control over fallen humanity, Christ's victory has been won. Satan offered Him the kingdoms of the world in the wilderness temptations (Matthew 4; Luke 4), but He refused. Instead, He chose to die on the cross as a blood offering for humanity's sins. He then arose, and returned victoriously to heaven, where the Father gave Him His inheritance. All He has to do now is return and claim it.

The psalmist saw this prophetically and declared, "The One enthroned in heaven laughs; the Lord scoffs at them. Then he rebukes them in his anger and terrifies them in his wrath, saying, 'I have installed my King on Zion, my holy hill'" (Psalm 2:4-6, *NIV*). He then goes on to declare that this King will rule with an "iron scepter" (v. 9, *NIV*), dashing His enemies to pieces.

"Our vision of hope goes beyond better schools, spiritual revival in the culture, or an improved political situation. We have an eternal hope—the kingdom of God."
—David C. Cooper

Even though Satan runs a regime on earth today, we shouldn't assume that the Lord is not reigning over His kingdom. Revelation 3:21 says Christ is enthroned with His Father, and He "must reign till He has put all enemies under His feet" (1 Corinthians 15:25, *NKJV*). The Kingdom is presently in the spiritual realm, but we have access to it. We are like American citizens living in a foreign country, but still having the same rights, privileges and responsibilities of any other Americans.

"Alleluia"

B. The Worship of the Elders (vv. 16, 17)

16. And the four and twenty elders, which sat before God on their seats, fell upon their faces, and worshipped God,

17. Saying, We give thee thanks, O Lord God Almighty, which art, and wast, and art to come; because thou hast taken to thee thy great power, and hast reigned.

As we saw in our last lesson, the elders again leave their thrones and throw themselves prostrate before the Lord. They have appeared seven times prior to this moment in Revelation. They sing a song of praise, much like the one that was sung in Revelation 4:8, 11. They exalt the "great power" of God. The Greek word here is *dynamis*, from where we get the English word *dynamite*, indicating explosive power. "God's power here is demonstrated in the sense of authority as well as in the sense of ability to accomplish His will" (John F. Walvoord, *The Revelation of Jesus Christ*).

The power exerted here is much different from the power Jesus exerted while on the earth. He taught the power of humility (see Matthew 3:11), the power of forgiveness (9:4-8), and the power of self-sacrifice (John 10:17, 18). Also, after His ascension, Jesus gave His followers the power of the Holy Spirit (Acts 1:8; 2:4) to accomplish His calling on their lives. The power that He gives us is not for destroying our enemies. He will do that. Rather, we are empowered to do the works of the Kingdom.

The elders sing a song of thanksgiving. Giving thanks is a necessary ingredient of Christian living. Paul said in Philippians 4:6 that we should "be careful for nothing; but in every thing by prayer and supplication with thanksgiving let [our] requests be made known unto God." As stated earlier, if a promise is from God, then whether it be visible before our eyes or not, we can still know it will come to pass. Thus, we can give thanks with total trust.

Both Daniel and Zechariah prophesied that a time will come when the Lord's kingdom will destroy the kingdoms of this world. Daniel 2:44 says, "In the days of these kings shall the God of heaven set up a kingdom, which shall never be destroyed: and the kingdom shall not be left to other people, but it shall break in pieces and consume all these kingdoms, and it shall stand for ever." Zechariah 14:9 declares, "The Lord shall be king over all the earth: in that day shall there be one Lord, and his name one." Because of the integrity of the Word, we can give thanks just as the elders do about the coming reign of Christ.

C. Table of Contents (v. 18)

18. And the nations were angry, and thy wrath is come, and the time of the dead, that they should be judged, and that thou shouldest give reward unto thy servants the

Talk About It:
What is the reason for the elders' particular act of worship here?

"Take Jesus out of the Bible—and it is like taking . . . truth out of history, matter out of physics . . . numbers out of mathematics. . . . Through this book the name of Jesus —the revealed, the redeeming, the risen, the reigning, the returning Lord—runs like a glimmering light."
—Robert G. Lee

prophets, and to the saints, and them that fear thy name, small and great; and shouldest destroy them which destroy the earth.

Here we are given a preview, or table of contents, for the remainder of the Book of Revelation. Three points are discernible:

1. *The nations are angry because they want to have their own way.* They set themselves against the Lord's rule. "Like adolescent children, the nations want to cast off all restraint; and God will permit them to do so" (*The Bible Exposition Commentary*). Romans 1:25 tell us of rebellious humanity "who changed the truth of God into a lie, and worshipped and served the creature more than the Creator."

2. *The nations cast off all restraint.* This is a reflection of Psalm 2:2, 3: "The kings of the earth set themselves, and the rulers take counsel together, against the Lord, and against his anointed, saying, Let us break their bands asunder, and cast away their cords from us." This attitude will bring them together to fight against God at the Battle of Armageddon.

3. *The time for judgment of the wicked dead has finally come.* This is carried out in Revelation 20:11-15. Also referred to here is the judgment of the righteous, or the judgment seat of Christ. This will not be a judgment of sins, but rather one of rewards for works done for the Lord.

The reference to "them which destroy the earth" (11:18) is interesting. These are those who absolutely refuse to submit to God. Instead, they worship the earth and all its pleasures as their only home. Ironically, they are bringing on the destruction of the very thing they are grasping.

D. The Temple in Heaven (v. 19)

19. And the temple of God was opened in heaven, and there was seen in his temple the ark of his testament: and there were lightnings, and voices, and thunderings, and an earthquake, and great hail.

Before this point in Revelation 11, the temple in Jerusalem during the Great Tribulation is referenced (see vv. 1, 2). Now a different temple opens up. "Though the earthly temple may have been desecrated by the Beast, its counterpart in heaven reflects the righteousness and majesty of God" (Walvoord). This likely is not a physical building, because Revelation 21:22 declares, "I did not see a temple in the city, because the Lord God Almighty and the Lamb are its temple" (*NIV*). "What John was seeing is the place where God dwells and the ark of the covenant, which had always symbolized God's presence" (*Life Application Commentary*).

The song of Revelation 11:15, which we continue to sing

Talk About It:
1. Who will be rewarded?
2. Who will be condemned?

"Eternity to the godly is a day that has no sunset; eternity to the wicked is a night that has no sunrise."
—Thomas Watson

Talk About It:
1. What item did John see in heaven, and why would it be there?
2. What does God send upon the earth?

today, is that there is a time in the future when "the kingdoms of this world are become the kingdoms of our Lord, and of his Christ." These words were immortalized in the "Hallelujah Chorus" of Handel's grand work, *The Messiah*. This reminds us also of the one prayer that saints through the ages have prayed and which has yet to be fully realized. Jesus taught it as part of the model prayer when He said, "Thy kingdom come. Thy will be done in earth, as it is in heaven" (Matthew 6:10). Spiritually and invisibly, the Kingdom already exists in the hearts of believers who make up the church, as well as in God's overall control of life on the earth. With the blowing of the seventh trumpet, the ultimate fulfillment of Christ's kingdom will be one step closer.

> "Judgment is real. Mark Twain said, 'It is not the parts of the Bible I don't understand that trouble me; it's the parts I do understand.' The awesome judgment of God is a troubling reality."
> —David C. Cooper

II. OUR GOD REIGNS (Revelation 19:1-6)
A. The Saints' Roar (vv. 1-3)

1. And after these things I heard a great voice of much people in heaven, saying, Alleluia; Salvation, and glory, and honour, and power, unto the Lord our God:

2. For true and righteous are his judgments: for he hath judged the great whore, which did corrupt the earth with her fornication, and hath avenged the blood of his servants at her hand.

3. And again they said, Alleluia. And her smoke rose up for ever and ever.

These verses describe the celebration that marks the end of the destruction of Babylon the Great (chs. 17 and 18). "Babylon was the source of all religious deception and confusion; Babylon has caused the death of multitudes of God's saints; and now Babylon has been destroyed" (*The Bible Exposition Commentary*). We see again the heavenly throne John viewed at the beginning of chapter 4. The throngs in heaven are praising God for His victory. Throughout the first eight verses of chapter 19, four "Hallelujah choruses" are sung by the multitudes in anticipation of Christ's return to the earth. The sounds of praise are louder than the screams of blasphemy on the earth. The apostate church and political system—the great harlot whose false teaching has corrupted the people of the earth—has now been judged.

The word *alleluia* is a translation of the Greek *allelouia,* which comes from the Hebrew word *hallelujah.* It appears four times in Revelation 19, and no other place in Scripture. "*Hallelujah* is taken directly from the Hebrew and is made up of two words: *hallel,* meaning 'praise,' and *jah,* a basic word for God" (*The Wycliffe Bible Commentary*). In addition to the alleluias, four other praise words are heard: *salvation, glory, honor* and *power.* "All that there is of honor, glory, power, in the redemption of the world belongs to God, and should be

Talk About It:
1. How will God prove Himself to be the perfect judge (vv. 1, 2)?
2. Explain the smoke in verse 3.

> "Belief in God and in immortality gives us the moral strength and ethical guidance we need for virtually every action in our daily lives."
> —Wernher von Braun

ascribed to Him. This is expressive of the true feelings of piety always; this will constitute the song of heaven" (*Barnes' Notes*).

B. "Amen" and "Alleluia" (v. 4)

4. And the four and twenty elders and the four beasts fell down and worshipped God that sat on the throne, saying, Amen; Alleluia.

Talk About It:
What do the 24 elders and four creatures say here, and why?

The elders and beasts worship here with the same reverence they did in the earlier scene of chapter 4. The fact that their worship is described separately from that of the "great multitude" (v. 1, *NIV*) may indicate that the elders represent the raptured church, while the multitude make up the martyred saints of the Great Tribulation. Whatever the case, they all praise God, falling on their faces in absolute humility and submission. The elders' and creatures' cry of "Amen" affirms all that God has done, and they echo the multitudes' cry of "Alleluia."

This rejoicing brings up the question as to whether we should rejoice at our enemies' downfall, especially in light of the admonitions of the Lord to "love your enemies" (Luke 6:27, 35). The call for rejoicing of the saints and heavenly hosts over Babylon's fall, however, was issued in Revelation 18:20. These wicked are not our enemies, but enemies of Christ. David said, "The Lord said to my Lord, 'Sit at My right hand, till I make Your enemies Your footstool'" (Psalm 110:1, *NKJV*). "So, as the evil systems of earth explode, God's people exclaim in praise, 'Amen! Hallelujah!'" (*Life Application Commentary*).

C. The Final Alleluia (vv. 5, 6)

5. And a voice came out of the throne, saying, Praise our God, all ye his servants, and ye that fear him, both small and great.

6. And I heard as it were the voice of a great multitude, and as the voice of many waters, and as the voice of mighty thunderings, saying, Alleluia: for the Lord God omnipotent reigneth.

Talk About It:
Describe the unity seen in these two verses.

Joining the praises of the throngs, along with the 24 elders and the four beasts, is suddenly a voice from "out of the throne" (v. 5). This is likely the voice of a heavenly being near the throne, calling *all* of God's servants, both human and celestial, from smallest to greatest, to praise God. The word *fear* indicates reverence for God.

The antiphonal cry of the multitude is a rejoicing that the Lord God now reigns over all. Everything is in submission to Him. "In His sovereignty, He has permitted evil men and evil angels to do their worst; but now the time has come for God's will to be done on earth as it is in heaven" (*Bible Exposition Commentary*).

During the time of John's vision, Domitian was the emperor

on the Roman throne. One of the titles he carried for himself was "Lord and God." John, as well as his readers, would have rejoiced to know that such wicked self-assumption would one day be judged, for only Jehovah is worthy of such praise.

III. UNITED WITH CHRIST FOREVER (Revelation 19:7-10)
A. The Marriage Supper of the Lamb (vv. 7, 8)

7. Let us be glad and rejoice, and give honour to him: for the marriage of the Lamb is come, and his wife hath made herself ready.

8. And to her was granted that she should be arrayed in fine linen, clean and white: for the fine linen is the righteousness of saints.

Marriage in ancient Israel generally included three distinct events. First was the contract arranged by the two sets of parents. This often took place when the bride and groom were still children. Second, at a suitable point when the partners were older and ready for marriage, the groom, accompanied by his friends, would go to the house of the bride and escort her to his home (see the parable of the 10 virgins in Matthew 25:1-13). Finally, there would be a marriage supper at the new couple's home, such as Jesus attended a wedding in Cana (John 2:1-11).

Matching this up symbolically, we see that the marriage contract between the church and Christ is made when men and women come to know Christ as Savior. When Christ returns for the church in the Rapture, the second phase of the wedding will be carried out. Finally, the Marriage Supper announced in our present passage is the third phase of this holy wedding.

In Revelation 19:7 the multitude rejoices that the marriage will take place and that the Bride has now readied herself. The concept that Christians are the Bride can be seen clearly in two of Paul's passages. First, "Husbands, love your wives, just as Christ loved the church . . . to present her to himself as a radiant church, without stain or wrinkle or any other blemish, but holy and blameless" (Ephesians 5:25, 27, *NIV*). Second, "I am jealous for you with a godly jealousy. I promised you to one husband, to Christ, so that I might present you as a pure virgin to him" (2 Corinthians 11:2, *NIV*). Our present text is the only place in Scripture where "the marriage of the Lamb" is found. In Matthew 9:15, Christ says, "How can the guests of the bridegroom mourn while he is with them? The time will come when the bridegroom will be taken from them; then they will fast" (*NIV*). He also made a similar reference in 22:2: "The kingdom of heaven is like a king who prepared a wedding banquet for his son" (*NIV*).

B. Blessed Participants (vv. 9, 10)

9. And he saith unto me, Write, Blessed are they which

Talk About It:
1. What is "the marriage of the Lamb" (v. 7)?
2. Who is the bride, what is she given to wear, and why (v. 8)?

"Our teaching and preaching should focus on a loving God who demands holiness because He knows it is the only way to flourish and prosper as a human being."
—Dale Coulter

are called unto the marriage supper of the Lamb. And he saith unto me, These are the true sayings of God.

10. And I fell at his feet to worship him. And he said unto me, See thou do it not: I am thy fellowservant, and of thy brethren that have the testimony of Jesus: worship God: for the testimony of Jesus is the spirit of prophecy.

The angel who had made known to John many of the events of the last days told him to write a beatitude. That he commanded John to write indicates that the words are very important. The beatitude is a promise of blessing to those who are invited to the wedding supper of the Lamb.

Of the marriage supper, William Barclay wrote: "There is at the back of this conception a very ancient Jewish idea. They believed that when the Messiah came, God's people would, as it were, be entertained by God at a great messianic banquet. Isaiah speaks of God preparing for His people 'a feast of fat things, a feast of wines on the lees, of fat things full of marrow, of wines on the lees well refined' (Isaiah 25:6). Jesus speaks of many coming from the north and the south and the east and the west and sitting down with the patriarchs in the kingdom of God (Matthew 8:11). The word which is used for *sitting down* is the word for reclining at a meal. The picture is one of all men sitting down at the messianic banquet of God. When Jesus was with His men at the Last Supper, as He drank of the cup, He said that He would not again drink of it, until He drank it new in His Father's kingdom (26:29). That was Jesus looking forward to the great messianic banquet in the kingdom of God."

John gave assurance that this beatitude is true. He vowed that these are the words of God. They are reliable.

John was so impressed by the presence and the message of the angel that he fell at his feet to worship him. Can you put yourself in John's place? How would you react if a being from heaven appeared and spoke to you?

The angel cautioned John that he was not to be worshiped. He identified himself with John and the other believers as a fellow servant of God. Since God is the Creator of all—men and angels—all have the duty as well as the privilege to serve Him.

God alone is to be worshiped. Others may be admired and respected, but none but the Lord deserve the homage of worship. He is worthy of all the honor and praise that we can possibly render unto His great name. We should be careful to show Him the adoration He deserves.

The authority of the message of prophecy rests on the testimony of Jesus. While John was on the island of Patmos for his "testimony of Jesus," he "was in the Spirit" and received his commission to write this prophecy (Revelation 1:9-11). Thus he sees Christ as the authority behind his words.

Talk About It:
1. Who are called "blessed" (v. 9)?
2. What did the angel tell John not to do, and why not (v. 10)?
3. Explain the statement "The testimony of Jesus is the spirit of prophecy" (v. 10).

Reason Enough
One day the telephone rang in the pastor's office—the church where President Roosevelt attended. A voice inquired, "Are you expecting the President in church tomorrow?"

"That," replied the pastor, "I cannot promise, but we expect God to be there, and we hope that will be incentive enough for a large attendance."
—Al Bryant

CONCLUSION

A number of years ago I was returning home on the last leg of a journey to Israel. There had been a number of flights on large commercial aircraft during the trip, all of which were comfortable and accommodating. This last flight was different, however. It was an old, small prop plane that seemed rickety and worn out. Suffering from sheer exhaustion, I suddenly became fearful when we left the ground. Would I make it home? Could I trust this airplane? I looked out the window and saw written on the side of the engine "Rolls Royce." That changed everything. It didn't matter what the plane looked like—the integrity of the name on its engine told me everything would be fine.

In Revelation 11, we hear proclaimed that "the kingdoms of this world have become the kingdoms of our Lord and of His Christ" (v. 15, *NKJV*). We also see this doesn't fully occur until later in Revelation. However, the integrity of the name of the Lord lets us know we can live with confidence. The Lord God is in control.

GOLDEN TEXT CHALLENGE

"I HEARD A GREAT VOICE OF MUCH PEOPLE IN HEAVEN, SAYING, ALLELUIA; SALVATION, AND GLORY, AND HONOUR, AND POWER, UNTO THE LORD OUR GOD" (Revelation 19:1).

As Revelation 19 opens we are taken down the corridors of heaven. There we are surrounded by the sound of a great multitude as they rejoice. We are reminded of what a beautiful place heaven is. It is difficult to picture an environment in which there is constant joy. Peace, love, beauty and worship are as common there as they are uncommon here on earth.

We must never get the notion that we can save ourselves, or that we can sustain our salvation in our own strength. Salvation is of God. Our hope rests in our trust in Him to do for us what we cannot do for ourselves. Christ died to make that possible.

The voices from heaven also ascribe glory, honor and power to the Lord. God's glory should remind us of His majesty. It was for His pleasure that we were created and that we exist. In Him, as Paul said, we "live, and move, and have our being" (Acts 17:28). If we live at His will, then we ought to live according to His will. We have no right to dictate our own actions; we should act only as we are directed of the Lord.

Awareness of the power of God should awaken within us a confidence to face whatever life may bring. As Paul asked, "If God be for us, who can be against us?" (Romans 8:31).

Daily Devotions:
M. God's Throne Is Everlasting
   Psalm 93:1-5
T. God's Throne Is Righteous
   Psalm 97:1-12
W. God's Everlasting Kingdom
   Daniel 4:1-3
T. Christ's Superior Reign
   Hebrews 1:1-9
F. Power to Reign
   Revelation 11:15-19
S. Reign With Christ Forever
   Revelation 22:1-5